THE CAMBRIDGE WORLD HISTORY OF
SEXUALITIES

Volume II focuses on systems of thought and belief in the history of world sexualities, ranging from early humans to contemporary approaches. Comprising eighteen chapters, this volume opens with a chapter on the evolutionary legacy and then delves into the sexualities of ancient Egypt, the Near East, Greece, and Rome, continuing with pre-modern South Asia, China, Japan, Africa, the Americas, and Oceania. Chapters include an examination of sexuality in the religious traditions of Buddhism, Judaism, Christianity, and Islam, and also look at more recent approaches, including scientific sex, sexuality in socialism and Marxism, and the intersections between sexuality, feminism, and post-colonialism.

MERRY E. WIESNER-HANKS is Distinguished Professor of History Emerita at the University of Wisconsin–Milwaukee. She acted as general editor for the seven-volume *Cambridge World History* published in 2015. Other notable works include *A Concise History of the World*, *Women and Gender in Early Modern Europe*, and *Christianity and Sexuality in the Early Modern World*.

MATHEW KUEFLER is Professor of History Emeritus at San Diego State University. He is a broadly trained medievalist who specializes in gender and sexuality and in LGBTQ+ history. From 2004 to 2014, he was the editor of the *Journal of the History of Sexuality*. Notable works include *The Manly Eunuch*, *The Making and Unmaking of a Saint*, and *The History of Sexuality Sourcebook*.

THE CAMBRIDGE WORLD HISTORY OF
SEXUALITIES

General Editors

MERRY E. WIESNER-HANKS, *University of Wisconsin–Milwaukee*
and
MATHEW KUEFLER, *San Diego State University*

Split into four volumes, *The Cambridge World History of Sexualities* examines sexualities across time and around the world at varying geographic and chronological scales. Featuring over eighty contributions from scholars across more than twenty countries in a number of disciplines, the volumes represent a cross-disciplinary approach that characterizes the history of sexuality as a field in itself. The first volume combines historiographical essays with general overviews of important topics and themes. The second evaluates sexuality in systems of thought and belief, from early humans to contemporary feminism. The third targets specific locations at different times to navigate further the lived experience of individuals and groups. Lastly, the fourth examines the intersection of modernity and human sexuality on issues such as colonialism and consumerism. Thorough and authoritative, the collection is a much-needed addition to the world history of sexualities.

Volume I General Overviews
EDITED BY MERRY E. WIESNER-HANKS AND MATHEW KUEFLER

Volume II Systems of Thought and Belief
EDITED BY MERRY E. WIESNER-HANKS AND MATHEW KUEFLER

Volume III Sites of Knowledge and Practice
EDITED BY MERRY E. WIESNER-HANKS AND MATHEW KUEFLER

Volume IV Modern Sexualities
EDITED BY MERRY E. WIESNER-HANKS AND MATHEW KUEFLER

THE CAMBRIDGE WORLD HISTORY OF SEXUALITIES

*

VOLUME II
Systems of Thought and Belief

*

Edited by
MERRY E. WIESNER-HANKS
University of Wisconsin–Milwaukee

and

MATHEW KUEFLER
San Diego State University

Shaftesbury Road, Cambridge CB2 8EA, United Kingdom

One Liberty Plaza, 20th Floor, New York, NY 10006, USA

477 Williamstown Road, Port Melbourne, VIC 3207, Australia

314–321, 3rd Floor, Plot 3, Splendor Forum, Jasola District Centre, New Delhi – 110025, India

103 Penang Road, #05–06/07, Visioncrest Commercial, Singapore 238467

Cambridge University Press is part of Cambridge University Press & Assessment, a department of the University of Cambridge.

We share the University's mission to contribute to society through the pursuit of education, learning and research at the highest international levels of excellence.

www.cambridge.org
Information on this title: www.cambridge.org/9781108842099

DOI: 10.1017/9781108896016

© Cambridge University Press & Assessment 2024

This publication is in copyright. Subject to statutory exception and to the provisions of relevant collective licensing agreements, no reproduction of any part may take place without the written permission of Cambridge University Press & Assessment.

First published 2024

Printed in the United Kingdom by TJ Books Limited, Padstow, Cornwall

A catalogue record for this publication is available from the British Library.

A Cataloging-in-Publication data record for this book is available from the Library of Congress

ISBN – 4 Volume Set 978-1-108-89618-4 Hardback
ISBN – Volume I 978-1-108-84208-2 Hardback
ISBN – Volume II 978-1-108-84209-9 Hardback
ISBN – Volume III 978-1-108-84210-5 Hardback
ISBN – Volume IV 978-1-108-84211-2 Hardback

Cambridge University Press & Assessment has no responsibility for the persistence or accuracy of URLs for external or third-party internet websites referred to in this publication and does not guarantee that any content on such websites is, or will remain, accurate or appropriate.

Contents

List of Figures in Volume II   *page ix*
List of Contributors to Volume II   *x*
Editors' Preface to the Series   *xiii*

1 · Human Sexuality: The Evolutionary Legacy of Mating, Parenting,
and Family Formation   *1*
KAREN L. KRAMER AND RYAN SCHACHT

2 · Sexuality in Ancient Egypt: Pleasures, Desires, Norms,
and Representations   *22*
UROŠ MATIĆ

3 · Sexuality in the Systems of Thought and Belief of the
Ancient Near East   *43*
ILAN PELED

4 · Sexuality in Traditional South Asian Systems of Thought and Belief   *63*
JAYA S. TYAGI AND TARA SHEEMAR MALHAN

5 · Discourses of Desire in Ancient Greece and Rome   *87*
ALLISON GLAZEBROOK

6 · Writing a History of Sexuality for Pre-Modern China   *114*
HSIAO-WEN CHENG

7 · Sexuality in Traditional Systems of Thought and Belief in
Pre-modern Japan   *136*
HITOMI TONOMURA

8 · African Traditions of Sexualities   *158*
YAARI FELBER-SELIGMAN

VII

Contents

9 · Sexuality in the Traditional Systems of Thought and Belief
of the Americas *181*
ROSEMARY A. JOYCE

10 · Oceanic Sexualities: Persistence, Change, Resistance *201*
MARGARET JOLLY

11 · Sexuality in Buddhist Traditions *228*
KALI NYIMA CAPE

12 · Sexuality in Jewish Traditions *250*
CHARLOTTE ELISHEVA FONROBERT

13 · Sexuality in Christian Traditions *271*
ADRIAN THATCHER

14 · Sexuality in Islamic Traditions *293*
SERENA TOLINO

15 · Scientific Sex in the Modern World *314*
HOWARD CHIANG

16 · Sexuality in Marxism and Socialism *340*
JILL MASSINO

17 · Feminism and Modern Sexuality *366*
VICTORIA HESFORD

18 · Post-Colonialism and Sexuality *388*
ANNE HARDGROVE

Index *411*
Tables of Contents to Volumes I, III, and IV *425*

Figures in Volume II

5.1 Marble plinth with phallic bird in relief surmounted by an oversize
phallus. Temple of Dionysus, Delos, *c.* 300 BCE *page* 98

5.2 Fresco of Priapus in the entryway of the House of the Vettii, Pompeii,
79 CE 99

5.3 Fresco from the suburban baths, Pompeii, showing group sex
with a foursome and threesome engaged in oral and rear entry
sex, 79 CE 100

5.4 Frontal view of a sleeping Hermaphroditus in marble,
first century BCE 103

5.5 Kylix depicting a seated youth reaching to kiss a standing male figure 105

15.1 A plate illustrating the psychological relations of the brain
(phrenology) (1851) 319

15.2 ACT UP demonstrators protest and take over the Food and Drugs
Administration headquarters in Rockville, Maryland, USA
(October 1988) 336

Contributors to Volume II

KALI NYIMA CAPE is Assistant Professor at Georgia State University, USA. She received her PhD in Buddhist Studies at the University of Virginia. Her research focuses on women in Tibetan Buddhism. Her research has been funded by the Tsadra Foundation, Fulbright-Hays and Ford Foundation Fellowship.

HSIAO-WEN CHENG is Associate Professor of Chinese history and religion at University of Pennsylvania, USA. She is the author of *Divine, Demonic, and Disordered: Women without Men in Song Dynasty China* (University of Washington Press, 2021).

HOWARD CHIANG is the Lai Ho and Wu Cho-liu Endowed Chair in Taiwan Studies, Professor of East Asian Languages and Cultural Studies, and Director of the Center for Taiwan Studies at the University of California, Santa Barbara, USA. Between 2019 and 2022 he served as the founding chair of the Society of Sinophone Studies.

YAARI FELBER-SELIGMAN is Assistant Professor at the City College of New York, USA. Their research and teaching explores histories of early Africa, comparative world, and sexual and gender diversity. They have published articles in *African Arts*, *History in Africa*, and the *International Journal of African Historical Studies*.

CHARLOTTE ELISHEVA FONROBERT teaches in the Department of Religious Studies at Stanford University, USA. She is the director of Jewish Studies and the programme Feminist, Gender, and Sexuality Studies. She has published widely on the intersection of Jewish tradition and sexuality, including the award-winning *Menstrual Purity: Rabbinic and Early Christian Reconstructions of Biblical Gender* (Stanford University Press, 2000).

ALLISON GLAZEBROOK is Professor of Classics at Brock University, USA. Her research focuses on women, slavery, gender, and sexuality in ancient Greece. Recent publications include *Sexual Labor in the Athenian Courts* (University of Texas Press, 2021) and *Themes in Greek Society and Culture: An Introduction to Ancient Greece,* 2nd edition (Oxford University Press, 2022, coedited with C. Vester).

ANNE HARDGROVE trained as an anthropologist and historian and is Associate Professor of History at the University of Texas at San Antonio, USA. She is a past president of the

List of Contributors to Volume II

Society for Advancing the Study of South Asia, an affiliate organization of the American Historical Association.

VICTORIA HESFORD is Associate Professor of Women's, Gender, and Sexuality Studies at Stony Brook University, USA. Her research focuses on post-1945 US feminist and queer history and culture. She is the author of *Feeling Women's Liberation* (Duke University Press, 2013), and numerous essays on feminist and queer history and culture.

MARGARET JOLLY is Emerita Professor at the Australian National University. A transdisciplinary scholar of gender and sexuality in Oceania, she is a Fellow of the Academy of Social Sciences in Australia, an Australian Research Council Laureate Fellow from 2010 to 2016, and a Member of the Order of Australia since 2020.

ROSEMARY A. JOYCE is Distinguished Professor of Anthropology at the University of California, Berkeley, USA. She has received an Honorary Doctorate from Leiden University and is the recipient of the 2022 A. V. Kidder Award for Eminence in American Archaeology.

KAREN L. KRAMER is Professor of Anthropology at the University of Utah, USA, whose research focuses on the evolution of human sociality and behavior, with particular interests in cooperative breeding, parenting, and childhood. Her three field sites are all small-scale horticultural and hunter-gatherer societies.

TARA SHEEMAR MALHAN teaches history at Janki Devi Memorial College, University of Delhi, India. She is the author of *Plunging the Ocean: Courts, Castes and Courtesans in the Kathāsaritsāgara* (Primus Books, 2017) and has various other publications related to her research interests, including gender, sexuality, religious praxis, and courtly culture.

JILL MASSINO is Associate Professor of History at University of North Carolina at Charlotte, USA, where she teaches on modern European and comparative history. She is the author of *Ambiguous Transitions: Gender, the State, and Everyday Life in Socialist and Postsocialist Romania* (Berghahn Books, 2019) and numerous chapters and articles on gender in socialist and post-socialist Romania.

UROŠ MATIĆ is a research associate of the Austrian Archaeological Institute, Austrian Academy of Sciences in Vienna. He was a co-chair of Archaeology and Gender in Europe community of the European Research of Archaeologists from 2016 to 2019. Among other interests, he specializes in violence and gender in ancient Egypt.

ILAN PELED is Lecturer of Hebrew, Aramaic, and Middle Eastern Studies at the Leiden University Institute for Area Studies, Netherlands. He is the author of *Masculinities and Third Gender* (Ugarit, 2016) and *Law and Gender in the Ancient Near East and the Hebrew Bible* (Routledge, 2019).

List of Contributors to Volume II

RYAN SCHACHT is Assistant Professor of Anthropology at East Carolina University, USA. He applies both ethnographic and demographic methods to study the social and ecological determinants of health across both 'small' and 'big' data.

ADRIAN THATCHER is Honorary Professor of Theology at the University of Exeter, UK, and Editor of the theological journal *Modern Believing*. His most recent book is *Gender and Christian Ethics* (Cambridge University Press, 2020).

SERENA TOLINO is an Associate Professor of Islamic and Middle Eastern Studies and Co-Director of the Institute for the Study of the Middle East and Muslim Societies at the University of Bern, Switzerland. Her main research interests include history of gender and sexuality, Islamic law, and the history of the Middle East.

HITOMI TONOMURA is Professor of Japanese History and Women's and Gender Studies, and University Diversity and Social Transformation Professor at the University of Michigan, USA. She was director of the Eisenberg Institute for Historical Studies, A/PIA Studies Program, and Center for Japanese Studies. Her research interests are gender, war, and masculinities.

JAYA S. TYAGI is Professor of History at the University of Delhi, India. She has been the director of Women's Studies and Development Center for Advanced Studies, University of Delhi and a Fellow at the Indian Institute of Advanced Study at Shimla, India.

Editors' Preface to the Series

Sexuality – the range of acts related to erotic desire, romance, and reproduction, and the meanings attached to them – lies at the centre of human existence. This has been as true throughout human history as it is today. From the customs of marriage and family life to rules about inheritance and status, from the pronouncements of philosophers and religious leaders to the lived daily experience of persons across society, from the global impact of commercialized sex to local regulations on sexual diversity – sexuality touches all areas of life.

Historians have included discussions of sexuality and its impact on human history in their writings since antiquity, often using sexual customs or actions to highlight differences between their own culture and others, praise or censure those they were writing about, or provide the moral guidance that was so often a part of history. In the nineteenth century, advocates of women's and gay rights sought to uncover the historical roots of oppression and to find exceptions to patriarchal and homophobic traditions. Anthropologists and social theorists also linked the varied sexual customs of modern peoples with patterns derived from the past. In the first half of the twentieth century, social historians focused on marriage and kinship in their examinations of the lives of ordinary people, and a few even concentrated explicitly on sexual issues.

The women's and gay liberation movements of the 1960s and 1970s inspired the first professional historians of sexuality. Many of them specialized in the modern histories of Europe and the United States, and they theorized mainly from the modern Western experience. This is beginning to change: the field has expanded to incorporate pre-modern histories and histories in all regions of the world, becoming increasingly transhistorical and global. World and global histories have encouraged broad cross-cultural comparisons and the study of *longue durée* trends, developments now also seen in the history of sexuality. Historians can now move beyond concentrated specializations in one time and place to create a more comprehensive image of sexuality in human history.

The Cambridge World History of Sexualities reflects these recent trends in the history of sexuality. It is made up of four volumes. The first volume offers historiographical essays on past, present, and future directions of the field, along with general overviews of central topics in the long history of human sexuality. The second volume contains essays on sexuality in systems of thought and belief from the world's regions and cultural and intellectual traditions, beginning with the earliest human groups and ending with contemporary approaches. The third volume targets specific times and places to more closely investigate the lived experience of individuals and groups and to highlight the diversity of human sexualities. The fourth volume examines the intersections of modernity and human sexuality through the forces, ideas, and events that have shaped the modern world, and the challenges we in the modern world have faced and continue to face. Across the four volumes, the series offers chapters at varying geographic and chronological scales, providing depth of coverage along with breadth of vision.

Our aim is to produce a useful reference for scholars, advanced students, and interested general readers, as well as for those who specialize in the history of sexuality. As with other Cambridge World Histories, this collection is intended to be the best and most detailed source of reliable, up-to-date information on the field. It will also provide readers with opportunities to make their own comparisons and contrasts between chapters and volumes. It is not exhaustive: despite our best efforts, the global crisis of the pandemic obliged some contributors to withdraw on short notice, and we were unable to replace them. We particularly regret the absence of chapters on Indigenous Australian sexualities, on the impact of slavery on sexuality, on LGBTQ+ rights and activism in the modern world, and on sex in film, television, and digital media.

This series reflects the best of contemporary scholarly discussions of sexuality. We recognize that 'sexuality' is a modern word and that some historians choose to avoid it when discussing the past, arguing that it is anachronistic. Investigations of the past are always informed by more recent understandings and concerns, however, and using modern concepts can often provide great insights. We also recognize that 'sexuality' is a Western invention and may not accurately reflect the cultural diversity even of modern societies across the globe. Yet we do not wish to draw too firm a line between the systems of sexual knowledge in modern European and European-influenced societies and those of other human traditions. As many of our contributors do, we reject the sharp distinction that the French historian of sexuality and philosopher Michel Foucault drew between *scientia sexualis* (sexual science) in the West and *ars erotica* (erotic arts) in the rest. So we use the term 'sexuality' with these caveats and have intentionally chosen the plural 'sexualities' in our title to signal the enormous diversity on all matters relating to sex across time and space.

A similar caveat must be made about the range of terms possible to describe gender and sexual diversity in history. Most of our contributors have used LGBTQ+ (lesbian, gay, bisexual, transgender, queer, and other) for these identities, or individual terms from within the list, even when referring to the distant past, and have used the pronoun 'they' for gender diverse individuals. Some have included historical terms used to identify such persons and groups, some of which might be considered derogatory or exclusionary today. Some authors have chosen to use terms from the language of the people they study, explaining what these mean rather than attempting a translation. Forms of gender and sexual diversity extend far beyond those covered by the LGBTQ+ label, and our intention is always to be as inclusive as possible.

We are very pleased with the broad scope of the series and have worked hard to make it truly diverse and interdisciplinary. Most chapters range widely across time and place and demonstrate the richness of a comparative approach. The series is diverse in other ways as well. The contributors live and work in more than twenty different countries, and their backgrounds and education represent about twice that number, providing a global perspective on many topics. They range in gender and sexual identity and in age. Their voices are those of distinguished senior scholars, mid-career researchers, and up-and-coming scholars, thus those who have shaped the field's history and those who will shape it long into the future. In addition to professional historians, some contributors are trained and teach in anthropology, archaeology, cultural studies, social sciences, languages and literatures, religious studies, theology, philosophy, area studies, communications, education, women's studies, and gender studies.

We acknowledge gratefully the work of the staff at Cambridge University Press and the support of our families. Most of the work on the series took place during the global pandemic, and we salute the perseverance of the scholars who contributed, despite personal and professional challenges that were unimaginable when we first invited them. This series is dedicated to those around the world who faced or still face persecution because of their perceived or actual sex, gender, sexuality, and/or gender identity.

I

Human Sexuality: The Evolutionary Legacy of Mating, Parenting, and Family Formation

KAREN L. KRAMER AND RYAN SCHACHT

Ascribing universal characteristics to human sexuality is rife with contention due to both methodological and ideological disagreements, as well as debate over what is 'typical' given variation in its expression. For example, Margaret Mead's investigation into the sexual lives of Samoan adolescents during the 1920s found that teenagers engaged in pre-marital sex, often having multiple partners before marriage. The results, presented in *Coming of Age in Samoa*, were heavily criticized both by scientists for being too subjective and by religious organizations that claimed Mead was attempting to legitimize her own beliefs on sexuality.[1] Nonetheless, Mead's pioneering work galvanized a growing number of researchers, who began to systematically investigate sexual and reproductive behaviour by way of time-intensive, cross-cultural inquiry. Yet, while long-studied, how best to characterize human sexuality remains challenging.

Given human placement in the primate order, we approach mating, parenting, and family formation from a comparative perspective to better understand the physical and behavioural traits that are either shared across or distinct from our closest living relatives. We will additionally draw on examples from contemporary small-scale societies, also referred to as traditional societies. Small-scale societies are not relics of the past, but they do exemplify a more representative, diversified, and inclusive view of human courtship, marriage, and family life, and thus provide valuable insights into human sexuality. Mating, parenting, and family life have changed substantially in just the last few centuries through industrialization, globalization,

---

1 Margaret Mead, *Coming of Age in Samoa: A Psychological Study of Primitive Youth for Western Civilization* (New York: William Morrow, 1928); Paul Shankman, *The Trashing of Margaret Mead: Anatomy of an Anthropological Controversy* (Madison, WI: University of Wisconsin Press, 2009).

and the shift from a subsistence-based to a cash-based economy. For example, small, nuclear families consisting of parents and their dependent children are the norm today in the developed world. Yet for most of human history, as well as in contemporary small-scale societies, they are not.[2] Rather, patterns of mating, parenting, and family formation occurred in a much broader social context and were both varied in their expression and flexible to situational needs.

This chapter reviews what can be gleaned about human sexuality from the evolutionary and ethnographic record. We cannot, of course, observe what ancestral human sexuality was like since it leaves neither fossil nor archaeological evidence. However, inferences about how humans mated, consorted, parented, formed partnerships, and aggregated into families can be drawn from two large and growing bodies of work. The first are anatomical and biological indicators of ancestral mating patterns inferred from fossil evidence as well as observations from non-human primates. The second is ethnographic research across an array of contemporary human societies, which highlights variation in mating, marriage, and family structure. Together, biological indicators and cross-cultural patterns shed light on the legacy, constraints, and possibilities carried forward into the diverse and variable expression of human sexuality today.

Ancestral Human Mating Systems

Chimpanzees, the great ape genetically most closely related to humans, have long been assumed as the behavioural model best resembling mating and childrearing patterns of the deep human past going back more than 4 million years. Chimpanzees live in multi-male/multi-female polygynandrous (both sexes mate with multiple partners) groups. However, the assumption that our ancestors lived in polygynandrous groups has more recently ceded to debate about whether they instead were organized in polygynous, gorilla-like harems, or had a hamadryas baboon-like structure with a single male and his consorts living within a larger group. These differences in group structure directly affect the possible kinds of relationships that can form between individuals of the same and opposite sex. Despite debate over the specific social organization from which the

---

2 Karen L. Kramer, 'The Human Family: Its Evolutionary Context and Diversity', *Social Science* 10, no. 6 (2021): 1–17.

hominin line (all modern humans, our immediate ancestors, and extinct human species) developed, most researchers agree that group living and multi-male/multi-female societies are ancient features of human sociality.

Differences between males and females within and across species offer insight into ancient and contemporary selection pressures. Sexual selection is a widely recognized evolutionary force that influences behavioural and physical traits across animal taxa. Anatomical and biological features are less plastic than cultural traits and as such hint at ancestral selection pressures and the mating patterns that underlie them. Three traits are commonly examined in reference to primate breeding systems: sexual dimorphism, testis size, and concealed ovulation. Each provides evidence that helps to explain current mating patterns.

Sexual dimorphism refers to male and female differences in size or appearance, other than differences in the sexual organs themselves. Although many exceptions exist, across primates, and mammals generally, sexual dimorphism is correlated with breeding systems. For example, monogamy is associated with low rates of inter-male competition, as with our lesser-ape relatives the gibbons, and minimal differences between males and females in body weight and canine tooth size (used for fighting among primate males, not for eating meat).[3] In contrast, in species that have polygynous mating systems, inter-male competition is high and size differences tend to be much more pronounced. In polygynous primates, competition among males to take over and maintain a harem can be intense, and stakes are high since winners have much to gain. Among mountain gorillas, dominant males monopolize sexual access to a group of females and perform up to 70 per cent of all copulations.[4] Gorillas exhibit high levels of reproductive skew, that is, variation across individuals in reproductive success, and males are nearly twice the size of females.[5] For primates who live in multi-male/multi-female groups, such as chimpanzees, body size dimorphism tends to be intermediary between monogamous and polygynous species.[6]

---

3 Alexander H. Harcourt, Paul H. Harvey, Susan G. Larson, and Roger V. Short, 'Testis Weight, Body Weight and Breeding System in Primates', *Nature* 293 (1981): 55–7.

4 Tara S. Stoinski, Staceu Rosenbaum, and Katie Fawcett, 'Patterns of Male Reproductive Behaviour in Multi-Male Groups of Mountain Gorillas: Examining Theories of Reproductive Skew', *Behaviour* 146 (2009): 1193–215.

5 Steven R. Leigh and Brian T. Shea, 'Ontogeny and the Evolution of Adult Body Size Dimorphism in Apes', *American Journal of Primatology* 36 (1995): 37–60.

6 Alan F. Dixson, *Sexual Selection and the Origins of Human Mating Systems* (Oxford: Oxford University Press, 2009).

Given the relationship between size dimorphism and mating systems, what evidence of sexual dimorphism is there in the hominin anatomical record? The general consensus is that height dimorphism was greater in the past and has diminished over time. *Australopithicine* (fossil hominins who lived from about 4 to 2 million years ago) males are estimated to be in the order of 50 per cent taller than females, and in *Homo erectus*-grade species (fossil hominins from about 2 million to 40,000 years ago), males are about 25 per cent larger. It is important to note, however, that determining size dimorphism from fossils is intensely debated due to differences in researcher interpretations, in part because isolated finds do not represent the actual distribution of a trait in a population. What can be measured with greater certainty is stature dimorphism in contemporary humans, among whom males are on average between 5 and 10 per cent taller than females, depending on population. This is often interpreted to indicate that size dimorphism has decreased over the course of hominin evolution as inter-male competition relaxed in conjunction with a prevalence of monogamy.

When the reduction in stature dimorphism occurred in the past, and its mating system implications, however, are not fully understood. Most researchers agree that humans today express relatively small size differences not only in stature, but also in other measures of body size when compared with closely related polygynandrous and polygynous species. For example, human dimorphism in weight averages about 1.15 (in other words, males are about 15 per cent heavier) than females, while the chimpanzee estimate is 1.3 and orangutans and gorillas are near 2 or more.[7] Although body weight dimorphism is slight in modern humans compared with these species, it is double that for monogamous gibbons, who exhibit very little difference in weight by sex (1.07).[8] These comparisons suggest that modern humans are less dimorphic than polygynandrous and polygynous species, but more dimorphic than expected for a monogamous species.

Added complexity arises when attempting to ascribe meaning to size dimorphism. Males may compete for female favour in other ways besides physical contest. Focus on body size dimorphism as an indicator of the

---

7 J. Micheal Plavcan and Carl P. van Schaik, 'Intrasexual Competition and Canine Dimorphism in Anthropoid Primates', *American Journal of Physical Anthropology* 87 (1992): 461–77.

8 Lesley A. Willner, *Sexual Dimorphism in Primates* (London: University College London Discovery Press, 1989).

intensity of inter-male competition may significantly underestimate the many and particularly human ways that males may compete, such as through wealth, intelligence, social reputations, and political power. While the attenuation of body size differences is often used to signify a reduction in male competition, male reproductive skew, and polygyny, it may instead indicate an evolutionary shift from physical to social forms of competition.

Testes size, as an indicator of sperm production and competition, is another commonly used metric of a species' mating system. Large testes relative to body size is positively correlated with the frequency that females mate with multiple partners, with males responding by producing and delivering more sperm to outcompete other males. Adjusting for body size, human testes are smaller than those of polygynandrous chimpanzees, yet are similar relative to polygynous gorillas.[9] At the same time, human testes are somewhat larger than those of other monogamous primates.

While testes size is a predictor of the extent to which females mate with multiple partners, it cannot discriminate between monogamy and polygyny because in both cases females mate with a single male, resulting in relatively low sperm competition.[10] Thus, the ratio of testes to body size complicates a simple story of ancestral mating derived from sexual dimorphism alone because human values are within the range of variation found among gorillas and orangutans – great ape species with polygynous mating systems. Therefore, the tempered interpretation is that human testes size is consistent with a pairbonded polygynous species.

Human females also lack obviously visible or easily detectable signs of ovulation, particularly in comparison to the conspicuous sexual swellings of, for example, chimpanzees and baboons.[11] Several functional arguments have been proposed to explain this phenomenon, called concealed ovulation. In many primate species, female receptivity to sexual advances is limited to oestrus, when females are ovulating. In chimpanzees, oestrus swellings are an unambiguous sign of the potential for conception and concentrate the

---

9 Geoffrey A. Parker, 'The Evolution of Expenditure on Testes', *Journal of Zoology* 298 (2016): 3–19; Harcourt et al., 'Testis Weight'.

10 Robert D. Martin and Robert M. May, 'Outward Signs of Breeding', *Nature* 293 (1981): 7–9.

11 Kelly Rooker and Sergey Gavrilets, 'On the Evolution of Visual Female Sexual Signaling', *Proceedings of the Royal Society, B: Biological Sciences* 285 (2018), https://doi.org/10.1098/rspb.2017.2875; Birgitta Sillén-Tullberg and Anders P. Moller, 'The Relationship between Concealed Ovulation and Mating Systems in Anthropoid Primates: A Phylogenetic Analysis', *American Naturalist* 141 (1993): 1–25; Beverly I. Strassmann, 'Sexual Selection, Paternal Care, and Concealed Ovulation in Humans', *Ethology and Sociobiology* 2 (1981): 31–40.

attention of multiple males during the short window of fecundity.[12] Concealed ovulation, however, limits information about fecundity to males, and even to females themselves. One common explanation for concealed ovulation and the constant sexual receptivity of women is that these traits interacted to favour monogamy. If males do not know when females are fecund, they are more likely to be continuously attentive, favouring monogamy through mate defence and/or paternal care.[13] Concealed ovulation might also ease tensions by dampening inter-male competition, and is thought to facilitate the formation of stable pairbonds within multi-male /multi-female societies.[14] Yet, it is increasingly evident from comparative study that concealed ovulation is not only characteristic of humans, but also of many polygynous female primates who likewise do not display overt signs of ovulation.[15]

In sum, the preceding biological traits, when interpreted singly, prompt different perspectives on ancestral mating in humans. For example, while men are larger on average than women, weight and canine tooth dimorphism are slight compared with that of polygynous gorillas and are more comparable to monogamous gibbons.[16] These differences suggest diverging sexual selection histories among the great apes (gorillas, orangutans, chimpanzees, and humans) with respect to male reliance on physical competition for reproductive success. Yet, while size dimorphism may suggest an evolutionary attenuation of male–male competition, testes size suggests that if there was a trend towards pairbonding, it may not have been expressed as fastidious adherence to monogamy. Relative testes size implies that sperm competition is lower than expected for a promiscuous primate, but higher than for a monogamous species. Human testes size (accounting for body size) is more similar to gorillas who live in polygynous societies. While concealed ovulation was once thought to be a human-specific adaptation that coevolved

---

12 Barbara B. Smuts and Robert W. Smuts, 'Male Aggression and Sexual Coercion of Females in Nonhuman Primates and Other Mammals: Evidence and Theoretical Implications', *Advances in the Study of Behavior* 22 (1993): 1–63.

13 Ryan Schacht and Adrian Bell, 'The Evolution of Monogamy in Response to Partner Scarcity', *Scientific Reports* 6 (2016), https://doi.org/10.1038/srep32472.

14 Frank W. Marlowe and J. Colette Berbesque, 'The Human Operational Sex Ratio: Effects of Marriage, Concealed Ovulation, and Menopause on Mate Competition', *Journal of Human Evolution* 63 (2012): 834–42.

15 Birgitta Sillén-Tullberg and Anders P. Moller, 'The Relationship between Concealed Ovulation and Mating Systems in Anthropoid Primates: A Phylogenetic Analysis', *American Naturalist* 141 (1993): 1–25.

16 J. Michael Plavcan, 'Implications of Male and Female Contributions to Sexual Size Dimorphism for Inferring Behavior in the Hominin Fossil Record', *International Journal of Primatology* 33 (2012): 1364–81.

with monogamy, it is common among anthropoid primates who express different breeding systems.

If the story thus far seems somewhat unclear that is because it is unsettled. Nonetheless, when moving beyond the interpretation of traits singly to viewing them as a suite of interrelated attributes, some general claims can be made. The lack of dramatic size dimorphism and large testes size to body size appears to rule out an ancestry of early humans living in highly promiscuous societies. Yet because sexual dimorphism and testes size relative to body size are larger than expected for a strictly monogamous species, it also suggests that if early humans were monogamous, it was imperfect.

Living in Multi-Male/Multi-Female Societies

Although societies composed of multiple males and females are found among a few other primates, including chimpanzees and some baboons, several features distinguish male and female relationships in human communities.

First, human societies can be generally described as composed of adult males and females living in pairbonded family units that are embedded within larger groups. This represents no small evolutionary or social feat, and it cannot be stressed enough how unusual it is in animal societies for sexual boundaries to be, in general, amicably respected. Explanations usually given as to why this rarely occurs in other species centre on rivalries between males competing for females prohibiting social cohesion.

Second, in all human societies, pairbonds are socially recognized through marriage unions. Those marriage unions express a wide range of configurations that vary across groups and the individuals within a society. Some marriages are monogamous (one male/one female), others are polygynous (one male/multiple females), and some are polyandrous (one female/multiple males). In each of these marriage systems, males and females are pairbonded.

Third, across human societies, men, women, and children perform different tasks, target different resources, and share the fruits of their labour. Although this takes many forms, and details vary widely across cultures, the age and gender division of labour is foundational to human subsistence and childrearing. While the age and gender division of labour is not unique to humans, the combination of individuals pursuing different subsistence activities, cooperating in joint activities, and sharing childcare, food, and other resources in humans is unmatched when compared with other primates. The division of labour and the complementary inter-reliance of men and women, and adults and children affect many aspects of male–female relationships.

Fourth, adults often maintain lifelong relationships with their natal families and move easily between neighbouring groups. This fluidity rarely occurs among other great apes. For example, among chimpanzees, individuals who attempt to emigrate from other troops are met with violence and sometimes death. Explanations for why humans cultivate social bonds across multiple groups have centred on building networks to exchange food, raw materials, labour, information, and marriage partners.[17]

In sum, social organization with respect to men and women is novel in the hominin line in several notable ways. Humans came to live successfully, for the most part, in communities of coresidential households and in socially recognized monogamous, polygynous, or polyandrous pairbonds. Human social organization is also unusual in that family groups are integrated through cooperation and that men and women maintain ties with their natal group and can fluidly move between communities.

Human Mating Cross-Culturally

Frank Boas, a pioneer of early anthropology, and a teacher and mentor to Margaret Mead, noted the following: 'Courtesy, modesty, good manners, conformity to definite ethical standards are universal, but what constitutes courtesy, modesty, good manners, and definite ethical standards is not universal. It is instructive to know that standards differ in the most unexpected ways.'[18] Societal norms become internalized through the process of enculturation, which establishes informal guidelines for appropriate behaviours. As the preceding quotation suggests, though, what is considered appropriate varies widely across groups, indicating a broad range of norms across human societies. For example, in many industrialized nations, the nuclear family with a husband/wife pairbond at the centre is the assumed norm. Yet the nuclear family is just one of many sexual and household arrangements, and is likely a recent norm. The human family exhibits remarkable flexibility within and across populations in ways that differ

---

17 Karen L. Kramer, Ryan Schacht, and Adrian Bell, 'Adult Sex Ratios and Partner Scarcity among Hunter-Gatherers: Implications for Dispersal Patterns and the Evolution of Human Sociality', *Philosophical Transactions of the Royal Society, B: Biological Sciences* 372, no. 1729 (2017), https://doi.org/10.1098/rstb.2016.0316.

18 Franz Boas, forward in Mead, *Coming of Age in Samoa*, xiv.

from the nuclear family model.[19] For instance, in the United States, 18.6 per cent of households were nuclear in 2020, down from 40 per cent in 1970.[20]

Across the animal kingdom, species-typical labels (e.g., monogamy, polygyny, or polygynandry) are regularly applied to describe male–female mating interactions. But no simple or single designation characterizes humans. Instead, diverse mating systems are variably present both across and within societies. Representative data from a range of societies, known as the Standard Cross-Cultural Sample, show that polygynous marriage is allowed in most societies (about 85 per cent).[21] Within these societies, however, the majority of marriages are monogamous.[22] For example, among the Savanna Pumé, South American hunter-gatherers, while polygyny occurs (20 per cent of women and 11 per cent of men are polygynously married at some point during their lives), most marriages are monogamous, and this is consistent with other similar groups.[23] Nevertheless, over the life course, individuals often re-enter the marriage market due to asymmetries in the cessation of fecundity (women cease being fertile around the age of forty-five; men's fecundity also declines with age, but somewhat later), divorce, and spousal death. This results in serial monogamy, where both men and women have multiple partners over their adult lives.

Marriage occurs in all human societies as a socially recognized union that separates some – a couple or a small group – from other members of a society. Although marriage is often thought of as the institution that legitimizes sexual activity, it might be more aptly seen, at least historically, as the institution that confines it. As a universal human trait, marriage publicly acknowledges who has sanctioned sexual access to whom, with divorce often resulting from extra-marital relationships. Many exceptions exist.

---

19 Kramer et al., 'Adult Sex Ratios'; Rebecca Sear, 'The Male Breadwinner Nuclear Family Is Not the "Traditional" Human Family, and Promotion of This Myth May Have Adverse Health Consequences', *Philosophical Transactions of the Royal Society, B: Biological Sciences* 376, no. 1827 (2021), https://doi.org/10.1098/rstb.2020.0020.

20 U.S. Census Bureau, *Current Population Survey, Annual Social and Economic Supplement*, 2021.

21 George P. Murdock and Douglas R. White, 'Standard Cross-Cultural Sample', *Ethnology* 8 (1969): 329–69.

22 Mark V. Flinn and Bobbi S. Low, 'Resource Distribution, Social Competition and Mating Patterning in Human Societies', in *Ecological Aspects of Social Evolution: Birds and Mammals*, ed. Daniel I. Rubenstein and Richard W. Wrangham (Princeton, NJ: Princeton University Press, 1986): 217–43.

23 Kramer et al., 'Adult Sex Ratios'.

Amazing, from a comparative primate perspective, is that men largely recognize the sexual exclusivity of other men and their partners and respect the bounds of a pairbond. If they did not, humans could not have transitioned to living in multi-level societies, where biological families exist within extended families, which exist within kin groups, and kin groups within communities.

While pairbonds and marriage are acknowledged in all societies, sex and parenthood are not necessarily restricted to marriage. In some societies, pre- and extra-marital relations must be clandestine because they are punishable transgressions if individuals are caught. In other cases, uncommitted sexual liaisons are socially permissible, which generally fall under two well-documented ethnographic contexts. The first occurs prior to first marriage when adolescent girls are in a life stage when they have a low probability of conceiving and are given freedom to explore different pre-marital relationships. For example, among the Makushi of Guyana, sexually mature adolescents engage in pre-marital sex,[24] an opportunity for young people to learn about mutual mate choice and to identify possible long-term mates. Once married, however, conventions abruptly shift, and sexual fidelity is generally expected.

Socially sanctioned sex outside marriage also occurs in the context of either partible paternity or spouse sharing under certain situations. For instance, among some lowland South American Indigenous groups, married women may have extra-marital partners.[25] This most commonly occurs where more than one man is perceived to contribute to a baby's development. While these relationships are not formalized through marriage, these non-spousal fathers customarily protect and invest in children. In other societies, both men and women may maintain several sexual partners at the same time. Historic ethnographic accounts of the Inuit (Arctic hunter-gatherers), for example, describe 'wife swapping' among monogamous couples.[26] Husbands and wives both consent to these relations, the duration of which varies, but often results in long-term social and sexual partnerships. In other cultural situations, extra-pair relationships are clandestine because of the

---

24 Ryan Schacht, 'Cassava and the Makushi: A Shared History of Resiliency and Transformation', in *Food and Identity in the Caribbean*, ed. H. Garth (London: Berg, 2013), 15–29.

25 Stephen Beckerman and Paul Valentine, eds., *Cultures of Multiple Fathers: The Theory and Practice of Partible Paternity in Lowland South America* (Gainesville, FL: University of Florida Press, 2002).

26 Arthur J. Rubel, *Partnership and Wife-Exchange among the Eskimo and Aleut of Northern North America* (Fairbanks, AK: University of Alaska Press, 1961).

threat of consequent penalties, violence, or ostracism if revealed. Even so, the ethnographic record has many examples of men willing to exchange resources for extra-marital sex. Although sex outside of marriage no doubt occurs to some extent in all societies, extra-pair paternity appears to be relatively low in human societies compared with other monogamous species. Estimates of non-paternity rates range from 0 to 11 per cent across human societies with median values falling between 1.7 and 3.3 per cent, while among monogamous birds these rates regularly exceed 20 per cent, and 5 per cent among mammals overall.[27]

In sum, a simple classification of a human-typical mating system would overly simplify the variety of pairing strategies observed. Monogamous, polyandrous, and polygynous marriages, as well as short-term sexual relationships, are found across contemporary human societies, with most societies exhibiting multiple kinds of marriages and mating relationships. What can be most simply distilled from this is that humans, generally, form long-term pairbonds. And while polygynous and polyandrous marriages are found in many societies, ethnographic evidence indicates that most individuals within a society live in monogamous marriages that are usually, but not always, sexually exclusive. It is important to emphasize that these unions are commonly serially monogamous and that this likely would have been the case in the past due to high rates of spousal mortality.

Parenting and Family Systems

The diversity of marriage and mating arrangements ultimately stems from a shared human reproductive biology and life history. Non-human great ape mothers nurse their young on average for four to six years. Comparatively, in societies without bottle feeding, mothers fully wean babies between the ages of two and three. This relatively young age at weaning results in shorter birth intervals (the time between births) compared with our closest primate relatives. Consequently, in natural fertility societies – those populations where women do not use birth control – children are spaced, on average, three years apart, a birth interval two to three times shorter than that of other great apes.[28]

27 Kermyt G. Anderson, 'How Well Does Paternity Confidence Match Actual Paternity?' *Current Anthropology* 47 (2006): 511–18.
28 Karen L. Kramer, 'How There Got to Be So Many of Us: The Evolutionary Story of Population Growth and a Life History of Cooperation', *Journal of Anthropological Research* 75, no. 4 (2019): 472–97.

Compared with close kin, human children are also more likely to survive. For example, in hunter-gatherer societies, a child is almost 40 per cent more likely to reach maturity than a chimpanzee juvenile.[29] Most explanations for the higher probability of survival point to the effects of caring for and provisioning children. Among other great apes, after weaning, food sharing is minimal between adults and offspring, and juveniles provision their own calories. Along the hominin line, a different life history strategy was favoured: infants were weaned earlier, but rather than fending for themselves, weanlings were fed by group members.

The combination of a fast reproductive pace and a good probability of children surviving commits human mothers to raising multiple dependents of different ages – something incredibly rare among non-human mothers. This pattern, which took millions of years to evolve, poses a time allocation and economic problem for mothers: how to find the time and resources to care for multiple dependents of different ages.[30] How this was solved, in many ways, sets human parenting apart and, ultimately, sent family formation on a trajectory distinct from other primates. How to support multiple dependents of different age shaped the central dilemma human mothers faced, to which the family, a small cooperative group, became a solution. Two divergent ideas about human parenting and family structure have developed, one focused on male parental care and the other on cooperative childrearing. While often presented as conflicting theories, they can be viewed as complementary means to support children.

With respect to male parental care, in few mammalian species do females and males parent together. The key limitations are paternity confidence – that is, a male's certainty that he is the father – and whether paternal care positively affects offspring outcomes. Consequently, habitual male care is typically associated with pairbonding, the combination of monogamy and fathering that occurs in only about 5 per cent of mammalian species. Although more common in the primate order, male parental care is not observed in chimpanzees and bonobos, species to whom humans are most closely related, and is uncommon in other great apes. At some point in the

---

29 Michael Gurven and Hillard Kaplan, 'Longevity among Hunter-Gatherers: A Cross-Cultural Examination', *Population and Development Review* 33, no. 2 (2007): 321–65.

30 Karen L. Kramer and Erik Otárola-Castillo, 'When Mothers Need Others: The Impact of Hominin Life History Evolution on Cooperative Breeding', *Journal of Human Evolution* 84 (2015): 16–24.

hominin line, fathering emerged, and while some posit that it is an ancient trait, its timing is ardently debated.

In some species, the need for male help is suggested to be the predominant pressure driving monogamy, and is a common argument made for humans. However, recent research makes a strong case that paternal investment is a consequence rather than a cause of the evolution of monogamy.[31] In fact, nearly half of monogamous mammals have no evidence of paternal care.

The investment of fathers in their offspring is well documented across human societies, and often argued to be a hallmark of family formation and human social evolution. While a division of labour between males and females is an efficient means to manage a household and raise young, how it comes about is disputed. Although fathers generally help little with childcare, they are important economic contributors in many societies.[32] In both traditional and industrialized societies, their help is linked to improved offspring survival and well-being.

As an evolutionary argument, the focus on male investment may oversimplify reasons why families formed in the first place. The division of labour argument overwhelmingly has emphasized men's specialization in hunting in foraging societies. But the contribution of meat to the diet is too highly variable across foraging societies to be broadly explanatory, and ignores the many other ways that the division of labour figures into daily lives. For example, among Savanna Pumé foragers, terrestrial game constitutes only about 5 per cent of the diet, and rather than being about meat, the division of labour is driven by the foods that women provide, such as fruit and roots, as well as food processing and other domestic tasks. Focus on the sexual division of labour as the impetus for family formation also overshadows the importance of the age division of labour, which is critical in incorporating older and younger generations into family groups,[33] and neglects the many individuals besides fathers who help with childrearing.

---

31 Dieter Lukas and Timothy H. Clutton-Brock, 'The Evolution of Social Monogamy in Mammals', *Science* 341 (2013): 526–30.

32 Karen L. Kramer and Amanda Veile, 'Infant Allocare in Traditional Societies', *Physiology and Behavior* 193 (2018): 117–26; Kim Hill and A. M Magdalena Hurtado, 'Cooperative Breeding in South American Hunter-Gatherers', *Proceedings of the Royal Society B: Biological Sciences* 276 (2009): 3863–70; Frank W. Marlowe, 'Hunting and Gathering: The Human Sexual Division of Foraging Labor', *Cross-Cultural Research* 41, no. 2 (2007): 170–95.

33 Karen L. Kramer, 'The Evolution of Human Parental Care and Recruitment of Juvenile Help', *Trends in Ecology and Evolution* 26, no. 10 (2011): 533–40.

Although male parental care is often assumed to be the basis for family formation, cooperative childrearing offers an alternative view. In many situations fathers of course do help mothers, though in a natural fertility society, where mothers may have six or more children, parents alone would find it difficult to meet their children's needs. In Maya families, for example, fathers spend as much time supporting children as do mothers. Even so, their work effort is insufficient to meet family consumption.[34] In the Maya case, their children help fill the gap. Recognition that others help mothers beside fathers – such as other children and other kin – led to an important recent shift in thinking about family systems.

Scholars refer to the reproductive and social system in which offspring are cared for by non-parental group members as cooperative breeding. Rather than focusing solely on the parent–child unit, a cooperative breeding framework is inclusive of the many caregivers who help mothers.[35] Across the ethnographic record, children are cared for and economically supported by a diverse range of people.[36] In addition to a woman's other children and her mother, aunts (usually mother's sisters), other relatives, and even nonrelatives provide care, food, shelter, and assistance to mothers and children. Children are well adapted to having a diversity of caretakers, which has a positive effect on their psychological and social abilities.[37] Because cooperative breeding is relatively rare – it is found in only 3 per cent of mammalian species – and because mothers are almost exclusively responsible for raising offspring in other great apes, cooperative childrearing marks a significant evolutionary departure in human reproductive and parenting strategies.

While shared parenting is a universal feature of human reproduction, the other individuals who help mothers besides fathers vary culturally, demographically, and situationally. Since Turke's seminal study among Micronesian

---

34 Karen L. Kramer, 'Does It Take a Family to Raise a Child?', in *Substitute Parents: Biological and Social Perspectives on Alloparenting in Human Societies*, ed. Gillian Bentley and Ruth Mace (New York: Berghahn Books, 2009), 77–99.

35 Sarah B. Hrdy, *Mother Nature: Maternal Instincts and How They Shape the Human Species* (New York: Pantheon Books, 1999); Paula K. Ivey, 'Cooperative Reproduction in Ituri Forest Hunter-Gatherers: Who Cares for Efe Infants?', *Current Anthropology* 41, no. 5 (2000): 856–66; Karen L. Kramer, 'Cooperative Breeding and Its Significance to the Demographic Success of Humans', *Annual Review of Anthropology* 39 (2010): 414–36; Ruth Mace and Rebecca Sear, 'Are Humans Cooperative Breeders?', in *Grandmotherhood: The Evolutionary Significance of the Second Half of Female Life*, ed. Eckart Voland, Athanasios Chasiotis, and Wulf Schiefenhövel (New Brunswick, NJ: Rutgers University Press, 2005), 143–60.

36 Karen L. Kramer, 'The Human Family: Its Evolutionary Context and Diversity', *Social Science* 10, no. 6 (2021): 1–17.

37 Judith M. Burkart, Sarah B. Hrdy, and Carel van Schaik, 'Cooperative Breeding and Human Cognitive Evolution', *Evolutionary Anthropology* 18 (2009): 175–86.

islanders first introduced humans as cooperative breeders, shared parenting has become a central explanation for the evolution of human life history and sociality.[38] Cooperative childrearing connects many behavioural, cognitive, and biological traits that are associated with the emergence of *Homo sapiens*, such as the age and gender division of labour, food sharing, the human pattern of growth and development, prosociality (behaviours intended to benefit others rather than oneself), and a long life span.

One key way in which mothers benefit from the help they receive is that it attenuates time constraints. For example, Maya mothers who raise large families only provide about 40 per cent of what their family consumes, and only about 50 per cent of infant care. The balance is met by the help of their children and husbands.[39] In managing the competing demands of supporting multiple dependents, mothers in many societies find the extra time to devote to young children, particularly nursing children, by downwardly adjusting the time they spend in other activities – foraging for food, time spent in agricultural work, domestic activities, or wage employment, depending on their livelihood. The help mothers receive also has a demonstrated positive effect on children's health, growth, and well-being.[40]

Although grandmothers, siblings, and fathers often are treated as mutually exclusive sources of help, they may be key at different points in the family life cycle, and under different ecological and demographic conditions. For example, early in a mother's reproductive career, when she has young children, both Savanna Pumé and Hadza women (both groups are hunter-gatherers from Venezuela and Tanzania, respectively) prefer to live in their natal camps with female relatives. They may shift to live near paternal kin as children grow up and benefit less from childcare and more from the food and other economic resources that male relatives can provide. Because both male and female labour and resources are important to human subsistence, there is strategic value for mothers to have access to a range of helpers.

In sum, recognition that others help mothers has led to an important shift in thinking about human reproductive systems not as exclusive units of parents and children living in nuclear families, but as cooperative networks in which

38 Paul W. Turke, 'Helpers at the Nest: Childcare Networks on Ifaluk', in *Human Reproductive Behavior: A Darwinian Perspective*, ed. Laura Betzig, Monique Borgerhoff Mulder, and Paul Turke (Cambridge: Cambridge University Press, 1988), 173–88. See also Hrdy, *Mother Nature*; Ivey, 'Cooperative Reproduction'; Kramer, 'Cooperative Breeding'; Mace and Sear, 'Are Humans Cooperative Breeders?'.

39 Karen L. Kramer, *Maya Children: Helpers at the Farm* (Cambridge, MA: Harvard University Press, 2005); Kramer and Veile, 'Infant Allocare'.

40 See Kramer, 'Cooperative Breeding'.

parenting is shared among many caregivers. What do helpers get out of it? Assured paternity for fathers, and for daughters or grandmothers, kin-selected benefits by leveraging their non-fertility into a higher reproductive potential for their mothers and daughters.[41]

Additional Noteworthy Aspects of Human Sexuality

Testosterone, a key hormone associated with differences between males and females, is responsible for the development of male secondary sexual characteristics, reproductive function, and behavioural profiles associated with mating, parenting, and competition. Consequent to the latter, testosterone is often implicated in aggression and violence. The 'challenge hypothesis' articulates this relationship and proposes that testosterone mediates the trade-off between the time and energy men devote to competition versus parenting.[42] Specifically, circulating levels of testosterone are thought to reflect the evolved hormonal regulation of male investment in mating versus parenting behaviours, which are sensitive to individual factors and local conditions. In humans, a feedback loop appears to have been selected in order to modulate testosterone levels in response to relationship status and men's exposure to young children. For example, a longitudinal study tracking Filipino men across time found that testosterone levels decline when men enter into committed relationships, and further decline with fatherhood.[43] Moreover, testosterone levels are associated with caregiving, and are lowest in men who spend the greatest amount of time caring for their children. A number of other studies corroborate these findings, collectively indicating that testosterone levels are associated with marital status, being lower among married men, and are lowest among men who provide paternal care.[44]

Across animal species, testosterone is also associated with aggression by males against females. Specifically, mate guarding is one key tactic that males

---

41 Karen L. Kramer and Andrew F. Russell, 'Kin-Selected Cooperation without Lifetime Monogamy: Human Insights and Animal Implications', *Trends in Ecology & Evolution* 29, no. 3 (2014): 600–6.

42 John C. Wingfield, 'The Challenge Hypothesis: Where It Began and Relevance to Humans', *Hormones and Behavior* 92 (2017): 9–12.

43 Lee T. Gettler, Thomas W. McDade, Alan B. Feranil, and Christopher W. Kuzawa, 'Longitudinal Evidence That Fatherhood Decreases Testosterone in Human Males', *Proceedings of the National Academy of Sciences* 108, no. 39 (2011): 16194–99.

44 Peter B. Gray, Sonya M. Kahlenberg, Emily S. Barrett, et al., 'Marriage and Fatherhood Are Associated with Lower Testosterone in Males', *Journal of Evolution and Human Behavior* 23, no. 3 (2002): 193–201; Martin N. Muller, Frank W. Marlowe, Revocatus Bugumba, and

Human Sexuality

employ to constrain female choice and defend their paternity certainty. While variable by species and locale, through mate guarding, males attempt to limit sexual access to females and control their movement. For those few mammalian species among whom males provide paternal care, infidelity is costly and males have evolved sophisticated anti-cuckoldry tactics to increase their certainty of paternity.

Following from the non-human literature, mate guarding is expected to be particularly pronounced in human societies where men invest in fathering, support spouses, and/or bequeath wealth and resources to spouses and children. Mate guarding takes a wide variety of forms, being quite muted in some societies while much more prevalent in others. Variation in the expression of mate guarding is correlated in large part with how wealth is accrued. In many hunter-gatherer societies, men do not accumulate asset wealth and women typically have autonomy in decisions about sexual activity, and who and when they marry. Marriage alliances are flexible, and both men and women can instigate divorce and remarriage. With the advent of agriculture and pastoralism, and consequent heritable and divisible forms of wealth (e.g., money, land), the historical record indicates that the reach of reproductive control over women was expanded. Depending on cultural norms or individual circumstances, men might control the ownership and flow of wealth and places where women and girls can go, how they dress, and who they associate with. They also might be concealed or secluded at puberty, be veiled, have separate eating and socializing places, or live in segregated structures or quarters. When extreme wealth was at stake, as among upper classes in the ancient Chinese, Greek, Aztec, and Incan empires, even more severely restrictive forms of control emerge (such as nunneries, foot binding, corseting), which themselves became symbols of purity, wealth, and status. Suitors favoured these qualities, and as a result, parents and families encouraged and enforced women's compliance. The extent to which men were either willing or able to enforce codes of extreme reproductive control was limited, however, to the very wealthy because few men or families could afford to have wives and daughters unable to engage in necessary economic activities (e.g., working in the fields, gathering food).

To better understand ancestral human sexuality and variation in marriage systems, this chapter has focused on heterosexuality as displayed both by our

Peter T. Ellison, 'Testosterone and Paternal Care in East African Foragers and Pastoralists', *Proceedings of the Royal Society, B: Biological Sciences* 276, no. 1655 (2009): 347–54.

closest relatives and across societies. While heterosexual marriage is the predominate form cross-culturally, homosexuality has existed throughout human history and has been noted in our closest genetic relatives.[45] In some societies, for example, homosexual behaviour is described as 'ritualized' and is expected for masculine development, and is practised willingly by men who also maintain heterosexual marriages.[46] In other societies, however, overt sexual behaviour between those of the same sex invites social sanctions, ostracism, legal action, imprisonment, or execution.[47] Common as well across societies are gender identities that allow individuals to adopt opposite gender roles, typically referred to as transgender, or to occupy a third or fourth gender, such as Indigenous two-spirits.[48]

An important point to highlight is that gender identity and sexual orientation are often inappropriately conflated. The former is, typically, the adoption of a social role and its associated behaviours, and the latter refers to physical attraction and sexual relationships. For example, marriage between women is documented in over forty pre-colonial African societies and permitted women to expand and strengthen their economic alliances, social status, rights, and authority.[49] Whether these were also sexual relationships is unknown. Likewise, two-spirit relationships in Indigenous North American societies describe a preference for men to perform women's social roles and tasks, rather than a desire for a particular type of sexual activity.

Moreover, while sexual orientation was traditionally thought of as binary, it is increasingly recognized that sexual orientation falls along a continuum. On one end is 'exclusive heterosexual orientation' and on the other end is 'exclusive homosexual orientation'.[50] For example, across nearly a century of study in the United States, research findings indicate that while 'exclusive

---

45 Evelyn Blackwood, ed., *Anthropology and Homosexual Behavior* (New York: Haworth, 1986).

46 Thomas M. Ernst, 'Onabasulu Male Homosexuality: Cosmology, Affect and Prescribed Male Homosexual Activity among the Onabasulu of the Great Papuan Plateau', *Oceania* 62, no. 1 (1991): 1–11; Gilbert H. Herdt, 'Ritualized Homosexual Behavior in the Male Cults of Melanesia, 1862–1983', in *Ritualized Homosexuality in Melanesia* (Berkeley, CA: University of California Press, 1984), 1–81.

47 Michael J. Maher, 'A Voice in the Wilderness: Gay and Lesbian Religious Groups in the Western United States', *Journal of Homosexuality* 51, no. 4 (2006): 91–117; Heather Simmons, 'Dying for Love: Homosexuality in the Middle East', *Human Rights and Human Welfare* (2014): 160–72.

48 Sandra E. Hollimon, 'Native American Two Spirits', in *The International Encyclopedia of Human Sexuality* (New York: John Wiley & Sons, 2015), 819–30.

49 Beth Greene, 'The Institution of Woman-Marriage in Africa: A Cross-Cultural Analysis', *Ethnology* 37, no. 4 (1998): 395–412.

50 Simon LeVay, *Gay, Straight, and the Reason Why: The Science of Sexual Orientation* (Oxford: Oxford University Press, 2010).

homosexuality' is rare, engagement in homosexual sex is not, particularly during adolescence.[51]

As a final point, homosexual behaviour is not limited to humans and is found across a wide variety of animal species. Among bonobos, for instance, both males and females regularly engage in homosexual sex, including fellatio and genital rubbing, with females engaging in these behaviours more frequently than males.[52] This research highlights the importance of sex for resolving disputes and strengthening social relationships, and offers insight into its role beyond conception in heterosexual relationships.

Conclusion

This chapter highlights the evolutionary backdrop that gave rise to the current range of human sexual and reproductive behaviours. Humans have a deep ancestry in a social structure of males and females living in social groups together. While today we likewise live in communities of multiple adult males and females, how humans organize themselves is structurally different from anything observed in our closest relatives. Not only do families form around long-term pairbonds in all societies, but there is also a great deal of flexibility in who constitutes the pairbond, the families that surround them, and in the prevalence of extra-pair relationships.

Further Reading

Anderson, Kermyt G. 'How Well Does Paternity Confidence Match Actual Paternity?' *Current Anthropology* 47 (2006): 511–18.

Beckerman, Stephen, and Paul Valentine, eds. *Cultures of Multiple Fathers: The Theory and Practice of Partible Paternity in Lowland South America.* Gainesville, FL: University of Florida Press, 2002.

Brown, Gillian R., Kevin N. Laland, and Monique Borgerhoff Mulder. 'Bateman's Principles and Human Sex Roles'. *Trends in Ecology and Evolution* 24 (2009): 297–304.

51 Robert E. Fay, Charles F. Turner, Albert D. Klassen, and John H. Gagnon, 'Prevalence and Patterns of Same-Gender Sexual Contact among Men', *Science* 243 (1989): 338–48. https://doi.org/10.1126/science.2911744.

52 Liza R. Moscovice, Martin Surbeck, Barbara Fruth et al., 'The Cooperative Sex: Sexual Interactions among Female Bonobos are Linked to Increases in Oxytocin, Proximity and Coalitions', *Hormones and Behavior* 116 (2019), https://doi.org/10.1016/j.yhbeh.2019.104581.

Buston, Peter M., and Stephen T. Emlen. 'Cognitive Processes Underlying Human Mate Choice: The Relationship between Self-perception and Mate Preference in Western Society'. *Proceedings of the National Academy of Sciences* 100, no. 15 (2003): 8805–10.

Chapais, Bernard. 'Monogamy, Strongly Bonded Groups, and the Evolution of Human Social Structure'. *Evolutionary Anthropology* 22 (2013): 52–65.

Primeval Kinship. Cambridge, MA: Harvard University Press, 2008.

Eagly, Alice H., and Wendy Wood. 'The Origins of Sex Differences in Human Behavior: Evolved Dispositions versus Social Roles'. *American Psychologist* 54 (1999): 408–23.

Ellis, Jackie, Chris Dowrick, and Mari Lloyd-Williams. 'The Long-term Impact of Early Parental Death: Lessons from a Narrative Study'. *Journal of the Royal Society of Medicine* 106, no. 2 (2013): 57–67.

Fromhage, Lutz, Mark A. Elgar, and Jutta M. Schneider. 'Faithful without Care: The Evolution of Monogyny'. *Evolution* 59 (2005): 1400–5.

Gray, Peter B., and Kermyt G. Anderson. *Fatherhood: Evolution and Human Paternal Behavior*. Cambridge, MA: Harvard University Press, 2010.

Gurven, Michael, and Kim Hill. 'Why Do Men Hunt? A Reevaluation of "Man the Hunter" and the Sexual Division of Labor'. *Current Anthropology* 50 (2009): 51–74. https://doi.org/10.1086/595620.

Guttentag, Marcia, and Paul Secord. *Too Many Women?* Beverly Hills, CA: Sage, 1983.

Hrdy, Sarah B. *Mothers and Others: The Evolutionary Origins of Mutual Understanding*. Cambridge, MA: Harvard University Press, 2009.

Kinsey, Alfred C., Wardell. B. Pomeroy, Clyde E. Martin, and Paul M. Gebhard. *Sexual Behavior in the Human Female*. Philadelphia: W. B. Saunders, 1953.

Kramer, Karen L. 'Cooperative Breeding and Its Significance to the Demographic Success of Humans'. *Annual Review of Anthropology* 39 (2010): 414–36.

Kramer, Karen L., and A. F. Russell. 'Was Monogamy a Key Step on the Hominin Road? Reevaluation of the Monogamy Hypothesis in the Evolution of Cooperative Breeding'. *Evolutionary Anthropology* 24 (2015): 73–83.

Kramer, Karen L., R. Schacht, and A. Bell. 'Adult Sex Ratios and Partner Scarcity among Hunter-Gatherers: Implications for Dispersal Patterns and the Evolution of Human Sociality'. *Philosophical Transactions of the Royal Society, B: Biological Sciences* 372, no. 1729 (2017). https://doi.org/10.1098/rstb.2016.0316.

Lancaster, Jane B., Hillard Kaplan, Kim Hill, and A. Magdalena. Hurtado. 'The Evolution of Life History, Intelligence and Diet among Chimpanzees and Human Foragers'. In *Perspectives in Ethology: Evolution, Culture and Behavior*, Vol. 13, ed. Francois Tonneau and Nicholas S. Thompson, 47–72. New York: Kluwer Academic, 2000.

Masquelier, Adeline. 'Nomads Who Cultivate Beauty: Wo'daa'be Dances and Visual Arts'. *International Journal of African Historical Studies* 35 (2002): 157–9. https://doi.org/10.2307/3097380.

Schacht, Ryan, and Adrian V. Bell. 'The Evolution of Monogamy in Response to Partner Scarcity'. *Scientific Reports* 6, no. 1 (2016): 1–9.

Schacht, Ryan, and Karen L. Kramer. 'Are We Monogamous? A Review of the Evolution of Pair-bonding in Humans and its Contemporary Variation Cross-culturally'. *Frontiers in Ecology and Evolution* 7 (2019): Article 230.

'Patterns of Family Formation in Response to Sex Ratio'. *PLOS ONE* 11, no. 8 (2016). https://doi.org/10.1371/journal.pone.0160320.

Schacht, Ryan, Huong Meeks, Alison Fraser, and Ken R. Smith. 'Was Cinderella Just a Fairy Tale? Survival Differences between Stepchildren and Their Half-siblings'. *Philosophical Transactions of the Royal Society B* 376, no. 1827 (2021): 20200032.

Sear, Rebecca, and Ruth Mace. 'Who Keeps Children Alive? A Review of the Effects of Kin on Child Survival'. *Evolution and Human Behavior* 29 (2008): 1–18.

Smuts, Barbara B., and Robert W. Smuts. 'Male Aggression and Sexual Coercion of Females in Nonhuman Primates and Other Mammals: Evidence and Theoretical Implications'. *Advances in the Study of Behavior* 22 (1993): 1–63.

Starkweather, Katherine E. 'Shodagor Family Strategies'. *Human Nature*, 28, no. 2 (2017): 138–66.

Tovee, Martin J., Viren Swami, Adrian Furnham, and Roshila Mangalparsad. 'Changing Perceptions of Attractiveness as Observers are Exposed to a Different Culture'. *Evolution and Human Behavior* 27 (2006): 443–56.

2

Sexuality in Ancient Egypt: Pleasures, Desires, Norms, and Representations

UROŠ MATIĆ

The meanings ascribed to sex in ancient Egypt, and the gender power relations that regulated them, differed significantly from period to period. There were many changes from what is usually seen as the 'beginning' of ancient Egypt with the development of a state and the appearance of a script *c.* 3200 BCE, to its 'ending', variously defined as transformation into a Roman province (30 BCE), Christianization (33 CE to the fourth century CE), or the Arab conquest (646 CE). The number and the background of the sources are very different in specific periods, with access to many sources limited by the long history of the censorship of erotica and archaeological finds ending up in private collections.[1]

Discussions in the field of Egyptology seem to focus on very specific topics, such as sex in the creation myths (cosmogonies), sex and fertility, 'love' poetry, festival sex, prostitution, and same-sex desire.[2] Taking inspiration from the late works of Michel Foucault, Lynn Meskell has argued that 'sexuality did not exist as a discursive category in New Kingdom Egypt' and she adds that 'sex was a practice rather than a discourse'.[3] She further notes that there was no word for sexuality, which is true, and in her opinion this is not surprising considering that sexuality is 'a specific

---

1 Philippe Collombert and Youri Volokhine, '*De Aegyptiacis rebus doctorum verecundia* ou "Let's Talk About Sex!"', *Egypte, Afrique et Orient* 40 (2005): 45–56.
2 Charlotte Booth, *In Bed with the Ancient Egyptians* (Stroud, UK: Amberley, 2015); Lise Manniche, *Sexual Life in Ancient Egypt* (London: KPI, 1987); Karol Myśliwiec, *Eros on the Nile*, trans. Geoffrey L. Packer (1998; London: Duckworth, 2004).
3 Lynn M. Meskell, 'Re-em(bed)ding Sex: Domesticity, Sexuality, and Ritual in New Kingdom Egypt', in *Archaeologies of Sexuality*, ed. Robert A. Schmidt and Barbara L. Voss (London: Routledge, 2000), 253–62, at 253, 261.

Western construction'.[4] Yet there were no words in ancient Egyptian for many phenomena that Egyptologists argue to have existed, such as art, religion, or decorum. Furthermore, when certain words are translated into modern languages, they are associated with meanings that they did not necessarily convey originally. For example, we associate the word 'love' with romantic feeling, an experience of 'loving someone', but as argued by several Egyptologists, this is not what ancient Egyptians meant with the word *mri* 'to love'. They understood 'love' as being 'something *forced* on someone by the obvious qualities of someone else'.[5]

Meskell has argued that sexual regimes such as 'bodily controls, medicalized practices and so on' highlighted by Foucault in his analyses of Greek and Roman sexualities did not exist in ancient Egypt as 'strictly articulated discourses'.[6] No one has actually explored this question thoroughly yet, however. If we understand discourses as 'practices that systematically form the objects of which they speak',[7] then sex discourses did exist in ancient Egypt, as I will demonstrate throughout this chapter. For example, there are examples in Demotic (first millennium BCE ancient Egyptian script) papyri of medicalized practices in which male discourse of the female body is presented through magico-medical practices, dealing with different aspects of female sexuality.[8] Thus, following Giulia Sissa, in this rather short overview of a complex topic I will attempt to 'abandon the clichéd language of sexuality and start talking about, on the one hand, sex – in order to capture ancient materialism – and, on the other, sensuality – if we are to grasp the full range of attitudes the ancients adopted in relation to *eros*'.[9]

---

4 Lynn M. Meskell, *Archaeologies of Social Life: Age, Sex, Class et cetera in Ancient Egypt* (Oxford: Blackwell, 1999), 97.
5 Gerald Moers, 'Why "the" Egyptians Never Said I Love You', in *Sex and the Golden Goddess*. Vol. 2: *World of the Love Songs*, ed. Hana Navrátilová and Renata Landgráfová (Prague: Czech Institute of Egyptology, 2015), 61–70.
6 Meskell, *Archaeologies of Social Life*, 96.
7 Michel Foucault, *The Archaeology of Knowledge*, trans. A. M. Sheridan Smith (1969; London: Routledge, 2002), 54.
8 Demotic papyrus Berlin P 13602, from the end of the first century BCE or beginning of the first century CE. Alexandra von Lieven and Joachim Friedrich Quack, 'Ist Liebe eine Frauenkrankheit? Papyrus Berlin 13602, ein gynäkomagisches Handbuch', in *Hieratic, Demotic and Greek Studies and Text Editions: Of Making Many Books There Is No End: Festschrift in Honour of Sven P. Vleeming*, ed. Koenraad Donker van Heel, Franscisca A. J. Hoogendijk, and Cary J. Martin (Leiden: Brill, 2018), 257–74.
9 Giulia Sissa, *Sex and Sexuality in the Ancient World*, trans. George Staunton (1996; New Haven, CT: Yale University Press, 2008), 6.

UROŠ MATIĆ

Ars Erotica? Desire and Pleasure in Ancient Egypt

What was considered desirable and for whom? Several authors have already emphasized that beginning with the Old Kingdom (*c.* 2543–2120 BCE) representations of sexual power in ancient Egypt contrasted the clothed male body and the naked and revealed female body.[10] This assertion, although correct in general terms, has to be observed contextually. Children of both sexes are more often than not depicted nude, and some men, such as workers and fishermen, are also depicted nude in scenes from private tombs.[11] Libyan enemies are depicted with their penises visible but flaccid. This is related to their feminization in Egyptian texts and to their actual mutilation in war, when Egyptians sometimes cut off the shafts of their penises.[12] Therefore, a nude or partly revealed body is not always a desired body; the context determines the meaning of nudity.

One Thirteenth Dynasty (*c.* 1759–1630 BCE) papyrus mentions twenty young women who have not yet given birth (*nfr.wt*) and twenty fishnets brought to them to wear instead of clothes, which would visually please the king. In fact, dresses made out of bead-nets are known as well.[13] New Kingdom (*c.* 1539–1077 BCE) 'love' poems inform us about the desirable female body from a very specific male perspective, as the protagonists of these poems can be described as unmarried adolescents.[14] One Twentieth Dynasty (1190–1077 BCE) love poem describes the beloved woman as long of neck, luminous of chest, with hair of true lapis, arms of gold, and fingers like lotuses.[15] Another New Kingdom poem describes a woman imagining how she is bathing in front of her desired lover, wearing a dress of the finest

---

10 Gay Robins, 'Male Bodies and the Construction of Masculinity in New Kingdom Egyptian Art', in *Servant of Mut: Studies in Honor of Richard A. Fazzini*, ed. Sue D'Auria (Leiden: Brill, 2008), 208–15; Lynn M. Meskell and Rosemary A. Joyce, *Embodied Lives: Figuring Ancient Maya and Egyptian Experiences* (London: Routledge, 2003), xvii.

11 Julia Asher-Greve and Deborah Sweeney, 'On Nakedness, Nudity, and Gender in Egyptian and Mesopotamian Art', in *Images and Gender: Contributions to the Hermeneutics of Reading Ancient Art*, ed. Silvia Schroer (Fribourg: Academic Press and Göttingen: Vandenhoeck & Ruprecht, 2006), 125–76.

12 Amarna period (*c.* 1353–1334 BCE) papyrus British Museum EA74100 and reliefs of Medinet Habu temple of Ramesses III (1187–1157 BCE) depict Libyan enemies with penises in a flaccid state. Uroš Matić, *Body and Frames of War in New Kingdom Egypt: Violent Treatments of Enemies and Prisoners* (Wiesbaden: Harrassowitz, 2019), 61, 149.

13 Papyrus Westcar. Rosalind Janssen, 'Ancient Egyptian Erotic Fashion: Fishnet Dresses', *Kmt: A Modern Journal of Ancient Egypt* 6, no. 4 (1995–6): 41–7.

14 Deborah Sweeney, 'Gender and Language in the Ramesside Love Songs', *Bulletin of the Egyptological Seminar* 16 (2002): 27–50, at 32.

15 First 'love' poem of Papyrus Chester Beatty I Group A (No. 31). John C. Darnell, 'The Rituals of Love in Ancient Egypt: Festival Songs of the Eighteenth Dynasty and the Ramesside Love Poetry', *Die Welt des Orients* 46 (2016): 22–61, at 28.

royal linen, drenched with fragrant unguent.[16] One Late Period stela, an inscription in honour of a princess Mutirdis dating around 700 BCE, informs us that hair blacker than the black of night, teeth whiter than gypsum and fibres of flax (?), and breasts set firm on the bosom were considered attractive in women.[17] Therefore, we can indeed speak of a *longue durée* of an ideal female beauty, though we should not forget that this is a product of the tastes of literate Egyptian elite.

Not only unmarried adolescents enjoyed the poems and not only they desired the bodies described in them. Married and older people could also have heard the poems, as they were performed in front of an audience.[18] They could have directly influenced people to conform to beauty ideals propagated in the poems. Thus, contrary to Meskell's view, there were discourses in ancient Egypt that regulated bodies and desires, although, interestingly, we are not informed much in texts about the desirable male body.

How was pleasure achieved, where, and by whom? The term 'sexscape' describes 'making sense of the spatialities, mobilities and regulation of sex, sexuality and/or commercialized sex'.[19] Different people used different sexscapes, dependent on the actors and the contexts. According to Charlotte Booth, the ancient Egyptian houses excavated at sites such as Tell el-Amarna (Amarna period), Deir el-Medina (New Kingdom), and El Lahun (Late Middle Kingdom, *c.* 1939–1760 BCE) were overcrowded, which indicates that ancient attitudes were different from modern ones so that 'sex was not something performed in seclusion but through stolen moments and opportunity' and that 'sex was not a particularly private event in Ancient Egypt'.[20] Sex could certainly have happened in stolen moments and opportunity, but the idea that it was not performed in seclusion is overly generalist and erroneous. For example, the protagonists of the previously mentioned 'love' poems are in many cases not able to fulfil their desires because their

---

16 Ostracon Cairo 25218 (8–14, A, 3). Renata Landgráfová and Hana Navrátilová, *Sex and the Golden Goddess*. Vol. 1: *Ancient Egyptian Love Songs in Context* (Prague: Agama, 2009), 178.

17 Joachim Friedrich Quack, 'Where Once Was Love, Love Is No More? What Happens to Expressions of Love in Late Period Egypt?' *Die Welt des Orients* 46 (2016): 62–89, at 64–5.

18 Heidi Köpp-Junk, 'The Artist behind the Ancient Egyptian Love Songs: Performance and Technique', in *Sex and the Golden Goddess*, Vol. 2, ed. Navrátilová and Landgráfová, 35–60.

19 Paul J. Maginn and Christine Steinmetz, 'Spatial and Regulatory Contours of the (Sub) urban Sexscape', in *(Sub)urban Sexscapes: Geographies and Regulation of the Sex Industry*, ed. Paul J. Maginn and Christine Steinmetz (London: Routledge, 2015), 1–16, at 1.

20 Booth, *In Bed with the Ancient Egyptians*, 15.

beloved is at home surrounded by relatives and they could not have the privacy they wanted.[21]

'Love' poetry in many cases contextualises erotic encounters in marshy and bucolic environments such as festive orchards or booths, tents, or beer huts.[22] This is certainly connected to the motif of the Sun Eye goddess (see following section) returning and appearing in a marshy setting. In one New Kingdom 'love' poem, the place of encounter between the lovers is a marsh in which the girl hunts birds that she is supposed to bring to her mother; instead, she comes back empty handed after being captivated by the love of her desired man.[23] Some of the 'love' poems use architectural and spatial images tied to settlements and houses. The lover's house is desired, and the opening of the house is the desired but unfulfilled outcome, either because the lover's siblings are there or because the bolt keeps the door closed. Furthermore, some metaphors, such as opened 'double doors' or fluid entering 'her gate', refer to a vagina.[24] The first story of Setne, a Demotic text from the Ptolemaic period (305–30 BCE, when Egypt was ruled by the Macedonian Greek dynasty of the Ptolemies) informs us that the street was one of the places where flirtatious encounters could have occurred. Setne meets Tabubu in the street, and offers her a substantial sum to spend an hour with him.[25] In a second century BCE graffito from the temple of Amun-Re at Karnak, the writer threatens to anally penetrate a certain Ptolemaios in the street.[26] We can only imagine that this threat was aiming at diminishing the status of Ptolemaios in the eyes of many.

Procession as a place of encounter is attested in a papyrus from the late first or early second century CE, involving a priest of the god Horus of Pe and

---

21 Steve Vinson, 'Behind Closed Doors: Architectural and Spatial Images and Metaphors in Ancient Egyptian Erotic Poetic and Narrative Literature', in *Sex and the Golden Goddess*, Vol. 2, ed. Navrátilová and Landgráfová, 121–44.

22 Darnell, 'The Rituals of Love'.

23 Papyrus Harris 500 (Recto 4,1–6,2). Alexandra von Lieven, 'Papyrus Harris 500 Recto 4,1–6,2', in *Peregrinations avec Erhart Graefe: Festschrift zu seinem 75. Geburtstag*, ed. Anke Ilona Blöbaum, Marianne Eaton-Krauss, and Annik Wüthrich (Münster: Zaphon, 2018), 317–32, at 319–20.

24 Renata Landgráfová, 'Breaches of Cooperative Rules: Metaphors and Parody in Ancient Egyptian Love Songs', in *Sex and Gender in Ancient Egypt: 'Don your wig for a joyful hour'*, ed. Carolyn Graves-Brown (Swansea: Classical Press of Wales, 2008), 71–82; Vinson, 'Behind Closed Doors'.

25 Quack, 'Where Once Was Love', 66–7.

26 Tom Sapsford, 'The Wages of Effeminacy? *Kinaidoi* in Greek Documents from Egypt', *Eugesta* 5 (2015): 103–23, at 118.

Nebese and the daughter of a priest of the goddess Neith.[27] A river in which a woman takes a bath is also attested as a place of encounter on one papyrus from 50–150 CE.[28] The battlefield as a place of encounter between lovers (Prince Petekhons and Serpot, Queen of the Amazons) is also attested in a papyrus from *c.* 50 CE, although the story is entirely fictional.[29] All these places are not the places where sex occurs, however, but rather where attraction is communicated. There are also stories that tell us where sex happens. The wife of the priest Webaoner, in a story from Papyrus Westcar, commits adultery in a pavilion specially prepared for that in her own garden.[30] In the Story of Petese, son of Peletum, from the late first or early second century CE, the mother of a young man dared to commit adultery with a soldier in her own home, although she was caught in the act by her son.[31]

The introduction of public bathhouses in Ptolemaic and Roman Egypt[32] brought new sexscapes, as evidenced by erotic figurines found in them possibly indicating sexual activities, such as those from a bathhouse in the city of Athribis during the reign of Ptolemy VI (186–145 BCE).[33] Bathhouses of Ptolemaic and Roman period Egypt separated male and female spaces, or had different times of access to the bathhouse for different genders.[34] Thus bathhouses were often places of same-sex encounters. In the Roman world bathhouses were spaces where normative Roman male-to-male sexuality could be subverted, and age or class background played less of a role.[35] (For

---

27 Papyrus Carlsberg 165 (x+8?, 4–30); Quack, 'Where Once Was Love, 67.

28 Papyrus Carlsberg 459+PSI Inv. D52; Quack, 'Where Once Was Love', 67.

29 Papyrus Vindobona D6165 and 6165a. These Amazons are the same supposed ethnic group as described by the ancient Greeks, transmitted from their cultural traditions to Ptolemaic Egypt. The names Petekhons and Serpot correspond to Achilles and Penthesilea. Quack, 'Where Once Was Love', 67.

30 Marc Orriols-Llonch. 'Women's Role in Sexual Intercourse in Ancient Egypt', in *Women in Antiquity: Real Women across the Ancient World*, ed. Stephanie Lynn Budin and Jean MacIntosh Turfa (London: Routledge, 2016), 194–203, at 195–6.

31 Papyrus Carlsberg 165, x+6, 22–30; Quack, 'Where Once Was Love', 67.

32 Thibaud Fournet and Béragère Redon, 'Bathing in the Shadow of the Pyramids: Greek Baths in Egypt, Back to an Original Bath Model', in *Collective Baths in Egypt. Vol. 2: New Discoveries and Perspectives*, ed. Béragère Redon (Cairo: Institut français d'archéologie orientale, 2017), 99–137.

33 Myśliwiec, *Eros on the Nile*, xv–xvi; Karol Myśliwiec, *The Twilight of Ancient Egypt: First Millennium B.C.E.* (Ithaca, NY: Cornell University Press, 2000), 202–3.

34 Monika Trümper, 'Gender-Differentiation in Greek Public Baths', in *Spa sanitas per aquam: Tagungsband des Internationalen Frontius-Symposiums zur Technik-und Kulturgeschichte der antiken Thermen, Aachen, 18.-22. März 2009*, ed. Ralf Kreiner and Wolfram Letzner (Leuven: Peeters, 2012), 37–46.

35 A. Asa Eger, 'Age and Male Sexuality: "Queer Space" in the Roman Bathhouse?', *Journal of Roman Archaeology* 65 (2007): 131–52.

more on Roman norms about sex, see Chapter 2 by Aven McMaster in Volume III of this work.) Furthermore, as indicated by a third century CE lead tablet with a magical spell from Hermopolis in Middle Egypt, bathhouses were imagined as places where women could burn in desire for other women, as in the case of Gorgonia who desired Sophia and wanted to enchant her.[36] We can also only assume that despite rules separating the sexes, in stolen moments and given the opportunity, those who were not married or married people who engaged in sex with people other than their spouse could have used bathhouses to fulfil sexual desires. The new sexscapes of Ptolemaic and Roman Egypt probably challenged the notion of clear-cut differences between Egyptian, Hellenic, and Roman sex.[37]

The Use of Pleasure: Public Sex and Festivals

One sexscape emerged during religious festivals, especially those celebrating the return of the Sun Eye goddess. According to the Myth of the Sun Eye, the daughter of Re (Sun Eye) fled her father to the far south and/or far west and was returned by a monkey, the god Thoth in disguise. She is transformed from the enraged lion-goddess Sekhmet into the pacified cat-goddess Bastet or the goddess Hathor. To celebrate the return of the goddess, ancient Egyptians organized festivals in which drunkenness, dance, and sexual intercourse were ways of honouring the goddess.[38]

A hall of drunkenness is known from the Eighteenth Dynasty (c. 1539–1292 BCE) temple of Mut at Karnak.[39] Such halls are also attested in later periods, as are sexually charged encounters taking place in them between people intoxicated with alcohol, music, and the festival atmosphere. Just as some people were born in temples in various myths and legends, others were conceived in their vicinity.[40] How these festivals looked is indicated by a depiction on one

---

36 PSI I 28. Dominic Montserrat, *Sex and Society in Graeco-Roman Egypt* (London: Routledge, 1996), 158.

37 See Tatiana Ivleva and Rob Collins, eds., *Un-Roman Sex: Gender, Sexuality, and Lovemaking in the Roman Provinces and Frontiers* (London: Routledge, 2020).

38 Alexandra von Lieven, 'Wein, Weib und Gesang – Rituale für die Gefährliche Göttin', in *Rituale in der Vorgeschichte, Antike und Gegenwart: Neue Forschungen und Perspektiven von Archäologie, Ägyptologie, Altorientalistik, Ethnologie und vergleichender Religionsgeschichte, Interdisziplinäre Tagung vom 1.-2. Februar 2002 in Berlin*, ed. Cornelia Metzner-Nebelsick (Leidorf: Rahden 2003), 47–55.

39 Betsy M. Bryan, 'Hatshepsut and Cultic Revelries in the New Kingdom', in *Creativity and Innovation in the Reign of Hatshepsut: Papers from the Theban Workshop 2010*, ed. José M. Galán, Betsy M. Bryan, and Peter F. Dorman. (Chicago: Oriental Institute of the University of Chicago, 2010), 93–124.

40 Darnell, 'The Rituals of Love in Ancient Egypt'.

Late Period steatite bowl where a procession of figures who play musical instruments approaches a columned building. One of the female figures slaps her buttocks, and between the two lotus-formed columns is a depiction of the face of goddess Hathor. On the bowl is a Demotic text indicating a connection to the lord of the city of Coptos, the god Min.[41]

A Demotic papyrus from early second century CE from the city of Tebtunis also informs us about sexual intercourses happening during the feasts of drunkenness for the goddess Bastet.[42] In the mid-fifth century BCE, the Greek historian Herodotus describes the festival of Bastet and how on their way to Bubastis in the eastern delta, men and women go in large numbers in boats. Some women play rattles and pipes, and other women and men sing and clap their hands. Whenever they come near to any town, they get close to the riverbank; some shout, mocking the women of the town, and others stand up and expose their genitals. When they reach Bubastis, they make sacrifices and drink more wine than in the whole rest of the year.[43] Religious festivals seem to be a sexscape that continued over a long time.

The Economy of Sex: Prostitution in Ancient Egypt

Most of the secure evidence for prostitution comes from Ptolemaic and Roman Egypt. This is because for the earlier periods scholars struggle with the proper translation of some words and their interpretation.

The word *ḥnm.t* (plural *ḥnm.wt*) is often translated as 'prostitute'. It is attested in a papyrus of the Nineteenth Dynasty (1292–1191 BCE) in which it is said that one's ear is death because of pleasures, but his heart lives with *ḥnm.wt* whom he took for friends.[44] Another New Kingdom papyrus mentions potential death causes, and among them death through a *ḥnm.t*.[45] In a passage of a hymn for the enthronement of the pharaoh Ramesses IV (1156–1150 BCE) from an ostracon (a piece of pottery with writing on it), it is stated that *ḥnm.wt* are

---

41 British Museum (No. 47992); A. F. Shore, 'A Rare Example of Dedicatory Inscription in Early Demotic', *British Museum Quarterly* 29, nos. 1/2 (1964–5): 19–21.

42 Papyrus Carlsberg 69+PSI D99+Papyrus Tebtunis Tait 10+ Papyrus British Museum 10861. Papyrus Vienna D 4869 (x+2, 1–16) (after the second century CE) also describes a sexual encounter during the feast of Bastet. Joachim Friedrich Quack, 'Herodot, Strabo und die Pallakide von Theben', in *Tempelprostitution im Altertum: Fakten und Fiktionen*, ed. Tanja Scheer and Martin Lindner (Berlin: Antike, 2009), 154–82.

43 Manniche, *Sexual Life*, 10.

44 Papyrus Anastasi V (17, 4–5); Quack, 'Herodot, Strabo und die Pallakide'.

45 Turin PR (121, 10); Quack, 'Herodot, Strabo und die Pallakide'.

shouting as they tune their cheering.[46] In a speech of the goddess Isis to the god Osiris, from the supplementary chapter of the *Book of the Dead*, she says that his phallus is in *ḥnm.wt*. According to Joachim Friedrich Quack, the word here includes a determinative – a hieroglyph that more closely explains or classifies the words in which they are written – with a phallus sign, which could indicate the activities of these women.[47] Egyptian texts contrast *ḥnm.wt* and widows to married women, so perhaps one should think of *ḥnm.wt* as women who are like *hetairai* of classical Athens – mobile, independent, sexually available women who charge for sex, thus the opposite of the controlled wife – *gyne* in Greek.

The evidence about the sale of sex from Ptolemaic and Roman Egypt is more secure. The Greek words used to describe prostitutes in Egypt are *porne*, *paidiske*, and *hetaira*, with the differences between them not being as clear-cut as in, for example, classical Athens. (For more on sex in classical Athens, see Chapter 1 by James Robson in Volume III of this work.) *Hetaira* is a term used for Irene and Thaïs, royal mistresses of Ptolemy I (367–283 BCE), and Hippe, the mistress of Ptolemy IV (244–204 BCE), but because of their connections with the ruler these women should be differentiated from other women designated as *hetaira*. The offer of Setne to Tabubu to pay for pleasure, attested in the first story of Setne mentioned earlier, confirms that such arrangements were possible. One papyrus from the town of Fayum, dated to 265 CE, indicates that some enslaved women worked in brothels run by men.[48] The Romans introduced a tax on prostitutes, the principal innovation of Roman rule in terms of the sale of sex. We do not have evidence for it before 65 CE, after which it was paid annually by prostitutes in Upper Egypt; the amount was 4 drachmas. Collectors also took fees from prostitutes, granting them special official permissions to engage in prostitution on a specified day, perhaps at a festival.[49] We have seen that festivals were occasions when sexual activity was celebrated by many.

Contrary to the common Orientalist trope, there is no evidence for temple or sacred prostitution in ancient Egypt. There are certainly no Egyptian sources that would indicate this, and the only reference to its existence is

---

46 Ostracon Turin 57001. Quack, 'Herodot, Strabo und die Pallakide'.
47 The supplementary chapter was numbered 162 by Willem Pleyte. See Quack, 'Herodot, Strabo und die Pallakide'.
48 Papyrus PSI IX 1055a. Montserrat, *Sex and Society in Graeco-Roman Egypt*, 107–9.
49 Roger S. Bagnall, 'A Trick a Day to Keep the Tax Man at Bay? The Prostitute Tax in Roman Egypt', *Bulletin of the American Society of Papyrologists* 28 (1991): 5–12; C. A. Nelson, 'Receipt for Tax on Prostitutes', *Bulletin of the American Society of Papyrologists* 32, nos. 1/2 (1995): 23–33, at 31.

found in the writings of the Greek geographer Strabo, who describes a consecration of one of the most beautiful girls of a most illustrious family to the temple of Zeus in Thebes (Amon temple). She is referred to as *pallacide*, meaning a woman consecrated to a god, and has intercourse with whomever she wishes until the purification of her body takes place, that is, until menstruation. After this she is given in marriage to a man. However, no payment is mentioned and the function of the girl as *pallacide* is temporary.[50]

Representations of Sexual Intercourse, or Rather the Lack of Them

Compared with other cultures, ancient Egypt did not produce numerous representations of sex. There are no such depictions from known elite palaces and houses, no such images on pottery, no such images among small finds such as cosmetic vessels or jewellery. Sex acts are completely absent from state-sponsored art such as temples or palaces. There are not many depictions of sexual intercourse in non-elite contexts either. The representations of the sex acts of deities related to creation are known,[51] but these should not be confused with the representation of sex between humans. Therefore, the assertion that ritual and sexual were not separate spheres has to be contextualized.[52] We have seen that sex was part of festival celebrations in honour of certain goddesses, but that does not mean that sex was part of every festival.

The rare representations of sex are found in the visual culture of commoners that was not sponsored by the state. There is one possible hieroglyph (actually now erased) from the Middle Kingdom, depicting a man and a woman on a bed presumably having sex.[53] The rest of the known depictions are a handful of New Kingdom ostraca with depictions of male–female intercourse or graffiti and the famous Papyrus Turin 55001, about which more in the following text. Later in the Ptolemaic and Roman period there are figurines of men with giant penises and women with spread legs with

---

50 Quack, 'Herodot, Strabo und die Pallakide', 172–4.

51 Atum masturbating on a relief from the temple of Darius at Kharga oasis; Isis in form of a falcon flying around the penis of dead Osiris, temple of Seti I, 1290–1279 BCE, Abydos. Myśliwiec, *Eros on the Nile*, 21.

52 Meskell, *Archaeologies of Social Life*, 102; Lynn Meskell, *Private Life in New Kingdom Egypt* (Princeton, NJ: Princeton University Press, 2002), 115; Meskell and Joyce, *Embodied Lives*, 104.

53 Tomb 140 of Khety at Beni Hasan. Collombert and Volokhine, 'De Aegyptiacis rebus', 49–50.

clearly indicated vaginas, and also male–female couples having sex.[54] Coitus *a tergo* between a man and a woman is depicted on ostraca and on a graffito that is difficult to date, although it is not always clear if it is vaginal or anal.[55] The missionary position is depicted on an ostracon from the Egyptian Museum in Cairo and on another ostracon found in the tomb of Puimre. Here we observe more intimacy, including touching and kissing.[56]

The Late New Kingdom Papyrus Turin 55001 is an exception as to the choice of the medium and the complexity of the erotic representations. Instead of depicting one couple, as on the ostraca or graffiti, here either one couple is depicted repeatedly in different positions or several couples are depicted simultaneously. The heavily damaged papyrus is over eight feet long, and shows twelve different sexual positions. Among the positions are coitus *a tergo*, with the woman on a chariot, bent and with her arms and head to the ground resembling depictions of goddess Nut and the man holding her hair as if he is holding the harness; the missionary position, in which the man stands and penetrates the woman he holds or the woman sits on a chair and inserts the penis of the man herself. One position depicts the man on the ground and the woman on top, with both resembling the god Geb and the goddess Nut in cosmogonic scenes. Egyptologists do not agree on the interpretation of individual figures nor on the overall interpretation of the papyrus. Whereas some interpret the men as having different occupations, such as soldiers, others interpret them all as priests or more specifically as priests of Hathor; the women are interpreted either as prostitutes from a brothel or as priestesses of Hathor impersonating various goddesses or women in a festival.[57]

Although sex acts other than those related to cosmogonies are not depicted in state-sponsored art, there are depictions that allude to sex. This is the case with the divine birth cycle, a sequence of images and texts central to which is the birth of the divine king and the child god. The divine king is fathered by the main god, Ra or Amun (depending on the period), and a human woman, wife of the ruling king. There are fifteen known attestations of the divine birth cycle from the Old Kingdom to the Roman period, with changes over time that have to be acknowledged and interpreted in their

---

54 Myśliwiec, *Eros on the Nile*, 54, 74, 121–4.
55 Graffito on the east wall of the tomb 504 at Deir el-Bahari. Christine Hue-Arcé, 'Les graffiti érotiques de la tombe 504 de Deir el-Bahari revisités', *Bulletin de l'Institut français d'archéologie orientale* 113 (2013): 193–202.
56 Ostracon no. 11198 from Egyptian Museum in Cairo. Manniche, *Sexual Life*, 17.
57 Jiří Janák and Hana Navrátilová, 'People vs. P. Turin 55001', in *Sex and Gender in Ancient Egypt*, ed. Graves-Brown, 63–70.

Sexuality in Ancient Egypt: Pleasures, Desires, Norms, and Representations

social and political context.[58] The iconographic programme of some temples, such as the mortuary temple of the female king Hatshepsut (1479–1458 BCE) and perhaps also the Middle Kingdom temple of the goddess Satet at Elephantine, have a depiction of curious couples. In the latter case the couple are King Senwosret I (1920–1875 BCE) and Satet. Unfortunately, not much is preserved of the scene, so it is not clear what this represents. In the case of Hatshepsut, the couple depicted are her mother Ahmose and her divine father Amun. That the scene in question has an erotic connotation is indicated in the accompanying hieroglyphic text. The text states that 'they' (the king and the god in one body) found the queen Ahmose resting in the palace. She awoke smelling the god and smiled seeing the king who let her see him in his divine form. She rejoiced seeing his *nfr*, which is usually read as beauty, but in some texts is also the penis of a god. His love went into her body and the palace was flooded with the scent of the god.[59] The word choice might not seem overtly sexual to us, but it might have been understood as such at the time. We have also seen that Osiris is attested as having sex with *ḥnm.wt*-women.

Sexual intercourse between human men and goddesses is not attested in Egyptian texts, however. We know from the Middle Kingdom 'Tale of the Herdsman' that encounters between men and goddesses were frightening and dangerous.[60] It can be argued that the reason why divine male–human female intercourse was encouraged and the divine female–human male intercourse was considered dangerous has to do with ancient Egyptian ideas about gender and its connection to status.[61] When a god impregnates

---

58 Hannah Sonbol, 'Und für welche Geschichte entscheiden Sie sich? Der Geburtzyklus und seine unterschiedlichen Narrative', in *Narrative: Geschichte – Mythos – Repräsentation, Beiträge des achten Berliner Arbeitskreises Junge Aegyptologie (BAJA 8) 1.12.–3.12.2017*, ed. Dina Serova, Burkhard Backes, and Matthieu W. Götz (Wiesbaden: Harrassowitz, 2018), 145–61.

59 Uroš Matić, 'The Sap of Life: Materiality and Sex in the Divine Birth Legend of Hatshepsut and Amenhotep III', in *Perspectives on Materiality in Ancient Egypt: Agency, Cultural Reproduction and Change*, ed. Érika Maynart, Carolina Velloza, and Renan Lemos (Oxford: Archaeopress, 2018), 35–54, at 40.

60 John C. Darnell, 'A Midsummer Night's Succubus: The Herdsman's Encounters in P. Berlin 3024, the Pleasures of Fishing and Fowling, the Songs of the Drinking Place, and the Ancient Egyptian Love Poetry', in *Opening the Tablet Box: Near Eastern Studies in Honor of Benjamin R. Foster*, ed. Sarah Melville and Alice Slotsky (Leiden: Brill, 2010), 99–106.

61 Uroš Matić, 'Ägyptische Gottheiten und *ars erotica*: Ein Versuch der ontologischen Anthropologie erotischer Netzwerke im alten Ägypten', in *Funktion/en: Materielle Kultur-Sprache-Religion, Beiträge des siebten Berliner Arbeitskreises Junge Ägyptologie (BAJA 7) 2.12–4.12.2016*, ed. Alexandra Verbovsek, Burkhard Backes, and Jan Aschmoneit (Wiesbaden: Harrassowitz, 2018), 141–60, at 154–5.

a human woman, a divine child is born to rule on earth, as the pharaoh. If a human man would impregnate a goddess, would the child have human or divine rights? Given ideas about ancient Egyptian gods and goddesses, such an ontological breach would be very problematic.

Same-Sex Intercourse

There are no words in ancient Egyptian for heterosexuals, homosexuals, bisexuals, or lesbians. According to Foucault, the non-existence of such terms 'should be neither underestimated nor overinterpreted'.[62] Contrary to ancient Greece and Rome, for example, same-sex intercourse was not much discussed in ancient Egypt before Ptolemaic and Roman rule. That of course does not mean that it was not practised. It seems that there was more concern with male–male sex acts than female–female sex acts. But not all same-sex acts were about pleasure. For example, in an often-told myth, the gods Horus and Seth contended with one another, a conflict that involved sex. In the Old Kingdom Pyramid Texts the sex act is reciprocal. However, in several sources dating from the Twelfth Dynasty (1991–1802 BCE) to the reign of Ramesses V (1149–1146 BCE), Seth tries to prove his domination by attempting to penetrate Horus. Instead, the trick is on Seth as Horus collects Seth's semen in his hand, and then with the help of his mother Isis places his own semen on the lettuce in Seth's garden so that after eating the lettuce Seth ends up being 'penetrated' by Horus.[63] At least in cosmogonic myths resulting in impregnation,[64] semen ingestion formed a connection between performing oral sex and being penetrated.

Meskell somewhat optimistically wrote that ancient Egyptian sexualities were seen as 'fluid and multiple'.[65] This is actually not supported by the available data. Normative desire was that of men for women, and of women for men, as we have seen in the case of the Ramesside 'love' poems. There are derogative terms for passive men in sexual intercourse, including *ḥmj.w*, a term variously translated by different Egyptologists.[66] Bearing in mind

---

62 Michel Foucault, *The History of Sexuality*. Vol. 2: *The Use of Pleasure*, trans. Robert Hurley (1984; New York: Vintage Books, 1990), 3.

63 Beate Schukraft, 'Homosexualität im Alten Ägypten', *Studien zur altägyptischen Kultur* 36 (2007): 297–331, at 308–10.

64 Marc Orriols-Llonch, 'Semen Ingestion and Oral Sex in Ancient Egyptian Texts', in *Proceedings of the Tenth International Congress of Egyptologists, University of the Aegean, Rhodes, 22–29 May 2008*, vol. 1, ed. Panagiotis Kousoulis and Nikolaos Lazaridis (Leuven: Peeters, 2015), 839–48.

65 Meskell, *Archaeologies of Social Life*, 106.

66 See Uroš Matić, *Violence and Gender in Ancient Egypt* (London: Routledge, 2021).

Sexuality in Ancient Egypt: Pleasures, Desires, Norms, and Representations

that the word *ḥmj.w* derives from the verb *ḥmj* which means 'to drive back; to repel', the translation 'back turner' by Richard Parkinson seems to keep both the etymological background and the gender connotation of passivity and therefore effeminacy, from a normative ancient Egyptian point of view.[67] The phallus determinative in *ḥmj.w* indicates that the term had a sexual aspect. Similarly, *nkk.w* is a term variously translated by Egyptologists as 'homosexual', 'fucked man', or 'sodomite'. The word clearly derives from the verb *nk* 'to have sex/to penetrate' so the most accurate translation would be 'penetrated man'. It is attested in Chapter 125 of the Book of the Dead, a funerary text from the New Kingdom. This chapter contains a series of negative confessions through which the deceased declares that he/she did not commit inappropriate deeds. One of these is: 'I did not penetrate a *nkk.w*', but there are also instances in which the deceased states 'I did not perform fellatio (*nwḥ*) on a *nkk.w*'. Fellatio as an act was not considered problematic when performed as autofellatio by gods such as Geb, but it was for humans.[68] Finally, we have to return to the previously mentioned contending of Horus and Seth. After he tried to show to the divine council that because he was the one who penetrated Horus, he should claim the dominion and the throne, Seth's trick backfires as he unknowingly ate the sperm of Horus. Upon hearing the claim Seth made about penetrating Horus, the deities cried out and spit in front of him, clearly not approving of him being passive in this intercourse.[69]

Meskell argues that words such as *ḥmj.w* and *nkk.w* refer to practices rather than individuals and that these did not serve to 'demarcate Egyptian individuals as homosexual or heterosexual', which is simply not true.[70] They contrast to *ṯ3y*, a man who penetrates women or other men, so clearly refer to individuals. Do these terms indicate the existence of sexuality as a facet of identity?[71] Self-identification as *ḥmj.w* or *nkk.w* is not attested. These are derogative terms attributed to them by others. But although we cannot speak of heterosexuality and homosexuality in our sense of these words, we can speak of normative sex, which involved penetrating women and men for men and being penetrated by men for women. The existence of derogatory

---

67 Richard B. Parkinson, 'Boasting about Hardness: Constructions of Middle Kingdom Masculinity', in *Sex and Gender in Ancient Egypt*, ed. Graves-Brown, 115–42, at 117.

68 Orriols-Llonch, 'Semen Ingestion'.

69 Schukraft, 'Homosexualität im Alten Ägypten', 309.

70 Meskell, *Private Life*, 144; Meskell, *Archaeologies of Social Life*, 94, 106.

71 Kathryn Babayan and Afsaneh Najmabadi, 'Preface', in *Islamicate Sexualities: Translations across Temporal Geographies of Desire* (Cambridge, MA: Harvard University Press, 2008), vii–xiv, at xi.

terms for those practising non-normative sex, even without individuals identifying with such terms in official documents, does not mean that these terms do not refer to individuals. English terms such as 'faggot' or 'queer' were derogatory terms before they were taken over in a subversive way by those to whom they referred. This brings me to another possible case of using terms in a subversive way. Socially accepted relations of same-sex friendships in ancient Egypt, expressed with the words ḥnms (male) or ḥnms.t (female) 'friend', but also sn 'brother' could also have been used as euphemisms to express something more than just friendship.[72]

Same-sex intercourse is not known from the rather poor corpus of visual representations of sex, contrary to ancient Greece and Rome. It is even questionable to what extent some cases of depictions of male–male intimacy, such as those from the unique Fifth Dynasty (2435–2306 BCE) tomb of Niankhkhnum and Khnumhotep in Saqqara, can be interpreted as an indication of sexual practices, identities, or romantic affinities. Whereas some authors argue that these two men, who also had wives and children depicted in their shared tomb, were lovers, others argue that they were brothers[73] or that we should seriously reflect on the reasons we attribute sexual connotations to male–male intimacy, even in cases such as touching or kissing. The reason we may unconsciously make such associations are rooted in our own heteronormative society in which male–male intimacy is discouraged or carefully regulated from childhood on.[74] But in ancient Egypt, even intimacy among family members or male–female couples, such as couples hugging or holding hands, is very rarely depicted. The depictions of Ramesses III tickling young girls under their chin or draping his arm around their shoulders on the reliefs of Medinet Habu temple are an exception. The reason for this lack of portrayal could have been decorum, but also Egyptian ideas of the afterlife, as showing 'people kissing may have necessitated obscuring parts of the face', and such depictions were avoided because they could affect the completeness of the person in the afterlife.[75] The Amarna period iconography of the royal

---

72 Beryl Büma and Martin Fitzenreiter, '"Spielt das Lied der beiden göttlichen Brüder": Erotische Ambiguität und "große Nähe" zwischen Männern im Alten Reich', *Studien zur Altägyptischen Kultur* 44 (2015): 19–42; Helmut Satzinger and Danijela Stefanović, 'The Middle Kingdom *xnmsw*', *Studien zur Altägyptischen Kultur* 41 (2012): 333–43, at 343.

73 Vera Vasiljević, 'Embracing His Double: Niankhkhnum and Khnumhotep', *Studien zur Altägyptischen Kultur* 37 (2008): 363–72.

74 Uroš Matić, 'Out of Touch: Egyptology and Queer Theory (or What This Encounter Should Not Be)', in *Von der Quelle zur Theorie: Vom Verhältnis zwischen Objektivität und Subjektivität in den historischen Wissenschaften*, ed. Anne-Sophie Naujoks and Jendrik Stelling (Leiden: Brill, 2018), 183–97.

75 Booth, *In Bed with the Ancient Egyptians*, 19, 91.

family is exceptional in this regard, as intimacy, including kissing and touching, becomes more elaborately depicted.[76]

Other terms for those not really conforming to normative gender expectations for men and women appear over time.[77] Many of them, such as ʿḥȝwty-z-ḥm.t, are still problematic to interpret. It has been argued that this term stands for effeminate men, but this argument is based on an erroneous reading of one sign in the word as the phallus determinative.[78] Furthermore, some expressions, such as 'woman-boy' (ḥm.t-ḥrd), are attested only in a few sources, which do not really say anything except that having sex with people described in these terms should be avoided. Here the problem is not so much the same-sex act, however, but rather the undistinguishable desire of the 'woman-boy'.[79]

It is clear, however, that by the time the Christian polemicist Clement of Alexandria wrote his *Paedagogus*, a manual on good behaviour for rich urban Christians, in the third century CE, individuals termed *kinaidoi* were a common site in urban spaces in Egypt. The problem with this term is that although in a literary context it is a derogatory term for feminine men assuming the penetrated role in intercourse with men, in official documents, including self-issued ones such as those from the temple of Isis on Philae in the first century BCE, *kinaidoi* are a type of performer, similar to flute-players (*auletes*).[80] Clearly, ancient norms concerning sex produced discourses about non-normative behaviour that used real-life individuals as referents. Perhaps in some cases men who were *kinaidoi* did have sex with men, but they did not necessarily look and act as the derogatory discourse describes them. Such stereotypes are similar to modern heteronormative discourses that attribute effeminacy to all male hairdressers or those who work in fashion such as designers and models, despite the fact that not all of them are effeminate or gay.

There is some evidence for women desiring women in Roman Egypt. We have already seen that a woman named Gorgonia wanted to enchant a woman named Sophia in the third century CE. One papyrus from

---

76 Arlette David, *Renewing Royal Imagery: Akhenaten and Family in the Amarna Tombs* (Leiden: Brill, 2020).

77 Mark Depauw, 'Notes on Transgressing Gender Boundaries in Ancient Egypt', *Zeitschrift für Ägyptische Sprache und Altertumskunde* 130 (2003): 49–59.

78 Uroš Matić, 'Gender in Ancient Egypt: Norms, Ambiguities, and Sensualities', *Near Eastern Archaeology* 79, no. 3 (2016): 174–83.

79 Maxim 31 of the Maxims of Ptahhotep. James P. Allen, *Middle Egyptian Literature: Eight Literary Works of the Middle Kingdom* (Cambridge: Cambridge University Press, 2015), 208–9.

80 Sapsford, 'The Wages of Effeminacy?'

the second century CE criticizes the famous poet Sappho for being a woman-lover (*gynaikerastria*), a critique imagined from a masculine point of view, as Sappho is said to be *erastes* of women, that is a dominant penetrating partner.[81]

Masculine Domination: Sex and Violence

Sexual violence such as assault and public degradation is extremely hard to find in ancient Egyptian texts. We seem to know more about the violent sexual misconduct of gods than men. Very often in complaints of men about the adultery of their wives, for example, the information on the woman's consent is missing. Therefore, one should consider that some adulteries were not consensual. When sexual assault is concerned, we do not have the perspective of the victim and the reactions of the victim are never described. Even the terms used are ambiguous, although there is an ancient Egyptian verb ($\underline{h}^c$), which was used for physical acts with a sexual background that most probably involved at least some force if not also physical violence ending in sexual assault.[82]

Cases of sexual assault in the divine world are less ambiguous. Horus' assault of Isis is attested in a papyrus of New Kingdom date. A series of episodes of sexual violence are repeatedly attested in a papyrus from the seventh century BCE. Alexandra von Lieven argues that these are sexual encounters either because unambiguous terms that indicate physical violence are used or because the reaction of the victim is defensive or frantic. These sexual encounters also result in abortion, although 'normally the birth of a child was considered desirable'.[83] The possibility of the god Geb's sexual assault of the goddess Tefnut is much discussed in Egyptology.[84] Clear

---

81 Papyrus Oxyrhynchos XV 1800. Montserrat, *Sex and Society in Graeco-Roman Egypt*, 160.

82 Matić, *Violence and Gender*, 70–1.

83 Horus assaulting Isis is attested in Magical Papyrus Harris (7, 10–11). Numerous sexual assaults are attested in Papyrus Brooklyn 47.218.84, also known as the 'Mythological Manual of the Delta'. Alexandra von Lieven, 'Antisocial Gods? On the Transgression of Norms in Ancient Egyptian Mythology', in *Lotus and Laurel: Studies on Egyptian Language and Religion in Honour of Paul John Frandsen*, ed. Rune Nyord and Kim Ryholt (Copenhagen: Museum Tusculanum, 2015), 181–207, at 184–7.

84 Especially concerning the text on the naos of El-Arish, see Ursula Verhoeven, 'Eine Vergewaltigung? Vom Umgang mit einer Textstelle des Naos von El Arish (Tefnut-Studien I)', in *Religion und Philosophie im Alten Ägypten: Festgabe für Philippe Derchain*, ed. Ursula Verhoeven and Erhard Graefe (Leuven: Peeters, 1991), 319–30, at 330; Orell Witthuhn, 'Zur Deutung einer Textpassage aus dem "Mythos von den Götterkönigen" im Kontext der Hermopolisstele Nektanebos' I (Kairo, Ägyptisches Museum JE 72130)', *Göttinger Miszellen* 251 (2017): 143–8, at 148.

indications are found in texts, and the act can be inferred from the context on the text of the El-Arish naos, a Ptolemaic shrine from the Thirtieth Dynasty (380–343 BCE).[85] Real-life and mythological sexual violence is accompanied by sexual metaphors for feminized enemies. For example, the previously mentioned term ḥmj.w (back turner) was used to designate enemies during the Middle and New Kingdom.[86]

Concluding Remarks

It is not surprising that no Egyptologist has yet written a comprehensive history of sex and sexuality in ancient Egypt. Like many other aspects of ancient Egyptian life, these are often considered to be static and 'natural', not matters of historical development. Still, although the differences between ancient Egyptian sex experiences and ours have to be acknowledged, sexual satisfactions were known in ancient Egypt, and therefore it cannot be said that they are a product only of modern times and our consumer culture.[87] Although the number of representations is rather small, throughout the pharaonic history there was a way of dealing with intimacy and sex in state-sponsored and elite-produced art that was socially codified and ordered by decorum, whereas the expressions of commoners were less restricted. Explicit sex acts in state-sponsored art are reserved to deities, usually in cosmogonies, and do not have the connotation of erotic depictions communicating pleasure. Still, model phalli were offered to goddess Hathor and people enjoyed sex during festivals in honour of the Sun Eye goddess for two millennia.[88]

Therefore, although sexuality was not like that in modern European discourse, it was still a discourse, but one that we have not yet explored fully. And there was change. For just one example, from its earliest attestations in the New Kingdom, nkk.w was an identity ascribed from outside to an existing practice, male sexual passivity. There is no evidence that a nkk.w was necessarily effeminate, however, although other texts indicate that passivity was considered to be feminine. However, in Roman Egypt some

---

85 Lieven, 'Antisocial Gods?', 191. That Geb indeed sexually assaulted Tefnut is corroborated by the 'Mythological Manual Florence' (PSI inv. I 72 x+4, 12–18) from the Roman period, and by the 'Mythological Manual of the Delta'. Lieven, 'Antisocial Gods?', 187; Dimitri Meeks, *Mythes et legends du Delta d'apres le papyrus Brooklyn 47.218.84.* (Cairo: Institut français d'archéologie orientale du Caire, 2006), 269.
86 Matić, *Violence and Gender*, 114–5.
87 Quack, 'Where Once Was Love'; Zygmund Bauman, *Liquid Love: On the Frailty of Human Bonds* (Cambridge: Polity, 2003), 12.
88 Geraldine Pinch, *Votive Offerings to Hathor* (Oxford: Griffith Institute, 1993).

men could have willingly taken on the identity of a *kinaidos* as an occupation or as a sexual orientation, despite the derogatory discourse on *kinaidoi*. The question is if those who had previously *acted* as the passive male partners for other men had to accept the effeminacy ascribed to them by others in order to *be* something they could not *be* before? This and other questions may ultimately be answered once a full history of sex, pleasure, desire, and ultimately sexuality is written for ancient Egypt.

Further Reading

Booth, Charlotte. *In Bed with the Ancient Egyptians*. Stroud, UK: Amberley, 2015.

Bryan, Betsy M. 'Hatshepsut and Cultic Revelries in the New Kingdom'. In *Creativity and Innovation in the Reign of Hatshepsut: Papers from the Theban Workshop 2010*, ed. José M. Galán, Betsy M. Bryan, and Peter F. Dorman, 93–124. Chicago: Oriental Institute of the University of Chicago, 2010.

Büma, Beryl, and Martin Fitzenreiter. '"Spielt das Lied der beiden göttlichen Brüder": Erotische Ambiguität und "große Nähe" zwischen Männern im Alten Reich'. *Studien zur Altägyptischen Kultur* 44 (2015): 19–42.

Darnell, John C. 'A Midsummer Night's Succubus: The Herdsman's Encounters in P. Berlin 3024, the Pleasures of Fishing and Fowling, the Songs of the Drinking Place, and the Ancient Egyptian Love Poetry'. In *Opening the Tablet Box: Near Eastern Studies in Honor of Benjamin R. Foster*, ed. Sarah Melville and Alice Slotsky, 99–106. Leiden: Brill, 2010.

'The Rituals of Love in Ancient Egypt: Festival Songs of the Eighteenth Dynasty and the Ramesside Love Poetry'. *Die Welt des Orients* 46 (2016): 22–61.

Förster, Frank, Stan Hendrickx, and Uroš Matić. 'Violence, Sex and Humiliation in a Unique Dynasty 0 Rock Art Scene at Wadi Ameyra, SW-Sinai'. In *Early Egyptian Miscellanies: Discussions and Essays on Predynastic and Early Dynastic Egypt*, ed. Gunnar Sperveslage, 35–51. Berlin: Internet Beiträge zur Ägyptologie und Sudanarchäologie and Golden House Publications, 2022.

Graves-Brown, Carolyn. *Sex and Gender in Ancient Egypt: 'Don your Wig for a Joyful Hour'*. Swansea: Classical Press of Wales, 2008.

Lieven, Alexandra von. 'Antisocial Gods? On the Transgression of Norms in Ancient Egyptian Mythology'. In *Lotus and Laurel: Studies on Egyptian Language and Religion in Honour of Paul John Frandsen*, ed. Rune Nyord and Kim Ryholt, 181–207. Copenhagen: Museum Tusculanum, 2015.

'Papyrus Harris 500 Recto 4,1–6,2'. In *Peregrinations avec Erhart Graefe: Festschrift zu seinem 75. Geburtstag*, ed. Anke Ilona Blöbaum, Marianne Eaton-Krauss, and Annik Wüthrich, 317–32. Münster: Zaphon, 2018.

'Wein, Weib und Gesang – Rituale für die Gefährliche Göttin'. In *Rituale in der Vorgeschichte, Antike und Gegenwart: Neue Forschungen und Perspektiven von Archäologie, Ägyptologie, Altorientalistik, Ethnologie und vergleichender Religionsgeschichte, Interdisziplinäre Tagung vom 1.–2. Februar 2002 in Berlin*, ed. Cornelia Metzner-Nebelsick, 47–55. Leidorf: Rahden 2003.

Lieven, Alexandra von, and Joachim Friedrich Quack. 'Ist Liebe eine Frauenkrankheit? Papyrus Berlin 13602, ein gynäkomagisches Handbuch'. In *Hieratic, Demotic and Greek Studies and Text Editions: Of Making Many Books There Is No End; Festschrift in Honour of Sven P. Vleeming*, ed. Koeenraad Donker van Heel, Franscisca A. J. Hoogendijk, and Cary J. Martin, 257–74. Leiden: Brill, 2018.

Manniche, Lise. *Sexual Life in Ancient Egypt*. London: KPI, 1987.

Matić, Uroš. 'Ägyptische Gottheiten und *ars erotica*: Ein Versuch der ontologischen Anthropologie erotischer Netzwerke im alten Ägypten'. In *Funktion/en: Materielle Kultur-Sprache-Religion, Beiträge des siebten Berliner Arbeitskreises Junge Ägyptologie (BAJA 7) 2.12–4.12.2016*, ed. Alexandra Verbovsek, Burkhard Backes, and Jan Aschmoneit, 141–60. Wiesbaden: Harrassowitz, 2018.

'Gender-Based Violence'. *UCLA Encyclopedia of Egyptology*. 2021. https://escholarship .org/uc/item/118752mp.

'Out of Touch: Egyptology and Queer Theory (or What This Encounter Should Not Be)'. In *Von der Quelle zur Theorie: Vom Verhältnis zwischen Objektivität und Subjektivität in den historischen Wissenschaften*, ed. Anne-Sophie Naujoks and Jendrik Stelling, 183–97. Leiden: Brill, 2018.

'The Sap of Life: Materiality and Sex in the Divine Birth Legend of Hatshepsut and Amenhotep III'. In *Perspectives on Materiality in Ancient Egypt: Agency, Cultural Reproduction and Change*, ed. Érika Maynart, Carolina Velloza, and Renan Lemos, 35–54. Oxford: Archaeopress, 2018.

Violence and Gender in Ancient Egypt. London: Routledge, 2021.

Meskell, Lynn. *Archaeologies of Social Life: Age, Sex, Class et cetera in Ancient Egypt*. Oxford: Blackwell, 1999.

Private Life in New Kingdom Egypt. Princeton, NJ: Princeton University Press, 2002.

Meskell, Lynn, and Rosemary Joyce. *Embodied Lives: Figuring Ancient Maya and Egyptian Experiences*. London: Routledge, 2003.

Montserrat, Dominic. *Sex and Society in Graeco-Roman Egypt*. London: Routledge, 1996.

Myśliwiec, Karol. *Eros on the Nile*. Trans. Geoffrey L. Packer. London: Duchworth, 2004.

Navrátilová, Hana, and Renata Landgráfová, eds. *Sex and the Golden Goddess*. Vol. 1: *Ancient Egyptian Love Songs in Context*. Prague: Agama, 2009.

Sex and the Golden Goddess. Vol. 2: *The World of the Love Songs*. Prague: Charles University in Prague, 2015.

Orriols-Llonch, Marc. 'Semen Ingestion and Oral Sex in Ancient Egyptian Texts'. In *Proceedings of the Tenth International Congress of Egyptologists, University of the Aegean, Rhodes, 22–29 May 2008*, Vol. 1, ed. Panagiotis Kousoulis and Nikolaos Lazaridis, 839–48. Leuven: Peeters, 2015.

'Women's Role in Sexual Intercourse in Ancient Egypt'. In *Women in Antiquity: Real Women across the Ancient World*, ed. Stephanie Lynn Budin and Jean MacIntosh Turfa, 194–203. London: Routledge, 2016.

Parkinson, Richard B. 'Boasting about Hardness: Constructions of Middle Kingdom Masculinity'. In *Sex and Gender in Ancient Egypt*, ed. Carolyn Graves-Brown, 115–42. Swansea: Classical Press of Wales, 2008.

Parra Ortiz, José Miguel. *La vida amorosa en el Antiguo Egipto*. Madrid: Editorial Alderaban, 2001.

Quack, Joachim Friedrich. 'Herodot, Strabo und die Pallakide von Theben'. In *Tempelprostitution im Altertum: Fakten und Fiktionen*, ed. Tanja Scheer and Martin Lindner, 154–82. Berlin: Antike, 2009.

'Where Once Was Love, Love Is No More? What Happens to Expressions of Love in Late Period Egypt?' *Die Welt des Orients* 46 (2016): 62–89.

3

Sexuality in the Systems of Thought and Belief of the Ancient Near East

ILAN PELED

The association between sexuality, society, and culture is a prominent feature in one of the most famous episodes from an ancient Near Eastern literary composition: the encounter at the beginning of the 'Epic of Gilgamesh' between the prostitute Shamhat and Enkidu, the beastly man who lives in the wild. This episode has been interpreted by modern scholars from numerous angles, but its main force seems to have been the idea that the untamed and uncivilized was introduced and indoctrinated into the basics of Mesopotamian civilization by means of sexual intercourse. Indeed, Akkadian verbs such as *edû* ('to know') and *lamādu* ('to learn') had the additional meaning of knowing someone sexually. Similarly, in the Hebrew Bible, the same verb for 'to know' (*lada'at*) also meant 'to have sexual intercourse'. Even in modern English, the term 'to know' may have a sexual connotation. All this is surely not coincidental; sexuality forms a distinct knowledge in its own right, a knowledge that is often culturally specific.

The term 'ancient Near East' has several different aspects: geographical, chronological, and cultural. In terms of geography, it corresponds to the core area of the modern Middle East, mainly modern Iraq and its surrounding countries and regions. As to chronology, the history of the region begins with the invention of writing in the city of Uruk, at around 3300 BCE. The periods that predate writing supply interesting archaeological data, but since they yield no written records, they are of a lesser value for understanding ancient social concepts of human sexuality. There is no exact point in time where the history of the ancient Near East ends; one may consider the Persian conquest of Babylon (539 BCE) as the end of independent Mesopotamian political rule; or the beginning of the

Hellenistic era (*c.* 330 BCE) as a marker of real cultural change in the region. Whenever it ended, the documented history of the ancient Near East lasted for some three millennia.[1] During this long duration of time, numerous social and cultural groups lived in different parts of this vast region. This spatial, chronological, and cultural diversity must be taken into account when offering a discussion on such a broad theme as 'sexuality in the ancient Near East'.

We must also bear in mind the opposite considerations: while contextualization is vital when assessing any historical evidence, and every ancient Near Eastern source must be considered against the specific background of its time and place, continuity and cultural diffusion characterized the history of the ancient Near East. Texts from first-millennium BCE Assyria and Babylonia usually reflect traditions already millennia-old, so what was true to societies which existed in the fourth and third millennia sometimes continued to be true in other parts and periods of the ancient Near East. For these reasons, even when the sources discussed in this chapter are explicitly dated, this does not mean that the historical reality they reflect was exclusively limited to their own time.

Where does our knowledge concerning the ancient Near East come from? Our sources of information are both archaeological and historical. The non-textual sources are mainly iconographic: statues, figurines, and wall reliefs. The written evidence, however, is by far more abundant and revealing: hundreds of thousands of clay tablets, written in the complex logosyllabic script scholars call 'cuneiform' (Latin for 'wedge-shaped'). These tablets were – and still are – found by archaeologists, and reveal a fascinating ancient world. Monumental writing is also found: royal inscriptions engraved in wall reliefs, stelae, and statues. The literary genres documented in the cuneiform texts cover almost any aspect of human life: diplomatic, bureaucratic, economic, ritual, cultic, mythological, and legal. Many languages were spoken by the different peoples who inhabited the ancient Near East, but the most widespread of these was Akkadian, a Semitic language similar to modern

---

1 The history of the ancient Near East is usually divided by modern scholars into millennia and the periods they included. This division can roughly be outlined as follows: the third millennium – Sumerian (*c.* 3300–2300 BCE), Old Akkadian (*c.* 2300–2100 BCE), and Ur III (*c.* 2100–2000 BCE); the second millennium – Old Babylonian/Assyrian (*c.* 2000–1600 BCE), Hittite (*c.* 1650–1200 BCE), Middle Babylonian (*c.* 1600–1150 BCE), and Middle Assyrian (*c.* 1400–950 BCE); and the first millennium – Neo-Assyrian (*c.* 900–612 BCE), Neo-Babylonian (627–539 BCE), and Late Babylonian (from the Persian conquest of 539 BCE on).

Hebrew, and Arabic. Less documented, but more ancient, was Sumerian, an isolated language that is still not entirely understood. Many other languages were documented in these texts, though to a lesser extent, most notably Hittite, Eblaite, Ugaritic, Hurrian, and Elamite.

One of the most significant sources of information concerning sexuality in the ancient Near East are legal documents, in which sexuality and its numerous social aspects and implications are mentioned or alluded to. The most important texts in this regard are several official law collections, which contain numerous references to sexual matters, and frequently demonstrate a one-sided perspective, clearly favouring males over females. These collections were composed in three different languages (Sumerian, Akkadian, and Hittite) and at different times and places. They obviously reflect much cultural and chronological diversity – but also millennia of continuity of legal traditions throughout the ancient Near East. It is not entirely clear to what extent these collections were enforced in everyday life, however, if they were at all. And, as with all ancient legal codes, we do not know the extent to which the concerns of legislators matched those of others, that is, whether laws codified values widely shared or were intended to re-shape behaviours to match the values of the lawmakers. In other words, they reflect assumptions, norms, and customs supported by those who wrote and collected them, but are not a depiction of everyday life.

Another important source are literary compositions, texts that we may dub 'tales', 'myths', or 'legends'. These frequently contain episodes that refer to sexual matters, but the morals such texts convey are often indirect and insinuated, so they require the modern scholar to resort to speculation and conjecture as to their actual meaning. Additional important sources of information derive from the realm of cult: religious ceremonies and magical rituals. The former texts reflect how organized religion influenced people's sexuality, and, in return, was influenced by it, while the latter ones usually demonstrate how people dealt with difficulties in their sex lives.

When we read these ancient texts and try to understand notions that concern human sexuality as reflected in them, we must bear in mind that the majority of ancient Near Eastern populations could not read or write. Texts were produced by expert scribes, mostly for the sake of the circles of royalty, nobility, and the social elite. It is therefore questionable whether certain texts reflect the everyday life of society at large. Even royalty and nobility lived and emerged within their larger societies, however, and one should not assume that no connection existed between the upper and lower social echelons.

As to the topics discussed in this chapter, a selection had to be made when covering the infinite subject of 'sexuality in the ancient Near East'. Indeed, as in Oscar Wilde's immortal words, 'to define is to limit', and choosing several topics of discussion inevitably entailed leaving others out. The presentation of each theme in this chapter begins with an overview and general explanations ('What are we looking at?'), continues with a presentation of the pertinent sources of information ('How do we know it?'), and then moves on to the discussion of the theme ('What do we know?'). The discussion is organized by sources and textual genres rather than historical periods, because not all periods are necessarily represented by the sources pertaining to each theme. More importantly, because of the cultural continuity that characterized ancient Near Eastern history, sources from one period were usually relevant to many others, and thus chronological sub-divisions might be anachronistic and misleading. Not all types of sources are equally relevant to all topics, and therefore some types were used more than others.

Sex and Reproduction

Sexual relations were very often associated with reproduction, though they also had other meanings and functions. Our knowledge of the association between sex and reproduction in the Ancient Near East derives from numerous sources, including artistic and iconographic representations, and, most significantly, legal, literary, and ritual texts.

Iconographic sources from the ancient Near East occasionally allude to sexual intercourse, and at times explicitly portray it. Naturally, not all depictions of sexual encounters were necessarily related to reproduction: one may associate sex with desire, eroticism, or prostitution, none of which has anything to do with procreation. But when no alternative interpretation is readily available, modern scholars of the ancient Near East tend to assume that portrayals of sexual intercourse in objects found in the public domain reflected aspired fertility.

A few cases in point may be mentioned. A group of Old Babylonian and Middle Assyrian clay and lead plaques depict couples engaged in sexual intercourse, frequently *a tergo*, at times while the woman drinks beer from a straw. Such objects were found in both private and palatial contexts, and their meaning and purpose are unclear. One of the best-known examples is a group of several lead pieces from the palace of the Assyrian king Tukulti-Ninurta I (*c.* 1240–1200 BCE), where men and women were depicted having intercourse in various sexual positions. Another example was found on an

Old Hittite (*c.* 1500 BCE) vase from the site of Inandik, which was covered by decorations of people engaging in preparations for a ceremony, preparing food, dancing, and playing musical instruments. As part of all these depictions, we can see a couple engaged in sexual intercourse. While both are clothed, the genitalia of the man, who stands behind the bending woman, are clearly visible.[2]

From a legal perspective, the importance of descendants is apparent in rules of inheritance. Since children formed the lineage continuation, they were the natural heirs of their parents, and many official laws were decreed in order to establish this situation as a legal fact. Other official means, such as transactions and contracts, were utilized for the same purpose, establishing descendants as heirs to their parents.[3]

The importance of reproduction, that is, men and women's desire to have children, is evident in several ancient Near Eastern literary compositions. One of the famous examples in this regard is found in a passage from the composition 'Gilgamesh, Enkidu and the Netherworld', where the two heroes, Gilgamesh and Enkidu, meet after the latter has died. Gilgamesh asks his friend about the different people he met in the realm of the dead, and Enkidu replies by describing each of them. Thus, a man with only one child is described as complaining, a man with two children is described more positively, and the pattern continues until the man who had seven children; the more offspring a dead man had, the better his fate in the Netherworld. But then the dialogue turns to people who had no descendants at all. None of them was portrayed in a particularly flattering manner: a man who had no heir was as nourishing as bread as hard as a brick; a eunuch was uselessly propped aside; and a woman who did not give birth was ignored by all, and no man was interested in her.[4]

A different relevant example is found in the Hittite literary composition 'Appu and His Two Sons'. This tale portrays the protagonist – a man named Appu – as a rich person who is miserable because he has no children. Appu's misery at not having children is explicitly associated with his inability to properly conduct sexual intercourse with his wife, who even publicly insults him for it: 'Appu's wife started asking the servants: "He has never had

---

2 F. A. M. Wiggermann, 'Sexualität (Sexuality). A. In Mesopotamien', in *Reallexikon der Assyriologie und Vorderasiatischen Archäologie*, Vol. 12, ed. M. P. Streck G. Frantz-Szabó, M. Krebernik, D. Morandi Bonacossi et al. (Berlin: De Gruyter, 2010), 410–26.

3 Ilan Peled, *Law and Gender in the Ancient Near East and the Hebrew Bible* (London: Routledge, 2020), 77–80.

4 Alhena Gadotti, *'Gilgamesh, Enkidu, and the Netherworld' and the Sumerian Gilgamesh Cycle* (Berlin: De Gruyter, 2014), 159.

intercourse. Did he have intercourse now?!" She went, the woman, and lay down to sleep with Appu clothed. Appu awoke from sleep, and his wife started asking him: "You have never had intercourse. Did you have intercourse now?!"[5] Later on, Appu indeed manages to sire two sons, thanks to the help of the gods.

A major aspect of cultic life in the ancient Near East was the performance of numerous magical rituals. These were meant to ward off perceived metaphysical evil, heal illnesses, and treat different types of problems. Some magical rituals pertained to sexuality and reproduction, mainly in treating impotence and infertility. The most prominent group of rituals that were supposed to treat impotence were called *šà-zi-ga*, Sumerian for 'rising of the heart', insinuating sexual desire and potency. These rituals included the uttering of incantations and pleas for the gods, and the use of various substances in an attempt to restore a man's potency.[6]

Several Hittite magical rituals addressed a variety of issues relating to human sexuality and reproduction. 'Tunnawi's ritual' was meant to treat reoccurring miscarriages and male and female infertility; 'Anniwiyani's Ritual' was probably aimed at a man who was engaged in passive homosexual intercourse, aspiring to instil in him active penetrative sexual inclinations; and 'Paskuwatti's Ritual' was performed in order to restore a man's sexual potency.[7]

Sex and the Body

The human body is obviously a major aspect of sexuality. This section evaluates representations of nudity, the question of castration, and the employment of eunuchs in the ancient Near East, for which the most pertinent sources of information are legal texts. As before, we begin this section with non-written sources: figurines, seal impressions, and wall reliefs that display the naked human body.

One of the most significant aspects of the relation between sexuality and the human body is the presentation of nudity. Depictions of naked people in visual media are usually highly suggestive of sexual

---

5 All translations are by the author unless otherwise indicated.

6 Robert D. Biggs, *ŠÀ.ZI.GA: Ancient Mesopotamian Potency Incantations* (New York: J. J. Augustin, 1967).

7 I. Peled, 'The Use of Pleasure, Constraints of Desire: Anniwiyani's Ritual and Sexuality in Hittite Magical Ceremonies', in *Acts of the VIIth International Congress of Hittitology, Çorum, August 25–31 2008*, ed. A. Süel (Ankara: T. C. Çorum Valiliği, 2010), 627–34.

Sexuality in the Systems of Thought and Belief of the Ancient Near East

intercourse, whether actual intercourse is shown or not. Therefore, when it comes to sex and the body in the ancient Near East, the role of iconography and artistic representations is no less important than that of written sources. Even though ancient Near Eastern iconography does not abundantly portray nakedness and exposed genitalia, we still have quite a few relevant examples.

Figurines of naked females with exaggerated hips and pronounced breasts and vulva, which begin in prehistoric times, have been interpreted by scholars as representations of 'mother goddesses' or 'fertility goddesses'. (For more on these figurines, see the Chapter 19 by Y. Yvon Wang in Volume I of this work.) This so-called 'Naked Goddess' motif reoccurs in different media throughout the history of the ancient Near East, on seals and their impressions, figurines, plaques, and images. Many seals produced throughout the entire history of the ancient Near East contained icono-graphic representations of naked female deities, usually Inanna/Ishtar, the goddess of war and sexuality. Such depictions are taken by modern scholars as markers of divine feminine fertility, or divine feminine patronage of eroticism and sexuality.

Male bodies were also displayed, though differently. A group of clay figurines and plaques from the Ur III and Old Babylonian periods depict nude male figures, which were interpreted by scholars to have been persons engaged in cultic worship. At times these persons are clearly portrayed as non-human, since they wear a horned cup, a prominent ancient Near Eastern iconographic emblem of divinity. Ancient Near Eastern rulers sometimes commissioned the production of wall reliefs and other artistic works to commemorate their military triumphs. Such triumphant portrayals included at times images of naked male enemies and war prisoners, as a display of subordination and humiliation.[8]

We may gain a different perspective on the association between sexuality and the human body in the ancient Near East by considering the issue of eunuchs and castration. Most of the relevant sources in this regard derive from the legal sphere. The matter of castration and employment of eunuchs in ancient Near Eastern courts is a debated one. Most scholars agree that at least in certain times and places, castrated men were indeed used as high-ranking palace officials, and sometimes even as military leaders.

---

8 U. Seidl, 'Nacktheit. B. In der Bildkunst', in *Reallexikon der Assyriologie und Vorderasiatischen Archäologie*, Vol. 9, ed. D. O. Edzard, M. Krebernik, J. N. Postgate, W. Röllig et al. (Berlin: De Gruyter, 1998), 66–68; and Christoph Uehlinger, 'Nackte Göttin. B. In der Bildkunst', in *Reallexikon*, 53–64.

Neo-Assyrian artistic representations of beardless men are almost unanimously taken by scholars as portrayals of eunuchs.

Textual evidence is usually implicit, but it is sufficient in order to convince even the most sceptical scholars that in the Neo-Assyrian courts the officials who bore the Akkadian title *sha-reshi* (Sumerian *lú.sag*) were eunuchs. Compelling evidence suggests that the same was true in the Middle Assyrian period as well. In addition, the Middle Assyrian Laws decree castration as a corporal punishment for adultery with a married woman:

> MAL A §15:[9] If a man seizes a man upon his wife . . . They shall kill both of them. If the woman's husband kills his wife, then he shall kill the lover; if he cuts off the nose of his wife, he shall turn the lover into a eunuch, and they shall mutilate his entire face; and if he releases his wife, he shall release the man.

They also decree castration as a punishment for same-sex relations:

> MAL A §20: If a man penetrates anally his fellow, and they prove him guilty and convict him: they shall penetrate him anally and turn him into a eunuch.

Needless to say, castration as a corporal punishment is a different matter altogether from the practice of employing castrated men as palace officials. While the former was an extreme sanction aimed at one's masculinity, the latter constituted a privilege, allowing certain men access to some of the highest positions in the state bureaucracy.

Many scholars also assume that eunuchs existed in Hittite courts, but the evidence in this respect is less unequivocal. It might be suggested, therefore, that the practice of employing castrated males as palace officials was local to Assyria and its neighbouring Hittite kingdom, but perhaps did not exist in Babylonia. Our view of the situation in Babylonia in this respect, however, must be made with caution, because it is based simply on a lack of evidence.[10]

---

9 The following abbreviations are used in this chapter for designating statutes from ancient Near Eastern law collections: LUN (Laws of Ur-Namma, *c.* 2050 BCE), LLI (Laws of Lipit-Ishtar, *c.* 1930 BCE), LE (Laws of Eshnunna, *c.* 1770 BCE), LH (Laws of Hammurabi, *c.* 1750 BCE), HL (Hittite Laws, *c.* 1650 BCE), and MAL (Middle Assyrian Laws, *c.* 1350 BCE).

10 On eunuchs and castration in the ancient Near East, see Ilan Peled, *Masculinities and Third Gender: The Origins and Nature of an Institutionalized Gender Otherness in the Ancient Near East* (Münster: Ugarit-Verlag, 2016), 203–37.

Gender Norms and Inequality

Sexuality cannot be discussed entirely separately from gender. While the term 'sex' usually refers to the physical and biological aspects of intercourse, reproduction, and genitalia, 'gender' usually refers to matters of psychological and social constructs attached to it, such as behaviour, identity, relationships, and human dynamics. This section supplies a brief overview of the intersection between sex and gender in the ancient Near East, focusing on matters of inequality between men and women in terms of norms, rights, privileges, and obligations. Since such issues were embedded in official records, the most relevant sources of information in this regard are legal, economic, and administrative documents, while additional evidence is found in literary compositions.

As the dominant gender in society, men enjoyed many advantages and privileges that were denied to women. Women were not legally independent, and their lives were governed by a male figure; depending on marital status, this male governing figure could have been their father or husband. Gender inequality was especially visible when it concerned extra-marital sex. Women were prohibited from having sexual intercourse with a man to whom they were not married. Hence, pre-marital sex was forbidden for women, and female virginity was extremely important; an unmarried girl lived under the auspices of her father and was obliged to remain a virgin until her marriage. Breaching these rules could lead to harsh sanctions. For example, an adulterous woman would face execution according to official law. These restrictions were never applied to men. A man who had sex with a woman married to another would suffer a punishment, but only because his act infringed on the rights of another man. Otherwise, a man who had sex with a woman other than his wife would face no official consequences.[11]

Women were expected to function primarily as wives and mothers – both roles that were the obvious result of sexuality attached to gender. Because of laws restricting women's economic independence and mobility, men did more of the work outside of the home, as merchants or artisans, occupations that necessitated one to be engaged with the public domain, while women worked more often within the domestic sphere, at tasks such as spinning and weaving. And men were the only ones who held the highest posts in the palace and military organizations.

---

11 Peled, *Law and Gender*, 26–30.

Sexuality and gender asymmetry are alluded to in several ancient Near Eastern literary compositions. For example, in the Hittite/Ugaritic tale 'Elkunirsha and Ashertu', Ashertu, wife of the god Elkunirsha, attempts to seduce the god Baal. Rejecting her, Baal reports it to her husband, and the two male gods agree that she should be humiliated by Baal, who kills her children. Following this, the humiliated Ashertu seeks to take revenge on Baal. Somewhat similarly, in the 'Epic of Gilgamesh', the goddess Ishtar tries to seduce the heroic Gilgamesh, who rejects her approaches. The rejected and enraged goddess tries to take revenge on Gilgamesh by sending the heavenly bull to kill him.

In both episodes we encounter a female deity who behaves in a manner that did not fit with the gender expectations of women in ancient Near Eastern societies: adulterous (Ashertu) or seductive (Ishtar). In both cases, the male figure (Baal and Gilgamesh) is portrayed as morally superior because he rejected the inappropriate sexual approaches.[12]

Sex and Marriage

In the ancient Near East, the institution of marriage supplied the primary socially and legally permitted frame for sexual intercourse. Sex outside of marriage could meet with harsh consequences, including public denunciation and severe legal sanctions, though these restrictions did not always apply to men. For example, under certain circumstances, married men could have officially sanctioned sex with their female slaves, and prostitutes did not serve only unmarried male customers.

Marriage was, by and large, an economic institution. Men and women were not usually free to choose their partners; instead they were chosen by the parents of both sides. In this sense, marriage was used to strengthen ties between families and to secure the economic future of the bride, groom, and their children. Therefore, marriage was established as a financial agreement, accompanied by legal documents and witnesses. For these reasons, the most significant sources of information at our disposal concerning the different implications of marriage in the ancient Near East are legal ones.

A wife's adultery undermined the essence of marriage, which related to sexual exclusivity: the moral and legal right of an individual man to be

---

12 I. Peled, 'Contempt and Similar Emotions in Akkadian and Hittite Literary Texts', in *Handbook of Emotions in the Ancient Near East*, ed. K. Sonik and U. Steinert (London: Routledge, 2022), 608–9. Outside of legal texts, references to human females who violated gender expectations through adultery or attempted seduction are rare.

granted exclusive access to his wife's sexuality. For a woman, to be married meant to be obliged to her husband and forbidden from having sex with any other man. Married men who had extra-marital intercourse would suffer no consequences, as long as their female partners were not married themselves – for example, prostitutes, enslaved women, divorcées, or widows. But, as noted earlier, married women who had extra-marital intercourse were regarded as adulteresses, and could suffer severe legal sanctions, even execution, as could their lovers. Young women were expected to remain virgins until they married.

Rape was considered a serious crime, not necessarily because of the harm it caused to the female victim, but because of the damage it caused to her male guardian – either her father or her husband. Attitudes to rape were strongly associated with attitudes to female chastity, virginity, and adultery. According to several law collections, a distinction was made between cases of rape or abduction involving married women and those involving unmarried women. Further distinction existed between cases of consent or the lack of it.

As discussed earlier, consensual sexual intercourse between a married woman and a man other than her husband was regarded as adultery, for which both paramours were punished, possibly executed. Consensual intercourse with an unmarried woman would have been problematic had she been a prepubescent girl, in which case the man who slept with her was considered a seducer, and had to pay a fine to her father and marry her. The lack of consent would change the nature of the crime from pre-/extra-marital sex to rape, in which only the male perpetrator would have been held responsible for performing a criminal act. Here again the law distinguished between a married and an unmarried rape victim. If she was married, she bore no legal liability, and her rapist was punished. But if she was an unmarried prepubescent girl, her rapist was required to pay her father a heavy fine, and her father was to decide whether the rapist and the girl were to be married or not.

The law was not always clear as to how the difference between rape and consensual intercourse was established. Women were expected to resist any illicit sexual intercourse. If such intercourse occurred in an inhabited place, it was assumed that the woman's shouting would suffice for deterring a rapist, so rape could be assumed had the intercourse occurred in an isolated place. Had the intercourse occurred in an inhabited place, it could have been assumed to be consensual. These assumptions, however, are only made explicit in HL §197 (similar to biblical law), and we are therefore ignorant as to whether similar assumptions governed the distinction between rape, seduction, and consent in other parts of the ancient Near East.

Lastly, we should also consider polygyny. While monogamy was the general rule, polygyny was legally permitted, but probably rarely practised. Polyandry – having more than one husband – is unattested in ancient Near Eastern texts. Legal sources allow for a man to marry a second wife in case his first wife became ill, acted immorally (by squandering his property or disrespecting him), or could not have children. Levirate marriage – in which a man married his brother's widow and any children that she had were regarded as her dead husband's – was also permitted under certain circumstances.[13]

Sex and Slavery

Since slaves were considered to be their owners' property, most of our information about the status and handling of slaves derives from legal texts – first and foremost, the different law collections. As property of their owners, enslaved people enjoyed very few legal rights. And although several law collections decreed certain legal provisions that protected slaves from abuse by their masters, most of the legislation that concerned slaves was meant to standardize their handling as human commodities, as people owned by someone else.

The treatment of slaves as property is alluded to in LUN §8, a very early law from 2050 BCE: 'If a man seduces by deception an unmarried slave-woman and takes her into (his) household: that man shall pay five shekels of silver.' Because the enslaved woman did not belong to her seducer, he was required to compensate her owner for the financial damages caused to him and pay him her full value. The sum – five shekels of silver – was indeed the price of an enslaved woman, as is evident from the court decision NSGU 45, dated to a few decades after the LUN. The crime committed was thus the infringement of the owner's property rights.

A development in the attitude to such a felony can be seen in LE §31, a statute issued three centuries later: 'If a man deflowers a(nother) man's slave-woman: he shall pay twenty shekels of silver, and the slave-woman (shall remain) of her master.' We can see, therefore, that in later legislation, the seducer was required to return the enslaved woman to her rightful

---

13 Peled, *Law and Gender*, 82–3, 94–7.

owner, and in addition to pay a fine four times greater than the payment specified in LUN §8.

The association between sexuality and slavery in the ancient Near East mainly concerns the relationships between female slaves and their male masters. Laws covered what happened if a married man had sex with an enslaved woman who belonged to him, and more importantly, what happened if she gave birth to his children. This was a legal matter that mostly concerned financial issues: property law, debt-slavery, and the inheritance rights of children born to such relationships.

For example, LLI §25 from *c.* 1930 BCE states: 'If a man marries a wife, she bears him a child, the child lives, and a slave-woman also bears a child to her master: the father shall free the slave-woman and her children; the children of the slave-woman shall not divide the household with the children of the master.' According to this statute, an enslaved woman and the children she bore to her master were to obtain their freedom, but the children were not entitled to their father's inheritance.

The legal implications of interclass marriages in the ancient Near East were especially significant in cases of marriage between a male slave and a free woman. Because of the androcentric nature of ancient Near Eastern societies, marriages between free men and female slaves were hardly considered problematic: men were the dominant gender in society, so marrying women of an inferior social class was easily tolerated. But for a man of an inferior rank to marry a woman of a superior rank was, in effect, a reversal of social standards; it created a situation where male gender superiority was threatened by the fact that the man was seen as inferior to his female spouse.

Official legislation addressed such potentially imbalanced situations several times, and did not always tolerate them. A case in point is found in LUN §E6, according to which an enslaved man who married his female owner was to be executed. Another statute from the same collection – LUN §5 – did permit marriages between slave and free, as long as the enslaved man married a free woman who was not his owner. According to HL §32, from *c.* 1650 BCE, in case such marriage reached a divorce, the couple would divide their joint property equally, but most of their children will remain with the free mother, the enslaved husband being entitled to take only one child with him. In contrast, the allocation of children between the parents was reversed if the father was free and his wife was enslaved (HL §31). Questions arise, however, concerning the legal status of children born from marriages in which the father was enslaved. The aforementioned LUN §5, as well as the much-later LH §175, determined that such children would be free and have inheritance rights to the wealth of their parents, and the owner of their father had no legal right to enslave them. In these cases, the higher social status of the free mother took precedence over the higher gender status of the male father in establishing the legal status of their children.[14] Marriage between slaves was legally permitted, but they remained the property of their owner, and so were their children, who inherited their enslaved status from their parents.

Whether such interclass marriages indeed took place cannot be inferred from the law collections alone. A few contract documents portray a wife giving her husband one of her female slaves in marriage, so the latter could bear him children. This situation changed the slave's status from slavery into concubinage, but she remained a secondary wife, with lesser privileges than those of the primary wife.[15]

Sex and Politics

Sexuality played a role even in the political domain. To begin, ruling dynasties across the ancient Near East were mostly hereditary. The heir to the throne would normally have been the eldest son of the ruling monarch. When there was no clear heir, internal political strife could break out between the competing fractions. For example, it is possible that the end of the Hittite Empire came about as a result of internal struggles between several opposing branches of the royal family. Throughout the history of the ancient Near East, civil wars occasionally broke out between brothers who each had claims to the throne. Some of the most famous cases occurred in the final decades of the Neo-Assyrian Empire, when King Sennacherib appointed his son Esarhaddon as his heir even though the latter was younger than his brothers, and later on, Esarhaddon himself repeated this action by appointing his younger son Ashurbanipal as crown-prince. On both occasions, the appointed heir had to survive attempted coups and civil wars in order to establish his rule.

Another aspect of the role of sexuality in politics was diplomatic marriages. Royal courts occasionally strengthened their bonds by marrying a princess of one side with a prince of the other side, or even with the king, who could marry more than one wife. Examples of this practice abound, especially from

---

14 Peled, *Law and Gender*, 61–2.

15 R. Westbrook, 'The Female Slave', in *Gender and Law in the Hebrew Bible and the Ancient Near East*, ed. Victor H. Matthews, Bernard M. Levinson, and Tikva Frymer-Kensky (Sheffield: Sheffield Academic Press, 1998), 214–38.

the second part of the second millennium BCE, when several geopolitical superpowers ruled the region: Egypt, Hatti, Assyria, and Babylonia. The courts of these kingdoms occasionally established joint ties based on such marriages. In addition, empires strengthened their influence over smaller kingdoms using such marriages, by inserting their own people into the ruling elites of these vassal states.

An interesting example for the implications of sexuality in the realm of politics is found in a passage from a vassal diplomatic treaty signed between the Hittite king Suppiluliuma I (*c.* 1350–1320 BCE) and Huqqana, ruler of the small kingdom of Hayasa (probably located somewhere in the highlands of today's northeast Turkey). This treaty solidified the relationships between the two kingdoms, and was accompanied by the diplomatic marriage of the sister of Suppiluliuma to Huqqana. Because the Hittite woman was to be sent to live in a foreign land, her brother cautioned his subordinate king to guard her, because, according to the Hittite king, the people of Hayasa had unacceptable social norms concerning sexuality:

> In Hatti an important rule is followed: a brother does not take [sexually] his sister or his [female-]cousin. It is not right! However, he who does it – such a thing – he will not live in Hatti, [but] will be killed here! Because your land is barbaric, it is in disarray: one regularly takes his sister or his [female-] cousin. But in Hatti it is not right! ... When you go to the land of Hayasa, you take [sexually] the wives of your brother, that is, your sisters. In Hatti it is not right![16]

The Hittite king views his people as culturally superior because they hold higher moral standards concerning sexual behaviour than the immoral people of Hayasa, whose sexual immorality derives from their basic cultural inferiority, and, in turn, heightens this inferiority. This passage supplies valuable information to the modern historian. It shows us how sex played a role in the construction of a collective political identity, as here the Hittite king defines his own people as superior to the Hayasa because of their sexual practices.

---

16 *Hittite Diplomatic Texts*, trans. Gary M. Beckman (Atlanta, GA: Scholars, 1996), 27–8. See also I. Peled, 'Gender and Sex Crimes in the Ancient Near East: Law and Custom', in *Structures of Power: Law and Gender across the Ancient Near East and Beyond* (Chicago: Oriental Institute of the University of Chicago, 2017), 31.

Sex and Religious and Cultic Practices

Different aspects of sexuality were quite prominent in matters of religion and cultic practices across the ancient Near East. Our main sources of information concerning these issues are legal and cultic texts that shed light on ancient Near Eastern institutionalized religion. Many of these issues are controversial, however, and a matter of ongoing debates between scholars.

One aspect of the role of sexuality in religious practices is related to the requirement that temple attendants were to remain pure and refrain from any defilement while performing their tasks in the temple. Sexual intercourse was sometimes associated with impurity, mainly because bodily fluids such as semen, sexual secretions, and menstrual blood were perceived as unclean and defiling. For example, the Middle Assyrian Palace Decree no. 7 (c. 1240–1200 BCE) obliged menstruating women to keep away from the king before he made sacrifices for the gods. Even more explicit are several passages from a set of Hittite instructions stipulated for temple personnel in which these persons were obliged to wash themselves after having sexual intercourse, before returning to the temple. Anyone ignoring these instructions would have faced possible execution.[17]

One of the more controversial associations between sexuality and religion in the ancient Near East involves the cult of Inanna/Ishtar, the goddess of sexuality, eroticism, and war. Because this goddess was the patron of human sexuality, it has been assumed by many scholars that her cult also involved the performance of sexual intercourse. The evidence in this regard, however, is mostly inconclusive. For example, a large group of male personnel acted as temple attendants of this goddess, but whether they engaged in same-sex intercourse as part of their service to the temple is not clear; actual evidence in this respect is almost non-existent.[18]

Another aspect of this debate concerns the interrelated issues of 'sacred prostitution' and 'sacred marriage'. While these are sometimes confused by scholars, they should be discussed separately. 'Sacred prostitution' is a custom reported by the fifth-century BCE Greek historian Herodotus (in *Histories* I.199): every Babylonian woman was required once in her life to have sex outside of the temple of Mylitta (a variation of the name Mulissu, a manifestation of Ishtar), and the coin she received for her sexual favours was dedicated to the goddess. Nowadays most scholars reject these

---

17 Peled, *Law and Gender*, 56–7.
18 For alleged male 'sacred prostitution' in the ancient Near East, see Peled, *Masculinities and Third Gender*, 157–8 and nn. 647–8, with previous literature.

descriptions of Herodotus as distorted accounts triggered by the biased views of the Greeks, who considered themselves culturally and morally superior to the decadent civilizations of the Near East.

More historically grounded was the ceremony of 'sacred marriage', which may have formed the vague historical background against which the fictional 'sacred prostitution' can be understood. 'Sacred marriage' was a rite during which the king and a female companion (the high priestess or the queen) had sexual intercourse, symbolizing the union between Inanna / Ishtar and her spouse Dumuzi / Tammuz. This ceremony was conducted at the beginning of the new year and symbolized the renewal of the king's legitimacy to rule over the land. Such ceremonies are documented several times, with the most complete of these descriptions the so-called 'Iddin-Dagan A' or 'The Hymn of Iddin-Dagan', after the name of the king who features in it (*c.* 1900 BCE).[19]

A unique phenomenon, only documented from the Old Babylonian period, was that of a specific class of priestesses called *nadītus*. These priestesses were dedicated to the Sun-god Shamash, and lived in secluded cloisters. Because of their dedication to the deity, they were not allowed to bear children. They thus accumulated significant wealth, but had no biological children who could inherit it, so they developed an interesting system of adoption. By adopting people as 'sons', the inheritance was not lost, but these 'sons' could have been adults, and at times even other *nadītu*-priestesses, rather than children. Our knowledge concerning the *nadītus* derives from different types of sources: private letters, administrative documents, transactions, adoption-contracts, and much more.[20]

Sex and Criminal Law

Law collections are primarily concerned with sexual issues related to marriage and inheritance, but a few of them also mention other sexual matters, generally to prohibit them. Somewhat surprisingly, incest is not frequently mentioned in ancient Near Eastern texts, and the law collections rarely

19 The scholarly literature over the themes of 'sacred prostitution' and 'sacred marriage' in the ancient Near East is vast; see Stephanie L. Budin, *The Myth of Sacred Prostitution in Antiquity* (Cambridge: Cambridge University Press, 2008). For the role of Iddin-Dagan A in this discussion, see I. Peled, 'Religious Practice in the Ancient Near East and Biblical Interpretation', in *Handbook of Historical Exegesis: The Use of Background Data in Biblical Interpretation*, ed. S. E. Porter and D. J. Fuller (Cambridge: Cambridge University Press, forthcoming).

20 On the *nadītus*, see Rivkah Harris, 'The Organization and Administration of the Cloister in Ancient Babylonia', *Journal of the Economic and Social History of the Orient* 6, no. 2 (1963): 121–57.

addressed it. One statute in the Laws of Ur-Namma (LUN §E5) decreed execution for a man who married the widow of his deceased older brother, while five clauses in the Laws of Hammurabi banned a man from having sex with his daughter (LH §154), daughter-in-law (LH §§155, 156), mother (LH §157), and stepmother (LH §158). The punishments varied: banishment, financial fines, disinheritance, and execution. The Hittite Laws stand out as the sole collection to have contained a detailed list of forbidden incestuous unions, both within the nuclear family and in the extended one. This collection forbade a man from conducting sexual relations with his biological mother, daughter, and son (HL §189), stepmother (while the father is alive; after the death of the father these relations were licit; HL §190), free sisters and their mother at the same time (HL §191), brother's wife while the brother is alive, stepdaughter, mother-in-law, and sister-in-law (HL §195). The sanction for all these illicit acts was probably execution.

Same-sex relations are almost never mentioned in the law collections. The sole exception is found in two consecutive clauses in the Middle Assyrian Laws:

> (MAL A §19): If a man has spread rumours in secret over his fellow thus, 'They are (all) penetrating him anally!', or in a quarrel before the public says to him thus, 'They are (all) penetrating you anally!' (and further) thus, 'I shall prove you!', (but) he is unable to prove, (and) does not prove: they shall strike that man 50 (times) with rods; he shall perform the king's service for one full month; they shall cut him off; and he shall give 1 talent (=3,600 shekels) of lead.[21]
>
> MAL A §20: If a man penetrates anally his fellow, they prove him (guilty), they convict him: they shall penetrate him anally, they shall turn him into a eunuch.

Both sources suggest real animosity towards same-sex relations among men. In contrast, same-sex relations among women are never mentioned in the extant sources.

References to bestiality are very rare: only the Hittite Laws address this issue. Several different animals are specified as prohibited for human copulation (cow, sheep, pig, and dog), and when a sanction is specified, it is the death penalty. Bestiality was considered in these laws as defiling, because the perpetrator was also forbidden from approaching the king, lest his sinful acts defile the king.

---

21 The phrase 'cut him off' probably refers to the man's hair or beard.

As a rule, the male partner was regarded by the law as the initiator of any illicit sexual act. The wording of the laws almost always opened with the formulaic conditional phrase 'If a man . . .', viewing him as the superior party and responsible for the consequences of the act.[22]

Conclusion

This chapter surveys several themes relating to sexuality in the different societies of the ancient Near East. We saw that legal documents – especially official law collections – were supposed to regulate people's sexual behaviour, while literary compositions reflected existing social values, and cultic rituals and ceremonies offered the means for handling sexuality in public and private domains. We saw that sexuality was gendered, and men enjoyed more privileges – but also bore more responsibilities – than women. The regulation of sex also established hierarchical relations within society, including between social ranks, and outside of it, between cultures. As in any part of human history, sexuality was one of the most fundamental aspects of human life in the ancient Near East. It therefore attracted much attention, and its numerous aspects are documented in a myriad of sources deriving from the entire history of the ancient Near East, covering a time-span of some 3,000 years.

Further Reading

Ackerman, Susan. *When Heroes Love: The Ambiguity of Eros in the Stories of Gilgamesh and David*. New York: Columbia University Press, 2005.

Biggs, Robert D. *ŠÀ.ZI.GA: Ancient Mesopotamian Potency Incantations*. New York: J. J. Augustin, 1967.

Bolger, Diane, ed. *Gender through Time in the Ancient Near East*. Lanham, MD: AltaMira, 2008.

Budin, Stephanie Lynn. *Fertility and Gender in the Ancient Near East*. New York: Routledge, 2014.

The Myth of Sacred Prostitution in Antiquity. Cambridge: Cambridge University Press, 2008.

Budin, Stephanie Lynn, and Jean MacIntosh Turfa, eds. *Women in Antiquity: Real Women across the Ancient World*. New York: Routledge, 2016.

Budin, Stephanie Lynn, Megan Cifarelli, Agnès Garcia-Ventura, and Adelina Millet Albà, eds. *Gender and Methodology in the Ancient Near East: Approaches from Assyriology and Beyond*. Barcelona: Universitat de Barcelona, 2018.

---

22 Peled, *Law and Gender*, 91–107.

Chavalas, Mark, ed. *Women in the Ancient Near East: A Sourcebook*. New York: Routledge, 2013.

Graef, Katrien de, Agnès Garcia-Ventura, Annes Goddeeris, and Beth Alpert Nakhai, eds. *The Mummy under the Bed: Essays on Gender and Methodology in the Ancient Near East*. Münster: Zaphon, 2022.

Harris, Rivkah. 'The Organization and Administration of the Cloister in Ancient Babylonia'. *Journal of the Economic and Social History of the Orient* 6, no. 2 (1963): 121–57.

Henshaw, Richard A. *Female and Male: The Cultic Personnel; The Bible and the Rest of the Ancient Near East*. Allison Park, PA: Pickwick, 1994.

Lafont, Sophie. *Femmes, Droit et Justice dans l'Antiquité orientale: Contribution à l'étude du droit pénal au Proche-Orient ancien*. Fribourg: Éditions Universitaires, 1999.

Leick, Gwendolyn. *Sex and Eroticism in Mesopotamian Literature*. New York: Routledge, 1994.

Lion, Brigitte, and Cécile Michele, eds. *The Role of Women in Work and Society in the Ancient Near East*. Berlin: De Gruyter, 2016.

Lipka, Hilary, and Bruce Wells, eds. *Sexuality and Law in the Torah*. London: T. & T. Clark, 2020.

Marsman, Hennie J. *Women in Ugarit and Israel: Their Social and Religious Position in the Context of the Ancient Near East*. Leiden: Brill, 2003.

Matthews, Victor H., Bernard M. Levinson, and Tikva Frymer-Kensky, eds. *Gender and Law in the Hebrew Bible and the Ancient Near East*. Sheffield: Sheffield Academic Press, 1998.

Nissinen, Martti. *Homoeroticism in the Biblical World: A Historical Perspective*. Minneapolis, MN: Fortress, 1998.

Parpola, Simo, and Robert M. Whiting, eds. *Sex and Gender in the Ancient Near East*. Helsinki: University of Helsinki Press, 2002.

Peled, Ilan. 'Contempt and Similar Emotions in Akkadian and Hittite Literary Texts'. In *Handbook of Emotions in the Ancient Near East*, ed. K. Sonik and U. Steinert, 597–613. London: Routledge, 2022.

'Gender and Sex Crimes in the Ancient Near East: Law and Custom'. In *Structures of Power: Law and Gender across the Ancient Near East and Beyond*, ed. I. Peled, 27–40. Chicago: Oriental Institute of the University of Chicago Press, 2017.

Law and Gender in the Ancient Near East and the Hebrew Bible. London: Routledge, 2020.

Masculinities and Third Gender: The Origins and Nature of an Institutionalized Gender Otherness in the Ancient Near East. Münster: Ugarit-Verlag, 2016.

Stol, Marten. *Birth in Babylonia and the Bible: Its Mediterranean Setting*. Groningen: Styx, 2000.

Women in the Ancient Near East. Trans. Helen and Mervyn Richardson. Berlin: De Gruyter, 2016.

Uehlinger, Christoph. 'Nackte Göttin. B. In der Bildkunst'. In *Reallexikon der Assyriologie und Vorderasiatischen Archäologie*, Vol. 9, ed. D. O. Edzard, M. Krebernik, J. N. Postgate, W. Röllig et al., 53–64. Berlin: De Gruyter, 1998.

Westbrook, Raymond, ed. *A History of Ancient Near Eastern Law*. Leiden: Brill, 2003.

Wiggermann, Franz. A. M., 'Sexualität (Sexuality). A. In Mesopotamien'. In *Reallexikon der Assyriologie und Vorderasiatischen Archäologie*, Vol. 12, ed. M. P. Streck, G. Frantz-Szabó, M. Krebernik, D. Morandi Bonacossi et al., 410–26. Berlin: De Gruyter, 2010.

4

Sexuality in Traditional South Asian Systems of Thought and Belief

JAYA S.TYAGI AND TARA SHEEMAR MALHAN

Cultural perspectives and sensibilities in South Asia relating to sexuality reflect divergent beliefs and practices. The word 'sexuality' itself is seen to have emerged in the nineteenth-century West, but it does not mark the sudden emergence of that to which it refers. 'Sexuality, whether in the erotic flourishes of Indian art and in the Dionysian rituals of its popular religion, or in the dramatic combat with ascetic longings of Yogis who seek to conquer and transform it into spiritual power, has been a perennial preoccupation of Hindu culture.'[1]

The religious tradition that today is called Hinduism involves a diverse set of practices and beliefs that developed over many centuries. These include rituals that might allow a person to achieve union with the ultimate unchanging reality that is the source of the universe, known as *Brahman*. Brahmanical traditions are recorded in sacred works, epics, hymns, philosophical treatises, and ritual texts called the Vedas, created during the period from roughly 1500 BCE to 500 BCE, an era that in Indian history comes to be known as the Vedic period. Reaching *Brahman* also involved living a moral life, what became known as *dharma*, a Sanskrit word with many shades of meaning, involving piety, moral law, ethics, order, duty, mutual understanding, justice, and peace.

There is considerable ambiguity in the discussions on sexual desire in Brahmanical traditions: sexual acts are not regarded as separate, but one of many indulgences. The word *kāma* reflects an intense desire for all pleasurable things, the urge to satisfy all sensory stimuli. *Kāma* led to creation and was one of the reasons for human existence, but it was this pursuit of desire,

---

1 Sudhir Kakar, *Intimate Relations: Exploring Indian Sexuality* (New Delhi: Penguin Books, 1989), 21.

according to the South Asian religious thinker who became known as the Buddha, which created a thirst that led to a deep but illusory attachment to people, things, and life itself, and was the cause of all sorrow. (For more on sexuality in Buddhist traditions, see Chapter 11 by Kali Nyami Cape in this volume.) Literary traditions of South Asia prescribe heteronormative relations within the institution of marriage, but a closer scrutiny of early texts and visual traditions reveal that while grappling with sexuality, the representations have undercurrents of anxiety and contrary opinions, sometimes within a single tradition itself.

In early Vedic and Brahmanical thought systems, the emphasis was on reproduction – sex was regarded as a sacral, ritual act. The anxiety related to paternity and 'purity of the progeny' is reflected in the need to control women's sexuality in texts that were written after the Vedas, including the Dharmaśāstras (second–seventh centuries CE), and in the large body of epics and other types of literature known as the Purāṇas. However, Brahmanical traditions were not homogenous or monolithic, and there have been intense debates on sexuality and on what construes as sexual propriety within them. Some traditions take fairly stringent views on celibacy, accompanied with an obsessive preoccupation with the human body, particularly women's bodies. This preoccupation is found in different 'heterodox' traditions in South Asia, such as Buddhism, Jainism, and the Ājīvika school, all of which emerged in the middle of the first millennium BCE. These ostensibly diverged from the Brahmanical thought systems, but converged when it came to discussions on the sexuality of women. These beliefs, bordering on misogyny, eschewed women and marriage, although Buddhist and Jaina monastic orders did take the radical step of including women. On the other end of the spectrum were the 'materialists', the followers of the Cārvākas school of thought, who promoted self-indulgence and must have had a substantial following, given the many references to them and their followers. This chapter will attempt to map some of the focal aspects of discussions on sexuality in multiple South Asian traditions, with the caveat that, given the complexity of the subject, any such discussion cannot be exhaustive.

The Pre- and Proto-Historic Context

Some of the earliest prehistoric paintings in South Asia depict activities such as hunting, fishing, and dancing along with sexual activities. When women are shown, they are shown doing specific tasks such as carrying a basket with a child slung on their back. Men and women are shown together, pointing towards a 'casual' and natural approach to sexuality, with some concern about fertility. Rock paintings at Kathotia, Bhimbetka, Kharwai, and Adamgarh in Central India from Upper Palaeolithic and Mesolithic levels (roughly 25,000–10,000 BCE) have cultic scenes, such as the men shown with erect penises in Kathotia. (Art historians refer to such figures as 'ithyphallic'.) Animals were painted in a more elaborate manner than humans, some in x-ray style with a foetus in the womb. The vivid depiction of an ejaculating boar from a site in Jaora seems to indicate preoccupation relating to fertility and some mystique or even rituals related to progenitors and lineage.

Historically, one can trace shifts in attitudes towards sexuality and women when the female body begins to be given unwavering attention and is represented in an isolated manner, as separate figurines, without any clearly discernible context. In South Asia, female figurines have been found in terracotta, bronze, and other material from the archaeological site of Mehrgarh, where we also get the earliest evidence of domestication of plants and animals, around the sixth millennium BCE. The connection between the domestication of plants and animals and the creative urge to depict the female form seems to suggest a 'heightened consciousness, an anxiety about reproductivity, fecundity, conception, labour and birth'.[2] The figurines from Mehrgarh are from different periods and found from several stratigraphical levels, beginning from the earliest ones in Period I (pre-7000 BCE–5500 BCE), which are very rudimentary, to more sophisticated ones later in Period VI (*c.* 3000 BCE), which include figurines with prominent breasts with nipples, and elaborate individual coiffures. From Period VII (2600 BCE–2000 BCE) onwards male figurines begin to be found, some of them with children and adorned with 'phallic type' jewellery.

While female figurines have been referred to in a generic manner as 'Venus type' figurines or even 'Mother Goddesses', we cannot group all figurines together. (For more on 'Venus figures', see Chapter 19 by Y. Yvon Wang in Volume I of this work.) Giving them the dual identity of 'mother' and 'goddess' is presumptive – they may well be 'icons', reflecting the sexuality and aesthetics of the time rather than procreation or religion. When women are depicted, however, they do often represent fertility and sexuality as well as societal notions of pleasure and cultural aesthetics. The making of a figurine is itself an act of seeking control, revealing an intent to document the feminine form, to sexualize it, and possibly to control it. It

---

2 Gregory Possehl has described their society as an internally differentiated, structurally specialized social system where gender made a difference. Gregory Possehl, *The Indus Civilization: A Contemporary Perspective* (New Delhi: Vistaar, 2002), 177.

indicates that the site of the female body was becoming one of cultural expression, representing the ideology and aesthetics of that culture, as well as its beliefs. But we do not know who was making these figurines – men, women or both – which makes the figures all the more intriguing.

The artefacts from the Indus Civilization (its mature period was between 2500 and 1750 BCE) tell us about the importance of fertility, as figurines of women carrying children have been found from the two Indus sites of Harappa and Mohenjo-daro. Some figurines are clearly female, depicted with breasts and hips, while males are shown with beards and, in some, with the genitalia clearly visible. Often figurines do not have very prominent features, however, or they have androgynous features, probably deliberately so. Not all depictions can be interpreted conclusively. For example, the so-called 'Pasupati' seal, a stone seal uncovered at Mohenjo-daro, has been variously identified as a seated bull, a woman deity, an ithyphallic male figure, or even androgynous. This shows that the different artefacts may represent varied beliefs, and that given the extent of the Harappan civilization, there must have been multiple practices. Harappan seals often depict scenes of fertility; one of them shows a plant emerging from a woman's womb, underlining the association of nature's fertility with the reproductivity of women in their thought systems. One of the exceptions to this emphasis on fertility is a Mohenjo-daro dancing girl, a vibrantly expressive figurine in which the girl is standing with one hand on a raised hip, coiffured head tilted to the side and the other hand laden with bangles from wrist to upper arm in a nonchalant, confident posture. Since only one other such figurine has been found among all the Indus sites, however, one cannot really say whether the figurine is representative of Harappan thought systems or attitudes towards sexuality.

Male figurines from Harappa and Mohenjo-daro include ithyphallic ones, many of which are nude and potbellied; the Harappan script remains undeciphered, however, so that in the absence of literary sources that we can read it is difficult to interpret their significance.[3] Objects shaped like male and female genitalia – *lingas* or *lingams* and *yonis* – in the Harappan sites are often associated with fertility cults, but whether they can even be called *lingas* and were used for pleasure or worship is not clear. The *linga* represents the male phallus and while its worship emerged in a considerable way in later times in South Asia, the socio-cultural manifestation and conceptualizations relating to *linga* iconography are fairly complex. In later times the phallus is often

3 Possehl, *The Indus Civilization,* 119.

depicted with the *yoni* (the vagina) around it – depicting the *linga-in-yoni* – suggestive of experiencing (and venerating) a perspective from within the womb wherein the entire world is the womb and the sexual act is a cosmic event.

Asexual Creation, Incest, and Heteronormativity: Vedic–Brahmanical Thought Systems

The earliest textual traditions in South Asia are the Vedas, which have cosmological theories and discuss cosmic processes of creation and procreation through the use of metaphors describing asexual reproduction. They also refer to copulation and sexual acts (such as that between the Father Sky and Mother Earth), revealing that ideas relating to sexuality were used for explaining complex cosmic phenomena. According to the earliest of these texts, the *Ṛg Veda* (1800 BCE onwards), the universe emerged from 'the One', and was created from the thought of the Creator. In the beginning there was 'nothing' and it was the beginning of desire, *kāma*, that led to creation.[4] The hymn ends in an open-ended manner stating that no one knows how Creation happened and only the Creator knows, and whether he also knows is not known.

In the myth of the *Ṛg Veda* relating to the primordial twins Yama and Yamī, the latter approaches her brother to initiate intimacy between them, but Yama chides his sister for suggesting something that is against the cosmic moral order and against the prevailing norm, *ṛta*. The dialogue between the twins is in a stylized form, and could have been recited as part of a ritual, suggesting connections between myth, memory, and primordial practices. The passage reflects changing sexual norms – but also has an undercurrent of disapproval of female desire and how there is need to control it.[5]

Dominant masculinity vis-à-vis recipient femininity is constantly reiterated in the Vedas. There are 250 hymns in the *Ṛg Veda* that invoke Indra, a virile masculine deity and warrior par excellence. These hymns are in contrast with the softer (and much fewer) hymns dedicated to goddesses such as Uṣas (Dawn). Progeny were defined by the father and the role of semen is underlined, as there are chants for strengthening of the seed and terms for those who possess virility. In the Atharva Veda, there is a valorizing of the male organ as it was seen as a source of the embryo. Polyandrous practices in

---

4 The Nāsadīya hymn, *Ṛg Veda* 10.129, in Ralph T. H. Griffith, *The Hymns of the Rg Veda*, 2 vols. (1896; Varanasi: Chowkhamba Sanskrit Series, 1971), 2: 575.
5 *Ṛg Veda* 10.10, in Griffith, *The Hymns*, 2: 391–4.

the Vedas hint at earlier practices of group marriage, for in the text 'paired marriages', that is, those between a man and a woman, are solely for the purpose of having a son.[6] In another hymn that has been interpreted in different ways, the goddess Indrāṇī complains to her husband, the superior god Indra, about the sexual liberties taken with her by his friend Vṛṣākapi (literally, monkey bursting with seed; or promiscuous monkey). In a vitriolic domestic spat, Indrāṇī accuses Indra of being too indulgent towards his friend and being dismissive of and trivializing his wife's angst.[7]

Instances of polygyny, homosexuality, and certain other sexual practices in later Vedic and Brahmanical texts (1000–500 BCE) are projected as transgressive and it is heteronormative sexual behaviour that is encouraged. Myths play on anxieties and categorize sexual relationships on the basis of what is acceptable and unacceptable, attempting to control norms of moral propriety. However, that they are even included in normative traditions means they socialize the audience into thinking about disparate expressions of sexuality, and perhaps accepting elite, royal, and male entitlement to a wide range of sexual practices: if the gods and sages could indulge in such activity, then so could the elite.

Celibacy, Asceticism, and Misogyny: Early Historic Heterodox and Epic–Purāṇic Traditions

In the middle of the first millennium BCE, in the post-Vedic Brahmanical Upanishads and what are termed the 'heterodox' traditions, philosophical discussions on the nature of life and death and on sexuality became more intensive. The emphasis on celibacy and abstention was reinforced, as celibacy was believed to be the 'highest state of purity' and it was thought that sexual abstention led to a concentration of virile energy, allowing the mind and body to attain special powers. These ideas were further reinforced by the followers of the religious thinker Mahāvīra, born in the sixth century BCE, who went on to formulate the Jaina order, and also by the Buddha and his followers; they were developed further by yogic practitioners.

The Jaina and Buddhist monastic orders were a refuge for men and women. Particularly for the nuns, monasticism, with the promise of soteriological escape, was not only an escape from the household, but also from societal expectations of sexual and reproductive roles. The *Therīgāthā* – the

---

6 *Ṛg Veda* 1.116.5, in Griffith, *The Hymns*, 1: 154.
7 *Ṛg Veda* 10.86, in Griffith, *The Hymns*, 2: 507.

songs of nuns – emphasize the need to go beyond the limits of physical existence. The *Vinaya Piṭaka*, the Buddhist canonical text on monasticism, refers to the fact that sexual intercourse was taboo for monks and nuns and denies ordination to non-conforming men and women. Studies have shown, however, that monastics were known to transgress these rules, and that homosexuality and homoerotic friendship were often a part of monastic life. A 'hierarchy of penalties' are mentioned in the text; masturbation of one monk by another and non-orgasmic contact were supposedly 'relatively minor' transgressions. Bestiality is condemned, and references to *paṇḍakas* – generally defined as 'one without testicles' or a 'weak, pusillanimous' person – were probably indicative of disapproval of homosexual behaviour. *Paṇḍakas* were also mentioned in earlier texts such as the Atharva Veda as a distinct group, different from 'ordinary males and females, and apparently transvestites'. In the *Mahāvagga*, one of the chapters of the Buddhist text called the Vinaya Piṭaka, it is said in reproach that the 'followers of Buddha are *paṇḍakas*' and that is why the Blessed One (Buddha) said that *paṇḍakas* should not be ordained and if they have been ordained, they should be expelled. Similarly, the *Cullavagga*, another chapter in the same Buddhist text, mentions that lesbians should be denied ordination as nuns.[8]

In these texts, it is female sexuality that is particularly problematic, however. Buddha is reputed to have said that it is better for a foolish man to put his male organ into the 'mouth of a terrible and poisonous snake' or a charcoal pit rather than enter a woman. When it comes to discussions on sexual abstention, the discussions about the woman's body are particularly harsh. The nuns seem to have internalized these notions and saw their own bodies as 'a hunter's snare'; some even went to the extent of self-mutilation in order to de-sexualize themselves. The texts refer to episodes related to the nun Subhā Jivakambavanikā who, revolted by the advances of a 'rogue', compares her body to a corpse rotting in the cemetery, and also talks about the impermanence of the body and material wealth.[9] When the man praises her beautiful eyes, she wrenches the eye from its socket and hands it over to him in a violent act of total detachment from her body. This suggests that

---

8 Quotations from Leonard Zwilling, 'Homosexuality as Seen in Indian Buddhist Texts', in *Buddhism, Sexuality and Gender*, ed. José Cabezón (Albany, NY: State University of New York Press, 1992), 203–13.

9 Therigāthā 366–99, in Kathryn Blackstone, *Women in the Footsteps of Buddha* (Delhi: Motilal Banarsidass, 1998), 59–81, at 57. See also Liz Wilson, *Charming Cadavers: Horrific Figurations of the Feminine in Indian Buddhist Hagiographic Literature* (Chicago: University of Chicago Press, 1996).

nuns were also vulnerable to sexual and other forms of violence for having adopted this alternative lifestyle.

The epics and Purāṇas were popular traditions, read, recited, and performed in diverse regions in South Asia and beyond. These texts contain myths in which sexual identity and gender orientation were linked to distinctive mannerisms, expressions, speech, hair, and even clothes. In the epics *Mahābhārata* and *Rāmāyana*, representations of gender bending and transsexuality exist. Arjuna/Bṛhannaḍā, Ambā/Sikhaṇḍin, and Ila/Ilā are some protagonists with fluid identities, but in many ways these only serve to reinforce notions of masculinity and femininity. The myth of Ila, a man who is transformed into a woman (Ilā) for daring to venture into the pleasure gardens of the deities Shiva and Pārvatī, reinforces the importance of conjugal intimacy and notions of masculinity and femininity, while projecting womanhood as a 'punishment'. The irony is that as Ilā she gives birth to King Purūravā, the founder of the lunar dynasty from which great kings were supposed to have descended.

Women's sexuality is discussed with considerable anxiety in most of the early texts, whether it is the epics, the legal text *Mānava Dharmaśāstra* (also known as the *Manusmṛti*), the law codes of Manu (*c.* 200 BCE–200 CE), or the Buddhist folk tales known as the *Jātaka* texts. The incoming bride is sought to be controlled and her potent sexuality channelled in the *Gṛhyasūtras*, Vedic texts prescribing various domestic rituals, of which the early ones come from *c.* 800–500 BCE. The texts show how the bride is introduced in the household with apprehension, as one who can be inauspicious and bring death and destruction. The *Gṛhyasūtras* refer to girls to be avoided while arranging marriages, including girls who would be a destroyer of progeny, a destroyer of animals, or a destroyer of her husband. Instead, these texts prescribe that she should become the destroyer of her lover, revealing the anxiety related to her sexuality and the possibilities of unwanted liaisons before or after the marriage. In these texts, the sacral character of the household with the householder as head is emphasized, and giving birth is a sacred task. The reproductive role of the wife in the marriage rites and those related to conception and childbirth is carefully recorded and the terms used for the wife all underline her sexual role. In the *Mānava Dharmaśāstra*, the wife's status is described as the same as a field owned by the husband; women are equated with the field while the seed is believed to be masculine. Concerns relating to the paternity of the progeny are constantly reiterated, even while epics such as the *Mahābhārata* describe all kinds of measures to obtain progeny, include levirate marriage, paired marriage, and boons from deities.

In these texts, women bore the brunt of elite male power games, to be fought over, abducted, used for one-upmanship, and as pawns in the display of boorish masculinity. For example, after being pawned off in a game of dice by her own husband in the presence of hapless elders and courtiers, Princess Draupadi in King Dhṛtrāṣtra's court, the wife of rival cousins, is disrobed and dragged by her hair, even while she is menstruating, though she puts up a spirited defence. Notions of masculinity were fairly stringent: kings are shown to be weakened by sexual desire and despite having many wives, as unable to conceive children and depending on Brahmanical rituals rather than their libido. The texts project elite male entitlement by describing sages' expectations of hospitality when they went on visits where young daughters of the host would take special care of them. Legends also refer to sexual violence and men forcing themselves upon protesting women.

Codifying and Institutionalizing Heteronormative Sexuality: The *Dharmaśāstra* Traditions

The dissonance in the approach towards young girls' sexuality reveals male-centric beliefs. Even when girls were being used as sexual pawns by kinsmen for furthering their political and personal interests, channelling the girls' sexuality was a major concern, which was addressed by marrying them off early. In the texts which codify *dharma*, the *Dharmaśāstras*, the notion of *kanyādāna*, the gift of the virgin, entailed a contract among males – the father of the bride and the groom. According to the *Mānava Dharmaśāstra*, the right age for marriage for a thirty-year-old man was a girl of twelve years, or for an eighteen-year-old man, an eight-year-old girl, or even younger.[10] While eight forms of marriage are included in varied texts, these are arranged in a hierarchical order, and the patriarchal nature of marriage as an institution is evident in that only those marriages which have the consent of the male elders and where the girl is 'given away' in a formal manner as a virgin are considered the 'best'. The first four are the most respected ones, in which the 'bedecked bride' is given by the father to the groom. The last two are clearly cases of abduction, although the fact that they are included in the forms of marriage, albeit at the bottom of the hierarchy, shows an attempt to give legal sanction to such relationships. Among the eight forms of heterosexual

---

10 *Mānava Dharmaśāstra* 9.94, in Patrick Olivelle, *Manu's Code of Law: A Critical Edition and Translation of* Mānava Dharmaśāstra (Oxford: Oxford University Press, 2010), 194.

unions, only one refers to a consensual union between the husband and wife – the *gāndharva* type of marriage.

Gradually, the emphasis in the *Dharmaśāstras* turns to endogamy, that is, marriages within the same *varṇa*, or caste category. The norms for this evolve over time: while the early *Dharmaśāstras* allow hypergamy (i.e., upper category men with lower category women), the reverse, hypogamy, was considered taboo. However, the later *Mānava Dharmaśāstra* frowns upon both these types of marriages, and states that the children from such marriages fall in status due to the 'contamination' of mixing categories.

Anxiety related to sexuality and the need to control women superseded all other ethical codes in these texts, as the primary role of a husband was to keep his wife in control, just as the primary role of the wife was to keep herself in control. The *Mānava Dharmaśāstra* states: 'Day and night men should keep their women from acting independently: for, attached as they are to sensual pleasures, men should keep them under their control.' Gods and ancestors do not partake of offerings if a wife plays a leading role in 'divine, ancestral, and hospitality rites'.[11]

The *Dharmaśāstras* evolved into compendia-type texts, and in a comprehensive attempt to encompass and rationalize all states of existence, discussed the four stages or *āśramas* included in a single person's life: celibacy, householdership, forsaking the material world, and asceticism. Among these stages, only the second stage, that of the householder, was envisaged as one where sexuality was expressed and experienced, while the other three stages were supposed to be celibate. In the householder stage, people were expected to marry and observe *dharma* within the family, with sexual pleasure, fulfilling religious obligations, and having children regarded as the three purposes of marriage.

This belief in stages of life existed alongside that of the *puruṣārthas*, the four reasons for human existence. These were: upholding of moral order (*dharma*); acquisition and management of wealth and resources (*artha*); experiencing all kinds of sensory pleasures (*kāma*); and preparing for the final soteriological escape (*mokṣa*). The concepts of the four stages and four reasons allow for sexuality to be an essential part of human existence, but only one part. Norms for men involved *puruṣa*, a sense of self, whereas women were expected to follow men in their choices, and serving their husband was a sacred observance (*pativratā*). These norms were reiterated frequently in texts about the ideal notion of womanhood, with the anxiety

---

11 *Mānava Dharmaśāstra* 9.2,3, in Olivelle, *Manu's Code*, 190.

and concerns relating to 'controlling' women's sexuality revealing how critical it was believed to be for the social order and also that not all women (and men) conformed to these normative directives.

Conceptualizing and Controlling Desire: The *Kāma* Tradition

In this section, we will narrow down our discussion about sexuality to a study of the erotic and its treatment in 'traditional' thought. Here the popularized and well-known work on erotics, the *Kāmasūtra* of the philosopher Vatsyayana (third–fourth century CE) is placed within the textual tradition that produced 'the science of *kāma*' (*kāmaśāstra*). Sexual pleasure as produced in these texts is not coterminous with the term 'sexuality'. The latter emerged in modern usage as an attribute deep in the human psyche; a biological principle connected with individual identity that can be examined, confined, or liberated. In the traditional Indic 'science of pleasure', sexuality was placed under the rubric of pleasure (*kāma*) and connected to the other goals of human existence. *Kāma* refers to wishing, longing, desire, and pleasure, especially sensual pleasure, and love (*prīti*) and enjoyment (*rati*), qualities that are also represented as the wives of Kāmadeva (the God of Pleasure). The pleasures related to the senses were also stigmatized, however, as a group of 'six enemies' along with anger, greed, pride, stupefaction, and excitement, which were to be controlled according to the 'ethical' codes of disciplined conduct in courtly manuals.

Erotic love formed the preferred subject of many of the Sanskrit literary compositions termed *kāvyas* (a genre of literature including poetry, drama, narratives, and biography), which had *śṛngāra rasa* (erotic/love sentiment) as a primary aesthetic experience. Poets and other writers who wrote *kāvyas* depended upon conventions of *kāma* found in the *kāmaśāstra*, while the latter texts borrowed heavily from literary conventions to supplement their theories about love and lovers. The science of erotics and courtly literature shows overlapping in the division of male and female types into *nāyakas* (romantic heroes) and *nāyikās* (romantic heroines). The definition of desire codified in the *Kāmasūtra* was integrated into relations of power, and focused on the heterosexual desires of upper class men rather than those of women or lower-class men. The *Kāmasūtra* is oriented towards the viewpoint of the male protagonist known as the *nāgaraka* or 'man-about-town', assuming an official male voice.

The 'science of *kāma*' outlines the ideal life of the male protagonist, defines the norms of heterosexual intercourse, locates intercourse within the context of marriage, expounds on the pursuit of pleasure outside marriage particularly with prostitutes and married women, and lists aphrodisiacs and magical spells to enhance potency. A comprehensive list of luxuries is provided as the setting for erotic encounters, including the personal grooming of the man-about-town, along with substantial sensual accoutrements. Though the concerns of hierarchy are not paramount, and varna does not find mention, the norms of Brahmanical patriarchy are clearly reflected in the androcentrism of desire, the wife's subordination, and what appears as a general vulnerability of women. Pleasure is to be enjoyed homogamously, that is, marriage within one's class, according to the texts, and for the purpose of reproducing sons. Intercourse is forbidden with women of higher classes and the wives of others (although this clause is entirely abandoned in a section on seducing other men's wives), but allowed with courtesans, 'second-hand women' (women who have cohabited with men before), women of the lower classes, 'loose' women who assist men, widows, wandering women ascetics (although this is forbidden at another place in the text), servants, daughters of a courtesan, and women of the 'third nature' (*tṛtiya prakṛti*), a phrase which has often been interpreted to mean those attracted to individuals of their own sex.[12]

The *kāma* tradition as represented in the *Kāmasūtra* attempted to unravel the feminine sexual psyche and physiology, discussing the duration of sexual pleasure experienced by women, as compared with that of men, and the necessity of female climax for conception (2.1.7–21). There is a striking inclusion of considerable violence in descriptions of sexual acts, a kind of sado-masochism, where the provision for reciprocity and female domination in intercourse is qualified with a reference to the natural propensity of men as dominating and women as submissive. This can be seen in the descriptions of kissing, biting, scratching, and the different kinds of marks these leave, and ascription of more intensely violent sexual activities to 'people whose sexual energy is fierce', though caution is advised and extremes are to be avoided (2.2.29–2.3.8, 2.5.11–29, 2.5.11–29). In projecting male violence as acceptable, the text, 'would have provided the means for enforcing what was conceived

---

12 *Kāmasutra*, 1.5, trans. Wendy Doniger and Sudhir Kakar (Oxford: Oxford University Press, 2002), 23–8. Further references will be noted in the text.

as the structure of sexual relations'.[13] The 'men-in-power' are warned to maintain restraint as they were under public scrutiny, but the section on regional practices reveals the sexual privileges of powerful men as being able to access ordinary women through various devices. These disclose an attitude towards sex that calls for being rid of 'prudish' notions, but also displays the connection between power and pleasure, implicating the powerful in its abuse (5.5.32–5.6.2).

At various places – explicitly and implicitly – Vatsyayana takes into account female desire. Thus, the *Kāmasūtra* acknowledges that women of the harem are unsatisfied because they share one husband and then goes on to list certain practices that they follow for sexual gratification, including adultery, homoeroticism, and fetishism (5.5.32–5.6.2–24). Descriptions of the efforts made to win over a newly married virgin's trust and winning over a young girl show some sensitivity (3.2.6–80, 3.3.1–89). However, the girl is advised not to be forthcoming since it would destroy her 'luck in love'. A married woman may take on a lover, it notes, due to the dull sexual energy of the husband and qualities such as jealousy, ingratitude, or stinginess (5.4.3–14). The later texts of the *kāmaśāstra* tradition demonstrate that the female protagonist remained a subject, but she was classified according to her sexual ties with a man – the virgin and wife being accessible to a single man, the wife of another and the remarried woman being accessible to two men, the courtesan being accessible to all men, and inaccessible women barred on grounds of incest, taboo, or class/caste restrictions. The number of restrictions placed on the wife were numerous, or she risked being called 'loose' by her husband.

The *kāma* tradition is at variance with the dharma texts, which ignore or stigmatize homosexual activity. The Sanskrit words traditionally translated as 'eunuch', generally referring to a man who did not act like a man or a defective male, are not used in the *Kāmasūtra*. Fellatio is the defining homosexual activity: it could be performed on the 'man-about-town' by persons of the 'third nature' (*tṛtīyā prakṛti*), male masseurs, promiscuous women, 'loose women', servant girls, and masseuses (2.9.1–45). In the *Kāmasūtra*, *tṛtīyā prakṛti* are described as one of two types: male-bodied individuals who dress and act feminine, and engage in oral sex, making their living from it as well as getting arousal from it; and male-bodied individuals who dress and act masculine, making their living as masseurs or by selling sex. (Whether any of these individuals were what we would today

---

13 Kumkum Roy, 'Unravelling the Kamasutra', in *The Power of Gender and the Gender of Power: Explorations in Early India History* (New Delhi: Oxford University Press, 2010), 294–342.

understand as trans or queer is not known.) Receiving fellatio does not make a *nāgaraka* a man of the 'third nature', but is simply something he indulges in for sheer pleasure. Thus patriarchal values connected with the hierarchizing that privileged elite heterosexual masculinity can be seen even in same-sex activity.

Several genres of Sanskrit courtly literature, whose earliest examples date between the fourth and seventh centuries, evoke contexts set out in the later books of the *Kāmasūtra*, particularly the dramas, courtesan-centred *kāvyas*, and satirical monologues. The dramas combine erotic and political fantasy, but also reveal serious psychic and social anxieties that attended sexual relationships in noble households. The satirical monologues of the Gupta and early medieval period (fourth–tenth centuries CE) set out some counter-attitudes towards the rigid code of valorized righteous behaviour that centred on the self-restraint and reasoning of the male and the compliance of the dutiful wife in the *Dharmaśāstras*. Instead, they highlight hedonism and pleasure-seeking, while exposing the hypocrisy of the pretentious elite or the renunciant through satire, witty dialogues, and lampooning.

The sexually and culturally accomplished *nāgaraka* pleasure-seeking ideal formed the discourse of urbanism rooted in Sanskrit *kāvyas*, with their vision of the city as centre of the culture of *kāma* or an ethic of pleasure. This city-centred culture featured repeated characters such as the libertine as an authentic exponent of *kāma*, the king with his tempered sexual prowess, the courtesan as culturally accomplished but socially degraded, the veiled *kulastrī* (noble family woman) with her sexuality under parental control and then channelled into legitimate reproduction, and the paradoxical depiction of high-born women in illicit love affairs even within the confines of the household. Various contradictory representations were one of the traits of early India, where along with love poetry, sensuous art, and scholarly works on pleasure there was also a strong tradition that emphasized the elimination and control of desire.

Expressing Femininity: Non-Sanskrit Love Poetry

We find explorations of erotic themes in other non-Sanskrit literary compositions, particularly from the peninsular part of the subcontinent – the Prakrit *Gāthā Sattasaī* or *Gāthāsaptaśati* (*Sat*) and the old Tamil love poetry (*akam*). The *Sat*, composed by an obscure Sātvāhana king named Hāla (first century CE) is primarily an anthology of love poems suffused with *śṛingāra rasa* (the erotic/love flavour/sentiment). The poems are in couplets and were probably sung, or recited, the language being a form of Prakrit, which evolved its grammar under the influence of Sanskrit. The erotic flavour is revealed in its sub-variants of love in union and in separation. It is usually a woman who is the first-person voice and she addresses others: her mother, friend, lover, or husband. The society of the *Sat* was rural, based on agriculture and animal husbandry. It was transitioning from a tribal to a class / caste-based society which was not completely Brahmanized, though the process had begun. The *Kāmasūtra* and the *Sat* represent two totally different world-views of love and sex, the former being concerned with theory and the urban milieu, the latter with the life experiences and rural milieu. The *Sat* has been contrasted with the *Kāmasūtra* where 'everything is docketed and programmed' and concerned with classification, while the *Sat* confronts theory with the 'untidy reality of life'.[14]

Some poems seem expressive of adolescent romance in which the boy and girl exchange glances, and a number of them deal with the village boy's fascination with the female body. Various poems deal with the secret meetings of lovers, along with descriptions of the natural setting. Some couplets deal with wrong choices and disappointments in love, and with the messengers used by lovers (usually a close friend of the girl). The conjugal relationship is the topic of many poems, with anxieties relating to experience, tenderness, establishment of sexual intimacy, sexual advances of the younger brother-in-law, and so on. There is plenty of descriptive love-play, with embracing and kissing. And there are topics that are otherwise rarely considered: the incompatibility of husband and wife, sex during menstruation (which was otherwise prohibited, and women were supposed to smear their face with a mixture of clarified butter and red dye as a sign that they were menstruating), and sadomasochism, beating with a twig as foreplay, a practice said to be popular among farmers whose courting habits are considered to lack subtlety. There are quarrels between lovers and also adultery, though, overall, there is more romantic love reflected in the poems, as in this example: 'I will never forget how she shook her head / When I tried to kiss her lips / And her tresses flew in all directions'.[15] The women of the poems appear as very expressive, sexually and emotionally, eager to engage in passionate, often adulterous love affairs.

---

14 Peter Khoroche and Herman Tieken, *Hāla's Sattasaī: Poems of Life and Love in Ancient India* (New Delhi: Motilal Banarsidass, 2014), 3–4.
15 Khoroche and Tieken, *Hāla's Sattasaī*, 68.

Old Tamil Caṅkam literature consists of eight anthologies of short poems, and a work on grammar and poetics. The poems, possibly composed under influence of Sanskrit poetics, are divided into two categories, namely love poetry of *akam* (interior), and heroic poetry of the *puram* (exterior). *Akam* poetry describes the erotic achievements of the leisure class, but also provides an idealized picture of ordinary people. Scenes of *akam* are set in small villages, with poor villagers as protagonists. The literary device called *ullurai uvamam*, or 'indirect suggestion', was used in the love poems of the *akam*, which explored the inner world of emotions/mind.[16] The poems are also very evocative of the landscape appropriate to the mood of the love that they want to depict. Women were the loci of sacred power and express their thoughts implicitly through a set of conventions. The five landscapes (*tinai*) – farmland, forests, mountains, wasteland, and seashore – have corresponding flowers/plants, time of day, seasons and moods of love.

Women are the chief voice in the *akam* poems, whose subject matter is chiefly the phases of pre-marital love, marital love, and extra-marital love. The characters include the heroine, her friend, mother, foster-mother, the hero, his friend or bard, the concubine, her friend, and a passersby. *Kuriñci*/hill stands for a meeting between lovers because of the secrecy hills made possible. The Tamil poems speak of two kinds of love: pre-marital love (*kalavu*) and marital love (*karpu*). Among the causes given for the separation of the man from his wife is consorting with courtesans, along with such causes as the pursuit of wealth or service to the king. Landscape symbolism is also used in the fifth-century CE Tamil epic *Cilappatikāram*, which explores aspects of marital and extra-marital love in the relationship of the hero Kōvalaṉ with his wife Kaṇṇaki and the courtesan Mātavi. The first book explores love in all its dimensions using the conventions of Tamil erotic poetry:

> In the bedroom
> Mātavi's couch was sown with homegrown
> Mullai petals, musk jasmine
> And other flowers. Undone was her red,
> Coral girdle that blazed over her mound
> Of love, and the fine garment unwound
> From her waist. Then to the open, moonlit terrace

---

16 *The Cilappatikāram: The Tale of an Anklet*, trans. R. Parthasarathy (Gurugram, India: Penguin Books, 2004).

> She stepped on, and with a heart bursting
> With passion drowned herself in Kōvalan.[17]

In patriarchy, female sexuality remained a threat, particularly that of the wife. Thus, Kaṇṇaki silently puts up with indignity and grief as a faithful wife, but after the death of her husband turns into an outlaw, ritually unsexing herself. She breaks her anklet, a symbol of chastity, acknowledging the end of married life, and releases her sexual energy into vengeance. With her husband gone she has no use of sex, which is further reinforced when she cuts off her breast, an embodiment of sexual power.

The evolution of *bhakti* (devotional) spiritualism in the south, under the leadership of wandering saint-poets devoted to the gods Shiva and Vishnu, had implications for the erotic-love tradition. The poets transformed the concept of *bhakti* by infusing it with a more personal desire for the god, 'an insistence on actual physical and visual presence, a passionate transference and counter transference'.[18] The gender stereotype of women as gentle, sacrificing, and loving became the model for all worshippers, and men imitated women in *bhakti*. A new stereotype emerged of the woman who defied conventional society to pursue her religious calling. Andal, an eighth-century Vaishnav saint, fantasized about her union with Vishnu as his divine consort until he finally took her as his bride. The love of Andal for Krishna, the eighth incarnation of Vishnu, is said to be the best example of *madhuri bhakti*, the love of a woman for her beloved, and has been termed 'bridal mysticism'. Andal's mystic vision of her marriage is described in her poetry, which is at places deeply sensual, but inevitably followed with separation, and pangs of one-sided love:

> How fortunate is the conch
> Which Kannan takes to his lips
> Andal enquires of it how they taste
> Does it have the flavor of camphor
> The sweet smell of the lotus?
> Does it taste sweet
> that handsome mouth of coral hue?[19]

Our purpose here is not to examine *bhakti* itself, but to see how notions related to sexuality shifted and transformed, as new ideas come into being.

---

17 *The Cilappatikāram*, 42.
18 Wendy Doniger, *The Hindus: An Alternative History* (New Delhi: Speaking Tiger, 2015), 343–4, 353–8.
19 Vijaya Ramaswamy, *Walking Naked: Women, Society and Spirituality in South India*, 2nd edn (Simla, India: Indian Institute for Advanced Study, 2007), 126.

Theism was to influence Sanskrit poetics as well and in this we can briefly discuss the *Gitagovinda* (The Song of Govinda), written by the twelfth-century Hindu poet Jayadeva, which is supposed to have folk origins and resemble the vernacular language known as Apabhraṁśa. The text is part of the *prema* or love tradition in Sanskrit, dealing with reciprocity and emotions, which is distinguishable from *śṛṅgāra* or eroticism, with its hegemonic masculinity and objectification of women. It centres on Krishna, mischievous love-play being his forte. Radha was his lover when he was an adolescent cowherd, and she an older married cowherd, though he also had love-play with a host of other female cowherds. Radha's relationship with Krishna can be seen as the adulterous love of a mature woman for an adolescent, but mutually passionate and equal, picked up from the Prakrit Apabhraṁśa poetry from north India and turned into an extraordinary Sanskrit *kāvya* by Jayadeva. The Radha–Krishna relationship transcended the usual male–female representation in Sanskrit erotic poetry. In the climax of her union with Krishna, Radha is referred to as the 'one whose lover is in her power', also a type of *nāyikā*, or romantic heroine. The poem overturns the representation of adulterous women by elevating the union of Radha and Krishna.

Consecrating the Body: Tantric Ritualized Sex and the Visual Medium

Tantra was a system of belief and ritual practice that gained widespread patronage in the early medieval period. Generally, Tantric systems shared a secretive – ritualistic, esoteric, soteriological – training which resulted in the gaining of super-human powers that were executed on the material realm. The Goddess-centred Tantric systems were particularly heterodox, and utilized substances in ritual (wine, meat, sexual fluids) that had come to be regarded as 'impure' in the orthodox Hindu mainstream. The participation of women in Tantrism is connected with the philosophical prominence of the feminine principle as *śaktī*, seen as more prominent among the early Goddess-centred Tantric systems.

Sex was both dangerous and central to Tantrism; the nomenclature of *vāma* (left/woman) feminized and stigmatized the sexual ritual and women came to be carefully controlled. Women were sexual partners as well as channellers of the goddess, and thus were objects of ritual worship. The Tantras describe techniques through which the divine *yoginīs* could be pleaded to either internally and symbolically through visualization, or externally through rituals with human *yoginīs*. Certain human women were selected as consorts, including one's wife, a courtesan, or an outcaste woman.

The expressions *dūtī* and *śakti* are used for female participants in sexual rites. *Yoginī* may designate women as autonomous ritualists or even living goddesses, and could also designate a female practitioner (*sādhaka*), and not ritual consort. The original Tantric sources on sexualized ritual seldom mention pleasure, though the later texts do speak of bliss. The Tantric rituals had both literal and metaphoric meanings. The early medieval Kashmir philosophers sublimated the physical ritual into meditative and ritual techniques, with the fundamental goal of expansion of consciousness, a divine state of mind homologous to the bliss produced in sexual orgasm. The more extreme cults continued with physical ritual practices in worship of the goddess, and persisted as underground traditions.

Buddhism came under the influence of Tantric ideas and the conceptualization of the feminine underwent transformation in Tantric Buddhist cosmology. In Tantric imagery there is an elaborate pantheon of female Buddhas, and numerous female enlighteners known as *ḍākinīs*. Tantric Buddhists eulogized the body as an 'abode of bliss', and the Tibetan Buddhist texts attribute the attainment of enlightenment by the Buddha to the bliss he experienced with his wife Gopā. The iconography includes the couple in an amorous embrace. Buddhist Tantric texts give explicit instructions on sexual techniques to be practised either during empowerments or yogic practice. The texts are prone to figurative as well as literal reading, making it possible to understand sexual imagery as the enlightenment experience in which knowledge of spiritual mysteries and great bliss are combined. Also, all aspects of the world, including the passions, are considered inherently pure. Worship of the female organ, sexual pleasure, and satisfaction was part of medieval Buddhist Tibetan Tantrism which has a gynocentric perspective, describing erotic experience from a female point of view. The texts also provide a number of oral techniques, and a catalogue of sexual positions to stimulate the flow of the woman's sexual fluid, which is supposed to contain special potency for nourishing the psychic anatomy.

Thus, ritualized Tantric sexual practices involve a consecration of the body and sexuality, with the consequence that pleasure, including sexual pleasure, is not demeaned or suppressed. The ritualized sexuality of Tantra may provide a means and a model for understanding how men and women might relate to each other without the ego, regarding each other as divine.

Visual art in South Asia, especially sculptural depictions, including narrative sculpture, contained a focus on beauty, desire, leisure, the female and male body, and couples from the early centuries CE onwards or even earlier. The *kāma* culture formed the subject matter of visual art within the imagined urban spaces of palaces, gardens, and balconies. There were depictions of *mithuna* figures, a man and woman in amorous embrace, a theme that continues in Indic art in later periods. The sculptural depictions took up various themes from literature, exploring their visual possibilities. In early medieval western Deccan, for example, we find portrayal of the pleasures of Lanka, the island fortress of King Ravana from the *Ramayana*, and of love in union. There appears to be a general trend towards portrayal of eroticism in the early medieval period, and a diminished interest in comedy or satire. Depiction of 'unseemly sexual acts' and oral sex is a regular topic in the sculptures of temples from the eleventh century. In the architectural scheme these depictions existed at the 'periphery' or 'margins', which was the visual counterpart to the social imagination of the courtly world, where 'low' characters were connected with baser human desires, debauchery, and humour. By the early medieval period, theatre and sculpture came to complement each other. The portrayal of sex and eroticism on temple walls also developed under the influence of Tantrism, with its belief in the magical and ritualistic powers of sex, which gave further impetus to the already prevalent exaltation of the erotic sentiment in literature. Sensuous imagery at sacred sites was imbued with auspicious ideas and considered indispensable.

Later Developments

Islam spread into South Asia gradually beginning in the seventh century, but even more so beginning in the twelfth century, when the first states ruled by Islamic rulers were established in the subcontinent. At that time devotional cults that were offshoots of Islamic and Hindu beliefs became very popular. Sufi and Bhakti cults promoted the notion of sublime desire and oneness with God wherein the idea of the lover and God could be interchanged. Spirituality was expressed in the language of eroticism and the boundaries between the spiritual and the physical became fluid–physical, tactile contact was replaced with abstract notions of intimacy and the divine contact of the souls.

This was in contrast with the accounts and chronicles written in the Muslim courts in the subcontinent, including the court of the Mughal Empire that controlled much of South Asia between the sixteenth and the nineteenth centuries. They discuss sexuality in different ways, imposing strict codes on the courtiers and issuing regulations concerning marriage. They developed norms for male body comportment and had considerable tolerance towards homosexuality. Sexuality was complicated, with conjugality, intense desire, and platonic love differentiated from physical lust. The Mughal emperor Babur's (1483–1530) love for a young boy has been represented as a sublime, platonic appreciation of his beauty which brought Babur closer to divinity, but at the same time he condemned sodomy and the predilection for young boys among older, powerful men, some of whom were his immediate family. *Hijrās* (individuals outside the gender binary) were employed in the inner, private quarters, and there are varied references to fluid identities, including cross-dressing, with women dressing up as men for battles and men dressing up as women to slay enemies. While masculinity and femininity were not defined strictly in a binary manner, court chroniclers such as Abu'l Fazl (1551–1602) presented manly virtue that emphasized the inner purity and masculine perfection of their bodies; this notion of perfection was extended to their roles in imperial households and the Mughal court. This was in contrast to accounts of lust and sexuality from regional courts such as that of the Deccan region in the South. (For more on sexuality within Islamic traditions, see Chapter 14 by Serena Tolino in this volume.)

South Asia was gradually conquered by European powers, particularly the British, and became part of their empire. While colonial writers of the eighteenth and nineteenth centuries imagine and described the *zenana*, the women's quarters, as a space for perverse sexual pleasure, scholars have more recently demystified it as a space full of activities and varied possibilities. It was a political, social, and cultural space, a place for political and strategic deliberations as much as one for sexual, reproductive, familial, and childcare activities.

Victorian notions of propriety and conduct began dominating the discourse in colonial writings about South Asia in the eighteenth and nineteenth centuries, with notions of puritanism on the one hand and Westernization on the other. The colonial state was depicted as powerful and masculine, while the colonized, native population were viewed as effeminate and weak. The British sought to control sexuality and domesticity through discussions and regulations on the age of consent, child marriage, restitution of conjugal rights, and elite polygamy. The legal ramifications of associating sexual deviance with criminality can be seen in colonial regulations on sexuality. The British sought to regulate prostitution through the Communicable Diseases Act of the 1850s and to restrict *hijrās*, who they called eunuchs, with the Criminal Tribes Act of 1871. They outlawed sexual acts 'against the order of nature' in 1861 with Section 377 of the penal code, a law that was used to prosecute homosexual activity. This was only lifted in 2018 in India and remains in the penal codes of Pakistan and Bangladesh.

The National Movement for freedom against British colonial rule gained ground in the late nineteenth and early twentieth centuries and ushered in its own dynamics regarding sexuality. Traditions were challenged due to Western education, but this did not always spell reform for women. Women were expected to be the vanguards of traditional value systems and in fact there was a 'revivalist' fervour for what were viewed as ancient Indian value systems. To throw off the mantle of being weak, macho nationalism was celebrated, although women also began to enter public spaces in a public manner. Among all this, Mahatma Gandhi's projection of celibacy and abstinence as a symbol of power and control over one's own body and mind may have made an already moralistic society look at expressions of sexuality in a disapproving manner. His 'experiments', in which he slept next to women without engaging in sex, were connected with long-standing practices of the 'alchemy of the libido' that sublimated sexuality into spirituality, viewed semen as the elixir of immortality, considered sexuality as 'cataclysmic depletion' and celibate *brahmacarya* (sexual abstinence) as the ideal for any person in public life.[20]

Media portrayals in the post-colonial period show certain trends in Indian sexuality, most of which are rooted in the past systems of thoughts and traditions. Indian cinema has played a major role in setting the tone for stereotypical depictions; until the turn of the millennium, wooing and winning over a protesting woman, force, and even rape were familiar motifs for the titillation of the male audience, reminiscent of the violence of the *kāma* tradition, when a woman's words were ignored or taken to mean the affirmative.

Sexuality and violence have a social and historical context; sexual violence, rampant in all modern societies has some specific qualities in South Asia. Women have equal suffrage rights in the Indian Constitution (in place since 1950) and are in theory worshipped as goddesses, but preference for boy children and male-centric attitudes in society have led to the rampant practice of pre-natal sex selection and the elimination of girl children in the womb. This has led to a skewed sex ratio in which there are more men than women. Conservative attitudes, misogyny, and the inability to handle women's sexuality sometimes translates into ill treatment of women in public spaces.

20 Kakar, *Intimate Relations*, 121.

Comments or lewd gestures towards women are ironically termed 'Eve teasing', a practice which is illegal but still quite common. Issues connected with women's 'purity', implying virginity until marriage, have remained an obsession for a long time and there are restrictions on the mobility of young women, especially in rural areas. These are just some of the challenges that women negotiate even to this day.

Further Reading

Ali, Daud. 'Censured Sexual Acts and Early Medieval Society in India'. In *Sexual Diversity in Asia, c. 600–1950*, ed. Raquel A. G. Reyes and William G. Clarence-Smith, 47–66. Oxford: Oxford University Press, 2012.

'The Erotic "World" of the *Kamasutra*'. In *A Companion to World Literature*, Volume 1, ed. Ken Seigneurie, 1–12. Chichester, UK: Wiley Blackwell, 2020.

'Towards a History of Courtly Emotions in Early Medieval India, c. 300–700 CE'. *South Asian History and Culture* 12, nos. 2/3 (2021): 129–45.

Anooshahr, Ali. 'The King Who Would Be Man: The Gender Roles of the Warrior King in Early Mughal History'. *Journal of the Royal Asiatic Society* 18, no. 3 (2008): 327–40.

Blackstone, Kathryn. *Women in the Footsteps of Buddha*. Delhi: Motilal Banarsidass, 1998.

Cabezón, José, ed. *Buddhism, Sexuality and Gender*. Albany, NY: State University of New York Press, 1992.

Collett, Alice. *Lives of Early Buddhist Nuns: Biographies as History*. Oxford: Oxford University Press, 2016.

Women in Early Indian Buddhism: Comparative Textual Studies. Oxford: Oxford University Press, 2013.

Custodi, Andrea. '"Show you are a Man!" Transsexuality and Gender Bending in the Characters of Arjuna/Brhannaḍā and Ambā/Sikhanḍin/ī'. In *Gender and Narrative in the Mahābhārata*, ed. Simon Brodbeck and Brian Black, 208–29. London: Routledge, 2021.

Dehejia, Vidya. *The Body Adorned: Dissolving Boundaries between Sacred and Profane in India's Art*. New York: Columbia University Press, 2009.

Doniger, Wendy. *Tales of Sex and Violence: Folklore, Sacrifice, and Danger in the Jaiminiya Brahmana*. Chicago: University of Chicago Press, 1985.

Dunn, Laura M. 'Yoginīs in the Flesh: Power, Praxis, and the Embodied Feminine Divine'. *Journal of Dharma Studies* 1, no. 2 (2019): 287–302.

Hatley, Shaman. 'Sisters and Consorts, Adepts and Goddesses: Representations of Women in the Brahmayāmala'. In *Tantric Communities in Context*, ed. Nina Mirnig, Marion Rastelli, and Vincent Eltschinger, 47–80. Vienna: Austrian Academy of Sciences Press, 2019.

Hinchy, Jessica. *Governing Gender and Sexuality in Colonial India: The Hijra c.1850–1900*. Cambridge: Cambridge University Press, 2019.

Jaini, Padmanabh. *Gender and Salvation: Jaina Debates on Spiritual Liberation*. Berkeley, CA: University of California Press, 1992.

Kāmasutra. Trans. Wendy Doniger and Sudhir Kakar. Oxford: Oxford University Press, 2002.

Kaul, Shonaleeka. *Imagining the Urban: Sanskrit and the City in Early India*. New Delhi: Permanent Black, 2010.

Lal, Ruby. *Domesticity and Power in the Early Mughal World*. Cambridge: Cambridge University Press, 2005.

O'Flaherty, Wendy Doniger. *Women, Androgynes and Other Beasts*. Chicago: University of Chicago Press, 1980.

O'Hanlon, Rosalind. 'Kingdom, Household and Body History: Gender and Imperial Service under Akbar'. *Modern Asian Studies* 41, no. 5 (2007): 889–923.

Pradhan, Shruti S. 'The Yama-Yamī Sūkta: New Perspectives'. *Annals of the Bhandarkar Oriental Research Institute* 71, no. 1/4 (1990): 109–38.

Roy, Kumkum. *The Power of Gender and the Gender of Power: Explorations in Early India History*. New Delhi: Oxford University Press, 2010.

'Sectional President's Address: Towards a History of Reproduction'. *Proceedings of the Indian History Congress* 69 (2008): 19–69. www.jstor.org/stable/44147166.

Sahgal, Smita. 'Gathasaptashati: Retelling Intimate History of Ancient Deccan'. *Advances in Social Sciences Research Journal* 6, no. 2 (2019): 467–74.

Seema Bawa, ed. *Locating Pleasure in Indian History: Prescribed and Proscribed Desires in Visual and Literary Cultures*. New Delhi: Bloomsbury, 2021.

Shah, Shalini. *Love, Eroticism and Female Sexuality in Classical Sanskrit Literature: Seventh-Thirteenth Centuries*. New Delhi: Manohar, 2009.

Shaw, Miranda. *Passionate Enlightenment: Women in Tantric Buddhism*. Princeton, NJ: Princeton University Press, 1994.

Trautman, Thomas. 'Marriage in the *Dharmasastra*'. In *Dravidian Kinship*, 238–315. Cambridge: Cambridge University Press, 1982.

Tyagi, Jaya. *Contestation and Compliance: Retrieving Women's 'Agency' from Puranic Traditions*. Delhi: Oxford University Press, 2014.

Engendering the Early Household. New Delhi: Orient Longman, 2008.

Vanita, Ruth, and Saleem Kidwai, eds. *Same-Sex Love in India: A Literary History*. New Delhi: Penguin Books, 2008.

5

Discourses of Desire in Ancient Greece and Rome

ALLISON GLAZEBROOK

As first noted by Kenneth Dover, the ancient Greeks had no specific term to denote 'sexuality'. The closest equivalents were *ta aphrodisia* ('things of Aphrodite') and *ta erotika* ('things of Eros'). The goddess Aphrodite and the god Eros (Venus and Cupid to the Romans) in turn personified physical desire (Greek: *erōs*; Latin: *cupido* and also *amor*) and its expression. Moreover, no single canonical text or religious moral code existed that prescribed sexual relations. Instead, we rely on the rich textual and visual culture of Greece and Rome to reconstruct sexual norms, attitudes, and practices. Rather than a belief system, we more accurately talk about discourses of ancient sexualities. Gender and status were key components in any sexual relations: a citizen woman was limited to sex with a husband; a citizen man had legitimate access to sex labourers, enslaved people in his household, and so on, in addition to his wife; enslaved persons were denied autonomy over their sexuality and compelled to have sex with their enslavers. Sex work was legal and practised openly. Some scholars have suggested that the Greeks and Romans had no concept of sexuality as an identity, so terms such as 'homosexual' are often avoided, with 'homoerotic', 'same-sex', 'pederastic', 'heteroerotic', 'bisexual' as common alternatives. We know the most about the sexuality of elite male citizens, since the majority of texts and visual objects were created by and for them.

This chapter presents a survey of key views on erotic desire and its management as well as common practices and norms in ancient Greece and Rome from the seventh century BCE to the third century CE. Although ancient discussions of desire frequently served as a form of social and political commentary, especially among the Romans, the focus here is reconstructing the sexualities from a variety of sources. The first section surveys *erōs* and its representation in literature by genre. The second documents its presence in the visual landscape. The third unpacks these discourses of sexuality in relation to status and gender. What emerges is a complex and even conflicting view of desire and sexual relations. (See also Chapter 1 by James Robson and Chapter 2 by Aven McMaster in Volume III of this work.)

Conceiving *Erōs*

Epic

In the Greek poet Hesiod's *Theogony* (*c.* 700 BCE), Eros is a primordial god alongside Chaos and Gaia ('Earth', 116–22). The god's presence at the coming-into-being of the universe is necessary because of his generative power. Without Eros there would be no night, no day, no sky, no other gods, no mortals. Reproduction is both asexual and sexual. His role in instilling desire, however, only arose with the birth of Aphrodite, the goddess of love (183–206). He accompanied her to Mount Olympus, from where, along with the god Himeros ('longing'), he carried out her bidding in the mortal realm, and in later traditions became known as Aphrodite's son. Hesiod appears to combine two different traditions about Eros in his poem: as a major deity and as a secondary god to Aphrodite. In both traditions the divinity of *erōs* means it is unavoidable. At first mention, Hesiod describes Eros as 'most beautiful', as one who 'relaxes the limbs', but who also 'in the breasts of all gods and men, subdues their reason and prudent counsel'.[1] This intersection of beauty, pleasure, and dominance is fundamental to ancient conceptions of *erōs*.

Erōs is also destructive. The most poignant example is the mythical story of Helen and the Trojan War: Paris, a Trojan prince, abducted the beautiful Helen from her husband Menelaus, the Spartan king; this act started the war between the Greeks and Trojans and ended with Troy's downfall. In Homer's account of the war in the *Iliad* (*c.* 750 BCE), Agamemnon and Achilles quarrel over ownership of the captured woman Briseis, and their dispute results in death and destruction for many Greeks at Troy (1.148–89; 9.131–4). In Homer's *Odyssey* (*c.* 700 BCE) on the meandering return of one of

---

1 Hesiod, *Theogony*, trans. J. Banks (Center for Hellenic Studies), https://chs.harvard.edu/primary-source/hesiod-theogony-sb/. Except when quoted, references to ancient Greek and Roman sources will be given in the main body of the text in standard numerical citations, and in English translation.

the Greek warriors at Troy, *erōs* causes Aegisthus and Clytemnestra to murder Agamemnon upon his homecoming (11.405–11), prompts Odysseus to forget about his return and stay with the enchantress Circe (10.469–75), but it is also a positive force in Odysseus and Penelope's marriage (11.440–51; 23.205–30). In Virgil's *Aeneid* (19 BCE), the pre-eminent Latin epic about another warrior's travels after the Trojan War, the forgetting caused by desire becomes a neglect of duty. Aeneas' intimate involvement with Dido, the Carthaginian queen, threatens his mission to establish a new homeland for the Trojan refugees and he must be reminded by the gods to resume his destiny for the future of his son and for the founding of Rome (4.265–76). When he breaks off the relationship with Dido, she curses him as she commits suicide, vowing revenge from a future generation (4.617–29). In this telling, the mythical account merges with the historical Punic Wars in the second century BCE and implicates *amor* and *cupido* in Rome's wars with Carthage.[2]

Lyric and Elegy

Eros is more fully explored as both a positive and a negative force in archaic Greek lyric and elegy (late seventh to sixth century BCE). In contrast to epic, this poetry can be inherently personal in tone, with desire and longing for boys as well as women as dominant themes. The beauty of the beloved and the pleasure desire brings are all celebrated. Here Eros the god is an overwhelming force that can have destructive consequences. In the *Theognidea*, Eros is 'merciless', possessing a recklessness that brought down Troy, emboldened Theseus to abduct Persephone from Hades, and led the hero Ajax to rape Cassandra in Apollo's temple (1231–4). The vulnerability of the lover is laid bare with forceful imagery. The poet Archilochus exclaims: 'Wracked with desire I lie, / deathless, pierced through the bone / by the crushing pains of the gods.'[3] In this example, desiring is compared to defeat in combat. In the poems of Anacreon, Eros is also a blacksmith who pounds the lover with his hammer. These verses present Eros as a subduer against whom the lover is helpless and *erōs* as akin to a kind of madness.[4]

---

2 Ingrid E. Holmberg, 'Sex in Ancient Greek and Roman Epic', in *A Companion to Greek and Roman Sexualities*, ed. Thomas K. Hubbard (Malden, MA: Blackwell, 2014), 314–34.

3 All translations for this section, except of Sulpicia, are by Peter Bing and Rip Cohen, ed. and trans., *Games of Venus: An Anthology of Greek and Roman Erotic Verse from Sappho to Ovid* (New York: Routledge, 1991).

4 Archilochus, fragment 193. Numbering follows M. L. West, *Iambi et Elegi Graeci*, Vol. 1 (Oxford: Clarendon, 1971); Anacreon 413. All numbering for Anacreon's verses follow the numeric system of D. L. Page, ed. *Poetae Melici Graeci* (Oxford: Clarendon, 1964). See

Sexual relations between mortal individuals also commonly express a power dynamic although the imagery is more subdued. The poetic persona is subject to his male beloved, who like a rider 'hold[s] the reins of my soul', as Anacreon wrote.[5] Yet these same poets also privilege the poetic persona as the dominant partner in sexual relations with women, who, regardless of status, are meant to submit to the male lover and be conquered. Anacreon reproaches a girl who runs away from him, calling her a 'Thracian filly' and boasting: 'I could fit you deftly with a bridal, and, holding the reins, could steer you past the end posts of our course.' At the same time, women who submit are despised for doing so. Anacreon disparagingly refers to 'Herotima, whom all men ride', and Archilochus calls Neobole unable to 'get enough'.[6]

In the fragments that survive from the lyrics of the late seventh- and early sixth-century BCE female poet Sappho, Eros 'shakes up my heart / like a mountain wind smashing into oaks', demonstrating the power of desire. But in another set of verses the poetic persona bypasses Eros and calls on the goddess Aphrodite to turn a beloved in her favour, even making the one being pursued into the pursuer. The relationship with desire is less adversarial or competitive, and mostly pleasurable. In another fragment, both partners share the experience of sexual pleasure. Sappho's poetic persona addresses her beloved, who is upset at having to part from her against her will. She describes what they have experienced as 'beautiful things' and recreates an idyllic scene of the lovers adorned with wreaths of flowers, garlands of blossoms, and myrrh, lying on 'plush beds' where the beloved 'satisfied her longing'. In this account, there is no dominant or submissive partner.[7]

These works of the Greek archaic period were seminal in the creation of a concept of *erōs* and its divine personification that persisted and was imitated

---

Margaret Williamson, 'Eros the Blacksmith: Performing Masculinity in Anakreon's Love Lyrics', in *Thinking Men: Masculinity and its Self-Representation in Classical Antiquity*, ed. Lin Foxhall and John Salmon (New York: Routledge, 1998), 71–82, at 72–4.

5 Anacreon 360. Also Theognis, 1283–94, 1341–4.

6 Anacreon, 417, 346 fragment 1; Archilochus, *First Cologne Epode*; Williamson, 'Eros the Blacksmith', 80; Kirk Ormand, *Controlling Desires: Sexuality in Ancient Greece and Rome*, 2nd ed. (Austin, TX: University of Texas Press, 2018), 42–4.

7 Sappho, fragments 47, 1, 94, All numbering for Sappho's poetry follows the numeric system of E. Lobel and D. L. Page, *Poetarum Lesbiorum Fragmenta* (Oxford: Clarendon, 1955). See Ellen Greene, 'Subjects, Objects, and Erotic Symmetry in Sappho's Fragments', in *Among Women: From the Homosocial to the Homoerotic in the Ancient World*, ed. Nancy Sorkin Rabinowitz and Lisa Auanger (Austin, TX: University of Texas Press, 2002), 84–96.

through the classical, Hellenistic, and Roman periods that followed. The paradox of *erōs* as a source of pain as well as pleasure found a place in the Latin elegists: Catullus, Tibullus, Propertius, and Ovid, who compared it to a disease and even to madness, and construed it as a competition to be won, like a wrestling match. Like the Greek poets, they associated sexual desire with leisure, but over-indulging it feminized the lover and was therefore an affront to duty, even anti-Roman, as in Roman epic. They also conflated the experience of desire with slavery, a rare topos in earlier periods, as well as with war. These themes developed further the connections between domination, aggression, and even violence in sexual relations, imagining the experience of *amor* and *cupido* to be a degrading one. In Tibullus, for example, Venus restrains and whips the male lover, so the lover can be dominated, but now by a female partner and not by the god. Such reversals can be suddenly overturned, however, or used to highlight the social alienation of the poet's persona, and so may still enforce the traditional expectation of male sexual dominance of women and others. Sulpicia, a rare Roman woman poet from the first century BCE whose work survives, shares many of these tropes of her contemporaries, but her poetic persona's relationship with *amor* is less combative. Like Sappho she is favoured, in this case by Venus, and she claims to be *digna cum digno* ('a worthy woman with a worthy man'), seemingly rejecting any hierarchy.[8]

For the poets, *erōs* is a divine force against which the lover is often helpless. Although descriptive and vivid, they offered little guidance for managing the strong emotions associated with desire – for this we turn to philosophy.

Philosophy

The first extensive philosophical treatment of Eros is Plato's *Symposium*, written in the fourth century BCE. The setting is an Athenian symposium or banquet where, instead of the regular entertainment of heavy drinking and

---

8 Love as disease and madness: Catullus 76.20–22; Propertius 1.1.2; Ovid, *Loves* 1.2.1–8; as competition: Catullus 66.13–14; Propertius 2.15.17–20; as feminizing: Propertius 1.7.19; as anti-Roman: Catullus 51.13–16; as slavery: Catullus 85; Tibullus 2.4.1–4; as war: Ovid, *Loves* 1.9; as domination: Tibullus 1.8.5–6; Catullus 68.68, 156; Tibullus 2.41–4. Sulpicia 3.17, 3.13.3.13.4–5, 3.13.10. See Barbara K. Gold and Genevieve Liveley, *A Guide to Latin Elegy and Lyric* (Malden, MA: Blackwell, 2021), 7–12, 101–4, 122–32, 134; E. Greene, 'Gender and Roman Elegy', in *A Companion to Roman Love Elegy*, ed. Barbara K. Gold (Malden, MA: Blackwell, 2012), 357–71; Paul Mugatroyd, '*Militia amoris* and the Roman Elegists', *Latomus* 34 (1975): 59–79; Paul Mugatroyd, '*Servitium amoris* and the Roman Elegists', *Latomus* 40 (1981): 589–606; and Richard Rawles and Bartolo Natoli, 'Erotic Lyric', in Hubbard, *A Companion*, 339, 341–2.

music, the guests – who are all illustrious members of the Athenian elite – decide to offer speeches in honour of Eros. Three speeches stand out: Pausanias provides what is considered by scholars to be the general Athenian view of love; Aristophanes recounts a fable that remains controversial, since it suggests the ancient Athenians had a concept of sexual identities akin to today; and Socrates presents the view that Plato wishes to advance with this dialogue. Socrates' telling will be the focus here (see later the speeches of Pausanias and Aristophanes).

Socrates offers no praise of Eros himself, but instead relates an encounter he had with Diotima, a woman and possibly a priestess, whom he consulted on love. Her Eros is a young god instead of the primordial god of Hesiod. He was conceived at a party celebrating Aphrodite's birth, where Poverty seduced Plenty, drunk on wine (203c). Born from such opposites, Diotima's Eros is a liminal deity, between goodness, beauty, wisdom, and immortality, and their opposites; not an incarnation of these qualities but the longing for them (201e–202d, 203e–204a). *Erōs* is still associated with physical desire and sexual reproduction, but is also elevated to an abstract concept that resides in the soul instead of the body and gives birth to the Supreme Good, including wisdom, moderation, justice, and virtue, all of which, she argues, have truer immortality than any offspring (206b, 208e–209e). The goal of Diotima's *erōs* then is the Good. But this philosophical *erōs* is not distinct from physical desire. According to Diotima, sexual arousal or longing is a necessary step towards the Good. The most noble *erōs* is desire for a beautiful boy, which, if managed appropriately, transforms into a desire for supreme beauty that can transport the soul to a higher realm of knowing (211d–212a). In Plato's text, *erōs* becomes a productive force for personal growth within the soul when divorced from the animal instinct of the body (210a–e). Similar views are presented in Plato's *Phaedrus* (250b–252c, 254a–256b).[9]

Plato's emphasis on *erōs* ensured that the philosophical schools that followed also engaged with the topic. The Hellenistic philosopher Zeno of Citium, founder of Stoicism (*c.* 300 BCE), valued the pederastic relationship, like Plato, as a means to approach the Good, the prime motivation for which he believed was beauty (Diogenes Laertius, *Life of Zeno* 129–30). Unlike Plato and the poets, the Stoics did not view *erōs* as sent from the gods, defining it instead as the simple recognition of beauty in another. Such beauty creates

---

9 Martha C. Nussbaum, '*Erōs* and Ethical Norms: Philosophers Respond to a Cultural Dilemma', in *The Sleep of Reason: Erotic Experience and Sexual Ethics in Ancient Greece and Rome*, ed. Martha C. Nussbaum and Juha Sihvola (Chicago: University of Chicago Press, 2002), 55–94.

bonds of friendship or *philia*, which, although not devoid of physical pleasure, did not have sex as its aim. The relationship was a venue for the lover to practise the Good and develop virtue in the beloved. Sexual activity was productive only when undertaken as a means to friendship, so sex in and of itself was immaterial to virtue (Stobaeus, *Eclogues* 2.115, 11s and 2.65–6, 5b9). Those who experienced *pathos* ('intense passions') and obsessive desires were considered fools incapable of obtaining the Good. Although Zeno discussed *erōs* in the context of pederasty (Athenaeus, *The Learned Banqueters* 563e), neither he nor other Stoics valued it above other relationships, and intimate friendships between a man and a woman were seen as equally productive for virtue. The Roman Stoics Seneca and Musonius Rufus, both of whom lived in the first century CE, however, promoted marriage alone as the ideal context for *erōs* (Musonius, *Discourses* 12–14). For them, reproduction through sexual intercourse does not appear devalued as it does in Plato. For the Stoics in general, *erōs* aimed at friendship and, if devoid of *pathos*, was key to virtue which, in turn, enabled the good life for individuals and ensured the well-being of the community. The Roman Stoics thereby laid the foundation for the Christian emphasis on procreation.[10]

Another philosophical school of the Hellenistic period, Epicureanism, considered pleasure essential to happiness, but since Epicureans defined pleasure as the absence of pain, the duality of *erōs* could not be easily reconciled with their philosophy. Epicurus (341–271 BCE) rejected the Platonic use of *erōs* in the pursuit of the Good, as well as the pederastic context for it. Like the Stoics, he did not believe *erōs* was sent from the gods, and as a result it could be more easily controlled. But while the Stoics remained indifferent to *erōs*, Epicurus suggested it should be rejected altogether as unnecessary for survival (Diogenes Laertius, *Life of Epicurus* 10.118). Yet, he also accepted sexual activity as natural and recognized it was pleasurable. Casual sex in the right circumstances, that is, in the absence of harm to personal wealth, property, health, others, institutions, breaking of laws, and upsetting of good customs, was acceptable, but Epicurus remained doubtful such circumstances could

---

10 Kathy Gaca, *The Making of Fornication: Eros, Ethics, and Political Reform in Greek Philosophy and Early Christianity* (Berkeley, CA: University of California Press, 2003), 93, 111–16. See also Christopher Gill, 'Stoic *Erôs* – Is There Such a Thing?', in *Erôs in Ancient Greece*, ed. Ed Sanders, Chiara Thumiger, Christopher Carey, and Nick Lowe (Oxford: Oxford University Press, 2013), 143–61, at 147–9, 151–2; James Jope, 'Platonic and Roman Influences on Stoic and Epicurean Sexual Ethics', in Hubbard, *A Companion*, 417–30, at 419, 421; Nussbaum, '*Erōs* and Ethical Norms', 76–9; Marilyn B. Skinner, *Sexuality in Greek and Roman Culture* (Malden, MA: Blackwell, 2005), 161–2.

commonly be met. The Roman Epicurean Lucretius, who lived in the first century BCE, concurred with this negative valuation of *erōs*, but recognized that the avoidance of sexual relationships could give rise to other difficulties. As a result, he was less sceptical of sexual relationships: men and women can and should learn to yield to the body without passionate love (*On the Nature of Things* 4.1191). He was thus able to recommend marriage, unlike Epicurus, who considered it unnecessary and rarely acceptable (Diogenes Laertius, *Life of Epicurus* 10.119).[11]

Platonism, Stoicism, and Epicureanism became popular intellectual movements from their foundations and their ideas and approaches to *erōs* remained influential throughout antiquity and beyond.

Medical Writers

With the exception of Aristotle, the philosophical schools were not interested in the biology of desire. For this we turn to the medical writers. The most famous physician of antiquity was the Greek Hippocrates of Cos, who lived in the late fifth and early fourth centuries BCE. The writings of Hippocrates and his followers are known collectively as the Hippocratic corpus. Not practising dissection, their knowledge was limited to observation alone. They described the female body as wet, loose, and porous like a sponge. The male body, in contrast, was hard, dense, and dry (*On Diseases of Women* 1.1; *On Glands* 16). Since women were spongy, they were prone to an excess of moisture from eating and drinking. A healthy female body purged this excess fluid regularly through menses to avoid illness (*Epidemics* 3.17, Case 11). Prepubescent girls were considered particularly susceptible to disease and even madness, for which the Hippocratics recommended marriage and first intercourse to open the pathway for the menses to flow out, and regular sexual intercourse to keep the menses flowing and the womb moist (*On Diseases of Girls* 8.466–70). A dried out womb was even riskier than the absence of menstrual flow: if too dry, it would move around the body in search of moisture and could cause suffocation if it blocked the breathing passages – what became known as the wandering womb theory (*On Diseases of Women* 1.7). Beginning or continuing sexual intercourse with the goal of menses or pregnancy was thus a common treatment for women's ailments. In contrast, men might be prescribed less intercourse.[12]

---

11 Jope, 'Platonic and Roman Influences', 423–24; Nussbaum, '*Erōs* and Ethical Norms', 73–5, 91 n. 50; Skinner, *Sexuality*, 163.

12 Leslie Dean-Jones, 'The Cultural Construct of the Female Body in Classical Greek Science', in *Women's History and Ancient History*, ed. Sarah B. Pomeroy (Chapel Hill,

When it came to sexual reproduction, the Hippocratics believed that both men and women contributed seed, which they released at orgasm. Both male and female bodies ejaculated seed into the womb where it intermingled (*On Diseases of Women* 1.17). They never discussed the role of the clitoris, however, or how to bring a woman to orgasm, but instead projected the male experience of pleasure onto the female body. The resulting pregnancy was evidence enough, in their minds, that the woman had reached a sexual climax.[13]

Although Aristotle (*c.* 460–*c.* 370 BCE) does not discuss *erōs* at length in any of his works, he was interested in its biology, as seen in his treatise *The Generation of Animals*. At times he responded directly to claims made by the Hippocratics. Aristotle argued against the idea of the wandering womb, for example, claiming instead that it was fixed in place (716b32–3, 720a12–4). While the Hippocratics understood male and female bodies as different in kind, Aristotle argued they were different only by degrees. Instead of dense versus porous flesh, Aristotle distinguished male and female bodies by the heat generated by each. Men's bodies were more efficient and effective in heating up and could use this heat to concoct seed, which in turn passed on his form in the creation of a new being (725a11–12). Female bodies were not able to get hot enough to transform blood in this way, but they could turn it into nourishment for the male seed (730b2–4). Because of its coolness and inability to concoct seed, Aristotle concluded the female body was a 'deformed male' that lacked fully formed sexual organs (737a25–8, 727a5–7). The uterus, for example, corresponded to the testicles but remained less developed (716b32–3, 728b18–31). Although Aristotle thought women could experience orgasm, he did not consider it necessary for conception (727b8, 738a29).[14]

Hellenistic and Roman practitioners generally favoured Aristotle's theories of the female body and its role in reproduction and developed these ideas more fully with the aid of dissection. Like Aristotle, they claimed the female did not provide seed for conception but rather menstrual fluid as nourishment for the male seed, and they continued to describe female sexual organs by analogy with male body parts. Herophilus of Alexandria in Egypt, who

---

NC: University of North Carolina Press, 1991), 111–37, at 114–17, 121–2; Leslie Dean-Jones, 'Medicine: The "Proof" of Anatomy', in *Women in the Classical World*, ed. Elaine Fantham et al. (Oxford: Oxford University Press, 1994), 183–205; Ann Ellis Hanson, 'The Medical Writer's Woman', in *Before Sexuality: The Construction of Erotic Experience in the Ancient Greek World*, ed. David M. Halperin et al. (Princeton, NJ: Princeton University Press, 1990), 309–38, at 318–20.

13 Hanson, 'Medical Writer's Woman', 316.

14 Dean-Jones, 'Cultural Construct', 118–20; Dean-Jones, 'Medicine', 190–4.

lived in the late fourth and early third centuries BCE, concluded that the ovaries corresponded to the testes and that the fallopian tubes were akin to the seminal ducts of the penis (Galen, *On Seed* 11.1). Soranus, a Greek physician in imperial Rome in the early second century CE, described the cervix and vagina as akin to the penis and prepuce (*Gynecology* 1.12, 1.16). Like the male, the female had to desire intercourse and be aroused for conception to take place, since without arousal the male seed would not be taken up. Like the Hippocratics, Soranus believed a woman's desire and arousal were 'product-oriented' and not necessarily observable during intercourse (*Gynecology* 1.37).[15] Following Aristotle, he argued the womb did not wander, but he still linked it to disease and erratic behaviour, as the Hippocratics had. He believed in a condition caused by the constriction of the womb, which he referred to as 'hysterical suffocation', but did not recommend intercourse as its treatment (*Gynecology* 2.26). Galen, born in Pergamum in Asia Minor and active at Rome in the mid- to late second century CE, also assimilated male and female sexual organs and argued further that the lack of heat in females was the reason these organs remained inside the body: they did not have enough heat to push them outwards (*On the Usefulness of the Parts of the Body* 14.6). Galen's female body was imperfect because of its lack of heat.

Overall, as the female body merged with the male body in the minds of medical writers, women's health and treatment was no longer directly connected to menses and intercourse but resembled more the diets and regimes prescribed for males. This change also resulted in a less positive view of menstruation and pregnancy than the Hippocratic one.[16] Like the philosophers, the views of the medical writers reflected more widespread social attitudes and practices about male superiority and female inferiority, but gave such views a biological justification.

Visualizing Desire

Erotic images in the Greek and Roman worlds appeared in both public and private contexts, covering pots, walls, lamps, mirrors, dedications, and more. Such imagery was part of the daily experience of space and interaction with objects regardless of gender, age, and status: they were not censured for women and children, in some cases produced for male and female viewers

---

15 Hanson, 'Medical Writer's Woman', 314–15.

16 Hanson, 'Medical Writer's Woman', 320–1, 330–3; Dean-Jones, 'Medicine'; and Lesley Dean-Jones, *Women's Bodies in Classical Greek Science* (Oxford: Oxford University Press, 1994), 157–60.

alike. The ubiquity of sexual imagery suggests that such images were not normally considered obscene. Instead, they were to entertain, to poke fun, to ward off evil, to mark status, as well as to arouse.

Phallic Imagery

Eva Keuls described classical Athens as the 'reign of the phallus' on account of the many representations of phalluses in Athenian visual culture and highlighted their use as visual markers of male power, authority, and dominance.[17] Houses, city gates, market places, gymnasia, and temples were regularly guarded by a herm, commonly the head of the god Hermes on a square stone plinth with a phallus, often erect, in relief in the middle of the stone. Such figures likely had a protective function. Athenian vase paintings humorously depicted phalluses with wings, also known as phallic birds. The padded costumes of Old Comedy included a dangling penis that could be raised and lowered by the actor and suggest that the male member, especially when erect, was also the butt of jokes and even an object of ridicule. Furthermore, the phallus was a sign of a lack of self-control: the mythological satyrs (part horse, part human), known for their excessive behaviours, were commonly shown with enlarged and erect penises in art of the late archaic and early classical periods. Images of the penis were far more common in these periods than female genitals and breasts, which were usually concealed. The incorporation of phallic imagery and objects in cults, especially in honour of the god Dionysus, suggest the phallus was an important signifier of fertility.

Such visual imagery was also common in the Hellenistic and Roman periods. Monumental marble phalluses with scrota on plinths are part of a dedicatory monument called the Stoibadeion adorning the Temple of Dionysus on the island of Delos (Figure 5.1). At Rome, phallic imagery was also common in jewellery, hanging ornaments, wall painting, and sculpture. Phallic amulets were worn by children, while the god Priapus with his enlarged penis adorned entry ways and gardens (Figure 5.2). In these uses, the phallus was likely an apotropaic symbol used to ward off the evil eye and ensure prosperity.[18]

---

17 Eva C. Keuls, *The Reign of the Phallus: Sexual Politics in Ancient Athens* (Berkeley, CA: University of California Press, 1985).

18 Catharine Johns, *Sex or Symbol? Erotic Images of Greece and Rome* (New York: Routledge, 1982), 62–75.

Figure 5.1 Marble plinth with phallic bird in relief surmounted by an oversize phallus. Temple of Dionysus, Delos. *c.* 300 BCE. Source: Buena Vista Images/Photodisc/Getty Images, 1395939311.

Visual representations of sex were also ubiquitous. Perspicuous depictions of couples engaged in sex appear on objects in the Hellenistic period – including objects typical to women, such as mirrors, and inexpensive items likely purchased by those without much wealth – and became common during the Roman imperial period. Some of the most explicit examples are wall paintings adorning the brothel and suburban baths at Pompeii. Images in the brothel most certainly added to the erotic ambience. More enigmatic are the images from the baths, since they depict unusual positions, including threesomes and foursomes. They decorate the changing room (*apodyterium*) and may have served as reminders to clients, who could be male or female and from any social class, on the location of their clothes. But they may have also been intended to provoke laughter, which released any tension upon entering the baths, and to keep away the evil eye when bathers were at their most vulnerable (Figure 5.3). Erotic images of lovemaking also appear in the private rooms (*cubicula*) and in more public areas, including gardens, of the grander Pompeiian houses (e.g., the House of Caecilius Iucundus, the House of the Centenary, and the House of the Vettii). They were likely intended to be arousing and presented sex as an acceptable form of recreation. Sexually explicit images continue on everyday objects, such as lamps, mirrors, and

Figure 5.2 Fresco of Priapus in the entryway of the House of the Vettii, Pompeii, 79 CE. His enlarged phallus ensures and protects the wealth and prosperity of the household. Source: Vincenzo Lombardo/Photodisc/Getty Images, 1214902556.

cups: again, some mass produced, such as clay lamps, and others elite luxury goods, such as the Warren Cup (crafted in silver 30 BCE–30 CE), which depicts sex between a male couple on one side and between a man and a boy on the other.[19]

Male Bodies

Male nudity was common in Greek culture: free males exercised at gymnasia and competed in athletic competitions in the nude. In addition to the minor arts, the earliest Greek sculpture represented male figures fully

---

19 John R. Clarke, 'Sexuality and Visual Representation', in Hubbard, *A Companion*, 509–33, at 511–20; John R. Clarke, *Looking at Lovemaking: Constructions of Sexuality in Roman Art 100 B.C.–A.D. 250* (Berkeley, CA: University of California Press, 1998), 212–40; Sarah Levin-Richardson, *The Brothel of Pompeii: Sex, Class, and Gender at the Margins of Roman Society* (Cambridge: Cambridge University Press, 2019), 64–79.

Figure 5.3 Fresco from the suburban baths, Pompeii, showing group sex with a foursome (left) and threesome (right) engaged in oral and rear entry sex, 79 CE. Source: Eric Vandeville/Gamma-Rapho/Getty Images, 108548356.

naked. Whether funerary monuments or temple dedications, the figures were idealized forms. Such nudity, often termed 'heroic', celebrated and eroticized the male body, with muscular bodies and athleticism highlighting a freedom of movement as well as youthfulness. The male genitalia are conventionally undersized as a way to indicate self-restraint and modesty, qualities important in male citizens and youths. Such genitalia contrast with the enlarged, commonly erect phalluses associated with satyrs and non-Greeks, characterized in myth and literature by their excessive appetites and lack of self-control.[20] After their conquest of the Hellenistic kingdoms, the Romans embraced Greek art and adapted the male nude to their own purposes, copying Greek originals and adapting them into portrait statues. By the imperial period, the portrait head of a mature Roman man on an idealized youthful body became a standard type.[21] Such nudes highlighted

---

20 Andrew Lear and Eva Cantarella, *Images of Ancient Greek Pederasty* (London: Routledge, 2008), 24–5, 64–5.
21 Caroline Vout, *Sex on Show: Seeing the Erotic in Greece and Rome* (Berkeley, CA: University of California Press, 2013), 78–82.

virility and connected Romans, including emperors, with the cultural authority of the Greeks.

Female Bodies

While nudity was common for women depicted at *symposia* on painted Athenian pottery from the archaic period onwards, depictions of women more generally were shown fully clothed, regardless of medium, to highlight their modesty. Over the course of the classical period, drapery grew more transparent and highlighted the female form, but it was not until the late classical period that the first female sculptural nude appeared. Praxitales' statue of Aphrodite of Knidos from the fourth century BCE showed her completely naked with just a hand reaching to cover her pubis area, though the other extends towards a garment with which to cover herself. The gestures eroticize the statue and highlight Aphrodite's connection with sexuality and desire, as recognized even in antiquity: the Roman writer Pliny the Elder told a story that a stain on the statue came from a man who was so aroused he embraced it sexually (*Natural History* 36.20). From the fourth century BCE forward, the goddess was more commonly shown nude in monumental sculpture and could be admired by men and women alike. Depictions of nude mortal women remained rare, however, until the Imperial period. By the late first and early second centuries CE, wealthy Romans and freedmen were commissioning portrait statues of their wives in the likeness of a nude or partially clothed Aphrodite. Such statues highlighted the productive sexuality of these women, and, like those of Roman men, their sophistication.[22]

Transgender Bodies

The mythical blind seer Teiresias spent seven years as a woman and his power and status as a clairvoyant was said to have resulted from his experiences of and transitions between male and female. Aristophanes' fabulist account of *erōs* in Plato's *Symposium* (189d–192a) includes intersex beings labelled *androgunos* (man/woman) and attributes the origin of heterosexual attraction to such beings. Other mythical accounts reference Hermaphroditus, a child of Hermes and Aphrodite, who had both male and female genitalia. The most extensive account of this myth is Ovid's *Metamorphoses* (4.274–388), where

---

22 Eve D'Ambra, 'Nudity and Adornment in Female Portrait Sculpture of the Second Century AD', in *I Claudia II: Women in Roman Art and Society*, ed. Diana E. E. Kleiner and Susan B. Matheson (Austin, TX: University of Texas Press, 2000), 101–14; and Vout, *Sex on Show*, 82–5.

Hermaphroditus is originally assigned a sex as male until the river naiad Salmacis, smitten with desire, merged her being with his as he bathed in her waters (Martial, *Epigram* 14.174). In other traditions, Hermaphroditus' intersexuality is a gift of their parents (Diodorus Siculus 4.6.5–6). The *Salmakis Inscription* (second century BCE) also attributes the institution of marriage to Hermaphroditus and suggests the origin myth symbolized harmony, unity, and cooperation between men and women (*Supplementum Epigraphicum Graecum* 48.1330). Yet Hermaphroditus does not appear to reflect historically attested intersex individuals who, at least by Hellenistic times, were seen at worst as abominations and at best as oddities (Diodorus Siculus 32.12.1; Phlegon, *On Marvels* 2; Pliny the Elder, *Natural History* 7.23) and sometimes killed at birth (Livy, *History of Rome* 27.11.4).

As early as the fourth century BCE intersex beings appear as terracotta figurines. They are represented standing with full breasts and raise their garments to expose male genitalia. Figures of Hermaphroditus begin to appear in sculpture in the Hellenistic period as standing figures, sleeping figures, and in group scenes. Although initially rendered as adolescent males with breasts, the figures became feminized in the waist, hip, and thighs, especially in the Roman context, where they are a common representation in wall paintings and gardens in Pompeiian houses (Figure 5.4). Their popularity in domestic contexts recalls Hermaphroditus' connection to marriage and may express a desire for marital harmony.[23] They may have fulfilled an apotropaic function, warding off evil, much like phallic imagery.[24] Aileen Ajootan attributes their protective power to their intersexuality: what she calls 'a third, transcendent gender'.[25] They may have also generated surprise and resulted in laughter and fear, especially where the intersex body was not obvious from every viewing angle.[26] Or the presence of both male and female sexual traits might have been a visual encapsulation of what Linnea Åshede calls 'the entire spectrum of erotic attraction' in the Graeco-Roman world, and their accompanying eroticism a testament to the erotic appeal of gender-fluid bodies.[27]

---

23 Katharine T. von Stackelberg, 'Garden Hybrids: Hermaphrodite Images in the Roman House', *Classical Antiquity* 33 (2014): 175–202.
24 Vout, *Sex on Show*, 77–8.
25 Aileen Ajootan, 'The Only Happy Couple: Hermaphrodites and Gender', in *Naked Truths: Women, Sexuality, and Gender in Classical Art and Archaeology*, ed. A. O. Koloski-Ostrow and C. E. Lyons (New York: Routledge, 1997), 220–42, at 228.
26 Clarke, *Looking at Lovemaking*, 50–5.
27 Linnea Åshede, 'Neutrumque et utrumque videntur: Reappraising the Gender Role(s) of Hermaphroditus in Ancient Art', in *Exploring Gender Diversity in the Ancient World*, ed. A. Surtees and J. Dyer (Edinburgh: Edinburgh University Press, 2020), 81–94, at 90–1.

Discourses of Desire in Ancient Greece and Rome

Figure 5.4 Frontal view of a sleeping Hermaphroditus in marble, first century BCE. National Museum, Rome. Source: Werner Forman Archive/N. J. Saunders, Heritage Images/Getty Images, 2624101.]

Everyday Love

Epic, lyric, elegy, philosophy, the medical writers, and visual imagery combined reflect complex attitudes towards sexuality and desire in the ancient world. But although *erōs/amor* was commonly overwhelming and destructive in Graeco-Roman thought, abstinence was rarely practised or prescribed in everyday life. Instead, moderation and self-control in the face of desire was the ideal. Citizen males displayed their masculinity in exhibiting such control: an inability to control sexual desire was associated with being female (and slavish) and feminized any man who did not conform to this ideal. Given the nature of the sources, the focus of the following discussion is free individuals primarily of elite status.

Male Sexuality

The views of the philosophical schools reflect a widespread valuation of self-control in Greek society that was typically associated with masculinity. Being in control of self also meant dominating others in sexual interactions, constructing sex as hierarchical. The male citizen, particularly when elite, had access to a variety of sexual partners both male and female, including wives, sex labourers, enslaved members of his household, and boys, but he was expected to remain in control and dominate in any relationship. According to Kenneth Dover, such dominance equated first and foremost with penetration: anal, oral, or vaginal. Instead of designating sexual identity on the assigned sex of one's sexual partner (equivalent to modern notions of asexual, bisexual, heterosexual, or homosexual), the distinction was drawn between the active and passive partner, the penetrator versus the penetrated. Although Dover was writing about ancient Greeks, other scholars have applied his penetrative model to the Romans. Sexual penetration, whether in elite poetry at Rome (as in Catullus 16) or everyday graffiti at Pompeii, was a common analogy for subduing another person and exerting one's masculinity.[28] Michel Foucault popularized these views in his *History of Sexuality*, and further emphasized that ancient Greeks and Romans lacked a sexual identity in the conception of self and as such had no concept of sexuality as understood today. Amy Richlin has argued strongly against this conclusion and suggests instead that Graeco-Roman culture did indeed recognize sexual orientations based on this model of penetration.[29]

The focus of Dover's work was the pederastic relationship (Figure 5.5). In ancient Greece, such relationships were between an older man (normally twenty to thirty years of age) and a prepubescent boy of similar status; the relationship regularly had the approval of the boy's father, since it could lead to social advancement for the family. In the poetry of Theognis, the relationship is a means of education with the *erastēs* (man or older lover) acting as mentor and adviser to his *erōmenos* (boy or younger beloved). In Plato's *Symposium*, speakers praise this type of relationship as the ideal, especially Pausanias (184d–e) but even Aristophanes (191e), who otherwise jokes about the practice in his comic plays (such as *Clouds* and *Wealth*). Although likely originally an elite practice in many regions, by the fourth century BCE the institution was more widespread among free citizens, at least in democratic Athens.[30] Most commonly a man courted a boy with gifts, who, upon accepting the lover, was expected to be faithful and not appear too eager. Dover interpreted the boy's modesty as not becoming sexually aroused and in refraining from anal intercourse. He deemed it problematic for the boy,

---

28 Pompeii graffiti: *Corpus Inscriptionum Latinarum* 4.2175, 2188, 2288, 8171. See also Kenneth J. Dover, *Greek Homosexuality* (1978; Oxford: Bloomsbury, 2016), 67–8, 75–6, 107–9); Paul Veyne, 'L'homosexualité à Rome', *Communications* 35 (1985): 26–33; Craig A. Williams, 'Greek Love at Rome', *Classical Quarterly* 45 (1995): 517–39 and 'Sexual Themes in Greek and Latin Graffiti', in Hubbard, *A Companion*, 493–508, at 498; Levin-Richardson, *The Brothel*, 102–6 and Appendix B.

29 Amy Richlin, 'Not before Homosexuality: The Materiality of the *Cinaedus* and the Roman Law against Love between Men', *Journal of the History of Sexuality* 3, no. 4 (1993): 523–73.

30 Nick Fisher, 'Athletics and Sexuality', in Hubbard, *A Companion*, 244–64, at 248–9, 254–6.

Figure 5.5 Kylix depicting a seated youth reaching to kiss a standing male figure. The image challenges Dover's conclusion that the youth should not appear too eager or sexually engaged. Red-figure cup by the Carpenter Painter. *c.* 510–500 BCE. Source: Sepia Times/Universal Image Group/Getty Images, 1157394383.

a future full citizen, to submit sexually to the penetration even of his male lover. Based on images on Attic vases, he argued that the older lover would instead pleasure himself between the boy's thighs, what he termed 'intercrural intercourse'. Some of Dover's conclusions have been challenged, but not his understanding of classical Greek pederasty overall.[31]

Although still practised in the Hellenistic period, pederasty began to give way to marriage as the ideal union. The Romans adopted the institution of pederasty from the Greeks with one major change: lovers of equal status were not the norm. Instead, enslaved and foreign youths more commonly served as boys and so the mentoring aspect of such relationships was no longer important. Although pederasty still dominates discussion of ancient

---

[31] Dover, *Greek Homosexuality*; see also James Davidson, 'Dover, Foucault, and Greek Homosexuality: Penetration and the Truth of Sex', *Past and Present* 170 (2001): 3–5.

Greek and Roman sexuality, scholars now recognize that same-sex relations were more variable and could sometimes be long lasting, as in the case of Pausanias and the tragic poet Agathon of classical Athens, as seen in Plato's *Symposium* (183d–184a, 193c). Peer homosexuality, for example, or sexual relationships between males equal in age and status, has become more widely recognized as also practised in the Greek and Roman worlds.[32]

A man in Greece who did not conform to accepted standards of masculinity was known as a *kinaidos*, a term that was denigrating in intent. In his *Gorgias* (494e–495a), Plato related the term to deviant pleasures. An ancient anonymous author mistaken for Aristotle maps it onto the appearance, voice, and deportment of the body (*Physiognomics* 808a, 813a–b). The Athenian orators used it to attack opponents: in the fourth century BCE, Aeschines labelled the famous orator Demosthenes a *kinaidos* on account of his clothing (Aeschines, *Against Timarchus* 1.131, 181; 2.88, 99, 151). Scholars differ widely in interpreting the specifics of this terminology. Based on the penetration model, David Halperin and John Winkler believe it was used for an adult male who enjoyed being penetrated sexually. Yet as Mark Masterson points out, evidence linking the term with anal penetration is vague; James Davidson defines it instead as an inability to exhibit self-control over any appetite (not just the sexual). The Latinized form *cinaedus* was equally complex and derogatory among the Romans, as used by the poet Juvenal in his satires in the late first or early second century CE (9.130–3). Craig Williams argues that it described an adult male who submitted to anal penetration, or one who was delicate, or one who was attractive to women, but most commonly one who lacked something of manhood. Although *kinaidos* and *cinaedus* are difficult to define, they are evidence that the Greeks and Romans experienced anxiety around male sexuality and behaviours. Certain sexual practices were problematic. Both cultures, for example, denounced performing oral sex as degrading and considered it a passive behaviour as well as polluting. But the joking and insults are also evidence that some men may have rejected conventions of normative masculinity and its accompanying sexuality.[33]

---

32 Craig A. Williams, *Roman Homosexuality: Ideologies of Masculinity in Classical Antiquity* (Oxford: Oxford University Press, 1999), 63–7; Amy Richlin, *The Garden of Priapus: Sexuality and Aggression in Roman Humor* (New Haven, CT: Yale University Press, 1983), 220–6; Thomas K. Hubbard, 'Peer Homosexuality', in Hubbard, *A Companion*, 128–47, at 132–4; and Richlin, 'Not before Homosexuality'.

33 James Davidson, *Courtesans and Fishcakes: The Consuming Passions of Classical Athens* (London: Fontana, 1997); David Halperin, 'The Democratic Body: Prostitution and Citizenship in Classical Athens', in *One Hundred Years of Homosexuality: And Other Essays*

Female Sexuality

The Hippocratic writers, as noted earlier, pathologized female bodies as prone to excess and as being less efficient than the male body. Their writings reflect the widespread Greek belief that women, unlike men, were innately unable to control their appetites. Hesiod (*c.* 700 BCE) in *Works and Days* describes the first woman as sexually insatiable, in addition to being greedy and lazy (65–8). Semonides in his poem on women (*c.* 650 BCE) equates them with various animals, from sows to weasels, with excessive appetites for food and sex. In the comic plays of Aristophanes (*c.* 446–386 BCE), women are the brunt of sexual jokes that present them as untrustworthy and always desirous of sex (e.g., *Lysistrata* 1–240). Given these inabilities, their bodies had to be controlled by external forces instead: a male guardian, marriage, and veiling. Otherwise, female sexuality could become dangerous: destructive for the female, emasculating for the male, and disruptive to the social order. As women gained prominence in the Hellenistic period and their bodies began to be equated with male bodies in the medical writings of Herophilus, Soranus, and Galen, they gained some agency over their desires. In the Roman Republic and Imperial periods, female sexual agency is much more in evidence. In Livy's account of the rape of Lucretia, written at the end of the first century BCE, Lucretia calls together the men of her household and has them promise to enact revenge on her rapist, Sextus Tarquinius. She then commits suicide so as not to be an example of infidelity to other women (*History of Rome* 1.58). Although a disturbing tale, Livy's narrative presents her as an ethical subject who can decide about her own sexual virtue.[34]

Marriage among the free was considered essential in all these periods. For citizen women, it was the primary outlet for sexual expression. In contrast to male citizens who had access to a variety of partners, a woman's sexual partner was her husband alone (but see later on female homoeroticism). This double standard meant that citizen women competed with others for sexual attention, even within their own households. Visual and material evidence suggest that Greek and Roman women used cosmetics and clothing to enhance their appearance and sexual appeal, though they were criticized

---

on *Greek Love* (New York: Routledge, 1990), 88–112; Mark Masterson, 'Studies of Ancient Masculinity', in Hubbard, *A Companion*, 17–30, at 21; Richlin, 'Not before Homosexuality'; R. Taylor, 'Two Pathic Subcultures in Ancient Rome', *Journal of the History of Sexuality* 7 (1997): 319–71; Williams, *Roman Homosexuality*, 176, 183, 197; John J. Winkler, 'Laying Down the Law: The Oversight of Men's Sexual Behaviour in Classical Athens', in *Before Sexuality*, ed. Halperin et al., 171–210, at 177.

34 Rebecca Langlands, *Sexual Morality in Ancient Rome* (Cambridge: Cambridge University Press, 2006), 23.

for it by many male writers, from Xenophon in the fourth century BCE (*Economics* 10.13) to Seneca and Valerius Maximus in the first century CE (Seneca, *Controversies* 2.7.3–4 and excerpt; Valerius Maximus, *Memorable Deeds and Sayings* 9.1.3). The expression of female desire and female sexual pleasure was considered acceptable in the context of marriage, where it could be monitored and controlled. As noted earlier, the Hippocratics and Soranus expected women to climax in order to conceive. The figure of Ischomachus in Xenophon's *Oeconomicus* prefers sex with his wife to that with the enslaved members of his household because she can be a willing and desirous partner rather than compelled (10.12). Roman sources speak about the pleasure of sex between a husband and a wife (e.g., in Catullus 61.22, 165–72; or in Pliny the Younger, *Letter* 7.5). While sex could be pleasurable for free women, its primary goal in marriage was still reproduction.

The emphasis on marriage and reproduction meant the primary virtue for free women in both Greece and Rome was sexual virtue (*sōphrosunē* in Greek and *pudicitia* in Latin), interpreted as sexual loyalty to a family and husband. Athenian women demonstrated their *sōphrosunē* by remaining socially invisible; Roman women, in contrast, were expected to display their *pudicitia* publicly in the community. Women in both cultures were expected to demonstrate such virtue by veiling themselves with their cloaks when out in public – although veiling was not strictly enforced in the Imperial period, and it had probably mostly existed among elite women, since it would likely have hindered a woman from working in the fields or marketplace. Women might also avert their eyes in the presence of men. These gestures not only indicated a woman's modesty, but also protected her from the male gaze, which was thought to have a physical component akin to touching, and to stimulate a reciprocal response, as in Plato's *Phaedrus* (255c–d). (It also safeguarded the one looking, who was at risk of being dominated by the object of the gaze.[35]) Since Greek and Roman societies were patrilineal in descent and inheritance, the sexual loyalty of female kin was cause for unease. Their seduction or rape by another man damaged a patriarch's honour, since he was expected to keep his wife and other female relatives under control and protect them, and it could compromise the paternal line without his knowledge. For this reason, sex with another citizen's female kin was a serious sexual transgression and punished in both Greek and Roman cultures. Women were also open to constant

---

35 Claude Calame, *The Poetics of Eros in Ancient Greece* (Princeton, NJ: Princeton University Press, 1992), 20–3, 188.

scrutiny by their husbands and others, including other women. Yet the dividing line between sexual propriety and impropriety was highly subjective and easily manipulated.[36]

The paucity of female voices from the Graeco-Roman world means that much of what scholars know about female sexuality is filtered through the elite male, who rarely wrote about the female experience. The Greek poet Sappho and the Roman poet Sulpicia provide the fullest accounts of female desire. Their poetry disrupts the penetrative model discussed earlier by positioning women as desiring subjects. Sappho is also important because her erotic poetry is directed at other women. Some scholars argue that Sappho's relationships reflected the pederastic model of relations and provided mentorship, since Sappho was possibly the elder partner in her relationship with young girls prior to their marriage.[37] Yet Sappho's liaisons differ from pederasty in that she sought a relationship in which pleasure was shared and not focused on one partner, and in this respect it may resemble lesbianism in the contemporary world.[38] Her writing thus hints that women may not have conceptualized their sexual relationships as having dominant and passive partners. The Hellenistic poet Nossis, who lived in the early third century BCE, was inspired by Sappho's poetry, and Kathryn Gutzwiller argues that Nossis' celebration of 'the beauty of individual women, the sensual appeal of objects prized in their world' recalls Sappho's homoeroticism.[39]

Greek male writers only rarely considered same-sex relations between women. Alcman, who lived in the seventh century BCE, normalized erotic desire between women at Sparta in his *Partheneia*, written to be performed by a female chorus. In Plato's *Symposium*, the playwright Aristophanes gives a speech on love that ends with a reference to sexual unions between men,

36 Allison Glazebrook and Nicola Mellor, 'Bodies and Sexuality', in *A Cultural History of Women in Antiquity*, ed. Janet H. Tulloch (London: Bloomsbury, 2013), 38–45; Lloyd Llewellyn-Jones, *Aphrodite's Tortoise: The Veiled Women of Ancient Greece* (Swansea: Classical Press of Wales, 2003); Kelly Olson, *Dress and the Roman Woman: Self-Presentation and Society* (New York: Routledge, 2008).

37 Claude Calame, *Les choeurs de jeunes filles in Grèce archaique*. Vol. 1: *Morphologie, fonction religieuse et sociale* (Rome: Edizioni dell'Ateneo e Bizzarri, 1977), 372.

38 Jane Snyder, *Lesbian Desire in the Lyrics of Sappho* (New York: Columbia University Press, 1977), 14–25; Contra Sandra Boehringer, *Female Homosexuality in Ancient Greece and Rome*, trans. Anna Preger (New York: Routledge, 2021), 38–43.

39 Ellen Greene, 'Apostrophe and Women's Erotics in the Poetry of Sappho', in *Reading Sappho: Contemporary Approaches* (Berkeley, CA: University of California Press, 1996), 233–47; Kathryn Gutzwiller, *Poetic Garlands: Hellenistic Epigrams in Context* (Ithaca, NY: Cornell University Press, 1998), 75–80; Alison Keith, '*Tandem venit amor*: A Roman Woman Speaks of Love', in *Roman Sexualities*, ed. Judith P. Hallett and Marilyn B. Skinner (Princeton, NJ: Princeton University Press, 1997), 295–310.

between men and women, and between women (191d–e). The specific comment on love between women is neutral in tone, but the passage makes it clear that the most valued relationship is that between two males. Scholars differ on how to interpret the dearth of references in male-authored sources: either such relations between women were not common in Greece or men did not care if women had intimate relations with each other, since their relations had no political or social importance. By the Hellenistic period, same-sex relations between women met with some disapprobation, as in the third-century BCE poet Asclepiades (*Palatine Anthology* 5.207). To the Romans, such relations were a perversion and even threatening. Ovid refers to such desire as unnatural (*Metamorphoses* 9.727) and the first-century CE poet Martial directs some of his most damning invective against such women (*Epigrams* 1.90, 7.67, 7.70). According to Judith Hallett, the Romans saw female homo-eroticism as a Greek practice not common among Roman women and imagined such relations as still involving some kind of penetration. They thus masculinized such women, even claiming they also penetrated boys and men, emphasizing an unnaturalness to such relations.[40]

Sexuality and the Enslaved

In addition to exploiting sexually those claimed as property with impunity, an enslaver also controlled their sexual interactions with each other. Xenophon spoke of maintaining separation between enslaved males and females and only sanctioning the most loyal to form bonds and have children (*Economics* 9.5). Sex was thus a reward for good behaviour and another form of social control, since it was thought that an enslaved person with a partner and family was more likely to do as an enslaver commanded. Most likely such a system was designed to benefit and content enslaved males since the consent of the woman was not important, as noted by the fourth-century BCE Greek playwright Menander (*The Hero* 40–5) and by the second-century BCE Roman statesman Cato the Elder (*On Agriculture* 143). The first-century CE Roman agronomist Columella recommends that overseers of estates be given a female companion (*On Rural Affairs* 1.8.5). Such unions had a specific name under the Romans, *contubernium*, but they were not formally recognized in law. Despite the precarity of these relationships, which could be ended by the enslaver at any time, they were likely as meaningful to the enslaved partners as marriage was to free

---

40 Judith P. Hallett, 'Female Homoeroticism and the Denial of Roman Reality in Latin Literature', in Hallett and Skinner, *Roman Sexualities*, 179–97. See further Boehringer, *Female Homosexuality*.

individuals and there is evidence of such relations continuing even after one or both individuals gained their freedom.[41]

Like free women, enslaved women were also valued for their reproductive capacities. The Romans encouraged sex between enslaved people as a way to increase the enslaved population of their estates, as Varro did in the first century BCE (*On Agriculture* 2.1.26). Fertility was a consideration when purchasing a woman and giving birth to children was one way a woman might obtain her freedom: her children replaced her lost labour. Women might also be freed as companions. The Greek orators speak of clients freeing and then living with female sex labourers (Demosthenes 48.53). In Rome a man could legally free an enslaved woman for the purpose of marriage, as noted by legal expert Gaius in the second century CE (*Institutes* 1.18–19) and Ulpian in the third (*Digest of Justinian* 40.2.13). Sex with free men could thus result in social advancement when an enslaved woman was able to tolerate or cultivate the affection of a lover. The sexual harassment of enslaved people was rarely condemned, however, and sexual violence was an approved strategy during the sacking of an enemy city for subduing captive women and children destined for slavery.[42]

The ancient sex market provided an opportunity for enslaved individuals, at least males, to assert the sexual agency normally denied them. Male and female sex labourers were commonly available in brothels, taverns, and on the streets, where enslaved individuals could purchase sex as did their free male counterparts. The average price of sex with a sex labourer was cheap: three obols at Athens and two *asses* at Pompeii. The low prices meant sex labourers, many of whom were enslaved themselves, were available to almost everyone, including other enslaved persons. In Greek and Roman comedy, enslaved characters purchase sex and visit brothels, from Aristophanes' *Thesmophoriazusae* (1190–8) and *Wasps* (500–1) in the fifth century BCE to Plautus' *Poenulus* (269–70) in the second century BCE. The purpose-built brothel at Pompeii, known as the Lupanar, provided a sexual experience where enslaved individuals, not just free persons, could dominate

---

41 Jason Douglas Porter, 'The Sexual Agency of Slaves in Classical Athens', in *Slavery and Sexuality in Classical Antiquity*, ed. Deborah Kamen and C. W. Marshall (Madison, WI: University of Wisconsin Press, 2021), 89–101; and Allison Glazebrook, 'Gender and Slavery', in *The Oxford Handbook of Greek and Roman Slaveries*, ed. Stephen Hodkinson, Marc Kleijwegt, and Kostas Vlassopoulos (Oxford: Oxford University Press, 2017).

42 Kathy L. Gaca, 'Ancient Warfare and the Ravaging of Martial Rape of Girls and Women: Evidence from Homeric Epic and Greek Drama', in *Sex in Antiquity: Exploring Gender and Sexuality in the Ancient World*, ed. Mark Masterson et al. (New York: Routledge, 2015), 278–97.

sexually and perform roles otherwise denied them outside the brothel.[43] Enslaved men spending their money on sex was likely acceptable to enslavers, who may have encouraged it or at least turned a blind eye if it did not interfere with the work and wealth of the household. In an extreme case, Cato supposedly trafficked his enslaved women to their male counterparts for a profit (Plutarch, *Life of Cato the Elder* 21.2). Visits to brothels may also have occurred without the knowledge and permission of the enslaver.

Conclusion

In modern popular culture, the ancient Greeks are regularly characterized as sexually permissive on account of their same-sex practices and acceptance of sex work, whereas the Romans are depicted as sexually excessive and deviant.[44] But despite these differing generalizations, the Greeks and Romans followed strict social codes and legislated against what they perceived as sexual transgressions. Desire represented a paradox: while a source of pleasure and essential to a person's well-being, it was also feared for its intensity and seen as a destructive force. Its management centred on the control of desire. Masculinity was synonymous with self-control, controlling the sexuality of others, and sexual dominance. The intersectionality of sexuality, gender, and status meant that sexual expression, agency, and autonomy varied between men, women, and intersex, and free and enslaved. While most literary and visual culture privilege the elite male's view of sexuality, looking beyond the dominant public discourse, it appears that some women and other subaltern groups found ways to experience and express desires. The variety and paucity of the evidence means that scholars remain divided on important questions.

Further Reading

Bing, Peter, and Rip Cohen. *Games of Venus: An Anthology of Greek and Roman Erotic Verse from Sappho to Ovid.* New York: Routledge, 1991.

Boehringer, Sandra. *Female Homosexuality in Ancient Greece and Rome.* Trans. Anna Preger. New York: Routledge, 2021. Orig. published as *L'Homosexualité féminine dans l'Antiquité grecque et romaine.* Paris: Les Belles Lettres, 2007.

---

43 Levin-Richardson, *The Brothel*, 101–8.

44 Sir Kenneth Dover, *Greek Popular Morality in the Time of Plato and Aristotle* (Oxford: Basil Blackwell, 1974), 205; Monica S. Cyrino, 'Ancient Sexuality on Screen', in Hubbard, *A Companion*, 613–28.

Discourses of Desire in Ancient Greece and Rome

Calame, Claude. *The Poetics of Eros in Ancient Greece*. Princeton, NJ: Princeton University Press, 1992.

Campanile, Domitilla, Filippo Carlà-Uhink, and Margherita Facella, eds. *TransAntiquity: Cross-Dressing and Transgender Dynamics in the Ancient World*. New York: Routledge, 2017.

Cantarella, Eva. *Bisexuality in the Ancient World*. Trans. Cormac Ò Cuilleanáin. New Haven, CT: Yale University Press, 1992.

Carson, Anne. *Eros, the Bittersweet: An Essay*. Princeton, NJ: Princeton University Press, 1984.

Clarke, John R. *Looking at Lovemaking: Constructions of Sexuality in Roman Art 100 B.C.–A.D. 250*. Berkeley, CA: University of California Press, 1998.

Dean-Jones, Lesley. *Women's Bodies in Classical Greek Science*. Oxford: Oxford University Press, 1994.

Gold, Barbara K., ed. *A Companion to Roman Love Elegy*. Malden, MA: Blackwell, 2012.

Golden, Mark, and Peter Toohey, eds. *A Cultural History of Sexuality in the Classical World*. London: Bloomsbury, 2011.

Hallett, Judith H., and Marilyn B. Skinner. *Roman Sexualities*. Princeton, NJ: Princeton University Press, 1997.

Hubbard, Thomas K., ed. *A Companion to Greek and Roman Sexualities*. Malden, MA: Blackwell, 2014.

Johnson, Marguerite, and Terry Ryan. *Sexuality in Greek and Roman Society and Literature: A Sourcebook*. New York: Routledge, 2005.

Jones, Catherine. *Sex or Symbol? Erotic Images of Greece and Rome*. New York: Routledge, 1982.

Kamen, Deborah, and C. W. Marshall, eds. *Slavery and Sexuality in Classical Antiquity*. Madison, WI: University of Wisconsin Press, 2021.

King, Helen. *Hippocrates' Woman: Reading the Female Body in Ancient Greece*. New York: Routledge, 1998.

Lear, Andrew, and Eva Cantarella. *Images of Ancient Greek Pederasty: Boys Were Their Gods*. New York: Routledge, 2008.

Masterson, Mark, Nancy S. Rabinowitz, and James Robson, eds. *Sex in Antiquity: Exploring Gender and Sexuality in the Ancient World*. New York: Routledge, 2015.

Nussbaum, Martha C. *The Therapy of Desire: Theory and Practice in Hellenistic Ethics*. Princeton, NJ: Princeton University Press, 1994.

Ormand, Kirk. *Controlling Desires: Sexuality in Ancient Greece and Rome*, 2nd ed. Austin, TX: University of Texas Press, 2018.

Rabinowitz, Nancy Sorkin and Lisa Auanger, eds. *Among Women: From the Homosocial to the Homoerotic in the Ancient World*. Austin, TX: University of Texas Press, 2002.

Sanders, Ed, Chiara Thumiger, Chris Carey, and Nick J. Lowe, eds. *Erôs in Ancient Greece*. Oxford: Oxford University Press, 2013.

Skinner, Marilyn B. *Sexuality in Greek and Roman Culture*. Malden, MA: Blackwell, 2005.

Surtees, Allison, and Jennifer Dyer, eds. *Exploring Gender Diversity in the Ancient World*. Edinburgh: Edinburgh University Press, 2020.

Thorsen, T. S. *The Cambridge Companion to Latin Love Elegy*. Cambridge: Cambridge University Press, 2013.

Vout, Caroline. *Sex on Show: Seeing the Erotic in Greece and Rome*. Berkeley: University of California Press, 2013.

Williams, Craig. *Roman Homosexuality: Ideologies of Masculinity in Classical Antiquity*. Oxford: Oxford University Press, 1999.

6

Writing a History of Sexuality for Pre-Modern China

HSIAO-WEN CHENG

Sex as a naturalized universal phenomenon and an object of modern scientific study was introduced to China only in the early twentieth century.[1] So, what exactly do historians look for when writing about the history of sexuality in pre-modern China? How do they determine what is relevant and what is not? What if a sexual reference (i.e., a reference that we now consider related to sex) was not distinguished categorically from a non-sexual matter in a certain historical context?

This chapter begins with a discussion of the terminology and conceptual frameworks that are useful for contextualizing pre-modern Chinese cases. It then surveys institutions and practices that have been well studied, including sex manuals, concubinage, female chastity, illicit sex, and literary representations of homoeroticism. The second half of the chapter is a methodological reflection, which begins with my observations of three phenomena in works on the history of sexuality of pre-modern China, namely retrospective sexology, the censorship hypothesis, and the assumption of sex as a given. The chapter concludes with a short review of scholarly approaches to comparing China with other (mostly Western) cultures and a proposal of the ways in which a comparative history of sexuality can be productive.

---

[1] An old term, *xing*, was used to translate this new concept and has become the standard term for both sex and sexuality in modern Chinese. In pre-twentieth-century Chinese, *xing* means the nature or the innate qualities of someone or something. For the intellectual processes of this translation and coinage, see Leon Antonio Rocha, '*Xing*: The Discourse of Sex and Human Nature in Modern China', *Gender & History* 22, no. 3 (2010): 603–28.

114

Writing a History of Sexuality for Pre-Modern China

Terminology and Epistemology

As in pre-nineteenth-century Europe (and perhaps elsewhere too), there was no single and neutral term in pre-twentieth-century Chinese that specifically and exclusively denoted sex. A few terms frequently used in technical texts – such as *jiāo* (intercourse; interaction; exchange), *hé* (conjoin; meet), *jiāohé* (intercourse), *jiāotōng* (communicate), and *jiāojiē* (contact; associate) – are all general terms which can refer to sexual and non-sexual matters, and whose precise meaning depends on context. Among the euphemisms and dysphemisms for sex, most refer only to specific forms of sex, and none is used exclusively for its sexual connotation. *Xiáni*, for instance, usually indicates that a man and a woman share intimacy beyond a legitimate relationship, but it can also describe non-sexual but improperly close relationships. *Jiān*, often seen in legal texts, refers to illicit sex, but legal codes of different regimes defined *jiān* differently.[2] In non-legal texts and in everyday language, *jiān* often means illicit sex or describes those who engage in illicit sex, but also applies to all kinds of other illicit activities and treacherous persons. *Luàn* and *yín* are two other terms that can refer to illicit sex, but the sexual meaning is only determined by context: in isolation, *luàn* means disorder in general, and *yín* excess. 'A man and a woman *luàn*' can be understood as saying that the man has illicit sex with the woman, while 'General so-and-so *luàn*' means that the general rebels. A '*yín* act' usually refers to illicit sex, but a '*yín* shrine' is an illegitimate or unorthodox shrine.[3] There are also a few words in late imperial vernacular literature that were (and some still are) used to describe the act of sexual penetration in a rather vulgar context, but they are in no ways comparable to an all-encompassing, neutral term such as 'sex'. References that we now consider sexual may not be distinguished in nature from other non-sexual matters and must always be evaluated in context.

The alignment and classification of bodily and affective experiences and expressions in one context could be radically different in another. The best example is perhaps the usage of the word *yù*, meaning 'to drive (a chariot)' in classical Chinese. The word was used to describe both 'any kind of action by

---

2 For instance, the new legal definition of *jiān* in the eighteenth century reflected the Qing court's concerns over the growing number of impoverished single men. Matthew H. Sommer, *Sex, Law, and Society in Late Imperial China* (Stanford, CA: Stanford University Press, 2000).

3 The word *yín* appears in pre-modern Chinese texts in two variants: one with a 'water' radical and the other a 'woman' one. The former is used in all contexts, while the latter tends to occur in more specifically sexual contexts. The latter still refers only to men's inappropriate relationship with women. This *yín* is a different and unrelated word from *yīn* as in *yin–yang*.

an emperor with regard to one of his inferiors (the emperor's control of his people)' and 'a man's sexual intercourse with a woman'.[4] A second-century scholar defined the term as such: 'What the Son of Heaven [the emperor] causes to advance is called *yù. Yu* means "to be advanced". Whatever clothing he added to his body, or drink and food he brings to his mouth, or consorts and concubines he receives in his bedchamber, are all called *yù*.'[5] What this passage defines is a very specific relationship between a supreme man and his subjects. No real distinction is made, at least within this passage, among objects and consorts in relation to an emperor. This is about what makes an emperor the emperor. The political, ritual, and physical significance of an emperor's intercourse with his consorts is fundamentally different from that of an ordinary person. *Yù* is also a common term in the 'bedchamber arts' literature, that is, ancient Chinese sex manuals, in which it refers mostly to men having intercourse with women (*yù nǚ*), suggesting the intrinsic power relations and the ultimate goal of making a supreme man.

Another example is the way in which the human body was perceived and organized in the numerologist and theorist Jing Fang's (77–37 BCE) *zāiyì* system, which did not create a separate category for the 'sexual body' as it exists today. *Zāiyì* (lit. catastrophe and anomaly) was a complex and heterogeneous interpretive system that treated calamities and anomalous incidents in the natural and human worlds as political portents. It originated in the Warring States period (408–221 BCE), when the Central Plain of China was divided among multiple competing states, and was systematized in various ways during the unifying Western Han dynasty (202 BCE–8 CE), the first long-reigning Chinese Empire. Sex change ('women turning into men' and 'men turning into women') was a common kind of anomaly included in this interpretive system, often indicating the subversion of political order. In Jing Fang's theory, men turning into women and women turning into men signified the same thing as did incidents of resurrection. Deformities potentially related to sexual body parts (expressed as the reverse of the 'upper' and the 'lower body parts') were neither singled out as a distinctive category nor assigned sexual meanings. The omen that pointed to the ruler's sexual decadence was not an anomaly of a sexual body part but of 'giving birth to a different kind'.[6]

---

4 Paul R. Goldin, *The Culture of Sex in Ancient China* (Honolulu: University of Hawai'i Press, 2002), 42–3.
5 Translated in Goldin, *The Culture of Sex*, 43.
6 Hsiao-wen Cheng, 'Before Sexual and Normal: Shifting Categories of Sexual Anomaly from Ancient to Yuan China', *Asia Major* 31, no. 2 (2018): 1–39.

Yet another example comes from an early thirteenth-century Daoist text, which teaches the adepts how to reach the ultimate Daoist goal – to become a 'transcendent' (*xiān*), which in a general Daoist context means someone who has 'ascended to links in the chain higher than those occupied by even the best human beings'.[7] In this text, the author describes the 'eight leaks' that practitioners should avoid during their thousand-day fast: 'Tears leak [energy from] the liver. Nasal mucus leaks the lungs. Saliva leaks the kidneys. Sweat leaks the hearts. Night sweat leaks the small intestines. Drooling during sleep leaks the brain. Dreaming of intercourse with ghosts leaks the *shén*-spirit. Lust [for women] leaks the body.'[8] To a modern reader, some of those 'leaks' are simply ordinary bodily functions. That was the case to the thirteenth-century Chinese readers as well. 'Dreaming of intercourse with ghosts' was an established category of illness/symptom in pre-modern Chinese medical texts, as was night sweat, which could happen to anyone.[9] 'Lust' here most likely refers to ordinary intercourse with women, rather than excessive or particularly strong desire. What is problematic here, for Daoist practitioners, is not anything unusual, excessive, or illicit, but precisely what is ordinary: they aimed for the extraordinary. No fundamental distinctions were made between ordinary bodily discharges (sexual or non-sexual) and medically problematic ones (sexual or non-sexual).

The links that we tend to draw between sexually related matters or between sexually related matters and other realms of life were not always obvious. Ancient bedchamber arts authors considered 'intercourse with ghosts' a symptom of men and women's lack of sexual contact with the other sex, while medical authors prior to the thirteenth century generally treated it as a result of ordinary bodily depletion. 'Intercourse with ghosts' was only frequently associated with sexual desire in medical treatises after the thirteenth century, along with a rising medical interest in female emotions and desire.[10]

---

7 Robert F. Campany, *To Live as Long as Heaven and Earth: A Translation and Study of Ge Hong's* Traditions of Divine Transcendents (Berkeley, CA: University of California Press, 2002), 5.

8 Hsiao-wen Cheng, *Divine, Demonic, and Disordered: Women without Men in Song Dynasty China* (Seattle: University of Washington Press, 2021), 62.

9 Illnesses and symptoms were not separate categories in ancient Chinese medicine; both were 'conditions requiring medical attention'. See Donald Harper, *Early Chinese Medical Literature: The Mawangdui Manuscripts* (London: Kegan Paul International, 1998), 72. A distinct concept *zhèng* (pattern; manifestation; sign), which is often (mis-) translated as 'symptom' in the modern context, refers to sets of the diagnostic signs that include pulse manifestations, tongue, and facial complexions, as well as more commonly observed symptoms such as fever and pain.

10 Yi-Li Wu, 'Ghost Fetus, False Pregnancies, and the Parameters of Medical Uncertainty in Classical Chinese Gynecology', *Nan Nü* 4, no. 2 (2002): 170–206; Shigehisa Kuriyama,

Medical writers prior to the twelfth century rarely associated men's and women's reproductive bodies with sexual desire. Authors of bedchamber arts manuals always spoke of successful conception and bodily cultivation through sexual intercourse between men and women as mutually exclusive. When a twelfth-century physician opined that women without sexual contact with men could become sick because of unchannelled desire, and that desire was related to their reproductive bodies, he was an anomaly in his own time.[11]

Two modern concepts are often misused in writing histories of pre-modern sexuality: normalcy and nature. In the nineteenth century, the English word 'normal' came to mean *both* a 'statistical regularity derived from quantitative analysis' and an 'evaluative judgement attached to a model or type', but these two meanings were often confused.[12] The emergence of the modern concepts of the norm and normalcy was closely related to developments in statistics and their application to the social sciences in the West.[13] In pre-twentieth-century China, health was not the average condition of the superior part of the population but viewed on a spectrum of sick–healthy–healthier – and, for those who believed in it, even immortality.[14] Norms were not established on a statistical basis. What was considered correct, orthodox, or healthy was not conflated with what was common or average.[15]

Turning to 'nature': in pre-modern China, nature was not the antonym of culture. Some ancient Chinese thinkers deemed the natural world mechanical and irrelevant to human society. Others argued that the universe followed an ultimately ethical principle that human society should mirror. Still others believed that there was some personified divinity that governed both

'Angry Women and the Evolution of Chinese Medicine', in *National Health: Gender, Sexuality and Health in a Cross-Cultural Context*, ed. Michael Worton and Nana Wilson-Tagoe (London: University College London Press, 2004), 179–89; Hsiu-fen Chen, 'Between Passion and Repression: Medical Views of Demon Dreams, Demonic Fetuses, and Female Sexual Madness in Late Imperial China', *Late Imperial China* 32, no. 1 (2011): 51–82; Cheng, *Divine, Demonic, and Disordered*, ch. 2.

11 Hsiao-wen Cheng, 'Manless Women and the Sex–Desire–Procreation Link in Song Medicine', *Asian Medicine* 13 (2018): 69–94.

12 Karma Lochrie, *Heterosyncrasies: Female Sexuality When Normal Wasn't* (Minneapolis, MN: University of Minnesota Press, 2005), 3.

13 Amy Hollywood, 'The Normal, the Queer, and the Middle Ages', *Journal of the History of Sexuality* 12, no. 3 (2006): 173–9.

14 Yan Liu, *Healing with Poisons: Potent Medicines in Medieval China* (Seattle: University of Washington Press, 2021), 4–6.

15 Two words in classical Chinese, *gui* and *ju* (meaning a pair of compasses and a carpenter's square, respectively, also norms and principles), served a similar function as the Latin word *norma*, the origin of the English 'norm'.

the natural and the human worlds. For those who asserted that social hierarchies, including gender, accorded with cosmic principles, or the 'pattern of Heaven and Earth', those principles were not what nature *is* but what it *should be*; the universe required humans' active engagement to recover or maintain its proper functioning. When an anomaly occurred, for instance, in the natural or the human world, codified values, rather than observations of nature, determined whether such an anomaly was divine, demonic, or irrelevant. Asking whether a certain form of gender performance or sexual behaviour was 'natural' or 'unnatural' in pre-modern China is often a wrong question, because 'nature' was almost never the standard by which bodies and actions were judged.

Institutions and Practices

With the preceding discussion in mind, we may now proceed to survey several aspects of Chinese sexuality that are well studied, including ancient sex manuals and sexual cultivation practice, the institutions of concubines and courtesans, the promotion and complexity of female chastity, legal definitions and proceedings of illicit sex, celibacy beyond widow chastity, and literary representations of homoeroticism.

Ancient Chinese sex manuals were first made known to the Western world by the Dutch scholar Robert Hans van Gulik (1910–67). What van Gulik calls the 'handbooks of sex' is a unique genre of sexual cultivation manuals from ancient and early medieval China, or what traditional bibliographies referred to as the 'bedchamber' (*fángzhōng*) literature. They include graphic discussions of sexual positions, signs of arousal, anatomy of the genitalia, injuries and disorders related to sexual intercourse, and the treatment thereof. Taken out of context, it could seem as if ancient China was a sexual utopia that prioritized pleasure – the 'Chinese formula' of *'plaisir–désir–(acte)'*, in the words of the French philosopher Michel Foucault.[16] Reading critically and contextually, however, scholars have convincingly argued that such texts are gendered. They were written mainly for upper-class men either to secure progeny or to nourish their own bodies. The two purposes were mutually exclusive because both utilized 'essence' (*jīng*), or the source of men's life and longevity. A basic principle (for men), to 'retain the essence and fortify the brain', was thus to withhold ejaculation. The (male) practitioner must not

---

16 Leon Antonio Rocha, '*Scientia Sexualis* versus *Ars Erotica*: Foucault, van Gulik, Needham', *Studies in History and Philosophy of Biological and Biomedical Sciences*, 42 (2011): 328–43, at 333.

lose control and must stay focused and closely observe his female partner's bodily signs. Descriptions of male and female sexual 'pleasure' were thus designed to help male practitioners achieve this.[17]

A small fraction of socially and economically superior men in traditional China had more than one officially recognized sexual partner, but with few exceptions in extreme circumstances, a man was only allowed to marry one wife (*qī* or *díqī*, principal wife) at a time. The number of concubines (*qiè*) a man could take depended on his political and economic standing. The privileged status of the wife vis-à-vis concubines was secured both legally and ritually in most parts of Chinese history. The wife was the hostess of the household and the legal mother of all her husband's recognized children. Only the wife had a standing position in the family ritual and in front of her husband's ancestors. Only the wife's relatives were recognized as affines.[18] Polyandry was never legal, though we see some evidence of it among the poor in late imperial China.[19]

The institution of concubinage underwent significant change during the Song dynasty (960–1279 CE) – concubines who had children became formal family members. The change was inseparable from the institution of courtesans and the changing economy in the eleventh and the twelfth centuries. The line between courtesans and concubines and that between concubines and maids had always been blurry. Government courtesans served in government banquets, while well-off families often kept courtesan-concubines for their own social events. The legal status of a concubine in a household was similar to that of a maid; they could both be bought and sold. The rise of the money economy and the difficulty of securing government positions for one's sons caused much anxiety among the Song elite. Families in serious financial crisis could end up selling their daughters and even wives as concubines, maids, or even courtesans. To arrange marriage for one's daughter as a principal wife required dowry, and the escalation of dowry became a real

---

17 Charlotte Furth, 'Rethinking Van Gulik: Sexuality and Reproduction in Traditional Chinese Medicine', in *Engendering China: Women, Culture, and the State*, ed. Christina K. Gilmartin, Gail Hershatter, Lisa Rofel, and Tyrene White (Cambridge, MA: Harvard University Press, 1994), 125–46; Paul R. Goldin, 'The Cultural and Religious Background of Sexual Vampirism in Ancient China', *Theology and Sexuality* 12, no. 3 (2006): 285–308; Cheng, 'Manless Women', 82–6.

18 Debby Chih-Yen Huang and Paul R. Goldin, 'Polygyny and Its Discontents: A Key to Understanding Traditional Chinese Society', in *Sexuality in China: Histories of Power and Pleasure*, ed. Howard Chiang (Seattle: University of Washington Press, 2018), 16–33.

19 Matthew H. Sommer, *Polyandry and Wife-Selling in Qing Dynasty China* (Berkeley, CA: University of California Press, 2015).

financial burden. The anxiety about downward mobility and monetary transactions associated with marriage in a rapidly changing economy prompted some to reform family ritual and finance. The result was a gradual recognition of concubines as formal family members in order to keep the family together and to reject the idea of marriage as monetary transactions.[20]

There was no real distinction between prostitutes and courtesans and other professional entertainers. Prostitution was never illegal in the (often hereditary) entertainment households. Song dynasty government courtesans were not supposed to be 'privatized', but no law forbade independent courtesans to also provide sexual service. When the Mongol Yuan dynasty (1271–1368 CE) established its own bureau to oversee the households of entertainers in the late thirteenth century, all courtesans became 'on call', with no distinction between government and independent ones. The Yuan law also forbade inter-marriage between entertainers and musicians (referred to as 'base people') and ordinary commoners (referred to as 'good people'), though this was never very effective.[21] Evidence from the seventeenth century shows that it was not unusual for husbands in the 'music households' to act as their wives' pimps, but among 'good people', it was illicit for any husband to pimp his wife or concubine. The Yongzheng emperor's (r. 1722–35) reform in the early eighteenth century 'freed' the 'base people' and extended the laws regulating 'good people' to them. No husband was allowed to pimp his wife or concubines. Heads of households could from then on be (mildly) punished for having sex with their married servants, and men from 'base households' enjoyed the same sexual monopoly over their wives as those from 'good households' did.[22]

Remarriage was never seen as positive for women, but it was not unusual for either elite or commoner women to divorce or remarry during the Song.[23] In men's writing, women's fidelity to their husbands was often juxtaposed with men's loyalty to the state.[24] The change of property laws in the Yuan, which continued in later dynasties, made it financially more difficult for

---

20 Patricia B. Ebrey, 'Women, Money, and Class: Sima Guang and Song Neo-Confucian Views on Women', in *Papers on Society and Culture of Early Modern China* (Taipei: Institute of History and Philology, Academia Sinica, 1992), 613–69; Patricia B. Ebrey, *The Inner Quarters: Marriage and the Lives of Chinese Women in the Sung Period* (Berkeley, CA: University of California Press, 1993); Beverly Bossler, *Courtesans, Concubines, and the Cult of Female Fidelity: Gender and Social Change in China, 1000–1400* (Cambridge, MA: Harvard University Asia Center, 2013).
21 Bossler, *Courtesans, Concubines*, 295–304.   22 Sommer, *Sex, Law, and Society*.
23 Ebrey, *The Inner Quarters*, 204–16.   24 Bossler, *Courtesans, Concubines*, 250–89.

widows to remarry because the law then stipulated that a widow must leave her dowry to her late husband's family if she remarried or returned to her natal home, and the late husband's family then had the right to receive betrothal gifts when arranging a remarriage for their widowed daughter-in-law.[25] Meanwhile, from the fourteenth century onward, a state-recognized 'faithful widow' could retain significant resources (including social status) both for herself and for her family.[26] This emphasis on female sexual fidelity even came to be extended to courtesans. In a popular tradition seen in dramas and vernacular novels during the late sixteenth and early seventeenth centuries, a courtesan who committed suicide for her lover was elevated to the same level as a chaste widow who died for her late husband or an honorable man who died for his country.[27]

Legal documents from the eighteenth century show that the Qing state had a strong interest in promoting chastity among people of all social classes. Rape was defined as penile penetration, and the victim could be a woman as well as a young man. Rape against women was considered a violation against female chastity, while rape against men was a pollution of masculinity.[28] Victims of sexual assault or harassment were only recognized as victims if they resisted to the extent of causing serious physical injuries to themselves or even death. Cases show that quite a number of female victims of sexual harassment protested by committing suicide when judges did not punish the perpetrators seriously enough; in those cases, the perpetrator was then sentenced to death, and the woman was considered a chaste heroine.[29]

Both men and women were expected to marry and to produce offspring, but it was more difficult for men with fewer resources to afford a wife, whereas it was less likely for lower-class women to be able to afford not to marry. Most of the documented eminent Buddhist monks in pre-modern

25 Jennifer Holmgren, 'The Economic Foundations of Virtue: Widow-Remarriage in Early and Modern China', *Australian Journal of Chinese Affairs* 13 (1985): 1–27; Bettine Birge, *Women, Property, and Confucian Reaction in Sung and Yüan China, 960–1368* (Cambridge: Cambridge University Press, 2002).

26 Susan Mann, 'Widows in the Kinship, Class, and Community Structures of Qing Dynasty China', *Journal of Asian Studies* 46, no. 1 (1987): 37–56; Siyen Fei, *You dianfan dao guifan: Cong Mingdai zhenjie lienü de bianshi yu liuchuan kan zhenjie guannian de yangehua* (From Exemplary to Regulatory Norms: Identification and Circulation of Female Fidelity in the Ming Dynasty) (Taipei: Guoli Taiwan daxue wenshi congkan, 1998). Bossler, *Courtesans, Concubines*, 381–2.

27 Dorothy Ko, *Teachers of the Inner Chambers: Women and Culture in Seventeenth-Century China* (Stanford, CA: Stanford University Press, 1994), 81.

28 Sommer, *Sex, Law, and Society*, 66–165.

29 Janet M. Theiss, *Disgraceful Matters: The Politics of Chastity in Eighteenth-Century China* (Berkeley, CA: University of California Press, 2004).

China were men of humble backgrounds who had never married, whereas most Buddhist nuns who had a biography written about them were widowed elite women. Discourses on men's desire for women and on women's desire for men also differed. There was a long tradition of praising men who had little desire for women, including their wives.[30] Women's desire for men, on the other hand, was mainly discussed in the contexts of women's jealousy and men's bodily or affective sublimation. Marriage was never about fulfilling or regulating sexual desire for men or for women, but women who made their sexual bodies unavailable to their husbands were often subject to suspicion and scrutiny. Medical and anecdotal sources from the Song period portrayed women who stayed away from their husbands as sick and/or possessed by spirits, although the same set of 'symptoms' was regarded as signs of women's divinity in several Buddhist and Daoist hagiographies. Disinterest in one's wife, by contrast, was never considered problematic for men.[31]

Male homoeroticism was a popular theme in vernacular fiction as well as quasi-ethnographies from the seventeenth and the eighteenth centuries. Scholarly opinions differ about whether or not depictions of male homoeroticism as a 'southern fad' were accurate reflections of reality.[32] Some scholars find traces of egalitarian relations between men in this body of literature, analogous to the egalitarian relations between 'chivalric' men and women that were praised in elite writings during this time.[33] Others see the reinforcement of traditional values such as chastity and filial piety in this body of literature.[34] Scholars agree that the Ming state (1368–1644 CE) was no more tolerant towards male homosexuality than the later Qing; the Ming dynasty outlawed male homosexual intercourse, while Qing laws targeted homosexual assault.[35]

Earlier scholarship attributed Qing statutes against homosexual sex to a 'disgusted' reaction against 'decadence' among the elite of the preceding

---

30 Cheng Yu-yu [Zheng yuyu], *Xingbie yu jiaguo: Han Jin cifu de chusao lunshu* (Gender and the State: The Discourse of Chu Songs in Han-Jin Rhapsodies) (Taipei: Le Jin Books [Liren shuju], 2000), 11–73.

31 Cheng, *Divine, Demonic, and Disordered*.

32 Sophie Volpp, 'The Discourse on Male Marriage: Li Yu's "A Male Mencius's Mother"', *Positions* 2, no. 1 (1994): 113–32; Sophie Volpp, 'Classifying Lust: The Seventeenth-Century Vogue for Male Love', *Harvard Journal of Asiatic Studies* 61, no. 1 (2001): 77–118; Giovanni Vitiello, *The Libertine's Friend: Homosexuality and Masculinity in Late Imperial China* (Chicago: University of Chicago Press, 2011), 15–52.

33 Keith McMahon, 'Sublime Love and the Ethics of Equality in a Homoerotic Novel of the Nineteenth Century: *Precious Mirror of Boy Actresses*', *Nan Nü* 4, no. 1 (2002): 70–109; Vitiello, *The Libertine's Friend*, 53–92.

34 Volpp, 'The Discourse on Male Marriage'; McMahon, 'Sublime Love'.

35 Sommer, *Sex, Law, and Society*, 114–65.

Ming dynasty, but Matthew Sommer demonstrates that it was not until a century into the Qing dynasty, in the early eighteenth century, when the rapidly growing number of poor single men became a source of concern to the state, that a paradigm shift from 'status performance' to 'gender performance' took place in the judicial system and practice. Male homosexual intercourse was assimilated to heterosexual offences under the rubric of 'illicit sex' (*jiān*) for the first time, along with changes including the curtailment of the sexual use of woman servants by their masters and new penalties for a number of variations of rape.[36]

Female homoeroticism was extremely rare in pre-modern Chinese sources and almost only seen in vernacular fiction in late imperial times. Compared to sexual intercourse between men, that between women was trivialized both in law and in literature.[37]

Limitations in the Scholarship

While scholars have made insightful observations of specific aspects related to sexuality in Chinese history, it is more difficult to define one's subject matter for the history of sexuality in general. I observe three phenomena in surveys of and introductions to the history of sexuality of pre-modern China: a retrospective sexology, the censorship hypothesis, and the assumption of sex as a given.

Sexology, as a modern way of 'scientifically' analysing sexual practices and habits, set up standards by which a given sexual practice could be evaluated and judged to be either healthy and normal or deviant and perverted. Here I use 'retrospective sexology' to refer to scholarship that applies the approaches or assumptions of sexology to historical subjects. Van Gulik's pioneering works on sexuality in traditional China, *Erotic Colour Prints of the Late Ming Period* (1951) and *Sexual Life in Ancient China* (1961), are perhaps the most obvious examples of retrospective sexology in twentieth-century sinology.[38] *Sexual Life in Ancient China* was intended for the 'Sexual Life'

---

36 Matthew H. Sommer, 'The Penetrated Male in Late Imperial China: Judicial Constructions and Social Stigma', *Modern China* 23, no. 2 (1997): 140–80; Sommer, *Sex, Law, and Society*.

37 Tze-lan D. Sang, *The Emerging Lesbian: Female Same-Sex Desire in Modern China* (Chicago: University of Chicago Press, 2003), 37–95.

38 For introductions to and critiques of the two works, see Charlotte Furth, 'Rethinking Van Gulik'; Paul R. Goldin, 'Introduction', in Robert Hans van Gulik, *Sexual Life in Ancient China: A Preliminary Survey of Chinese Sex and Society from ca. 1500 B.C. till 1644 A.D.* (1961; Leiden: Brill, 2003), xiii–xxv; James Cahill, 'Introduction to R. H. Van Gulik, *Erotic Colour Prints of the Late Ming Period*', in Robert Hans van Gulik, *Erotic Colour Prints of the*

Writing a History of Sexuality for Pre-Modern China

series published by Routledge.[39] The renowned Sinologist Joseph Needham (1900–95) was invited to contribute a volume on ancient China. Needham liked the idea, saying that, 'there is a debt which has not yet been paid to Chinese civilisation' because 'Chinese sexology was of an extremely healthy, human and non-sadistic character, comparing favourably with the sexual theory and practices of other Asian peoples, and indeed with all other peoples in the world.'[40] He recommended van Gulik for the task. Van Gulik did not entirely share Needham's sanguine point of view: in *Erotic Colour Prints of the Late Ming Period*, he had observed a kind of 'sexual perversion' – which he termed 'sexual vampirism' – in ancient Chinese sex manuals, aimed at 'stealing' the 'vital energy' of one's sexual partners through intercourse in order to enrich one's own.[41] But he was convinced otherwise by Needham, and in his preface to *Sexual Life in Ancient China*, writes:

> For writing that preface [to *Erotic Colour Prints*] I needed some knowledge of ancient Chinese sexual life and habits. In my Chinese studies I had till then always shirked this subject, because I felt that this was a field best left to qualified sexologists – especially since I had gathered from casual remarks in older and later Western books on China that *pathologia sexualis* [sexual pathology] was largely represented there . . . The ancient Chinese had indeed no reason for hiding their sexual life. Their handbooks of sex prove clearly that their sexual habits were healthy and normal – at any rate by the norms of the polygamic system that has prevailed in China from the oldest known times till recent years.[42]

The 'handbooks of sex' referred to the aforementioned 'bedchamber arts' literature, wherein van Gulik found evidence of sexual vampirism. Whether they found sex in ancient China to be healthy or perverted, both Needham and van Gulik approached their subject as contemporary sexologists.

Late Ming Period with an Essay on Chinese Sex Life from the Han to the Ch'ing Dynasty, B.C. 206–A.D. 1644, Vol. 1 (1951; Leiden: Brill, 2004), ix–xxv; J. S. Edgren, 'A Bibliographical Note on Van Gulik's Albums of Erotic Colour Prints', in van Gulik, *Erotic Colour Prints*, xxvii–xxx; Wilt L. Idema, '"Blasé Literati": Lü T'ien-Ch'eng and the Lifestyle of the Chiang-nan Elite in the Final Decades of the Wan-li Period', in van Gulik, *Erotic Colour Prints*, xxxi–lix.

39 Rocha, '*Scientia Sexualis*'.   40 Quoted in Rocha, '*Scientia Sexualis*', 336.

41 van Gulik, *Erotic Colour Prints*, 11–13, 68–72. Van Gulik identified such practice as '[D]aoist black magic', though there was no hard evidence that such practices or the other sex manuals were produced or promoted by any Daoist institution; in fact, the earliest documented Daoist community (the Celestial Masters) explicitly condemned such practices. On sexual vampirism in ancient China, see also Goldin, 'The Cultural and Religious Background'.

42 van Gulik, *Sexual Life in Ancient China*, xxxi–xxxii.

Scholars have since challenged much of van Gulik's work, from his use of sources to the anachronism of applying standards of modern sexual pathology to ancient China, as well as his old-fashioned Orientalist tendencies. For example, Charlotte Furth has noted van Gulik's assumption that

> discussions of sexual practices, wherever they may be found, are evidence for the historical presence of a discrete erotic domain: a self-consciously understood cultural sphere for the experience and understanding of sexual pleasure, in and of itself. The presence of such a domain is assumed to be the natural by-product of human instinct, and this universal category of experience leaves its historical traces as *ars erotica* [erotic arts].[43]

Furth also points out that ancient Chinese sex manuals, which belonged to the distinct genre of 'bedchamber arts', did not celebrate female sexual pleasure as van Gulik claimed; instead, 'pleasure was a means to other ends', benefitting men. Men were advised to observe their female partners' bodily reactions closely in order to maintain the power of control and to nourish their own bodies.[44] In addition to the anachronism of labels such as 'repression' or 'perversion', Paul R. Goldin has found that van Gulik's definition of 'perversion' was idiosyncratic even among sexologists of his own time.[45] Bret Hinsch notes that van Gulik clearly considered male homosexuality to be pathological, but also developed 'a private fantasy of the Zhou dynasty (1045–256 BCE) as a lesbian utopia', even though there is little hard evidence of female same-sex relations in ancient China.[46]

Sinologists now no longer depict ancient China as a sexual utopia; nor do we label anything in traditional China as 'repressed' or 'perverted'. However, we rarely question people's sexual practices and habits as the legitimate, go-to subject for the history of sexuality, despite the acknowledged lack of sources. In his pioneering work on male homosexuality in Chinese history, *Passions of the Cut Sleeve* (1990), for example, Bret Hinsch defines his subject matter as 'the [male] homosexual tradition' (i.e., the long literary tradition of writing about eroticism between men) rather than homosexual people, because 'in all periods lacunae outnumber surviving records, making systematic social history almost impossible'.[47] Yet when discussing 'the particular nature of

---

43 Furth, 'Rethinking Van Gulik', 129.   44 Furth, 'Rethinking Van Gulik', 133.
45 Goldin, 'Introduction', xvi–xvii.
46 Bret Hinsch, 'Van Gulik's *Sexual Life in Ancient China* and the Matter of Homosexuality', *Nan Nü* 7, no. 1 (2005): 79–91.
47 Bret Hinsch, *Passions of the Cut Sleeve: The Male Homosexual Tradition in China* (Berkeley, CA: University of California Press, 1990), 2–3.

Writing a History of Sexuality for Pre-Modern China

homosexuality in China', he seems to fall back into a retrospective sexual ethnography:

> On a physical level, surviving literature depicts anal intercourse as the preferred form of homosexual intercourse ... Among the references to homosexuality that mention explicit sexual positions, anal intercourse is most common by far; references to mutual masturbation, intercrural intercourse, fellatio, and other forms of intercourse are relatively rare.[48]

Here he is analysing texts as if they were describing actual sexual practices, and adopts a typology developed by David Greenberg, which puts social expressions of homosexuality outside of the modern West into four categories (transgenerational, transgender, class-structured, and egalitarian), and matches them with Chinese examples.[49]

Paul Goldin also recognizes the lack of sources for actual sexual practices, and in *The Culture of Sex in Ancient China* (2002) defines his subject matter as follows:

> This is a study of intellectual conceptions of sex and sexuality in China from roughly 500 B.C. to A.D. 400 ... The sources for this book are primarily philosophical, literary, and religious texts. *This work is not intended as a history of sexuality or sexual behavior (and the material on which it is based sheds very little light on people's sexual practices).* Historians have begun to question whether any such history can – or should – be written; and in any case, for ancient China, the extant sources are not sufficiently informative for that purpose. The sources do reveal, however, that Chinese authors wrote earnestly about sexual activity and expected their readers to consider the subject thoughtfully. Sexual intercourse constituted a fundamental source of imagery and terminology that informed the classical Chinese conception of social and political relationships.[50]

Goldin implies that his focus on the literary and intellectual tradition ('the culture of sex') might not constitute a history of sexuality, but from my point of view, illuminating the ways in which discourses of sexual intercourse and those of social and political relations intertwined and informed each other is precisely the strength of a proper history of sexuality. Goldin argues convincingly, for example, that, with the rise of China's early empire during the Qin and Han dynasties (221 BCE–220 CE), 'unregulated or illicit sexual activity was associated with, or construed as symptomatic of, unregulated or illicit

48 Hinsch, *Passions of the Cut Sleeve*, 8.
49 Hinsch, *Passions of the Cut Sleeve*, 11–13. For the typology itself, see David F. Greenberg, *The Construction of Homosexuality* (Chicago: University of Chicago Press, 1988), 25.
50 Goldin, *The Culture of Sex*, 1. Emphasis mine.

political activity'.[51] In another example of the intertwining of sexual and political discourses, during the Southern Song (1127–1279 CE), when the Jurchens and the Mongols in the north were a constant threat to the dynasty, writers began to celebrate female fidelity not on the basis of a woman's loyalty to her husband but rather her 'refusal to submit to rape by bandits or invaders'. Beverly Bossler argues that this was because raped women's bodies were associated with invaded territories.[52]

Susan Mann begins her *Gender and Sexuality in Modern China* (2011), a survey that focuses on modern China but makes reference to all periods of Chinese history, also by discussing the problem of sources:

> Does sex have a history? Almost any teenager coping with a parent who still lives in the dark ages will assure you that it does. *But the history of sex is surprisingly difficult to study. Why? Lack of evidence.* Most people keep their sex lives to themselves. What people write down, publish, and circulate may be sexual fantasy or invention, with plot lines designed to sell copy. This evidence can tell us a lot about what people like to read or watch or imagine, but *little about what they actually do.* Ironically, the most reliable evidence for a history of sex is the mass of material (by government officials, religious leaders, parents, doctors, and so on) telling people what not to do. We can be certain that *some* people were doing *some* of that.[53]

In contrast to van Gulik's conviction that 'the ancient Chinese had indeed no reason for hiding their sexual life', Mann sees that 'most people keep their sex lives to themselves'. She also mentions a disproportion of the quantity and the types of sources: 'sometimes the historical record on sex becomes very noisy, but at other times it is quiet'.[54] She makes a similar assumption that the history of sex should be about 'what [people] actually do'.

Mann notes that this lack of evidence was not limited to China, a point with which Howard Chiang agrees:

> [It is] not surprising that surviving documentation of human sexual experience from the past is scattered and incomplete. When people disclose information about their sexual lives in a factual manner or metaphorically, *public record – usually censored in one way or another – rarely captures the true extent of what happened in the bedroom (or elsewhere).* This poses a significant degree of methodological difficulty for studying the history of sexuality. Furthermore, different social groups leave behind disproportional measures

---

51 Goldin, *The Culture of Sex*, 3 and ch. 3.   52 Bossler, *Courtesans, Concubines*, 288.
53 Susan Mann, *Gender and Sexuality in Modern Chinese History* (Cambridge: Cambridge University Press, 2011), xv. Emphasis mine, except in the last sentence.
54 Mann, *Gender and Sexuality*, xv.

of historical voice, making it a challenge to deduce broader generalizations about erotic desire and sexual practice in a particular region or a given time period.[55]

Here, again, 'what happened in the bedroom (or elsewhere)' is considered the first-and-foremost subject of the history of sexuality.

We now know that van Gulik's sources, even supplemented with newly excavated materials that he never had a chance to see, cannot really tell us what people actually did.[56] A common explanation for this lack of sources is political or ideological censorship. As Weijing Lu notes:

> Van Gulik attributed the disappearance of these texts [the 'arts of the bedchamber' manuals] to the censorship of neo-Confucian ideology, which dominated the last centuries of imperial history. He argued that after the thirteenth century, 'Confucian puritanism gradually restricted the circulations of literature of this genre'.[57]

Lu does not tell us whether she agrees, nor does she offer an alternative explanation for the disappearance of the bedchamber arts manuals. Mann, on the other hand, suggests that censorship might also contribute to rather than reduce the production of sources about sex because it led to sources about 'what not to do'. She notes that recent scholarship using such sources has productively taken up the question: 'When, where, and why do certain kinds of sex, or certain kinds of sexual relationships, become problematic?'[58]

Other explanations of the 'lack of evidence' for sex in Chinese history have touched upon considerations of print technology and the publishing industry, changes in the social structure and the population of those who read and write, and elite men's trivialization of certain forms of sex. For instance, Ping Yao points out that the kind of subjects and type of sources that survive from each time period have much to do with what the literati at that time were interested in.[59] Tse-lan Sang argues that 'the complete absence of female-female eroticism from traditional Chinese moral and legal codes suggests that it did not constitute a significance source of anxiety for men. Literature

---

55 Howard Chiang, ed., *Sexuality in China: Histories of Power and Pleasure* (Seattle: University of Washington Press, 2018), 6. Emphasis mine.

56 Such as the Mawangdui manuscripts. See Donald Harper, 'The Sexual Arts of Ancient China as Described in a Manuscript of the Second Century BC', *Harvard Journal of Asiatic Studies* 47, no. 2 (1987): 539–93.

57 Weijing Lu, 'Introduction', *Journal of the History of Sexuality* 22, no. 2 (2013): 201–6, at 203.

58 Mann, *Gender and Sexuality*, xv.

59 Ping Yao, 'Between Topics and Sources: Researching the History of Sexuality in Imperial China', in *Sexuality in China: Histories of Power and Pleasure*, ed. Howard Chiang (Seattle: University of Washington Press, 2018), 34–49.

further shows that men often trivialized female–female intimacy rather than treating it punitively or prohibiting it.'[60]

If writing a history of sexuality for traditional China is difficult, it is perhaps not solely because of the lack of sources but also because we have not thought seriously enough about what we have been looking for and why. Most scholarship takes sex as a given, a self-evident human phenomenon. When we say, 'sex/uality has a history', we often mean that the social institutions and cultural expressions of something that we *already* know is sex have a history. Even in the best scholarship, generalizations about 'sex' tend to refer to *certain* sexual activities under *certain* conditions. For instance, Mann describes China as 'a culture where sex was never coupled with [the Christian concept of] sin'.[61] Nonetheless, certain forms of sex could be severely punished in some if not all periods, such as wives' adultery or a man having sex with the wife of a superior man. Summarizing Ping Yao's analysis of two Tang dynasty (618–907 CE) erotic texts, Weijing Lu states that they 'are regarded as a manifestation of Tang society's openness with regard to sex'.[62] And yet the works of erotica can only manifest Tang society's openness to the kind of 'elegant' sex that elite men performed as a demonstration of their sophisticated tastes, along with equally elegant wine, music, and poetry.[63] (For more on sex in Tang China, see Chapter 4 by Ping Yao in Volume III of this work.) Goldin writes that in ancient China, 'sex was usually treated openly, even by today's standards. Ancient Chinese writers discussed sex seriously, as one of the most important topics of human speculation, and freely adopted sexual metaphors in discussing social, political, and religious relationships'.[64] As Goldin makes clear elsewhere, however, 'sex' here refers only to the kinds of sex that were meaningful to ancient Chinese writers.

The paucity of 'evidence' may also be an epistemological problem – both for us and for our historical subjects. For example, if in certain historical sources, such as in medical and anecdotal writings of the seventh through thirteenth centuries, female sexuality was legible and explicable almost exclusively in relation to men, we may broaden our search beyond *what* women were doing with or without men, to *how* people described the

---

60 Sang, *The Emerging Lesbian*, 21.   61 Mann, *Gender and Sexuality*, xvii.
62 Lu, 'Introduction', 204.
63 Ping Yao, 'Historicizing Great Bliss: Erotica in Tang China (618–907)', *Journal of the History of Sexuality* 22, no. 2 (2013): 207–29.
64 Paul R. Goldin, 'Sexuality: Ancient China', in *The International Encyclopedia of Human Sexuality*, ed. Patricia Whelehan and Anne Bolin (Chichester, UK: John Wiley & Sons, 2015), 3.

Writing a History of Sexuality for Pre-Modern China

mysterious and the inexplicable. What is interesting is no longer just how people wrote about what they knew but also how they wrote – or struggled to write – about what they did not know or did not know for sure.[65]

Comparative Histories

Needham and van Gulik were convinced that ancient Chinese sexology was superior to that of the rest of the world. Van Gulik's *Sexual Life in Ancient China* informed Michel Foucault's imagination of China as *the* example of *ars erotica*.[66] (For more on Foucault, see Chapter 6 by Michael Behrent in Volume I of this work.) While admitting in an interview that he had made a mistake in creating a false dichotomy between *scientia sexualis* and *ars erotica*, sexual science versus erotic arts, Foucault insisted that China had an *ars erotica*:

> The Greeks and Romans did not have any *ars erotica* to be compared with the Chinese *ars erotica* ... The Chinese 'formula' would be *plaisir–désir–(acte)*. Acts are put aside because you have to restrain acts in order to get the maximum duration and intensity of pleasure. The Christian 'formula' puts an accent on desire and tries to eradicate it.[67]

After van Gulik, sinologists have adopted different approaches to making comparisons. Some try to prove that China had something similar to *scientia sexualis* as well. Others argue that China is or was still different, but in other ways. Charlotte Furth's critique of van Gulik's reading of the bedchamber arts manuals is an example of the former. Furth convincingly argues that the bedchamber arts manuals were not about pleasure but rather the regulation of reproduction and the distinction of sexual difference, placing them broadly in line with the aims of *scientia sexualis*.[68] According to Furth, medical views of female sexuality in the Song dynasty also served ends more similar to *scientia sexualis* than *ars erotica*: 'the woman's sexual body was not separated from her generative and gestational body, and desire in both sexes was naturalized as a manifestation of the intentionality of Heaven and Earth rather than psychologized as erotic pleasure'.[69]

---

65 Cheng, *Divine, Demonic, and Disordered*.   66 See Rocha, 'Scientia Sexualis'.
67 Quoted in Rocha, 'Scientia Sexualis', 333.
68 Furth, 'Rethinking van Gulik'.
69 Charlotte Furth, *A Flourishing Yin: Gender in China's Medical History, 960–1665* (Berkeley, CA: University of California Press, 1999), 91. What Furth observes here is mainly the opinion of the Song physician Chen Ziming (1190–1270), which I believe to be an anomalous rather than common opinion in Song medicine. See Cheng, *Divine, Demonic, and Disordered*, ch. 1.

Among those who emphasize difference, both Mann and Goldin make a case for the absence of the Christian concept of sin in Chinese history. In Mann's words:

> [I]n a culture in which sex was never coupled with sin – in which Adam and Eve had no role in the cultural or historical explanations for sexual desire and its consequences – the Chinese conviction that sexual activity is an essential part of a healthy human life softened and defused the conflicts about homoerotic desire, and about homosexual and transgendered identities, that feed homophobia and even violence in many modern cultures.[70]

It is debatable whether Chinese society, in history or in the present, is indeed less homophobic than the Christian world. (Can homophobia even be quantified?) But Mann's assumption seems to be that homophobia in modern societies is mainly a result of the Christian concept of sin. Goldin's comparison is somewhat different. In an encyclopaedia entry for sexuality in ancient China, in the section titled 'No Christian concept of sin', Goldin explains: 'sex was not regarded as inherently shameful. To be sure, various powers ... sought to limit the permissible partners and locations for sexual intercourse ... But sexuality – especially if not "immoderate" (*yín*) – was never laden with anything like a Christian conception of sin.'[71] Indeed, although by this standard, maybe nothing was inherently shameful: acts were made problematic by their participants, their locations, and their purposes. If 'sex' was not a distinct category, as discussed earlier, how could it be 'inherently' anything? Some ascetic traditions (such as Quanzhen Daoism, active in north China in the twelfth and thirteenth centuries) even considered sex between husband and wife problematic – not shameful, but dangerous and destructive.[72] Desire, for almost all Chinese traditions that sought some form of transcendence, was always dangerous – not excessive or inappropriate desire, but desire itself.

After critically reviewing scholarship in both Chinese and European languages regarding whether or not ancient Chinese sexual culture could be considered *ars erotica*, Leon Rocha concludes that, 'assumptions concerning the "essential features" of "Chinese civilisation" precede the act of producing knowledge about China. In figuring out whether China is similar or different from the West, we have often already decided *that* China is similar or

---

70 Mann, *Gender and Sexuality*, xvii.
71 Goldin, 'Sexuality: Ancient China', 3. This *yín* is the same word as that explained in note 3; it is a different and unrelated word from *yīn* as in *yin–yang*.
72 Louis Komjathy, 'Sun Buer: Early Quanzhen Matriarch and the Beginnings of Female Alchemy', *Nan Nü* 16, no. 2 (2014): 171–238; Cheng, *Divine, Demonic, and Disordered*, 147–8.

different from the West.'[73] So what is the point of making comparisons, and should we still do it at all? If there is no way for historians to avoid making comparisons, as I would argue, it becomes all the more important for us to keep asking ourselves what matters to us and why. We often hear historians (especially historians of non-Western cultures) advocate that we ought to understand something on its own terms. Yet how is this epistemically possible? What reference point can we possibly use, if not our own world and language? What is the point, really, of studying the history of sexuality without any interest in the gender dynamics and sexual politics of our own world? There is no escape from comparative history, because even if we are not comparing two historical subjects to each other we are comparing them to our own world. If we accept the fact that it is almost impossible to 'understand something on its own terms', perhaps we can defamiliarize both our historical subjects and ourselves by persistently questioning both. For instance, while it may be tempting to say, 'China has no Christian concept of sin and so is less homophobic', we can keep asking whether the Christian concept of sin is and has been truly the main reason for homophobia. I would also like to urge readers of this work, especially those who are not specialists in Asia, to read more about Chinese history and not to be discouraged by Foucault's or others' mistakes. Historians of China alone cannot answer questions such as 'whether the Christian concept of sin is the true reason for homophobia', nor all the other fascinating questions that a comparative study of 'sexuality' – however it is defined and understood – raises.

Further Reading

Bossler, Beverly. *Courtesans, Concubines, and the Cult of Female Fidelity: Gender and Social Change in China, 1000–1400*. Cambridge, MA: Harvard Asia Center, 2013.

Cheng, Hsiao-wen. 'Before Sexual and Normal: Shifting Categories of Sexual Anomaly from Ancient to Yuan China'. *Asia Major* 31, no. 2 (2018): 1–39.

Divine, Demonic, and Disordered: Women without Men in Song Dynasty China. Seattle: University of Washington Press, 2021.

Chiang, Howard, ed. *Sexuality in China: Histories of Power and Pleasure*. Seattle: University of Washington Press, 2018.

Ebrey, Patricia B. *Women and the Family in Chinese History*. London: Routledge, 2003.

73 Rocha, *'Scientia Sexualis'*, 341.

Furth, Charlotte. 'Androgynous Males and Deficient Females: Biology and Gender Boundaries in Sixteenth- and Seventeenth-Century China'. *Late Imperial China* 9, no. 2 (1998): 1–31.

'Rethinking Van Gulik: Sexuality and Reproduction in Traditional Chinese Medicine'. In *Engendering China: Women, Culture, and the State*, ed. Christina K. Gilmartin, Gail Hershatter, Lisa Rofel, and Tyrene White. Cambridge, MA: Harvard University Press, 1994.

Goldin, Paul R. 'The Cultural and Religious Background of Sexual Vampirism in Ancient China'. *Theology and Sexuality* 12, no. 3 (2006): 285–308.

The Culture of Sex in Ancient China. Honolulu: University of Hawai'i Press, 2002.

Hay, John. 'The Body Invisible in Chinese Art?' In *Body, Subject and Power in China*, ed. Angela Zito and Tani Barlow, 42–77. Chicago: University of Chicago Press, 1994.

Hinsch, Bret. *Passions of the Cut Sleeve: The Male Homosexual Tradition in China*. Berkeley, CA: University of California Press, 1990.

Huntington, Rania. 'Foxes and Sex in Late Imperial Chinese Narrative'. *Nan Nü* 2, no. 1 (2000): 78–128.

Jia, Jinhua, Xiaofei Kang, and Ping Yao, eds. *Gendering Chinese Religion: Subject, Identity, and Body*. Albany, NY: State University of New York Press, 2014.

Lu, Weijing. *True to Her Word: The Faithful Maiden Cult in Late Imperial China*. Stanford, CA: Stanford University Press, 2008.

ed. 'Sexuality in Chinese History'. Special issue of the *Journal of the History of Sexuality* 22, no. 2, (2013): 201–331.

Mann, Susan L. *Gender and Sexuality in Modern Chinese History*. Cambridge: Cambridge University Press, 2011.

McMahon, Keith. *Misers, Shrews, and Polygamists: Sexuality and Male-Female Relations in Eighteenth-Century Chinese Fiction*. Durham, NC: Duke University Press, 1995.

Polygamy and Sublime Passion: Sexuality in China on the Verge of Modernity. Honolulu: University of Hawai'i Press, 2009.

Rocha, Leon Antonio. '*Scientia Sexualis* versus *Ars Erotica*: Foucault, van Gulik, Needham'. *Studies in History and Philosophy of Biological and Biomedical Sciences*, no. 42 (2011): 328–43.

'Xing: The Discourse of Sex and Human Nature in Modern China'. *Gender & History* 22, no. 3 (2010): 603–28.

Rouzer, Paul. *Articulated Ladies: Gender and the Male Community in Early Chinese Texts*. Cambridge, MA: Harvard University Asia Center, 2001.

Sang, Tze-lan D. *The Emerging Lesbian: Female Same-Sex Desire in Modern China*. Chicago: University of Chicago Press, 2003.

Sommer, Matthew H. *Sex, Law, and Society in Late Imperial China*. Stanford, CA: Stanford University Press, 2000.

Theiss, Janet. *Disgraceful Matters: The Politics of Chastity in Eighteenth-Century China*. Berkeley, CA: University of California Press, 2005.

Vitiello, Giovanni. *The Libertine's Friend: Homosexuality and Masculinity in Late Imperial China*. Chicago: University of Chicago Press, 2011.

Volpp, Sophie. 'Classifying Lust: The Seventeenth-Century Vogue for Male Love'. *Harvard Journal of Asiatic Studies* 61, no. 1 (2001): 77–118.

'The Discourse on Male Marriage: Li Yu's "A Male Mencius's Mother"'. *Positions* 2, no. 1 (1994): 113–32.

Yao, Ping. *Women, Gender, and Sexuality in China: A Brief History*. London: Routledge, 2021.

Zeitlin, Judith T. *The Phantom Heroine: Ghosts and Gender in Seventeenth-Century Chinese Literature*. Honolulu: University of Hawai'i Press, 2007.

7

Sexuality in Traditional Systems of Thought and Belief in Pre-modern Japan

HITOMI TONOMURA

This chapter conceptualizes 'sexuality' broadly and explores its various manifestations in the historical sources of pre-modern Japan from the seventh to the sixteenth centuries. This is not an easy task, because the English word 'sexuality' finds no direct correspondence in the pre-modern Japanese lexicon nor do historical sources mention sexuality as a discreet subject.[1] Consequently, we seek to capture 'sexuality' through the modulated filter of the modern lens, by searching for expressions, concepts, and symbols that resonate with our general sense of sexualities, including actions and affects associated with real and imagined bodily organs and their functions, as well as the psychological and emotional states, such as copulation, birth, assaults or desires, longing, pleasure, excitement, loathing, and pain. This endeavour necessarily poses a methodological challenge. First, *their* contemporary senses and expressions that reflect or shape sexuality may fail to trigger *our* sensibility and bypass our notice because of our unfamiliarity with them or our insufficient imagination. On the other hand, words that typically incite, normalize, define, and govern today's sexuality may be non-existent in the pre-modern vocabulary, and we may fail to capture and appreciate the meaning of that absence in our analysis.

With these caveats, we look for sexualities as manifested in systems of thoughts and beliefs which came to be rooted in pre-modern Japanese society while themselves transforming in meaning throughout the centuries. First is the *Kami* (deity) Way, which celebrates a myriad of 'native' deities, although

---

[1] In modern Japanese, sexuality is often rendered in *katakana*, an alphabet used for borrowed foreign words, thus 'sekushuarithi'.

Sexuality in Traditional Systems of Thought and Belief in Pre-modern Japan

some are actually of foreign origin.[2] Often called 'local cults', the *Kami* Way in our discussion is distinguished from Shinto, which developed later, and aimed to 'impose a unifying framework upon disparate kami cults, or at creating a distinct religious tradition by transforming local kami cults into something bigger'.[3] We consider representation of sexuality in the *Kami* Way by considering the action and symbolic meanings associated with deities who appear in Japan's earliest writing, the *Kojiki* (Records of Ancient Matters), compiled in 712 CE.[4]

The second system of thought to be examined is Buddhism, in particular, Mahāyāna Buddhism, which arrived in Japan from continental East Asia in the sixth century CE. While the *Kojiki* shows little influence of Buddhist ideas, *kami*-worship and Buddhism soon became hardly distinguishable to most lay people. According to the theory of *honji suijaku*, Buddhist bodhi-sattvas, compassionate beings who were far along on the path to enlighten-ment, and *kami* were merged as mutually supportive and interchangeable manifestations of the same spirit, or *kami* were 'transformations of the

---

2 Michael Como, *Weaving and Binding: Immigrant Gods and Female Immortals in Ancient Japan* (Honolulu: University of Hawai'i Press, 2009).

3 Mark Teeuwen and Berhard Sheid, 'Tracing Shinto in the History of Kami Worship, Editor's Introduction', *Japanese Journal of Religious Studies* 29, no. 3/4 (2002): 195–207, at 200; Anna Andreeva, *Assembling Shinto: Buddhist Approaches to Kami Worship in Medieval Japan* (Cambridge, MA: Harvard University Asia Center, Harvard University Press, 2017), 1–16. Richard Bowring, *The Religious Traditions of Japan, 500–1600* (Cambridge: Cambridge University Press, 2005), esp. 'The Emergence of Shintō', 344–62. Shinto refers either to a theoretical school focused on the Ise Shrine developed by a medieval ritualist family, Watarai (and later Yoshida), or (more commonly) a belief associated with the modern Japanese state in the nineteenth century, often with a nationalistic strain.

4 A larger corpus of this mythology dating from roughly the same period includes the *Nihon shoki, Fudoki*, and myth fragments in the *Manyōshū*. But the *Kojiki* is best suited for our purposes because of its unique effort to preserve and represent the vernacular vocabulary, rather than the Chinese used by others. David T. Bialock, *Eccentric Spaces, Hidden Histories: Narrative, Ritual, and Royal Authority from* The Chronicles of Japan *to* The Tale of the Heike (Stanford, CA: Stanford University Press, 2007), ch. 4. Robert Borgen and Marian Ury compare *Nihon shoki* (compiled in 720) and the *Kojiki* in 'Readable Japanese Mythology: Selections from *Nihon shoki* and *Kojiki*', *Journal of the Association of Teachers of Japanese* 24 no. 1 (1990): 61–97. Yamaguchi Yoshinori and Kōnoshi Takamitsu, comp., *Kojiki: Shin Nihon koten bungaku zenshū* 1 (1997; Tokyo: Shōgakkan, 2007); and Kurano Kenji and Takeda Yūkichi, comp., *Kojiki Norito: Nihon koten bungaku taikei*, Vol. 1 (Tokyo: Iwanami Shoten, 1958). I have relied on the newest review of the wide range of interpretations of the text's meaning given in Ignacio Quiros, in cooperation with Kate Wildman Nakai, trans., *Kojiki gaku* (Studies on the *Kojiki*) 3 (2017): 1–12; 4 (2018): 1–6; 5 (2019): 1–27; 6 (2020): 1–64; 7 (2021): 1–61; *Kokugakuin daigaku kenkyū kaihatsu suishin kikō kiyō* (Kokugakuin University Transactions of the Organization for Advancement of Research and Development) 14 (2022): 23–96; also http://kojiki.kokugakuin.ac.jp. Donald L. Philippi, trans., *Kojiki* (Tokyo: University of Tokyo Press, 1968) has been the standard translation.

Buddhas manifested in Japan to save all sentient beings'.[5] Eighth-century sources even record deities wishing to convert to Buddhism and escape their *kami*'s body.[6] Locally many shrines, the architectural home of deities, and Buddhist temples shared rituals and ceremonies. Some material objects of worship that pre-dated the writing of the *Kojiki*, such as the male and female genitals carved into stone or wood, acquired additional Buddhist meanings.[7] In addition to this elastic adoptability, the difficulty for our study in examining Buddhist sexuality is the very diversity of ideas promoted by various schools or sects, which evolved along with the emergence of new religious leaders, each of whom proposed his or her own theory.[8] Their teachings and attitudes towards aspects of sexuality greatly differed, creating a cacophony of a polyvocal chorus. Our attempt will be to capture the taste of this variety while marking what seemed the most dominant and influential in the actual lives of people, rather than in doctrinal debates.

Finally, we will describe briefly a third system of thought, called Confucianism in English, which also arrived in Japan alongside Buddhism in the sixth century. Confucianism is not a religion but a system of ideas for creating an orderly society and the rule of a state. For the Yamato family and its allies, the rising elites on the Japanese archipelago in this period, Confucianism offered a remarkable range of the instruments of statecraft, such as a written script (Chinese), laws, taxation method, administrative division of land, bureaucracy, and, not least, the idea of *tennō*, or the monarch that heads the realm. A new, sophisticated system of rule emerged, some elements of which would last throughout Japan's history, despite modification. Confucian ideas imposed stricter boundaries on human conduct, including matters related to sexuality, marriage, and family. Sexuality exists within

5 John Breen and Mark Teeuwen, 'Introduction: Shinto Past and Present', in *Shinto in History: Ways of the Kami*, ed. John Breen and Mark Teeuwen (Honolulu: University of Hawai'i Press, 2000), 5; Mark Teeuwen and Fabio Rambelli, 'Introduction: Combinatory Religion and the *honji suijaku* Paradigm in Pre-modern Japan', in *Buddhas and Kami in Japan: Honji Suijaku as a Combinatory Paradigm*, ed. Mark Teeuwen and Fabio Rambelli (London: Routledge, 2003), 1–53. Citing Kuroda Toshio, 'Shinto in the History of Japanese Religion', trans. James C. Dobbins and Suzanne Gay, *Journal of Japanese Studies* 7, no. 1 (1981): 1–21, at 18.

6 Andreeva, *Assembling Shinto*, 19.

7 On statues, see Junko Habu, *Ancient Jomon of Japan* (Cambridge: Cambridge University Press, 2004), 150–8; Stephen Turnbull, *Japan's Sexual Gods: Shrines, Roles and Rituals of Procreation and Protection* (Leiden: Brill, 2015), 57–62.

8 The first to travel to Korea to learn Buddhist teachings in the seventh century were three women. Barbara Ruch, 'Woman to Woman: Kumano *bikuni* Proselytizers in Medieval and Early Modern Japan', in *Engendering Faith: Women and Buddhism in Premodern Japan*, ed. Barbara Ruch (Ann Arbor, MI: Center for Japanese Studies, University of Michigan, 2002), 537–80, at 538.

Sexuality in Traditional Systems of Thought and Belief in Pre-modern Japan

the structure of gendered awareness that often corresponds to the broader dynamic of power disparities. The meaning of gender differentials intensified with Buddhism in ways that were both structural and spiritual. Confucianism systematically employed gender hierarchy in sexual matters as one of its most potent instruments of moral guidance.

The Way of *Kami*

Among the expressions of sexuality, copulation or coitus is its clearest and most legible form. The scene of intercourse between two deities, Izanaki and Izanami, described early in the *Kojiki*, establishes a foundational attitude towards sexuality. As a creation story, it is sometimes compared to the book of Genesis. The comparison is useful in highlighting the features that are more contrasting than similar. Notable is the positive function that desire plays in bringing the two deities together and the unabashed clarity of anatomical engagement. Broadly viewed, the deities' sexual act is part of the natural and generative world. Intercourse fits in a larger blueprint for creating the realm, including islands, the sea, and deities who in turn propagate more deities. As a component of a cosmological scheme to 'create', sex acquires a cultural meaning that is inseparable from the natural environment and cosmological wonders in which deities dwell. Finally, the story is an early segment of a larger 'historical explanation' of the rise of the Yamato imperial lineage through its divine beginning, generational continuity, and eternal spiritual authority. As such, genitalia and coitus acquire a sacred and ritualistic meaning associated with the throne.[9] The copulation of Izanaki and Izanami marks a specific point in the evolving process of creation in the *Kojiki*. By tracing what precedes it, we can appreciate its full meaning. The plot begins by establishing the habitat. First, heaven and earth became activated, and a number of deities appear in the High Celestial Field. These deities lacked the capacity to reproduce because they were 'solitary and their bodies were hidden'. They were without sexual partners and without the proper or recognizable anatomical parts that could be mobilized for intercourse. But matters improved. The next batch of deities to emerge came in heterosexual pairs and had visible bodies. Izanaki and Izanami, whose names mean 'the male who beckons' and 'the female who beckons',

---

9 The *Kojiki* has three volumes. Izanaki and Izanami appear early in volume one. In volumes two and three, the narrative transitions to the human descendants of deities who, as quasi-historic and historic rulers, presided over the newly established imperial bureaucracy, and ends with the reign of the female Emperor Suiko (r. 592–628).

appeared. Izanami, the female, is noted as Izanaki's 'sister' (*imo*), a term that also means 'female sexual partner' or 'lover', suggesting what we would call an incestuous relationship.[10] A consortium of celestial deities orchestrate the process, including the emergence of other deities; at no time is there a concentration of creative authority in one figure or one God.[11] Soon, our protagonist pair is commissioned to 'complete and solidify this drifting land' and is entrusted with a heavenly jewelled halberd, an item suggestive of a phallus. In response, they stand on the heavenly floating bridge and lower the halberd into the liquid salt and stir the substance, making a churning sound, a motion suggesting sexualized energy. When they pull up the halberd, salt drips from its tip, which piles up and hardens. The pile takes shape and forms the first island.[12] Izanaki and Izanami descend on this island and 'bring into view' or 'let emerge' a celestial pillar and a palace that is broad-spanned and spacious, an architectural environment that itself evokes an image of the male and female reproductive organs.[13] Although scholars have debated the precise shape of the structures and how they emerged, their metaphoric meaning seems inescapable.[14] As the two consider their mission, they ponder how it is done. Izanaki takes the initiative to ask his sister/lover: 'How is your body formed?' Izanami's answer points to the process of her body 'becoming' and its final shape, for she says: 'My body has been formed and is formed; but there is one place that does not completely come together' (成り合わぬ *nariawanu*). Izanaki responds: 'My body has been formed and is formed; but there is one place that is formed in excess' (成り余れる *nariamareru*). Having thus acknowledged the anatomy of each deity's matured form and irregularities, Izanaki proposes: 'So, I am thinking to take the part that is excessive in my body, insert it in your body's

---

10 The term *imo* reflects a fluid concept of incest or the notion of consanguinity in the absence of a firm notion of family or marriage in early Japan, but in later chapters, words from the Confucian style patrilocal and patrilineal marriage begin to appear. In world myths, paired deities are often mother and son or father and daughter. Brother and sister pairs are common in East Asia. Yao Shaodang, 'Ki-ki shinwa ni okeru nishin sōsei no keitai' (Cosmogony by the Two Deities in the Kojiki and Nihon shoki), *Chūgoku gengo bunka kenkyū* (Study of Chinese Literary Culture) 7 (July 2007): 1–20, at 2–3.

11 The group atmosphere likely reflects the realistic condition of the political system in which the imperial family, considered mere *primus inter pares*, necessarily worked collaboratively with powerful ministerial families, each of whom claimed descent from a deity mentioned in the myth.

12 Yamaguchi and Kōnoshi, *Kojiki*, 31.   13 Yamaguchi and Kōnoshi, *Kojiki*, 31.

14 Various interpretations of the pillar and the palace are possible, from the notion of *axis mundi* that supports the world, introduced by Mircea Eliade in *The Sacred and the Profane*, to one closer to Japan's folklore, that celebrates pillars and tree trunks or rocks of a certain shape as sacred symbols of fertility. Quiros and Nakai, *Kojiki* 6, 5–8. Translations hereafter largely follow Quiros and Nakai.

Sexuality in Traditional Systems of Thought and Belief in Pre-modern Japan

incompletely joined part, and block (塞 *sai* or *fusagu*) it, thereby bringing land/country into existence. How would that be?' Izanami responds, 'That is good!' What follows this agreement is not intercourse but a motion that is suggestive of sexual foreplay. Izanaki proposes to encircle the heavenly pillar from opposite directions: 'You go around from the right and meet me; I will go around from the left and meet you.' After encircling the pillar, they meet, prompting Izanami to utter: 'Oh! what a good-looking man!' Izanaki's immediate response is to echo Izanami's adoration: 'Oh, what a good-looking woman!' But once each has thus spoken, Izanaki realizes the inappropriateness of Izanami's initiative and quickly declares: 'The woman spoke first. That is not good!' a phrase that scholars typically attribute to Confucian influences. But they proceed to copulate and give birth to a 'leech-child' whom they put on a reed boat which floats away.[15]

At this juncture, the two deities discuss the situation and conclude that 'the child we bore was not good. We should consult the Celestial deities.' The Celestial deities, after divination, reconfirm what Izanaki had already said: the woman spoke first. They command Izanaki and Izanami to repeat the act, starting with encircling the celestial pillar, voicing adoration for each other upon meeting in the proper order that gives Izanaki the first word. Then, once again, their genitals come together (見合い *miai*). After copulation, they give birth to fourteen islands in succession.[16] The verb used for the act of parturition here is 生む *umu*, a transitive verb that means 'to give birth' or 'to generate'. The verb suggests it is Izanami's body from which the offspring is delivered, although the involvement of both deities in the birthing process could be inferred.[17] Following the birth of islands, the two turn to producing deities, including those of rocks, domiciles, roofs, and of the sea and inlets. The last pair in turn produce eight more deities of various natural forces, such as the wind and the river.[18] Fecundity and vitality permeate the action of the three generations of birth-givers. The next development reveals both the power and the vulnerability of the female body engaged in vaginal birth (*umu*). Though the narrative describes the pair together 'giving birth', the Fire Deity (Hinokagutsuchi no kami), is clearly

---

15 Yamaguchi and Kōnoshi, *Kojiki*, 31–3.
16 Each island's name is associated with an actual geographical place and a deity with a distinct alternate name.
17 Yamaguchi and Kōnoshi, *Kojiki*, 35–7. As is standard for Japanese sentences, the verb has no subject.
18 Quiros and Nakai, *Kojiki* 6, 39–41. Yamaguchi and Kōnoshi, *Kojiki*, 41.

born through Izanami's vaginal opening.[19] As a result of this birth, Izanami's 'august genitalia' (御陰 *mihoto*) are scorched, and she falls ill. From her vomit, faeces, and urine, different deities are born. Then she departs the realm in 'divine departure'.[20] The segment likely reflects the social awareness and observation of the realistic results of sexual intercourse, which leads to birthing, often with grave consequences on the woman's body and life. This story echoes the widespread prehistoric interest in carving statues of female bodies that accentuate reproductive organs, a protruding stomach, a nursing breast, and the vagina, and for the male, a phallic-shaped stone or wood. The *Kojiki*'s presentation of *hoto*, or genitalia, and the symbolic phallus in the form of halberd and the pillar may reflect people's wishes and prayers for fertility that were materially evident by the fourth century BCE and noted in local histories.[21]

Desire, Impurity, and Gender

This segment briefly highlights different themes in the *Kojiki* and looks ahead to our discussion of Buddhism that follows, in which similar themes are prominent in the teaching and practice of some schools. We have already noted the role of desire in the process leading to copulation, but we will expound on the power of desire in Izanaki's next initiative. The notion of pollution or impurity is a powerful concept that often defines the parameter of one's action in both the *Kami* Way and Buddhist teachings, albeit with important differences between the two; the *Kami* Way is explanatory, rather than didactic as are most Buddhist teachings.

After Izanami 'departed', Izanaki feels a deep longing for Izanami but is overwhelmed by a sense of rage against the Fire Deity, the child responsible for the destruction of his loved one. He draws his sword and chops off the child's head. But this violent manoeuver is generative. From the gushing blood and other body parts, many new deities emerge. Izanaki's desire for Izanami impels him to visit her in the land of Yomi to which Izanami has gone. Izanaki marshals his masculine authority by lighting a 'male pillar', or the end tooth of his comb, for seeing into the dark space. Izanami is not 'dead', and she actively retaliates against Izanaki who violates her command not to look at her, but the

---

19 As do many other deities, this deity has three names. Each of the three names has a meaning associated with the rapidity, brightness, and smell of fire.
20 Quiros and Nakai, *Kojiki* 7, 8. The meaning and direction of Izanami's 'departure' continues to be debated. Many consider her to have died, but the next segment shows her lively action.
21 Habu, *Ancient Jomon*, 150–8; Turnbull, *Japan's Sexual Gods*, 57–62.

space she resides in is full of contaminants. Izanami's body, too, is full of maggots. Leaving behind the dramatic chase and the land of Yomi, Izanaki returns and washes away the pollutant from his left eye, right eye, and his nose. In the process of cleansing, he produces offspring on his own, what he calls 'three noble children'. They are Amaterasu (Sun Goddess), Susanoo (Storm Deity), and Tsukiyomi (Moon Deity). We understand that the vaginal birth that cost Izanami her vitality is replaced by a single male deity's generative power, without the involvement of a female partner. Nor is there any sign of a reproductive organ. The process of creation has been elevated from a method that engages the tangible and perilous body to one that defies it. In the myth sequence that ensues, Susanoo, the brother, challenges Amaterasu for a contest perhaps over the land Amaterasu is assigned to rule. The proposed method for determining the winner is the gender of offspring each produces. The method of reproduction is through chewing and spitting material things belonging to the opponent. Amaterasu, the female, is not presented with the feminine physiology in possession of *hoto*, or vagina. Amaterasu, the progenitor of the imperial family, is free of the burden of that which makes female deities (and humans) vulnerable and, especially in later Buddhist language, impure.

Readers of Japan's creation story have tended to view it as validation of female authority and power. It was written in the historical time prior to the penetration of the continental system of marriage and family that was based on patrilineal and patrilocal principles. Without the institutional framework of marriage that governed women more strictly than men, the unbound desire between Izanaki and Izanami rightfully operates on emotional parity. The *yin–yang* style of meeting of the body parts establishes the two deities as complementary players. But gender hierarchy lurks in various features of the story. It prioritizes the male in the order of naming and in the order of speaking, as well as the centrality of referents to 'sister' (but not 'brother') in which the main subject is obviously the male. The vulnerability of the female body contrasts with the stable and unspoken presence of the phallic masculinity, which could be deployed aggressively even if unintentionally. Instances of sexualized violence in the *Kojiki* are cases of this aggression, even if the phallus is not the actual perpetrator. For example, Susanoo's gross misdeed causes a weaving maiden to die from being struck in the genitals by a shuttle. But the *Kami* Way also illuminates female initiatives in loving a man and in naming children. The genealogical authority of Amaterasu, whether or not we call it sexual, offers a vision of the gender-sexual axes that are far from simple. In later centuries, Amaterasu, especially in its turbulent spirit (*aramitama*), would acquire an additional portfolio in the view of various Buddhist thinkers as not only 'the supreme deity of esoteric Buddhism, Dainichi, but also Dainichi's fiercer manifestations, such as the esoteric wisdom kings, Aizen and Fudō, or even darker divinities, the female demons Dakiniten'.[22]

Buddhism

Buddhism is represented by a large corpus of texts produced by leaders from across the globe and over a long span of time. In addition, literate women and men who were not Buddhist preachers also left abundant writings. Consequently, heterogeneity and polyvalence characterize Buddhist thought. The writings transmit divergent ideas in numerous formats, from doctrines, polemical literature, ritual manuals, laws, and dialogues to poetry, diaries, prayers, and *setsuwa* (narrative stories) to paintings. What appears in canonical texts, which themselves often present contradictory ideas, can contrast with what is conveyed in *setsuwa* tales, aimed at appealling to the public through relatable narrative. Women's diaries contain reflections or descriptive passages that illuminate their understanding of Buddhist spirituality. As Bernard Faure states, sex is not an independent and isolated category of discussion in Buddhism, and no text is able to summarize Buddhist notions of sexuality.[23] In view of the extraordinary richness of the field, we adopt a modest and limited approach by highlighting a few notable themes: desire and salvation, the body and gender, purity and pollution, and male–male sex.

Desire and Salvation

Desire or delusion is the greatest obstacle to salvation. Salvation or enlightenment, also described as rebirth, is achieved by being liberated from the cycle of suffering and transmigration, which is caused by ignorance and delusion, including sexual desire.[24] The working of desire appears in the oldest Buddhist *setsuwa* collection, commonly known as *Nihon ryōiki* (Miraculous Tales from Japan's Buddhist Traditions), compiled by the monk Kyōkai (or Keikai) in about 822. The stories fall in the category of

---

22 Andreeva, *Assembling Shinto*, 35.
23 Bernard Faure, *The Red Thread: Buddhist Approaches to Sexuality* (Princeton, NJ: Princeton University Press, 1998), 10.
24 Delusion, a craving, leads a person to become mired in worldly matters, such as honor, disgrace, aggression, love, hate, power, and so on, and endlessly suffer from the law of karmic causation.

Sexuality in Traditional Systems of Thought and Belief in Pre-modern Japan

vernacular Buddhism, disseminated by itinerant preachers who entertained their audiences along the roadways for donations and proselytizing.[25] In the first story, a man is overcome by lust while engaged in a holy activity of copying a religious text. In the second, a woman with an excessive sexual desire for men neglects to breastfeed her children. The details are as follows.

In 771, Tajihi, a copier of scripture, was invited to copy the *Lotus Sutra*, an important Buddhist text, at Nonakadō temple. Female devotees also gathered to add purified water to the ink for copying scriptures. The sky suddenly darkened and a shower sent people indoors to shelter. Tajihi sat alongside the women and felt strong lust. 'He crouched behind a young woman, lifted her skirt, and had intercourse with her. As his penis entered her vagina, they died holding each other's hand. The woman died foaming at the mouth.' The author observes that this was the punishment given by the guardian of the Buddhist law (*dharma*): 'However intensely your body and heart may burn with the fire of lust, do not, because of the promptings of a lewd heart, commit a filthy deed.' The sin was so great that the author likens the act to a moth jumping into a fire, and that 'a person with a soft spine would masturbate with his own mouth'. The tale admonishes that if one understood the Law of Five Desires, or knew the essence of the five kinds of desire, which arise out of attachment to colour, voice or sound, smell or fragrance, taste, and touch, one would not find any pleasure in them nor remain a slave to them.[26]

Temples were considered pure spaces. Scribes of sutra, who were not priests, were to avoid all defilements by purifying their bodies, following strict no-meat diets, avoiding defilement from death and illness, taking baths, and donning pure robes (*jōe*).[27] For Tajihi, all this preparation was for naught,

25 Keller Kimbrough and Hank Glassman, 'Introduction: Vernacular Buddhism and Medieval Japanese Literature', *Japanese Journal of Religious Studies* 36, no. 2 (2009): 201–8.

26 Kyoko Motomochi Nakamura, trans., *Miraculous Stories from the Japanese Buddhist Tradition: The Nihon ryōiki of the Monk Kyōkai* (Cambridge, MA: Harvard University Press, 1973), 3: 245–46 (Tale 18); Ikegami Jun'ichi, ed., *Nihon ryōiki: Nihon koten shinsho* (Miraculous Stories from the Japanese Buddhist Tradition: New Japanese Classics) (Tokyo: Sōeisha, 1978), 334–6. A similar story, with greater emphasis on the culpability of the scribe, appears in Yamada Takao et al., eds., *Konjaku monogatarishū*. Vol. 3: *Nihon koten bungaku taikei* (Tales of Times Now Past. Vol. 3: Compendium of Japanese Classical Literature) (Tokyo: Iwanami Shoten, 1980), 312–13. Brian D. Lowe, 'The Discipline of Writing: Scribes and Purity in Eighth-Century Japan', *Japanese Journal of Religious Studies* 39, no.2 (2012): 201–39, at 219–20.

27 Lowe, 'The Discipline', 209–19. Lowe cautions the reader that *kegare* (pollution) as a formal concept only appeared in the late ninth century: 211, n24.

for he committed the worst act in the sacred space. Despite his effort to attain purity and gain numinous rewards by copying sutras, he received karmic punishment. The female who 'participated' was also culpable. For her action, not intention, she died with foam coming out of her mouth.

The second story is narrated as an event dreamt by a dharma master, Jakurin, who was travelling in search of the Buddha's Law. In the dream, Jakurin meets a woman who was suffering from a swollen breast, which hung down with pus dripping. As the woman squatted on the grass, she wailed how painful was her breast. Responding to Jakurin's query, she explained she was the mother of Narihito. 'When I was young, I had sex with many men, absorbed by my sexual desires, and ignored my infants. For many days, children, especially Narihito, were starving for milk.' She admitted this punishment came from this sin. Jakurin asked how she might be relieved of this suffering, and she responded that Narihito's forgiveness would be able to do this. So, Jakurin looked for Narihito, found him and his sister, both of whom forgave their mother and said: 'Our mother had such good features that she was loved by men, kept company with them, and begrudged giving her breasts to us.' The children atoned for her sin by copying sutras and creating Buddha's images. The mother was released from her sin. The tale concludes by giving this advice: 'A mother's tender breasts, though capable of bestowing great benefits, can, on the contrary, become a source of sin if she begrudges offering them to her little ones.'[28]

Both stories convey the inherently destructive power of desire when unleashed unwisely. Violation of the sacred space of the temple and the scripture copying practice called for the harshest punishment. The desire of the mother of Narihito brought suffering to her children by her failing to perform her maternal function. Her sexual desire subordinated the expected function of the maternal body. Unlike Tajihi, her remorse over her past action met with her children's benevolence and she was forgiven. Both stories consider the danger of a lustful heart that harms others or the environment, but neither condemns sexual intercourse. The location and the circumstance of Tajihi's action called for karmic punishment. For the mother, children's words show an understanding for why the mother would have had many lovers. It was not the excessive sexual activity but her neglect of her maternal function that was culpable. Lust or desire that dwells in one's heart was the source of their misconduct, but the stories

---

28 'On a Licentious Woman Whose Children Cried for Milk, Receiving an Immediate Penalty', in Ikegami, *Nihon ryōiki*, 326–30; Nakamura, *Miraculous Stories*, 242–3.

Sexuality in Traditional Systems of Thought and Belief in Pre-modern Japan

criminalize how desire is deployed. In these tales, sexuality itself does not seem to be condemned or considered unconditionally evil, harmful, or shameful.

For religious leaders, sex with women was considered transgression. Shinran (1173–1262), the leader of Jōdo Shinshū (Shin Buddhism, or True Pure Land), acquired a wife and started a family. Shinran had a dream in which a bodhisattva appeared in the form of a priest. The priest said that if any practitioner commits *nyobon* (sex with women – and therefore non-compliance with monastic precepts), he would take on the bodily form of a 'precious stone woman' or *gyokunyo*, and make sure the sinful ones are reborn in the Land of Bliss. Scholars have debated the meaning of this dream: if it is about sexual release specifically for Shinran's needs; if *nyobon* stood metaphorically for the generalized human suffering which called for Buddha's attention; or if it legitimated Shinran's marriage and blood lineage. In Shinran's time, strict sexual isolation of priests was unrealistic. Clerics maintained households and families, especially in and around the settlements near the temple. Precepts about celibacy were only sporadically followed, although officially, *nyobon* was considered transgressive.[29]

Of interest to our inquiry into sexuality is a heterodox and even heretical tradition known today as Tachikawaryū. It is famous for 'a graphic and detailed explanation of a Skull Ritual involving necromancy and the use of sexual fluids of both male and female'.[30] Until recently, modern scholars have described Tachikawaryū as having accepted the idea that 'passions are enlightenment' literally, and 'equated sexual bliss with the achievement of Buddhahood in this very body (*sokushin jōbutsu*)'.[31] Banned in the 1470s, its treatises were destroyed. However, *Juhō yōjinshū* (Notes on Precautions to Be Taken When Receiving Teaching) written by a Shingon monk named Shinjō in 1268, refers to Tachikawaryū. Rappo states that in the following centuries, the original construct received continual addition and revision from various monks, turning it into something that was likely different from the original.[32] A recent reading of this text by Nobumi Iyanaga concludes that 'the

29 Galen Amstutz, 'Sexual Transgression in Shinran's Dream', *The Eastern Buddhist*, new series 43, nos. 1/2 (2012): 225–69, at 225–54.
30 Bowring, *Religious Traditions*, 359.   31 Bowring, *Religious Traditions*, 358.
32 Gaétan Rappo, '"Deviant Teachings": The Tachikawa Lineages as a Moving Concept in Japanese Buddhism', *Japanese Journal of Religious Studies* 47, no. 1 (2020): 103–33.

infamous reputation of the Tachikawaryū as a lineage that taught heretical and sexual doctrines and rituals is without any foundation'.[33]

The Body and Instability of Gender

As heterogeneous as Buddhist texts and literature are, so are the concept and image of the body that they portray. In the diaries of aristocratic women, the body nearly disappears underneath the copious description of massive clothing and the culture the clothes represent.[34] In *setsuwa*, the description of the flesh and bodily movements may give a sense of corporeality. The biological differences between women and men often become highlighted in reference to copulation, parturition, or violation of the genitals. Medical texts, based on Chinese classics, have a view based on *yin* and *yang* – female and male – which are balanced and complementary.[35] For Bernard Faure, the body in Buddhism 'is ephemeral, condemned to dissolve into its constitutive aggregates; it is what makes us fall into illusion, succumb to the temptation of the senses, and what chains us to *samsāra*, the continual whirl of karmic retribution'. Moreover, 'if the body is generally deficient in every respect, the female body is even worse'.[36]

This last characterization of the body resonates with the frequently cited Devadatta chapter of the *Lotus Sutra*, in which the daughter of the dragon king transforms into a man and attains Buddhahood:

> Sāriputra, a disciple of Buddha, said to the eight-year-old dragon girl, 'You suppose that in this short time you have been able to attain the unsurpassed way. But this is difficult to believe. Why? Because a woman's body is soiled and defiled, not a vessel for the Law ... The road to Buddhahood is long and far-stretching ... How then could a woman like you be able to attain Buddhahood so quickly?' The answer was that the dragon girl had a precious jewel worth as much as the thousand millionfold world. She presented this to the Buddha, who accepted it. Then she said: 'Employ your supernatural power and watch me attain Buddhahood'. At that moment the members of the assembly all saw the dragon girl in the space of an instant change into a man and carry out all the practices of a bodhisattva. He immediately proceeded to the Spotless World of the south, took a seat on a jeweled

33 Nobumi Iyanaga, 'Secrecy, Sex and Apocrypha: Remarks on Some Paradoxical Phenomena', in *The Culture of Secrecy in Japanese Religion*, ed. Bernhard Scheid and Mark Teeuwen (London: Routledge, 2006), 204–28, at 213.
34 Rajyashree Pandey, *Perfumed Sleeves and Tangled Hair: Body, Woman, and Desire in Medieval Japanese Narratives* (Honolulu: University of Hawai'i Press, 1968).
35 Charlotte Furth, *A Flourishing Yin: Gender in China's Medical History, 960–1665* (Berkeley, CA: University of California Press, 1999), 52.
36 Faure, *Red Thread*, 55.

Sexuality in Traditional Systems of Thought and Belief in Pre-modern Japan

lotus, and attained impartial and correct enlightenment. He expounded the wonderful Law for all living beings everywhere in the ten directions.[37]

This passage first establishes an undisputed premise that the woman's body is soiled. Women are hindered by the five obstructions, and their bodies are polluted from menstruation and childbirth. But a woman only needs to transform into a man; the mutability of the gendered state enabled a woman's body (*mi*) to become a man's through the power of the *Lotus Sutra*. The *Vimalakirti Sutra* asserts that the Buddhist doctrine of nonduality made maleness or femaleness unstable and fluid categories; what seems a stable reality is always transformative, for there are no immutable essences or traits. One only appears to be female or male.[38]

Karmic transmigration and rebirth in different body forms is a common theme in *setsuwa*. The vulnerability of the vagina that was present in the *Kojiki* reappears in this story, which is about the efficacy of drugs:

A daughter of a wealthy household in the province of Kawachi, during the time of Emperor Jun'nin [r. 758–64], in summer of 759, climbed a mulberry tree to harvest leaves. [Mulberry leaves are fed to silkworms.] A large snake emerged and began climbing the tree where the girl was. A passerby saw this and warned the girl. Alarmed, the girl fell from the tree to the ground, as did the snake. The snake coiled itself around the girl and crept into her vagina. The girl, shocked, fainted. The parents called a doctor, put the daughter and the snake on one board and placed it on the yard's ground. The doctor created a solution mixing millet stalks, boar's hair, and other things. He hung the girl on stakes by her head and feet and poured the solution into her vagina. The snake came out, was killed and discarded. The snake's babies, white and similar to tadpoles, with boar's hair stuck to them, came out. He poured some into her mouth and all the babies came out. The girl awoke from her stupor, and said 'I felt like I was dreaming, but now I am awake and feel as before'. Since drugs work effectively, we should deal with them very carefully. Three years later, the girl was again penetrated by a snake and died. Her love [for the snake] was deep and she declared that she would see the snake again in the other world.[39]

37 Ōsumi Kazuo, 'Historical Notes on Women and the Japanization of Buddhism', trans. and adapted by Cecilia Segawa Seigle and Barbara Ruch, in *Engendering Faith: Women and Buddhism in Premodern Japan*, ed. Barbara Ruch (Ann Arbor, MI: Center for Japanese Studies, University of Michigan, 2002), xxix.

38 Pandey, Perfumed Sleeves, ch. 1; Hitomi Tonomura, 'Black Hair and Red Trousers: Gendering the Flesh in Medieval Japan', *American Historical Review* 99, no. 1 (1994): 129–54, at 133.

39 My interpretation follows Ikegami, *Nihon ryōiki*, 266.

The author of the tale offers this wisdom. According to the law of karmic causality, one is reborn as a snake, horse, cow, dog, or bird, or falls in love with a snake depending on the evil deeds done in the past life, or is born in the form of a ghostly creature. Sensual attachments are not all the same.[40]

Purity and Pollution

In the *Kojiki*, when Izanaki returned from having visited the land of Yomi, to which his lover Izanami had departed, he washed off the pollution that he acquired in Yomi. Out of the process of washing, three noble children, including Amaterasu, were born. Pollution, or defilement, and the need to wash to eradicate it, would be reconceptualized, expanded, and formalized into governmental procedural rules, called *Engishiki* in the tenth century. *Engishiki* defined what was polluted, polluting, and for how long. For each category of pollution, the government set forth a specific number of days for avoiding sacred spaces, such as the imperial palace. Death of a person, the most potent source of pollution, called for thirty days of abstinence after encountering it; seven days for the birth of a person; five days for the death of and three days for the birth of a domestic animal (except chickens); three days for eating meat; and thirty days for encountering the sick, or for having an abortion or miscarriage in the fourth month or later.[41] Such rules initially affected a small percentage of people with close affiliation with the imperial court and shrines, but in the late thirteenth century and after, rules were adopted by many of the country's religious institutions and the rules themselves became harsher.[42] The change occurred as the *Kami* Way reasserted itself through a self-conscious discourse that provided intellectual justification for putting the *Kami* Way on a basis equal or even superior to Buddhism. The Ise or Watarai shinto school 'discovered' that Mahāvairocana (a cosmic Buddha) and Tenshō Daijin (another name for Amaterasu) were one and the same deity. Deities no longer were the traces of a Buddhist original.[43]

---

40 'On a Woman Who Was Violated by a Large Snake but Survived, Due to the Power of Drugs', in Ikegami, *Nihon ryōiki*, 264–9; Nakamura, *Miraculous Stories*, 213–15. Tonomura, 'Black Hair', 143; Yamada et al., *Konjaku monogatari*, 24–9.

41 Hitomi Tonomura, 'Rewriting the Ubuya (Parturition Hut): Its Historicity and Historiography', in *Writing Histories of Japan: Texts and Their Transformations from Ancient through the Meiji Era*, ed. James C. Baxter and Joshua A. Fogel (Kyoto: International Research Center for Japanese Studies, 2007), 41–84, at 52–3. Felicia Bock, trans., *Engi-shiki: Procedures of the Engi Era, Books I–V* (Tokyo: Sophia University, 1970), 117–18.

42 The concept of pollution itself underwent transformation over time, becoming more severe for women-specific causes. Tonomura, 'Ubuya', 53.

43 Bowring, *Religious Traditions*, 352.

Though the *Engishiki* initially mattered only in the interactions of a limited group of people within the sacred space defined by the *Kami* Way, its provisions advanced the conceptual connection between bodily functions and pollution, especially as local shrines began to adopt them. Moreover, the popularization of a new sutra, *Ketsubonkyō* or Blood-bowl Sutra, redefined the meaning and risk of women's biological functions, specifically those enabling fertility and procreation. Even before the Blood-bowl Sutra became well known in the fifteenth century, there was an understanding that women who died in childbirth carried the burden of sinful karma and would be sent to a special hell.[44] Hank Glassman explains that the sutra's intended use to rescue women from the hell changed over time, from a memorial for the deceased mother to a preventive or prophylactic, and to a talismanic function. Initially a deceased woman's relatives would copy and recite the sutra. Soon, women themselves initiated the process as insurance against the fall. In the Tokugawa period (1600–1868), the sutra gained a more comprehensive function of providing benefits in this life when women carried it as an amulet. Promoting these activities, especially in their later phases, were itinerant nuns, such as the 'nuns of Kumano', variously described as singing nuns, prostitutes, preachers, and proselytizers who used pictures to explain the horror of the Blood Pool and the path to salvation.[45]

Male–Male Sex

For priests in Buddhist institutions, religious awakening (*hosshin*, or a sincere and strenuous effort to attain enlightenment) was desirable even if it meant breaking the vow of celibacy by having sex with a woman or a young boy. Many stories feature initiates being lured into having sex with a beautiful woman, only to discover the woman was in fact a bodhisattva on a pedagogical mission. Other stories portray priests' sexual engagement with *chigo*, acolytes aged from about seven to seventeen. *Chigo* stories were produced in a large number in the fifteenth and sixteenth centuries, when monastic institutions gained economic and political power from land and commerce. These stories portray *chigo* with long hair, similar to women's, make-up and blackened teeth, and special clothes. These were features that constituted the

---

44 Caroline Hirasawa offers a thorough explanation of Buddhist hells in 'The Inflatable, Collapsible Kingdom of Retribution: A Primer on Japanese Hell Imagery and Imagination', *Monumenta Nipponica* 63, no. 1 (2008): 1–50.

45 Hank Glassman, 'At the Crossroads of Birth and Death: The Blood Pool Hell and Postmortem Fetal Extraction', in *Death and the Afterlife in Japanese Buddhism*, ed. Jacqueline Ilyse Stone and Mariko Namba Walter (Honolulu: University of Hawai'i Press, 2008), 179–83. Ruch, 'Woman to Woman', 557–76.

elements of an esoteric ritual, called *chigo kanjō*, that transformed the boy into an avatar of buddha / *kami*. *Chigo* were liminal, symbolically standing on the boundaries of child and adult, male and female, as well as sacred and profane.[46]

The pattern of male–male sex in Japan is probably best known through *chigo* stories, and from relationships among men and boys in Buddhist institutions. But the practice was common long before the *chigo* stories became popular. *Manyōshū* (Collection of Ten Thousand Leaves; compiled in the seventh or eighth century) contains love poems exchanged between men with a sensibility similar to that expressed in poems of heterosexual lovers.[47] The aristocratic literature of the Heian period (ninth to twelfth century), such as *The Tale of the Genji*, a magnum opus written by a female author, Murasaki Shikibu, describes male–male love. (On the Heian era, see also the chapter by Joshua Mostow in Volume III of this work.) *Ōjōyōshū* (Treatises on Rebirth), written in 985 by Genshin (942–1017), a priest at a Buddhist monastery on Mount Hiei, describes human activities worthy of entry into Nirvana or doomed to hell. It imagines eight hells: the third hell has sixteen sub-sections, and one of them is a special hell to which a man who forced himself on another man's *chigo* would fall and suffer terribly.[48] Some men recorded their real experiences in a journal format. The aristocrat Fujiwara Yorinaga (1120–56) wrote in his journal, *Taiki*, about his having visited the Tennōji temple in Kōyasan. He wished to have sex with one of the ritual dancers. The place being a temple, he did not because he dreamt of pollution from their intercourse.[49]

Margaret Childs has studied the religious dimensions of the production of *chigo* stories. Many of them have a sad ending in which the *chigo* becomes separated, abused, or dies. Because of it, 'the intensity and power of the Buddhist concept of transience (*mujō*), a sense of the uncertainty of life, and personal loss' may lead the priest to 'accept the futility of all attachments to this world'. The suicide of the protagonist *chigo* in *Aki no Yo no Nagamonogatari* (A Long Tale for an Autumn Night, 1377), for example, likely triggered a religious awakening.[50]

---

46 Tanaka Takako, *Seiai no Nihon chūsei* (Sexual Love in Medieval Japan) (Tokyo: Yōsensha, 1997), 12–15.

47 Iwata Jun'ichi, *Honchō nanshokukō: danshoku bunkenshoshi* (Thoughts on Male–Male Love in Japan: Bibliography of Scholarly Titles on Male–Male Love) (Tokyo: Hara Shobō, 2002), 12–14.

48 Iwata Jun'ichi, *Honchō nanshokukō*, 18–20.   49 Iwata Jun'ichi, *Honchō nanshokukō*, 39.

50 Margaret H. Childs, '*Chigo monogatari*: Love Stories or Buddhist Sermons?', *Monumenta Nipponica* 35, no. 2 (1980): 128–9. Recent readers have noted the need to avoid romanticizing the relationships, as these were based on power differentials and included outright sexual violence. Tanaka Takako, *Seiai no Nihon chūsei*, 9–12.

Not all stories end in sorrow. A priest who is poor falls in love with a boy of about sixteen or seventeen years old. Other priests also admire the boy. But the boy announces he is pregnant. The priest is upset and wonders how to explain the matter to others. The boy gives birth and leaves the baby. The baby turns out to be a large nugget of gold. The priest chips fragments from it little by little and becomes wealthy. He thinks the boy must have been an incarnation of the guardian god of four directions, who provided him with a reward.[51] Perhaps such was the wishful thinking of some priests in real life.

Confucianism

Confucianism in English refers to a large assortment of philosophical ideas and moral prescriptions that structure and guide human behaviour. Confucian ideas were valuable for rulers in constructing and promoting orderly social and political systems based on the hierarchy of status, gender, age, and occupation. Japan's first set of laws, from the eighth century and modelled after Chinese laws, include the 'seven grounds for divorce of a wife by her husband', which were being childless (i.e., not having a male child), having committed adultery, being disobedient to one's parents-in-law, talking too much, stealing, being jealous, and having a serious disease.[52] These provisions were not enforced, however, for Japanese society in the eighth century had no firm organization called the 'family', no patrilineage, and no powerful household heads. Sexuality operated to some degree without the restricting framework of marriage or well-defined kin relations. Only gradually did the notion of family, or household, develop to contain sexuality within the boundaries specified by both law and custom.

In later centuries, Confucianism had more of an impact in Japan. Economic, political, and spiritual authority evolved to be concentrated more in the male, though class differences were evident for each gender. Confucian ideas began to affect ordinary people's lives noticeably beginning in the fourteenth century, and more deeply when the level of violence increased in the fifteenth and sixteenth centuries, leading to calls for stricter boundaries around human conduct, including matters related to sexuality, marriage, and family.

51 Takao et al., *Konjaku*, 3: 567–70; Tonomura, 'Black Hair', 149.
52 David J. Lu, *Japan: A Documentary History*. Vol. 1: *The Dawn of History to the Late Tokugawa Period* (Armonk, NY: East Gate Books, 1996–7), 35.

Confucianism began to burden women with the responsibility of maintaining stable sexual relations in the context of the institution of marriage, which also gained administrative clarity. Monogamy for women was seen as upholding the institutional arrangement of the marital household dictated by political authorities. Women's instructional texts, *jokunsho*, which incorporated Confucian ideal behaviour, first appeared in the Tokugawa period (1603–1867). These trends coincided with the spread of the knowledge of the Blood-bowl Sutra and the intensified legal requirements to regulate adulterous relations. The goal of such new provisions was not necessarily control over the women's body or sexuality, however. The ultimate objective was order, for adultery might lead to feuds, and perhaps even to battle.

Confucian principles also governed men's behaviour, including their obligations to their household and the lord. Confucian virtues, especially those previously associated with the samurai, such as loyalty and honour, were now embraced by men of various statuses. In particular, these notions affected the idealized mode and the language surrounding male–male relationships. Popular writers of the time featured the power of the vow between two male lovers, which would be proven by self-mutilation of one's fingers or even seppuku (disembowelment).[53] Despite the spread of some Confucian ideas, the spiritual force of *kami* and boddhisattvas remained intact, while themselves undergoing transformation. Confucianism, then, had an impact on formalized behavioural norms, but did not lead to a condemnation of sex in itself.

Conclusions

I have examined sexuality in the *Kojiki*, and certain select aspects within the Buddhist framework. In the centuries that followed its arrival, Mahāyāna Buddhism assimilated to local culture and Buddhist temples shared rituals and ceremonies with shrines and deities. Even so, Buddhism differed from the *Kojiki* in its approach to sexuality through its views about the denial or pursuit of certain forms of sexual desire, pleasure, and fulfilment. The concept of sin governed forms of sexual acts, for example, prohibiting priests from desiring or engaging with women sexually, while largely permitting or even admiring male–male

---

53 Ihara Saikaku, *The Great Mirror of Male Love*, trans Paul Gordon Schalow (Stanford, CA: Stanford University Press, 1990), 28.

sex. Confucianism did not address sexuality per se but valued hierarchically organized human relations and subordinated sexuality to these. But the fundamental acceptance of sexuality that began as part of the larger natural force of universe, as depicted in the *Kojiki*, remained in force.

In other ways as well, Japanese ideas about sexuality remained distinct. No custom of artificially 're-shaping' male or female sexual organs developed, as was the case with eunuchs in China, Korea, and other empires in Asia. There was no concern over women's virginity. There seemed to have been no vocabulary for virginity or any value in men getting the first access to a woman's hymen. Even at the height of warfare, apart from punishing adulterers, few restrictions were placed on the sexual body or on sexual practices such as masturbation and same-sex relations. Sexuality was not caged within the moral institutions of family and marriage as much as it was in other historical societies, nor was it particularly limited by religious ideals.

Further Reading

Andreeva, Anna, and Dominic Steavu, eds. *Transforming the Void: Embryological Discourse and Reproductive Imagery in East Asian Religions*. Leiden: Brill, 2016.

Ambros, Barbara R. *Women in Japanese Religions*. New York: New York University Press, 2015.

Atkins, Paul S. '*Chigo* in the Medieval Japanese Imagination'. *Journal of Asian Studies* 67, no. 3 (2008): 947–70.

Blair, Heather. 'Mothers of the Buddhas: The Sutra on Transforming Women into Buddhas (Bussetsu Tenno Jōbutsu Kyō)'. *Monumenta Nipponica* 71, no, 2 (2016): 263–93.

Eubanks, Charlotte. 'Sympathetic Response: Vocal Arts and the Erotics of Persuasion in the Buddhist Literature of Medieval Japan'. *Harvard Journal of Asiatic Studies* 72, no. 1 (2012): 43–70.

Faure, Bernard. *The Power of Denial: Buddhism, Purity, and Gender*. Princeton, NJ: Princeton University Press, 2003.

Glassman, Hank. 'The Nude Jizō at Denkōji: Notes on Women's Salvation in Kamakura Buddhism'. In *Engendering Faith: Women and Buddhism in Premodern Japan*, ed. Barbara Ruch, 383–416. Ann Arbor, MI: Center for Japanese Studies, University of Michigan, 2002.

Goepper, Roger. *Aizen-Myōō: The Esoteric King of Lust, an Iconological Study*. Zurich: Artibus Asiae, Museum Rietberg, 1993.

Goodwin, Janet. *Selling Songs and Smiles: The Sex Trade in Heian and Kamakura Japan*. Honolulu: University of Hawai'i Press, 2007.

Katsuura, Noriko. 'Tonsure Forms for Nuns: Classification of Nuns according to Hairstyle', trans. Virginia Skord Waters. In *Engendering Faith: Women and Buddhism in Premodern Japan*, ed. Barbara Ruch, 109–30. Ann Arbor, MI: Center for Japanese Studies, University of Michigan, 2002.

Kawashima, Terry. *Writing Margins: The Textual Construction of Gender in Heian and Kamakura Japan*. Cambridge, MA: Harvard University Asia Center, 2002.

Kimbrough, R. Keller. *Preachers, Poets, Women, and the Way: Izumi Shikibu and the Buddhist Literature of Medieval Japan*. Ann Arbor, MI: Center for Japanese Studies, University of Michigan, 2008.

Laffin, Christina. *Rewriting Medieval Japanese Women: Politics, Personality, and Literary Production in the Life of Nun Abutsu*. Honolulu: University of Hawai'i Press, 2013.

Lurie, David. 'Myth and History in the *Kojiki*, *Nihon shoki*, and Related Works'. In *The Cambridge History of Japanese Literature*. Volume I: *The Ancient Period (Beginning to 794)*, ed. Haruo Shirane, Tomi Suzuki, and David Lurie, 22–39. Cambridge: Cambridge University Press, 2015.

Matisoff, Susan. 'Barred from Paradise? Mount Kōya and the Karukaya Legend'. In *Engendering Faith: Women and Buddhism in Premodern Japan*, ed. Barbara Ruch, 463–500. Ann Arbor, MI: Center for Japanese Studies, University of Michigan, 2002.

McCormick, Melissa. 'Mountains, Magic, and Mothers: Envisioning the Female Ascetic in a Medieval *Chigo* Tale'. In *Crossing the Sea: Essays on East Asian Art in Honor of Professor Yoshiaki Shimizu*, ed. Gregory P. A. Levine, Andrew M. Watsky, and Gennifer Weisenfeld, 107–33. Princeton, NJ: P. Y. and Kinmay W. Tang Center for East Asian Art, Department of Art and Archaeology, Princeton University, and Princeton University Press, 2012.

Meeks, Lori. *Hokkeji and the Reemergence of Female Monastic Orders in Premodern Japan*. Honolulu: University of Hawai'i Press, 2010.

Minamoto, Junko, and Hank Glassman. 'Buddhism and the Historical Construction of Sexuality in Japan'. *U.S.-Japan Women's Journal, English Supplement* 5 (1993): 87–115.

Nagata, Mizu. 'Transitions in Attitudes toward Women in the Buddhist Canon: The Three Obligations, the Five Obstructions, and the Eight Rules of Reverence', trans. Paul B. Watt. In *Engendering Faith: Women and Buddhism in Premodern Japan*, ed. Barbara Ruch, 279–96. Ann Arbor, MI: Center for Japanese Studies, University of Michigan, 2002.

Payne, Richard K. 'At Midlife in Medieval Japan'. *Japanese Journal of Religious Studies* 26, nos. 1/2 (1999): 135–57.

Porath, Or. 'The Cosmology of Male–Male Love in Medieval Japan: *Nyakudō no kanjinchō* and the Way of Youths'. *Journal of Religion in Japan* 4 (2015): 241–71.

Schalow, Paul Gordon. 'Kūkai and the Tradition of Male Love in Japanese Buddhism'. In *Buddhism, Sexuality, and Gender*, ed. José Ignacio Cabezón, 215–30. Albany, NY: State University of New York, 1992.

Schmidt-Hori, Sachi. *Tales of Idolized Boys: Male–Male Love in Medieval Japanese Buddhist Narratives*. Honolulu: University of Hawai'i Press, 2021.

Swanson, Paul L., and Clark Chilson, eds. *Nanzan Guide to Japanese Religions*. Honolulu: University of Hawai'i Press, 2006.

Tonomura, Hitomi. 'Sexual Violence against Women: Legal and Extralegal Treatment in Premodern Warrior Society'. In *Women and Class in Japanese History*, ed.

Sexuality in Traditional Systems of Thought and Belief in Pre-modern Japan

Hitomi Tonomura, Anne Walthall, and Wakita Haruko, 135–55. Ann Arbor, MI: Center for Japanese Studies, University of Michigan, 1999.

Wakita Haruko, *Women in Medieval Japan: Motherhood, Household Management and Sexuality.* Trans. Alison Tokita. Clayton, Australia: Monash Asia Institute and Tokyo: University of Tokyo Press, 2006.

8

African Traditions of Sexualities

YAARI FELBER-SELIGMAN

Tracing traditions of sexualities across time and cultures is a significant challenge, one compounded for African history due to circumstances of stereotyping and silencing. This chapter highlights instances of pre-twentieth-century sexualities in Africa and assumes the following: that categories such as 'sexualities', 'gender', 'class', and more are culturally constructed, and therefore inherently contingent and dynamic; that Africa's pasts were neither 'timeless' nor 'uniform'; and last but hardly least, that consideration of 'gender' must be central to any exploration of 'sexualities'.[1] Because other contributions in these volumes discuss North Africa, this chapter focuses on African societies located south of the Sahara. (For sexuality in ancient Egypt, see Chapter 2 by Uroš Matić in this volume, and for sexuality in nineteenth-century Cairo, see Chapter 15 by Mario Ruiz in Volume III of this work.)

Before turning to specifics, the respective topics of research challenges, changing perspectives, and recent interventions all merit mention. Scholars have grappled with Western culture and academia's fraught legacy that has spanned from racialized exoticism to outright erasure. Alongside infamous examples, such as the case of the Khoikhoi woman Sarah Baartman, publicly displayed and after her death dissected in nineteenth-century Europe, other subtle, but no less problematic, biases existed.[2] (For more on Sarah Baartman, see Chapter 11 by Jennifer Boittin in Volume I of this work.) These have

---

1 Sylvia Tamale, 'Researching and Theorising Sexualities in Africa', in *Sexualities in Africa: A Reader*, ed. Sylvia Tamale (Dakar, Senegal: Pambazuka/Fahamu, 2011), 11.

2 Clifton C. Crais and Pamela Scully, *Sara Baartman and the Hottentot Venus: A Ghost Story and a Biography* (Princeton, NJ: Princeton University Press, 2009); Catherine Cymone Fourshey, Rhonda Marie Gonzales, Christine Saidi, and Carolyn Vieira-Martinez, 'Lifting the Loincloth: Reframing the Discourse on Gender, Identity, and Traditions – Strategies to Combat the Lingering Legacies of Spectacles in the

included mistranslations that erased women's roles and past scholarship that censored sexualities that departed from recent Western ideas of what is appropriate, namely those found between a man and a woman in a monogamous marriage.[3] In addition, Africans – including scholars, politicians, and ordinary people – have all brought forward their own interpretations of earlier 'traditions'. In particular, the last two centuries have witnessed fierce debates about young people's initiations, women's styles of dress, and the acceptability of same-sex sexuality, topics that for many became entangled with questions of national unity and 'authentic' Africanness.[4] These dynamics inflect historical sources, particularly ones produced in recent centuries.

Scholars utilize varied sources to reconstruct earlier African history, including language vocabularies, material culture, art, and historic documents. Many of these preclude reconstructing an individual's experiences – often a focal point for studies of sexuality elsewhere. Narratives of collective practices and beliefs carry the risk of inadvertently flattening out individual choices.[5] More recent sources must also be used with care in interpreting more distant pasts. What was considered 'traditional' in the eighteenth or nineteenth century was often the outcome of substantial change that had happened recently, not a timeless custom from antiquity. During the past five centuries, Africans navigated the forces of the transatlantic slave trade, major political and economic changes on the continent, European colonialism, post-colonial nation building, and twenty-first century neo-liberal politics. All these developments shaped notions of 'sexualities' over the last century, and they also influence how Africans recall

---

Scholarship on East and East Central Africa', *Critique of Anthropology* 36, no. 3 (2016): 302–38.

3 Oyèrónkẹ́ Oyěwùmí, 'Making History, Creating Gender: Some Methodological and Interpretive Questions in the Writing of Oyo Oral Traditions', *History in Africa* 25 (1998): 263–305; Desiree Lewis, 'Representing African Sexualities', in *African Sexualities*, ed. Tamale, 199–216.

4 Works that consider the entanglement of ideas of the acceptability of same-sex intimacies with Western neo-colonialism and forms of capitalism include Neville Hoad, *African Intimacies: Race, Homosexuality, and Globalization* (Minneapolis, MN: University of Minnesota Press, 2007) and Brenna M. Munro, *South Africa and the Dream of Love to Come: Queer Sexuality and the Struggle for Freedom* (Minneapolis, MN: University of Minnesota Press, 2012).

5 David Schoenbrun, 'Gendered Themes in Early African History', in *A Companion to Gender History*, ed. Teresa A. Meade and Merry E. Wiesner-Hanks (Oxford: Blackwell, 2006), 249–72, at 250.

customs of an earlier past.[6] Given these challenges, this chapter takes particular care to limit generalizations, favouring instead specific examples.

In addition, this chapter departs from some earlier conventions when it considers historical figures whose gender was unclear or varied during their lifetime. Various African societies had flexible gender systems in which individuals might shift gender as they took on a new status or simultaneously hold multiple genders. For example, an Igbo biological man might serve as husband to his wife, father to his children, and female priestess to a spiritual deity, while certain life stages such as motherhood were regarded, in some communities, as discrete genders of their own.[7] Following the twenty-first-century convention of using gender neutral pronouns (such as the singular 'they') for such individuals avoids imposing either a Eurocentric or ahistorical interpretation, in contrast to what happens when scholars simply select 'he' or 'she' based on their estimate of an individual's biological sex.[8] This choice also has the advantage of mirroring many African languages, which did not use grammatical gender to distinguish humans.

Recent decades have witnessed a substantial expansion of scholarship on African sexualities, including many key contributions from scholars from the continent. As elsewhere in world history, however, the bulk of scholarship centres on the last three centuries, underscoring the continued need for research into earlier African pasts. This chapter proceeds thematically, highlighting examples from different eras and regions with the caveat that one chapter cannot be a comprehensive survey.

---

6 For example, Ndubueze L. Mbah masterfully traces how the last three centuries witnessed new forms of Biafran masculinities that arose because of the region's increased entanglement in Atlantic economies. Ndubueze L. Mbah, *Emergent Masculinities: Gendered Power and Social Change in the Biafran Atlantic Age* (Athens, OH: Ohio University Press, 2019).

7 Nwando Achebe, 'Igbo Goddesses and the Priests and Male Priestesses Who Serve Them', in *Igbo in the Atlantic World: African Origins and Diasporic Destinations*, ed. Toyin Falola and Raphael Chijioke Njoku (Bloomington, IN: Indiana University Press, 2016), 28–45, at 42; Oyèrónkẹ́ Oyěwùmí, *What Gender Is Motherhood? Changing Yorùbá Ideals of Power, Procreation, and Identity in the Age of Modernity* (New York: Palgrave Macmillan, 2016).

8 For a discussion of the analytic advantages of gender-neutral language for historians, see the introduction to Jen Manion, *Female Husbands: A Trans History* (Cambridge: Cambridge University Press, 2020). Oyèrónkẹ́ Oyěwùmí's scholarship has also explored how implied gender-assumptions from English-language publishing has created significant distortions: Oyěwùmí, *What Gender Is Motherhood?*; Oyèrónkẹ́ Oyěwùmí, 'Making History, Creating Gender: Some Methodological and Interpretive Questions in the Writing of Oyo Oral Traditions', *History in Africa* 25 (1998): 263–305.

Adolescence

Many historic Africans viewed young people's sexual explorations positively. For example, in many parts of Central East Africa in the late pre-colonial and early colonial period, young people played 'marriage', by building huts outside villages and engaging in sexual explorations. In a number of matrilineal cultures (those in which inheritance passed down through the female line), young women were expected to have sex with a lover following their initiations into adulthood.[9] Some cultures of southern Africa, such as the Zulu, endorsed non-penetrative sex (called *hlobonga*), as long as no pregnancy resulted. Others, such as the Shona, discouraged encounters between young men and young women but permitted solo sex and sex between young men.[10] Earlier examples of young women's same-sexuality are not as well documented. However, during the colonial era, Sotho adolescents formed 'mummy-baby' relations in which an older girl partnered with a younger teen, sharing intimacy, material gifts, and advice about preparing for marriage to men.[11]

Practices of initiations have a deep history. Many Africans considered them vital to transform youths into gendered adults. In the post-colonial era, some criticized initiations as demeaning to women, yet many women have endorsed initiations as a form of empowerment. Even today, some adults seek out initiation educators for marital advice.[12] Historically, initiations entailed a period of seclusion. Bantu societies, for example, which spread across central and southern Africa, repurposed existing Batwa rock shelters for this purpose, adding their own paintings.[13] During the time of initiation, educators taught adolescents about puberty, adult bodies, and strategies for mutual pleasure, hygiene, and morality. Instruction also included demonstrations of erotic and sexual practices. For example, from as early as 1,000 years

---

9 Christine Saidi, *Women's Authority and Society in Early East-Central Africa* (Rochester, NY: University of Rochester Press, 2010), 149.

10 Marc Epprecht, *Hungochani: The History of a Dissident Sexuality in Southern Africa* (Montreal: McGill-Queen's University Press, 2004), 32.

11 Judith Gay, '"Mummies and Babies" and Friends and Lovers in Lesotho', *Cambridge Journal of Anthropology* 5, no. 3 (1979): 36, 55.

12 Lynn M. Thomas, *Politics of the Womb: Women, Reproduction, and the State in Kenya* (Berkeley, CA: University of California Press, 2003); Signe Arnfred, 'Female Sexuality as Capacity and Power? Reconceptualizing Sexualities in Africa', *African Studies Review* 58, no. 3 (2015): 149–70; Sylvia Tamale, 'Eroticism, Sensuality and "Women's Secrets" among the Baganda', in *Women, Sexuality and the Political Power of Pleasure*, ed. Susie Jolly, Andrea Cornwall, and Kate Hawkins (New York: ZED Books, 2013), 265–85.

13 Cymone Fourshey, Rhonda M. Gonzales, and Christine Saidi, *Bantu Africa: 3500 BCE to Present* (New York: Oxford University Press, 2018), 52–3.

ago, Central Sabi people in today's Zambia emphasized the importance of ritual washing after sex and initiates were taught to use a special pot for this purpose.[14] Often, teachings combined songs, dance, and visual arts that all served as mnemonics.

In the last two centuries, the body modification practices involved with some initiations have provoked debates, particularly in regard to female genital cutting (also called 'female circumcision' or 'female genital mutilation').[15] Scholars have stressed that female genital cutting was often a more recent adaptation in African societies and a practice that should be understood in the context of transformative rituals to create adult, recognized women.[16] Male circumcision, in contrast, dates back at least 5,000 years in parts of Africa, such as among Bantu societies of the rainforests in central Africa. Yet, it was also not a timeless inheritance. Bantu speakers who migrated to eastern Africa, approximately 2,500 years ago, practised male circumcision, but some of their later descendants did not, such as Sabi and Botatwe communities, who dropped the practice when they moved into central southern Africa.[17]

Other body modifications have received less attention, but were also significant. These included decorative scarifications, tattooing, dental modifications, and labia lengthening (also called labia pulling). The latter was a custom that arose among Eastern Savannah Bantu about 3,000 years ago.[18] Bemba speakers (Bemba is one of the hundreds of Bantu languages) called it 'to grow the vagina' (ukuna masino), and many understood it to bring sexual pleasure to both partners as it encouraged foreplay and increased friction during penetrative intercourse. In the years leading up to their initiations, young girls would stretch their labia, sometimes on their own and sometimes with a close female friend using their fingers or small roots or leaves.[19] Recent

---

14 Saidi, *Women's Authority*, 131.
15 Male circumcision, too, has not been without its own debates. See Pamela Khanakwa, 'Reinventing Imbalu and Forcible Circumcision: Gisu Political Identity and the Fight for Mbale in Late Colonial Uganda', *Journal of African History* 59, no. 3 (2018): 357–79.
16 Obioma Nnaemeka, *Female Circumcision and the Politics of Knowledge: African Women in Imperialist Discourses* (Westport, CT: Praeger, 2005); Bettina Shell-Duncan and Ylva Hernlund, *Female 'Circumcision' in Africa: Culture, Controversy, and Change* (Boulder, CO: Lynne Rienner, 2000).
17 Christopher Ehret, *The Civilizations of Africa: A History to 1800* (Charlottesville, VA: University of Virginia Press, 2002), 157; Saidi, *Women's Authority*, 63.
18 Brigitte Bagnol and Esmeralda Mariano, 'Elongation of the Labia Minora and Use of Vaginal Products to Enhance Eroticism: Can These Practices Be Considered FGM?', *Finnish Journal of Ethnicity and Migration* 3, no. 2 (2008): 42–53; Saidi, *Women's Authority*, 158.
19 Saidi, *Women's Authority*, 153–9.

history also points to widespread interests in the uses of herbs to manage bodies and sexual pleasure. For example, in contemporary Zimbabwe, women turned to 'husband-taming herbs' (*mupfuhwira*) to retain their spouses' affection, ensure their fidelity, and improve marital harmony amid the pressures of rural poverty.[20]

Far from stereotypes of oppressed African women, many historic societies emphasized pleasure, consent, and harmony in sexual relations, themes emphasized during initiations. This was evident even in cultures that celebrated arranged marriages. Expected conduct featured in the epic of Sunjata, an oral tradition dating from the thirteenth century CE that scholars have likened to a living Manden constitution for parts of Western Africa. Through a narrative of the rise of Mali, the characters' behaviours in the epic related expectations of proper conduct. Sunjata's mother, for example, enters the narrative after she is given to two hunters as thanks for vanquishing a threat. When the hunters attempt to rape her, she defends herself with her innate *dalilu* (occult power):

> But when the elder brother, Danmansa Wulanba, got close to Sogolon, she did not accept his advances. She shot two porcupine quills from her chest and they stuck in him. He jumped up and fell on the ground. Afraid of her sorcery, he spent the rest of the night sleeping on the opposite side of the room.[21]

Customs found in later times also protected women. The Ba-Ila in twentieth-century Zambia regarded forced sex, even if it happened in a marriage, as one of the greatest offences.[22]

Marriages and Investments

Marriages could represent opportunities for families as well as individuals and were usually managed carefully. *Bridewealth* and *bride service* represented part of negotiations in which the suitor and their family paid material goods and/or labour to secure their rights to claim any resulting children; otherwise, children belonged to the mother's lineage. Many historic Africans saw affect, love, and economic exchange as interconnected. Bridewealth could express

---

20 Allison Goebel, '"Men These Days, They Are a Problem": Husband-Taming Herbs and Gender Wars in Rural Zimbabwe', *Canadian Journal of African Studies* 36, no. 3 (2002): 460–89.

21 David C. Conrad, ed. and trans., *Sunjata: A New Prose Version* (Indianapolis, IN: Hackett, 2016), 38.

22 Saidi, *Women's Authority*, 151.

affection as much as it allowed families to demonstrate their wealth. For instance, one contemporary Malagasy elder proudly related that her husband had 'even paid a bull for her'.[23]

In matrilineal cultures, bride service often reinforced female elders' authority, while in patrilineal societies (those in which inheritance passed down through the male line), particularly recently, it has bolstered patriarchy. Matrilineal authority and bride service share a deep antiquity. In certain Bantu cultures, the term for sororal groups (called *bumba) dates back to the second millennium BCE.[24] Among the Nsenga and the Central Sabi, suitors had to work for their intended's mother for a number of years prior to marriage. In contrast, bridewealth offered stable (and exchangeable) forms of wealth. Popular goods such as iron hoes received for a daughter's marriage could be saved to secure a son's wife. Bridewealth also solidified ties between families, creating social wealth.[25] Although bridewealth in cattle (*ilobolo*) became ubiquitous for the Zulu of southeastern Africa, this was not a timeless custom; rather, cattle represented an innovation due to the changing circumstances of the early second millennium.[26]

In historic Africa, some biological women, known as *female husbands*, also paid bridewealth to marry wives, a custom found in over thirty societies in the recent past. Usually, their wives took male lovers and the female husband claimed the resulting children as their own. In this manner, female husbands could increase their wealth and status – even if they, in turn, were a wife to a husband. The wives of female husbands often experienced greater freedoms than in marriages to biological men, such as retaining a male lover that a woman's family had rejected as a marital suitor. In some cases, female husbands were considered social males in their cultures. In others, kinship idioms explained their ties, such

---

23 Jennifer Cole and Lynn M. Thomas, eds., *Love in Africa* (Chicago: University of Chicago Press, 2009), 29, 21.

24 Saidi, *Women's Authority*, 76–7. The asterisk in the term *bumba identifies a historical term that scholars have reconstructed with the methodology of historical linguistics, and distinguishes it from contemporary African terms that may appear similar. Chapter 2 of Saidi's book provides an introduction to this historical method. On further research into matrilineal history, see Catherine Cymone Fourshey, Rhonda Gonzales, and Christine Saidi, 'About African Matrilineal Histories', *African Matrilineal Histories*, 2019. https://africanmatrilinealhistories.blogs.bucknell.edu/.

25 Abigail Joy Moffett, Tim Maggs, and Johnny van Schalkwyk, 'Breaking Ground: Hoes in Precolonial South Africa – Typology, Medium of Exchange and Symbolic Value', *African Archaeological Review* 34, no. 1 (2017): 1–20.

26 Raevin Jimenez, '"Slow Revolution" in Southern Africa: Household Biosocial Reproduction and Regional Entanglements in the History of Cattle-Keeping among Nguni-Speakers, Ninth to Thirteenth Century CE', *Journal of African History* 61, no. 2 (2020): 155–78.

as the use of 'mother-in-law' and 'daughter-in-law' for female husbands in communities that lived near Lake Nyanza (Lake Victoria) in eastern Africa.[27]

Scholars agree that female husbands and their wives sought the advantages that marriage and claims to children provided, just as husbands and wives did in most historic marriages. Yet significant disagreement exists over whether female husbands and their wives shared forms of intimacy, a debate illustrative of the challenges of conceptual translation. Some have castigated scholars for suggesting the possibility of 'lesbian' sexuality, while others question categorical denials of this given the limited historical documentation of women's sexualities and desires in any form of marriage.[28] The debate is more complicated than assumptions, however. Few historic Africans saw gender differences as biologically based, making many possible 'female' same-sexualities actually relationships between a woman and a social male. Furthermore, Africans' ideas of what constituted sex varied, which calls into question how scholars categorize and compare intimacies. For instance, in recent times, many Sotho women in southern Africa felt 'you can't have sex unless someone has a *koai* [penis]'.[29] They saw caresses, touching, and even genital contacts between women not as sex, but as how they expressed their love.

Recent centuries have brought significant changes to the politics and forms of marriage. Global economies and an expansion of domestic slavery in Africa eroded women's power, especially the status of wives.[30] Wealthy Africans and large states incorporated an increased number of dependents, often through fictive kin ties. One telling example is the case of the West African woman Abina. Taken captive in the Asante Empire, Abina escaped to the Gold Coast, where the British had just established the Gold Coast Colony

27 Joseph M. Carrier and Stephen O. Murray, 'Woman–Woman Marriage in Africa', in *Boy-Wives and Female-Husbands: Studies in African Homosexualities*, ed. Stephen O. Murray and Will Roscoe (New York: Palgrave for St. Martin's Griffin, 1998), 255–66, at 261.

28 Ifi Amadiume, *Male Daughters, Female Husbands: Gender and Sex in an African Society* (Atlantic Highlands, NJ: Zed Books, 1987), 7; Carrier and Murray, 'Woman-Woman Marriage', 262–6. See also Ashley Currier and Thérèse Migraine-George, '"Lesbian"/ Female Same-Sex Sexualities in Africa', *Journal of Lesbian Studies* 21, no. 2 (2017): 133–50.

29 K. Limakatso Kendall, '"When a Woman Loves a Woman" in Lesotho: Love, Sex, and the (Western) Construction of Homophobia', in *Boy-Wives*, ed. Murray and Roscoe 223–41, at 228–9.

30 Akinwumi Ogundiran, *The Yoruba: A New History* (Bloomington, IN: Indiana University Press, 2020); Mbah, *Emergent Masculinities*. For East Africa, see the last chapters of Rhiannon Stephens, *A History of African Motherhood* (Cambridge: Cambridge University Press, 2013).

(which later expanded into Ghana). There, Abina brought a lawsuit against her former captors. Although she did not win, her case brought her protection from re-enslavement. Yet, for Abina, the case was not about securing her freedom alone. Despite the fact her husband had sold her into slavery, she wanted to regain the respect accorded to a married woman, not remain a 'slave girl'.[31] Abina was not alone in finding creative solutions when kin networks ruptured. Captives rescued by the British in East Africa and placed in mission schools, for example, embraced the affective kinship offered by these spiritual communities and went on to form lifelong friendships, find spouses, and found villages of their own.[32] For many Africans, adopting European ideals of marriage brought opportunities in the colonial governments, yet these changes were not universally welcomed, especially by those in power who had benefited from earlier forms of marriages.[33]

Children, Parenthood, and Status

For many historic Africans, children were the desired outcome of sexual relationships and they featured prominently in family politics, as examples illustrate from various kingdoms in historic Uganda. Between the eighth and twelfth centuries, North Nyanza peoples emphasized *social motherhood* as the ideal. It could be achieved through raising biological, fostered, or adopted children or even by mothering the children of one's co-wives. In the Busoga Kingdom, a woman who became *senior wife* (**kaidu*) in a household was assured motherhood (either biological or through adoption), and thus guaranteed security in her old age. Yet, in Buganda, chances for such security became limited after the thirteenth century, when ideal motherhood was redefined as being the biological mother of the family's chosen heir. Their contemporaries in South Kyoga disagreed and continued to emphasize social motherhood, for mothering orphans and fostering newcomers' children helped to integrate immigrants arriving in the region.[34]

---

31 Trevor R. Getz and Liz Clarke, *Abina and the Important Men: A Graphic History*, 2nd ed. (Oxford: Oxford University Press, 2016), 77.

32 Andreana C. Prichard, *Sisters in Spirit: Christianity, Affect, and Community Building in East Africa, 1860–1970* (East Lansing, MI: Michigan State University Press, 2017).

33 See Charlotte Walker-Said, 'Christian Marriage between Tradition and Modernity: Catholic and Protestant Women and Marriage Education in Late Colonial Cameroon, 1939–1960', *Gender & History* 29, no. 3 (2017): 544–69; and Robert Ross, *Status and Respectability in the Cape Colony, 1750–1870: A Tragedy of Manners* (Cambridge: Cambridge University Press, 1999).

34 Rhiannon Stephens, 'Birthing Wealth? Motherhood and Poverty in East-Central Uganda, c. 700-1900', *Past and Present*, 215 (2012): 235–68, at 237; Stephens, *Motherhood*.

While it was considered a problem if a young woman became pregnant before she had completed her initiation, societies that practised matrilineal and patrilineal descent regarded pre-marital children differently. Generally, patrilineal societies expected a child's social father to be their biological father and discouraged children before marriages. Yet in some matrilineal societies it was regarded favourably if a woman had already had children prior to marriage, for it confirmed her fertility. Among the Nyanja-Cewa of eastern Africa, it was only after a woman's first child that she became a full adult. In recent centuries, this milestone was celebrated with a second initiation ceremony and permission to have a cook fire and to thresh grains.[35]

Becoming a recognized parent often involved obtaining the approval of elders and in-laws. In the late pre-colonial period and perhaps also earlier, communities in southern Uganda developed the ceremony of *okwalulá abaana*, which translates literally as the 'hatching of children'. The ceremony incorporated *enkejje*, a type of maternal mouthbrooding fish native to Lake Nyanza, as a ritual food and metaphor for a mother's role. In the multi-step ceremonies, senior women symbolically tested the infant and evaluated the mother's conduct. As part of the ceremony, the senior women took the infant's preserved umbilical cord, coated it with ghee, and placed it in water. If it floated (which a liberal amount of ghee would guarantee), the child was welcomed as legitimate; if it sank, the recriminations could be harsh. This practice rewarded mothers who demonstrated good conduct, regardless of their origins, and it represented an important means of social integration in this multi-ethnic context.[36]

Yet, motherhood was not without hierarchies. In recent centuries in Buganda, poverty significantly limited lower-class women's fertility, thus restricting their chances to gain the high status of becoming the mother to the household's heir. Alongside the impact of poverty on health, lower-class women lacked the advocacy offered by more powerful lineages, which supported a woman's bid to have her child named heir. Over time, infertility became associated with poverty and viewed harshly: in the vocabulary of nineteenth-century Bugandans, the noun *ñgujuubaà* could mean 'carefree, irresponsible person', 'completely destitute person', or a 'woman without children'.[37]

---

35 Saidi, *Women's Authority*, 103–4.
36 Jennifer L. Johnson, 'Fish, Family, and the Gendered Politics of Descent Along Uganda's Southern Littorals', *History in Africa* 45 (2018): 445–71, at 463–4, 461.
37 Stephens, 'Birthing Wealth?', 242, 251, 259, 263.

Elite Alliances, Politics, and Lovers

Sexualities, when managed well, offered individuals as well as kin groups opportunities for biological as well as social, political, and economic reproduction. Often Africans lived in contexts where land was plentiful and populations low, which made attracting dependents a priority for leaders, hence the widespread African strategy of 'wealth in people as wealth in knowledge'.[38] Marriages as well as less formal sexual relations played significant political roles in creating alliances. Some of the earliest examples come from 5,000 years ago, as Bantu speakers migrated into the rainforests of Central Africa near Cameroon. There they formed alliances of trade and inter-marriage with the autochthonous Batwa that provided links to their practical and spiritual knowledge of these environments.[39]

Centuries later, marriage alliances offered other African elites opportunities during the uncertainties of changing geopolitics. For example, faced with an expanding rival kingdom, in 1428 the Ethiopian emperor Yishak sought an alliance with the king of Aragon in present-day Spain through a proposed double marriage. Although it did not come to pass, the marriage would have paired the king's daughter with the emperor and the king's son with Yishak's daughter, allying two Christian kingdoms facing the perceived threat of Muslim states.[40] As the Portuguese began exploring the West African coast in the fifteenth century, some Africans pursued sexual and marriage relations. They and their descendants formed Eurafrican societies, which soon rivalled the Portuguese Crown for control of regional trade. Europeans' high mortality in the tropical climate and African inheritance customs meant that much of this trade wealth remained within the African families who had voluntarily formed these relationships.[41] In the seventeenth century and after, some European men sought to circumvent the restrictions of matrilineal inheritance by marrying enslaved Africans. Slaves lost their claims to protection from their natal kin groups. This meant that when people married slaves instead of free spouses, they gained exclusive claims to the resulting children,

---

38 Jane I. Guyer and Samuel M. Eno, 'Wealth in People as Wealth in Knowledge: Accumulation and Composition in Equatorial Africa', *Journal of African History* 36, no. 1 (1995): 91–120.

39 Kairn Klieman, *'The Pygmies Were Our Compass': Bantu and Batwa in the History of West Central Africa, Early Times to c. 1900 C.E.* (Portsmouth, NH: Heinemann, 2003).

40 David Northrup, *Africa's Discovery of Europe: 1450–1850* (Oxford: Oxford University Press, 2002), 4.

41 George Brooks, *Eurafricans in Western Africa: Commerce, Social Status, Gender, and Religious Observance from the Sixteenth to the Eighteenth Century* (Athens, OH: Ohio University Press, 2003).

property, and inheritance. This also provided opportunities for European men stationed at African forts, as well as for affluent African men, to increase their power. Over time such dynamics expanded patriarchy in societies such as the Biafran Igbo.[42]

Marriages also bolstered rulers' claims of legitimacy, particularly in the era of expanding states from the thirteenth to the nineteenth centuries. The oral tradition of Nachituti's Gifts explained the Kazembe kingdom's claim to the prosperous fisheries of Lake Mweru and the Mofwe lagoon on rivers in present-day Zambia. Nachituti was the sister of the local ruler. According to a twentieth-century version of the tale, after the ruler caught Nachituti's son with the ruler's favourite wife, he killed the son in a jealous rage. When Nachituti discovered the murder, she asked Kazembe, the ruler of the neighbouring kingdom, for help avenging her son. In gratitude, Nachituti gave Kazembe rights to produce from the land and fish from its waterways. She also stayed with him, a decision that conveyed her acceptance of a subordinate relationship (and implied marriage).[43] Whether this narrative originated in the eighteenth century as Kazembe expanded or became popular subsequently, claiming this tie to Nachituti justified the new political order.

Marriages and consorts also helped align new rulers with expectations. Thwarting local politics and Portuguese proto-colonialism amid the burgeoning economy of Atlantic slavery, the savvy leadership of the gender diverse *Ngola* (ruler) Njinga Mbandi (1582–1663) saw them sometimes fight the Portuguese and sometimes ally with them. Born into one of the many competing elite families in Ndongo, part of today's Angola, Njinga grew up as an elite woman and took the throne, despite local and Portuguese opposition in 1624. Later they ritually became a man, led the Imbangala army (a powerful, mercenary group), and fought the Portuguese with a series of military battles and strategic alliances with other Africans and the Dutch. Ultimately, Njinga secured the relative autonomy of the kingdoms of Ndongo and Matamba. Later in life, Njinga identified as a Christian woman, allied with Capuchin missionaries, and formed a lasting peace with the Portuguese in 1661. During Njinga's life, they reportedly had lovers and

42 Natalie Everts, 'Motley Company: Differing Identities among Euro-Africans in Eighteenth Century Elmina', in *Brokers of Change: Atlantic Commerce and Cultures in Precolonial Western Africa*, ed. Toby Green (New York: Oxford University Press, 2012), 53–69; Mbah, *Emergent Masculinities*.

43 David M. Gordon, *Nachituti's Gifts: Economy, Society, and Environment in Central Africa* (Madison, WI: University of Wisconsin Press, 2006), 31–3.

consorts of multiple genders (including some who appeared biologically male but wore women's clothes at court). Such sexual relationships, along with savvy politics and battle strategies, all helped Njinga cement their rule and align with the shifting gendered expectations associated with leaders in this period.[44]

Eroticism, of course, also factored into elite politics. For example, in the nineteenth-century kingdom of Rwanda, Nyiramongi, a queen, and Rugaju, a male lover, battled to control the *mwami* (king). Both Nyiramongi and Rugaju employed intimate assets, using erotic acts, emotions, and sex in their quests to influence court politics and win primacy with this leader. Ultimately, Nyiramongi prevailed, a victory best attributed to her skilful use of politics and eroticism, as well as to the period's gendered limitations on power. The position of an *umugabekazi* (queen mother), which Nyiramongi ultimately obtained, had come to require a biological rather than only a social basis for motherhood, which precluded her male rival.[45]

At times, leaders also strategically limited sexuality. Shaka Zulu, the founder of the Zulu state in nineteenth-century South Africa, refused to marry or have children and expected his regiments to remain celibate until they earned the right to marry.[46] In Buganda in recent centuries, the king's biologically female children (*àbàmbejja*) were forbidden to marry, lest such marriages give competing nobles too much influence in the ruling family. Instead, *àbàmbejja* exerted authority through the political sphere, where they were considered male in local cosmologies. They had considerable sexual freedom and could take lovers and travel throughout the kingdom, making them ideal as royal spies. Others became wives to the kingdom's deities (*lubaale*), which linked the king to centres of public healing that had previously rivalled the state.[47]

---

44 Heywood offers the most detailed biography to date. Linda M. Heywood, *Njinga of Angola: Africa's Warrior Queen* (Cambridge, MA: Harvard University Press, 2017). See also Doris Wieser, 'A Rainha Njinga no diálogo sulatlântico: género, raça e identidade' (Queen Njinga in a South-Atlantic Dialogue: Gender, Race, and Identity), *Iberoamericana* 17, no. 66 (2017): 31–53.

45 Sarah E. Watkins, '"Tomorrow She Will Reign": Intimate Power and the Making of a Queen Mother in Rwanda, c.1800–1863', *Gender & History* 29, no. 1 (2017): 124–40, at 136, 137.

46 Murray and Roscoe, *Boy-Wives*, 177.

47 Neil Kodesh, *Beyond the Royal Gaze: Clanship and Public Healing in Buganda* (Charlottesville, VA: University of Virginia Press, 2010), 156–7.

Intimate Partnerships

Beyond marriages and politics, examples in African history reveal a wide range of relationships shaped by forms of intimacy. Young people often held their own ideas about whom they should marry. Between the eighth and thirteenth centuries, North Nyanzans criticized the custom of eloping with the verbs **-hambuka* for women and **-hambula* for men. The etymology of these words referred to young people's act of seizing themselves, a form of social violence that precluded the possibility of a formal marriage between the families. In Uganda, this critique endured over many centuries. Those living in the nineteenth-century kingdom of Bugwere said similarly that those who eloped had 'forced their way through' (**-bandúká* or **-bandúlá*).[48] While language vocabularies conveyed this collective disapproval, the existence of these terms also spoke to the frequency with which young people made independent choices.

Intimate same-sex partnerships also existed in various societies, with the best-documented examples from recent centuries.[49] Many historic Africans understood gender, sex, and sexuality according to their own cosmologies, which seldom used biological difference as a category.[50] The use of same-sex here is for clarity with comparative history, not to imply historic African categorizations. Even today, while some Africans embrace lgbtqi labels (and many prefer lowercase letters to avoid reifying Western forms of these identities), others maintain distinctive identities such as the *'yan dandu* in Nigeria that describes men who see themselves as men but act 'like women'.[51]

Historically, same-sex desires did not always meet disapproval, despite some politicians' recent claims to the contrary.[52] For Shona in southeastern

---

48 Stephens, *Motherhood*, 47, 156.

49 Among others, Serena Owusua Dankwa, *Knowing Women: Same-Sex Intimacy, Gender, and Identity in Postcolonial Ghana* (Cambridge: Cambridge University Press, 2021); Currier and Migraine-George, '"Lesbian"/Female Same-Sex Sexualities'.

50 Nwando Achebe, *Female Monarchs and Merchant Queens in Africa* (Athens, OH: Ohio University Press, 2020); Oyěwùmí, *What Gender Is Motherhood?*

51 Rudolf P. Gaudio, 'Male Lesbians and Other Queer Notions in Hausa', in *Boy Wives*, ed. Murray and Roscoe, 116; Rudolf Pell Gaudio, *Allah Made Us: Sexual Outlaws in an Islamic African City* (Hoboken, NJ: Wiley-Blackwell, 2009).

52 Margrete Aarmo, 'How Homosexuality became "Un-African": The Case of Zimbabwe', in *Female Desires: Same-Sex Relations and Transgender Practices across Cultures*, ed. Evelyn Blackwood and Saskia Wieringa (New York: Columbia University Press, 1999), 255–80; Marc Epprecht and S. N. Nyeck, eds., *Sexual Diversity in Africa: Politics, Theory, and Citizenship* (Montreal: McGill-Queen's University Press, 2013). Despite highly publicized statements of homophobia, activists have made significant progress in a number of countries, Marc Epprecht, *Sexuality and Social Justice in Africa: Rethinking Homophobia and Forging Resistance* (London: Zed Books, 2013).

Africa in the late pre-colonial era, such relationships could exist, provided participants exercised discretion, and also usually participated in marriages to produce children. Close male–male friendships (called *sahwira*) were considered typical at that time and did not carry any connotation of same-sexuality. Yet for those inclined towards male–male sexual intimacy, they provided a layer of privacy. In other cases, however, Shona spiritual cosmologies helped with acceptance of same-sex and gender diverse desires. A man possessed by a spirit of a woman would be expected to desire to marry a man. Such couples were endorsed so long as the possessed individuals took on the roles associated with their new gender. A biological man who took on women's roles in this manner was called a *murumekadzi* and a biological woman who took on male roles was a *mukadzirume*. In still other cases, beliefs that some individuals were inexplicably stricken with bad luck (*chitsina*) could help communities overlook those who (for whatever reason) refused to marry.[53]

Sotho women in the late pre-colonial and colonial era often had intimate relationships with each other that involved caresses, kissing, and contact between mouths, breasts, and genitals. Women in these relationships described themselves as *batsoalle*. They understood these relationships to be about love, not sex, a distinction that enabled these relationships to coexist with their marriages to men. Mpho 'M'atsepo Nthunya, for instance, recalled her long-term love of a woman named Malineo in twentieth-century Lesotho: 'When a woman loves another woman, you see, she can love with her whole heart.' Their husbands celebrated the women's relationship with two ritual feasts that involved food, dancing, and the exchange of gifts. 'It was like a wedding', Nthunya shared.[54] In recent decades, however, more Western (and more homophobic) reframing of *batsoalle* has caused the custom's decline.[55]

Elsewhere, historic Africans made explicit connections between female intimacies and the possibilities for same-sex sexuality. In Ethiopia in the late seventeenth century, the hagiography of Saint Wälättä Petros (1592–1642) included a key moment that reveals tacit acceptance of such desires. Saints were held to rigorous standards of asceticism, so acceptance could only be conveyed through the language of negation. Wälättä Petros took part in

---

53 Epprecht, *Hungochani*, 35–8.
54 Quoted in K. Kendall, 'Mpho 'M'atsepo Nthunya and the Meaning of Sex', *Women's Studies Quarterly* 26, nos. 3/4 (1998): 220–4, at 220.
55 K. Limakatso Kendall, 'Women in Lesotho and the (Western) Construction of Homophobia', in *Same-Sex Relations*, ed. Blackwood and Wieringa, 157–78.

a long-term intimate relationship with her female co-leader, Ǝḫǝtä Krǝstos. Their emotional love for each other was accepted and even encouraged by some, including the abbot who first introduced them. Yet, desiring sex (or engaging in it) was not acceptable for nuns or saints due to their vows of celibacy. A key moment came late in Wälättä Peṭros's life when she caught younger nuns having sex and she related that 'my heart caught fire'. When asked if they would be 'damned', Wälättä Peṭros replied: 'Nobody from among them will be condemned, nor anyone [from my community] before them or after them.'[56]

The twentieth and twenty-first centuries have made possible still other forms of relationships, alongside forms of Christian marriage that conformed more closely to European ideals. New economies allowed young people greater autonomy. In Tanzania, for example, young women sought opportunities in big cities such as Dar es Salaam and lived together in supportive, although not evidently sexual, relationships. They also engaged in new forms of leisure, including the contentious dance halls where they pursued young men outside of their kin's oversight.[57] (For discussion of sex in late nineteenth- and early twentieth-century Lagos, Nigeria, see Chapter 18 by Ndubueze Mbah in Volume III of this work.) Urban living also offered opportunities for sex work, such as in Nairobi, where contrary to Western stereotypes, such work remained under the sex worker's control.[58] Monetized sexual relationships in some cases also served as new preludes to formal marriages.[59] Many young men used caravan porterage or urban wage-work to save money and marry sooner (sometimes without the approval of their elders).[60] In other instances, such as where mine labour created all-male environments, some men formed same-sex partnerships

---

56 Wendy Laura Belcher's research provides a nuanced discussion of these desires and the literary conventions. See Wendy Laura Belcher, 'Same-Sex Intimacies in the Early African Text Gädlä Wälättä Petros (1672): Queer Reading an Ethiopian Woman Saint', *Research in African Literatures* 47, no. 2 (2016): 20–45. For these key passages from the text, see Wendy Laura Belcher and Michael Kleiner, eds. and trans., *The Life and Struggles of Our Mother Walatta Petros: A Seventeenth-Century African Biography of an Ethiopian Saint by Gälawdewos* (Princeton, NJ: Princeton University Press, 2015), 113–15, 255–57.

57 Emily Callaci, 'Dancehall Politics: Mobility, Sexuality, and Spectacles of Racial Respectability in Late Colonial Tanganyika, 1930s–1961', *Journal of African History* 52, no. 3 (2011): 365–84.

58 Luise White, *The Comforts of Home: Prostitution in Colonial Nairobi* (Chicago: University of Chicago Press, 1990).

59 Jennifer Cole, *Sex and Salvation: Imagining the Future in Madagascar* (Chicago: University of Chicago Press, 2010); Gaudio, 'Male Lesbians'.

60 Stephen J. Rockel, *Carriers of Culture: Labor on the Road in Nineteenth-Century East Africa* (Portsmouth, NH: Heinemann, 2006).

organized by age, in which the older partner took the sexually insertive role and paid the junior bridewealth to formalize the relationship. The junior partner was expected to use this bridewealth later to secure a marriage to a wife.[61]

Sexual Power, Protection, Healing, and Danger

Many Africans perceived profound connections between bodies, sexualities, and power. In southern African, ancient San rock art emphasized ties between bodies, rainmaking, healing, and channelling power. Paintings that showed bodily fluids related shamans' abilities. Because of their abilities to give birth, historic San saw women as closer to the spiritual world and depictions of menstrual blood and amniotic fluid communicated their power.[62]

Even average individuals utilized the power of sexuality during key life transitions. For instance, Bemba parents in South Central Africa protected infants by engaging in ritual sex two months after the child's birth and then abstaining until the child was weaned. Having ritual sex with a relative of one's late spouse, in turn, helped widows or widowers cleanse themselves of the loss before marrying another. Among nearby Central Sabi societies this custom may date back a thousand years.[63]

Women's sexuality could be used to chastise, punish, or even defeat enemies. Women waged war on behalf of the Asante state using a form of spiritual warfare called *mmomomme*, enacted with ritual chants, processions in partial nudity, and sometimes by pounding empty mortars with pestles. Menstrual blood also protected the Asantehene's stool (the symbol of royal authority) by charging it with power.[64] Even in more recent history, women used their sexuality as a political force. For example, Nsukka Igbo women's societies protected the women's interests and could discipline abusive or neglectful spouses. They would gather in the marketplace, insult the

61 T. Dunbar Moodie, 'Migrancy and Male Sexuality on the South African Gold Mines', *Journal of Southern African Studies* 14, no. 2 (1988): 228–56; Epprecht, *Hungochani*.

62 J. David Lewis-Williams, *San Rock Art* (Athens, OH: Ohio University Press, 2013), 41–9; Anne Solomon, '"Mythic Women," A Study in Variability in San Rock Art and Narrative', in *Contested Images: Diversity in Southern African Rock Art Research*, ed. Thomas A. Dowson and David Lewis-Williams (Johannesburg, South Africa: Witwatersrand University Press, 1994), 331–72.

63 Saidi, *Women's Authority*, 151–2.

64 Emmanuel Akyeampong and Pashington Obeng, 'Spirituality, Gender, and Power in Asante History', in *African Gender Studies: A Reader*, ed. Oyèrónké Oyěwùmí (New York: Palgrave Macmillan, 2005), 23–48 at, 30, 33.

offending spouse, and then drag him out of his home, strip him, and sit on him nude. Here female nudity was a potent curse, for one's mother's nakedness held the potential to give life or take it away. In the Onyonyo Muru Nwanga Women's War, for example, women protested the Nigerian colonial government's conscription of their sons. Nsukka women tied up the warrant chiefs, who had condoned the policy, and forced them to view their nakedness, then they followed this with a sit-in at the Nsukka colonial office until officials wisely agreed to end the policy.[65]

Many Africans understood sexuality to have the power to influence the success or failure of creative endeavours. Iron working represented one of the quintessential examples. Alongside their sophisticated technological knowledge (ironworkers in Africa produced some of the highest calibre carbon steel prior to the Industrial Revolution), smelters also ritually managed the furnace's fecundity. Smelters served as husbands and midwives to the furnace, who conceived and then birthed the child: iron. The process of ritual management involved far more than sexual prohibitions that required smelters abstain from sex during the process or menstruating women avoid the furnace. The former's sexuality and the latter's negation of fertility (menstruation) could influence the smelt's outcome. Many furnaces across Africa were created with features of adult, fertile women and included clay breasts, vaginal openings, and waist beads that enhanced sexuality (*mutimwi*).[66] Male smelters increased the furnace temperature using tuyeres and blow pipes, understood as analogous to a penis and testicles. The head smelter also managed the furnace's internal sexuality by adding medicines to increase fertility and thwart malevolent forces that could disrupt the smelt.[67]

Sexual power also extended beyond the actions between individuals. Many communities perceived profound connections between individual and collective well-being. Healers' sexuality often related directly to their power, and many conceptualized their partnerships with ancestral or regional spirits as marriages. By the early second millennium, societies in the region of Lake Nyanza developed beliefs that linked creative power with healing centres.[68]

---

65 Nwando Achebe, *Farmers, Traders, Warriors, and Kings: Female Power and Authority in Northern Igboland, 1900–1960* (Portsmouth, NH: Heinemann, 2005), 176–7, 183–4.

66 Peter R. Schmidt, 'Tropes, Materiality, and Ritual Embodiment of African Iron Smelting Furnaces as Human Figures', *Journal of Archaeological Method and Theory* 16 (2009): 262–82, at 268–9.

67 Schmidt, 'Tropes'. See also Eugenia W. Herbert, *Iron, Gender, and Power: Rituals of Transformation in African Societies* (Bloomington, IN: Indiana University Press, 1993).

68 A history detailed by David Schoenbrun in *A Green Place, a Good Place: Agrarian Change, Gender, and Social Identity in the Great Lakes Region to the 15th Century* (Portsmouth, NH: Heinemann, 1998).

Here communities expected spirit wives to remain chaste so that their fertility could be redirected on behalf of supplicants. Such healers often exerted key political as well as social and spiritual roles. For example, by the late pre-colonial period, fertility had become a key concern at the healing centres in Buganda. By dedicating wives to them, families cemented their ties with these influential sites. Bugandans understood fertility not only in the narrow sense of conceiving children, but also in the social sense of raising children who were accepted by broader society. The latter possibility became especially important for marginalized individuals in the nineteenth century. These wives and often their children became part of shrines' political forces that rivalled the state's power.[69]

Elsewhere, engaging in rather than abstaining from sexuality could enhance healers' ability to transfer power to their clients. Although sex appeared infrequently in ancient rock art, one image suggested this connection. In Zimbabwe, a painting depicted male–male sex in an image scholars estimate to be about 2,000 years old.[70] Given certain healers' use of sex documented in later periods of southern African history, it is possible that this rock art reflected similar uses of the power of sexuality. For instance, in the seventeenth century, examples from Namibia and Angola indicated the prevalence of biologically male diviners who channelled female spirits and engaged in anal sex by taking the enclosing role with their petitioners to transfer healing energy and prosperity. Called by multiple terms in local languages, including *chibanda*, this practice was important enough to certain enslaved Africans that they replicated it in the Americas.[71]

In other cases, healers (of any gender) were expected to marry a wife who was understood to be the wife of one of the healer's ancestors, who lent power to the healer. In the recent history of South Africa, such marriages were expected to be strictly celibate between the healer (called a *sangoma*) and their ancestral wife. Nonetheless, some South African healers find that these partnerships have supported discrete same-sex sexual relationships.

---

69 Kodesh, *Beyond the Royal Gaze*, 75, 169–71.
70 'The earliest known image from Africa south of the Sahara that depicts young men apparently engaged in anal or thigh sex dating from an estimated 2,000 years ago. Like many Bushman cave paintings, its exact location in the Harare area is kept secret in order to protect it from vandalism'; Epprecht, *Hungochani*, ix, 26. Epprecht's analysis of this rock art suggests this intimacy may have been 'playful', yet other details from his work suggest other connections, discussed in the following text.
71 Epprecht, *Hungochani*, 41–2.

Nkunzi Nkabinde, for example, identifies as a lesbian *sangoma* and is guided by a male ancestral spirit and married to a wife.[72]

Sexuality's power, in the wrong hands, could be a source of danger, for many believed that an individual's sexual choices affected others. For example, Sabi in South Central Africa considered a husband's adultery during a woman's pregnancy especially dangerous for it could harm the foetus and make the birth difficult. In turn, Sabi believed that a woman's infidelity could cause health problems after an infant's birth.[73] Knowing when to engage in sexual relations was an important aspect of adult knowledge, particularly when participants in a relationship engaged in creative or dangerous work. Among the Chikunda of eastern Africa, for example, sex the night before a hunt was a taboo for it polluted the forest and brought dire consequences. While hunters were away, their wives also had to abstain from sex, lest such adultery adversely affect the hunt or weaken their husbands. Chikunda oral traditions recalled that husbands often used a medicine called *likanko* as a precaution. A husband would place this medicine secretly in his wife's food. If a wife then saw a lover while the husband was away, this sexual contact would transfer the medicine and make the lover fatally ill.[74]

Discourses of taboo sexualities also related cosmologies of political power, particularly the boundaries between subjects and rulers, the latter who might gain power through illicit sexual acts, such as incest. Some accounts of Danhomè, a powerful empire in West Africa that arose in the seventeenth century, attributed the founder's might to having broken taboos prohibiting both incestuous and human–leopard sex. This symbolism conveyed a political warning: that members of the royalty 'were not like other humans'.[75]

Even in recent decades, discourses about dangerous sexuality presented avenues for citizens to voice critiques and allude to less accepted desires. Accounts of supernatural sex in the twentieth and twenty-first centuries illustrate this well. For instance, in parts of West Africa, fears about supernatural

---

72 Nkunzi Nkabinde with Ruth Morgan, '"This has happened since ancient times . . . it's something you are born with": Ancestral Wives among Same-Sex Sangomas in South Africa', in Ruth Morgan and Saskia Wieringa, *Tommy Boys, Lesbian Men, and Ancestral Wives: Female Same-Sex Practices in Africa* (Johannesburg: Jacana Media, 2005), 231–60. See also her autobiography, Nkunzi Zandile Nkabinde, *Black Bull, Ancestors and Me: My Life as a Lesbian Sangoma* (Auckland Park, South Africa: Fanele, 2008).

73 Saidi, *Women's Authority*, 149.

74 Allen F. Isaacman and Barbara S. Isaacman, *Slavery and Beyond: The Making of Men and Chikunda Ethnic Identities in the Unstable World of South-Central Africa, 1750–1920* (Portsmouth, NH: Heinemann, 2004), 90.

75 Suzanne Preston Blier, 'The Path of the Leopard: Motherhood and Majesty in Early Danhomè', *Journal of African History* 36, no. 3 (1995): 391–417, at 415.

'penis-snatching' and male impotency, more generally, provided discourses through which Africans reflected on unstable relationships between manhood and post-colonial states.[76] For others in Tanzania, discourses about supernatural sexual attacks formed safe ways to hint at desires that had become less accepted in mainstream, popular culture. Using the language of negation where one was 'overcome or seduced' by *Popobawa*, a shapeshifter with an enormous penis, various Swahili criticized restrictions on female sexuality and voiced interest in same-sex desires.[77]

Conclusions

This chapter attests to key contributions of African history to the field of sexualities. Examples here challenge conventional academic categories, revealing the intersections between aspects personal and societal, romantic and transactional, and even sacred and sensual. Despite the pervasiveness of stereotypes, earlier history yields examples far more expansive than some contemporary Africans' views of 'traditions' suggest. Ideally, future research on sexualities would complement the nuance that scholars have brought to the study of gender in African history, revealing the previously overlooked political power of many women, the shifting notions of femininity and masculinity, and the care scholars must take to avoid inadvertently replicating historic or contemporary Western assumptions.[78] Similarly, sexualities research for earlier eras might probe the shifting customs and associations with forms of sexuality as it varied by life stage, class, political circumstances, economics, and more. Other research might trace the changes surrounding Africans' ideas of typical and atypical sexuality from the forms associated with healers and elites to customs of more ordinary inhabitants. In contemporary

---

76 Jane Bryce, 'The Anxious Phallus: The Iconography of Impotence in *Quartier Mozart & Clando*', in *Men in African Film and Fiction*, ed. Lahoucine Ouzgane (Woodbridge, UK: James Currey, 2011), 11–27, at 12.

77 Katrina Daly Thompson, *Popobawa: Tanzanian Talk, Global Misreadings* (Bloomington, IN: Indiana University Press, 2017). The decline of acceptance of male same-sexuality was a change from earlier periods of acceptance in eastern Africa; see Deborah P. Amory, '*Mashoga, Mabasha*, and *Magai*: "Homosexuality" on the East African Coast', in *Boy-Wives*, ed. Murray and Roscoe, 67–90.

78 See Nwando Achebe, *Female Monarchs*; Christine Saidi, 'A History of African Women from Origins to 800 CE: Bold Grandmas, Powerful Queens, Audacious Entrepreneurs', in *The Palgrave Handbook of African Women's Studies*, ed. Olajumoke Yacob-Haliso and Toyin Falola (Cham, Switzerland: Springer International, 2021), 1027–44; Oyěwùmí, *What Gender Is Motherhood?*; Stephan F. Miescher, 'Masculinities', in *A Companion to African History*, ed. William H. Worger, Charles Ambler, and Nwando Achebe (Medford, MA: John Wiley & Sons, 2019), 35–58; Fourshey et al., 'Lifting the Loincloth'.

sexuality studies, a turn to the topic of pleasure has substantially broadened the field. This innovation urges similar investigations for the more distant past including attention to love outside of marriages, practices of play and pleasure, desire and materiality's many intersections, and the broad spectrum of relationships found between the poles of strictly sexual and non-sexual.[79]

Further Reading

Achebe, Nwando. *Female King of Colonial Nigeria: Ahebi Ugbabe*. Bloomington, IN: Indiana University Press, 2011.
Female Monarchs and Merchant Queens in Africa. Athens, OH: Ohio University Press, 2020.
Arnfred, Signe. 'Female Sexuality as Capacity and Power? Reconceptualizing Sexualities in Africa'. *African Studies Review* 58, no. 3 (2015): 149–70.
Cole, Jennifer, and Lynn M. Thomas. *Love in Africa*. Chicago: University of Chicago Press, 2009.
Currier, Ashley, and Thérèse Migraine-George. '"Lesbian"/Female Same-Sex Sexualities in Africa'. *Journal of Lesbian Studies* 21, no. 2 (2017): 133–50.
'Queer Studies/African Studies: An (Im)Possible Transaction'. *GLQ: A Journal of Lesbian and Gay Studies* 22, no. 2 (2016): 281–305.
Dankwa, Serena Owusua. *Knowing Women: Same-Sex Intimacy, Gender, and Identity in Postcolonial Ghana*. Cambridge: Cambridge University Press, 2021.
Epprecht, Marc. *Heterosexual Africa? The History of an Idea from the Age of Exploration to the Age of AIDS*. Athens, OH: Ohio University Press, 2008.
Hungochani: The History of a Dissident Sexuality in Southern Africa. Montreal: McGill-Queen's University Press, 2004.
Epprecht, Marc, and S. N. Nyeck. *Sexual Diversity in Africa: Politics, Theory, and Citizenship*. Montreal: McGill-Queen's University Press, 2013.
Fourshey, Catherine Cymone, Rhonda Marie Gonzales, and Christine Saidi, 'About African Matrilineal Histories', *African Matrilineal Histories*, 2019. https://africanmatri linealhistories.blogs.bucknell.edu/.
Fourshey, Catherine Cymone, Rhonda Marie Gonzales, Christine Saidi, and Carolyn Vieira-Martinez. 'Lifting the Loincloth: Reframing the Discourse on Gender, Identity, and Traditions – Strategies to Combat the Lingering Legacies of Spectacles in the Scholarship on East and East Central Africa'. *Critique of Anthropology* 36, no. 3 (2016): 302–38.
Hoad, Neville. *African Intimacies: Race, Homosexuality, and Globalization*. Minneapolis, MN: University of Minnesota Press, 2007.

---

79 See Nkiru Nzegwu, '"Osunality" (or African Eroticism)', in *African Sexualities*, ed. Tamale, 253–70; Arnfred, 'Female Sexuality'; Goebel, '"Men These Days"'; Sheryl McCurdy, 'Fashioning Sexuality: Desire, Manyema Ethnicity, and the Creation of the 'Kanga, ca. 1880-1900', *International Journal of African Historical Studies* 39, no. 3 (2006): 441–69. Belcher, 'Same-Sex Intimacies', urges consideration of a much broader range of intimacies beyond dichotomies of sexual/non-sexual.

Jimenez, Raevin. '"Slow Revolution" in Southern Africa: Household Biosocial Reproduction and Regional Entanglements in the History of Cattle-Keeping among Nguni-Speakers, Ninth to Thirteenth Century CE'. *Journal of African History* 61, no. 2 (2020): 155–78.

Johnson, Jennifer L. 'Fish, Family, and the Gendered Politics of Descent Along Uganda's Southern Littorals'. *History in Africa* 45 (2018): 445–71.

Kendall, K. Limakatso. 'Women in Lesotho and the (Western) Construction of Homophobia'. In *Female Desires: Same-Sex Relations and Transgender Practices across Cultures*, ed. Evelyn Blackwood and Saskia Wieringa, 157–78. New York: Columbia University Press, 1999.

Macharia, Keguro. 'Queering African Studies'. *Criticism* 51, no. 1 (2009): 157–64.

Magadla, Siphokazi, Babalwa Magoqwana, and Nthabiseng Motsemme. 'Thirty Years of *Male Daughters, Female Husbands*: Revisiting Ifi Amadiume's Questions on Gender, Sex and Political Economy'. *Journal of Contemporary African Studies* 39, no. 4 (2021): 517–33.

Mbah, Ndubueze L. *Emergent Masculinities: Gendered Power and Social Change in the Biafran Atlantic Age*. Athens, OH: Ohio University Press, 2019.

Munro, Brenna M. *South Africa and the Dream of Love to Come: Queer Sexuality and the Struggle for Freedom*. Minneapolis, MN: University of Minnesota Press, 2012.

Murray, Stephen O., and Will Roscoe. *Boy-Wives and Female Husbands: Studies in African Homosexualities*. Albany, NY: State University of New York Press, 2021.

Ocobock, Paul. *An Uncertain Age: The Politics of Manhood in Kenya*. Athens, OH: Ohio University Press, 2017.

Onah, Chijioke K. 'Naked Agency: Genital Cursing and Biopolitics in Africa'. *Research in African Literatures* 52, no. 1 (2021): 205–6.

Oyěwùmí, Oyèrónke. *Gender Epistemologies in Africa: Gendering Traditions, Spaces, Social Institutions, and Identities*. New York: Palgrave Macmillan, 2011.

What Gender Is Motherhood? Changing Yorùbá Ideals of Power, Procreation, and Identity in the Age of Modernity. New York: Palgrave Macmillan, 2016.

Saidi, Christine. *Women's Authority and Society in Early East-Central Africa*. Rochester, NY: University of Rochester Press, 2010.

Saidi, Christine, Catherine Cymone Fourshey, and Rhonda M. Gonzales. 'Gender, Authority, and Identity in African History: Heterarchy, Cosmic Families and Lifestages'. In *The Palgrave Handbook of African Women's Studies*, ed. Olajumoke Yacob-Haliso and Toyin Falola, 1257–73. Cham, Switzerland: Springer International, 2021.

Schoenbrun, David. 'Gendered Themes in Early African History'. In *A Companion to Gender History*, ed. Teresa A. Meade and Merry E. Wiesner-Hanks, 249–72. Oxford: Wiley Blackwell, 2006.

Shell-Duncan, Bettina, and Ylva Hernlund. *Female 'Circumcision' in Africa: Culture, Controversy, and Change*. Boulder, CO: Lynne Rienner, 2000.

Stephens, Rhiannon. 'Birthing Wealth? Motherhood and Poverty in East-Central Uganda, c. 700–1900'. *Past & Present* 215, no. 1 (2012): 235–68.

A History of African Motherhood: The Case of Uganda, 700–1900. Cambridge: Cambridge University Press, 2015.

Watkins, Sarah E. '"Tomorrow She Will Reign": Intimate Power and the Making of a Queen Mother in Rwanda, c. 1800–1863'. *Gender & History* 29, no. 1 (2017): 124–40.

9

Sexuality in the Traditional Systems
of Thought and Belief of the Americas

ROSEMARY A. JOYCE

This chapter discusses societies in North and South America prior to European colonization in the sixteenth century. This is a vast expanse, and the chapter makes no pretence to cover every possible example, rather, it selectively presents examples of societies where scholars, primarily historians, art historians, and archaeologists, have engaged with questions of sexuality in order to illuminate some repetitive themes in sexuality in the Precolumbian Americas. It should be noted from the outset that it is a fundamental part of most such studies to also draw on historical resources after European powers entered the scene in the late fifteenth and early sixteenth centuries and on contemporary information from descendant societies. A major consideration must be how to grapple with the specific transformations that took place through colonization and Indigenous strategies and tactics for survivance. On the one hand, the continuity of Indigenous societies provides scholars with insights that would be difficult if only the Precolumbian sources were available. Yet it is clear that one of the challenges Indigenous societies confronted was defending themselves against European dismissal of sexuality that could be very far from what the colonial authorities felt was legitimate. Thinking about sexuality in these Indigenous societies, then, requires us to begin with a critical perspective on sources and their biases.

Sources and Sources of Bias

Three distinct kinds of sources have been used productively by scholars interested in gender in the Indigenous societies of the Americas, and through those interests, in sexuality. The first of these sources are texts, written in both European and Indigenous languages, especially those from the first century of colonization. Most of these texts are preserved in European archives or the archives of former colonies, where they were situated as part of administrative efforts. Some early narrative sources, such as Diego de Landa's (1524–79) *Relación de las Cosas de Yucatan*, were compiled to present a summation of knowledge of a colonized society by a colonial administrator. Landa, a Franciscan missionary assigned to Yucatan in 1549, describes men's and women's life courses, including rituals through which the maturation of children was marked in Maya towns in Yucatan. He offers comments that characterize some dances in the context of rituals as lascivious, pointing to a public display of sexuality in Maya society that exceeded what the Spanish cleric expected. Here, the temptation to take seriously the claims of authors to adequately summarize social worlds for which they were first or early witnesses must be countered by a consideration of the position of those authors, their likely access to and dependence on certain kinds of informants, and their biases in approaching their self-appointed task. Landa, for example, was recalled to Spain to stand trial for excesses committed in attempting to convert Maya people, and wrote his account as part of his defence.[1]

Perhaps the most extensive scholarly analysis of such a source is provided by the many commentaries on the work of Fray Bernardino de Sahagún (*c.* 1499–1590), another Franciscan, who participated in efforts at conversion of the Indigenous people of central Mexico, the centre of the former Mexica (Aztec) empire, starting in 1529. Sahagún compiled a series of works that have sometimes led to his identification as the first ethnographer of Mexican Indigenous life. His motivation was not to gain an empathetic understanding of the worldview of the Mexica so as to understand them from something close to their own perspective, as would be the case with a modern ethnographer; rather, he began his work by eliciting word lists, using drawings and the help of converted assistants, so as to make it possible to proselytize effectively. He followed this initial stage of elicitation with a second phase of collecting narratives, orations, and even poetry, again through his converted assistants, in order to have examples of rhetorical structures to be used by Spanish religious. In a series of volumes, published in English translation as the *Florentine Codex*, Sahagún himself writes that he reproduces certain speeches as examples of rhetorical achievement, and leaves out other information

---

1 Diego de Landa, *Relación de las Cosas de Yucatan*, trans. Alfred M. Tozzer (Cambridge, MA: Peabody Museum of Archaeology and Ethnology, Harvard University, 1941).

Sexuality in the Traditional Systems of Thought and Belief of the Americas

because it was, in his view, of Satanic inspiration. Rather than a comprehensive account of Mexica life, his work is a valuable, and rich, body of fragments of speech, recorded in the original Nahuatl, edited to remove material that might well have included relevant topics for a consideration of sexuality.[2]

To Sahagún's own bias, we also need to add the biases of the assistants who actually collected these narratives, and the bias of sampling that marks their sources. The assistants who worked with Sahagún were converted young men, who began their lives in Mexica society but were extracted from it. They were engaged in actively translating two worlds in which they were suspended. We can expect that this would include the kind of post-hoc explication of originally unexamined practices and habits that modern ethnographers often encounter. These middlemen themselves apparently drew on a specific set of informants, who specialists believe were adult men of the noble class who had previously ruled the city of Tenochtitlan.[3]

We thus begin with three layers of potential editing and shaping of what is arguably one of the richest narrative sources available for the earliest encounter of Europeans with an Indigenous society on the mainland, any one of which might be expected to systematically eliminate much that is relevant to understanding sexuality. The adult noble men describing their former lives did offer descriptions of the cycle of marriage, childbirth, and maturation, but these are provided from the perspective of the elders of property-holding families, invested in the survival of this group through reproduction, a heteronormative lens. Some of the poetry that was provided as examples of the work of noble authors in the work of Sahagún and other early Spanish observers includes sexual expressions. Some of the proverbial sayings recorded in the *Florentine Codex* point towards both normative sexuality and sexual practices sanctioned by men of this class. The younger male assistants who recorded such narratives, poems, and sayings were in a position to leave out anything that they chose. Finally, Sahagún himself eliminated from the collected texts content he judged not worthy of recording.[4]

---

2 Bernardino de Sahagún, *Primeros Memoriales* (Norman, OK: University of Oklahoma Press, 1993); Bernardino de Sahagún, *Florentine Codex: General History of the Things of New Spain*, trans. A. J. O. Anderson and C. E. Dibble, 12 vols. (Salt Lake City, UT: University of Utah Press, 1950–82).

3 Alfredo Lopez Austin, 'The Research Method of Fray Bernardino de Sahagún: The Questionnaires', in *Sixteenth-Century Mexico: The Work of Sahagún*, ed. M. Edmonson (Albuquerque, NM: University of New Mexico Press, 1974), 111–49.

4 John Bierhorst, *Cantares Mexicanos: Songs of the Aztecs* (Stanford, CA: Stanford University Press, 1985); Camilla Townsend, '"What in the world have you done to me, my lover?" Sex, Servitude, and Politics among the Pre-Conquest Nahuas as Seen in the *Cantares*

Most glaring, all the individuals involved in these exchanges were male. This is not always the case with early documents; and indeed, specialists have identified poems originating with Mexica women in the extant body of documents from the sixteenth century.[5] Yet the imbalance of authorship by gender must be kept in mind, especially when these sources turn to judgements about the sexuality of women.

Still, the most problematic sources of bias preventing scholars from adequately dealing with women's sexuality are not those of the noble men and their Spanish counterparts who collaborated to produce the historical records on which modern scholars depend; rather, it is twentieth-century scholars who project a heteronormative framework on the original sources that has proven most difficult to dislodge. Modern scholars used contemporary understanding of words that historically meant something else; for example, interpreting the use of the word 'virgin' in colonial sources as support for an Indigenous value of preventing women from engaging in sexual experience.[6] They have ignored entries in dictionaries testifying to the existence of same-sex relations of both men and women. Twentieth-century scholarship routinely employed androcentric binarisms in analysis of societies which do not really conform to these gender ideologies.

Three fruitful approaches to Indigenous sexuality counter these forms of bias. First, re-reading sources, including where possible returning to the original Indigenous languages, offers scholars access to new insights. Sexual actions, characterizations of sexuality, poetic expressions of desire, all are discernible. In some cases, this explicitly comes from considering new kinds of texts; reviewing dictionaries for the sentences offered to gloss words, for example, or reading legal cases that describe sexual situations, rather than centring attention on the more interpretive narrative sources. Finally, scholars have taken into account sources that entirely predate the period of European colonization, using objects and images created by Indigenous societies as resources to understand sexuality. The interpretation of the meanings of Indigenous representational media has to be undertaken with

---

Mexicanos', The Americas 62, no. 3 (2006): 349–89. See also Rosemary Joyce, Gender and Power in Prehispanic Mesoamerica (Austin, TX: University of Texas Press, 2000), 156–62, 185; Sharisse McCafferty and Geoffrey McCafferty, 'Spinning and Weaving as Female Gender Identity in Post-Classic Mexico', in Textile Traditions of Mesoamerica and the Andes, ed. J. C. Berlo, M. Schevill, and E. B. Dwyer (New York: Garland, 1991), 19–44.

5 Miguel Leon-Portilla, Fifteen Poets of the Aztec World (Norman, OK: University of Oklahoma Press, 1992).

6 Interpretive commentary by Tozzer, in footnotes in Landa, Relación de las Cosas de Yucatan.

Sexuality in the Traditional Systems of Thought and Belief of the Americas

self-conscious awareness of binarism built into contemporary Euro-American scholarship, beginning with the binarism of normative pronouns and the conflation of variation in sexuality into a claimed biological dichotomy said to be imposed by the demands of reproduction. Yet this is still a very productive avenue, since there is no chance that the authors of these works were modifying them to fit into a restrictive definition of sexuality by new political and religious authorities, as is definitely the case in sixteenth-century narrative documents written in European script.

Much of the work that engages with sexuality in Indigenous societies of the Americas emerged originally from concerns with women's lives by feminist scholars, queer theorists, and scholars of gender. They show that visual images can be analysed as evidence of women's social prominence, or of the way a desirable body was shaped and represented. In order to address questions about desirable bodies, it is helpful to have a working definition of sexuality that is broad, including actions or practices that were shaped by desire and that framed inter-personal bodily relationships. We can begin with an extended example of how analysis can proceed from concern with women's lives, to understanding embodiment, subjectivity, and interpersonal attraction and engagement in one area, the zone extending from Central Mexico to Central America that scholars refer to as Mesoamerica.

Mexica and Maya in Mesoamerica

Mesoamerica is the scholarly term for the network of societies that were distributed from present-day central Mexico to western Honduras and El Salvador. Although these societies were not united under a single political administration, and were made up of speakers of many different languages, they shared a suite of values and practices that distinguish them from neighbouring social groups. These people lived in villages, towns, and cities from at least 1500 BCE, relied on agriculture, including the staple crop, maize, and engaged in exchange of raw materials used for tools, such as the volcanic glass obsidian, and for luxuries, such as jade and other green stones. Most significant, they employed a common set of calendars in which local histories were recorded, individual birth dates were expressed, and biographical events were commemorated. In some of the Mesoamerican societies, this calendrical knowledge was expressed in written texts, with the most complete and extensive documents coming from Maya-speaking peoples of the modern regions of Chiapas, Guatemala, Belize, and western Honduras. Yet even where writing was used less extensively, as among the Mexica, records

185

of names of people and places, and dates of events in which they participated, are found, juxtaposed to drawings in which actions by the named individuals are portrayed. The earliest preserved written texts date long before 100 BCE; after that date, preserved texts in the form of stone monuments, drawings on pottery, carvings on bone, shell, and wood, and even a few examples of barkcloth and deerskin manuscripts form an abundant visual and textual resource.[7] These sources routinely represent people who can be identified as adult men and women, less commonly children, and sometimes people whose gender status is non-binary. They include explicit scenes of sexual actions, as well as providing grounds to infer broader aspects of desire and pleasure.

Studies of sexuality in Mesoamerican societies can be illustrated by two extended examples: the Postclassic to early colonial Mexica (*c.* 1300–1600 CE); and the Classic and Postclassic Maya (*c.* 600–1500 CE). In both cases, scholars routinely shift back and forth between Precolumbian sources and others created after colonial disruption. In both cases as well, scholars use sources that primarily reflect the perspective of a political and economic class exercising control over others. With these limitations clearly indicated, we can review what these case studies can tell us about sexuality.

Beginning with Mexica sexuality: Sahagun's informants offered narrative accounts of how children were socialized in Tenochtitlan. These parallel visual images in an early colonial manuscript, the *Codex Mendoza*, created for colonial administrators by Indigenous artists working after political control was established in Central Mexico.[8] By juxtaposing the visual images with the narrative sources, scholars have shown that from birth, for Mexica people, adults worked to point children towards specific, normative adult roles. This began with the presentation to the child of tools of adult work, for boys, a shield and weapons, for girls, spinning and weaving tools. In the *Codex Mendoza*, year by year images show parallel training for boys by adult men, leading in their teenage years to residence with other youths in special schools for the arts of war. Girls, meanwhile, are shown being trained by adult women in spinning and weaving, by implication, at home. As young adults, these boys and girls are shown being married in household

---

7 Rosemary A. Joyce, 'Mesoamerica: From Culture Area to Networks of Communities of Practice', in *Mesoamerican Archaeology: Theory and Practice*, 2nd ed., ed. J. A. Hendon, L. M. Overholtzer, and R. A. Joyce (Malden, MA: Blackwell, 2021), 1–31.

8 Frances Berdan and Patricia Anawalt, *The Codex Mendoza* (Berkeley, CA: University of California Press, 1992).

ceremonies witnessed by elder men and women, to carry on the next generation of the household.

This highly normative schema is, however, not without some non-conforming imagery. Even at the moment when babies were presented with adult tools, a third option is shown, in which some children are dedicated to move as young adults into service in temples. Teenage boys who are sent to the school for the arts of war (literally called 'the house of youths' or the 'house of song', as much concerned with their learning music and dancing as to practise warfare) have distinctive items of costume and hair styles that distinguish them. So also do teenage girls who are shown remaining at home as new weavers, and as young wives. The boys and girls who are sent to live in religious communities have other hairstyles that do not distinguish the girls from the boys, but rather, set off these celibate youths from those intended to pursue marriage and reproduction.[9]

Thus, we could speak of a spectrum of gender and certainly a range of sexuality predicated for children even in these highly edited, highly normative, texts created by and for ruling personages. Celibacy and sexuality was one pole of difference in the experiences of youths; so was the choice between marriage or single life. Returning to the normative career painted for young men, this actually included the option of the man remaining in the house of youths as an elder, unmarried, and thus no longer part of their family of birth. Indeed, to retrieve a youth from the house of song, members of the natal family undertook a ceremony in which they were symbolically cut free from their bonds to their all-male cohort.

The men who remained together as a military academy, and the youths who spent years with them, were not celibate. They were expected to engage in sexual activity. This was normatively figured as taking place with special women, who Spanish priests and authorities, and scholars overly reliant on them, later characterized as prostitutes or 'loose women'.[10] There is no reason to accept the pejorative characterization of this category of women. Instead, we can accept that in Mexica society, there was a route of adult life, separate from the heteronormative household, in which some women pursued sexual exchanges with men which bound neither of the two parties.

---

9 Rosemary A. Joyce, 'Girling the Girl and Boying the Boy: The Production of Adulthood in Ancient Mesoamerica', *World Archaeology* 31, no. 3 (2000): 473–83.

10 Margaret Arvey, 'Women of Ill-repute in the Florentine Codex', in *The Role of Gender in Precolumbian Art and Architecture*, ed. V. E. Miller (Lanham, MD: University Press of America, 1988), 179–204.

Perhaps the most arresting part of undertaking this kind of re-reading of these normative sources is the fact that they also clearly record the existence of men whose preferred or occasional sexual partners were other men, and women who preferred or occasionally had sex with women. These practices mainly emerge from statements condemning those who had these sexual preferences.[11] At the same time, while sources written by European priests represent this condemnation as about the forms such sexual liaisons took, the primary texts recorded in Nahuatl seem much more concerned with the way that this freedom might undercut the continued survival of the family, or the decorum expected of Mexica adults.[12]

What were the sexual acts involved? Here, we may deal with sources that cannot be treated as reliable – the confessional prompts of European priests who imagined all kinds of sexual behaviour. Much of this licence, these informants suggest, took place in and around sweat baths, a household facility prized by the Indigenous people for its effects on health, including reproductive health.[13] Dancing was also seen as encouraging what these sources saw as licentious behaviour.[14] In both cases, sexuality and its excess was not something limited to those marginalized from the heteronormative family life that was presented as the ideal goal. Rather, these moments of sexual expression involved youths and older adults who were otherwise part of the normative structures of family life from which those expressing same-sex desire were systematically excluded. Indeed, as scholars have noted, the normative activity of the young women kept at home, spinning thread and weaving cloth, itself served as the metaphoric language for sexual inter-course. As the Mexica proverb went, the spindle gathering up cotton thread was the body of the young woman dancing in the marketplace, ending as a pregnant person.

Turning to Maya sex and sexuality: the relationship between textile working and sexuality is also seen in the Maya descendant people who

11 Pete Sigal, 'Queer Nahuatls: Sahagún's Faggots and Sodomites, Lesbians and Hermaphrodites', *Ethnohistory* 54 (2007): 9–34; Pete Sigal, 'The *Cuiloni*, the *Patlache*, and the Abominable Sin: Homosexualities in Early Colonial Nahua Society', *Hispanic American Historical Review* 85 (2005): 555–94.

12 Arvey, 'Women of Ill-repute'; Rebecca Overmyer-Valazquez, 'Christian Morality Revealed in New Spain: The Inimical Nahua Woman in Book Ten of the Florentine Codex', *Journal of Women's History* 10, no. 2 (1998): 9–37.

13 Susan Toby Evans, 'Sexual Politics in the Aztec Palace: Public, Private, and Profane', *Res: Anthropology and Aesthetics* 33 (1998): 166–83; Lisa Overholtzer, '"So that the baby not be formed like a pottery rattle": Aztec Rattle Figurines and Household Social Reproductive Practices', *Ancient Mesoamerica* 23, no. 1 (2012): 69–83.

14 Evans, 'Sexual Politics'; Joyce, *Gender and Power*, 157–9; Townsend, 'Sex, Servitude and Politics'.

today live in the highlands of Guatemala.[15] Here, it is the interweaving of threads that creates a new being, rather than the dancing of the spindle in the marketplace. Yet the shared metaphoric equation of what has come to be seen as the defining work of women with sexual relations remains, and reminds us to beware of overly literal surface understandings of these societies as well.

Archaeologists and art historians, drawing on the distribution of sometimes quite elaborate spinning and weaving tools around the houses of noble families in Classic Maya cities, have proposed that the same kind of training of girls to be textile producers that was documented for the later Mexica existed among the Classic Maya. The intersection of this form of work with social class is significant in both cases; cloth produced by young women was more than simply a necessity for their domestic group. It was a social currency, used to pay tribute to political hierarchs. In these cases, women weaving were engaged in social reproduction to a profound degree, and families of the noble class would have had strong incentives to maintain that discipline.[16]

Young men are depicted in Classic Maya visual media in ways that suggest a similar normative life course as in the case of the Mexica.[17] They are dressed in ways that reveal much of their body, and are shown in muscular poses, in action as ballplayers, dancers, and engaged in at least theatrical enactment of violence against other men. Older adults, both men and women, are shown gazing at the bodies of these young men.[18] A sexualization of the male body as an object of desire for both men and women, a sexualization that was in no way sanctioned or obscured, is powerfully evident.

The actual practice of sex acts was more rarely captured. Unusual images appear to show male victors lying on the bodies of women, perhaps violently

---

15 Martin Prechtel and Robert S. Carlsen, 'Weaving and Cosmos amongst the Tzutujil Maya of Guatemala', *Res: Anthropology and Aesthetics* 15 (1988): 122–32.

16 Traci Ardren, T. Kam Manahan, Julie Wesp, and Alejandra Alonso, 'Cloth Production and Economic Intensification in the Area Surrounding Chichen Itza', *Latin American Antiquity* 21 (2010): 274–89; Arlen F. Chase, Diane Z. Chase, Elayne Zorn, and Wendy Teeter, 'Textiles and the Maya Archaeological Record: Gender, Power, and Status in Classic Period Caracol, Belize', *Ancient Mesoamerica* 19, no. 1 (2008): 127–42; Julia A. Hendon, 'Spinning and Weaving in Pre-Hispanic Mesoamerica: The Technology and Social Relations of Textile Production', in *Mayan Clothing and Weaving through the Ages*, ed. B. Knoke de Arathoon, N. L. Gonzalez, and J. M. Willemsen Devlin (Guatemala City: Museo Ixchel del Traje Indígena, 1999), 7–16.

17 Rosemary A. Joyce, 'A Precolumbian Gaze: Male Sexuality among the Ancient Maya', in *Archaeologies of Sexuality*, ed. B. L. Voss and R. A. Schmidt (London: Routledge, 2000), 263–83.

18 Joyce, 'A Precolumbian Gaze'; Rosemary A. Joyce, 'Desiring Women: Classic Maya Sexualities', in *Ancient Maya Gender Identity and Relations*, ed. L. Gustafson and A. Trevelyan (Westport, CT: Greenwood, 2002), 329–44.

sexually exploiting them – although the characterization of the facial expression of one such woman as showing 'lust' raises cautions about contemporary scholarly projection onto these scenes. An unusual set of images from inside a cave shows individual men with erect penises apparently engaged in masturbation. Clustered with these images is a third, where a standing figure with an exposed, erect penis pulls a second figure towards him, as if to initiate penetration. Originally characterized as a scene of male–female sex, this image was subsequently recognized as showing two people with male bodies, one dressed in a transgender way, suggesting the existence of a more varied range of sexual actions in Classic Maya society.[19]

Male–male sexuality is also suggested by slightly later images from sites in Yucatan. These, it has been suggested, may relate to institutions such as the Mexica house of youths. Phallic imagery of an exaggerated nature is part of the ornamentation of these sites and specific buildings in them. Late manuscript sources painted by Maya scribes before European contact actually show scenes in which a group of young men are bound together by a rope running through their erect penises.[20] Whether accepted as a normative practice or simply something that happened in certain contexts, stages of life, or individual circumstances, Classic and Postclassic Maya youths apparently engaged in sexual activity in front of each other, with each other, and, potentially, with persons who occupied gender statuses beyond the binary.

In both Mexica and Maya society, despite the insistent presentation of Mesoamerican people as either normatively male, or normatively female (and usually, normatively heterosexual), there are many indications of the existence of non-binary individuals. Sometimes described as third genders or two-spirits (using a term from contemporary North American Native societies), these non-binary beings are complex. For the Mexica, scholars have long pointed to the existence of political-religious figures who were biological males referred to with a female title as consistent with the existence of a form of dual, or ambiguous, gender (ambiguous in the face of a European expectation that genders would be both defined and binary).[21] Also evident in

---

19 Stephen D. Houston, 'Decorous Bodies and Disordered Passions: Representations of Emotion among the Classic Maya', *World Archaeology* 33, no. 2 (2001): 206–19; Joyce, 'A Precolumbian Gaze'; Andrea J. Stone, *Images from the Underworld: Naj Tunich and the Tradition of Maya Cave Painting* (Austin, TX: University of Texas Press, 1995), 143–6.

20 Traci Ardren and David Hixson, 'The Unusual Sculptures of Telantunich, Yucatan: Phalli and the Concept of Masculinity among the Ancient Maya', *Cambridge Archaeological Journal* 16 (2006): 7–25; Joyce, 'A Precolumbian Gaze'.

21 Cecelia F. Klein, 'None of the above: Gender Ambiguity in Nahua Ideology', in *Gender in Pre-Hispanic America*, ed. C. F. Klein (Washington, DC: Dumbarton Oaks, 2001), 183–253.

Mexica ideology is the existence of supernatural beings whose sexual identification was non-binary, or varied depending on the stage in their existence.[22] Notably, maize was anthropomorphized as male or female depending on the stage in its growth and the part of the plant under discussion. Related debates have been prompted by Classic Maya images, where the divine being associated with corn appears as a youthful, androgynous figure wearing a skirt or kilt, a costume worn by both human men and women.[23]

The gender fluidity that these ceremonial and supernatural beings reflect is evident as well in the way that humans were treated. Mexica children were not born already divided into three categories with respect to adult sexuality: that effect was produced by adults through repeated actions. The dichotomous sexuality of boys and girls reached its peak with the married couple; as the couple aged, they became more alike, as an age-graded group of elders. Similarly, ancestors in contemporary Maya descendant communities are conceived of as a single merged category of mother/fathers.[24]

Gender fluidity does not of itself lead to fluidity in sexuality, of course. But it seems consistent with the hints given in Precolumbian visual sources, and in colonial documents, that sexuality was not actually reduced to a single male–female form of intercourse.[25] Among the Mexica, while surviving sources written from the perspective of men of the ruling class stigmatize male–male sexuality as abnormal, they simultaneously confirm that such acts were not uncommon. The vocabulary for sex acts recorded in colonial dictionaries for the Yukatek Maya language is varied, recording specific sexual positions and combinations. In the nineteenth century, some Yukatek dictionaries record words for sexual identity that recall the man–woman of North America, using terms that can be glossed as 'maidenly heart', and later 'maiden with a penis', for individuals engaged in non-binary sexuality.[26] (On

---

22 Joyce, *Gender and Power*, 166–75; Cecelia F. Klein, 'Gender Ambiguity and the Toxcatl Sacrifice', in *Tezcatlipoca: Trickster and Supreme Deity*, ed. E. Baquedano (Denver, CO: University Press of Colorado, 2015), 135–62.

23 Matthew G. Looper, 'Women-Men (and Men-Women): Classic Maya Rulers and the Third Gender', in *Ancient Maya Women*, ed. T. Ardren (Walnut Creek, CA: Altamira, 2002), 171–202; Mary Miller and Marco Samayoa, 'Where Maize May Grow: Jade, Chacmools, and the Maize God', *Res: Anthropology and Aesthetics* 33, no. 1 (1998): 54–72; Joyce, *Gender and Power*, 77–82, 192.

24 Susan D. Gillespie, 'Rethinking Ancient Maya Social Organization: Replacing "Lineage" with "House"', *American Anthropologist* 102, no. 3 (2000): 467–84.

25 Pete Sigal, *From Moon Godesses to Virgins: The Colonization of Yucatecan Maya Sexual Desire* (Austin, TX: University of Texas Press, 2000); Pete Sigal, *The Flower and the Scorpion: Sexuality and Ritual in Early Nahua Culture* (Durham, NC: Duke University Press, 2011).

26 Joyce, 'A Precolumbian Gaze', 276–8.

gender diversity in Indigenous North America, see later in this chapter and also Chapter 14 by Jen Manion in Volume I of this work.)

Archaeologists and bioarchaeologists have even suggested that specific individuals whose burials were confusing under the assumption of binary sex might represent transgendered or intersexed individuals. In Oaxaca, although spinning tools were normatively associated with female heterosexual status, some bodies identified by bioarchaeologists as male were buried with these symbolically significant items. This is the case for the principal individual in Tomb 7 from Monte Albán, which has been the subject of considerable debate due to the difficulty of rendering a decision on whether this was a female or male.[27] Another person encountered in a tomb constructed at Copán, Honduras, during the Classic Period has been identified as probably intersex by the bioarchaeologist working there.[28] This person was buried in the manner of a royal woman, but had a parry fracture typical of participants in warfare, and was accompanied by trophy skulls. The bioarchaeologist notes that skeletal features are not determinative for expectations of a male or female skeleton. In a second case from the Classic Maya site of Dos Barbaras, Belize, a bioarchaeological examination documented contradictory skeletal sexual indicators.[29] In this case, the mixed skeletal indicators were reinforced by distinctive burial treatment that led the analyst to conclude they were buried as an ancestor who had, in life, carried out 'gender-bending' ritual activities. These examples indicate that gender beyond a binary, rooted in gender fluidity, was of social significance in Mesoamerica. This has significant implications for lived sexuality.

Understanding Mexica and Maya gender fluidity and its implications for sexuality is informed not only by the contemporary products of Indigenous societies, but also by the texts written in European script that were products of the process of mutual translation under conditions of domination by European regimes that valorized normative heterosexuality. It is useful to explore how far researchers have been able to push considerations of sexuality in even earlier societies in Mesoamerica, for which colonial commentary

---

27 Sharisse McCafferty and Geoffrey McCafferty, 'Engendering Tomb 7 at Monte Albán: Respinning an Old Yarn', *Current Anthropology* 35, no. 2 (1994): 143–66; Geoffrey McCafferty and Sharisse McCafferty, 'Evaluation of Monte Albán's Tomb 7', in *Ancient Queens: Archaeological Explorations*, ed. S. Nelson (Walnut Creek, CA: Altamira, 2003): 41–58.

28 Rebecca Storey, 'Health and Lifestyle (Before and After Death) among the Copán Elite', in *Copán: The History of an Ancient Maya Kingdom*, ed. E. W. Andrews and W. L. Fash (Santa Fe, NM: School of American Research Press, 2005), 315–44.

29 Pamela Geller, 'Skeletal Analysis and Theoretical Complications', *World Archaeology* 37, no. 4 (2005): 597–609.

Sexuality in the Traditional Systems of Thought and Belief of the Americas

is lacking. The earliest societies for which researchers have discussed sex and gender come from what is called the Formative or Preclassic Period, starting with the earliest sedentary villages (by 1500 BCE) and ending with the emergence in many areas of more centralized and stratified states between 400 BCE and 100 CE. With such a long time frame and including the entire territory, Formative period visual sources represent sexuality in a diversity of ways, often varying from one village to the next.

Many analysts have approached these visual sources with the primary question about sex already framed in terms of a sexual binary, seeking to identify two categories: women and men. The materials being analysed in this way primarily consist of small, hand-modelled effigies of anthropomorphic form made of fired clay. More rarely, monumental stone sculptures exist that have anthropomorphic figures. Both kinds of images are known from Mexico's Gulf Coast region, where sites were part of the Olmec regional cultural area. Here, scholars have used a ratio of waist to hip measurements to label some figures, in both stone sculpture and small clay figurines, as female.[30] The figures identified as female in this way include many that do not have marked breasts. Based on this ratio, the majority of the small figurines are identified as likely images of female persons. At the same time, application of this analysis was tempered by the observation that variation by age might be more clearly marked than any distinction in binary sexual category.

This echoed other analyses in regions including Honduras and Mexico's Pacific Coast, where youthful bodies were distinguished from older adults in consistent, although varying, ways.[31] At some sites, such as Tlatilco in Central Mexico, two categories of youthful male and youthful female were foregrounded by this form of visual culture. At Paso de la Amada on the Pacific coast, scholars identified youthful bodies of women, sometimes apparently shown lacking arms, as a category contrasting with figurines of seated and

---

30 Billie J. Follensbee, 'Formative Period Gulf Coast Ceramic Figurines: The Key to Identifying Sex, Gender, and Age Groups in Gulf Coast Olmec Imagery', in *Mesoamerican Figurines*, ed. C. Halperin, K. Faust, R. Taube, and A. Giguet (Gainesville, FL: University Press of Florida, 2009), 77–118.

31 Rosemary A. Joyce, 'Burying the Dead at Tlatilco: Social Memory and Social Identities', in *New Perspectives on Mortuary Analysis*, ed. M. Chesson (Arlington, VA: American Anthropological Association, 2001), 12–26; Richard G. Lesure, 'Figurines and Social Identities in Early Sedentary Societies of Coastal Chiapas, Mexico, 1550–800 BC', in *Women in Prehistory: North America and Mesoamerica*, ed. C. Claassen and R. A. Joyce (Philadelphia: University of Pennsylvania Press, 1997), 227–48; Richard G. Lesure, 'Figurines as Representations and Products at Paso de la Armada, Mexico', *Cambridge Archaeological Journal* 9 (1999): 209–20; Ann Cyphers Guillén, 'Women, Rituals, and Social Dynamics at Ancient Chalcatzingo', *Latin American Antiquity* 4 (1993): 209–24.

masked men and women of apparently greater age. Quite a different situation existed at the contemporary site of Chalcatzingo, in Morelos, not far south of Tlatilco. There, scholars argue that most of the figurines are images of life stages of a developing female body, with particularly detailed rendering of changes in the body introduced by pregnancy. In all these analyses, while the researchers emphasize sexual differences, age-related distinctions are important cross-cutting dimensions of variation.

All these analyses treat one kind of feminine sexuality – youthful sexual maturity leading to heterosexual intercourse resulting in pregnancy and birth – as encompassing all forms of femininity. It is critical to note that the visual record is in no way comprehensive; themes foregrounded in one place may be entirely absent in another. It is also the case that beginning with the aim of identifying two distinct sexual categories guarantees that the visual images will be assigned to two, and only two, such categories. In an analysis of figurines from early Honduras, biological sex was only identified when either a bodily feature that was unambiguous (a vulva, in most cases) or an item of costume that seemed normally associated with female bodies (a pubic apron) or male bodies (a loincloth) was present.[32] This analysis identified the majority of figures as being either female bodied or of deliberately unmarked bodily sexuality. As in some of the other analyses of contemporary figurines from other sites, this analysis found that age-related bodily differences were more consistently thematized. Infants whose bodies either were supported by adults or depicted in reclining positions, youthful, apparently feminine, standing persons, and older seated figures, some with apparent female bodily markings, were identified by consistent features of pose, clothing, hair treatment and ornaments. In a comparison of this analysis with the others summarized earlier, an argument was made that sexuality of younger people was a public concern being displayed and commented on, while age and greater status served as an equally strong theme. The emphasis on sexuality as linked to reproduction in this medium tells us more about the concerns of village and family elders than it does about the range of experiences of living men and women. Not all Formative females can be assumed to have become mothers; not all Formative people with apparent female or male biology can be assumed to have engaged in exclusive or even intermittent heterosexual relations.

---

32 Rosemary A. Joyce, 'Making Something of Herself: Embodiment in Life and Death at Playa de los Muertos, Honduras', *Cambridge Archaeological Journal* 13 (2003): 248–61.

Sexuality in the Traditional Systems of Thought and Belief of the Americas

Queering Andean History

The same complexity documented for Mesoamerican societies is seen in other cases in the Americas. The Andean region extending along the western edge of the South American continent was home to a similarly long-lived network of societies, made up of towns, villages, and cities inhabited by people speaking different languages, some incorporated at particular historic periods into larger-scale political structures. The most extensive of these was the Inka tribute state that created a vast road network and administrative bureaucracy in the final centuries before European colonization began in the sixteenth century.

Scholars of Inka society have demonstrated that, as was the case for the Mexica, femininity and masculinity developed over the lifetime of humans. A cosmological warrant for the original androgyny from which humans developed, like that in the Mexica cosmology, has been identified in Andean materials as well.[33] Marked sexuality emerged from a more unified humanity in which sexuality did not distinguish people, a unity typical of very young and very old people. In Inka society, sexuality was rarely subject to state control, except in the famous example of the *aclla*, young women abstracted from the home communities and brought to weave cloth for the Inka state.[34] While some scholars emphasize the requirement that they remain celibate as if it reflected an Inka moral demand, feminist scholars point to the state interest in controlling the productive labour of these women as the basis for the monitoring of their sexuality.

The Pacific coast of the Andean region is the source of the single most extensive archive of visual representations of sex acts known from the Indigenous Americas. Produced by the pre-Inka Moche people, these images have been employed to create the most original and provocative arguments to date about how an ancient people of the Americas understood sexuality. Initially, Moche pottery was viewed as representing sexual dominance of women by men, based on the explicit representation of anal penetration and fellatio.[35] More recently, scholars have explored how the imagery on vessels

33 Carolyn Dean, 'Andean Androgyny and the Making of Men', in *Gender in Pre-Hispanic America*, ed. C. F. Klein (Washington, DC: Dumbarton Oaks, 2001), 143–82; Susan Niles, 'Pachamama, Pachatata: Gender and Sacred Space in Amantani', in *The Role of Gender in Precolumbian Art and Architecture*, ed. V. E. Miller (Lanham, MD: University Press of America, 1988), 135–52.

34 Irene Silverblatt 'Andean Women in the Inca Empire', *Feminist Studies* 4, no. 3 (1978): 37–61.

35 Susan E. Bergh, 'Death and Renewal in Moche Phallic-spouted Vessels', *Res: Anthropology and Aesthetics* 24 (1993): 78–94; Steve Bourget, *Sex, Death, and Sacrifice in Moche Religion and Visual Culture* (Austin, TX: University of Texas Press, 2006).

relates to ontologies of human development, with substances being transmitted inter-generationally through acts of feeding and sexual contact.[36] In this analysis, the multiplicity of sex acts shown is both an illustration of the breadth of sexual activity imagined by the Moche artists (and presumably, put into action by Moche people) and a broad testimony to the way in which sexualized bodies were shaped in fluid ways. While not all scholars accept these new analyses, they are consistent with the implications of materials from Mesoamerican and North American societies in which sexuality is emergent, fluid, a product of social relations, and open to shifting over the life course.

Revisiting Men–Women and Women–Men in North America

An important part of the studies of Indigenous North America has been the exploration of gender or sexuality beyond the binary. Initially framed as a search for third genders, and inspired by ethnographic and historical accounts from societies such as the Zuni, historical researchers argued that scholars needed to consider the potential presence of people who were not considered men or women. When noted in early European accounts, such individuals were often labelled with words corresponding to European models of heteronormative sexuality, such as *berdache* (a French word for young men in male–male sexual relations) or *joya* (a Spanish word with similar connotations, also meant to be pejorative). Some scholars, drawing on the language of contemporary Native American activists, have characterized these people as 'two-spirits'. Acknowledging that this term reflects a specific philosophical understanding of a gender beyond the binary as a combination of male and female, and recognizing that this was not the only way to conceptualize non-binary sexuality, other scholars used either Indigenous terms or translations of them. In many cases, non-binary people were categorically addressed using terms that can be rendered in English as 'man-woman' or 'woman-man', and this terminology was employed in the most comprehensive historical studies.[37] Archaeologists, and bioarchaeologists, in turn tended to describe these positions as third and/or fourth genders.

---

36 Mary Weismantel, 'Moche Sex Pots: Reproduction and Temporality in Ancient South America', *American Anthropologist* 106, no. 3 (2004): 495–505; Mary Weismantel, *Playing with Things: Engaging the Moche Sex Pots* (Austin, TX: University of Texas Press, 2021).
37 Sabine Lang, *Men as Women, Women as Men: Changing Gender in Native American Cultures*, trans. J. L. Vantine (Austin, TX: University of Texas Press, 1998).

Sexuality in the Traditional Systems of Thought and Belief of the Americas

These studies are interesting because they grapple with the actual diversity of bodily expressions of sex, treating sex as multiple and different sources of sexual identification in the body as potentially not congruent. Recognizing that chromosomal sexual variation absolutely involves more than two chromosomal states, that the expression of chromosomal sexuality in developing bodies is affected by the activities and environments in which a person matured, and that in many Native American societies sexuality was understood as fluid and a product of cultivation, these studies provide valuable insight into the breadth of sexual experiences present in the Indigenous Americas.

One of the earliest studies of this sort united bioarchaeological and mortuary analyses of Chumash people of southern California with a review of historical and ethnographic accounts in which a non-binary sexual status was recorded.[38] In this work, the archaeologist identified a few people whose burial treatment was ambiguous when compared to normative male and female patterns. These people shared attributes that suggested they might have participated in preparing and burying the dead. Historical sources documented that this was a role reserved for men who restricted their sexual activity to other men and for post-menopausal women. While Spanish sources used a derogatory term for the people involved, Chumash people who were said to belong to the category *aqi* were not socially marginalized. Instead, they played significant roles in the social treatment of the dead, and their transformation into ancestral beings after death, based on an acknowledged status of ritual power that came from their celibacy, engagement in sex that would not lead to pregnancy, and/or post-reproductive status.

Refraining from reproductive sexuality was not a universal characteristic of non-binary individuals in Indigenous societies. Among the historic Hidatsa of the North American plains, such individuals occupied distinctive houses, larger than those of others in the community, built on cosmologically charged models. People in Hidatsa and other North American societies historically were described as assembling families through sexual relations that could include same-sex and cross-sex relationships.[39] Consistent with

38 Sandra E. Hollimon, 'The Third Gender in Native California: Two-spirit Undertakers among the Chumash and Their Neighbors', in *Women in Prehistory: North America and Mesoamerica*, ed. C. Claassen and R. A. Joyce (Philadelphia: University of Pennsylvania Press, 1997), 173–88; Sandra E. Hollimon, 'Archaeology of the '*aqi*: Gender and Sexuality in Prehistoric Chumash Society', in *Archaeologies of Sexuality*, ed. Voss and Schmidt, 179–96.

39 Elizabeth Prine, 'Searching for Third Genders: Towards a Prehistory of Domestic Space in Middle Missouri Villages', in *Archaeologies of Sexuality*, ed. Voss and Schmidt, 197–219.

ideologies of sexuality that saw it as fluid, shifting, and developing over the life course, the non-binary persons in such societies were able to engage in a variety of sexual activities with people of multiple sexual expressions.

Conclusion

Across the Americas, sexuality was fluid, not circumscribed by a sex/gender binary. Sexual expression was fundamental to continuity of the cosmos. European colonizers, whether driven by religious goals, or simply by the desire to control the newly absorbed territory and its peoples, sanctioned many of the practices involved, and described them in ways that impede modern scholarship. Twentieth-century scholars approaching these colonial sources and viewing the primary documents available from these Precolumbian societies brought their own heteronormative sensibilities to them. Nonetheless, the monuments, artworks, and texts in which these experiences are documented resist erasure and serve today as openings to encounter this distinct history of sexuality. Yet even this work struggles with the inherent dichotomous language of European concepts of sexuality. Discussions of 'alternative' sexual cultures treat as non-normative the experiences that break out of the heteronormative framework, thus potentially reifying it. Working beyond the binary requires attention to intersecting forms of bodily difference, to avoid privileging one form of sexuality.

Throughout the Americas, scholars who attempt to avoid the initial dichotomization recognize traces of more varied sexual identities. These scholars often recognize cosmological or ontological understandings in which human potential is initially multiple, and is narrowed through specific actions, often not producing a permanent sexuality but an emergent one that can continue to change. European sources will often describe this in terms of the existence of androgynous, dual-gendered, or 'ambiguous' sexualities. Replacing these terms with an understanding of sexuality as a less tightly constrained, constantly unfolding set of relations that extend not only between sex partners but also between them and their generational predecessors and followers provides us insight into a way of doing sexuality that continues as the legacy of many Indigenous peoples today.

Sexuality in the Traditional Systems of Thought and Belief of the Americas

Further Reading

Burkhart, Louise M. 'Mexica Women on the Home Front'. In *Indian Women of Early Mexico*, ed. S. Schroeder, S. Wood, and Robert Haskett, 25–54. Norman, OK: University of Oklahoma Press, 1997.

Ghisleni, Lara, Alexis M. Jordan, and Emily Fioccoprile. 'Introduction to "Binary Binds": Deconstructing Sex and Gender Dichotomies in Archaeological Practice'. *Journal of Archaeological Method and Theory* 23 (2016): 765–87.

Gontijo, Fabiano S., Barbara M. Arisi, and Estêvão R. Fernandes, eds. *Queer Natives in Latin America: Forbidden Chapters of Colonial History*. Cham, Switzerland: Springer, 2020.

Holliman, Sandra E. 'The Archaeology of Nonbinary Genders in Native North America'. In *Handbook of Gender in Archaeology*, ed. Sarah Nelson, 435–50. Lanham, MD: AltaMira, 2006.

Jacobs, Sue-Ellen, Wesley Thomas, and Sabine Lang, eds. *Two-Spirit People: Native American Gender Identity, Sexuality, and Spirituality*. Champaign, IL: University of Illinois Press, 1996.

Joyce, Rosemary A. *Ancient Bodies, Ancient Lives*. London: Thames and Hudson, 2008.
Gender and Power in Prehispanic Mesoamerica. Austin, TX: University of Texas Press, 2001.

Kellogg, Susan. 'Woman's Room: Some Aspects of Gender Relations in Tenochtitlan in the Late Pre-Hispanic Period'. *Ethnohistory* 42 (1995): 563–76.

Klein, Cecelia F., ed. *Gender in Pre-Hispanic America*. Washington, DC: Dumbarton Oaks, 2001.

Lang, Sabine. *Men as Women, Women as Men: Changing Gender in Native American Cultures*. Trans. J. L. Vantine. Austin, TX: University of Texas Press, 1998.

Larco Hoyle, Rafael. *Checan: Essay on Erotic Elements in Peruvian Art*. Geneva: Nagel, 1965.

McCafferty, Geoffrey, and Sharisse McCafferty. 'The Metamorphosis of Xochiquetzal: A Window on Womanhood in Pre- and Post-Conquest Mexico'. In *Manifesting Power: Gender and the Interpretation of Power in Archaeology*, ed. Tracy Sweeley, 103–25. London: Routledge, 1999.

Meskell, Lynn M., and Rosemary A. Joyce. *Embodied Lives: Figuring Ancient Egypt and the Classic Maya*. London: Routledge, 2003.

Miller, Virginia E., ed. *The Role of Gender in Precolumbian Art and Architecture*. Lanham, MD: University Press of America, 1988.

Roscoe, Will. *Changing Ones: Third and Fourth Genders in Native North America*. New York: St Martin's Press, 1998.

Sigal, Pete. *The Flower and the Scorpion: Sexuality and Ritual in Early Nahua Culture*. Durham, NC: Duke University Press, 2011.
From Moon Goddesses to Virgins: The Colonization of Yucatecan Maya Sexual Desire. Austin, TX: University of Texas Press, 2000.
'Latin America and the Challenge of Globalizing the History of Sexuality'. *American Historical Review* 114, no. 5 (2009): 1340–53.

Silverblatt, Irene M. *Moon, Sun and Witches: Gender Ideologies and Class in Inca and Colonial Peru*. Princeton, NJ: Princeton University Press, 1987.

Slater, Sandra, and Fay A. Yarbrough. *Gender and Sexuality in Indigenous North America, 1400–1850*. Columbia, SC: University of South Carolina Press, 2011.

Sousa, Lisa. *The Woman Who Turned into a Jaguar, and Other Narratives of Native Women in Archives of Colonial Mexico*. Stanford, CA: Stanford University Press, 2017.

Stone, Andrea J. 'Keeping Abreast of the Maya: A Study of the Female Body in Maya Art'. *Ancient Mesoamerica* 22, no. 1 (2011): 167–83.

'Sacrifice and Sexuality: Some Structural Relationships in Classic Maya Art'. In *The Role of Gender in Precolumbian Art and Architecture*, ed. Virginia Miller, 75–103. Lanham, MD: University Press of America, 1988.

Voss, Barbara L., and Rob Schmidt, eds. *Archaeologies of Sexuality*. London: Routledge, 2000.

Weismantel, Mary. *Playing with Things: Engaging the Moche Sex Pots*. Austin, TX: University of Texas Press, 2021.

'Towards a Transgender Archaeology: A Queer Rampage through Prehistory.' In *The Transgender Studies Reader*, Vol. 2, ed. Susan Stryker and Aren Aizura, 319–34. New York: Routledge, 2013.

Williams, Walter L. *The Spirit and the Flesh: Sexual Diversity in American Indian Culture*. Boston: Beacon, 1986.

10

Oceanic Sexualities: Persistence, Change, Resistance

MARGARET JOLLY

Writing about Oceanic sexualities is oceanic in both senses: I am writing about sexualities across the Pacific and the horizon seems limitless. It involves vast travel in space and time to appreciate the striking diversities in Indigenous sexualities across Oceania and to witness how these have transformed over centuries in relation to and resistance against global influences, especially those originating in Euro-American imperialism.[1] To write about Oceanic sexualities also entails a prior question about what we mean by 'sexuality' given that most Oceanic languages and knowledges do not name this as a separate sphere of human life and/or see sexuality as sacred or taboo, although there were and are names for sexual practices and identities.[2] Thus, several researchers have suggested that there is a risk in imposing conceptions of 'sexuality' discussed in European texts of the nineteenth and twentieth centuries, culminating in influential theories such as those of Sigmund Freud and Michel Foucault. (On Freud, see Chapter 5 by Alison Downham Moore, and on Foucault, see Chapter 6 by Michael Behrent both in Volume I of this work.)

This chapter was originally envisaged as a co-authored collaboration with Mitiana Arbon and Katherine Lepani. Other commitments intervened but I am indebted to their work and our collaboration in teaching about gender and sexuality in the Pacific at ANU. For comments on earlier drafts I thank Nayahamui Rooney, Romitesh Kant, Katherine Lepani, Mitiana Arbon, Chris Ballard, and Carolyn Brewer. Huge thanks to Carolyn Brewer and Cambridge University Press for their meticulous copyediting. Any remaining errors and infelicities are mine alone.

1 I use Oceania rather than the Pacific to emphasize the vastness of the ocean and the historical and contemporary connections between islands, rather than their smallness and isolation. See Epeli Hau'ofa, *We Are the Ocean, Selected Works* (Honolulu: University of Hawai'i Press, 2008).

2 Jiojo Ravulo, 'Exploring the Role of Sexuality and Identity across the Pacific: Navigating Traditional and Contemporary Meanings and Practices', in *The Routledge International Handbook of Indigenous Resilience*, ed. Hilary N. Weaver (London: Routledge, 2022), 108–20.

Authors writing about sexualities in Oceania have grappled with questions of similarity and difference in ways that are entangled with imperial genealogies, which all too often presume Europeans are 'us' and Oceanic peoples are 'them'. Howard Chiang discerns a 'double alterity' in much sexology whereby the 'other' is seen at a distance in both space (remote, exotic) and in time (archaic, traditional).[3] So, observers on eighteenth-century European voyages of exploration in Oceania traced an arc from west to east and from savagery to civilization. On Cook's three voyages, the islands we now know as New Caledonia and Vanuatu were plotted as more 'savage' than those to their east, such as Tahiti and Hawai'i. Gender and sexual regimes were distinguished sharply – between western islands where males were seen to dominate women and jealously sequester women's sexuality and eastern islands where women were seen to have far more agency, including sexual licence, to engage with eager white sailors, officers, and scientists.[4]

Writing about Oceanic sexualities has thus entailed profound challenges of *translation* in the context of colonial power and decolonial resistance. Texts and images by foreign authors have often been hegemonic, as in late eighteenth-century views from the three voyages of the British explorer James Cook (1728–79). To fully appreciate the depth, diversity, and complexity of Oceanic sexualities we need Indigenous perspectives as expressed in contemporary practices and conversations, in oral histories, chants, poetry, and dance and in the materiality of clothing, housing, artefacts, and arts. Until the arrival of Europeans, and of Christian missionaries in particular, Oceanic peoples did not communicate across time and space through writing. Communication was rather oral/aural and through performances of poetry and dance and creative arts such as sculptures, masks, and textiles. When Indigenous languages were recorded and written down by Christian missionaries, they became a significant novel medium of communication. But the views and values about sexuality expressed therein were powerfully shaped

---

3 Howard Chiang, 'Double Alterity and the Global Historiography of Sexuality: China, Europe, and the Emergence of Sexuality as a Global Possibility', *e-pisteme* 2 no. 1 (2009): 33–52.

4 See Serge Tcherkézoff, *Le mythe occidental de la sexualité polynésienne, 1928–1999: Margaret Mead, Derek Freeman et Samoa* (Paris: Presses Universitaires de France, 2001); Serge Tcherkézoff, 'A Reconsideration of the Role of Polynesian Women in Early Encounters with Europeans: Supplement to Marshall Sahlins' Voyage around the Islands of History', in *Oceanic Encounters: Exchange, Desire, Violence*, ed. Margaret Jolly, Serge Tcherkézoff, and Darrell Tryon (Canberra: Australian National University Press, 2009), 113–59; A. Marata Tamaira, 'From Full Dusk to Full Tusk: Reimagining the "Dusky Maiden" through the Visual Arts', *Contemporary Pacific* 22, no. 1 (2010): 1–35; Margaret Jolly, 'Women of the East, Women of the West: Region and Race, Gender and Sexuality on Cook's Voyages', in *The Atlantic World in the Antipodes*, ed. Kate Fullagar (Newcastle, UK: Cambridge Scholars Press, 2012), 2–32.

by the fact that early Indigenous authors were often eager converts to Christianity.

I explore the historical complexities of Oceanic sexualities through three case studies: Hawai'i, Papua New Guinea, and Samoa, all places where there has been intensive research and equally intensive debate about persistence, change, and resistance in the context of colonialism and decolonization. I highlight two crucial questions: How do Oceanic people contrast old and new ways in their sexual lives and how is individual sexual experience situated in relational values embedding human life in the cosmos?

Hawai'i: Fluid Pleasures, Christian and Capitalist Enclosures, and Decolonial Prospects

Caroline Ralston has suggested that whereas Kānaka Maoli (Indigenous Hawaiians) saw sexuality as a source of 'great pleasure, aesthetic beauty and religious affirmation of life', Calvinist missionaries from New England saw sexuality as 'a source of shame, anxiety and frustration'.[5] This invidious contrast is supported by J. Kēhaulani Kauanui's path-breaking analysis.[6] Yet, Kauanui also reveals the complex paradoxes in the radical restructuring of gender and sexual regimes from ancient pre-colonial Hawai'i, to the Hawaiian Kingdom of the nineteenth century, to the prospects of sovereignty and decolonization in the present. Building on many earlier works, she documents how the chiefly class, including the royals of the united Hawaiian Kingdom from 1810, struggled to relinquish their Indigenous sexual pleasures even as they proclaimed conversion to the Christian and capitalist values of individualism and property, crucial to the international recognition of their sovereign monarchy. King Kamehameha I (c. 1758–1819) violently subjugated island chiefs under his rule and, after his death, two of his female partners, Kēopūolani (1778–1823) and Ka'ahumanu (1768–1832), introduced Christian patriarchal norms throughout the realm, promoted by foreign missionaries who first arrived from Boston in 1820. The last queen, Lili'uokalani (1838–1917), was overthrown in 1893 and Hawai'i was ultimately

---

5 Caroline Ralston, 'Changes in the Lives of Ordinary Women in Early Post-contact Hawaii', in *Family and Gender in the Pacific: Domestic Contradictions and the Colonial Impact*, ed. Margaret Jolly and Martha Macintyre (Cambridge: Cambridge University Press, 1989), 45–64, at 61.

6 J. Kēhaulani Kauanui, *Paradoxes of Hawaiian Sovereignty: Land, Sex and the Colonial Politics of State Nationalism* (Durham, NC: Duke University Press, 2018). The discussion that follows draws significantly from this book.

MARGARET JOLLY

annexed by the United States in 1898. A novel regime of 'heteropatriarchal' law was secured and has persisted.[7]

In ancient Hawai'i, rank eclipsed gender and this hierarchical configuration pervaded sexuality and reproduction. There were three main strata – *the ali'i nui* (the high chiefs), the *kaukau ali'i* (the middle, mediating stratum), and the *maka'āinana* ('people of the land', ordinary Hawaiians, or 'common people'). The *ali'i nui* embodied the divine power of the gods (*akua*). Their *mana* was demonstrated by making things *kapu* (taboo, a word that comes from *kapu/tapu*), as in gender-segregated eating, whereas lowly ranked people were seen as *noa* (unrestricted). Kauanui highlights the power of female deities, such as Pele, the goddess of the volcano, on the largest island of Hawai'i. Women could be powerful paramount chiefs, priests, and prophets while some assisted men in battle. Women of all ranks were strong, active agents in relation to land and in their associations with men. Kinship was bilateral, recognizing both maternal and paternal lines, and residence was usually matrilocal. Marriage was a flexible arrangement; lifelong partnerships were not expected. Biological parenting was complemented by fostering and adoption.

The sexual and reproductive lives of the *ali'i nui* were distinctive – both men and women often had multiple heterosexual partners. Although this was described by missionaries as 'polygyny' and 'polyandry', these polyamorous relations were not marriages in the Christian sense. Long-standing attachments between a man (*kāne*) and a woman (*wāhine*) were bound by love, compassion, and care (*aloha*) rather than law. High-ranking women avoided sex with low-ranking men: a potential child would lose rank.

The highest chiefs safeguarded their rank by partnering with close consanguineal kin, half-siblings, or even full brothers and sisters. This practice of *pi'o* was legitimated by the epic story *Kumulipo* about primordial humans, the half-siblings Wākea (Sky Father) and Papa Hanāumoku (Earth Mother), whose cosmological coupling was powerful and generative: she birthed the islands. *Pi'o*, pervasive among royals in the nineteenth century, concentrated their divine power. Christian missionaries condemned such practices as 'incest' and refused baptism even to high-ranking royals who persisted in this or other 'debauchery'.

Kauanui relates the saga of King Kamehameha III (1814–54) and his full sister Nahi'ena'ena (1815–36) whose intermittent sexual relationship extended over several years though they tried to conceal it. In 1834, Nahi'ena'ena was

---

7 Kauanui, *Paradoxes of Hawaiian Sovereignty*, 116.

Oceanic Sexualities: Persistence, Change, Resistance

accused of drunken debauchery, enjoying hula, and 'listening to Hawaiian chants' and was eventually excommunicated from the church. Theirs is a poignant saga: his attempts at suicide, her turmoil, oscillating between defiance and remorse, her marriage to another chief and the birth and (barely a few hours later) the death of a child fathered by either her husband or her brother. She died soon after; both King Kamehameha III and her husband were present at her funeral, but she was buried by her brother next to their mother, Kēopūolani. The royal siblings endured anguish in the tension between ancestral practices and the Christian norms embraced by their mother. Kēopūolani was the highest chief in the archipelago and partner of Kamehameha I, but after his death in 1819 had moved to end the *'aikapu*, the restrictions based on gender and rank. Soon after his sister's death, Kamehameha III reconsidered Christian teachings and, though he never joined the church, married Kalama (1817–70), the daughter of a prominent chief, in a Christian ceremony, and had two children with her who died in infancy but adopted a child from his extra-marital affair with another woman.

As well as outlawing polyamory and royal incest, Christian missionaries attacked two other relationships expressive of sexual and gender fluidity, *aikane* and *mahu*. These words were first recorded on Cook's third voyage (1776–80), but their full meaning and significance often eluded foreigners. *Aikane* were described in the Cook voyage journals as a male chief's lovers, crucial in gaining access to the chief. Yet, *aikane* denotes not an identity but a relationship and, according to Mary Pukui and Samuel Elbert, an intimate same-sex friendship of a man *or* a woman which *may* involve sexual relations.[8] In 1832, the year before his relationship with his sister began, Kamehameha III began an *aikane* relation with a young man, Kaomi, a Protestant minister who had joined the Christian chiefs led by Ka'ahumanu. When Ka'ahumanu died in that same year, Kamehameha III rebelled against the Christian reforms; Kaomi left the ministry and became a joint ruler with him. In this partnership, Kamehameha III was perpetuating the same-sex relationships of his great grandfather, a paramount chief at the time of Cook's third voyage. But the missionaries blamed Kaomi for Kamehameha's lapse into 'savage sexuality'.

Although the word *aikane* is based on the word *kane* for man, it could also refer to close friendships and sexual intimacy between women. An epic poem about the goddess Pele tells of how her heroic younger sister Hi'iaka was in

---

8 Mary Kawena Pukui and Samuel H. Elbert, eds., s.v. 'aikane', *Hawaiian Dictionary*, rev. ed. (Honolulu: University of Hawai'i Press, 1986); Kauanui, *Paradoxes of Hawaiian Sovereignty*, 161.

a love relationship with a girl, Hōpoe. Their relationship is depicted in romantic language with hidden meanings (*kaona*), metaphors, and veiled allusions which intensified listeners' delight; blatant details were considered coarse. Same-sex relations were depicted as normal practices for which labels such as hetero/homo/bisexual identity were irrelevant.[9] Same-sex relationships between high-ranking women avoided the risk of pregnancy; desire could be fulfilled without danger.

Māhū has proved more difficult to translate, with several shifts in its meaning over time.[10] Early European explorers interpreted this as someone who was neither male nor female. Later scholars pondered whether it constituted a 'third sex/gender'.[11] In successive translations, meanings have diffused between signifying gender and sexual fluidity. In the twentieth century it was used for both homosexuals and intersex individuals, while more recently it has been reclaimed to mean transgender, especially transgender women.[12] Kaumakaiwa Kanakaʻole, a *māhū* singer, dancer, and activist, refuses to hitch it to either gender or sex, seeing it as a more transcendent spiritual state beyond the gender binary.[13]

Foreign missionaries were both appalled and overwhelmed by all such 'debauchery', especially among chiefs who were their main conduit to the mass conversion of Hawaiians. The early missionary and later Judge Lorrin Andrews recorded so many words for 'illicit intercourse' in the Hawaiian language that he said it was impossible to name them all. In Christian laws promulgated in 1827 and 1829, the injunction 'Thou shall not commit adultery' was translated as 'Thou shall not sleep mischievously'.[14]

Later Indigenous Christian authors appropriated the missionaries' language to describe the 'old ways' of ancient Hawaiʻi. In his history of the Hawaiian Kingdom, David Malo, writing in the 1840s, traced practices of 'sodomy' and intercrural sex to the ancient chief Liloa, but failed to speculate on its contemporaneous practice.[15] Samuel Kamakau, writing in the 1860s,

---

9 Noenoe K. Silva, 'Pele, Hiʻiaka, and Haumea: Women and Power in Two Hawaiian Moʻolelo', *Pacific Studies* 30, nos. 1–2 (2007): 159–81, at 167–8.

10 Kauanui, *Paradoxes of Hawaiian Sovereignty*, 178–83.

11 Niko Besnier, 'Polynesian Gender Liminality through Time and Space', in *Third Sex, Third Gender: Beyond Sexual Dimorphism in Culture and History*, ed. Gilbert H. Herdt (New York: Zone Books, 1994), 285–328.

12 Andrew Matzner, ed., *'O Au No Keia: Voices from Hawaiʻi's Mahu and Transgendered Communities* (Bloomington, IN: Xlibris, 2001).

13 Kauanui, *Paradoxes of Hawaiian Sovereignty*, 181.

14 Kauanui, *Paradoxes of Hawaiian Sovereignty*, 137–8, 170.

15 David Malo, *Hawaiian Antiquities (Moolelo Hawaii)*, 2nd ed. (1898; Honolulu: Bishop Museum, 1951).

described same-sex relations as an 'evil practice' whereby chiefs in the 'old days' 'defiled themselves'.[16] Both attacked homosexuality, royal 'incest', 'polygyny', 'polyandry', 'adultery', and *māhū* as evil relationships to be consigned to the darkness of the heathen past, as they embraced enlightened new norms: heterosexual, monogamous, lifelong Christian marriages.

Despite chiefly 'backsliding', the complicit influences of Christian conversion and colonizing capitalism led to a profound transformation in the gender and sexual regimes of Hawai'i. This occurred during a period of dramatic population decline. David Swanson's recent estimate for the population in 1778 is about 683,200, with people living well on the bounty of irrigated taro gardens, breadfruit, and fish cultivated in ponds or caught from rivers, shores, and the deep ocean.[17] Yet the census of 1900 counted only 29,799 'Native Hawaiians', which means that the population had declined by 73.7 per cent. There was increased mortality due to several major epidemics of diseases to which native Hawaiians had no or little immunity, including influenza, measles, and Hansen's disease (leprosy). Moreover, early European explorers brought venereal disease, both syphilis and gonorrhoea. As well as suffering and death, these caused infertility, fewer births, and infant mortality. The rapid decline in the health and fertility of people and place was seen in spiritual terms, since seasonal cycles and cosmological fertility were linked to the gods and the *mana* of those who ruled. Population collapse was thus likely a catalyst in the embrace of the one male god of Christianity.

After Kamehameha I's death in 1819, Kēopūolani and then Ka'ahumanu, who served as co-ruler (*kuhina nui*) with her sons Kamehameha II (r. 1819–24) and Kamehameha III, enacted many changes in Hawai'i to accord with Western values and Christian norms. Thus, we have one of the central paradoxes that Kauanui reveals: elite royal women, alongside other chiefly male converts, were crucial in establishing patriarchal laws in the kingdom, new laws privatizing land (such as the Māhele in 1848), and new laws for sex and marriage.[18] Both land and sexuality were thus enclosed. In the successive constitutions of the Hawaiian Kingdom, from 1840 to 1887, women were increasingly removed from the centre of governance. Although some chiefly women rose to royal status, such as Queen Lili'uokalani, women's broader role was circumscribed.

---

16 Samuel Manaiakalani Kamakau, *Ruling Chiefs of Hawaii*, rev. ed. (1866–71; Honolulu: Kamehameha Schools, 1991), 234.

17 David A. Swanson, 'A New Estimate of the Hawaiian Population for 1778, the Year of First European Contact', *Hūlili* 11, no. 2 (2019): 203–22.

18 See Kauanui, *Paradoxes of Hawaiian Sovereignty*, 80–99.

The proscription against adultery and fornication in the national laws enacted in 1827 and 1829 was directly modelled on a Massachusetts statute of 1784.[19] But the Hawaiian laws had a distinctive salience since they entailed a regulation of ordinary Hawaiian women's sexuality. Sexual liaisons between Hawaiian women and foreign men, often sailors, whalers, or traders, were not 'prostitution' as it was understood in the United States.[20] Ordinary women thereby gained foreign goods for their kin, evading chiefly monopolies in trade. Prohibiting such liaisons provoked anger and violence from foreign men who presumed their white male entitlement to 'Hawaiian women's bodies for sexual pillage'.[21] They saw white missionaries as authors of the ban rather than Ka'ahumanu, but she was adamant it was *her* authority. Eventually concessions were made and only three of the Ten Commandments became law: prohibitions against murder, theft, and adultery. Ka'ahumanu accused some male chiefly opponents of adultery although she flouted the prohibition herself by a furtive affair with a young Captain Lewis.

Christian marriage, formally solemnized by a missionary or a chief, became the only legal sexual relationship. Moreover, Christian marriage enforced the husband's primacy through the rule of coverture, whereby a wife came under her husband's authority in all matters (in line with English common law and enacted in 1841). A wife's legal rights and obligations were subsumed by her husband so that, unlike an unmarried woman, a wife had no rights to property or to make contracts without her husband's consent: 'by law she is civilly dead'.[22]

These legal and political reconfigurations were accompanied by Christian efforts to transform the family ('*ohana*), extended and inter-generational, into the European bourgeois ideal of a nuclear family in which the wife-mother did most domestic labour and childcare. Ideally the family was supported by men who worked for the market, but in fact, when the white missionary families established large sugar plantations, labour had to be sought from indentured immigrants: Japanese, Chinese, and Filipino. Missionaries regularly complained about Hawaiian women's coarse behaviour – their love of boxing, surfing, horse riding, dancing, playing cards, gambling, and smoking. The 'men of God' lamented local women's incapacity for subservience to

---

19 Sally Engle Merry, *Colonizing Hawai'i: The Cultural Power of Law* (Princeton, NJ: Princeton University Press, 2000).
20 Ralston, 'Changes in the Lives of Ordinary Women', 61.
21 Kauanui, *Paradoxes of Hawaiian Sovereignty*, 131.
22 Kauanui, *Paradoxes of Hawaiian Sovereignty*, 139.

their husbands, especially older high-ranking women who married younger men.

A tension thus continued between the legal status of women reflecting a Euro-American ideology of gender and sexuality and the Indigenous cultural valuation of women as powerful beings, endowed with sexual and reproductive agency and, for high-ranking women, replete with authority (*mana*) from the gods. Kauanui's analysis is focused on the radical transformations of the nineteenth-century kingdom. She and others have written about the equally profound changes in twentieth-century Hawai'i, reconfigured by Hawai'i's militarization, by the US Empire and the concurrent growth of mass tourism. This perpetuated an image of Hawai'i as a Pacific 'paradise', the feminization of the archipelago in tourist promotions focused on the alluring hula girl, and the eroticization of the islands for white heterosexual pleasure – all tropes which cloaked Hawai'i's pivotal significance in the geopolitics of the Second World War and as a continuing US military base. Teresia Teaiwa has dubbed this 'militourism'.[23]

Kauanui draws deep lessons from Hawaiian history for the contemporary struggles for sovereignty in Hawai'i and for decolonizing contemporary gender and sexual regimes. She criticizes the 2013 same-sex marriage act, passed after heated debate between Christian opponents, on the one hand, and groups such as Nā Mamo o Hawai'i, on the other, who pointed to same-sex cultural traditions as Indigenous to Hawai'i. Some have portrayed this law as coming 'full circle' back to ancient Hawai'i. Yet, for Kauanui, it instead perpetuates settler colonial continuity by assimilating same-sex relations to the terms of a patriarchal, proprietorial male–female marriage.[24] She seeks something beyond a continuation of a colonial biopolitics, what Jacqui Alexander has described as 'erotic autonomy'.[25] This entails a form of relationality vis-à-vis the land and sexuality that is not proprietary and celebrates an Indigenous corporeal, cultural, and spiritual presence.

In an old love chant composed for King Kalakaua (r. 1874–91) the land (*aina*) is likened to a lover. This is echoed in contemporary Hawaiian chants

---

23 See her essay on the perverse conjunction of Bikini atoll, site of US nuclear testing, and the bikini swimsuit – the 'atom bomb' of fashion, launched by Louis Réard in Paris 1946. Teresia Teaiwa, 'Bikinis and Other S/pacific/oceans', *Contemporary Pacific* 6, no. 1 (1994): 87–109.

24 Teaiwa, 'Bikinis and Other S/pacific/oceans', 186.

25 M. Jacqui Alexander, 'Erotic Autonomy as Politics of Decolonization: An Anatomy of the Feminist and State Practice in the Bahamas Tourist Economy', in *Feminist Genealogies, Colonial Legacies, Democratic Futures*, ed. M. Jacqui Alexander and Chandra Talpade (New York: Routledge, 1997), 63–100.

by modern musicians such as Israel Kamakawiwoʻole, Kealiʻi Reichel, and Halau Keʻalaokamaile in which the cliffs are sometimes likened to the shoulders of the lover and gushing waterfalls to sexual fluids. Creative expressions like this evoke a world where human sexuality is merged with the beauty and the fertility of the world and the cosmos. They articulate what Hawaiians call *ea*: 'the power and life force of interconnectedness among deities, ancestral forces, humans and all elements of the natural world'.[26]

Papua New Guinea: Persistence, Rupture, and Human Rights for Gender and Sexual Minorities

Unlike the Hawaiian archipelago where a common Indigenous language and culture prevails, Papua New Guinea is characterized by great linguistic and cultural diversity. It occupies the eastern half of the island of New Guinea, one of the world's largest islands, and smaller neighbouring islands. Papua New Guinea has 820 distinct living languages among its almost 10 million estimated inhabitants. (Tok Pisin is the main lingua franca.) Unlike Hawaiʻi, a state of the United States, Papua New Guinea is an independent country. But like Hawaiʻi, human sexual practices are often suffused with notions about the fertility of the world and of cosmic, sacred regeneration.

Papua New Guinea was one of the first places in the world where practitioners of the new field of anthropology studied local cultures, including their sexuality. The Polish-British anthropologist Bronisław Malinowski (1884–1942) conducted an ethnography of the Trobriand Islands in Papua New Guinea from 1914 to 1918, which exemplified the emergent practice of 'fieldwork' in anthropology, *in situ* observation over long periods, learning the local language, and trying to see from 'the native's point of view'.[27] His functionalist method, discerning the 'organic unity' of a culture, was displayed across many monographs, including studies of sexuality.[28] Sexologist Havelock Ellis celebrated him as the 'natural historian' of sexuality.[29] Malinowski, not averse to self-celebration, vaunted the superiority of his careful fieldwork against the speculations of 'armchair' anthropologists. He

---

26 Kauanui, *Paradoxes of Hawaiian Sovereignty*, 192.
27 Bronisław Malinowski, *The Sexual Lives of Savages in North-Western Melanesia* (1929; New York: Harcourt, Brace and World, 1932), 381.
28 Bronisław Malinowski, *Sex and Repression in Savage Society* (Cleveland, OH: Meridian, 1927); Malinowski, *Sexual Lives of Savages*.
29 Havelock Ellis, 'Preface', in Malinowski, *The Sexual Lives of Savages*, vii.

combined direct observation, conversations, interviews, photos, and recordings of dreams and myths. He challenged Freud's psychoanalytic analyses, particularly his claims for the universality of the Oedipus complex. Rather, Malinowski depicted a matrilineal society tracing descent through women; the mother's brother and not the father had authority over the son, conferring wealth and succession to rank. Rather than infantile male incestuous desire, as Freud had it, this family environment promoted a desire for power grounded in fear as young men vied for chiefly status. Malinowski also claimed Trobrianders denied physiological paternity: a baby was the conjoint creation of the mother's blood and the agency of a reincarnating ancestral spirit (*baloma*).[30] Fathers gave love and nurture, thus imparting an outward resemblance in their children.[31] Malinowski plotted a tension between mother right and father's love, especially pronounced for high-ranking male chiefs, such as those of the Tabalu subclan (*dala*) of Omarakana village where Malinowski pitched his tent.

In stark contrast with early European voyagers who witnessed sexual restraint in the western islands of Oceania, Malinowski assiduously documented how heterosexuality was celebrated in the Trobriands. From age five or six, children went off on excursions, independent of adult supervision, revelling in natural beauty, playing sensuous games, even imitating their parents making love at night. String figures with associated songs told bawdy stories: an ancestral woman with a gigantic clitoris, an ancestral man with a huge snaking penis. Adolescents, from around ten for girls and twelve for boys, were free to have sexual partners, often several in succession, in private trysts in shaded groves or in coral hollows. Serious couples retreated to a special house, taking turns on the bunks, or having intercourse discreetly at night. When a couple desired a long-term partnership, they proclaimed their marriage by sharing a meal together. Fathers were influential in opposing or approving marriages. Clans were exogamous, so sex within clans was considered incestuous, but unions should involve those of similar rank. The high-ranking *dala* of Tabalu inter-married with another high-ranking *dala* through reciprocal cross-cousin marriage. Marriage entailed mutual gifts flowing between the kin of the bride and groom.

Sexual unions were suffused with ideas of love, embracing romantic attraction and emotional attachment. Beauty for both sexes meant clean,

30 On the regeneration of matrilineal value/power, see Katherine Lepani, *Islands of Love, Islands of Risk* (Nashville, TN: Vanderbilt University Press, 2013).
31 Mark Mosko, *Ways of Baloma: Rethinking Magic and Kinship from the Trobriands* (Chicago: Hau Books, 2017).

glossy skin (bodily hair was shaved, including eyebrows), a full head of hair, a round face like a full moon, bright eyes, and teeth blackened with soot or betel nut juice. Moonlight, aromatic herbs, perfumed coconut oil, and ornamentation enhanced beauty, as for men and women who danced and sang at festivals such as *milamala*, celebrating the yam harvest when ancestral spirits returned. Erotic life followed the arc of seasons, phases of the moon, and the fertility of plants (such as valuable yams).

Men confided with Malinowski how they liked to make love, including as married partners. Pre-coital caresses involved biting lower lips (not kissing), nibbling eyelashes, and erotic scratching. Fellatio and mutual masturbation were rarer, preferably pre-coital. The preferred position for intercourse was for the man and woman to squat, directly facing each other, the woman resting her legs either on his hips or elbows. The man should wait for the woman to orgasm before he did and, mutually satiated, they should express loving endearments. In coitus, as in most other aspects of life, Malinowski discerned equality between men and women, despite gendered labour and the fact that only men were chiefs and voyagers in *kula* expeditions exchanging valuables. Men criticized how white men made love on top, inhibiting a woman's responsiveness. Beauty and desire were thought to wane with age, but long-lasting marriages might remain sexually active. Widows, widowers, and divorcees did not stay sexually quiescent. The island of Tuma, abode of ancestral spirits, was an erotic, perfumed paradise where no one needed to work.

Trobrianders' seeming 'sexual freedom' still entailed rules. Sexual excess or public displays were improper. Adultery, though frequent, was wrong, and if it infringed on the marriage of a high-ranking chief could occasion death. Since high-ranking chiefs were polygynous, this was a major proscription. (At the time of Malinowski's research, one high chief had twenty-four wives.) Male homosexuality and anal intercourse were thought repugnant, as this brought sex and faeces too close together.[32] Malinowski does not comment on sex between women. Incest, particularly between a brother and a sister, was *tabu*. From late childhood brothers and sisters eschewed physical proximity, eye contact and conversation, and any knowledge of their opposite siblings' sexual lives. As in Hawai'i, a canonical creation myth told of incest between a brother and a sister, who copulated many times, failed to drink or eat, and ultimately died in shame and remorse. In reflecting on this myth of

---

32 Mosko, *Ways of Baloma*, 377, 395–8.

'savage incest', Malinowski stressed how this reversal of accepted norms warned of the parlous consequences of incest.

After Malinowski's seminal work, other ethnographies of Papua New Guinea often rather chastely sequestered studies of sexuality in analyses of initiation rituals, pollution, or gender roles. But when HIV began spreading in epidemic waves across Papua New Guinea in the 1980s, anthropologists, biomedical specialists, epidemiologists, and public health professionals engaged in direct studies of sexual practices and knowledges across the country.[33] From this vast corpus I focus on two exemplary anthropological studies – Katherine Lepani with the Trobriand people and Gilbert Herdt with the Sambia people, his pseudonym for a group living in the Eastern Highlands of Papua New Guinea. They offer illuminating contrasts in Indigenous sexual values (pleasurable freedom versus anxious ritual regulation) and in patterns of persistence and rupture. But both studies sensitively consider individual and relational values in sexual lives.

Islands of Love, Islands of Risk by Katherine Lepani is a study of Trobriand Islanders in the context of the HIV epidemic in the early 2000s.[34] Married to a Trobriand man, Lepani challenges aspects of Malinowski's depiction of the Trobriands, dominated by the views of men and especially high-ranking men.[35] Instead, working with many female and male interlocutors across regional and rank divides, Lepani discerned strong continuities – women's expansive agency exercised through the value and practice of matriliny, the celebration of sexuality for both female and male adolescents, the pursuit of mutual pleasure in marriage, and the mutability of marriage in easy divorce. Christian influence had outlawed polygyny, so serial monogamy prevailed for most, though even some Christian chiefs remained defiantly polygynous.

From the late nineteenth century onwards, Trobrianders, like most people in the Milne Bay Province of Papua New Guinea, were exposed to diverse colonial agencies – traders and labour recruiters, planters, officials from the colonizing powers of Britain and Australia, and Christian missionaries from Samoa. Trobrianders were mostly converted to mainstream Christian denominations – Methodism and Catholicism – and despite recent reconversions to evangelical churches, most Trobrianders expressed a strong sense of

---

33 For example, National Sex and Reproduction Research Team (NSRRT) and Carol Jenkins, *National Study of Sexual and Reproductive Knowledge and Behaviour in Papua New Guinea* (Goroka: Papua New Guinea Institute of Medical Research, 1994).

34 Lepani, *Islands of Love, Islands of Risk*. The discussion that follows draws significantly from this book and her articles cited below.

35 See also Annette Weiner, *Women of Value, Men of Renown: New Perspectives in Trobriand Exchange* (Austin, TX: University of Texas Press, 1976).

continuity in their sexual and reproductive lives. Emblematic of these changes, imported cloth was incorporated alongside traditional banana leaf fibre bundles and skirts exchanged in the complex mortuary ceremonies (*sagali*) in which women play a central role.[36] These ceremonies ensure the movement of the dead to the island of Tuma as *baloma'*, spirits reborn as future children of the matrilineage, ensuring growth and cosmic regeneration. Inspired by a spiral dance performed by young children, and associated chants to an ancestral mother, Lepani represents this as a regenerative spiral, connecting past, present, and future, enacting a shared Indigenous ethos.

The 'islands of love' label generated by Malinowski, though locally criticized for its imperial exoticism, is still central to perceptions of Trobrianders and Papua New Guineans. The celebration of consensual and pleasurable heterosexuality, fundamental to forming and sustaining social life, persists, despite conversion to Christianity a century ago. Male and female homosexuality remains disapproved. Christianity has thus been profoundly Indigenized in the Trobriands, in contrast to the stark revolution in gender relations and sexuality which Kauanui charts for Hawai'i and which Herdt discerns for Sambia (see below).

With the advent of HIV in Papua New Guinea, especially from 1987, Trobriand sexual culture became a national concern, as a 'hot spot' in the public health response to the epidemic. Lepani's nuanced ethnography reveals how Trobrianders themselves interpreted HIV – grappling with the dissonances between an approach to sexuality which stressed danger and death rather than pleasure and fertility, and one that focused on individuals 'at risk' rather than relational persons. She clearly demonstrates how Trobrianders' understanding of HIV was profoundly influenced by pre-existing ideas of the body, of health and illness, of gender and sexuality. And though some outsiders called for the banning of the erotic dance *tapiokwa* for allegedly promoting sexual immorality, Lepani sees Trobrianders as sustaining a sex-positive culture through a reconceptualization of HIV prevention strategies. HIV was understood as manifesting symptoms akin to *sovasova* (incest) but could spread between persons (like other sexual diseases, *pokesa*). Rather than a bifurcated world in which Trobriand sexual life focuses on shared collective norms, relationality, and reciprocity, on the one hand, and biomedical public health in the context of HIV focuses on individuals, on the

---

36 Katherine Lepani, '*Doba* and Ephemeral Durability: The Enduring Material Value of Women's Work in the Trobriand Regenerative Economy', in *Sinuous Objects: Revaluing Women's Wealth in the Contemporary Pacific*, ed. Anna-Karina Hermkens and Katherine Lepani (Canberra: Australian National University Press, 2017), 37–59.

other, she argues that ideals of relationality and of individual autonomy are equally Indigenous.[37] Trobriand sexuality remains a powerful catalyst for exchange and reciprocity, creating and sustaining relations, not just mutual pleasure between living persons but the elemental divine power which regenerates life and the cosmos. Thus, there is here a strong sense of continuity between the 'old ways' and the 'new ways' in sexual life, rather than a sense of rupture.[38]

Gilbert Herdt's studies of Sambia sexuality in Papua New Guinea reveal a very different Indigenous configuration and pattern of transformation.[39] Herdt started research with the Sambia people in 1974, a year before Papua New Guinea became independent, and he continued ethnographic work over several decades. He entered a region where earlier anthropologists had reported a pervasive 'sexual antagonism' between men and women, endemic warfare and the celebration of male warriorhood, staunch patrilineal and patrilocal norms, pronounced male domination, and profound gender segregation. Herdt revealed deeper philosophies underlying both quotidian and ritual sexual practices. Fundamental was the notion that female and male bodies were ontologically different, in both their corporeal essences and their maturation, and that girls matured naturally and more quickly, generating the potent, polluting blood of menstruation and childbirth, while boys needed to ingest semen through fellatio with unmarried older men to become men. Semen expelled emasculating maternal blood, fostering mature masculinity and warrior capacity. Boys and younger men were fed the semen of older men in a complex series of ritual initiations starting from the age of seven through to early adulthood as married men and fathers. Ancestral spirits were crucial presences throughout, their voices heard in resonating flutes which symbolized phallic potency and seductive masculine beauty.

---

37 Katherine Lepani, "'I am still a young girl if I want": Relational Personhood and Individual Autonomy in the Trobriand Islands', *Oceania* 85, no. 1 (2015): 51; see also Holly Wardlow, *Wayward Women: Sexuality and Agency in a New Guinea Society* (Berkeley, CA: University of California Press, 2006).

38 See also Mosko, *Ways of Baloma;* Margaret Jolly, 'Animating the Ancestors in the Anthropology of the Trobriands', *Asia Pacific Journal of Anthropology* 20, no. 4 (2018): 362–8.

39 Gilbert H. Herdt, *Guardians of the Flutes: Idioms of Masculinity* (New York: McGraw-Hill, 1981); Gilbert H. Herdt, *The Sambia: Ritual and Gender in New Guinea* (Fort Worth, TX: Holt Rinehart and Winston, 1987). The discussion that follows draws significantly from these and from Herdt's other publications cited in the following text.

Herdt initially called this 'ritualized homosexuality',[40] but from the start stressed that homoerotic practice did not entail a homosexual identity for Sambia men but was rather a necessary precursor to heterosexual relations and fatherhood. His later phrase for this was 'boy insemination'.[41] These were secret, sacral rites, hidden from women and non-initiates. Pleasure and terror combined. He connected the domination of older men over younger boys with the forceful domination of men over women. Pre-marital heterosexuality was forbidden, and marital sex was an anxious affair, with persisting fears of the loss of bodily fluids and of mutual pollution – exacerbated if men were polygynous. Marital sex was ritualized, rule-bound, and saturated by taboos which prescribed the timing and duration of oral sex and later vaginal sex and their meanings and purposes. Rare in this period, Herdt engaged both women and men in conversations about their sexual pleasure. Whereas men saw oral sex from their wives as especially pleasurable, women preferred vaginal sex, and sometimes linked their erotic desires with the sensuality of breastfeeding.[42] In discussing Sambia sexual lives, Herdt writes not just of the Sambia as a whole, but also of named individuals – men, women, and an intersex person. He portrays initiation rituals not just as collective cultural performances but also as practices which engaged the subjectivities of individuals and indeed his own subjectivity.

In his latest publication on the Sambia, Herdt describes the profound ruptures in Sambia sexual lives over the four decades since his first research.[43] Pacification, colonization, out-migration, primary schooling, and especially conversion to Seventh-day Adventist Christianity combined to transform the highly ritualized and regulated male cult into non-ritualized, more individualistic sexual relations. The ritual homoerotic practices of the past were abandoned as sinful while heterosexual courtship, romance, and new monogamous Christian marriages celebrated a modern, mutual intimacy between couples. As Sambia now say, husbands and wives 'cuddle under one blanket'. Oral sex, once universal between husbands and wives, has largely disappeared from intimate relations. Women now have far more

---

40 Gilbert H. Herdt, ed., *Ritualized Homosexuality in Melanesia* (Berkeley, CA: University of California Press, 1984); see also Bruce Knauft, 'Whatever Happened to Ritualized Homosexuality?', *Annual Review of Sex Research* 14 (2003): 137–59.
41 Gilbert H. Herdt, 'Introduction', in *Ritualized Homosexuality in Melanesia*, 2nd ed. (Berkeley, CA: University of California Press, 1993), vii–xliv.
42 Gilbert Herdt and Robert J. Stoller, *Intimate Communications: Erotics and the Study of Culture* (New York: Columbia University Press, 1990).
43 Gilbert Herdt, 'Intimate Consumption and New Sexual Subjects among the Sambia of Papua New Guinea', *Oceania* 89, no. 1 (2019): 36–67.

agency in choosing partners and husbands and in their sexual and reproductive lives. Still, some past fears, and especially fears of mutual pollution, haunt the present and were reanimated by the appearance of HIV and what was called 'sikAIDS' in the Sambia Valley, as across many regions of Papua New Guinea, from the late 1980s.

So among the Sambia, in contrast to the Trobriands, there is little sense of continuity in sexual life but rather a pervasive sense of a sharp rupture between the Indigenous and the exogenous, the non-Christian and the Christian, the old ways and the new ways. Contemporary Sambia people deny the Indigeneity of male homoerotic practice and perceive male homosexuality as *ol somting blong waet man tasol* ('a practice only of white men' in Tok Pisin). But studies of sexuality in the national capital Port Moresby suggest that, across its diverse terrain, Papua New Guinea evinces greater sexual and gender fluidity than such a characterization allows. In a pathbreaking study, Christine Stewart shows the critical influence of colonial laws introduced from Australia in criminalizing both sex work and consensual relations between men.[44] She documents the chilling severity of punishment for both 'prostitution' and 'sodomy' in the colonial courts and those of independent Papua New Guinea. Based on media analysis and life history interviews with women selling sex, men who were having sex with other men, and transgender women, she documents their extreme persecution in everyday life and work, in violent punishments by both police and *raskol* gangs, and in vilification by the media. Deploying Foucauldian insights about the disciplining of deviants, she notes the power of middle-class and Christian norms in relegating these people to states of marginality and abjection.

Timothy Leach developed an innovative project based on long-term participatory research and advocacy in the capital of Port Moresby with stigmatized gender and sexual minorities.[45] He explores how human rights are understood and experienced by people living with HIV, men with diverse sexualities, and transgender women. He examines the emergence and progress of two organizations established by these communities – Igat Hope and Kapul Champions – and how they have limited the impacts of HIV on their members and others and promoted the human rights of their constituents. Leach consummately reflects on his own history with these organizations,

---

44 Christine Stewart, *Name, Shame and Blame: Criminalising Consensual Sex in Papua New Guinea* (Canberra: Australian National University Press, 2014).

45 Timothy Leach, 'Human Rights of People Living with HIV, Men with Diverse Sexualities and Transgender Women in PNG' (PhD thesis, Australian National University, 2021).

the community movements which built them, and his roles as both advocate and researcher. Grounded in sensitive participant observation and anonymized oral histories and interviews, his research documents regular violations of the human rights of his interlocutors but simultaneously their potent efforts to fight back. His interlocutors Indigenized global human rights discourse in a dynamic way, situating it in the terrain of inclusive relationality and shared kinship rather than of isolated individuals. Here, we see another move in connecting old ways and new ways.

Samoa: Promiscuity/Chastity, Mead-Freeman Controversy, and Decolonizing Sexuality

Finally, I turn to Samoa – or should I say the two Samoas, the independent state of that name, and American Samoa, still an unincorporated territory of the United States. Like Hawai'i, Samoa is characterized by a complex intersection of rank and gender which structures sexual life. Here as well, precolonial configurations have been dramatically influenced by colonization and especially Christianity, initially through the interdenominational Protestant London Missionary Society beginning in 1830.

In pre-Christian times the *ali'i*, men and women seen to be direct descendants of the gods, were far more elevated. They perpetuated their distinction by selective breeding, as male chiefs established alliances with other powerful families through polygynous marriages with high-ranking virgins (*taupou*) whom they manually deflowered in a public ritual and then made pregnant. Her virginity was seen as a 'gift' to honour her high-ranking husband.[46] Male *ali'i* were served by a male class of *tulāfale'*, orators, master builders, and tattooists. High-ranking women were also powerful chiefs with their own attendants, while in pre-Christian times there were female deities, priests, and spirit mediums. After marriage, a high-ranking woman would typically move to the village of her husband, but she never lost her status as a powerful daughter and sister in her natal village and might return there if her husband married another wife. A low-ranking woman was deflowered privately but also typically moved to her husband's village while her sexual and reproductive life was less constrained by strategic marriages. Women who were no

---

46 Penelope Schoeffel, 'Sexual Morality in Samoa and Its Historical Transformations', in *Sexualities in Anthropology: A Reader*, ed. Andrew P. Lyons and Harriet D. Lyons (Maldon, MA: Wiley Blackwell, 2011), 222–31.

longer virgins were far more sexually free.[47]

Kinship in Samoa was and is consanguineal: each descent group (*aiga*) recognizes founding ancestors, typically a brother–sister pair, and distinguishes between those women and men who descended from the sororal descent line (*tamafafine*) and those men and women descended from the fraternal descent line (*tamatāne*). In the past, the first were the *ali'i* and the second the *tulāfale*. Their relation was described as a *feagaiga*, a contract foundational to an idealized order of dignity and respect.

Significantly, this meaning of *feagaiga* has disappeared but this same word is still used to describe the relation of sister and brother. Brothers are vulnerable to the divine power of their sisters. In childhood and adolescence girls are given more domestic comforts and do lighter indoor work while boys do harder outdoor work. This distinction is accompanied by differential restrictions – boys roam freely, while girls are more sequestered and as adolescents are accompanied by chaperones. In the past strict avoidance characterized relations between brothers and sisters – no touching, no talking, and minimal interaction, lest the brother be divinely harmed. A brother should safeguard his sister's virginity and, if she were discovered in an illicit sexual relationship, he could beat her and take vengeance on her lover. The strength of these prohibitions and protocols has diminished but not disappeared.[48]

Although several Samoan creation stories recount divine brother–sister unions, in contrast to ancient Hawai'i, incest between living brothers and sisters was and is a terrible crime which would occasion divine retribution. This pivotal sibling relationship was extended to those linked as *tamafafine* and *tamatāne'*, who should mutually respect each other, with those from the fraternal line offering deference to those from the spiritually dangerous sororal line. Significantly, with the advent of Christianity the notion and value of *feagaiga* has been extended to the relation between the pastor and his congregation: he is a 'sister' to the congregation who is his 'brother'.[49] Hence the *feagaiga* assumed a more Judeo-Christian inflection as a covenant,

47 See Penelope Schoeffel, 'The Samoan Concept of *Feagaiga* and its Transformations', in *Tonga and Samoa: Images of Gender and Polity*, ed. Judith Huntsman (Christchurch, New Zealand: Macmillan Brown Centre for Pacific Studies, University of Canterbury, 1995), 85–109; Schoeffel, 'Sexual Morality in Samoa', 225.

48 Schoeffel, 'The Samoan Concept of *Feagaiga*'.

49 Schoeffel, 'The Samoan Concept of *Feagaiga*'; Latu Latai, 'Covenant Keepers: A History of Samoan (LMS) Missionary Wives in the Western Pacific from 1839–1979' (PhD thesis, Australian National University, 2015); Latu Latai, 'Changing Covenants in Samoa? From Brothers and Sisters to Husbands and Wives', *Oceania* 85, no. 1 (2015): 92–104.

symbolizing that between God and humanity created by Christ's supreme sacrifice.

Over time the *feagaiga* relation between *ali'i* and *tulafale* has become more muted and that between brother and sister more relaxed. But a complex relation between rank, gender, and sexuality persists. Serge Tcherkézoff consummately argues that Western interpretations of Samoa have been distorted by a binary view of gender focused on the conjugal relation of husband and wife, that Samoans privilege the brother–sister bond over the husband–wife, and that there is no singular notion of 'woman' in Samoa. The unmarried woman as sister is not a *fafine*; this term is reserved for wives and for females in animal reproduction. Its sexual connotations would be insulting to such women who are rather described as girls (*teine*) or ladies (*tama'ita'i*). When a woman marries, she still retains formal membership and status of her *'āiga'*, but as a wife she typically has no status in the female decision-making bodies of her husband's village, while low-ranking women resident in their husband's village, *nofotane*, often undertake hard labour, preparing food and serving their husband's sisters.[50]

Eurocentric premises about gender and sexuality have also pervaded discussion of *fa'afafine*. They have typically been seen as biological males who act in 'the manner of women' (which is what the term means) in their comportment, dress, and labour, and as lovers of Samoan men rather than other Samoan *fa'afafine*. Rev. George Pratt censored *fa'afafine* from the first edition of his grammar and dictionary of the Samoan language and the Samoan translation of the Bible (both in 1862). But in the second edition of his grammar and dictionary, Pratt included both *fa'fafine* and *fa'atane* with derogatory definitions and allusions. So like Hawaiian *aikane* and *mahu*, these are ancient words. Some scholars have suggested that, given the equality between men and women in traditional Samoan society and the powerful female rulers in its history, who were sometimes said to 'act as men' (*fa'atane*), those who wished to identify as women were honoured.[51]

This background provides the context for the (in)famous controversy about Samoan sexuality involving the American anthropologist Margaret Mead (1901–78) and the New Zealand anthropologist Derek Freeman

---

50 Serge Tcherkézoff, 'The Illusion of Dualism in Samoa: "Brothers-and-Sisters" are Not "Men-and-Women"', in *Gendered Anthropology*, ed. Teresa Del Valle (London: Routledge and Kegan Paul, 1993), 54–87; see also Kalissa Alexeyeff, 'Cinderella of the South Seas? Virtuous Victims, Empowerment and Other Fables of Development Feminism', *Women's Studies International Forum* 80 (2020): 1–9.

51 Reevan Dolgoy, '"Hollywood" and the Emergence of a Fa'afafine Social Movement', in *Gender on the Edge: Transgender, Gay, and Other Pacific Islanders*, ed. Niko Besnier and

(1916–2001). In 1927 Margaret Mead published a popular book, *Coming of Age in Samoa*,[52] suggesting a less traumatic transition to adulthood than American teenagers, with greater sexual freedom for both adolescent women and men. Her ethnographic research suggested that young women engaged in sexual adventures but secreted them from their elders. Young men were more public in aggressive heterosexual competition for young women. Five years after Mead's death, her analysis of Samoan adolescence, gender, and sexuality was denounced by Derek Freeman. He countered that adolescence in Samoa was instead 'full of conflict, aggression, and stress',[53] that the sexual culture of Samoa was tightly restrictive, and that pre-marital virginity was highly valued, for Samoan women at least.[54] His second book claimed that Mead had been 'hoaxed' into believing the testimony about women's nocturnal sexual adventures told by two young women, Fa'apua'a Fa'amū and Fofoa, while Mead was holidaying with them in March 1926.[55] Freeman's books, strategically published after Mead's death, generated a 'media feeding frenzy',[56] especially in the United States, where her distinguished reputation as a pioneering anthropologist, woman of science, and public intellectual was diminished, though others suggested there was little evidence for Freeman's claims, and offered a spirited defence of Mead.[57]

From the huge popular and media debate, I distil five main lines of contention. First, there are many contested details about the 'alleged hoaxing'. Freeman's allegations were based on an interview with Fa'apua'a in 1987 when she was eighty-six years of age and two subsequent interviews. Discrepancies between her three interviews suggest her memories were uncertain and she was neither acknowledged nor cited as a key informant by Mead, whose claims about adolescent sexuality rather

---

Kalissa Alexeyoff (Honolulu: University of Hawai'i Press, 2014), 56–72; Niel Gunson, 'Sacred Women Chiefs and Female "Headmen" in Polynesian History', *Journal of Pacific History* 22, no. 3 (1987): 141–2. Dan Taulapapa McMullin, 'Fa'afafine Their Story', in Yuki Kihara, *Paradise Camp*, ed. Nathalie King (Wellington: Creative New Zealand, Toi Aotearoa and Thames and Hudson Australia, 2022), 38–41.

52 Margaret Mead, *Coming of Age in Samoa* (New York: William Morrow, 1927).

53 Paul Shankman, 'The Mead-Freeman Controversy', in *International Encyclopedia of Anthropology*, ed. Hilary Callan (Hoboken, NJ: Wiley Blackwell, 2018), 3881–4.

54 Derek Freeman, *Margaret Mead and Samoa: The Making and Unmaking of an Anthropological Myth* (Cambridge, MA: Harvard University Press, 1983).

55 Derek Freeman, *The Fateful Hoaxing of Margaret Mead: An Historical Analysis of Her Samoan Research* (Boulder, CO: Westview, 1999).

56 Shankman, 'The Mead-Freeman Controversy', 3882.

57 Paul Shankman, 'The "Fateful Hoaxing" of Margaret Mead: A Cautionary Tale', *Current Anthropology* 54, no. 1 (2013): 51–70. This last article includes responses by Leasiolagi Malama Meleisea and Penelope Schoeffel, Nancy McDowell, and Virginia Yans.

primarily came from interviews with twenty-five Samoan girls on the island of Ta'ū.[58] Close examination of the unpublished interviews in Freeman's archive held in San Diego and of Mead's own fieldnotes and letters leads most commentators to conclude that all this 'shows Freeman manipulating evidence, misrepresenting quotations, and rigging interview questions – [via his unpublished archives] Freeman has become a damning witness against himself'.[59]

Second, there are debates about the significance of the *taupou*, the ceremonial virgin whose chastity was protected by a village and whose virginity was publicly tested by manual defloration when she married a high-ranking Samoan man. Freeman saw this traditional figure as emblematic of the value of virginity for *all* Samoan women; Mead saw it as important primarily for high-ranking women, not for most of lesser rank. In any case, *taupou* marriages had almost disappeared by the late nineteenth century with colonial and Christian pressures.

Third are debates about how Samoan conversion to Christianity, promoted by Samoans of high rank, reconfigured gender and sexual relations. As elsewhere across Oceania, Christian missionaries privileged the dyadic relation of husband and wife and promoted ideas of the domestic wife–mother. As Latu Latai has shown in his revolutionary history of high-ranking Samoans on evangelism in the mid-nineteenth century, the messages of white Christianity were early on creolized with *fa'a Samoa* (Samoan customs/ways).[60] As Leasiolagi Malama Meleisea and Penelope Schoeffel observe, 'Ancient norms of aristocratic virginity were gradually conflated with Christian doctrines of female purity which enjoin pre-marital chastity upon all unmarried girls.'[61]

Fourth are deep questions about the relations between nature and culture and individual and society, binaries which have saturated much Western scholarship. Mead was very interested in the interaction of nature and nurture, as can be seen in her later studies of gender in Papua New Guinea. Freeman's embrace of ethology and sociobiology entailed a faith in the

---

58 Shankman, 'The Mead-Freeman Controversy', 2.

59 Virginia Yans, response to Shankman, 'The "Fateful Hoaxing" of Margaret Mead', 66–7.

60 Latu Latai, 'From Open *Fale* to Mission Houses: Negotiating the Boundaries of "Domesticity" in Samoa', in *Divine Domesticities: Christian Paradoxes in Asia and the Pacific*, ed. Hyaeweol Choi and Margaret Jolly (Canberra: Australian National University Press, 2014), 299–324; Latai, 'Covenant Keepers'.

61 Meleisea and Schoeffel, response to Shankman, 'The "Fateful Hoaxing" of Margaret Mead', 66.

Oceanic Sexualities: Persistence, Change, Resistance

universal character of a biology of aggression and male domination, while his focus on the individual testimony of an elderly Samoan woman ignores a broader cultural analysis.[62]

Fifth and finally, the controversy can be situated in the longer and broader genealogy of foreign representations of Oceanic sexuality. As Tcherkézoff argues, Mead's interpretation of Samoan 'permissiveness' was potently influenced by earlier framings of Polynesian sexuality as untrammelled.[63] The success of *Coming of Age in Samoa* made Mead the greatest twentieth-century proponent of this myth.[64] Shankman concludes, by contrast, that 'Samoan sexual conduct was neither as restrictive as Freeman asserted nor as permissive as Mead suggested.'[65] Significantly, in this book, Mead only valorized heterosexual permissiveness, did not mention either *fa'afafine* or *fa'atane*, and used derogatory words such as 'pervert' and 'freak'.

Both the permissive and restrictive views have perpetuated an anthropological optic on Samoan sexuality which has been consummately challenged by Samoan scholars, novelists, poets, and artists. Albert Wendt, a distinguished scholar, poet, playwright, and novelist, has written a suite of essays and novels which offer a compelling Indigenous view of sexuality, kinship, and rank in past and contemporary Samoa, in the islands, and in the diaspora. He believes 'our quest should not be for a revival of our past cultures but for the creation of new cultures which are free from the taint of colonialism and based firmly in our own pasts'.[66] Wendt's novel, *The Mango's Kiss*, features a hybrid anthropologist Mardrek Freemeade, from Harvard University, who is hosted by Samoan pastor Mauta. Freemeade is also a medical doctor and saves the life of Mauta's wife Lalaga. Despite this debt, Mauta becomes increasingly angry with the anthropologist's performance of scientific objectivity, 'standing apart ... watching and not allowing anyone too close', and his 'inescapable voice' and 'irrefutable opinions' about 'the Samoans and their fascinating way of life'. Freemeade both celebrates *fa'a Samoa* and sees it as eviscerated by foreign things and capitalist values. Mauta sees Freemeade regularly disappearing at night and when he hears that

---

62 Serge Tcherkézoff, 'Is Anthropology about Individual Agency or Culture? Or Why "Old Derek" is Doubly Wrong', *Journal of the Polynesian Society* 110, no. 1 (2001): 59–78, at 62.

63 Tcherkézoff, 'A Reconsideration of the Role of Polynesian Women'.

64 Tcherkézoff, *Le mythe occidental de la sexualité polynésienne*.

65 Shankman, 'The Mead-Freeman Controversy', 3.

66 Albert Wendt, 'Towards a New Oceania', *Mana* 1, no. 1 (1976): 49–60, at 53. See also Albert Wendt, *The Mango's Kiss: A Novel* (Auckland: Vintage, 2003).

he has been asking young people about sex and indulging in the pleasures of 'being with other men', he summarily banishes Freemeade.[67]

Sia Figiel's novels explore Samoan sexuality from the viewpoint of an adolescent woman.[68] Her fiery poetry fights back against prurient visions of Polynesian women by tourists and film crews. Noumea Simi, later a prominent official in the Samoan government, wrote an excoriating poem, 'What are we', offering an explicit challenge to both Mead and Freeman. She protests about being guineafowls for 'slit-minded brain-washers': 'Leave us alone palagi [white] man'.[69]

A less full-frontal response is offered in a collection of essays and poems by writers and poets from Samoa and across Oceania written in response to an address by a revered cultural custodian and head of state in Samoa, Tui Atua Tupua Tamasese Ta'isi Efi. He suggests Indigenous religion has been diminished to whispers about ancestral deities and spirits, but that they embody the same divine power as the Christian God. Moreover, Indigenous religion was explicit about sexual pleasure, considered it sacred, and evinced no shame about naked bodies. Against human hubris he celebrates the equivalence of humans with other living creatures and with the animated world of earth and the sky, embracing all cosmic life.[70]

Another facet to this reinterpretation and reintegration of tradition can be seen in modern discussions by *fa'afafine*. The visual and performance artist Yuki Kihara, herself a *fa'afafine*, writes:

> As an artist and a *fa'afafine* (in this case a 'Pacific island woman of transgender experience'), the idea of beauty and harmony across the Pacific and specifically to Sāmoa is possessed through a dual combination of both male and

---

67 Wendt, *The Mango's Kiss: A Novel*.

68 Sia Figiel, *Where We Once Belonged* (Auckland: Pasifika, 1996); Sia Figiel, *Free Love* (Auckland: Little Island Press, 2018).

69 The first part of her poem reads:

> Do we know what we are / Mebbe mebbe not / Some palagi wommin / say we the childrun of free luv / shud be examples to prudish societies / But some palagi man / calls hisself a Free man / says No! / we the child run of violence / cause we play war on cricket pitches / Dis Free man even say / we are liars / but only to Mead and not to him / and dat is why his word is god's / for he alone know what we are

> Noumea Simi, 'What Are We?', in *Sails of Dawn=La folau ole vaveao: Poems* (Apia, Samoa: Samoa Observer, 1992), 46.

70 Tui Atua Tupua Tamaesese Ta'isi Efi, 'Whispers and Vanities in Samoan Indigenous Religious Culture', in *Whispers and Vanities: Samoan Indigenous Knowledge and Religion*, ed. Tui Atua Tupua Tamasese Ta'isi Tupuloa Tufuga Efi et al. (Wellington: Huia, 2014), 11–42.

female energy. Hence, the reason why people like myself are allowed to exist within the context of my Sāmoan culture is for living in the *vā* or space between men and women ... Through Sāmoa's encounter with introduced religion, colonialism and globalization, the dual energy has been challenged by the western binary opposition of gender and sexuality. My *Fa'afafine* series exposes and shatters these colonial constructions imposed upon many Indigenous cultures in the Pacific.[71]

Kihara's exposure and shattering of colonial constructions are most direct in an early triptych where she appropriates and subverts the figures of the 'dusky maiden' of the Pacific and Odalisques in European art traditions and colonial photography. In *Fa'afafine: In the Manner of a Woman*, Kihara consummately uses her own body. She offers critical and satirical assessments of colonial projections of gender and race in Samoa, but also honours ancestral values and Samoan spirituality in embodied performances and photographs. These simultaneously witness the past traumas of colonization and the contemporary challenges of disasters and climate crisis, as in a series of photographs where she appears as Salome, dressed in a tightly corseted black Victorian mourning gown.[72] Her work *Paradise Camp*, mounted at the Venice Biennale in 2022 before travelling to Sydney and Samoa, is designed simultaneously to subvert European myths of paradise in Oceania and to play creatively with the encounter between the gender and sexual regimes of Samoa and Europe. A suite of photographs staged with *fa'afafine* re-enact several scenes from Paul Gauguin's Tahitian paintings: expressly designed to empower *fa'afafine* and all Oceanic people who live 'beyond the binary', it also celebrates Kihara's *fa'afafine* ancestors.[73] She makes clear that she wants to be understood in Indigenous terms, rather than be labelled with Euro-American vocabulary, whether third gender, transgender, or LGBTIQ +. Those frames, as much as studies of heteronormative sexuality in Oceania, can reproduce an imperial lens.

---

71 Cited in Erica Wolf, 'Shigeyuki Kihara's *Fa'a fafine: In a Manner of a Woman*: The Photographic Theatre of Cross-cultural Encounter', *Pacific Arts* 10, no. 2 (2010): 23–33, at 24.

72 See Margaret Jolly, 'Spiralling Visions: The Decolonial Oceanic Arts of Yuki Kihara and Taloi Havini in the Anthropocene', in *Resurgence: Decolonizing the Anthropocene, Emerging Indigenous Futures*, ed. Margaret Jolly, Siobhan McDonnell, and Tammy Tabe, forthcoming.

73 Yuki Kihara, *Paradise Camp by Yuki Kihara*, ed. Nathalie King (Wellington: Creative New Zealand, Toi Aotearoa with Thames and Hudson, 2022). See also Dan Taulapapa McMullin and Yuki Kihara, *Samoan Queer Lives* (Auckland: Little Island, 2018).

Conclusion

In their path-breaking volume, Niko Besnier and Kalissa Alexeyeff argued that understanding Oceanic sexualities means appreciating not only intimate personal and domestic lives but also the wider world and how the region has been dramatically reconfigured in the geopolitics of colonialism, Christian conversion, and contemporary globalization.[74] Through our travels across time and space we have seen how true this is as Oceanic peoples in Hawai'i, Papua New Guinea, and Samoa have navigated old and new ways in their sexual lives, sometimes celebrating continuity between past and present, sometimes coping with rupture. Moreover, we have seen how the 'wider world' for Oceanic peoples is not just conceived in secular political terms but in a world cosmologically conceived, where sexuality might be seen as divine rather than shameful and as being crucial to the generation and regeneration of the world.[75] Hopefully navigating the futures of Oceanic sexualities will be a smoother voyage: Oceanic people often proclaim the past is ahead of them and not behind.

Further Reading

Camacho, Keith. 'Homomilitarism: The Same-Sex Erotics of the US Empire in Guam and Hawai'i'. *Radical History Review* 123 (2015): 144–75.

Côté, James. 'Was Mead Wrong about Coming of Age in Samoa? An Analysis of the Mead/Freeman Controversy for Scholars of Adolescence and Human Development'. *Journal of Youth and Adolescence* 21 (1992): 499–527.

Figiel, Sia. *Free Love*. Auckland: Little Island, 2018.

They Who Do Not Grieve. Auckland: Random House, 1999.

Grimshaw, Patricia. *Paths of Duty: American Missionary Wives in Nineteenth-Century Hawaii*. Honolulu: University of Hawai'i Press, 1989.

Holmes, Lowell D. *Quest for the Real Samoa: The Mead/Freeman Controversy and Beyond*. South Hadley, MA: Bergin and Garvey, 1987.

Jolly, Margaret. '*Braed Praes* in Vanuatu: Both Gifts and Commodities'. *Oceania* (special issue: *Gender and Person in Oceania*, ed. Anna–Karina Hermkens, Rachel Morgain and John Taylor) 85, no. 1 (2015): 63–78.

'Contested Paradise: Dispossession and Repossession in Hawai'i'. *The Contemporary Pacific* (special issue: *Repossessing Paradise*, ed. Kalissa Alexeyeff and Siobhan McDonnell) 30, no. 2 (2018): 355–78.

'Damming the Rivers of Milk? Fertility, Sexuality, and Modernity in Melanesia and Amazonia'. In *Gender in Amazonia and Melanesia: An Exploration of the Comparative*

---

74 Niko Besnier and Kalissa Alexeyeff, eds., *Gender on the Edge: Transgender, Gay and Other Pacific Islanders* (Honolulu: University of Hawai'i Press, 2014).

75 See Ravulo, 'Exploring the Role of Sexuality'.

Oceanic Sexualities: Persistence, Change, Resistance

Method, ed. Tom Gregor and Donald Tuzin, 175–206. Berkeley, CA: University of California Press, 2001.

'From Point Venus to Bali Ha'i: Eroticism and Exoticism in Representations of the Pacific'. In *Sites of Desire, Economies of Pleasure: Sexualities in Asia and the Pacific*, ed. Lenore Manderson and Margaret Jolly, 99–122. Chicago: University of Chicago Press, 1997.

Kame'eleihiwa, Lilikalā. *Nā Wāhine Kapu: Divine Hawaiian Women*. Honolulu: 'Ai Pohaku, 1999.

Native Land and Foreign Desires: Pehea Lā E Pono Ai? How Shall We Live in Harmony. Honolulu: Bishop Museum, 1992.

Kauanui, J. Kēhaulani. *Hawaiian Blood: Colonialism and the Politics of Sovereignty and Indigeneity*. Durham, NC: Duke University Press, 2008.

Linnekin, Jocelyn. *Sacred Queens and Women of Consequence: Rank, Gender and Colonialism in the Hawaiian Islands*. Ann Arbor, MI: University of Michigan Press, 1990.

Orans, Martin. *Not Even Wrong: Margaret Mead, Derek Freeman and the Samoans*. Novato, CA: Chandler and Sharp, 1996.

Osorio, Jonathan Kay Kamakawiwo'ole. *Dismembering Lahui: A History of the Hawaiian Nation to 1887*. Honolulu: University of Hawai'i Press, 2002.

Schoeffel, Penelope. 'Daughters of Sina: A Study of Gender, Status and Power in Western Samoa'. PhD thesis, Australian National University, 1979.

'Representing *Fa'afafine*: Sex, Socialization and Gender Identity in Samoa'. In *Gender on the Edge: Transgender, Gay and Other Pacific Islanders*, ed. Niko Besnier and Kalissa Alexeyeff, 73–90. Honolulu: University of Hawai'i Press, 2014.

Silva, Noenoe K. *Aloha Betrayed: Native Hawaiian Resistance to American Colonialism*. Durham, NC: Duke University Press, 2004.

Spiro, Melford E. *Oedipus in the Trobriands*. Chicago: University of Chicago Press, 1982.

Tengan, Ty P. Kāwika. *Native Men Remade: Gender and Nation in Contemporary Hawai'i*. Durham, NC: Duke University Press, 2008.

Trask, Haunani-Kay. 'Lovely Hula Hands: Corporate Tourism and the Prostitution of Hawaiian Culture'. In *From a Native Daughter: Colonialism and Sovereignty in Hawai'i*, 179–97. Monroe, ME: Common Courage, 1993.

Wardlow, Holly. 'Paradoxical Intimacies: The Christian Creation of the Huli Domestic Sphere'. In *Divine Domesticities: Christian Paradoxes in Asia and the Pacific*, ed. Hyaeweol Choi and Margaret Jolly, 325–44. Canberra: Australian National University Press, 2014.

Wendt, Albert. *The Adventures of Vela*. Wellington: Huia, 2009.

Leaves of the Banyan Tree. Auckland: Longman Paul, 1979.

Sons for the Return Home. Auckland: Longman Paul, 1973.

Williamson, David. *The Heretic: Based on the Life of Derek Freeman*. Melbourne: Penguin Books, 1996.

Young, Michael W. *Malinowski: Odyssey of an Anthropologist, 1884–1920*. New Haven, CT: Yale University Press, 2004.

ed. *The Ethnography of Malinowski: The Trobriand Islands, 1915–18*. London: Routledge and Kegan Paul, 1979.

II
Sexuality in Buddhist Traditions

KALI NYIMA CAPE

Buddhist sexualities range from celibacy, to altruistic sex, to tantric sexuality in India, the historical birthplace of Buddhism, and in Tibet. Buddhism emerged from the life and teaching of Siddhartha Guatama, a historical person who lived sometime between the early fifth and sixth century BCE. He renounced sex, wealth, and family life to go on a spiritual quest that led to his enlightenment, that is, insight into how things really are. He came to be known as the Buddha, which means 'the awakened one'. He taught that a path of liberation from human suffering could be achieved by living morally and searching for enlightenment through contemplation. The teachings of the Buddha were not written down during his life, but were passed on by oral tradition. The scriptures that make up Buddhist canonical literature came centuries later, recording the Buddha's teachings and stories about his life. Thereafter, Buddhist scriptures continued to be developed through Buddha-voiced texts from other figures regarded as enlightened or divine, and through commentarial literature, translations, and scriptural revelations that carried Buddhism into the international context. Over the centuries divergent traditions developed as different communities and religious thinkers emphasized different texts, rules, and practices.

Before beginning to define Buddhist sexualities, we will pause and consider the term 'Buddhism'. Here, 'Buddhism' refers to religious, philosophical, and cultural traditions that have taken varied forms ranging across geographical regions, historical periods, and languages. To think of Buddhism as a single tradition in its many forms in the pan-Asian context is an idea that can be traced back to the eighteenth century.[1] In the modern period, it has been interpreted as a religion comparable with other religions and with modern science, a definition that neglects significant cultural elements.

In Buddhism, attitudes towards sexual activity are culturally embedded, and as this chapter demonstrates, they vary dramatically based on the country, period, genre, and context. Yet, even contradicting arguments for Buddhist sexualities have something in common: the regulation and control of sexuality for common purposes, whether it be via celibacy or religious sexuality. All the arguments for Buddhist sexualities that will be addressed here have been conducted primarily within the context of heteronormativity and androcentrism, where women are subordinates, with rare exceptions. Also, for Buddhists, the regulation of sexuality was often about the regulation of other things. Whether it be attention to regulating mental states, increasing the life force, or cultivating harmony within the community, sexuality was not an end to itself, but instead an instrument for harnessing other forces.

The Problem with Sex

There is not one uniform set of moral imperatives shaping Buddhist sexualities.[2] Yet an important place to begin to define them is in Buddhist critiques of desire, sexuality, and reproduction found in the *Vinaya*. The *Vinaya*, the monastic discipline literature written in the Pāli language, is a cornerstone of Buddhist sexual ethics, focused on celibate monastics. As a scripture that is considered canonical by all schools of Buddhism, it remains an important reference point for Buddhist ethics today. The *Vinaya* was based on rules set by the Buddha and contains narratives and speeches of the Buddha on those rules, along with detailed lists of consequences for violating them. This literature is important to studies of sexualities in Buddhism because it is one of two places where sexual practice is described in detail in canonical Buddhist literature, the other being tantric literature, discussed later.[3] The *Vinaya* is also important because it documents the rules and

---

1 Donald S. Lopez Jr., 'Introduction', in *Critical Terms for the Study of Buddhism*, ed. Donald S. Lopez Jr. (Chicago: University of Chicago Press, 2005), 1–29, at 7.
2 Bernard Faure, *The Red Thread: Buddhist Approaches to Sexuality* (Princeton, NJ: Princeton University Press, 1998), 10; Amy Langenberg, 'Buddhism and Sexuality', in *The Oxford Handbook of Buddhist Ethics*, ed. Daniel Cozort and James Mark Shields (Oxford: Oxford University Press, 2017), 568; José Ignacio Cabezón, *Sexuality in Classical South Asian Buddhism* (Somerville, NJ: Wisdom, 2017), 10.
3 Janet Gyatso, 'Sex', in *Critical Terms for the Study of Buddhism*, ed. Donald Lopez (Chicago: University of Chicago Press, 2005), 271–90, at 275.

procedures governing monasticism. Although it is unclear to what extent this literature reflected actual historical events, it is a valuable record of influential views on the topic of sexuality and celibacy.

The *Vinaya* was considered to have been recorded by the First Council, a convening of senior monks after the Buddha's death traditionally dated to 483 BCE, although the historicity of this claim has been disputed. *Vinaya* literature is housed within a collection of Buddhist scriptures called the three baskets (*Tripiṭaka*) or three kinds of literature that compose the Buddhist canon, put into writing hundreds of years after the Buddha's life. There are numerous versions of these scriptures, with some of the most influential versions maintained in the Pāli, Chinese, and Tibetan languages.

The *Vinaya* literature frames sex in terms of the central problem of Buddhism – the concern with ending suffering. In this literature, sexuality was the subject of legal control and seen as a way to regulate mental states that lead to suffering. In particular, sex was regarded as the fuel for dangerous ignorance that would lead to being trapped in repeated cycles of being reborn in lifetimes of suffering (*saṃsāra*) and thus served as an obstacle to spiritual advancement. The result of this view was the production of practices to reduce and repress sexual desire and even to attain a state of complete desire-less-ness.[4]

The Celibate Ideal and *Vinaya* Literature

Early Indian Buddhist monasticism strictly forbade monks from engaging in sexual intercourse through the rules of monasticism, the *prātimokṣa* vows. There are multiple versions of these vows today – in Theravada Buddhism in Sri Lanka and Southeast Asia, in Chinese and Korean Buddhism, and in Tibetan Buddhism – and although there are differences, there is also substantial agreement among them.[5] The procedures for handling the violation of vows are described in the *Vinaya*, composed of laws and prohibitions couched within narratives of transgressions and the rules that were created in their wake.

The *Vinaya* frames sexual intercourse as the most serious violation of monastic vows, resulting in expulsion from the order, the end of

---

4 Cabezón, *Sexuality*, 91, 238.
5 Robert E. Buswell Jr. and Donald S. Lopez Jr., *The Princeton Dictionary of Buddhism* (Princeton, NJ: Princeton University Press, 2014), 667.

a monastic's career and life in the monastic community.[6] There are also lesser offences related to sex, listed as probationary offences but still considered severe infractions. These include: willingly emitting semen, engaging in lustful physical contact with a woman, using sexually inappropriate language towards a woman, praising sexual intercourse as a religious act, or even acting as a go-between in the arrangement of sexual liaisons.[7] The punishment for these offences included loss of privileges, being stripped of one's seniority, and not being able to leave the grounds without being accompanied by at least four monks.[8]

In the *Vinaya*, Buddha gives a paradigmatic rejection of sex. He says: 'It would be better for you, foolish man, that your male organ should enter the mouth of a black snake, than that it should enter a woman. It would be better for you, foolish man, that your organ should enter a charcoal pit, burning, ablaze, afire than it should enter a woman.'[9] The vivid rejection of sexuality dramatized in this passage is intertwined in the *Vinaya* literature with numerous other tropes, including a revulsion towards the householder's life, a married life, which was considered inferior to the monastic life. Celibacy is not just a matter of sexual ethics or praxis, but also serves multiple purposes for Buddhist institutions and societies, in the past and today. Some scholars have even argued that the main concern of *Vinaya* literature is internal social harmony and external reputation, not ethics.[10] Still, the *Vinaya* also makes clear that sex is not just a matter of keeping up social appearances, as it details how sexual misconduct still breaks the rule of celibacy even if the monk is not in robes or is wearing a disguise.[11]

In the *Vinaya*, sex is portrayed as an evil practice (*asaddhamma*) and low behaviour (*vasaladhamma*), an obstacle to what matters most to Buddhist monks, that is, the goal of enlightenment, freedom from suffering, and freedom from sensual entanglements.[12] Yet, in explaining how to practise celibacy, *Vinaya* literature also provides copious narratives about the many possible creative attempts to get around the rules, an elaborate and detailed discourse on human sexual impulses and activities. The abundant treatment of sensual acts and transgressions includes descriptions of having sex with

---

6 Charles S. Prebish, *Survey of the Vinaya Literature*. Vol. 1: *The Dharma Lamp Series* (New York: Routledge, 1996), 3; Langenberg, 'Buddhism and Sexuality', 574.
7 Buswell and Lopez, *Dictionary*, 753, 657.
8 Buswell and Lopez, *Dictionary*, 753.
9 Pārājika I.5, 10–11, in I. B. Horner, *The Book of the Discipline: Vinaya-Piṭaka*. Vol. 1: *Sutta Vibhaṅga* (London: Pali Text Society, 1949), 35.
10 Damien Keown, *The Nature of Buddhist Ethics* (London: Macmillan, 1992), 34; Prebish, *Survey*, 6.
11 Horner, *Discipline*, 53.   12 Horner, *Discipline*, 36–7.

animals, dolls, corpses, ghosts, or *nāgas* (semi-divine half-serpent beings); sex while wearing costumes; autoeroticism; prostitution; and also addresses the rape of monks and nuns. The rules of celibacy thereby appear to have incited an explosion of detailed discussions of sex.[13] The elaborate disciplinary tales serve as evidence of copious, nuanced, and complex discourse about sensuality and sexuality that reflect struggles against the control of sexuality and its expressions. *Vinaya* literature shows that this struggle takes place on multiple fronts: mentally in terms of desires and longings, socially in terms of interpersonal ties, and economically in terms of the consequences for abandoned wives and families.

Another telling example of this struggle is provided in the *Majjhima Nikāya*, which is also housed, alongside the *Vinaya* literature, within the collection of Buddhist scriptures known as the three baskets. Like the *Vinaya*, the *Majjhima Nikāya* holds discourses attributed to the Buddha, written down from the second to third century CE.[14] The *Majjhima Nikāya* describes sexual desire in dramatic similes which include a pit full of burning coal, a slaughterhouse, the point of a sword, and a snake's head.[15] These analogies dramatize the suffering that was thought to come from being ensnared by sexual desire, linking sexual desire to extreme pain and horror.

A strict definition of 'sex' in the early Buddhist literature is elusive, with the Buddha being quoted as offering only vague descriptions.[16] The *Vinaya* says:

> Sexual intercourse means: what is not verily *dhamma*, village *dhamma*, low-caste *dhamma*, wickedness, the final ablution, secrecy, having obtained in couples, this is called sexual intercourse. Indulgence means: whenever the male organ is made to enter the female, the male member to enter the female, even for the length of a fruit of the sesame plant.[17]

The passage declares that intercourse is not *dhamma* (the Pali spelling for *dharma*), that is, not virtuous because it is indulgence in sense pleasures, which are wicked. By describing it as 'village *dhamma*', the passage also refers to the other core problem with sexuality in the early literature, that procreative sex is linked to the life of a householder by metonymy with a village. Finally, the discussion of the male entering the female for the 'length of a fruit of the sesame plant', defines sex as penile–vaginal penetration. Indeed, the

---

13 Amy Paris Langenberg, 'Buddhism and Sexuality', in *The Oxford Handbook of Buddhist Ethics*, ed. Daniel Cozort and James Mark Shields (Oxford: Oxford University Press, 2017), 578.

14 Upinder Singh, *A History of Ancient and Early Medieval India: From the Stone Age to the 12th Century* (Delhi: Pearson India, 2009), 25.

15 Faure, *Red Thread*, 17.   16 Gyatso, 'Sex', 278.   17 Horner, *Discipline*, 47.

Vinaya literature's primary definition of sex is penetrative sex – vaginal, anal, or oral.

In the *Vinaya* literature however, an array of sexual acts are described. Penetrative sex which results in expulsion from the monastery includes descriptions of sex with animals, non-humans (such as spirits or ghosts), hermaphrodites, eunuchs, males, women who are awake, asleep, drunk, insane, dead (in any one of three states of decomposition), or even with a plaster decoration or a doll.[18] The case of a flexible monk who was able to take his own organ into his mouth or anus was also considered intercourse, resulting in expulsion.[19] Masturbation is also mentioned as an infraction, but not as serious as intercourse, as it did not involve penetration. What counts as an infraction the most is when an orifice, mouth, vagina, or anus is penetrated. The literature underscores this with tales that emphasize that it is not the ejaculation that counts,[20] but the penetration of forbidden orifices that resemble a female human vagina.[21] Homosexual intercourse is also considered a violation, including homosexual intercourse with a monk who is sleeping, awake, or not consenting. However, the primary concern of the monastic rules is heterosexual sex, as evidenced by more serious punishments for overtures towards women than towards men, animals, or *paṇḍakas* (a broad category for non-normative individuals, about which there are more details later).[22]

A notion of consent (*sādiyati*) is also present in *Vinaya* scriptures, once again emphasizing a concern with mental states. The *Vinaya* notes that a monk must consent to sex for the sex to be an offence that results in his expulsion.[23] Therefore if he is ignorant, has not agreed, is insane, is afflicted with pain or a beginner, then that intercourse does not result in the monk's expulsion.[24]

Today, celibate monasticism remains the standard ideal of elite Buddhist practice in many parts of the world. Nonetheless, this is not true everywhere, nor was it always true in the past. When Buddhism entered China hundreds of years after the Buddha's life, it arrived in a context where regular sexual activity was believed to have medical benefits and promote longevity, and the continuation of the family line was valued. Despite this, despite stories of scandals and avaricious monks that were stock figures in popular literature, an ideal of Buddhist celibacy was still developed in China. Chinese

---

18 Horner, *Discipline*, 39, 50, 54.   19 Horner, *Discipline*, 54.   20 Gyatso, 'Sex', 279.

21 Although Gyatso notes that this rule is not entirely consistent, based on some odd examples in the *Vinaya*. Gyatso, 'Sex', 278–80.

22 Gyatso, 'Sex', 280.   23 Horner, *Discipline*, 49.   24 Horner, *Discipline*, 51.

monasteries became centres of art and learning. In Japan, local traditions recast as forms of discipleship within Buddhist monasteries allowed for sexual relationships between the monks and their boy attendants, called *chigo* (see Chapter 6 by Joshua Mostow in Volume III of this work). By the nineteenth century, the requirement for celibacy among Japanese Buddhist priests was dropped, and in contemporary times up to 90 per cent of Japanese Buddhist clerics are married, with leadership of temples passed from fathers to sons.[25]

Rules for Lay Men

Although it was espoused as the supreme lifestyle for attaining enlightenment, celibate monasticism was not the only form of Buddhist practice even in early Indian Buddhism. Buddhist lay people were not expected to be celibate. They were not necessarily monogamous either, since men could have multiple wives and active extra-marital sex lives. Although monogamy was praised, men's promiscuity and the widely accepted practice of polygyny are abundantly attested to in the literature.[26] Lay sexual ethics developed in the first half of the first millennium CE, partly patterned on the monastic juridical literature, though with less detail.

Married lay people were expected to practise Buddhism by taking refuge vows (the vows that declare oneself to be a Buddhist), and by following a set of ethical guidelines known as the five precepts. The five precepts refer to avoiding killing, stealing, lying, using intoxicants, and engaging in sexual misconduct. In the early Buddhist literature, avoiding sexual misconduct meant avoiding adultery. One example is found in the *Dharmapadda*, a scripture of verses attributed to the Buddha, but recorded in written form hundreds of years after his life in the first century BCE. In the *Dharmapadda*, Buddha is said to have said, 'whoever goes to another's wife digs up his own root here in this very world'.[27] This passage dramatizes the negative social consequences of adultery.

Ideals of marital relationships were espoused for both men and women, although predominantly for men, with the five precepts as key factors that defined good relationships. Within the context of Buddhist beliefs in reincarnation, a married couple might even be thought of as connected together for

---

25 John Kieschnick, 'Celibacy in East Asian Buddhism', in *Celibacy and Religious Traditions*, ed. Carl Olsen (Oxford: Oxford University Press, 2007), 225–40, at 233.

26 Steven Collins, 'Remarks on the Third Precept: Adultery and Prostitution in Pāli Texts', *Journal of the Pali Text Society* 29 (2007): 263–84, at 263; Cabezón, *Sexuality*, 468.

27 *Dharmapadda* 3: 479–81, quoted in Collins, 'Third', 273.

lifetimes, or as wishing to be together for lifetimes. An example of this is the
life stories of the Buddha and his wife Yaśodharā, who he was married to
before renouncing his worldly life. There are many versions of the Buddha's
life story. Yaśodharā is usually his main wife, or his only wife depending on
the source.[28] Even though the Buddha left Yaśodharā for the renunciate life,
Young points out that in the literature concerning the past lives of the
Buddha, known as the *Jātaka* tales, Yaśodharā appears as a repeat character
wherever the Buddha has a wife in those past lives.[29] As such these stories
may be considered as a prototype for a type of ideal Buddhist couple that then
gets revised in later tantric reconfigurations of the Buddhist couple. Neither
the Buddhist sutras, scriptures considered records of Buddha's teachings, nor
the *Jātaka* tales give attention to details about sexual praxis in the ideal
marriage to the extent exhibited by the *Vinaya* descriptions of rules of
celibacy. Still, there are general concerns expressed in the Pāli Sutras and
Jātaka tales about male debauchery such as adultery, losing the family's
finances to gambling, and indulging in costly courtesans.[30]

In terms of sexual misconduct for lay people, the main concern was
with penetrative sex. For example, *Teaching on the Ten Non-Virtues*
(*Daśākuśalakarmapathanirdeśa*) by the Buddhist philosopher Aśvaghoṣa (first
or second century CE) defines lay people's sexual ethics as avoiding forbidden
partners (women who belong to others, men who belong to others such as
male slaves, and children), forbidden orifices (meaning non-procreative
forms of sex such as anal or oral sex), and unsuitable times and places.[31]
There are consequences for men for breaking these rules. For adultery, that
is, for a man to have sex with a woman married to someone else, the
consequences included being born in a torturous existence in the hell realm
for many hundreds of thousands of years, or being reborn as a woman, which
was considered a lower birth.[32]

Lay men were allowed to have sex with their wives, mistresses, courtesans, and prostitutes. Despite a monogamous ideal, visiting prostitutes did
not constitute sexual misconduct for lay men, nor did having sex with
another woman as long as she was not one of the forbidden partners.
Poetic literature directed to the leisure class portrayed men's sex lives as

---

28 He is sometimes portrayed with one, two, or three wives. Serenity Young, *Courtesans
    and Tantric Consorts: Sexualities in Buddhist Narrative, Iconography, and Ritual*
    (New York: Routledge, 2004), 88.
29 Young, *Courtesans*.   30 Cabezón, *Sexuality*, 453.
31 Cabezón, *Sexuality*, 471–2; Faure, *Red Thread*, 67; Young, *Courtesans*, 84.
32 Collins, 'Third', 274.

including multiple partners, but such a lifestyle required wealth, and non-elite men would not have had the resources necessary to maintain multiple partners.[33] For elite men, the list of possible suitable sexual partners is long: those purchased with money or possessions, chosen due to mutual affection, chosen by oaths, one's own slaves or former slaves, wars-captives, temporary wives, widows, and divorcees.[34] The tensions created by this rich extra-marital sex life of men is witnessed in poetry and narratives, which some-times frame wives as angry, jealous, or heartbroken, but otherwise portray them as relieved to have independence or as adulterers themselves.[35]

There were also lists of prohibited partners for Buddhist laymen. This included wives of other men, women who were betrothed or under protec-tion of relatives, and women under religious vows or under legal interdiction.[36] Missing from this list of unsuitable partners is mention of same-sex partners being forbidden for men, unless they belonged to others, such as male slaves.

Consent or volition is also discussed in the early literature, but it is unclear as to what exactly counted as consent. For example, although some mar-riages were by choice, other marriages were arranged marriages of young women around the age of their first menses, or women sold, given as gifts, taken in wars or even abducted, yet these were not classified as forbidden partners.[37] Also the degree of a man's sexual misconduct when having sex with a woman who did not consent was dependent upon the status of the woman. Sex with a virtuous woman, such as a nun or one on the Buddhist path to enlightenment, was a severe transgression, but sex with a less virtu-ous woman was not as bad, even if she did not consent. This distinction reflected women's vulnerability in an androcentric framework.[38]

Rules for Lay Women

Attitudes reflected in early Buddhist scriptures demonstrate that women were not considered equal to men, nor were they considered capable of becoming enlightened. This was reflected in the rules regarding acceptable sexual activity for women. For married lay women, there were no lists of forbidden partners, but that was because everyone was forbidden to them except for their husbands, who had exclusive rights to sexual access.[39]

33 Cabezón, *Sexuality*, 460.   34 Collins, 'Third', 265–6; Cabezón, *Sexuality*, 459, 467.
35 Cabezón, *Sexuality*, 463.   36 Young, *Courtesans*, 83; Cabezón, *Sexuality*, 457.
37 Cabezón, *Sexuality*, 464.   38 Collins, 'Third', 269.
39 Collins, 'Third', 265; Young, *Courtesans*, 85.

Cabezón notes that these restrictions reflect two concerns: protecting the virginity of girls, because a virgin was considered the ideal wife, and assuring the paternity of children.[40] For the rare unmarried woman living independently, such as prostitutes and courtesans, sex was permitted with any man except those who had made vows of celibacy.[41] Pāli literature suggests that women who were not married or betrothed could have sex with men freely.[42]

Going beyond theoretical prohibitions and ideals, however, narrative literature in the *Vinaya* and *Jātaka* tales depicts married women with active extra-marital sexual lives.[43] Married women are portrayed as promiscuous seductresses, morally depraved, and therefore sexually active beyond the marital context.[44] Narratives also include lustful sixteen-year-old girls, spinsters, and widows, all presented as dangers to monks.[45] It is unclear how much this represented reality and how much was merely the fears of the authors of this literature, but lustful women were certainly not beyond the realm of the imagination for these authors.

As an example of this, courtesans were venerated in the early literature, drama, poetry, and ritual as the subject of men's erotic desires. Courtesans appeared in the biographies of the Buddha, as do harem women and the demon Māra's daughters, who try to seduce the Buddha on the night of his enlightenment. These women all serve as personifications of ideas about desire, impermanence, and temptation. They serve as contrasts to ascetics, while also articulating an alternative type of freedom from the bonds of society.[46] In these texts, another kind of freedom was enjoyed by courtesans. They were educated, refined, and accomplished in the arts. They could also be wealthy, with their expensive fees and powers of seduction leading men to spend all their money, a reason why Pāli texts associated them with greed.[47] Yet although they were associated with defilement, they could also reform and become nuns, with stories of these transformations presented in the literature as positive examples.

Non-Normative Bodies and Sexual Activities

In its list of transgressions and prohibitions, the *Vinaya* includes sex with females, males, and three intersex persons, whether they are humans,

---

40 Cabezón, *Sexuality*, 466. 41 Young, *Courtesans*, 84. 42 Cabezón, *Sexuality*, 458.
43 Cabezón, *Sexuality*, 458. 44 Collins, 'Third', 270. 45 Collins, 'Third', 275.
46 Young, *Courtesans*, xxiii, 14, 106. 47 Collins, 'Third', 282.

non-humans, or animals.[48] It also mentions another category of forbidden partner, the *paṇḍaka*. *Paṇḍaka* is a term with no direct English translation, as it includes a wide variety of sexual and gender categories and activities: persons who are temporarily or permanently impotent; voyeurs; men who perform fellatio on other men or engage in other same-sex-activities; eunuchs, transvestites, or intersex individuals; homosexual prostitutes; and male courtesans.[49]

Paṇḍakas lacked the normative expectations of an adult male, and were thought to have become *paṇḍakas* due to negative karma incurred from misbehaviour in a past life.[50] The social stigma that they were assigned was due to their association with past wrong deeds, such as dressing as a woman or being a male prostitute for men.[51] They were said to be dominated by their unquenchable libido and other mental defilements and unable to achieve ethical progress; thus they were viewed as sharing characteristics with libidinous female temptresses.[52] *Paṇḍakas* were also portrayed as ethically, psychologically, cognitively, and soteriologically impaired. In terms of monastic law, however, sex with a *paṇḍaka* was considered less of an infraction than sex with a woman, underscoring that the greatest concern in prohibitions was procreative sex. *Paṇḍakas* were also excluded from the monastic order and considered unsuitable marriage partners.[53] Indeed, in order to become an ordained monk, part of the ritual was to inquire if the candidate was a *paṇḍaka*. Yet Vinaya literature demonstrates that there were some *paṇḍakas* who were ordained anyway.[54]

Although the idea of sexual orientation is undertheorized in these texts and appears to be a later development,[55] in early Indian Buddhist literature, there are distinctions between sexual acts and people who have an orientation towards certain types of acts. *Paṇḍakas* were considered promiscuous with a range of partners, with fluid sexual preferences, not necessarily exclusively homosexual.[56] Homosexual acts among monks and nuns frequently merited the same punishments as heterosexual activity. For example, in the *Vinaya*, the issue depended on the action, not the partner; penetration and ejaculation

---

48 Horner, *Discipline*, 48; Faure, *Red Thread*, 76.   49 Young, *Courtesans*, 138.
50 Cabezón, *Sexuality*, 382; John Powers, *Bull of a Man, Images of Masculinity, Sex, and the Body in Indian Buddhism* (Cambridge, MA: Harvard University Press, 2009), 95.
51 Cabezón, *Sexuality*, 382.
52 Leonard Zwilling, 'Homosexuality as Seen in Indian Buddhist Texts', in *Buddhism, Sexuality and Gender*, ed. José Ignacio Cabezón (Albany, NY: State University of New York Press, 1992), 203–14, at 205.
53 Zwilling, 'Homosexuality'.   54 Cabezón, *Sexuality*, 375–6.
55 Langenberg, 'Buddhism and Sexuality', 586.   56 Powers, *Bull of a Man*, 95.

with any person regardless of gender was cause for expulsion from the monastic order, whereas mutual masturbation among monastics was considered less of an offence.[57] In later Buddhist texts, homosexuality is sometimes regarded with greater antipathy. For example, the fifth-century CE Buddhist scholar Buddhaghosa associates homosexuality with decline and decadence.[58] On the other hand, there has also been a notable tolerance of homosexuality in Buddhism. Goldstein notes that homosexual relations between monks were tolerated in Tibet. Monasteries even tolerated some long-term relationships between men, not considering these a breach of the vow of celibacy if the sex was between the thighs rather than anal sex involving penetration.[59]

Altruistic Sexuality in Mahayana Literature

The *Vinaya* and other Pali texts offer one perspective on sexuality in Buddhism, and texts produced somewhat later offer other perspectives. Among these are texts that were part of Mahayana, a movement within Buddhism that emerged in North India in the first century CE. It spread into other parts of South Asia, Central Asia, China, the Himalayas, and ultimately into Korea, Japan, and much of Southeast Asia. Mahayana, which means 'Great Vehicle,' focused on *bodhisattvas*, compassionate beings who were far along on the path to enlightenment, but who stayed in the world to help other sentient beings on their own paths.

Bodhisattvas had altruistic love as their highest ideal, along with 'skilful means' (*upāya*), which is permission to engage in whatever means are necessary to liberate others. This *bodhisattva* ideal is thus sometimes at odds with a strict observance of celibacy and sexual renunciation. In their efforts to liberate beings from suffering, *bodhisattvas* are said to use sex, desire, and sexual pleasure to convert others to the Buddhist path, without this being considered a transgression. Sex may also be used to bring beings to enlightenment, as in the story of a female *bodhisattva* from *The Sūtra of the Revelations of Transforming Woman* (*Strīvivartavyākaraṇa Sūtra*), who led two merchants to enlightenment by giving the merchants pleasure. The merchants say: 'When someone is infected by the poison of a venomous snake, he or she is cured only by poison. Likewise, this woman has destroyed the poison of

---

57 Zwilling, 'Homosexuality', 207.   58 Zwilling, 'Homosexuality', 209.
59 Melvyn C. Goldstein, 'Tibetan Buddhism and Mass Monasticism', in *Des moines et des moniales dans le monde: La vie monastique dans le miroir de la parenté*, ed. Adeline Herrou and Gisele Krauskopff (Toulouse: Presses Universitaires de Toulouse le Mirail, 2010), 5.

our desire by using the poison of pleasure.'[60] This female *bodhisattva* is able to emanate as a man to please women or a woman to please men. When questioned by a monk about this method she says: 'there is no sentient being that I do not tame through these special methods of pleasuring'.[61]

Another example can be seen in 'Ascertaining the Vinaya: Upāli's Questions'.[62] This text explores the relationship between *bodhisattva* vows and monastic vows (*prātimokṣa*). Here the Buddha declares that *bodhisattvas* may be householders, and do not have to be celibate monks.[63] The same text ranks errors associated with anger as more harmful than those associated with desire, because the former forsakes beings and the latter brings them together.[64] Such texts reflect the Mahayana idea that every sentient being is on the path to enlightenment, not simply monks, and that women may also possibly obtain enlightenment without having to first become men. Tropes of *bodhisattva* sexuality existed in tension with the monastic celibate ideal, as evidenced in the writings of the third-century CE Mahayana scholar Asaṅga, who both defended the use of sex as skilful means in his treatment on ethics in the *Bodhisattvabhūmi* and also declared that such sexual 'skilful means' are not permitted for monastic *bodhisattvas*.[65]

Indian Tantra and Sacramental Sex

The next major development in literature on Buddhist sexualities was that of the tantric traditions of Buddhism, which developed alongside tantras of Hindus and Jains in India,[66] appearing as early as the third century CE but spreading centuries later.[67] (For more on tantric traditions within Hinduism, see Chapter 4 by Jaya S. Tyagi and Tara Sheemar Malhan in this volume.) Tantra was a system of belief that involved secretive and esoteric ritual practices thought to give one advantages in the spiritual and material realms. Like Mahayana literature, tantric literature developed long after the life of the Buddha, but was considered to be authoritative, and like *Vinaya*, tantras deal extensively with sexual practice. As in Mahayana texts, tantric literature was

---

60 Cabezón, *Sexuality*, 276; Faure, *Red Thread*, 121, 130.   61 Cabezón, *Sexuality*, 276.
62 'Ascertaining the Vinaya: Upāli's Questions', *84000: Translating the Words of the Buddha*, trans. UCSB Buddhist Studies Translation Group, https://read.84000.co/translation/toh68.html, verse 1.33.
63 'Ascertaining', verse 1.33.   64 'Ascertaining', verse 1.69.
65 Asaṅga, cited in Langenberg, 'Buddhism and Sexuality', 581.
66 Geoffrey Samuel, *Shamans: Buddhism in Tibetan Societies* (Washington, DC: Smithsonian Institution, 1993), 409.
67 Young, *Courtesans*, 135.

also more inclusive of women, positing that women could attain enlightenment and making female adepts a necessary part of tantric ritual and contemplative praxis. The literature featured female figures as *yoginīs* and *ḍākinī*, names for semi-human, semi-divine goddess-like figures which later came to be used as monikers for highly enlightened female teachers.

Tantras reframed sexual praxis as having ritual and soteriological purposes as evidenced in ritual sexuality or sacramental sexuality. Tantric literature featured reciting mantras (sacred words or syllables), visualization, and ritual as contemplative methods to attain liberation, along with practical benefits. These included magical powers (*siddhi*), curing disease, staving off demonic assault, or even delaying death. Early tantras developed in non-Buddhist groups and were characterized by transgressive rhetoric.[68] They offered views that differed from earlier forms of Buddhism regarding sexuality, the body, and soteriological trajectories, but they also shared much in common with early Buddhist literature. Common elements include a concern with the freedom from suffering, theories about mind and body, and concerns about the relationship between personal choices and communal consequences. They also shared a strategy of legitimizing theories of sexuality based on scriptural references, ritual logic, medical and biological ideologies, contemplative exigencies, and theories of desire. Tantric theories tend to focus on the transformation of experiences rather than the renunciation of experiences that characterized early Buddhist monastic literature. For tantras that developed in Indian Buddhism, that transformation was achieved through transgressive experiences such as breaking caste boundaries, eating forbidden foods, and breaking sexual taboos.[69]

The paradigmatic example of tantric literature is the *yoginī tantras*, Indian tantras composed from the eighth century CE onwards that featured sacramental sexuality and ritual sexual practices.[70] Religious sexuality was framed in this literature as an efficacious means for spiritual progress. Sacramental sexuality was possible because, in contrast to early Indian Buddhist classical literature, which emphasized the dangers of women, the *yoginī tantras*, texts such as *The Cakrasamvara Tantra* and *Hevajra Tantra*, placed emphasis on the ritual power and salvific potential of sexuality, practices that necessitated women's participation. The scriptures notably valorized the female in

---

68 David B. Gray, 'Eating the Heart of the Brahmin: Representations of Alterity and the Formation of Identity in Tantric Buddhist Discourse', *History of Religions* 45, no.1 (2005): 45–69, at 45.

69 Janet Gyatso, *Apparitions of the Self: The Secret Autobiographies of a Tibetan Visionary – A Translation and Study of Jigme Lingpa's Dancing Moon in the Water and Ḍākki's Grand Secret Talk* (Princeton, NJ: Princeton University Press, 1999), 186.

70 Gray, 'Eating the Heart', 50.

various ways – they included female divinities and female adepts in rituals and venerated female associated qualities – even while continuing to have androcentric and misogynistic themes. Female perspectives are glaringly absent from these texts and the inclusion of women is still focused on the male adepts' needs. For example, a passage from the *Hevajra Tantra* describes the ritual 'worship' of a female adept, performed in order to produce reproductive fluids which are then to be ingested for the attainment of magical powers: 'Kissing and embracing her, and touching her vulva, he should effect the drinking of the fertilizing drops of the "male nose" and of the honey down below ... He attains abundant powers and becomes the equal of all the Buddhas. White camphor [semen] is drunk there, and especially wine.'[71] The ingestion of reproductive fluids was thought to fill the adept with vital energy, an elixir of the life force. Sacramental sexuality was a practice within a series of ritual consecrations that involved bringing a female sexual partner to the religious leader, who then had sex with her in order to produce the ejaculated fluids ingested by disciples. Disciples also practised sexual yogas under the supervision of the religious leader, a method of a ritualized orgasm that involved visualizations and bodily exercises in order to experience somatic contemplative experiences called the four joys. It also involved the visualization of oneself and the partner as divinities.[72]

Another example of androcentrism is found in the *Cakrasamvara Tantra*, dating from the eighth to ninth century CE, a text central to the development of Buddhist tantra in India. In one of these tantras, in a female-voiced text, the male tantric adept is advised not to 'have disgust for a woman born of any class (*varna*), as she is the Blessed Lady Wisdom (*bhagavatī prajñā*) dwelling in conventional form'.[73] Yet such passages are still within the context of literature that provided instructions for subduing and controlling female figures, the *ḍākinī*. The social facts surrounding tantric practice also speak to inequalities, as the women in these rites were social subordinates from low-caste or outcaste groups. The texts speak of respect for women only in a limited role within a limited sphere – that of sexual yogic practices.[74]

The *Cakrasamvara Tantra* is concerned with rites that rely upon the sacramental consumption of sexual fluids as well as consumption of other

---

71 David Gordon White, *Kiss of the Yogini: Tantric Sex in Its South Asian Contexts* (Chicago: University of Chicago Press, 2006), 73.
72 Ronald M. Davidson, *Indian Esoteric Buddhism: A Social History of the Tantric Movement* (New York: Columbia University Press, 2002), 197–8.
73 David B. Gray, *The Cakrasamvara Tantra (The Discourse of Sri Heruli): Editions of the Sanskrit and Tibetan Texts* (New York: American Institute of Buddhist Studies, 2013), 95.
74 Gray, *Cakrasamvara*, 96–7, 103.

transgressive substances such as meat. It reads: 'Then the hero, having drunk the "flower water", should recollect this mantra. The adept should thus dance with his consort. At night one should enjoy consecrated meat and thus drinking with that and offering it, saying things like: "May bliss be produced!"'[75] The 'flower water' here refers to the mixture of seminal fluid, menstrual blood, and vaginal secretions which were used at that time in tantric practices as consecrating ritual substances. The *Cakrasamvara Tantra* says that by eating this 'water of bliss' one's karma is purified and the residue of past negative actions is destroyed.[76] Of note here is that in tantra there are instructions for contradictory practices of dealing with ejaculation, such as retention versus emitting it and eating it.

The tantras emerged from a subculture of *yogis*, *yoginīs*, and various renunciates who practised in a style that rejected cultural norms. These groups were influenced by non-Buddhist, Indian Śaiva groups (who worshipped the Hindu god Shiva), with rites similar to Hindu tantric rites of worshiping the vulva evident in Hindu texts, art, and architecture. These *yoginī tantra* texts provide rhetorical evidence of transgressive language, but the relationship between discourse and praxis is not entirely clear. Critiques of these practices suggest, however, that there was some degree of literal implementation or multiple interpretations of sexual yogas.[77]

The *yoginī tantras* reflect a continuity of Buddhist concerns about the regulation and control of sexuality, in this case regulated through tantric rituals involving intercourse rather than through celibacy, as was the case in the *Vinaya* texts. The Indian tantric literature served as an influential precursor to later Tibetan tantric literature which expanded upon sexual praxis, although an antinomian mindset that completely rejected social norms never really took hold as a widespread practice in Tibet.

Tibetan Reformulations

Buddhism emerged in Tibet from the sixth to the eighth centuries CE, and the primary form that took hold was Buddhist tantra. By the early modern period, Tibet was home to the largest monasteries in the world. Tibetan tantric sexualities included sacramental sexual praxis, which are the ritual sexual practices, as well as sexual yogas, which are physical and contemplative sexual exercises. Heteronormativity once again looms

---

75 Gray, *Cakrasamvara*, 120.   76 Gray, *Cakrasamvara*, 117.
77 Gray, *Cakrasamvara*, 104.

large there, as does the framework of binary sex, especially featured in prevalent imagery of the union of male and female Buddhas in sexual union. As tantric couples in embrace, these Buddhas are regarded as the personification of the union of skilful means and wisdom, the two ideals of tantric practice. The Tibetan tantric literature continued the legacy of androcentrism, with texts by male authors for the sake of male readers. Female figures are featured heavily in Tibetan tantric literature, however, and there are exceptions to androcentrism.

A defining characteristic of Tibetan tantra is the incorporation of female adepts who served as sexual partners or consorts, as well as female figures as teachers, guides, protectors – and also malevolent beings. Women were considered an essential part of sexual yoga practices, whether as real or imagined partners. The tantric ethical code (*dam tsig*) includes a proscription against the disparagement of consorts, but typologies of consorts often exhibit misogynistic views of women. The women in tantric literature were sometimes portrayed as human protagonists, such as the female exemplar Yeshe Tsogyal, a figure from the eighth and ninth centuries, who was positioned as an enlightened figure and teacher, one who had a significant role in the transmission of the Tibetan Buddhist lineage. Whether she was an actual historic person is debated, but in the hagiographic accounts of her life story, she was the student and consort of Padmasambhava, a tantric Buddhist master from India, but also a teacher in her own right. In later stories of her life, Tsogyal is a sexual agent who takes her own male consort. The story of Tsogyal served as a model for many female religious leaders in Tibet, who patterned their lives and identities after her hagiographies and were regarded as her reincarnations.

Sexual yoga refers to practices of Buddhist tantra in India and Tibet that approached sexuality in terms of the bodily and mental energies to be controlled and directed by somatic and physical exercises and visualizations. Sexual yogas are based on the tantric theories of embodiment in which the body was valorized as a landscape of liberation whose energies could be harnessed. Sexual yogas are posited as a set of techniques to control the life force and manipulate the physical, energetic, and mental body in contemplative praxis. Both sacramental and yogic sexuality transformed earlier discourses of Buddhist sexualities. Instead of viewing sex as a hindrance to enlightenment and a danger to society, they posited that sex was necessary for liberation and for regulating mental states and benefitted the community. Yet, despite the contrary views, similar themes were recruited to make the arguments for both celibacy and sexual yoga practices: regulation, control, and spiritual liberation.

Sexual yoga was practised in visualized forms or in literal forms by tantric couples.[78] It had multiple purposes, including health, an increase in vitality and by extension an increase of the life span. This link between sexual activity and cultivation of vitality is a pan-Asian concept that also appears in Daoism and Hinduism. Tibetan tantric literature drew on these influences and upon Indian Buddhist tantra.

Sexual yoga is centred on ideas of yogic physiology, also known as the subtle body. This is a somatic-sensory field of physical experience interpreted as a visual, somatic, and hydraulic system of channels (*tsa*), winds (*rlung*), wheels (Sanskrit *cakra*, Tibetan *'khor lo*), and vital nuclei (*thig-le*), all of which have a variety of meanings, including reproductive fluids, drops of energy, and visualized spheres of light. The network of channels and winds parallels the physical body's circulatory system: arteries, veins, capillaries, and so forth. The wheels along the central channels contain knots that must be loosened so that the wind and vital nuclei may be freed and redirected to increase bliss and spiritual realization.

Sarah Jacoby analyses the autobiography of a nineteenth-century female tantric consort and adept, Sera Khandro, and the instructions on sexual yoga that Khandro received in a religious revelation:

> The vital nuclei having arrived from the [woman's] secret space into the pollen bed of the lotus [the womb], the wind of the first time period dissolves and you attain the realization of the first ground ... this is traversing the excellent quick path in which liberation is instantaneous, not depending on all the gradual causes, results, grounds and paths.[79]

The purpose of sexual yoga in this passage is twofold, facilitating the attainment of enlightenment as well as assisting in practical vitality such as curing disease and extending the life span.

Yet sexual yoga has deeper purposes. It rests upon the idea of embodied praxis as liberatory, with the body as the support for liberation. This is described in terms of changing the flow of the bodily energies, loosening knots in the subtle body, redirecting these flows into the central column of the body, and uniting the male and female generative energies. These are all based on internal yogas focused on bodily experiences and manipulation of

---

78 Gyatso, *Apparitions*, 196.

79 Sarah H. Jacoby, *Love and Liberation, Autobiographical Writings of Tibetan Visionary Sera Khandro* (New York: Columbia University Press, 2014), 202.

the breath. Furthermore, sexual yoga is seen as having many other results, including the appearance of visions and the facilitation of scriptural revelations. Purification is said to happen through sexual yogas, including purification of negative karmas such as those from broken vows. Results can also include particular states of contemplative experience such as meditative stability.[80] Another example of a contemplative result of sexual yoga is the 'one taste' (ro gcig), in which appearances of the phenomenal world and mind have a single flavour, the state of bliss-emptiness.[81] These benefits of sexual yoga with an appropriate consort go even beyond individual benefits. In tantric practice, they are associated with the increase of wealth, food, friends, social harmony, and power, which are seen as benefits for oneself and for one's entire community.[82] In her study of sexual practice in the autobiography of the eighteenth-century tantric adept Jigme Lingpa, Gyatso notes that sexual yogas are linked with the notions of independence, autonomy, power, and confidence.[83]

These practices propose not only a transformation of desire through these complex somatic exercises, but also a transmutation of the process of orgasm. Tantric practice, which is usually described from the male's point of view, does not result in ejaculation, but instead retention of the seminal fluid and the reversal and redirection of it upwards, a key feature that distinguishes it from ordinary sexual activity. The seminal fluid is associated with spiritual power and vitality and its loss is associated with loss of vitality.[84] In Tibetan esoteric Great Perfection literature, sexual yoga culminates in the male *yogi* taking in the female *yoginī's* red vital essence (*thig le*). By drawing the red and white vital essence upward through the body in successive stages, the end result is that the tantric adept attains buddhahood.[85] However, in the autobiography of Sera Khandro, the process is also done by a woman, drawing the vital essence upward along the energy centres of the body.[86]

The basic theme of tantric theory overall is the transformation of human experiences. The twentieth-century Tibetan lama and tantric adept Thubten Yeshe declares that the function of tantra is to

> transform all pleasures into the transcendental experience of deep penetrative awareness. Instead of advocating separation from worldly pleasures the

---

80 Kali Cape, 'Anatomy of a Ḍākinī: Female Consort Discourse in a Case of Fourteenth-Century Tibetan Buddhist Literature', *Journal of Dharma Studies* 3 (2020): 349–71, at 364.
81 Gyatso, *Apparitions*, 195.   82 Cape, 'Anatomy', 364, 365.
83 Gyatso, *Apparitions*, 197.
84 Jacoby, *Love and Liberation*, 203; Young, *Courtesans*, 138.
85 Jacoby, *Love and Liberation*, 203.   86 Jacoby, *Love and Liberation*, 205.

way many other traditions do, tantra emphasizes that it is much more effective for human beings to enjoy themselves and channel the energy of their enjoyments into a quick and powerful path to fulfilment and enlightenment.[87]

Tantric logic acknowledges the trope, inherited from classical Indian Buddhist literature, in which desire is distortive, but it theorizes that the basic energy of desire can be harnessed for the purpose of spiritual awakening.[88] Desire can be used to fulfil soteriological aims, if it is experienced without grasping or clinging.[89] This is a paradox, since desire is associated with grasping in early Buddhist literature, but tantric literature posits that desire can be separated from grasping and transmuted into a bliss-emptiness through yogic exercises which are visual, somatic, and philosophical contemplations. Through such practices bliss in turn further consumes and transforms desire.[90]

Conclusion

The Buddhist ideas about sexuality described here come from literature that ranges from 500 BCE to the modern period, primarily in India and Tibet. Because Buddhism has taken so many forms over time and space, this is far from a complete account of Buddhist sexualities and traditions, which are extremely diverse. One thing that unites Buddhist sexualities, however, is meticulous attention to how sexuality can be harnessed for liberation from suffering and for actualizing buddhahood. This chapter has also shown how notions of ideal religious lives, gender, ethics and embodiment are intertwined with ideas about sexuality. These ideas were revised, contested, and reinterpreted from context to context, changes that continue within Buddhist cultures to the present time.

Further Reading

'Ascertaining the Vinaya: Upāli's Questions' (Āryavinayaviniścayopāliparipṛcchānā mamahāyānasūtra). *84000: Translating the Words of the Buddha*, fols. 115.a–131.a. https://read.84000.co/translation/toh68.html.

Cabezón, José Ignacio. *Sexuality in Classical South Asian Buddhism*. Somerville, NJ: Wisdom, 2017.

87 Lama Thubten Yeshe, *Introduction to Tantra: The Transformation of Desire*, 2nd ed., ed. Jonathan Landow (Boston: Wisdom, 2001), 17.
88 Yeshe, *Tantra*, 4.   89 Gyatso, *Apparitions*, 196.   90 Jacoby, *Love and Liberation*, 205.

Cape, Kali. 'Anatomy of a Ḍākinī: Female Consort Discourse in a Case of Fourteenth-Century Tibetan Buddhist Literature'. *Journal of Dharma Studies* 3 (2020): 349–71.

Collins, Steven. 'Remarks on the Third Precept: Adultery and Prostitution in Pāli Texts'. *Journal of the Pali Text Society* 29 (2007): 263–84.

Faure, Bernard. *The Red Thread: Buddhist Approaches to Sexuality*. Princeton, NJ: Princeton University Press, 1998.

Gayley, Holly. *Love Letters from Golok: A Tantric Couple in Modern Tibet*. New York: Columbia University Press, 2016.

'Revisiting the "Secret Consort"*(gsang yum)* in Tibetan Buddhism'. *Religions* 9, no. 6 (2018), https://doi.org/10.3390/rel9060179.

Goldstein, Melvyn C. 'Bouddhisme tibétain et monachisme de masse'. In *Des moines et des moniales dans le monde: La vie monastique dans le miroir de la parenté*, ed. Adeline Herrou and Gisele Krauskopff, 409–24. Toulouse: Presses Universitaires de Toulouse le Mirail, 2010.

Gray, David B. 'Eating the Heart of the Brahmin: Representations of Alterity and the Formation of Identity in Tantric Buddhist Discourse'. *History of Religions* 45, no. 1 (2005): 45–69.

Gyatso, Janet. *Apparitions of the Self: The Secret Autobiographies of a Tibetan Visionary; A Translation and Study of Jigme Lingpa's Dancing Moon in the Water and Ḍākki's Grand Secret Talk*. Princeton, NJ: Princeton University Press, 1999.

'Sex'. In *Critical Terms for the Study of Buddhism*, ed. Donald Lopez, 271–90. Chicago: University of Chicago Press, 2005.

Horner, I. B. *The Book of the Discipline: Vinaya-Piṭaka*. Vol. 1: *Sutta Vibhaṅga*. London: Pali Text Society, 1949.

Jacoby, Sarah H. *Love and Liberation: Autobiographical Writings of Tibetan Visionary Sera Khandro*. New York: Columbia University Press, 2014.

Junko, Minamoto, and Hank Glassman. 'Buddhism and the Historical Construction of Sexuality in Japan'. *U.S.-Japan Women's Journal, English Supplement* 5 (1993): 87–115.

Keown, Damien. *The Nature of Buddhist Ethics*. London: Macmillan, 1992.

Kieschnick, John. 'Celibacy in East Asian Buddhism'. In *Celibacy and Religious Traditions*, ed. Carl Olsen, 225–40. Oxford: Oxford University Press, 2007.

Klunklin, Areewan, and Jennifer Greenwood. 'Buddhism, the Status of Women and the Spread of HIV/AIDS in Thailand'. *Health Care for Women International* 26 (2005): 46–61.

Langenberg, Amy Paris. 'Buddhism and Sexuality'. In *The Oxford Handbook of Buddhist Ethics*, ed. Daniel Cozort and James Mark Shields, 567–91. Oxford: Oxford University Press, 2017.

'Sex and Sexuality in Buddhism: A Tetralemma'. *Religion Compass* 9, no. 9 (2015): 277–86.

Pommaret, Francoise, and Tashi Tobgay. 'Bhutan's Pervasive Phallus: Is Drukpa Kunley Really Responsible?' In *Buddhist Himalaya: Studies in Religion, History and Culture: Proceedings of the Golden Jubilee Conference of the Namgyal Institute of Tibetology, Gangtok, 2008*, ed. Anna Balikci-Denjongpa and Alex MacKay, 59–81. Gangtok, India: Namgyal Institute of Tibetology, 2011.

Powers, John. *Bull of a Man: Images of Masculinity, Sex, and the Body in Indian Buddhism*. Cambridge, MA: Harvard University Press, 2009.

Prebish, Charles S. *Survey of the Vinaya Literature*. Vol. 1: *The Dharma Lamp Series*. New York: Routledge, 1996.

Samuel, Geoffrey. *Shamans: Buddhism in Tibetan Societies*. Washington, DC: Smithsonian Institution, 1993.

Soh, C. Sarah. *The Comfort Women: Sexual Violence and Postcolonial Memory in Korea and Japan*. Chicago: University of Chicago Press, 2020.

Yao, Ping. 'Changing Views on Sexuality in Early and Medieval China'. *Journal of Daoist Studies* 8 (2015): 52–68.

Yeshe, Lama Thubten. *Introduction to Tantra: The Transformation of Desire*, 2nd ed., ed. Jonathan Landow. Boston: Wisdom, 2001.

Young, Serenity. *Courtesans and Tantric Consorts: Sexualities in Buddhist Narrative, Iconography, and Ritual*. New York: Routledge, 2004.

Zwilling, Leonard. 'Homosexuality as Seen in Indian Buddhist Texts'. In *Buddhism, Sexuality and Gender*, ed. José Ignacio Cabezón, 203–14. Albany, NY: State University of New York Press, 1992.

12

Sexuality in Jewish Traditions

CHARLOTTE ELISHEVA FONROBERT

For much of its history, Jewish culture has been shaped in profound ways by the intellectual traditions and teachings that were collected and edited into encyclopaedic anthologies by the rabbinic sages of late antiquity, both in Roman Palestine (modern Israel) and in Sasanian Mesopotamia (modern Iraq). Rabbinic teachings turned the biblical literature of ancient Israel, and especially biblical law, as it was transmitted to them, into a tradition they called *Torah*. They turned biblical tradition into what we have come to recognize as Jewish, as Jewish discourse, and as Jewish tradition. The *Torah* was meant to be studied and observed by a particular people ('Israel') and its sages. Between the first and seventh centuries CE, these teachings were assembled into works – Midrash collections, Mishnah, and Talmud – that in turn generated centuries of commentaries, rewritings, and codifications.

The norms derived from these writings, called *halakhah* (or Jewish law), still guide the daily lives of many Jewish communities, though in recent centuries the authoritativeness of Jewish law and of its judges has been profoundly diminished. While Jewish culture was always diverse, both geographically and intellectually, since the eighteenth century and the onset of secularization it has acquired even more profound diversity, including of its sexual cultures. These texts continue to be studied in Jewish communities around the world, and continue to provoke thought and practices even in postmodern contexts. Some are liturgical texts and are regularly recited in worship and continue to shape Jewish theological thinking.[1] Their import is felt even in post-traditional communities and continues to be observed, in whatever rudimentary forms.

I cannot hope to capture this long history and the diversity in any comprehensive way. In what follows, I focus on the classical rabbinic traditions and its discourses of sexuality, as well as the sexual practices they shaped. The rabbinic sages based their teachings in fundamental ways on the biblical traditions transmitted to and by them. The Hebrew Bible, whose precise shape was still under discussion in the first century CE, provided the rabbinic sages with ancient normative and legal traditions. It equally famously provided them with an archive of stories and myths, such as the canonized myth of human creation, in the two versions in Genesis, one emphasizing fertility as a fundamental human task,[2] the other emphasizing heteropartnership of husband and wife.[3] The rabbinic sages drew their inspiration for thinking and talking about sexual matters from the wells of biblical tradition.

At the same time, the rabbinic texts emerge from a particular historical context – one that we have come to refer to as late antiquity. Academic scholarship has shown how deeply these rabbinic teaching traditions were shaped by their historical and cultural context, in particular with regard to the discourses on sexuality. Thus, we have come to regard developments in Roman law as a meaningful context for early rabbinic legal discussions of marital law and sex. Equally, notions of ritual purity derived from the Zoroastrian religion of the Sasanian Empire, where the Babylonian Talmud was formulated, may have reinforced the biblical concept of embodied purity into an important framing for sexuality.[4]

A focus on the rabbinic discourses of sexuality that were formulated in late antiquity, therefore, provides us with a heuristic focus for presenting Jewish

---

1 The recitation of Leviticus 18, for example, including its indictment of sex between men among other forms of prohibited sexual relations, is recited during the Day of Atonement services. The liturgical recitation of this biblical chapter on the highest of holidays on the Jewish calendar goes back to Talmudic tradition (Babylonian Talmud, *Megillah* 31a). In modern liberal synagogues, alternative texts are read. (Throughout this chapter, references to the Bible, Talmud, and other canonical writings will use traditional systems of identification rather than refer to modern editions. Many will be cited within the text.)

2 Genesis 1:28: 'Be fruitful and multiply'.

3 Genesis 2:24: 'Hence a man leaves his father and mother and clings to his wife, so that they become one flesh.'

4 For male sexuality, emission of seminal fluid played a crucial role, and for women, menstrual and other vaginal fluids. See Charlotte Fonrobert, *Menstrual Purity: Rabbinic and Christian Reconstructions of Biblical Gender* (Stanford, CA: Stanford University Press, 2000); and Shai Secunda, *The Talmud's Red Fence: Menstrual Impurity and Difference in Babylonian Judaism and Its Sasanian Context* (Oxford: Oxford University Press, 2020).

discourses of sexuality. This runs the danger of keeping at the centre of cultural historiography a tradition that has marginalized women's sexual desires and practices, not to mention same-sex and other desires and practices. Unfortunately, for much of the pre-modern period of Jewish history we have only limited access to such perspectives. Nonetheless, the large archive of rabbinic traditions provides us with a tremendous wealth of representations of sexual practices, desires, and discourses, often in tension with each other, that reverberate throughout Jewish history. It further provides a framework and language for contemporary Jewish discourses of sexuality, including newly emerging identities, individual and communal, specifically for Jewish LGBTQ+ people. Three topics out of many possible have been selected in what follows: obligations of marriage, reproduction, and same-sex and queer sexualities. They represent three topics of perennial debate in Jewish traditions around the world. For each, rabbinic texts and especially the Talmud have played a pre-eminent role in shaping the debates over the centuries.

The Rise of Rabbinic-Jewish Heteronormativity: Marriage and Sex

Undoubtedly, the most prominent framework for rabbinic discussions of sexual practices and representations is (heterosexual) marriage. The biblical library on which the rabbinic sages of late antiquity built their own discourse by and large assumed the founding of a patriarchal household as a goal of a man's life. Biblical *narratives*, especially the stories of the Book of Genesis, prominently feature finding the proper wife as a central plot. Biblical *law* provides a smattering of specific laws for a man 'taking a wife' (e.g., Deuteronomy 22:14), a process that remains generally poorly defined, and certainly weakly institutionalized. Sexual intercourse obviously played a role in this process – 'when a man *takes* a wife and *comes upon* her' (Deuteronomy 22:13, my emphasis) – but is again weakly defined. At the same time, biblical legal texts had a rather expansive vocabulary about illicit sex: if a man 'lies with' a virgin who is engaged to someone else (or not, Deuteronomy 22:23, 22:28); he should not 'uncover his father's "garment"' (i.e., have sex with his father's wife) or 'uncover the "nakedness" of his father's wife' (Leviticus 18:7) or other close relatives, and more. It was left to the rabbinic sages to devote an enormous amount of hermeneutic and legislative activity to institutionalizing marriage.

An early rabbinic treatise dealing with the rules of engagement or 'sanctification' of a relationship between a man and a woman opens with the three ways in which 'a wife *is acquired*': 'she is acquired by money, by document, or by sexual intercourse'.[5] This teaching can be found in the Mishnah, a compendium of rabbinic teachings thought to have been assembled and edited in the late second and early third century CE in what was then Roman Palestine. Adopting the medium of normative or legal language, the Mishnah in due course provided the foundation for rabbinic learning in late antiquity, and Jewish intellectual history for centuries to come. Part of the Mishnah's organization of rabbinic normative traditions, significantly, is its attempt at the normativization of Jewish marriage, the kinship relations it enables, and the sexual acts and relationships that may alternately sustain or undermine it. Sexuality, sexual behaviour, and to some degree also sexual desires, became very much a matter of law and legal rhetoric in Jewish traditions. The laws of marriage thereby acted as a cornerstone of rabbinic legal discourse, and a platform for a Jewish dialogue that would span centuries.

Thus we find in the Mishnah the following tradition, attributed to an early second century CE rabbinic sage:

> The regular interval [of sexual intercourse owed by a husband to his wife] *mentioned in the Torah* [is this]:
> 'People of leisure' – daily
> Laborers – twice weekly
> Donkey drivers – once a week
> Camel drivers – once every thirty days
> And sailors – once every six months –
> the words of Rabbi Eliezer.
>
> (Mishnah, Ketubbot 5:6)[6]

Without dwelling on the details of the list, itself a well-known rabbinic teaching, we can tease out some of the cultural values and dynamics encapsulated in it that unfold over the course of centuries in the history of Jewish sexualities, including its reception in modern scholarship. Four points seem apt.

---

5 In this and subsequent quotations from the Mishnah, I use the translations in *The Oxford Annotated Mishnah: A New Translation of the Mishnah*, 3 vols., ed. Shaye J. D. Cohen, Robert Goldenberg, and Hayim Lapin (Oxford: Oxford University Press, 2022), 3: 306, my emphasis. See Judith R. Wegner, *Chattel or Person: The Status of Women in Mishnah* (Oxford: Oxford University Press, 1988), 276n79, who was the first to relate these three ways to Roman law, and specifically Gaius's *Institutes* 1:108–24.

6 *The Oxford Mishnah*, 2: 99, my emphasis.

First, in the early rabbis' reading of biblical law and lore, a husband's sexual debt within marriage was ordained by the Torah. After all, the Torah included a rule that a husband owes his wife not only provisions for her food and clothing, but also something called *onah* in biblical Hebrew, understood by the rabbinic sages as 'sexual debt' (Exodus 21:10). Rabbi Eliezer in this teaching took the concept to refer to the *frequency* of sexual intercourse expected within marriage, determined and limited by a husband's trade or occupation, as well as the locality of his work. According to the logic of the list, the more local an occupation, the greater a husband's sexual debt to his wife. To the rabbis, we might add, biblical theology in general and the creation myth of Genesis in particular certainly emphasized the sexual union of a man and a woman as a purpose of human creation as embodied. Hence, a commandment of regular sexual intimacy would make perfect sense.

Second, regular sexual intercourse is something that the rabbinic scholars of late antiquity understood to be a *quintessential* aspect of a marital relationship, which in turn was also taken to have been ordained by the Torah. The Mishnah prefaces Rabbi Eliezer's list with a dispute between the two major early rabbinic schools of thought at the time, the School of Shammai and the School of Hillel, about the question of how long a husband might temporarily foreswear sexual relations with his wife, if done 'by means of a vow'; according to the former up to two weeks, and to the latter maximally one week, so if any longer he would have to divorce her (Mishnah, *Ketubbot* 5:6). By early rabbinic understanding, then, a Jewish husband was not allowed to go completely celibate on his wife. Later rabbinic teaching traditions recorded in the Babylonian Talmud, in contrast, very much struggled with the obligation of the sexual debt as a burden,[7] as did some medieval philosophical and mystical traditions. The great medieval scholar Maimonides (d. 1204), for example, both a radically innovative philosopher influenced by the Aristotelian tradition and a codifier of rabbinic halakhic tradition in his *Mishneh Torah*, was beholden to a disdain for sexual pleasure that he partially inherited from his philosophical forbearer Aristotle. When discussing the importance of moderation and temperance in fulfilling one's physical needs, including sex, Maimonides explicitly states that pleasure should *not* be the goal, rather than a concern for health and 'propagation of the species':

---

7 Daniel Boyarin, *Carnal Israel: Reading Sex in Talmudic Culture* (Berkeley, CA: University of California Press, 1993), ch. 5; and Steven Fraade, 'Ascetical Aspect of Ancient Judaism', in *Jewish Spirituality: From the Bible through the Middle Ages*, ed. Arthur Green (New York: Crossroad, 1986), 56–88.

Sexuality in Jewish Traditions

'he should not have sex whenever he desires, but when he feels he needs to ejaculate for health reasons or to preserve the seed'.[8] The biblically ordained sexual debt appears only when discussing marital obligation, as a sort of contractual obligation that the husband was bound to observe for that reason alone, and not to satisfy his own pleasure.[9] Some devotees of the Jewish esoteric tradition called *Kabbalah* equally rejected the sexual obligation especially when understood as means of providing pleasure.[10] To such later Jewish intellectual formations, a commitment to the life of the body in marriage held great potential to detract from the life of devotion. In talmudic tradition, the rising value of the devotional study of Torah was perceived as competing with the obligation of marriage and family. The notion, possibly borrowed from Christian asceticism, took hold and found expression in a new economy of desire: desire for devotional study of Torah could excuse lengthy periods of a husband's absence from his home.[11] As much as devotion and domestic life came to move to opposite sides of the fence, however, rabbinic traditions never instituted a completely monastic life.

The pious misgivings of such scholastic inclinations notwithstanding, a husband's sexual debt was codified in Jewish law and remains valid to this day.[12] Modern scholars in turn have suggested that this normative commitment to the sexual debt in early rabbinic Judaism was a sign that sexual intercourse should be minimally understood as a means of establishing and maintaining the affect of the marital bond, and not merely as a necessary means for reproduction. Optimally, at least, late ancient rabbinic culture viewed sex and sexual intimacy as a fundamental aspect of human life. Rabbi

---

8 Maimonides, *Mishneh Torah, Hilkhot Deot* 3:2, 5:4–5. In *Hilkhot Issurei Bi'ah* (The Laws of Prohibited Sex), 21:9, Maimonides insists that the sole purpose of heterosexual sex was procreation. See also David Biale, *Eros and the Jews: From Biblical Israel to Contemporary America* (New York: Harper Collins/Basic Books, 1992), 92.

9 Maimonides, *Mishneh Torah, Sefer Nashim, Hilkhot Ishut*, 14:1. See also *Iggeret ha-Kodesh*, 98, described later. Maimonides adds that the halakhic tradition wisely restricted the number of a man's wives to four, so as to allow a husband to fulfil his sexual debt equitably and not be overwhelmed by it. Maimonides lived in Muslim lands. Jewish men living in Christian lands were forbidden to have more than one wife, according to a halakhic amendment (*takkanah*) attributed to Rabbenu Gershon (d. 1040), instituting monogamy but binding only on Jews in Christian lands.

10 Biale, *Eros and the Jews*, 109. He attributes the disdain for sexual pleasure with 'ecstatic Kabbalah', though other schools of esoteric thought did not exhibit that same tendency, on which see later.

11 Daniel Boyarin, 'The Married Monk: Babylonian Aggada as Evidence of Changes in Babylonian Halacha', in *A View into the Lives of Women in Jewish Societies: Collected Essays*, ed. Yael Azmon (Jerusalem: Shazar, 1995), 77–93.

12 Shulhan Arukh, *Even ha-Ezer*, 76:1–2, published in 1565 and still authoritative for orthodox Jews.

255

Eliezer's teaching then, maintained and upheld as it was through its reception in later Jewish cultures, considers sexual intimacy a value and religious norm in its own right – of course, within the framework of regulated, normative, and heterosexual marriage.

Third, the androcentric perspective embedded in the preceding Mishnah's text is palpable. It is the husband who is said to owe his wife the sexual debt within a marital relationship. With the biblical law (Exodus 21:10) as background, the list spells out *his* sexual debt to his wife. At first brush this might appear as a concern for the well-being or the rights of the wife. Yet the Mishnah does not present an equivalent ruling for a wife. Instead, she is said to owe him *labour* and particular kinds of work, implied in the contractual relationship that was rabbinic marriage: 'she grinds and bakes and cooks, launders and nurses her child, makes his bed and works in wool'.[13] A sexual debt as such is not included in *her* obligations to him or in the biblical concept of *onah*. On the contrary, her obligation in terms of marital sex is marked by prohibition, that is, the prohibition of sex during her menstrual period.[14] The wife thereby is considered responsible for guarding the observance of that biblical prohibition. At the same time, the Mishnah rules that if she 'rebels against her husband' (Mishnah, *Ketubbot* 5:7) she stands to lose her marital financial support. The talmudic tradition understands such rebellion to mean a refusal to be sexually available to him.[15] Thus although she does not have a biblically ordained sexual debt, talmudic tradition still holds her accountable as a sexual partner to her husband.[16]

Such rabbinic legal texts perhaps implement the gendered structure of sexual desire that the rabbinic interpretive traditions elicited from the biblical story of human creation, namely, through their reading of the divine punishment upon the primordial woman after the transgression of eating the

---

13 Mishnah, *Ketubbot* 5:5 (*The Oxford Mishnah*, 2: 98). These labours are codified into Jewish law beginning in the thirteenth century with Maimonides's *Mishneh Torah, Sefer Nashim, Hilkhot Ishut* 21:3.

14 Based on Leviticus 18 and 20. Rabbinic scholars devoted an entire treatise to the prohibition of menstrual sex, enmeshed with the priestly tradition of purity. Their halakhic language creates a category of personal status for her, *niddah*, 'the menstruating woman', which is also the title for the treatise. See Fonrobert, *Menstrual Purity*.

15 See Babylonian Talmud, *Ketubbot* 63a. This does not necessarily mean that the wife has to comply whenever a husband desires sex with her. Later legal authorities such as Maimonides hold that a husband should not have sex with his wife against her will.

16 Rachel Biale, *Women and Jewish Law: The Essential Texts, Their History and Their Relevance for Today*, 2nd ed. (New York: Schocken Books, 1995), 88–91; Michael L. Satlow, *Tasting the Dish: Rabbinic Rhetorics of Sexuality* (Atlanta, GA: Scholars, 1995), 282–6. For medieval permutations of this legal discussion see Avraham Grossman, *Pious and Rebellious: Jewish Women in Medieval Europe* (Waltham, MA: Brandeis University Press, 2004), 240–52.

forbidden fruit. According to the biblical text, Eve's punishment was that '*her* desire was to be *for* her husband' (Genesis 3:16, my emphasis), but apparently not his for her. As the medieval commentator Rabbi Shlomo bar Yitzhak, known as Rashi (d. 1104) glossed the biblical verse: her desire would be 'for *sex* [with her husband]'. He continues to paraphrase the divine intent: 'Nonetheless you [i.e., Eve, and perhaps every woman after her] will not have the temerity to demand [sex] verbally from him, but rather "he will rule over you" – everything will come from him and not from you.'[17] In this classic rabbinic interpretation, it is the cursed condition of women – wives, that is – to burn with desire, but not to have the courage ever to demand its satisfaction explicitly. Hence, the husband's sexual debt enjoined by rabbinic legal texts is intended to ameliorate that condition, while maintaining an obviously one-directional dynamic of sexual desire. Such representation of sexual desire within a married couple as a one-sided affair reflects the general androcentric perspective of rabbinic culture, including its preference for male control over sexual affairs. The husband pursues his desire and is to provide her with satisfaction; the wife waits for hers to be fulfilled.

Fourth and finally, as mentioned earlier, Rabbi Eliezer's list takes for granted what plays out in the cultural background from which it emerges, namely, that marriage became increasingly institutionalized in Jewish late antiquity. In biblical tradition the founding of a household is assumed to be one of the fundamental values of ancient, mostly patrilocal Israelite society: 'building the house Israel' (Ruth 4:11). The late ancient rabbis subsequently invested a concerted effort in making marriage the rock upon which Jewish society as they envisioned it was to be built. For the crucial early centuries CE, historians of Palestinian-Jewish life have pointed to the diversity of local jurisdictions to which Jews would have been subject and which Jews, including women, could rely on for settling marital disputes. The rabbis in turn invested a significant amount of hermeneutic and jurisdictional energy to normativize marriage in line with their interpretation of their ancient Torah. In the process, they may have slightly ameliorated the position of women, certainly in comparison to biblical law.[18] But in rabbinic hands marriage turned into a firmly androcentric institution, in which almost everything related to sexual matters assigned an active role to the husband and a passive role to the wife, including the structuring of sexual desire and its satisfaction. (The grammatical structure of all matters related to sex in rabbinic Hebrew

17 Rashi ad Genesis 3:16.
18 Judith Hauptman, *Rereading the Rabbis: A Woman's Voice* (Boulder, CO: Westview, 1998).

follows this pattern: he marries her, she is married to him, he acquires her, she is acquired, and so on.)

In sum, the Mishnah lays out the entire process of what it refers to with the biblical notion of the 'acquisition' (*kinyan*) of a wife by a husband, as well as with the rabbinic notion of 'sanctification' (*kiddushin*) of a wife. It traces the shifts of legal status and obligations of a couple starting with engagement and the marital contract owed a wife (*ketubbot*), to the possibility of the dissolution of the marital bond by formalized divorce (*gittin*). Fully one-sixth of this text is devoted to the laws of Jewish marriage and to the sexual relations establishing and threatening that bond, both licit and illicit. In the Mishnah, much more determinately than in biblical law, marriage itself is turned into the mainstay for regulating sexual relations. It may have taken some centuries before rabbinic courts actually gained jurisdictional control over Jewish marital relations, and for these laws and norms to take hold.[19] But in the early centuries following the Roman-Jewish wars (66–70 and 132–135 CE), the rabbis determined the criteria by which the formation of a marital bond would become one of the central and most enduring institutions of Jewish society, whether in the many centuries of diaspora or – since 1948 – in the State of Israel, which has ceded control of personal status law, including marital law, to the rabbinical courts. Modern and postmodern Jews may have marital arrangements as diverse as everyone else, but rabbinic traditions continue to reverberate into even the most egalitarian forms.

The Call of the Child: Sex and Procreation

Another and clearly related framework for rabbinic representations and discussions of sex and what is considered a supreme good in Jewish traditions all around is procreation. The divine command to the first humans to 'be fruitful and multiply' (Genesis 1:28) frames biblical literature from its very beginning. As modern scholars have shown, fertility is a concept that was central to biblical culture. Indeed, the quintessence of the biblical concept of 'blessing' is fertility, and to the priestly writers of the Bible, human fertility was both a sign of divine blessing as well as a reflection of the nature of the divine itself. That is, if humans are said to reflect the divine image and their

---

19 This is the current consensus of the field of the study of Jewish Late Antiquity in Roman Palestine, certainly since the publication of Seth Schwartz, *Imperialism and Jewish Society, 200 B.C.E. to 640 C.E.* (Princeton, NJ: Princeton University Press, 2001). In Sasanian Mesopotamia the political dynamics were slightly different.

charge is to be fertile, then the very being of the divine creator must include within itself the principle or force of fertility.[20]

Rabbinic traditions adopted this biblical penchant for fertility in a variety of ways. In rabbinic language the biblical grammatical imperative (*peru u-revu*, 'be fruitful and multiply') is turned into the very term for reproduction itself (*periyah u-reviyah*, literally, 'fruitfulness and multiplication'). While having children as such is not explicitly *prescribed* in biblical law, later classical rabbinic and medieval traditions picked up the prompt of the grammatical imperative of Genesis 1:28 and turned it into an aspirational Jewish norm. Thus, a popular medieval text listing the 613 biblical commandments forming the backbone of Jewish law, the *Sefer ha-Hinukh* (thirteenth century CE), starts with procreation as the very first biblical commandment (*mitzvah*), foundational for all the others, since it read the blessing as the divine creator's intent for the world to be populated.[21] After all, the biblical prophet Isaiah had also proclaimed in no uncertain terms that God 'created [the world] not for waste [*tohu*], but formed it for habitation [*yishuv*]'.[22] Already in the earliest rabbinic discussions this norm was considered binding for *every* Jewish 'person' (*'adam*). Thus the Mishnah insisted that '*no person* may desist from procreation, unless he [*sic*] has children [already]'. There follows a discussion of the number of children that could be considered sufficient to fulfil the norm, and which kind: 'The House of Shammai say: two males, but the House of Hillel say: A male and a female, as it is written: "male and female he created them".'[23] Early rabbinic Judaism insisted that *everyone* (at least every male) was enjoined to procreate.

Everyone? Curiously, women were not included in the biblical charge as the rabbis read it: 'The man/husband is commanded with respect to procreation but not the woman/wife' (Mishnah, *Ketubbot* 6:6). The best the rabbinic tradition has to offer in this regard is a dispute on this very issue in the Mishnah, offering a possible dissent: 'Rabbi Yohanan ben Beroka dissented: With regard to *both* of

20 Jeremy Cohen, *'Be Fertile and Increase, Fill the Earth and Master It': The Ancient and Medieval Career of a Biblical Text* (Ithaca, NY: Cornell University Press, 1989).

21 The *Sefer ha-Chinukh* is popular to this day in traditional Jewish circles. The author of the work is not entirely verifiable, but lived in thirteenth-century Spain. The Talmudic count of commandments in the Hebrew Bible is famously 613. The genre of using the commandments (*mitzvot*) as a way of organizing Jewish rabbinic teaching became particularly popular in medieval Europe. Maimonides in the twelfth century in his *Sefer ha-Mitzvot* lists the commandment of procreation as the 212th, with the comment that its intent was for the preservation of the species.

22 Isaiah 45:18, as quoted by the *Sefer ha-Hinukh* in its commentary on the first commandment. This is based on the Babylonian Talmud, *Gittin* 41b.

23 Mishnah, *Yevamot* 6:6, citing Genesis 5:2 (*The Oxford Mishnah*, 2: 33). See also Tosefta, *Yevamot* 8:3.

them [God] said: "Be fruitful and multiply"' (Mishnah, *Ketubbot* 6:6, my emphasis). This early rabbinic sage's dissent and its hermeneutic obviousness notwithstanding, the talmudic tradition of Jewish law and its later codification in the medieval period ended up siding with the first opinion. Again and again the medieval rabbis insisted that only a man, but not a woman, must reproduce. To cite the *Sefer ha-Hinukh*: 'This commandment [of procreation] does not apply to women.'[24] The exclusion of women from this particular biblical commandment seems curious, since a woman has an obvious role to play in its fulfilment. Numerous explanations have been offered in the long history of Jewish legal literature. We can posit that the restriction of the biblical obligation to procreate to men has consequences for understanding Jewish sexualities. In rabbinic-Jewish culture and its modern heirs, that is, fertility and procreative sex as circumscribed by law is turned into a masculine principle. In other words, male sex is bounded by the fertility principle, while female sex is not, or not necessarily.

Halakhic masculinity finds a certain culmination in procreative sex; women's sexuality is sidelined. Theoretically, this could have opened a window of opportunity, so to speak, for if women were not obligated, they might have had greater sexual freedom and options for sexual lives outside the law and outside of heteronormative marriage. To be clear, as far as we know this did not happen.[25] Certainly we do not have significant historical evidence in that regard until recently.

The notion of fertility and procreative sex as a masculine principle is further underwritten by rabbinically inspired theological theories. Indeed, the biblical insistence on the human as being in the image of God is in the rabbinic version instantiated in the charge of procreativity. A well-known rabbinic dialogue from the second century CE includes an emphatic voice on this issue: 'Rabbi Eliezer ben Azariah says: Whoever does *not* engage in procreation, [in fact] *diminishes the divine likeness*, as it is said: "for in the

---

24 *Sefer ha-Hinukh Bereishit* 1. See also Maimonides, *Mishneh Torah, Hilkhot Ishut* 15:2. In the Babylonian Talmud the rejection of Rabbi Yohanan ben Beroka's biblical argument links 'be fruitful and multiply' to the injunction 'to fill the land and conquer it', which – so the Talmud concludes – is self-evidently addressed to men only (Babylonian Talmud, *Yevamot* 65b). See Cohen, *The Ancient and Medieval Career of a Biblical Text*, 141–4.

25 Some rabbis made sure to make this understood. In his gloss on the Shulhan Arukh, Rabbi Moses Isserles (d. 1572) writes that 'a woman should not remain without a husband *to avert suspicion*' (Shulhan Arukh, *Even ha-Ezer* 1:13). In the contemporary world of reproductive technologies such as artificial insemination, the equivalent would be the possibility for women to bear children without husbands. For the rabbinic resistance to this, see Susan M. Kahn, *Reproducing Jews: A Cultural Account of Assisted Conception in Israel* (Durham, NC: Duke University Press, 2000).

image of God he created the human being [*'adam*]; be fruitful, then, and multiply".'[26] Procreative sex, therefore, to which now we can add *male* procreative sex, is considered a quintessential means of instantiating the divine image in human life.

Medieval Jewish mystical traditions picked up on this aspect of the earlier rudimentary theology of the rabbis and developed it in sometimes surprising directions. One of the medieval texts that has gained prominence in post-modern historiographies of Jewish sexuality is the so-called *Iggeret ha-Kodesh* or 'Holy Letter' from late thirteenth- or early fourteenth-century Spain. Its author presents a pious sex manual of sorts, instructing the addressee – his 'brother' – how 'a person [*'adam*] may consummate sexual union with his wife', not only for the sake of pleasure, but also to 'merit sons learned of the law, worthy of accepting the yoke of the kingdom of heaven'.[27] While this goal is conservative – to say the least – and falls squarely within the andro-centric rabbinic framework handed down from late antiquity, the language and means of accomplishing that goal through a perfect sexual union is innovative, endowing this text with a unique status in the intellectual history of Jewish sexualities. Importantly, the text insists against Maimonides and his love of the Aristotelian philosophical tradition that 'no one should think that sexual intercourse is ugly or loathsome, God forbid! … Rabbi Moses [Maimonides] is incorrect in praising Aristotle for stating that the sense of touch is shameful for us.'[28] The *Iggeret ha-Kodesh* therefore sets out to explain perfect timing for good sex: Friday night, the holy Sabbath. A good diet is indispensable to produce high-quality sperm, as are (mostly verbal) practices of foreplay to achieve the perfect physical union of husband and wife, based on a union of minds.[29] Maimonides, for whom the cognitive had to dominate completely and thereby erase physical passion, would surely have turned in his grave.

The *Iggeret ha-Kodesh* exercises its readers' imagination also for its esoteric dimension, extensively discussed among modern academic scholars. A perfect heterosexual union has a cosmic dimension and effect to it, with a clear androcentric focus on the production of the most wholesome and pure semen: 'for in being connected to his wife physically, and his

---

26 Tosefta, *Yevamot* 8:7 (my emphasis), citing Genesis 9:6–7, the restatement of the original divine command to the children of Noah. Cited also in the Babylonian Talmud, *Yevamot* 63b.

27 Seymour J. Cohen, *The Holy Letter: A Study in Jewish Sexual Morality, Ascribed to Nahmanides*, 2nd ed. (Northvale, NJ: Jason Aronson, 1993), 61.

28 Cohen, *The Holy Letter*, 72–4, with reference to Maimonides's *Moreh ha-Nevuhim*.

29 Cohen, *The Holy Letter*, 142.

thought cleaving to the "upper things", that very thought causes the "upper light" to descend and it hovers over that drop that it had thoughts about'.[30] That is, the divine and the human embodied spheres can, and according to this text should be joined in the moment of male ejaculation – during heterosexual marital union, of course – in an unlikely combination of cognitive and physical passion. The man is charged to connect cognitively to the divine sphere during the sexual union, thereby instrumentalizing it such that the divine presence will rest on the outcome, meaning both the sperm ('drop') as well as the perfect son. Thus medieval Jewish mystical traditions could take the rabbinic teaching about human (male) procreative sex in the image of God to a whole different spiritual level.

What all this amounts to is this: early rabbinic traditions did not make much room for alternative lifestyles, that is, alternative to the charge of procreation for a Jewish man, not even for devotional reasons. Celibacy, a complete refusal to beget children, including a refusal of marrying and mating, was never considered a value in and of itself in any of the pre-modern or early modern Jewish traditions. Modern scholarship has excavated proto- or extra-rabbinic exceptions to this rule. The proto-rabbinic Alexandrian-Jewish biblical interpreter and philosopher Philo Judaeos, for instance, may have imagined or described and idealized a Jewish asexual, monastic community in the first century BCE, the so-called Therapeutae. We do not know whether these Therapeutae ever existed, or whether they were merely the product of Philo's fantasy of a perfect, asexual community.[31] Regardless, none of this found reception in early rabbinic traditions. The one rabbinic exception to this rule appears in the dialogue between early rabbinic sages about procreation, mentioned previously. One of the sages, Shimon ben Azzai (who lived sometime in the second century CE), is outed as not even abiding by his own teaching about procreation as fulfilling a man's nature as the image of God, because he is known to have refused to do so. 'What can I do?', he is supposed to have replied. 'My soul thirsts for Torah, and *the world will be preserved* by others', that is, those who have children.[32] In the context of late antiquity, ben Azzai's excuse sounds 'Christian' in rabbinic garb: a desire for the Torah, for the divine, or for devotion to the divine in the form of love of Torah is considered as competing with, rather than as complementing, a commitment to the 'world' by having children. When all is said and

30 Cohen, *The Holy Letter*, 156.
31 Joan E. Taylor and Philip R. Davies, 'The So-Called Therapeutae of "De vita contemplativa": Identity and Character', *Harvard Theological Review* 91, no. 1 (1998): 3–24.
32 Tosefta, *Yevamot* 8:7, also Babylonian Talmud, *Yevamot* 63b.

done, however, ben Azzai's exclamation is merely an exception to the rabbinic rule inscribing procreation into male sexuality, an exception voiced by one sole scholar. No other Torah scholar cited in the talmudic tradition is reported as refusing the charge of procreation, nor being celebrated for it. Rabbinic culture early on rooted itself firmly in this particular aspect of the heritage of the biblical writings, and no Jewish cultural tradition since then ever promoted refusal of procreative sex as a religious ideal.

Modern scholarship has sought to complicate this general picture somewhat and has shown the attraction that celibate ideals exerted on late antiquity Jewish communities, certainly in later rabbinic circles of learning, both in Roman Palestine and in Sasanian Mesopotamia. These proved to be quite susceptible to the appeal that an undivided devotion held, especially for men. Talmudic literature, in fact, includes multiple stories of husbands losing themselves in their Torah studies for weeks and months, and neglecting the obligations to their home-lives, including the sexual debt to their wives.[33] Alternately, halakhic traditions weigh the obligations of domestic life against devotional life in the form of the question: when should a man marry so as to allow him to devote more time to study? Ben Azzai's conflict of desires is thus transformed into a permission to young men to delay the fulfilment of the command to procreate if they chose to engage in devotional study, reaffirmed in later writings.[34] But in the end none of this amounts ever to anything like the promoting of monastic ideals or the creating of communities based on them.

Same-Sex Relationships

The rabbinic investment in the normativization of marriage accounts for the enmeshment of sexual behaviour and sexual relations in *legal* discourse, rooted in the longer tradition of biblical law. Heteronormative marriage, once institutionalized, captured the social as well as theological imagination in a web of heteronormativity. At the same time, from early on its flip side was also generated, in the form of discussions of same-sex relations, in premodern traditions mostly – but not always – to the tune of prohibition.

---

33 Boyarin, *Carnal Israel*, ch. 5; Satlow, *Tasting the Dish*, 272–8; Jeffrey L. Rubenstein, *The Culture of the Babylonian Talmud*, 2nd ed. (Baltimore, MD: Johns Hopkins University Press, 2005), ch. 6.

34 See, for example, Maimonides, *Mishneh Torah, Hilkhot Ishut* 15:2. On the spread of the related phenomenon of child marriages in medieval Jewish communities in Europe, although focusing mostly on girls, see Grossman, *Pious and Rebellious*, 37–44.

Same-sex relations, specifically between men, entered the long history of Jewish halakhic discourse from biblical law. It forms part of the long list of prohibited sexual relations in the so-called Holiness Code, a section of the Book of Leviticus (chapters 17–26) considered by biblical scholars to be distinct stylistically and ideologically from the rest, in that it considers the entire people, rather than merely the priestly class, as subject to the requirement of 'holiness'. Addressing a male audience, it enjoins that 'With a male you shall not lie [the] lyings of a woman' (Leviticus 18:22, also Leviticus 20:13).[35] Both the phrasing and grammatical structure are famously obscure: for what are 'the lyings of a woman', and why are they in the plural? This prohibition has generated a long Jewish tradition of commentary and conflicting interpretations, from the earliest rabbinic traditions to modern scholarship on the Jewish history of sexualities. The spectrum of suggestions has extended all the way from reading the verse as a broad prohibition of any kind of male–male sexual or even erotic emotional connection, influenced by understandings and definitions of homosexuality, to a more restrictive reading of the verse as prohibiting only one act: male sexual penetration or anal intercourse. Whatever the biblical writers might have intended, the formulation minimally refers to some kind of sexual activity between two men.

Classical rabbinic tradition read the prohibition in Leviticus 18:22 mostly as a specific prohibition of the act of anal sex between men.[36] The Mishnah rules in no uncertain terms that the man who 'comes upon a male' or who commits other biblical sexual transgressions deserves capital punishment.[37] Rabbinic halakhic language shifts the biblical terminology from 'lyings of a woman' to 'lying of a male',[38] and early midrashic interpretations insist that both partners in the act are included in the biblical prohibition.[39]

---

35 The translation here is more 'literal' than the standard New Jewish Publication Society of America translation, which has: "Do not lie with a male *as one* lies with a woman." What precisely is meant by 'lyings of women' is by no means clear. Among the biblical legal collections, only the Holiness code in both its versions lists sex between men as punishable by death. The much shorter list of sexual transgressions in Deuteronomy 27:20–23 does not include it.

36 Anal sex between a heteronormative married couple was not prohibited, though it was discussed, as in the Babylonian Talmud, *Nedarim* 20b, where the metaphor of 'overturning the table' is used, which could also mean vaginal intercourse with the woman being on top. See Biale, *Women and Jewish Law*, 137–8; and Boyarin, *Carnal Israel*, 109–13.

37 Mishnah, *Sanhedrin* 7:4; see also Mishnah, *Keritot* 1:1.

38 For example, Talmud, *Sotah* 6:9.

39 Sifra, *Kedoshim* 9:14. Michael Satlow argues that the early rabbinic language of active and passive partner reflects an anxiety in particular about being penetrated as a male: *Tasting the Dish*, 186–8.

Sexuality in Jewish Traditions

In one of the more revealing moments in the early rabbinic discussions, the nature of the prohibited act is interpreted through a seemingly marginal case. The Mishnah includes a teaching about an intersex person, referred to in rabbinic language as an *androginos*,[40] or dually sexed person, as a sexual partner for a male person: 'Rabbi Eliezer [or El'azar] says: Regarding an *androginos*, the sages consider him liable for [capital punishment by] stoning, like a male' (*Yevamot* 8:6). A contemporaneous gloss adds: 'When does this apply? When he "comes upon" him by way of his "maleness" [*zakhrut*], but if he does not "come upon" him by way of his "maleness", he is exempt' from capital punishment (Tosefta, *Yevamot* 10:2). This text, which has been enormously generative for postmodern scholarship on Jewish sexuality, comes closest to naming male anal penetration as that which is entailed in the biblical prohibition. Remarkably, the tradition leaves open the possibility and even permissibility of vaginal sex with an *androginos*, a possibility that is not considered in rabbinic discussions until recently. Later talmudic discussions do analyse the prohibition at some length, in order to determine the precise conditions of the transgressive act, whether intentionality matters, and the question at which stage of the act the death penalty would be warranted.[41] Altogether, rabbinic tradition both intensified the prohibition within Leviticus 18:22 and restricted it significantly to the particular sexual act of male anal penetration.

As has long been pointed out, the Holiness Code in fact does not offer a parallel prohibition for sex between women, yet another lacuna with regard to women's sexuality. Little can be said about the biblical writers' intent, which has not precluded conjectures. Did they not consider sexual relations between women a possibility? Or did they not consider them as sex? Could it be possible that they did not consider such relations as prohibited? Regardless, the omission meant that same-sex relations between women has remained somewhat under the radar of the general androcentric orientation of halakhic tradition, albeit not entirely.

Rabbinic literature offers very few references to sexual activity between women: so few, in fact, that only the most recent scholarship in search of a Jewish queer 'tradition' has made them visible.[42] Early midrashic exegesis of

---

40 *Androginos* has often been translated as *hermaphrodite*, but the term has come to be considered as inappropriate. See Max Strassfeld, *Trans Talmud: Androgynes and Eunuchs in Rabbinic Literature* (Berkeley, CA: University of California Press, 2022).

41 Babylonian Talmud, *Yevamot* 54b; also Babylonian Talmud, *Sanhedrin* 55a.

42 Biale, *Women and Jewish Law*, 192–7; Bernadette Brooten, *Love between Women: Early Christian Responses to Female Homoeroticism* (Chicago: University of Chicago Press, 1996), 66–73; Miryam Kabakov, ed. *Keep Your Wives away from Them: Orthodox*

Leviticus 18 somewhat off-handedly mentions *marriage* between men as well as between women as examples of 'the practices of the land of Egypt ... and of the land Canaan' (Leviticus 18:3) mentioned in the preamble to the biblical list of prohibited sexual relations. The Midrash asks what precisely would have been intended by this divine warning and suggests: 'And what did they use to do? A man would *marry* a man, and a woman [would marry] a woman, a man would marry a woman and her daughter, a woman would marry two [men]. For this it was said, "and in their laws you should not go".'[43] Same-sex relations between women, along with polyandry, slip into the reading of the biblical list almost inadvertently, as a polemical tool to allow the rabbis to deepen the divide between Jewish and other people's sexual practices, whether specifically ancient Egypt and Canaan, or perhaps implying the rabbis' own contemporary Other, the Romans.[44] To this rabbinic tradition, Jewish difference accordingly consists in the refusal of same-sex *marriage*.

Talmudic discussions mention sexual activity between women only twice, both attributed to a third-century sage, Rav Huna, according to whom 'Women who are *mesolelot* with each other are prohibited from marrying a *kohen*.'[45] If the integrity of a woman's sexual body were compromised, so the androcentric reasoning of talmudic tradition goes, she would no longer be eligible for marriage with a priest (*kohen*), a relatively mild punishment. With a male sexual partner there is no question that she would lose her eligible status, but with another woman the question is how to gauge their sexual activity with each other, whether even to consider it sex or mere 'licentiousness'. The term for the sexual activity (*mesolelot*) is suggestive but not entirely transparent, since it is left unexplained. Translators have rendered it as anything from the Victorian sounding 'women that commit lewdness with each other',[46] to 'women who "rub" against'[47] or 'with each

---

  Women, Unorthodox Desires – An Anthology (Berkeley, CA: North Atlantic Books, 2010), 78–99. See also Satlow, *Tasting the Dish*, 188.

43 Sifra, *Aharei Mot* 9:8, citing Leviticus 18.3, trans. Beth A. Berkowitz, *Defining Jewish Difference: From Antiquity to the Present* (Cambridge: Cambridge University Press, 2012), 79.

44 Berkowitz, *Defining Jewish Difference*, 88.

45 Babylonian Talmud, *Shabbat* 65a.

46 The translation called the Soncino Talmud: *The Babylonian Talmud*, 18 vols., trans. Isidore Epstein (London: Soncino, 1935–52).

47 The popular translation called the Steinsaltz Talmud: *Koren Talmud Bavli*. Vol. 15: *Yevamot, Part Two*, commentary by Rabbi Adin Even-Israel Steinsaltz (Jerusalem: Shefa Foundation) can be found online at sefaria.org, which renders Rashi's comment as 'two women, who, in the manner of male-female sex rub their genitalia together' (Babylonian Talmud, *Yevamot* 76a).

other'.[48] Translations inspired by feminist sensitivities leave the term untranslated.[49]

It would seem therefore that in rabbinic law, at least in the Talmud, sexual activity between women is not particularly noteworthy, and certainly not considered a matter of biblical prohibition. Nonetheless, the medieval halakhist Maimonides opted for intensifying the rabbinic tradition and made women being *mesolelot* with each other a forbidden act, a 'deed of Egypt, potentially punishable by lashes', instructing husbands to be strict with their wives in this matter. While the punitive legal outcome is noxious, his concern also suggests that 'this matter' was common enough so as to prompt him to admonish husbands to 'prevent *the women known for these acts* from coming in for her, or her going out to them'.[50] Ironically, in his attempt to erase lesbians, Maimonides ends up providing one of the main medieval sources for modern Jewish lesbians to find themselves in the past.

Rabbinic halakhic traditions regarding same-sex relationships therefore appear to be suspended between a generally rather strong insistence on the prohibition of sexual union between men, and a general but not total silence with regard to the sexual relations between women. They generally seem to focus the punitive discourse specifically on (male) anal penetration, while the nature of women's sexual relations remains ambiguous at best.

In postmodern Jewish scholarship the question is how homosexuality can or should be read into this tradition. In the wake of second-wave feminism and LGBTQ+ liberation, most Jews initially assumed that Leviticus 18:22 along with the rabbinic tradition prohibited *homosexuality* in general, certainly in the case of gay sexuality. Lesbian sexuality remained more complex, given the history of silence, although even here rabbinic traditions were perceived as less than friendly.

The impact of modern scholarship on sexuality, as it started to intersect with Jewish scholarship in the 1990s, changed hermeneutic strategies and thinking about the history of sexualities in Jewish traditions. Michel Foucault's argument that 'homosexuality' is a modern episteme that cannot simply be retrojected into antiquity was mobilized in Jewish contexts to great effect. Following this logic, the biblical Holiness Code and its adaptations in the rabbinic tradition could not have prohibited homosexuality or gay

---

48 Satlow, *Tasting the Dish*, 190.
49 Elaine Chapnik, '"Women Known for these Acts" through the Rabbinic Lens: A Study of Hilchot Lesbiut', in Kabakov, *Keep Your Wives Away*, 78–98.
50 Chapnik, '"Women Known for these Acts"'; Maimonides, *Mishneh Torah*, *Hilkhot Issurei Biah* 21:8, repeated in the *Shulhan Arukh*, *Even ha-Ezer* 20:2.

sexuality, since it did not exist or was not conceptualized as such. Biblical and rabbinic traditions considered one specific sexual act to be prohibited, male anal penetration, but it was as a sexual act rather than as gay sexuality and identity. But neither biblical nor rabbinic traditions developed a discourse of prohibition on the broader range of same-sex *erotic* relations.

This shift, towards revealing what might be called the queer undercurrents of Jewish tradition writ large, allowed and continues to allow the opening of more space for a much fuller spectrum of human erotic relations *within* rabbinic and Jewish traditions, and thereby transforms and limits 'traditional' exclusionary practices. That space includes the narrative accounts of potentially erotic relationships in the biblical sources, such as the relationships between the biblical characters David and Jonathan, or Ruth and Naomi.[51] In both cases love is invoked, and reverberates powerfully through the narratives. In the case of rabbinic literature the dynamics of desire between male sages has also become more visible. Daniel Boyarin, *the* scholar of talmudic literature who has changed the historiography certainly of rabbinic and arguably of Jewish sexuality, has made this case to the greatest effect, by moving the wealth of narrative traditions about the relationship between men and between male sages in the Talmud to the foreground. Boyarin turned one of the well-known talmudic narratives of the genesis of a study partnership between two famous talmudic sages, Rabbi Yohanan and Resh Laqish (both of whom lived in the early third century CE), into one of the most iconic narratives about homoeroticism in the Talmud. Read in queer terms, Resh Laqish, the passionate, masculine man, falls for the effeminate, beardless Rabbi Yohanan, who channels the former's dangerous passion into a scholarly 'study-partnership', and has him marry his sister as the mediating tool for consummation of the one sexual activity the two men cannot engage in.[52] Ever since, it has become difficult not to read rabbinic and especially talmudic culture as infused with homoeroticism, and the rabbis as somewhat queer characters. Jewish men have thus gained an expansive history of not just hetero- but also profound homoerotics and queer desire. Women, on the other hand, lesbians and straight, possess only preciously few sources for their queer history.

---

51 Martti Nissinen, *Homoeroticism in the Biblical World: A Historical Perspective*, trans. Kirsi Stjerna (Minneapolis, MN: Fortress, 1998).

52 Daniel Boyarin, *Unheroic Conduct: The Rise of Heterosexuality and the Invention of the Jewish Man* (Berkeley, CA: University of California Press, 1997), ch. 3.

New Traditions in (Post-)Modernity

The advance of secularization in the modern world and, perhaps even more importantly, the civil liberation movements in the aftermath of the Second World War generally had the effect of diversifying the Jewish world, including traditions and cultures of sexuality. Jews as Jews became prominently involved in a variety of new intellectual, artistic, and institutional contexts. Synagogues helped to define the boundaries of Jewish communities and their reinterpretations of traditions, and turned into the religious movements as we know them now, with a wide spectrum of adaptations of the rabbinic traditions. Reform, Orthodox, and Conservative movements in Judaism, and the Reconstructionist movement later, did not split because of differing ideas about sexualities, but certainly these subsequently contributed to defining differences. As LGBTQ+ identities have become de-pathologized and more widely recognized, these Jewish movements have begun to accept and legitimize not only identities but also diverse marriages. At the same time, LGBTQ+ Jews have organized themselves into synagogal communities, for example, in the United States in New York (Congregation Beit Simchat Torah, founded in 1973) and in San Francisco (Sha'ar Zahav, founded in 1977). More recently, transgender, intersex, and other queer Jews have become more outspoken and visible in Jewish communities especially in the United States.

By way of conclusion, I point to what might be thought of as an anthological mode of writing that has significantly contributed, especially in recent years, to producing new Jewish traditions of sexualities, just as feminist Jews in the 1970s and 1980s produced anthologies to underwrite feminine and feminist ways of thinking and being Jewish. As collective forms of writing, anthologies such as *Keep Your Wives away from Them* by Jewish lesbians and their allies, *Balancing on the Mechitza* by transgender Jews and their allies, *Torah Queeries: Weekly Commentaries on the Hebrew Bible* by queer Jews, signal moments of consolidation of modern Jewish sexual identities as Jewish sexual traditions. It is these new postmodern traditions that point to the expansiveness of 'the' Jewish tradition.

Further Reading

Biale, David. *Eros and the Jews: From Biblical Israel to Contemporary America.* New York: Harper Collins/Basic Books, 1992.

Biale, Rachel. *Women and Jewish Law: The Essential Texts, Their History and Their Relevance for Today*, 2nd ed. New York: Schocken Books, 1995.

Boyarin, Daniel. *Carnal Israel: Reading Sex in Talmudic Culture*. Berkeley, CA: University of California Press, 1993.

　　Unheroic Conduct: The Rise of Heterosexuality and the Invention of the Jewish Man. Berkeley, CA: University of California Press, 1997.

Cohen, Jeremy. *Be Fertile and Increase, Fill the Earth and Master It: The Ancient and Medieval Career of a Biblical Text*. Ithaca, NY: Cornell University Press, 1989.

Drinkwater, Gregg, Joshua Lesser, and David Shneer, eds. *Torah Queeries: Weekly Commentaries on the Hebrew Bible*. New York: New York University Press, 2012.

Dzmura, Noach, ed. *Balancing on the Mechitza: Transgender in Jewish Community*. Berkeley, CA: North Atlantic Books, 2009.

Fonrobert, Charlotte. *Menstrual Purity: Rabbinic and Christian Reconstructions of Biblical Gender*. Stanford, CA: Stanford University Press, 2000.

　　'Regulating the Human Body: Rabbinic Legal Discourse and the Making of Jewish Gender'. In *Cambridge Companion to the Talmud and Rabbinic Literature*, ed. C. Fonrobert and M. Jaffee, 270–95. Cambridge: Cambridge University Press, 2007.

Greenberg, Steven. *Wrestling with God: Homosexuality in the Jewish Tradition*. Madison, WI: University of Wisconsin Press, 2004.

Grossman, Avraham. *Pious and Rebellious: Jewish Women in Medieval Europe*. Waltham, MA: Brandeis University Press, 2004.

Hauptman, Judith. *Rereading the Rabbis: A Woman's Voice*. Boulder, CO: Westview, 1998.

Kabakov, Miryam, ed. *Keep Your Wives Away from Them: Orthodox Women, Unorthodox Desires – An Anthology*. Berkeley, CA: North Atlantic Books, 2010.

Kiel, Yishai. *Sexuality in the Babylonian Talmud: Christian and Sasanian Contexts in Late Antiquity*. Cambridge: Cambridge University Press, 2016.

Nissinen, Martti. *Homoeroticism in the Biblical World: A Historical Perspective*. Trans. Kirsi Stjerna. Minneapolis, MN: Fortress, 1998.

Rosen-Zvi, Yishai. *Demonic Desires: 'Yetzer Hara' and the Problem of Evil in Late Antiquity*. Philadelphia: University of Pennsylvania Press, 2011.

Satlow, Michael L. *Tasting the Dish: Rabbinic Rhetorics of Sexuality*. Atlanta, GA: Scholars, 1995.

Secunda, Shai. *The Talmud's Red Fence: Menstrual Impurity and Difference in Babylonian Judaism and Its Sasanian Context*. Oxford: Oxford University Press, 2020.

Sienna, Noam. *An Anthology of Queer Jewish Texts from the First Century to 1969*. Philadelphia: Print-O-Craft, 2019.

Simcha DuBowski, Sandi, dir. *Trembling before G-d*. New Yorker Films, 2001. 1 hr 24 min.

Strassfeld, Max. *Trans Talmud: Androgynes and Eunuchs in Rabbinic Literature*. Berkeley, CA: University of California Press, 2022.

Wegner, Judith R. *Chattel or Person: The Status of Women in Mishnah*. Oxford: Oxford University Press, 1988.

Wheeler-Reed, David. *Regulating Sex in the Roman Empire: Ideology, the Bible, and the Early Christians*. New Haven, CT: Yale University Press, 2017.

13

Sexuality in Christian Traditions

ADRIAN THATCHER

Christian teaching about sexuality, marriage, the body, and gender, never uniform, has undergone many changes over time. This chapter begins with some teachings about sexuality from the New Testament or Christian Bible, and traces some lines of their development within the churches up to the present time.

Christianity in Antiquity

Jesus, his disciples, and Paul the Apostle were all Jews, so the Hebrew Bible, which Christians term the Old Testament, provides an important background to New Testament teaching about sexuality.[1] Christians rely on the Gospels for the teaching of Jesus, but these are already the products of churches a generation after his life. In a preserved saying (addressed to men) Jesus warns that 'everyone who looks at a woman with lust has already committed adultery with her in his heart' (Matthew 5:28). But *gunè*, 'woman', is just as easily translated as 'wife', so the verse need not be read (as it invariably was) as a general condemnation of sexual desire. Adultery was a property crime, 'a form of theft by one man of what belonged to another man and complicity in theft by that man's wife'.[2] But marriage itself and the possibility of divorce is contested in the Gospels. In Mark and Matthew, Jesus affirms marriage and its permanence: 'what God has joined together, let no one separate' (Matthew 19:6; Mark 10:9). But Jesus in Luke's Gospel roundly dismisses marriage as inconsistent with the new age (Luke 20:34–38). Paul, in

---

1 Although most scholars prefer the term 'Hebrew Bible', for the sake of familiarity the form 'Old Testament' is retained here.
2 William Loader, *Sexuality in the New Testament* (London: SPCK, 2010), 61.

a long argument, recommended singleness (1 Corinthians 7:25–39), permitting marriage reluctantly as a defence against male passion (7:36), while warning that 'those who marry will experience distress in this life' (7:28). Marriage cannot be a priority because 'the present form of this world is passing away' (7:31). Yet the later New Testament letters assume most Christians will be living in households headed by a married man with a wife, children, and slaves (Colossians 3:18–4:1; Ephesians 5:22–6:9; 1 Peter 2:18–3.7).

The earliest New Testament document to discuss sexual questions (1 Corinthians) was written between 53 and 57 CE, well before the consensus date of the first gospel (Mark, c. 70 CE) and by someone (Paul) who converted to Christianity after the death of Jesus and who never knew him. The Christian community in Corinth was coping with a number of issues related to sex, and asked Paul for advice. A church member is having sex with his stepmother (5:1–5), and another with a prostitute (6:15–20). At the other extreme the church asked Paul whether or not a man should 'touch' a woman (7:1) at all, while some worshippers found the practice of the spectacle of unveiled women praying and prophesying a disorder (11:2–16). Christians are in some material sense the many members of Christ's one body, Paul warned (12:12–28), so when a male believer has sex with a prostitute, Christ also has sex with her (6:15–16). The problem of liturgical disorder also had a solution: hierarchical order. The order is God–Christ–husband–wife (11:3). Wearing a veil is a sign of women's place in the hierarchy, and possibly protection from randy angels (those who had sex with women in Genesis 6:1–4) as well (11:10). More than this, the hierarchy is justified by a one-sided appeal to the idea of the 'image of God' (Genesis 1:27). In the Old Testament women and men alike share the image; in the New Testament only the man 'is the image and glory of God', while 'woman is the glory of man' (11:7).

A later letter attributed to Paul introduced the notion of love into the marriage relationship. It required husbands to love their wives 'as Christ loved the Church and gave himself up for her' (Ephesians 5:25), but this was a 'masterly' asymmetrical love, requiring from wives instead submission and obedience. 'Sexual acts and love were not associated.'[3] Gospel ambivalence about marriage together with Paul's preference for its avoidance 'left a fatal legacy to future ages'.[4] His gospel delivered converts from the obligation to

---

3 John T. Noonan, Jr., *Contraception: A History of Its Treatment by the Catholic Theologians and Canonists* (Cambridge, MA: Harvard University Press, 1986), 73.
4 Peter Brown, *The Body and Society: Men, Women and Sexual Renunciation in Early Christianity* (London: Faber & Faber, 1990), 55.

obey the Jewish law, but the holiness demanded by the Pentateuch (the first five books of the Hebrew Bible) and ritualized in Temple worship was instead to be relocated in the blameless lives of second- and third-generation Christian communities. In the absence of Christ's return, ascetic sexual conduct, or preferably no sexual contact at all, became an identifying character of the faith.

The male–female hierarchy in the later writings of the New Testament reflected Graeco-Roman beliefs about reproduction, sexuality, and gender. From Aristotle on it was widely believed that male sperm provided the 'form' or 'soul' of the embryo while the mother provided the *materia* or 'matter'[5] through her *katamenia* or menstrual blood.[6] Women were inferior versions of men, as the Christian philosopher and theologian Thomas Aquinas (1225–74) was later to insist as well. The human body was a default male body,[7] and human coupling re-enacted the ubiquitous view that men were born to be active, hard, and penetrators, and women passive, soft, and penetrated.[8] These antique assumptions also help to explain Paul's description of the 'degrading passions' of the Gentiles: 'Their women exchanged natural intercourse for unnatural, and in the same way also the men, giving up natural intercourse with women, were consumed with passion for one another' (Romans 1:26–7). Paul knew that the Holiness Code of the Old Testament (Leviticus 17–26) forbade men, on pain of death, to 'lie with a male as with a woman; it is an abomination' (Leviticus 18:22), but his version of the Christian faith emphasized freedom from the law. He is likely to have agreed that the 'abomination' was a gender infraction, since men are penetrators and women are penetrated. For a man to be penetrated is to consent, fatally, to the role of playing a woman. That explanation might account for the word *malakoi* ('softies') in the vice-list of 1 Corinthians 6:9 (though the meaning of *malakos* is broader: it means anything 'effeminate').[9] Later, in the East, John Chrysostom (347–407 CE) used this argument. Accusing a putative passive same-sex partner, he wrote

---

5 See Adrian Thatcher, *Redeeming Gender* (Oxford: Oxford University Press, 2016), 19–21.
6 Aristotle, *On the Generation of Animals*, trans. Arthur Platt (1912; last updated 2013), Book 4, Book 2.1, https://en.wikisource.org/wiki/On_the_Generation_of_Animals/.
7 Thomas Laqueur, *Making Sex: Body and Gender from the Greeks to Freud* (Cambridge, MA: Harvard University Press, 1990).
8 Mathew Kuefler, *The Manly Eunuch: Masculinity, Gender Ambiguity, and Christian Ideology in Late Antiquity* (Chicago: University of Chicago Press, 2001), ch. 1.
9 Dale B. Martin, *Sex and the Single Saviour: Gender and Sexuality in Biblical Interpretation* (Louisville, KY: Westminster John Knox, 2006), 47.

'For I should not only say that you have become a woman, but that you have lost your manhood.'[10]

Into the second century CE there was a growing revulsion among Christian male leaders, often later termed the 'Church Fathers', towards the bodies of women. A New Testament letter had already blamed Eve for bringing catastrophe into the world, and made the salvation of womankind depend on their willingness to become mothers (1 Timothy 2:14–15), while in the last New Testament writing a special place was reserved in heaven for exceptional Christian men 'who have not defiled themselves with women, for they are virgins' (Revelation 14:4). By the start of the third century the Church Fathers agreed that having sex during a woman's menstrual period led to the birth of deformed children.[11] The soul–body dualism of Greek thought inevitably devalued the human body because it was mortal, perishable and unruly, and within a gender hierarchy the bodies of women were further relegated: for centuries they were thought to betray a lack of form and mental capacity along with an excess of passion and emotion. The influential Marcion (85–c. 160), a Christian theologian, took literally the saying of Jesus that marriage belonged to a former age (Luke 20:34–36), and like the ascetic Christian sect the Encratites (from the Greek *enkrateia*, 'continence'), he required complete sexual abstinence from church members (a powerful motive for missionizing). Valentinus (100–160), another theologian and candidate for the bishop of Rome, that is, leader of its churches in 140, proclaimed a system in which the male–female binary manifest throughout the 'fallen world' would be redeemed not by restoration but by elimination. The female would become male. The last of 114 sayings of Jesus in the extracanonical Gospel of Thomas, roughly contemporaneous with Valentinus, conveys a similar sentiment: 'Every woman who makes herself male will enter the kingdom of heaven.'[12] These ideas are often termed 'Gnostic', and were soon to be regarded as a heresy.

The oft-quoted accusation by the prolific Christian theologian Tertullian (155–c. 240), that women 'are the Devil's gateway',[13] truthfully reflects the growing disdain of his (male) theological contemporaries for women's bodies and their depiction of womankind as temptresses. In the next century,

---

10 John Chrysostom, 'Homily 4', *Homilies on Romans*, www.newadvent.org/fathers/210 204.htm.

11 Uta Ranke-Heinemann, *Eunuchs for the Kingdom of Heaven: The Catholic Church and Sexuality* (London: Penguin Books, 1990), 21–3.

12 *Gospel of Thomas*, trans. Thomas O. Lambdin, 1988, www.marquette.edu/maqom/Gos pel%20of%20Thomas%20Lambdin.pdf.

13 Tertullian, *On the Apparel of Women*, 1.1, www.newadvent.org/fathers/0402.htm.

voluntary exile to the desert was one means whereby monks avoided women.[14] Many male leaders consciously contrasted their sexual renunciation with Roman masculinity, identifying it with the practice, if not display, of holiness. Origen (c. 184–253), the most notable Christian theologian of the third century, took literally the saying of Jesus about 'eunuchs who have made themselves eunuchs for the sake of the kingdom of heaven' (Matthew 19:12) and may have castrated himself.

Marriage had its cautious defenders. Some men and women attempted 'spiritual' or 'chaste' marriages,[15] but these were generally condemned. Clement of Alexandria (c. 150–c. 250) permitted married Christians to have sex, as the pagan Stoics did – but without passion and with due decorum, and only 'for the succession of children and for the completion of the world'.[16] This 'stark insistence' caused 'the delicate bloom' of any sense that pleasure or mutuality might be enjoyed by having sex, 'to vanish forever from late antique Christian thought'.[17] The theologian Jovinian (d. 405) was condemned as a heretic in 393 for arguing that celibacy and marriage were equally acceptable to God. The much more influential theologian Jerome (c. 347–420), who gave the Western Church its Latin Bible or Vulgate, retorted that while marriage replenishes the earth (citing Genesis 1:28), 'virginity fills paradise'.[18]

The theologian and bishop Augustine of Hippo (354–430), the most important Latin Church Father, constructed an awkward middle ground between these rival positions: 'It is good to marry, because it is good to beget children, to be a mother of a family: but it is better not to marry.'[19] He famously stated what Pope Pius XI in 1930 was still to call 'a splendid summary of the whole doctrine of Christian marriage'.[20] Marriage has 'three goods', Augustine wrote: 'offspring, faith[fulness], and sacrament'.[21] The first two are shared 'throughout all nations and men'. The third good, the sacramental bond which not even separation can dissolve, was declared the distinction between Christian and non-Christian marriage. The elevation of virginity did not preclude a gradual sacralization of marriage, prompted by the laity who

14 Brown, *Body and Society*, part 2.
15 Dyan Elliott, *Spiritual Marriage: Sexual Abstinence in Medieval Wedlock* (Princeton, NJ: Princeton University Press, 1993).
16 Clement of Alexandria, *Miscellanies*, 2, www.newadvent.org/fathers/02102.htm.
17 Brown, *Body and Society*, 133.
18 Jerome, *Against Jovinian*, 1.16, www.newadvent.org/fathers/30091.htm.
19 Augustine, *Of the Good of Marriage*, 9, www.newadvent.org/fathers/1309.htm.
20 Pope Pius XI, *Casti Connubii (On Chaste Marriage)* (1930), 10, www.vatican.va/content/pius-xi/en/encyclicals/documents/hf_p-xi_enc_19301231_casti-connubii.html.
21 Augustine, *Good of Marriage*, 32.

wished to marry and have sex, and by the twelfth century, marriage was *officially* declared one of the seven sacraments of the church.

Attitudes of Christian slave owners to their slaves were ambiguous. In Roman society free men had sexual access to their slaves, male and female. They 'played something like the part that masturbation has played in most cultures', while 'the commodification of sex was carried out with all the ruthless efficiency of an industrial operation'.[22] Slaves were included in many Christian churches and households, so Christian owners had to negotiate between regarding them as Christians and as property. On the one hand, *The Shepherd of Hermas* (written *c.* 120 CE) enjoined wealthy Christians to purchase the freedom of slaves, and the Greek theologian Gregory of Nyssa (*c.* 335– *c.* 395), unusually, condemned slavery outright.[23] On the other hand, Augustine held that slavery as an institution was divine punishment for sin, and yet permitted by God as part of the natural order, so that slaves by obedience acquired the virtue of humility. The desire for manumission, he taught, was a form of blasphemy.[24] There was contempt for slaves among many Christian owners and writers,[25] which contributed to the continued practice of slave ownership into the nineteenth century. A fifth-century Christian theologian blamed the fall of the Roman Empire on God's punishment of male slave owners who had sex with their slaves.[26] We have almost no evidence about how slaves fared from the slaves themselves. Bishops and the clergy who led the churches were expected not to have sex with their female slaves, but the practice was tolerated among laymen who married.[27] Christian slaves could marry only with their master's permission.

The long-standing influence of Augustine on subsequent centuries was not confined to marriage. His doleful sexual pessimism received doctrinal justification in the doctrine of original sin. In his semi-autobiographical *Confessions*, he lamented his pre-conversion sexual history, and candidly described his ongoing inability to control his erections. This inability, he adjudged, was due

---

22 Kyle Harper, *From Shame to Sin: The Christian Transformation of Sexual Morality in Late Antiquity* (Cambridge, MA: Harvard University Press, 2013), 26–7, 49.

23 D. Bentley Hart, 'The "Whole Humanity": Gregory of Nyssa's Critique of Slavery in Light of His Eschatology', *Scottish Journal of Theology* 54, no. 1 (2009): 51–69.

24 Augustine, *City of God*, 19.15, www.newadvent.org/fathers/120119.htm.

25 Kimberly Flint-Hamilton, 'Images of Slavery in the Early Church: Hatred Disguised as Love?', *Journal of Hate Studies* 2 (2003): 27–45.

26 Salvian of Marseilles, *De gubernatione Dei*. See C. L. De Wet, '"The Barbarians Themselves are Offended by our Vices": Slavery, Sexual Vice and Shame in Salvian of Marseilles' *De gubernatione Dei*', *HTS Teologiese Studies/Theological Studies* 75 no. 3 (2019): 1–8.

27 Mary E. Sommar, *The Slaves of the Churches: A History* (Oxford: Oxford University Press, 2020), 242.

not simply to carnal desire, but also to *weakness of will*. This was a deep-seated psychological flaw within him which he traced back to the 'original sin' of Adam and Eve and their resulting body-shame. They had no sex in the Garden of Eden, but since there is no sex without sinful desire, having sex becomes the means by which original sin is transmitted. Augustine was the first theologian to advocate a non-allegorical, that is, a literal, reading of Genesis. 'By making the story of Adam and Eve the central episode in the drama of human existence',[28] Augustine added to the current of misogyny its alleged source in the first temptress, Eve. 'I fail to see', wrote Augustine, 'what use woman can be to man if one excludes the function of bearing children.'[29] By emphasizing the universal wretchedness of the human condition, and the hell-bound destination of all the unelected and unbaptized, sexual pessimism was extended into every nook and cranny of mortal life. Its influence remains.

The escalating valuation accorded to lifelong male and female virginity could not be anticipated from the Old Testament, which did not value it at all. It finds expression in the belief that Mary the mother of Jesus was a virgin, then ever-virgin, and then officially declared the 'God-bearer' (*theotokos*) at the authoritative Council of Ephesus in 431. The legends describing the birth of Jesus in the Gospels of Matthew and Luke (Matthew 1–2; Luke 1:1–2:40) belong to a late stratum of New Testament writing. Matthew cites Isaiah 7:14 – 'A virgin shall conceive and bear a son' (Matthew 1:23) – but neither the Greek term, *parthenos*, found in the Septuagint (the Greek translation of the Hebrew Bible), nor the original Hebrew of Isaiah, *alma*, mean 'virgin'. The terms mean a 'young woman'. The attempted genealogies of Jesus in both Gospels assume Joseph's paternity (Matthew 1:16), Luke deliberately refuting any suggestion of a supernatural birth ('Jesus ... being the son (as was supposed) of Joseph' – 3:23, New Revised Standard Version, Anglicized). Jesus is unambiguously 'the carpenter's son' (Mark 6:3; Matthew 13:55) with four brothers and at least two sisters, while John's Gospel insists he is 'the son of Joseph' (1:45, 6:42).

But Christianity grew in a world that was at best suspicious of human bodies and their desires, and as the conviction grew that Jesus was 'truly God', the more it was felt necessary to assert that Jesus, while also 'truly human', must have avoided the impurities of sexual intercourse, and even, for some, conception and birth. Joseph 'knew her not till she had brought

---

28 Stephen Greenblatt, *The Rise and Fall of Adam and Eve* (New York: W. W. Norton, 2017), 121.
29 Augustine, *On the Literal Interpretation of Genesis*, 9.5.9.

forth her firstborn son' (Matthew 1:25, King James Version). This became 'Joseph knew her *not at all* and she had *only* a firstborn son.' In a Gnostic work of the mid-second century, Mary is already the 'Holy Mother of God': Joseph an old man with children charged 'to take into your keeping the virgin of the Lord'; and the midwife Salome, after an intimate examination of Mary's vagina following Jesus' birth, declares that she remains a virgin.[30] Jerome later declared Jesus' stepbrothers and stepsisters were *cousins*, thereby assuming the continued virginity even of Joseph.

That Mary is the Mother of God remains central to the worship and devotion of Roman Catholic and Orthodox Churches. Elements such as mystery, maternity, relationality, transcendence, respect for womankind, and obedience to God accompany devotion to Mary, and for millions of Christians these clearly outweigh the difficulties introduced by historical scholarship, feminist criticisms about Mary's passivity, the unattainability of Marian perfection, the impossibility of being a real mother while retaining all the attributes of a virgin, and modern doubts about the incompatibility of *any* miraculous virgin birth doctrine with belief in the complete humanity of the child born.[31]

Mary provided a model of virginity as well as of maternity for Christian women. There were undoubted advantages of virginity for women. They avoided the obvious perils of childbirth, the heartbreak of frequent child mortality, and payment of the 'marital debt' – the obligation to have sex with a demanding husband, authorized by Paul (1 Corinthians 7:3). Vowed virgins had a certain status within early Christian congregations, symbolized by exemption from veil-wearing in a minority of them, a practice angrily condemned by Tertullian.[32] But their status was double-edged, since theologians such as Jerome regarded virginal women as honorary men, 'making themselves male' by avoiding sex.

Jesus provided the model for male virginity, though it is much less frequently discussed among the Church Fathers. A question arose which expressed the deep unease of *male* virgins with their unruly bodies – nocturnal emissions of semen or, more colloquially, 'wet dreams'. How did they arise? Were they sinful? Since wet dreams were regarded as 'pollutions', lasting for a day before cleansing, could a clergyman performs the Christian

---

30 *Protevangelium of James*, 1, 9, 20, www.newadvent.org/fathers/0847.htm.

31 Elisabeth T. Vasko, 'The Difference Gender Makes: Nuptiality, Analogy, and the Limits of Appropriating Hans Urs von Balthasar's Theology in the Context of Sexual Violence', *Journal of Religion* 94, no. 4 (2014): 504–28.

32 Tertullian, *On the Veiling of Virgins*, www.newadvent.org/fathers/0403.htm.

rituals if he had ejaculated in the previous twenty-four hours?[33] John Cassian (d. c. 435) affirmed the prevailing view that they were caused by 'a surfeit of food', or 'a careless mind', or 'the snares of the mocking enemy'.[34] The answer of Augustine and Aquinas to the second question is they are not sinful per se, because they are involuntary: the will and reason are suspended during sleep. Nonetheless, the preceding causes may be sins. They may be caused physically by the discharge of excess 'seminal humour',[35] yet the origin of even these quasi-mechanical ejaculations may lie sinfully in the depths of the soul. Since the Desert Fathers of the third century, the 'Devil' or particular demons were perceived as enemies, able to pierce the armour of the Christian soul, to infiltrate all the senses, and even to manifest themselves through the bodies of real women.[36]

Christianity in Medieval Europe

It is highly likely that 'clerical efforts to disavow and distance themselves from their own fantasy lives' led to 'an institutional war against women, who were perceived as polluting the ministers of the altar'.[37] The Gregorian Reform in the Western churches of the eleventh century required priests to be celibate, and married priests to abandon their wives. Priestly celibacy was a major issue in the break between the Catholic and Orthodox Churches in 1054. 'In the high Middle Ages the intimate enemy (namely, erotic thoughts and their physiological consequences), unexamined and repressed internally, was ultimately externalized and began to walk abroad.'[38]

The woman and the demon became combined in the figure of the witch. The *Malleus Maleficarum* (Hammer of Witches, 1486), written by the Dominican monk and witch hunter Heinrich Kramer, must be one of the most distressingly misogynistic religious texts ever produced, insisting 'Any person, whatever his rank or position, upon such an accusation [of witchcraft], even if he confesses his crime, let him be racked.'[39] The Devil was believed to be able, by deploying *incubi* (male-bodied demons) and *succubi*

---

33 Dyan Elliott, *Fallen Bodies: Pollution, Sexuality, and Demonology in the Middle Ages* (Philadelphia: University of Pennsylvania Press, 1999), 14–34.
34 John Cassian, *Conferences*, trans. Boniface Ramsey (New York: Paulist Press, 1997).
35 Thomas Aquinas, *Summa Theologiae*, 2.2, q.154, art. 5, www.newadvent.org/summa/3.htm.
36 Elliott, *Fallen Bodies*.   37 Elliott, *Fallen Bodies*, 7.   38 Elliott, *Fallen Bodies*, 29.
39 Heinrich Kramer and James Sprenger, *The Malleus Maleficarum*, trans. Montague Summers (Whitefish, MT: Kessinger, 2003), 1.1, p. 6.

(female-bodied demons), to have sex with both men and women, and to bring about real pregnancies.[40]

The Gregorian Reforms also sparked a growing intolerance for men having sex with men. It was called the 'vice of sodomy', a term apparently coined in Peter Damian's *Book of Gomorrah* (1051), which reported on and condemned the many examples of sexual immorality among the clergy. Yet even as Damian wrote, in some of the churches of the East, rites of blessing for same-sex couples were authorized, and almost eighty manuscripts documenting these were published in 1995, generating unresolved controversy about their meaning.[41] Some historians propose there was 'a vibrant culture of same-sex interactions'[42] in the European Middle Ages, even among Christians, prior to this shift into intolerance.

Aquinas had already confirmed the inferior ontological status of women in his *Summa Theologiae*. Using the ancient but newly rediscovered biology of Aristotle, he asserted that individual women are 'defective and misbegotten, for the active force in the male seed tends to the production of a perfect likeness in the masculine sex; while the production of woman comes from defect in the active force or from some material indisposition, or even from some external influence; such as that of a south wind'.[43] Sex should happen only within marriage and only for the purpose of procreation, Aquinas argued.[44] The 'vice against nature' was not confined to men having sex with men, but was attached 'to every venereal act from which generation cannot follow'. At the same time, potentially procreative sexual acts, such as 'simple fornication', incest, and rape are *in accord with nature*, although wrong for other reasons (not least the disadvantage to any child who has an absent biological father). When kisses and caresses are enjoyed merely for 'delectation', they too are sinful. Unnatural vice, following Aquinas, was any sexual act not potentially procreative, which might include 'procuring pollution, without any copulation, for the sake of venereal pleasure' (i.e., masturbation, alone or with other persons – and still prohibited today by the Catholic Church as 'an intrinsically and gravely disordered action'[45]); or having sex

---

40 Kramer and Sprenger, *Malleus Maleficarum*, 1.3, p. 28.
41 John Boswell, *The Marriage of Likeness: Same-Sex Unions in Pre-Modern Europe* (London: HarperCollins, 1995).
42 Helmut Puff, 'Same-sex Possibilities', in *The Oxford Handbook of Women and Gender in Medieval Europe* ed. Judith Bennett and Ruth Mazo Karras (Oxford: Oxford University Press, 2013), 379–92, at 379.
43 Aquinas, *Summa Theologiae*, 1.92.1, www.newadvent.org/summa/1092.htm.
44 Thomas Aquinas, *Summa Theologiae*, 2.2.154.
45 *Catechism of the Catholic Church*, para. 2352, www.vatican.va/archive/ENG0015/__P85 .HTM.

with an 'undue species' (non-human animals), with an 'undue sex' (men with men, or women with women); or 'by not observing the natural manner of copulation' (men on top), 'undue means' (using an object other than the penis for penetration), or 'other monstrous and bestial manners of copulation' (including heterosexual anal or oral penetration and contraception).[46]

Handbooks of penance, or *Penitentials*, were used by confessors to assign punishments for sins to individual Christians from the sixth century CE onwards, assigning penalties in accordance with the gravity of the offence. The great majority of Christians were married, and faced with such regulation it is difficult to imagine how they coped with it. Expectations were varied. Sex was forbidden during feast days, holy days, and the three holy seasons of the Christian calendar (Lent, Advent, and Pentecost), before and after receiving communion, and in any position other than 'missionary'. It was to be fully clothed, and always in the dark. According to one model, this meant that married couples were allowed to have sex less than four times a month.[47] They were told that intercourse was inevitably polluting, and so spiritually dangerous, while those who ignored the Penitential recommendations may have been subject to fear and guilt at the prospect of imposed penance, humiliation, or worse: the thought of eternal punishment for unforgiven sin. Many people lived in a state of 'unmarriage', a term used to encompass the forgotten arrangements forged by people who could not, or would not, conform to the severe marital norm, including men of the Catholic clergy. Instead they formed secret or unlawful marriages.[48]

Once marriage had become a sacrament in the twelfth century, a more precise definition of it was needed. The theologian and bishop of Paris Peter Lombard (*c.* 1096–1160) held that consent alone made the marriage, though others held that it was consummation, in keeping with the idea that in marriage 'two become one flesh' (Matthew 19:5, quoting Genesis 2:24). This debate was already the outcome of a millennium of negativity about sex, exacerbated by a conundrum of the time: was the marriage of Mary and Joseph a real marriage? Believed never to have been consummated, 'this was one of the reasons why it was believed to be a perfect marriage'.[49] The final position in the Catholic Church was that consent makes the marriage valid

---

46 Aquinas, *Summa Theologiae*, 2.2.154, q.11.4.
47 See James A. Brundage, *Sex, Law and Marriage in the Middle Ages* (Aldershot, UK: Ashgate, 1993), 154–65.
48 Ruth Mazo Karras, *Unmarriages: Women, Men, and Sexual Unions in the Middle Ages* (Philadelphia: University of Pennsylvania Press, 2012).
49 Adrian Thatcher, *Marriage after Modernity: Christian Marriage in Postmodern Times* (Sheffield, UK: Sheffield Academic, 1999), 109.

(*ratum*) and the first (successfully completed) act of sexual intercourse rendered it indissoluble. Failure to consummate (*consummatum*) became a ground not for divorce but for annulment. Orthodox Churches took a different view. While remaining a sacrament, consent is already assumed at the marriage ceremony, and the 'making' of the marriage is the blessing conferred on the couple by the priest. Other more relational, embodied accounts of marriage were available in the West from ancient Roman discussions about what constituted marriage, such as a 'partnership for the whole of life' (*consortium totius vitae*) or the presence of 'marital affection' (*maritalis affectio*), but the influence of the allegedly sexless marriage of Mary and Joseph won the day in Western Christendom and has remained ever since.

Christianity in the Early Modern World

The Protestant Reformation in the sixteenth century 'brought a momentous change in direction in the Christian history of sexuality'.[50] The former Catholic monk and Protestant theologian Martin Luther (1483–1546) ridiculed celibacy, viewing it as impossible for most people, and an obvious source of much sexual immorality among the clergy. Following Paul (1 Corinthians 7) and in accordance with his famous doctrine of justification by faith alone, he thought marriage was the means provided by God for the discharge of sexual desire and protection against sin, and he could see no accrual of merit in struggling against it. The Calvinist Protestant tradition developed a covenant model of marriage based on biblical notions of a covenant between God and Israel, whereas the Anglican Protestant tradition produced the 'commonwealth' model, emphasizing the vital contribution of marriage to the patriarchal structure of the family, the wider society, and the created order.[51] Protestant clergy were allowed to marry, shedding the mystique attaching itself to the celibate priest who (at least theoretically) transcended the lusts of the flesh. Protestant clergy lived openly with their wives and children and became role models for the patriarchal family in most Protestant traditions. Marriage ceased to be a sacrament in Protestant countries. Since it was sacramentality that rendered marriage indissoluble, the ultimate ground for refusing divorce was removed. Modern Orthodox Churches, however, affirm

---

50 Diarmaid MacCulloch, *Reformation: Europe's House Divided, 1490–1700* (London: Penguin Books, 2004), 609.

51 See John Witte, Jr., *From Sacrament to Contract: Marriage, Religion, and Law in the Western Tradition* (Louisville, KY: Westminster John Knox, 1997).

marriage is a sacrament, yet allow divorce and further marriages up to three, on the grounds that the Church has the authority to declare the marital bond dissolved.[52]

Protestants did not interfere with the earlier legal basis of marriage as consent between two eligible persons. They did insist that marriage vows be taken in the present tense (*verba de presenti*).[53] Thus they objected to vows taken in the future tense (*verba de futuro*), which had commonly been done at a future couple's betrothal, and which were widely understood to be the beginning of marriage (the 'spousals'), but which could be done while the future couple were children (a child could be betrothed at the age of seven). Luther called this notion of betrothal a *Narrenspiel* or 'fools' game',[54] and both Protestants and Catholics moved against it, requiring parental consent in the case of minors and the presence of a priest or minister and other witnesses to establish a marriage's validity. Their replacement, a declaration of 'engagement', had no legal force. Marriages were now thought to begin with weddings (the 'nuptials') – a radical change which was much resented, at first ignored, and in many countries never fully accepted. The title of the marriage ceremony in the English Prayer Book ('The Solemnization of Matrimony'), for example, assumes a matrimonial state has already been achieved, waiting to be solemnized. Thus despite the fact that officially a marriage began with the wedding, betrothal 'constituted the recognized rite of transition from friends to lovers, conferring on the couple the right to sexual as well as social intimacy' for centuries after the Reformation.[55] One historian estimates that in some countries between 40 to 50 per cent of brides were pregnant when they came to the altar.[56] Pre-marital (i.e., pre-ceremonial) sex became a new category of sexual sin, however, now named by the biblical term 'fornication'.

Living together before or apart from marriage is now extremely common among Christians throughout the world, and the churches have not dealt with it. The assumption, growing since the sixteenth century, that marriages begin with weddings, impeded a more developmental or 'processual'

---

52 See Kallistos Ware, 'The Sacrament of Love: The Orthodox Understanding of Marriage and Its Breakdown', *Downside Review* 109, no. 375 (1991): 79–93.

53 Thatcher, *Marriage after Modernity*, 108–16.

54 Joel F. Harrington, *Reordering Marriage and Society in Reformation Germany* (Cambridge: Cambridge University Press, 1995), 30.

55 John Gillis, *For Better, For Worse: British Marriages, 1600 to the Present* (Oxford: Oxford University Press, 1985), 47.

56 Lawrence Stone, 'Passionate Attachments in the West', in *Perspectives on Marriage: A Reader*, ed. Kieran Scott and Michael Warren (New York: Oxford University Press, 1993), 171–9, at 176.

understanding of the beginnings of marriage. The Church of England attempted to accommodate cohabitation in a 1995 report,[57] which was poorly received, and has evaded the problem ever since. In 2015, Pope Francis took a different approach, citing poverty as an understandable reason why couples lived together before marriage, acknowledging some couples were simply delaying and not avoiding marriage, and observing that 'respect also can be shown for those signs of love [among such couples] which in some way reflect God's own love'.[58] A Synod of the Russian Orthodox Church in 2000 acted against rigorism about cohabitation and 'remind[ed] pastors that the Orthodox Church also respects common-law marriage'.[59]

While the Reformation was taking place in Europe, several European countries began exploring, colonizing, and exploiting whole continents. European Christianity was exported first to Central and South America, then to Africa, Asia, and North America. The missionaries took with them a strict understanding of marital and sexual morality, and a rigid gender binary. Both of these would clash with Indigenous moralities. While it is dangerous to generalize, 'indigenous peoples quickly noted that Christian conquerors and colonists – sometimes including the clergy themselves – did not practice what they preached, but raped local women, entered into bigamous marriage, or engaged in numerous sexual relationships'. Spanish men in the Americas 'had essentially polygamous households', while 'almost all European men in the Caribbean had sexual relations with slaves or free mixed-race women, and half of all slave children in Brazil were baptized with an unknown father'.[60]

Christian attitudes towards sex created sizeable stumbling blocks to the conversion efforts around the world. The missions struggled with polygamy, which was commonplace in Africa, the Muslim Middle East, and China. Indigenous cultures were sometimes more tolerant of same-sex relationships than the missionaries, in places such as Japan, the Pacific Islands, and North and Central America. Christians found respect for marriage throughout the world, but were slow to understand that their own emphases on individual

---

57 *Something to Celebrate: Valuing Families in Church and Society* (London: Church House, 1995).
58 Pope Francis, *Amoris Laetitia* (2015), para. 294, w2.vatican.va/content/dam/francesco/pdf/apost_exhortations/documents/papa-francesco_esortazione-ap_20160319_a moris-laetitia_en.pdf.
59 Russian Orthodox Church Department for External Church Relations, *The Basis of the Social Concept*, 10.2, https://mospat.ru/en/documents/social-concepts/.
60 Merry E. Wiesner-Hanks, *Christianity and Sexuality in the Early Modern World: Regulating Desire, Reforming Practice* (New York: Routledge, 2000), 143, 163.

consent and pre-marital chastity ignored the communitarian and familial dimension of marriage in colonized cultures.[61] Church insistence on couples refraining from sex prior to a wedding, for example, was incompatible with African traditional marriage. And while European Christians had long struggled with marriages between those of different faiths, Christians across the globe resisted interracial marriages. Today, ironically, many African and Asian Christian leaders see these imposed ideas about sex and marriage as culturally traditional, deploring liberalization in former colonized countries, and resisting the expectation of liberalization within their churches as neo-colonial interference.

Yet it is difficult to generalize too broadly about Christian notions of proper sex, as a few examples from North America will demonstrate. New England settlers were initially Protestant and Puritan, and sexually strict, but some Protestant groups deviated from the marital norm. Around 1747, Shakers established alternative communities which attempted to combine communal living with celibacy. In the eighteenth century, the Moravians established colonies in Pennsylvania and North Carolina. They saw marital sex as a sacramental union, a direct sharing in the union between Christ and His Church. Mystical experience, however, was also shared between persons of the same sex, and expressed itself in homoerotic acts among the Brethren.[62] In 1848, the first Oneida Community was established in New York, practising 'bible communism'. This included the sharing of wives in a practice called 'complex marriage'. Husbands practised *coitus reservatus*, refraining from ejaculation during intercourse, while communities later practised 'stirpiculture', pairing couples in order to create spiritually superior children.[63] The more numerous Mormons practised plural or polygamous marriage from the 1830s onwards across the United States, with the prospect of eternal or 'celestial' marriage for the most worthy.[64]

---

61 Benezeri Kisembo, Laurenti Magesa, and Aylward Shorter, *African Christian Marriage* (Nairobi: Paulines, 1977).

62 Paul Peucker, *Marriage and the Crisis of Moravian Piety in the Eighteenth Century* (University Park, PA: Pennsylvania State University Press, 2015).

63 Anthony Wonderley, *Oneida Utopia: A Community Searching for Human Happiness and Prosperity* (Ithaca, NY: Cornell University Press, 2017).

64 Kathryn M. Daynes, 'Celestial Marriage (Eternal and Plural)', in *The Oxford Handbook of Mormonism*, ed. Terryl L. Givens and Philip L. Barlow (Oxford: Oxford University Press, 2015), 334–49.

Modern Legacies of the Christian Tradition on Sex

The Christian traditions about sex have become increasingly less authoritative in the modern world. It is due in part to the ascendancy of scientific ideas about sex, to the assumption of regulatory powers over marriage and private life by the modern state, and to the decline overall in church adherence as well as the outright rejection of Christian belief by many in the regions of the world where it was strongest. Nonetheless, the legacy of Christian belief continues to inform modern persons in various and significant ways.

Attitudes towards homosexuality are a perfect example. From the 1920s there was a growing social tolerance of homosexuality in several Western countries, powered by the acknowledgement of the positive role of private intimacy in (heterosexual) marriage, the adoption of the 'medical model' of homosexuality which presumed a condition that was not chosen, and the increasing conviction that criminal law had no place in regulating private consensual behaviour.[65] A later medical and scientific consensus identified homosexuality 'as a normal variant within the spectrum of human sexual experience'.[66] The Stonewall riots in New York (1969) were a significant event in the formation of the gay liberation movement in the United States and around the world (including the adoption of the term 'gay' by homosexual people themselves). People living in the 1960s in the 'Western world' who are alive now have seen the social reframing of same-sex relations from criminality to matrimony. Some Christian leaders followed suit. The then Archbishop of Canterbury, Michael Ramsey, supported the passing of the 1967 Sexual Offences Act in Britain, partially decriminalizing consensual 'homosexual acts'. The growing conservative reaction was inevitable. Cardinal Joseph Ratzinger (prior to becoming Pope Benedict XVI) told all the Catholic bishops that while 'the particular inclination of the homosexual person is not a sin, it is a more or less strong tendency ordered towards an intrinsic moral evil', and 'an objective disorder', so that 'the living out of this orientation in homosexual activity' cannot be 'a morally acceptable option'.[67] Orthodox Churches remain opposed to same-sex marriage, although a Pew Research Centre poll found a majority of Orthodox Christians in Greece and the

---

65 See David Hilliard, 'Homosexuality', in *The Cambridge History of Christianity*. Vol. 9: *World Christianities c. 1914–c. 2000*, ed. Hugh McLeod (Cambridge: Cambridge University Press, 2003), 546–55, esp. 548–9.

66 Christopher C. H. Cook, 'Science and Theology in Human Sexuality', *Theology and Sexuality* 24, no. 3 (2018): 183–99.

67 Cardinal Joseph Ratzinger, *Letter to the Bishops of the Catholic Church on the Pastoral Care of Homosexual Persons* (1986), 3, www.vatican.va/roman_curia/congregations/cfaith/documents/rc_con_cfaith_doc_19861001_homosexual-persons_en.html.

United States do not condemn homosexuality.[68] A fractious meeting of the Lambeth Conference of Anglican bishops in 1998 condemned 'homosexual practice as incompatible with Scripture'.[69]

The bitter and disruptive arguments over homosexuality in the Churches are based on the diverse ways of interpreting the Bible. Sexual acts between men and between women are condemned by Paul as being contrary to nature (Romans 1:26–7). They are condemned in the popular second-century CE *Apocalypse of Peter*, which describes the eternal torments of sinners in hell. The punishment for 'men who defiled their bodies acting as women' and women who 'lay with one another as a man with a woman'[70] is to be hurled down a great cliff, driven back up, and then hurled down again, forever. The text, and others like it, clearly condemns both male and female homoeroticism, and the manner of the punishment endured confirms their sin was gender reversal or 'infraction', that is, because 'these men and women reversed their proper roles during their lifetimes, so too must they now pursue a ceaseless process of going up and coming down ... reversing their direction just as they reversed the gendered order of society'.[71] The condemnation of homosexuality was repeated in various ways throughout Christian history: it was non-procreative, non-marital, and non-hierarchical. Disapproval of homosexuality has lingered longer in the churches than belief in hell.

Attitudes towards contraception and masturbation are another excellent example of the modern legacy of long-standing tradition. The Protestant reformer John Calvin, commenting on the Old Testament story of Onan's 'spilling his seed on the ground' (Genesis 38), held that masturbation was tantamount to murder, an attempt 'to destroy a part of the human race'.[72] But there is no direct biblical prohibition of contraception or masturbation. The Onan story demonstrates instead what is probably the most commonly used contraceptive method worldwide: *coitus interruptus*. Fear of the negative consequences of masturbation reached a peak in the eighteenth century when it became a medical pathology, understood as a primary manifestation of excessive

---

68 Pew Research Centre, *Religion and Public Life* (2017), www.pewforum.org/2017/11/08/orthodox-take-socially-conservative-views-on-gender-issues-homosexuality/.

69 Resolution 1.10, *Anglican Communion*, www.anglicancommunion.org/resources/document-library/lambeth-conference/1998/section-i-called-to-full-humanity/section-i10-human-sexuality?author=Lambeth+Conference&subject=Human+sexuality.

70 *The Apocalypse of Peter*, 31, www.earlychristianwritings.com/text/apocalypsepeter-roberts.html.

71 Bernadette J. Brooten, *Love between Women: Early Christian Responses to Female Homoeroticism* (Chicago: University of Chicago Press, 1996), 306.

72 John Calvin, *Commentary on Genesis*, https://ccel.org/ccel/calvin/calcom02/calcom02.xvi.i.html.

individualism.[73] The memoir of John Cannon, a literate English farm labourer, between 1705 and 1719 shows he had pleasurable sexual relationships with three women, including mutual masturbation, yet he avoided intercourse with them all and considered them virgins when they later married other men.[74] No one knows how widespread the practice of bodily intimacies excluding sexual intercourse with ejaculation actually was.

The Christian objection to contraception was its frustration of the only licit purpose of intercourse: procreation. Gnostics who denied the goodness of creation and taught it was wrong to procreate sometimes used *coitus interruptus* or alternative forms of infertile sexual contact to prevent procreation, thereby associating contraception with heresy. Augustine confirmed the Manichees practised it for similar reasons in the fourth century,[75] as did the much-persecuted Cathars (or Albigensians) in the twelfth and thirteenth centuries. No Christian Church approved contraception until the Lambeth Conference of Anglican bishops in 1930,[76] provoking an angry retort from Pope Pius XI in the same year that it remained a 'grave sin' to frustrate the 'natural power' of marriage to 'generate life'.[77] Pope Paul VI's encyclical *Humanae vitae* (Of Human Life, 1968) shocked millions of Roman Catholics by upholding the ban on all 'artificial' forms of contraception, including condoms, diaphragms, and the newly invented birth control pill. He allowed 'that married people may … take advantage of the natural cycles immanent in the reproductive system and engage in marital intercourse only during those times that are infertile'.[78] Critics were swift to point out that 'natural family planning' of the sort that Pope Paul VI was recommending was contraception under another name.[79] In 1981 Pope John Paul II, in the face of much dismay and open disregard among the worldwide laity, reaffirmed the Catholic Church's ban, teaching that the 'total personal self-giving'[80] of *every* act of (marital) sexual intercourse was

73 Thomas W. Laqueur, *Solitary Sex: A Cultural History of Masturbation* (New York: Zone Books, 1984).
74 Tim Hitchcock, 'Redefining Sex in Eighteenth Century England', *History Workshop Journal* 41 (1996): 73–90.
75 Noonan, *Contraception*, 114.
76 Resolution 15, *Anglican Communion*, www.anglicancommunion.org/media/127734/1930.pdf?year=1930.
77 Pope Pius XI, *Casti connubii* (*Chaste Marriage*) (1930), 56, www.vatican.va/content/pius-xi/en/encyclicals/documents/hf_p-xi_enc_19301231_casti-connubii.html.
78 Pope Paul VI, *Humanae vitae* (*Of Human Life*) (1968), 12, www.vatican.va/content/paul-vi/en/encyclicals/documents/hf_p-vi_enc_25071968_humanae-vitae.html.
79 Gareth Moore, *The Body in Context: Sex and Catholicism* (London: Continuum, 1992), 163–5.
80 Pope John Paul II, *Familiaris consortio* (1981), section 11, www.vatican.va/content/john-paul-ii/en/apost_exhortations/documents/hf_jp-ii_exh_19811122_familiaris-consortio.html.

compromised by contraception – a partial withholding of each partner from the other, a failure to share the God-given power of fecundity. Prolonged opposition to the use of condoms in the time of HIV/AIDS caused countless lives to be lost. In 2016 Pope Francis, while not revoking previous teaching, has emphasized instead that 'decisions involving responsible parenthood' are firmly a matter of conscience: 'The parents themselves and no one else should ultimately make this judgment in the sight of God.'[81] The Orthodox Churches and most Protestant Churches accept contraception as a fact of married life.[82]

Abortion is a third obvious example of the weight of the Christian tradition on sex. The *Roe v. Wade* decision of the United States Supreme Court in 1973 intensified Catholic and Evangelical Protestant opposition to abortion. There had been a strong tradition against abortion from the *Didache* ('Teaching', written probably in the late first century) onwards, where it is associated with magic and witchcraft,[83] and the *Letter of Barnabas* (written between *c.* 70 and 132),[84] which adds 'Neither shalt thou kill it [a child] when it is born.'[85] The exposure of children after birth was the usual method of 'disposing' of them for the ancient Romans, and Christians were resolutely opposed to this. But there is also a 'counternarrative' which posits instead that abortion was 'viewed and judged variously in relation to fetal development and the woman's motivation, methods, and circumstances'.[86] Augustine distinguished between foetuses which were 'fully formed', and those which were not, expressing doubt whether the latter were human enough to rise from the dead at the end of time when all others would.[87] The various *Lives* of early Irish saints record abortion miracles in which male and female saints *cause* the unwanted pregnancies of chaste women to disappear.[88] Not surprisingly, later manuscripts gloss or omit these accounts. They may indicate an unusually tolerant attitude to abortion in medieval Ireland, together with a sanguine acceptance of

---

81 Pope Francis, *Amoris Laetitia*, 222.
82 William Basil Zion, *Eros and Transformation: Sexuality and Marriage: An Eastern Orthodox Perspective* (Lanham, MD: University Press of America, 1992), 239–62.
83 *Didache*, 2, www.newadvent.org/fathers/0714.htm.
84 *Letter of Barnabas*, trans. J. B. Lightfoot, 19.5, www.earlychristianwritings.com/text/barnabas-lightfoot.html.
85 *The Epistle of Barnabas*, 19.5.
86 Margaret D. Kamitsuka, *Abortion and the Christian Tradition: A Pro-Choice Theological Ethic* (Louisville, KY: Westminster John Knox, 2019), 24, 31.
87 Augustine, *Enchiridion*, 23.85, www.tertullian.org/fathers/augustine_enchiridion_02_trans.htm#C23.
88 Zubin Mistry, 'The Sexual Shame of the Chaste: "Abortion Miracles" in Early Medieval Saints' Lives', *Gender and History* 25, no. 3 (2013): 607–20.

unwanted pregnancies.[89] But they also reveal the value to women of chastity, even supernaturally restoring to them the virginal state of which they had been deprived, even at supreme cost to the unborn. Opposition to abortion is constant in Christian traditions, but the popular justification, that the foetus is a person from the moment of conception, is recent.

Sex, including homosexuality, contraception, and abortion, became the principal ground on which larger 'culture wars' were fought in the churches throughout the world over the authority of the Bible, modern biblical criticism, the legitimacy of theological development, and the role of science in matters of belief. The overturning of the *Roe v. Wade* decision by the Supreme Court of the United States in June 2022 effectively ended the constitutional right to an abortion for millions of women, and brought the culture wars in that country to new depths of rancour and harm. Although opposed by the majority of Americans, the decision was strongly supported by most Roman Catholic and Evangelical Protestant Christians.

Prioritizing these issues has deflected attention from other troubling sexual issues in the Churches, perhaps deliberately. Violence against women is rife throughout the world, leading some to speak of a generalized 'rape culture'.[90] While multi-causal, intersectional explanations of gender violence are needed, theological emphases on male 'headship', uxorial obedience, and scriptural justifications for continuing gender inequality, play their part in many churches.[91] The sexual abuse of minors in churches throughout the world, together with failed attempts at concealment, have led to widespread, angry, and astonished criticism of the patriarchal theology, preparation for ministry, and the dysfunctional ecclesiastical organization which was powerless to prevent it. Concealment of clergy misdemeanours has a long history, fuelled by the fear of causing scandal, leading to the tacit toleration of same-sex relations among clergy supposedly hidden from lay suspicion.[92] A leading Catholic commentator adjudges that the scandal has 'highlighted, in the most

---

89 Maeve Callan, 'Of Vanishing Fetuses and Maidens Made-Again: Abortion, Restored Virginity, and Similar Scenarios in Medieval Irish Hagiography and Penitentials', *Journal of the History of Sexuality* 21, no. 2 (2012): 282–96.

90 Caroline Blyth, Emily Colgan, and Katie B. Edwards, eds., *Rape Culture, Gender Violence, and Religion: Interdisciplinary Perspectives* (Cham, Switzerland: Palgrave Macmillan, 2018).

91 Elizabeth Koepping, *Spousal Violence among World Christians: Silent Scandal* (London: Bloomsbury Academic, 2021).

92 Dyan Elliott, *The Corrupter of Boys: Sodomy, Scandal, and the Medieval Clergy* (Philadelphia: University of Pennsylvania Press, 2020), esp. chs. 3 and 4.

Sexuality in Christian Traditions

shocking way possible, how a malignant nexus of sexuality and power could undermine a tradition so completely'.[93]

The dominant traditions of Christian sexual thought still posit firm binaries around sexuality: male–female (sex), masculine–feminine (gender), married–unmarried (status), and heterosexual–homosexual (desire, identity). A new ideology, complementarity, is deployed to endorse them.[94] Binary (and hierarchical) thinking lies behind the refusal of Catholic, Orthodox, and many conservative churches to ordain women. In 1994 John Paul II seemed to foreclose the possibility forever, causing distress to the many women throughout the world believing themselves called to priesthood.[95] But these binaries are increasingly problematic and even dangerous. One in 2,500 people is 'intersex' (once known as 'hermaphrodite'), and increasing numbers of people identify as 'transgender'. They feel their gender does not correspond with their biological sex.[96] There are *hijras* in India, *two-spirits* among Native Americans, *kathoeys* in Thailand, *leiti* in Tonga, *fa'afafine* in Samoa, all of whose gender does not conform to their biological sex. Missionaries generally failed to comprehend them and generally persecuted them. Intersex and transgender Christians are now developing their own theologies.[97]

Christian churches remain riven with controversy about sexuality (and gender), and the harm caused by the controversy still undermines the case for Christian belief.

Further Reading

Beardsley, Christina, and Michelle O'Brien, eds. *This Is My Body: Hearing the Theology of Transgender Christians*. London: Darton, Longman, and Todd, 2016.

Boswell, John. *The Marriage of Likeness: Same-Sex Unions in Pre-Modern Europe*. London: HarperCollins, 1995.

Bray, Alan. *The Friend*. Chicago: University of Chicago Press, 2003.

---

93 Linda Hogan, 'Conflicts within the Roman Catholic Church', in *The Oxford Handbook of Theology, Sexuality and Gender*, ed. Adrian Thatcher (Oxford: Oxford University Press, 2015), 323–39, at 336.

94 Adrian Thatcher, *Gender and Christian Ethics* (Cambridge: Cambridge University Press, 2021), 96–118.

95 'Ordinatio Sacerdotalis, 4, www.vatican.va/content/john-paul-ii/en/apost_letters/199 4/documents/hf_jp-ii_apl_19940522_ordinatio-sacerdotalis.html.

96 Susannah Cornwall, *Sexuality and Uncertainty in the Body of Christ: Intersex Conditions and Christian Theology* (London: Equinox, 2010); Thatcher, *Gender and Christian Ethics*, 149–52.

97 Megan K. DeFranza, *Sex Difference in Christian Theology: Male, Female, and Intersex in the Image of God* (Grand Rapids, MI: Eerdmans, 2015); Christina Beardsley and Michelle O'Brien, eds., *This Is My Body: Hearing the Theology of Transgender Christians* (London: Darton, Longman and Todd, 2016).

Brown, Peter. *The Body and Society: Men, Women and Sexual Renunciation in Early Christianity*. London: Faber & Faber, 1990.

Brownson, James V. *Bible, Gender, Sexuality: Reframing the Church's Debate on Same-Sex Relationships*. Grand Rapids, MI: Eerdmans, 2013.

Brundage, James A. *Law, Sex, and Christian Society in Medieval Europe*. Chicago: University of Chicago Press, 1987.

Bynum, Caroline Walker. *Holy Feast and Holy Fast: The Religious Significance of Food to Medieval Women*, 2nd ed. Berkeley, CA: University of California Press, 1992.

Clark, Anna. *Desire: A History of European Sexuality*. London: Routledge, 2008.

Coontz, Stephanie. *Marriage, a History: From Obedience to Intimacy or How Love Conquered Marriage*. New York: Viking, 2005.

Cornwall, Susannah. *Sexuality and Uncertainty in the Body of Christ: Intersex Conditions and Christian Theology*. London: Equinox, 2010.

Elliott, Dyan. *The Bride of Christ Goes to Hell: Metaphor and Embodiment in the Lives of Pious Women, 200–1500*. Philadelphia, PA: University of Pennsylvania Press, 2012.

  Fallen Bodies: Pollution, Sexuality, and Demonology in the Middle Ages. Philadelphia: University of Pennsylvania Press, 1999.

Foucault, Michel. *The History of Sexuality*. Vol. 1: *An Introduction*. Trans. Robert Hurley. Harmondsworth, UK: Penguin, 1976.

Greenblatt, Stephen. *The Rise and Fall of Adam and Eve*. New York: W. W. Norton, 2017.

Harper, Kyle. *From Shame to Sin: The Christian Transformation of Sexual Morality in Late Antiquity*. Cambridge, MA: Harvard University Press, 2013.

Kuefler, Mathew. *The Manly Eunuch: Masculinity, Gender Ambiguity, and Christian Ideology in Late Antiquity*. Chicago: University of Chicago Press, 2001.

Laqueur, Thomas. *Making Sex: Body and Gender from the Greeks to Freud*. Cambridge, MA: Harvard University Press, 1990.

Loader, William. *Sexuality in the New Testament*. London: SPCK, 2010.

MacCulloch, Diarmaid. *A History of Christianity*. London: Penguin, 2009.

  Reformation: Europe's House Divided, 1490–1700. London: Penguin Books, 2004.

Noonan, John T., Jr. *Contraception: A History of Its Treatment by the Catholic Theologians and Canonists*. Cambridge, MA: Harvard University Press, 1986.

Phillips, Kim M., and Barry Reay. *Sex before Sexuality: A Premodern History*. Cambridge: Polity, 2011.

Ranke-Heinemann, Uta. *Eunuchs for the Kingdom of Heaven: The Catholic Church and Sexuality*. London: Penguin Books, 1990.

Thatcher, Adrian, ed. *The Oxford Handbook of Theology, Sexuality and Gender*. Oxford: Oxford University Press, 2015.

Wiesner-Hanks, Merry. *Christianity and Sexuality in the Early Modern World: Regulating Desire, Reforming Practice*, 3rd ed. New York: Routledge, 2019.

Witte, John, Jr. *From Sacrament to Contract: Marriage, Religion, and Law in the Western Tradition*, 2nd ed. Louisville, KY: Westminster John Knox, 2012.

14
Sexuality in Islamic Traditions

SERENA TOLINO

In a well-known article, Afsaneh Najmabadi asked provokingly whether gender and sexuality could be useful categories of historical analysis when looking at the past and when looking 'beyond the Americas'. As she put it, 'if Foucault was right that the nineteenth-century transformations made sexuality the truth of our identification and the basis of our becoming subjects, have we in turn made sexuality the truth of our historiographies even beyond the temporal and geographical terms of that initial proposition?'[1] Her question was inspired by the debate that followed the publication of Foucault's *History of Sexuality* and by the emergence of feminist studies, which also came to influence Islamic studies. But her question was also made possible by the awareness that categories such as gender and sexuality emerged within scholarship that focused mostly on Western societies: universalizing them as epistemological and ontological categories and applying them elsewhere could represent a Eurocentric move.

In the case of an article about Islamic traditions, the risk is even bigger: as Aysha Hidayatullah points out, 'one inevitably risks the essentialization of a complex, multifaceted set of religious beliefs and practices'. Indeed, she adds, it is clear that '*there is no one Islam*, just as there is no *one* understanding of sexuality'.[2] Even within Islamic traditions, namely traditions in which

---

I would like to thank Ashraf Hassan for his support with locating primary sources and understanding difficult passages, and Helena Rust for our brainstorming on this chapter and its title.

1 Afsaneh Najmabadi, 'Beyond the Americas: Are Gender and Sexuality Useful Categories of Historical Analysis?', *Journal of Women's History* 18, no. 1 (2010): 11–21, at 17–18.

2 Aysha Hidayatullah, 'Islamic Conceptions of Sexuality', in *Sexuality and the World's Religions*, ed. David W. Machacek and Melissa M. Wilcox (Santa Barbara, CA: ABC Clio, 2003), 257–92, at 259.

Islam has a prominent role, a monolithic vision of gender and sexuality is not appropriate: we move within contested fields, with different institutional realms trying to impose control over them, even within the same historical context.

Nonetheless, recent research on gender and sexuality in and on Muslim-majority societies has proven that these still seem to be extremely fruitful and productive categories of analysis, even though historicizing, contextualizing, and reflecting on them is essential. In a recent book introduction, the editors propose four insights about sex and desire in the Middle East:

> (1) The variability of hierarchies shaping norms; (2) the multiplicity of sources of authority on gender and sexuality that always coexist; (3) the existence of realms of activity in which the quest for pleasure seems to take precedence over dominant ethical goal setting, sometimes producing its own framework of normative expectations; and (4) the limits of our capacity as historians and social-science researchers to give a full account of the experience of sexuality.[3]

In this chapter I would like to follow that approach when looking at Islamic traditions, putting religious aspects at the centre of my analysis but also trying to go beyond them. There are certainly specific normative characteristics that are shared across different regions and different historical periods when looking at sexuality in Islamic traditions. At the same time, norms are context-based: a scholar writing a book of Islamic jurisprudence in the twelfth century CE would not say the same things about sex that a scholar writing a book of literature in the same period would do, even if they both came from the same socio-cultural background. Recognizing this plurality of discourses is necessary if we want to understand what sexuality in Islamic traditions may look like.

In this chapter I will present an overview of the most relevant aspects related to sexuality in Islamic traditions, looking at how, especially in pre-modern societies, different normative systems coexisted beside each other. In this I am inspired by Thomas Bauer, who showed that in pre-modern Islamic history there was not one single register of truth, but many 'truths'. Islamic culture was characterized by tolerance for what Bauer calls 'cultural ambiguity', which should not be seen simply as 'norm and deviation'

---

3 Aymon Kreil, Lucia Sorbera, and Serena Tolino, 'Introduction: The Main Names of Desire; On the Study of Sexual Practices, Norms and Binaries in the Middle East', in *Sex and Desire in Muslim Cultures: Beyond Norms and Transgression from the Abbasids to the Present Day* (London: I. B. Tauris, 2021), 1–19, at 3.

(*Norm und Abweichung*), 'but more as a coexistence of different norms'.[4] Cultural ambiguity helps explain why sexual practices that were illegitimate from the perspective of *fiqh* (Islamic jurisprudence) were perfectly tolerated from a social perspective. I will also make use of Marshall Hodgson's term 'Islamicate', which he used to describe 'the social and cultural complex historically associated with Islam and the Muslims, both among Muslims themselves and even when found among non-Muslims' in Muslim-majority states, in contrast to 'Islamic', which only refers to the religion.[5]

Given the existence of different norms, this chapter focuses on different discourses on sexuality, beginning with the Qur'an, the Sunna, a term used to refer to the traditions of Islam, but more technically also to sayings and accounts of Muḥammad that gave advice on matters that went beyond the Qur'an, and the so-called *ḥadīths*, which provided a normative example of how to live. I then look at Islamic jurisprudence (*fiqh*), medicine, and books on *bāh* (coitus). Many of these sources were written by scholars of similar background, that is, men of the well-educated urban cosmopolitan elite, but they still presented different approaches to and ideas about sexuality, given the different aims of these genres. I will focus on those aspects of sexuality that were considered legitimate, and then on those sexual practices that were debated, such as masturbation, or considered completely illegitimate from the perspective of Islamic jurisprudence, such as same-sex relations. The chapter ends with a brief discussion of how traditional ideas have been reinterpreted and/or challenged by feminist approaches to Islam.

Although it is important to situate each source in its specific historical and social context, sources discussed in this chapter are taken from different historical periods, as this chapter aims at providing an overview of some of the shared Islamic traditions on sex/uality. Much has changed over these centuries, but Islamic traditions still play a role in how sexuality is understood. For example, the understanding of the contract of marriage in many contemporary Muslim-majority states is related to understandings of marriage in pre-modern *fiqh*. Indeed, when law was codified in many Muslim-majority countries during the colonial period and then the nationalist age,

---

4 Thomas Bauer, *Die Kultur der Ambiguität: Eine andere Geschichte des Islams* (Berlin: Verlag der Weltreligion im Insel, 2011). Trans. as *A Culture of Ambiguity: An Alternative History of Islam*, trans. Hinrich Biesterfeldt and Tricia Tunstall (New York: Columbia University Press, 2021).

5 Marshall G. S. Hodgson, *The Venture of Islam: Conscience and History in a World Civilization*. Vol. 1: *The Classical Age of Islam* (Chicago: University of Chicago Press, 1977), 59.

family law remained 'the last fortress of the Sharīʿa to survive the ravages of modernization'.[6] Thus along with change, continuities should be taken into account.

Sexuality in the Qurʾan and the Sunna

The Prophet Muḥammad (c. 570–632), the founder of Islam, experienced religious visions and revelations. His followers memorized these revelations and some wrote them down. Shortly after his death, memorized and written materials were collected and organized into an official version, known as the Qurʾan (literally 'recitation'), which Muslims revere as the direct word of God communicated to Muḥammad. The Qurʾan is organized into chapters called *suras*, which are divided into verses, so that references refer to chapter and verse. It addresses topics ranging from religious practices to the different phases of the human life, to the afterlife, to the organization of the early Muslim community, and much more. Therefore, it comes as no surprise that topics related to sexuality are mentioned and that the Qurʾan has a central place when it comes to understandings of sexuality within Islamic traditions.

The Qurʾan often stresses the relevance of marriage. For example, verse 24:32 says: 'And marry the unmarried among you and the righteous among your male slaves and female slaves. If they should be poor, Allāh will enrich them from His bounty, and Allāh is all-Encompassing and Knowing.'[7] The relationship between the spouses is depicted as one that is to be defined by kindness and compassion. For example, verse 7:189 states that: 'It is He who created you from one soul and created from it its mate that he might dwell in security with her. And when he [man] covers her, she carries a light burden [a pregnancy] and continues therein. And when it becomes heavy, they both invoke Allāh, their Lord, "If You should give us a good [child], we will surely be among the grateful."'[8] Similarly, verse 30:21 mentions: 'And of His signs is that He created for you from yourselves mates that you may find tranquillity in them; and He placed between you affection and mercy. Indeed in that are signs for a people who give thought.'

---

6 Wael Hallaq, *Sharīʿa: Theory, Practice, Transformations* (Cambridge: Cambridge University Press, 2009), 446.
7 All quotations from the Qurʾan are from the Saheeh International English translation.
8 'Light' in this passage refers to a pregnancy.

These and other verses show that while reproduction is viewed as a fundamental pillar of marriage, marriage is more than that. It is seen as a place to find love, compassion, and safety. Polygyny was common in Arab society before Muḥammad, though it was generally limited to wealthier families. The Qur'an restricted the number of wives a man could have to four, and prescribed that he treat them equitably (Qur'an 4:3). Sex is praised and considered a natural part of matrimonial life. For example, verse 2:187 states that 'It has been made permissible for you the night preceding fasting to go to your wives [for sexual relations]. They are a clothing for you and you are a clothing for them. Allāh knows that you used to deceive yourselves, so He accepted your repentance and forgave you. So now, have relations with them and seek that which Allāh has decreed for you.' Men are also specifically allowed to have sex with the enslaved women in their household.

Marriage is therefore generally praised, although marriage with specific categories of women is forbidden: 'Prohibited to you [for marriage] are your mothers, your daughters, your sisters, your father's sisters, your mother's sisters, your brother's daughters, your sister's daughters, your [milk] mothers who nursed you, your sisters through nursing, your wives' mothers, and your step-daughters under your guardianship [born] of your wives unto whom you have gone in' (Qur'an 4:23).

Married life is also, as pointed out by Abdelwahab Bouhdiba, 'hierarchized', with men clearly seen as superior to women.[9] Verse 2:228 mentions, for example, 'But the men [i.e., husbands] have a degree over them [in responsibility and authority].' Similarly, verse 4:34 mentions that 'Men are in charge of women by [right of] what Allāh has given one over the other and what they spend [for maintenance] from their wealth. So righteous women are devoutly obedient, guarding in [the husband's] absence what Allāh would have them guard. But those [wives] from whom you fear arrogance – [first] advise them; [then if they persist], forsake them in bed; and [finally], strike them [lightly], But if they obey you [once more], seek no means against them. Indeed, Allāh is ever Exalted and Grand.'

Traditional interpretations have seen this verse as the basis of men's authority over women, with two main aspects: *qiwāma*, referring to a husband's authority over his wife and his financial responsibilities, and *wilāya*, referring to the 'right and duty of male family members to exercise

---

9 Abdelwahab Bouhdiba, *Sexuality in Islam*, trans. Alan Sheridan (London: Saqi Books, 2012), 11.

guardianship over female members', which also 'grants fathers priority over mothers in guardianship of their children'.[10]

The Sunna agrees on these basic aspects. It also expands on the details of the marriage contract, including the payment of the *mahr* (dower), married life, and aspects related to it, or how a marriage could end, for example, with *ṭalāq*, a husband's repudiation of his wife. *Ḥadīths* are usually also condemnatory of celibacy. As can be seen in the many reports that show the Prophet advocating marriage, celibacy was certainly not something that Muḥammad appreciated. It is reported that he said: 'Whoever Allah provides with a righteous wife, Allah has assisted him in half of his religion. Let him fear Allah regarding the second half.' There were a few people who chose an ascetic life among Muḥammad's contemporaries and in the first century of Islam, but this was rare.

Muḥammad called for unity within the Muslim community, but shortly after his death his followers split over who was his proper successor. This dispute created a division within Islam between a larger group that would become known as Sunnis (taking their names from Sunna, which may be confusing as the Shi'a also follows the Sunna) and a smaller group known as Shi'a (from *Shi'at 'Alī*, the party of 'Alī, the cousin and son-in-law of Muḥammad, as they believed that he and his descendants should be the followers of Muḥammad). When coming to an understanding of sexuality, the main difference is that some Shi'i groups recognize the validity of a temporary marriage (*mut'a*), while Sunni scholars came to believe that it was accepted at the beginning of Islam but was later prohibited.

Marriage in Islamic Law

Muslim legal scholars built upon these basic aspects in their understanding of sex/uality. Sunni Muslim jurisprudence was divided into four schools of thought (*madhhab*), each named after the jurist regarded as their founder, but on most matters of sexuality they were fairly similar. They considered sex to be basically licit if it takes place between a man and a woman in a relation that is legitimized in two ways: either by marriage, or by slavery – though only men could have sex with the enslaved women they owned, and not women with enslaved men.

---

10 Ziba Mir-Hosseini, Mulki al-Sharmani, and Jana Rumminger, eds., 'Introduction', in *Men in Charge?: Rethinking Authority in Muslim Legal Tradition* (London: Oneworld, 2015), 1. The entire book engages with the question of how to read these verses in feminist ways.

Jurists considered marriage to be a natural part of human life and sex as permissible not only for reproductive purposes but also for pleasure; thus *coitus interruptus* was allowed, with most jurists requiring the wife to agree to it. The influential jurist, theologian, and mystic al-Ghazālī (d. 505/1111)[11] devotes one book of his monumental *Iḥyā' Ulūm al-Dīn* (The Revival of Religious Sciences) to marriage. Here he stresses that it is important that the husband takes care of his wife's desires and that he tries to sexually satisfy her.[12] He mentions that when the husband has obtained his sexual pleasure, he should devote himself to his wife until she reaches her orgasm (literally 'her need', *ḥājatuhā*). He mentions that he should respect the timing of her desire, as reaching orgasm together is preferable because a difference in that would cause disharmony in the marriage.[13]

We find scattered references such as al-Ghazālī's to women's desire in pre-modern Islamic sources, but most of these stress the fact that women should make themselves sexually available to men, and not the other way around. Moreover, once a man has been able to have sexual intercourse with his wife once, then intercourse ceases somehow to be her right.[14] Discussions about castrated and impotent men are quite instructive on this: according to most jurists, if a woman declares that her husband is not able to penetrate her, he has one year to be able to do so. If he is not able to do so, then the marriage is dissolved. If he does so at least once, then the marriage is not dissolved, but there is no mention of further measures to be taken for the woman's pleasure.[15] As put concisely by Kecia Ali, 'sex is, by and large, a male right and a female duty, according to *fiqh* texts, whatever the ethical importance of a husband's satisfying his wife and thus enabling her to keep chaste'.[16]

In *fiqh* texts marriage is first and foremost a contract between a man and a woman who are allowed to marry. It has three main elements: an offer, the acceptance of the offer, and the payment of the *mahr*, a sum of money or other valuables that the man pays to the woman in order to obtain sexual access to her. In this sense, sex is at the centre of the marital contract from the

---

11 When two dates are given in this chapter, the first is according to the Muslim *hijri* calendar and the second according to the Gregorian (Western) calendar.

12 Hidayatullah, 'Islamic Conceptions of Sexuality', 273.

13 See Abū Ḥāmid Muḥammad ibn Muḥammad al-Ghazālī, *Iḥyā' 'Ulūm al-Dīn*, ed. Badawī Ṭabānah, 4 vols. (Semarang, Indonesia: Maktabat Kriāṭa Futra, 1957), 2: 52.

14 Kecia Ali, *Sexual Ethics and Islam: Feminist Reflections on Qur'an, Hadith, and Jurisprudence*, 2nd ed. (2006; Oxford: Oneworld Academics, 2016), 13.

15 Ibn 'Abd al-Barr, *al-Istidhkār (The Memorization)*, ed. Sālim Muḥammad 'Aṭā and Muḥammad 'Alī Mu'awwaḍ, 9 vols. (Beirut: Dār al-Kutub al-'Ilmiyya, 2000), 6: 192; Al-Marghīnānī, *al-Hidāyah (The Guidance)*, 4 vols. (Cairo: Dār al-Salām, 2000), 2: 619.

16 Ali, *Sexual Ethics and Islam*, 9.

first moment. The marriage was supposed to take place in the presence of two witnesses, who basically testify that the marriage has taken place to the community. Moreover, for most jurists it is necessary for the woman's guardian (*walī*) to be present. With this contract, the man is granted sexual access, in exchange for the *mahr* and for paying to support the woman.[17] In return for support, a woman was supposed to be obedient to her husband. If she failed to do so, she entered a status of disobedience (*nushūz*) and lost her rights. This has been the traditional interpretation, although today feminist interpretations are pushing against this understanding of *nushūz*.[18]

The dower has a central position. It was already an established practice in pre-Islamic Arabia, given by a husband or husband's family to the wife's family. This changed in Islam, and the dower became the direct property of the wife. This gave married women in medieval Islamic societies much more opportunity to be financially independent than Christian women living in Europe during the same period, who generally had no right to hold property independent of their husbands. The dower payment was made either before or after the consummation of a marriage, either 'paid up front, deferred to death or divorce, or split between prompt and deferred'.[19] In any case, its payment is 'understood as a compensation in exchange for *milk al-nikāḥ*, the husband's exclusive dominion over the wife's sexual and reproductive capacity, which also conveys his sole right to dissolve the marriage tie by unilateral divorce'.[20]

Milk comes from the root *m-l-k*, which refers to possessing, but also to having authority over someone. As Kecia Ali points out, there are many parallels between slavery and marriage: both allow the man a kind of ownership that makes sex licit and cohabitation lawful. In both cases, there is the payment of a sum of money: either the price to buy the slave or the *mahr* in the case of marriage. In both, a man's right to sexual intercourse can cease, either by repudiation (*ṭalāq*) of the wife or by the manumission of the enslaved woman.[21] Until the abolition of slavery in the nineteenth and twentieth centuries, men in Islamic societies were also allowed to have sex with enslaved women, often described as 'what their right hand possessed' (in Arabic *milk al-yamīn*). Concubinage was widespread in the Mediterranean

---

17 See Hallaq, *Sharīʿa*, 271–80.
18 Ayesha S. Chaudhry, *Domestic Violence and the Islamic Tradition* (Oxford: Oxford University Press, 2013).
19 Ali, *Sexual Ethics and Islam*, 4.   20 Ali, *Sexual Ethics and Islam*, 5.
21 Kecia Ali, *Marriage and Slavery in Early Islam* (Cambridge, MA: Harvard University Press, 2010), 54, 164, 165.

Sexuality in Islamic Traditions

and Middle East before the rise of Islam, with wealthy men having many concubines, a practice that continued in many areas under Muslim rule.[22]

The main elements of the Islamic marriage are still valid in many Muslim-majority countries. European colonizers introduced new law codes in the nineteenth century, sometimes through the adoption of European-based codes, particularly in French colonies in the eastern Mediterranean. In British India, the translation of pre-modern *fiqh* texts into English brought about the creation of the so-called Anglo-Muhammadan law, which has been defined as a 'heavily distorted English legal perspective on Islamic law that was administered by Muslim individuals'.[23] Similar processes also happened in formerly Dutch Indonesia, with the codification of both *Shari'a* and customary law. The only part of law that was not subject to codification was what came to be understood as family law, which was 'sacralized' as a marker of religious and national identity. Thus laws related to marriage and family changed less than those about other aspects of life.

With the ending of colonialism and the creation of independent nation-states, most Muslim-majority countries used state law to re-shape family structures via the regulation of marriage, divorce, and inheritance, what came to be known as personal status. Even though jurists used different tools that allowed space for legal reforms, the main aspects of Islamic traditions related to sexuality found their way into the law of contemporary Muslim-majority countries. Beginning in the late twentieth century, women's rights expanded thanks to the pressure of the feminist movements, but this was limited by the codification of law.

Illicit Sex in Islamic Law

All forms of sex that are not legitimized by a valid marriage or by a relationship of slavery are considered illicit in Islamic traditions. This includes the broad category known as *zinā'*: *liwāṭ* (male–male intercourse), *siḥāq* (female–female intercourse), and also bestiality and necrophilia. *Zinā'* is the Arabic term used to refer to both fornication and adultery and refers to the penetration by a man of a woman without the main pre-requisite for legal intercourse: the right of *milk*. Depending on the *madhhab*, *zinā'* can also include other sexual acts involving penetration; for example, incest, rape, prostitution, and for some scholars also *liwāṭ* and bestiality.

---

22 Ali, *Marriage and Slavery*, 51.   23 Hallaq, *Sharī'a*, 377.

Zinā' constitutes one of the *ḥudūd*, the 'limits' posited by God so as to avoid the most serious offences in Islamic law. The term *ḥudūd* (sing. *ḥadd*) is used to refer to those crimes mentioned in the Qur'an, whose punishment is based either on the Qur'an or on Sunna, and that are considered an aggression against God's rights (*ḥuqūq Allāh*). Besides *zinā'*, *ḥudūd* also include slander (*qadhf*), the drinking of alcohol (*shurb al-khamr*), theft (*sariqa*), and highway robbery (*qaṭ' al-ṭarīq* or *ḥirāba*).[24] The punishment for all these crimes is extremely harsh, but the requirements to prove them are difficult, so actual punishment is rare and in most cases applied only because of a confession. It is also believed, however, that a person who commits *zinā'* but is not punished in this world would be in eternal hellfire after death.[25]

In jurisprudential discussions, one who commits *zinā'* should be punished either by flogging or by stoning, depending on their status. If the offender is *muḥṣan* (generally meaning adult, free, married, sane, and Muslim), and there was penetration, then the person should be stoned, while a non-*muḥṣan* should receive 100 lashes.[26] *Zinā'* is mentioned in the Qur'an, but only flogging is mentioned as a penalty.[27] The punishment of stoning is based instead on the Sunna. Indeed, according to a *ḥadith*, Muḥammad imposed this on an adulteress who was married.[28]

In order for a person to be punished for *zinā'*, there needed to be four trustworthy men who testified they had seen the two people having illicit sexual intercourse (including the actual penetration), or the accused needed to confess four times. Clearly, this was something very unlikely to happen. Moreover, if there was any discrepancy between the witnesses or the accuser could not find enough witnesses, then the accuser was to be punished for slander (*qadhf*) with eighty lashes.[29] There were other legal ambiguities that made prosecution for *zinā'* difficult, such as *shubha*, a legal principle according to which if an illegal act resembles a legal act, then the punishment cannot

---

24 For more details, see Rudolph Peters, *Crime and Punishment in Islamic Law: Theory and Practice from the Sixteenth to the Twenty-First Century* (Cambridge: Cambridge University Press, 2005), 53–65. For some jurists, rebellion (*baghī*) and apostasy (*ridda*) were also considered *ḥudūd*. Hallaq, *Sharī'a*, 310–11.

25 Hallaq, *Sharī'a*, 311.

26 The conditions that determined if someone was *muḥṣan* differed somewhat across legal schools, particularly over whether both people needed to fulfil the conditions. For an extensive treatment of *zinā'* in Islamic Law, see Peters, *Crime and Punishment*, 59–62. On rape as a form of *zinā'*, see Hina Azam, *Sexual Violation in Islamic Law: Substance, Evidence and Procedure* (Cambridge: Cambridge University Press, 2015); and Hina Azam, 'Rape as a Variant of Fornication (*Zina*) in Islamic Law: An Examination of the Early Legal Reports', *Journal of Law and Religion* 28, no. 2 (2013): 441–66.

27 Qur'an 24:2.   28 Peters, *Crime and Punishment*, 60.

29 Peters, *Crime and Punishment*, 64.

be applied. So, for example, if a man had illegal intercourse with a woman he thought he was legally married to, then they cannot be punished for *zinā*'.[30] All this meant that penalties for *zinā*' were applied extremely rarely in the past, if at all. They seem to have mostly been a deterrent, with the aim to establish a specific moral code. Indeed, as pointed out by Ziba Mir-Hosseini: 'The power and sanction of *zinā*' rulings, it must be stressed, lie not in their implementation, but in how they define the limits of permissible sexual conduct.'[31]

This changed in the modern period with Islamist movements that introduced elements of *ḥudūd* into national legal codes. Regulations on *zinā*' were part of this, accompanied by public rhetoric about immorality. This happened in Pakistan and Iran in 1979, and in a dozen other countries since then.[32] There were highly publicized public stonings of women for *zinā*' in Iran, and a few elsewhere. These were marketed as a 'return' to Islamic morals, an imprecise claim, as such punishments had been applied very rarely in the pre-modern Islamic world.

The situation with male same-sex relations (*liwāṭ*) and female same-sex relations (*siḥāq*) is quite similar. Both are fundamentally prohibited and considered crimes and sins by Muslim jurists.[33] *Liwāṭ* refers to the 'actions of the people of Lot',[34] from the story of Lot and the city of Sodom,

---

30 Peters, *Crime and Punishment*, 21–3; James E. Baldwin, 'Prostitution, Islamic Law and Ottoman Societies', *Journal of the Economic and Social History of the Orient* 55 (2012): 117–52, at 125.

31 Ziba Mir-Hosseini, 'Criminalising Sexuality: Zina Laws as Violence against Women in Muslim Contexts', *International Journal of Human Rights* 15 (2011): 7–33, at 18.

32 Elyse Semerdjian, 'Zinah', in *The Oxford Encyclopedia of the Islamic World* (Oxford: Oxford University Press, 2009), www.oxfordreference.com/view/10.1093/acref/97801 95305135.001.0001/acref-9780195305135.

33 A number of publications on these topics have appeared: Arno Schmitt, 'Liwāṭ im fiqh: Männliche Homosexualität?', *Journal of Arabic and Islamic Studies* 4 (2001–2002): 49–110; Mohammed Mezziane, 'Sodomie et masculinité chez les juristes musulmans du IXe au XIe siècle', *Arabica* 55 (2008): 276–306; Amr A. Shalakany, 'Islamic Legal Histories', *Berkeley Journal of Middle Eastern & Islamic Law* 1 (2008): 1–82; Camilla Adang, 'Ibn Ḥazm on Homosexuality: A Case-Study of Ẓāhiri Legal Methodology', *Al-Qanṭara* 24, no. 1 (2003): 5–31; Sara Omar, 'From Semantics to Normative Law: Perceptions of *Liwāṭ* (Sodomy) and *Siḥāq* (Tribadism) in Islamic Jurisprudence (8th–15th Century CE)', *Islamic Law and Society* 19 (2012): 222–56; Serena Tolino, 'Homosexual Acts in Islamic Law: *Siḥāq* and *Liwāṭ* in the Legal Debate', *GAIR-Mitteilungen* 6 (2014): 187–205; and Serena Tolino, 'Normative Discourses on Female Homoeroticism in Pre-Modern Islamicate Societies', in *Mediterranean Crossings: Sexual Transgressions in Islam and Christianity (10th–18th Centuries)*, ed. Umberto Grassi (Rome: Viella, 2020), 27–41.

34 See Serena Tolino, *Atti omosessuali e omosessualità fra diritto islamico e diritto positivo: Il caso egiziano con alcuni cenni all'esperienza libanese* (Naples: Edizioni Scientifiche Italiane, 2013), 21. See also Ibn Manẓūr, *Lisān al-'Arab* (The Tongue of the Arabs) (Beirut: Mu'assasa al-'ālamī li-l-maṭbū'āt, 2005), s.v. 'lwṭ'.

mentioned several times in the Qur'an in a slightly different version than that in the Hebrew Bible. In the Qur'an, Lot is a prophet and messenger sent by God to preach to the inhabitants of Sodom against their lustful and violent acts. The people did not listen, so God sent angels in the form of men to Lot's house; a crowd of men surrounding the house demanded Lot send his guests out, stating that they desired them. As he does in the Biblical story, Lot offered the crowd marriage to his daughters instead, but they turned this down and continued to demand the men, saying 'you know what we want'. Lot and his followers fled the city, and the angels destroyed Sodom (Qur'an 11:76–83). This represented a clear admonition to the people of Arabia and a warning about what could happen if they did not obey their Prophet Muḥammad. (For more on the story of Lot, see Chapter 12 by Dominic Janes in Volume I of this work.)

The 'people of Lot', that is, the residents of Sodom, committed several crimes, including lack of charity and violence against Lot and his household, but since at least the tenth century, the term *liwāṭ* in legal discourse has come to mean basically anal sex. (At roughly the same time, Christian scholars increasingly used the term 'sodomy' to refer to any form of non-reproductive sex, including anal sex and bestiality as well as same-sex relations.) The term is used in legal sources to refer to active and passive anal intercourse, while the term *ubna*, which only refers to being penetrated anally, is mostly used in medical sources.[35] The main point of discussion between jurists was whether *liwāṭ* should be punished with the same *ḥadd* as *zinā'* was. Most jurists considered that the two crimes should be punished in the same way or set an even higher punishment for *liwāṭ*.[36] A few jurists opted for a punishment set by the discretion of the judge.[37] The discussion about woman–woman relations was much shorter: jurists came to the conclusion that there was no *ḥadd* punishment, because there was no penetration, and a discretional

---

35 Franz Rosenthal, 'Ar-Rāzī on the Hidden Illness', *Bulletin of the History of Medicine* 52 (1978): 45–60; and Hans-Peter Pökel, 'Der sexualpathologische Diskurs über den penetrierten Mann in der arabisch-islamischen Medizin des 10. und 11. Jahrhunderts', in *Liebe, Sexualität, Partnerschaft: Paradigmen im Wandel; Beiträge zur orientalistischen Gender-Forschung*, ed. Roswitha Badry, Maria Rohrer, and Karin Steiner (Freiburg: Fördergemeinschaft wissenschaftlicher Publikationen von Frauen, 2009), 65–79.

36 According to the jurists al-Shafiʿī (d. 204/820) and Ibn Ḥanbal (d. 241/855), who gave their names to the Sunnī shāfiʿī and ḥanbalī schools of Islam jurisprudence, the person who committed *liwāṭ* (the *lūṭī*) should be stoned regardless of whether they were *muḥṣan* or not. See Tolino, *Atti omosessuali*, 98, 101.

37 Most jurists who recommended juridical discretion were from the ḥanafī *madhhab*, named after Abū Ḥanīfa al-Nuʿman ibn Thābit (d. 150/767).

punishment established by the judge (*ta'zīr*) should be applied.[38]

Legal sources were quite strict, but we know from literary sources that especially age-stratified same-sex relationships between men were socially accepted in Islamic society, as long as the adult man remained the active partner. Literary sources also point to the fact that homoeroticism was part of life. For example, in one of his treatises the author al-Jāḥiẓ (d. 255/868) depicts a controversy between a man having sexual intercourse with concubines and a man having sexual relations with adolescent boys, and analyses both the pros and the cons of the two kinds of intercourse.[39] This simultaneous rejection and acceptance of male same-sex relations supports Thomas Bauer's idea that in pre-modern Islamic societies ambiguities were accepted, and that legal norms and literary sources simply represented different discourses.[40] Because most sources that survived were written by men and focused on men, we know less about homoerotic relationships between women, but there is evidence that they were also tolerated.[41] (On pederastic sexual relations in sixteenth-century Istanbul, see Chapter 10 by Selim S. Kuru in Volume III of this work.)

Muslim jurists held a variety of opinions about masturbation, with the main reason for the diversity being the fact that there is no clear textual evidence in the Qur'an or the *ḥadīth* about it. Most jurists considered it permissible for men within marriage, based on the fact that the Qur'an commands that one safeguard the private parts of the body, except in front of a spouse or concubine. Others considered it prohibited or at least discouraged within marriage. The case of those men who could not marry or purchase a concubine was more complicated: some jurists still opposed masturbation, as they considered that a man could find other means to lessen his sexual desire, such as fasting, while others considered it allowed, viewing it as better than committing fornication. Jurists also discussed the case of women, stating that women can also be overcome by desire, some scholars

---

38 See Tolino, 'Homosexual Acts in Islamic Law', 198–9; and Omar, 'From Semantics to Normative Law'.
39 Serena Tolino, 'Homosexuality in the Middle East: An Analysis of Dominant and Competitive Discourses', *DEP: Deportate, Esule, Profughe* 25 (2014): 72–91, at 76.
40 Bauer, *Die Kultur der Ambiguität.*
41 Fedwa Malti-Douglas, 'Tribadism/Lesbianism and the Sexualized Body in Medieval Arabo-Islamic Narratives, in *Same Sex Love and Desire among Women in the Middle Ages*, ed. Francesca Canadé Sautman and Pamela Sheingorn (New York: Palgrave, 2001), 123–41; Sahar Amer, *Crossing Borders: Love between Women in Medieval French and Arabic Literatures* (Philadelphia: University of Pennsylvania Press, 2008); Sahar Amer, 'Medieval Arab Lesbians and Lesbian-Like Women', *Journal of the History of Sexuality* 118, no. 2 (2009): 215–36; Tolino, 'Normative Discourses on Female Homoeroticism'.

allowed them to use something that resembled a penis.[42] We also find a number of discussions on intercrural sex or sex between the thighs (*tafkhīd*), which was allowed when done within a licit sexual relation, and prohibited in other situations, although with milder punishment than that for cases of sexual acts that include penetration.[43]

Medicine and Erotology

Legal sources are obviously not the only ones to deal with sex and sexuality. Patrick Franke has pointed out that there was a specific field of knowledge in the Islamicate world, *'ilm al-bāh*, which was 'a hybrid discipline in which different fields of knowledge were merged. For the history of sexuality it is important because it can be considered, in one way at least, as a precursor to modern sexual science.'[44] *'Ilm al-bāh* is sometimes translated as the 'science of coitus', and sometimes as 'erotology', a rather obscure English word meaning the study of sexual stimuli and behaviour. Franke demonstrated that the term is wider than erotology, as 'there are many *bāh*-books that do not have erotological contents, and inversely, several erotological books not are related in any way to *'ilm al-bāh*'.[45] According to him, *bāh*-books can be basically divided in two groups: those from the medical tradition, which are based on Graeco-Arabic medicine, focus on 'sexual intercourse as a mere biological process'[46] and see sex as having a number of beneficial effects, and those from the erotic tradition, which seem to have as an explicit purpose the arousal of sexual desire, and are strongly influenced also by Indian and Persian erotological traditions.[47]

---

42 The Arabic term for masturbation is *istimnā'*, which means literally to cause one's semen to be released, or more rarely *jald 'Umayra*, which means 'the flogging of the little 'Umar', most often found in literary works but also in a few legal sources. See Sara Omar, 'Sexuality and Law: Masturbation', *The Oxford Encyclopedia of Islam and Law*, www.oxfordislamicstudies.com/article/opr/t349/e0011; and Omar Anchassi, 'The Churning in the Flogging of 'Umayra: Or, Towards a History of Masturbation in Premodern Islamic Law', *Studi Magrebini* 20, no. 2 (2022): 213–46.

43 Everett K. Rowson, 'The Categorization of Gender and Sexual Irregularity in Medieval Arabic Vice Lists', in *Body Guards: The Cultural Politics of Gender Ambiguity*, ed. Julia Epstein and Kristina Straub (New York: Routledge, 1991), 50–79, at 62. Peters pointed out that for Shi'i Muslim jurists and those from the Sunni Hanbalī school of jurisprudence, sexual acts without penetration are regarded as *ḥadd* offences to be punished with 100 lashes. See Peters, *Crime and Punishment*, 61.

44 Patrick Franke, 'Before *scientia sexualis* in Islamic Culture: *'ilm al-bāh* between Erotology, Medicine and Pornography', *Social Identities: Journal for the Study of Race, Nation and Culture* 18, no. 2 (2012): 161–73, at 162.

45 Franke, 'Before *scientia sexualis*', 163.   46 Franke, 'Before *scientia sexualis*', 167.

47 See Pernilla Myrne, 'Women and Men in al-Suyūṭī's Guides to Sex and Marriage', *Mamlūk Studies Review* 21 (2018): 47–67, at 48–9.

Medically oriented *bāh*-books were particularly influenced by Greek sources, which since at least the third/ninth century were translated into Arabic and became widely known by the cultural elite of the Islamicate world.[48] This included medical works; in particular, the works of Hippocrates from the fourth century BCE and also Galen and Rufus of Ephesus from the second century CE were held in high esteem. Many of the ideas on the benefits of sexual intercourse as formulated by Rufus and Galen are also quoted in Arabic sources.

For example, in his *Kitāb al-bāh* (The Book of Coitus), the physician, polymath, alchemist, and philosopher Muḥammad ibn Zakariyā al-Rāzī's (d. 313/925 or 323/935), known in the Western world as Rhazes, mentions the fact that an accumulation of sperm would be dangerous for men, as it would make their heads heavy, their bodies cold, and their movement difficult.[49] Both Galen and al-Rāzī believed that women also produced sperm, and thought that the accumulation of sperm was also dangerous for them, as it could lead to the 'suffocation of the womb'. Al-Rāzī discusses women's pleasure openly, and 'the author conveys an intriguing idea: not only is mutual sexual pleasure significant, but in fact the most powerful tool to accomplish and strengthen love is simultaneous orgasm'.[50] The manual devotes space 'to teach men how to treat women and how to make her desire compatible with his, so that they can together reach the highest form of pleasure'.[51] Here and in other medical sources, homoerotic desire is not pathologized per se; only the desire of a man to be anally penetrated, the so-called *ubna*, was seen as an illness to be cured.[52] Interestingly, al-Rāzī seems to mention the benefit of sexual intercourse mostly in his medical writings; in his ethical writings, 'sexual intercourse acquires entirely negative

---

48 On the translation of Greek works into Arabic, see Dimitri Gutas, *Greek Thought, Arabic Culture: The Graeco-Arabic Translation Movement in Baghdad and Early 'Abbasid Society (2nd–4th/5th–10th C)* (London: Routledge, 1998). For the impact of Greek medicine on Arab-Islamic medicine, see Ursula Weisser, *Zeugung, Vererbung und Pränatale Entwicklung in der Medizin des arabisch-islamischen Mittelalters* (Erlangen: Verlagsbuchhandlung Hannelore Lüling, 1983); and Sherry Sayed Gadelrab, 'Discourses on Sex Differences in Medieval Scholarly Islamic Thought', *Journal of the History of Medicine* 66, no. 1 (2011): 40–81.

49 Peter E. Pormann, 'Al-Rāzī (d. 925) on the Benefits of Sex: A Clinician Caught between Philosophy and Medicine', in *O ye Gentlemen: Arabic Studies in Science and Literary Culture. In Honour of Remke Kruk*, ed. Arnoud Vrolijk and Jan P. Hogendijk (Leiden: Brill, 2007), 115–27, at 118.

50 Pernilla Myrne, 'Pleasing the Beloved: Sex and True Love in a Medieval Arabic Erotic Compendium', in *The Beloved in Middle Eastern Literatures: The Culture of Love and Languishing*, ed. Alireza Korangy, Hanadi al-Samman, and Michael C. Beard (London: I. B. Tauris, 2018), 215–36, at 224.

51 Myrne, 'Pleasing the Beloved', 225.

52 Rosenthal, 'al-Rāzī on the Hidden Illness'; Pökel, 'Der sexualpathologische Diskurs'.

connotations, except for the preservation of the species'.[53] In this way, he 'adjusts what he says to the expectations of his audience',[54] yet another confirmation that Islamic norms of sexuality are context-situated. Even the same author can approach them differently when writing with different audiences in mind.

Ibn Sīnā (d. 428/1037), known in the Western world as Avicenna, also considered sexual issues in his monumental encyclopedia of medicine *al-Qānūn fī-l-Ṭibb* (Canon of Medicine), translated into Latin as *Liber canonis medicinae* and considered for centuries the medical standard work in both the Islamicate world and Europe. Among other issues, he includes a chapter on 'how to make the vagina smaller and the penis larger', mentioning that 'a small penis is often the reason why a woman does not experience pleasure'.[55] In a similar fashion, if the vagina is not 'small enough, then the husband will not satisfy her and she will not satisfy him, and he will look for an alternative'.[56] Female pleasure is considered important for Ibn Sīnā for two reasons: first, because it was seen in connection with the emission of female sperm, necessary for reproduction; second, because if a man did not satisfy the woman, then this 'will cause *musāḥaqa* [lesbianism] and women will meet among themselves because of their desire'.[57]

Turning from the medical *bāh*-books to the more erotic ones, we find a greater focus on love. The tenth-century *Jawāmī al-Ladhdha* (The Encyclopedia of Love) by 'Alī ibn Naṣr was the earliest of these erotic manuals in Arabic and widely influenced later authors. Pernilla Myrne points out how 'Alī ibn Naṣr describes two kinds of lovers: 'those who regard sex as a necessary component of a romantic relationship and those who maintain that sex and love are incompatible'.[58] Erotic *bāh*-books do not exclude homoerotic sex and love; indeed, according to 'Alī ibn Naṣr, 'love couples can comprise a man and a woman, a man and a man, or a woman and a woman. These categories are described in one section each, without denouncement.'[59] Once again, despite the fact that homoerotic relations were strongly prohibited in Islamic law, other sources considered them normative.

---

53 Pormann, 'Al-Rāzī (d. 925) on the Benefits of Sex', 126–7.
54 Pormann, 'Al-Rāzī (d. 925) on the Benefits of Sex', 127.
55 Ibn Sīnā, *al-Qānūn fī-l-Ṭibb* (Canon of Medicine), 3 vols. (Beirut: Dār al-Kutub al-'Ilmiyya, 1999), 3: 746.
56 Ibn Sīnā, *al-Qānūn fī-l-Ṭibb*, 2: 746.
57 Ibn Sīnā, *al-Qānūn fī-l-Ṭibb*, 2: 746. See also Tolino, 'Normative Discourses on Female Homoeroticism', 37.
58 Myrne, 'Pleasing the Beloved', 218.   59 Myrne, 'Pleasing the Beloved', 223.

Bāh-books declined in the nineteenth century and disappeared completely in the twentieth, as did many other genres of an erotic nature in Islamic traditions, including obscene poetry (*mujūn*), love poetry (*ghazal*), and philosophical treaties related to love.[60] This was one of many changes that happened to the Islamicate world after contact with the West and the anxieties that emerged from the colonial experience. These also included the abolition of concubinage, the introduction of Western medicine that gradually took the place of the Graeco-Arab medical tradition,[61] and a critique of gender segregation and the social exclusion of women. Age-stratified same-sex relationships between adult and adolescent males, which were common and visible in pre-modern Muslim societies, gradually disappeared from public view, seen as a sign of decadence in comparison to the West. However, neither the modernist project of the early twentieth century nor the nationalist one of the later twentieth century meant a complete transformation of how gender and sex/uality were conceptualized in the Muslim world. Continuities were (and are) as striking as ruptures. For example, discourses on homosexuality by contemporary Muslim scholars show conceptual categories that are much more similar to those of *liwāṭ* and *siḥāq* in pre-modern jurists than to the modern Western notion of homosexuality as a sexual orientation.

Feminist Interpretations

There is a vibrant movement of Muslim feminists, both in Muslim-majority countries and beyond, challenging traditionalist interpretations of Islamic sources. A feminist engagement with Islamic traditions on sexuality emerged especially in the 1990s and contributed to the field of gender history. For example, Leila Ahmed showed that women's position during the life of Muḥammad and in the early Islamic community was better than what it would be later, with a decline during the ninth and tenth centuries, when 'the body of Sunni Muslim legal thought and practice achieved final formulation in four schools of law'.[62] She recognized an egalitarian spirit in Islam, but also saw a patriarchal orthodoxy that became more and more important in later

---

60 Nadia Al-Bagdadi, 'Eros and Etiquette: Reflections on the Ban of a Central Theme in Nineteenth-Century Arab Writings', in *Sex and Desire in Muslim Cultures*, ed. Krell, Sorbera, and Tolino 113–30, at 113.

61 Franke, 'Before *scientia sexualis*', 170.

62 Leila Ahmed, *Women and Gender in Islam: Historical Roots of a Modern Debate* (New Haven, CT: Yale University Press, 1992), 90.

centuries. This was not simply the result of Islam, however, as 'Islam continued and reinforced an increasingly patriarchal shift that was already under way due to the Greek, Roman, and Christian periods that preceded Islam'.[63] (On women's status in the early Abbasid era, see Chapter 5 by Karen Moukheiber and Nadia Maria El Cheikh in Volume III of this work.)

Other scholars started to engage directly with Islamic traditions in order to reinterpret them. For example, in *Qur'an and Woman*, Amina Wadud criticized patriarchal interpretations of the Qur'an.[64] Asma Barlas supported a holistic reading of the Qur'an, arguing that the Qur'an could be read in 'anti-patriarchal modes if we ask the right sorts of questions of it', and that 'sexual inequality and discrimination do not derive from the Qur'an'.[65] This movement, known as 'Islamic Feminism' (though that term is contested) or gender *jihad*,[66] argues for a reinterpretation of divine sources in ways that challenge the patriarchal interpretations that had been developed in the past. As Margot Badran points out, these scholars engage 'in re/thinking or *ijtihad* (intellectual struggle to understand) and *jihad* (activist struggle)'.[67] In this sense, 'Islamic feminism promotes the idea and practice of full human equality in the public and private spheres. In an Islamic framework, the unequivocal assertion of human equality in family and society constitutes an historical breakthrough.'[68]

Campaigns for women's equality in the field of family law have also been championed by *Musawah*: Campaign for Justice in Muslim Family Laws, a global organization founded in 2009, which brings together advocates for family law reform from the Middle East, Africa, and South and Southeast Asia.[69] Ziba Mir-Hosseini, a founding member of *Musawah* and an anthropologist of law, stresses in her work a crucial element in the tradition of Muslim legal thought: the distinction between *Sharī'a*, in the sense of the path that brings one to God, as found in the Qur'an and the Sunna, and *fiqh*,

---

63 Saadia Yacoob, 'Islamic Law and Gender', in *The Oxford Handbook of Islamic Law*, ed. Anver M. Emon and Rumee Ahmed (Oxford: Oxford University Press, 2018), 75–101, at 83.

64 Amina Wadud, *Qur'an and Woman: Rereading the Sacred Text from a Woman's Perspective* (Oxford: Oxford University Press, 1999).

65 Asma Barlas, 'The Qur'an and Hermeneutics: Reading the Qur'an's Opposition to Patriarchy', *Journal of Qur'anic Studies* 3, no. 2 (2001): 15–38, at 22, 33.

66 Amina Wadud, *Inside the Gender Jihad: Women's Reform in Islam* (Oxford: Oneworld, 2006).

67 Margot Badran, 'Between Secular and Islamic Feminism/s: Reflections on the Middle East and Beyond', *Journal of Middle East Women's Studies* 1, no. 1 (2005): 6–28, at 16.

68 Margot Badran, 'Re/placing Islamic Feminism', *Critique internationale* 46, no. 1 (2010): 25–44, at 26.

69 *Musawah*, Home Page, www.musawah.org/.

the jurists' efforts to deduce laws from these textual sources.[70] She shows that there is always the possibility to propose new interpretations of *Sharī'a*, because interpretations are done by human beings, who are fallible. Other scholars that follow this approach include Asifa Quraishi-Landes and Azizah al-Hibri, who stress that women's oppression is often based on juristic interpretations that, while necessary to make *Sharī'a* concrete, are often biased because of patriarchal approaches.[71]

Final Remarks

This chapter has provided an overview of how different aspects related to sexuality are addressed in Islamic traditions, looking first at the Qur'an and Sunna, then at licit and illicit or controversial sex in Islamic legal sources. I then looked at how sex was discussed in some medical and erotological sources, and finally at how feminism is pushing against patriarchal interpretations of Islamic tradition. Aware of the risks of essentialism and over-simplification, I have tried to present a map of how sex was conceptualized in key Islamic texts and by pre-modern scholars in Islamic(ate) societies. Premodern texts can help to explain how sexuality is understood in Muslim-majority societies today, in which there are continuities along with great change.

If we really want to make sense of the history of sexuality in Muslim-majority societies and the meaning that sexuality in Islamic traditions has for Muslims today, then we need more local histories of sexuality in different historical contexts. Most scholarship has focused on Arabic-language sources from the heartland of Islam. A full picture of sexuality in Islam would need to take into account sources in all the languages in which Muslims of the past and of the present express themselves, in speaking, writing, and certainly also desiring.

Further Reading

Adang, Camilla. 'Ibn Ḥazm on Homosexuality: A Case-study of Ẓāhiri Legal Methodology'. *Al-Qanṭara* 24, no. 1 (2003): 5–31.

Ahmed, Leila. *Women and Gender in Islam: Historical Roots of a Modern Debate*. New Haven, CT: Yale University Press, 1992.

---

70 Ziba Mir-Hosseini, 'Islam and Gender Justice', in *Voices of Islam*. Vol. 5: *Voices of Change*, ed. Vincent J. Cornell and Omid Safi (Westport, CT: Praeger, 2007), 85–113, at 86.

71 See Yacoob, 'Islamic Law and Gender'.

al-Ghazālī, Abū Ḥāmid Muḥammad ibn Muḥammad. *Iḥyāʾ ʿUlūm al-Dīn*, 4 vols., ed. Badawī Ṭabānah. Semarang, Indonesia: Maktabat Kriāṭa Futra, 1957.

Ali, Kecia. *Marriage and Slavery in Early Islam*. Cambridge, MA: Harvard University Press, 2010.

  Sexual Ethics and Islam. Feminist Reflections on Qurʾan, Hadith, and Jurisprudence. Oxford: Oneworld Academics, 2016.

Amer, Sahar. *Crossing Borders: Love between Women in Medieval French und Arabic Literatures*. Philadelphia: University of Pennsylvania Press, 2008.

Anchassi, Omar. 'The Churning in the Flogging of ʿUmayra: Or, Towards a History of Masturbation in Premodern Islamic Law'. *Studi Magrebini* 20, no. 2 (2022): 213–46.

Azam, Hina. 'Rape as a Variant of Fornication (*Zinā*) in Islamic Law: An Examination of the Early Legal Reports'. *Journal of Law and Religion* 28, no. 2 (2012–13): 441–66.

Baldwin, James E. 'Prostitution, Islamic Law and Ottoman Societies'. *Journal of the Economic and Social History of the Orient* 55 (2012): 117–52.

Bauer, Thomas. *Die Kultur der Ambiguität: Eine andere Geschichte des Islams*. Berlin: Verlag der Weltreligion im Insel, 2011.

Bouhdiba, Abdelwahab. *Sexuality in Islam*. Trans. A. Sheridan. London: Saqi Books, 2012.

Declich, Lorenzo. 'L'erotologia araba: Profilo bibliographico'. *Rivista degli Studi Orientali* 68 (1995): 249–65.

Franke, Patrick. 'Before *scientia sexualis* in Islamic Culture: *ʿilm al-bāh* between Erotology, Medicine and Pornography'. *Social Identities: Journal for the Study of Race, Nation and Culture* 18, no. 2 (2012): 161–73.

Hallaq, Wael B. *Sharīʿa: Theory, Practice, Transformations*. Cambridge: Cambridge University Press, 2012.

Hidayatullah, Aysha. 'Islamic Conceptions of Sexuality'. In *Sexuality and the World's Religions*, ed. David W. Machacek and Melissa M. Wilcox, 257–92. Santa Barbara, CA: ABC Clio, 2003.

Kreil, Aymon, Lucia Sorbera, and Serena Tolino, eds. *Sex and Desire in Muslim Cultures: Beyond Norms and Transgression from the Abbasids to the Present Day*. London: I. B. Tauris, 2021.

Malti-Douglas, Fedwa. 'Tribadism/Lesbianism and the Sexualized Body in Medieval Arabo-Islamic Narratives'. In *Same Sex Love and Desire among Women in the Middle Ages*, ed. Francesca Canadé Sautman and Pamela Sheingorn, 123–41. New York: Palgrave, 2001.

Mezziane, Mohammed. 'Sodomie et masculinité chez les juristes musulmans du IXe au XIe siècle'. *Arabica* 55 (2008): 276–306.

Mir-Hosseini, Ziba. 'Criminalising Sexuality: Zina Laws as Violence against Women in Muslim Contexts'. *International Journal of Human Rights* 15 (2011): 7–33.

  'Islam and Gender Justice', in *Voices of Islam*. Vol. 5: *Voices of Change*, ed. Vincent J. Cornell and Omid Safi (Westport, CT: Praeger, 2007), 85–113.

Myrne, Pernilla. *Female Sexuality in the Early Medieval Islamic World: Gender and Sex in Arabic Literature*. London: I. B. Tauris, 2019.

  'Pleasing the Beloved: Sex and True Love in a Medieval Arabic Erotic Compendium'. In *The Beloved in Middle Eastern Literatures: The Culture of Love and Languishing*, ed. Alireza Korangy, Hanadi al-Samman, and Michael C. Beard, 215–36. London: I. B. Tauris, 2018.

Sexuality in Islamic Traditions

'Women and Men in al-Suyūṭī's Guides to Sex and Marriage'. *Mamlūk Studies Review* 21 (2018): 47–67.

Najmabadi, Afsaneh. 'Beyond the Americas: Are Gender and Sexuality Useful Categories of Historical Analysis?' *Journal of Women's History* 18, no. 1 (2010): 11–21.

Omar, Sara. 'From Semantics to Normative Law: Perceptions of *Liwāṭ* (Sodomy) and *Siḥāq* (Tribadism) in Islamic Jurisprudence (8th–15th Century CE)'. *Islamic Law and Society* 19 (2012): 222–56.

'Sexuality and Law. Masturbation'. In *The Oxford Encyclopedia of Islam and Law. Oxford Islamic Studies Online*, www.oxfordislamicstudies.com/article/opr/t349/e0011.

Pökel, Hans-Peter. 'Der sexualpathologische Diskurs über den penetrierten Mann in der arabisch-islamischen Medizin des 10. und 11. Jahrhunderts'. In *Liebe, Sexualität, Partnerschaft: Paradigmen im Wandel; Beiträge zur orientalistischen Gender-Forschung*, ed. Roswitha Badry, Maria Rohrer, and Karin Steiner, 65–79. Freiburg: Fördergemeinschaft wissenschaftlicher Publikationen von Frauen, 2009.

Rosenthal, Franz. 'Al-Rāzī on the Hidden Illness'. *Bulletin of the History of Medicine* 52 (1978): 45–60.

Shalakany, Amr. 'Islamic Legal Histories'. *Berkeley Journal of Middle Eastern & Islamic Law* 1 (2008): 1–82.

Tolino, Serena. 'Homosexuality in the Middle East: An Analysis of Dominant and Competitive Discourses'. *DEP: Deportate, Esule, Profughe* 25 (2014): 72–91.

'Normative Discourses on Female Homoeroticism in Pre-Modern Islamicate Societies'. In *Mediterranean Crossings: Sexual Transgressions in Islam and Christianity (10th–18th Centuries)*, ed. Umberto Grassi, 27–41. Rome: Viella, 2020.

Qur'an and Woman: Rereading the Sacred Text from a Woman's Perspective. Oxford: Oxford University Press, 1999.

Wadud, Amina. *Inside the Gender Jihad: Women's Reform in Islam*. Oxford: Oneworld, 2006.

15

Scientific Sex in the Modern World

HOWARD CHIANG

This chapter examines the origins and legacy of sexology – the scientific study of sexuality – in the modern world. First consolidated into a coherent programme in the late nineteenth century, sexology has its roots in the reorganization of knowledge about nature in the frameworks of taxonomy, evolutionism, and race. A pervasive preoccupation with heredity gave rise to powerful eugenics movements around the world. The interest in controlling variability and unlocking the secrets of the soul generated parallel developments in biomedicine, especially psychoanalysis and endocrinology. Sex experts worldwide converged in diagnosing cultural signs of homosexuality for the purpose of national modernization. As the centre of gravity in sexual science began to shift from Europe to North America, researchers gave growing support to the sex/gender distinction and redefined the meanings of normality. In the waning days of hereditarian theories, the rise of cultural anthropology coupled with a renewed scientific investment of colonial powers to reverse hierarchical templates of sexual practices and norms emanating from the metropoles. A public health crisis (HIV/AIDS), social movements (gender and sexual minority rights), and the systematization of research protocols (bioethics) shaped a comeback of biological sexology in the closing decades of the twentieth century.

Sexing Nature

A systemic shift in the empirical sciences of the eighteenth century pushed naturalists, botanists, zoologists, anatomists, and other thinkers to approach nature by prioritizing the premise of sexual difference. This shift was characterized by at least four features. First, scientific thinkers elevated *taxonomy* to an activity of pre-eminent empirical value. Second, they moved away from previous theories of the body based on humoral balance or cosmology and towards a *materialistic* approach. Third, with such activities, they renewed their understanding of *nature*, now conceptualized as a pre-ordained entity responsible for prescribing the laws of society. Though taking shape during the Enlightenment, this new conception of human–nature relations was inseparable from, fourth, the broader context of global geopolitics: European imperialism. Before the rise of evolutionism, science and medicine consolidated the taxonomic, materialistic, naturalistic, and imperialist tendencies of sexual knowledge.

Nowhere was the rise of taxonomy in natural history more evident than in the field of plant biology. The work of Swedish botanist Carl Linnaeus (1707–78) stood out, whose binomial nomenclature system is still widely employed today. In his *Systema naturae* (The System of Nature, 1735), Linnaeus proposed the classification of plants on the basis of sexual difference.[1] This taxonomic system differentiated flowers based on their male and female parts. Linnaeus divided the vegetable world into twenty-four *classes* based on the number, relative proportions, and position of stamens (the pollen-producing male parts). These classes were then subdivided into some sixty-five *orders* based on the number, relative proportions, and positions of pistils (the ovule-producing female parts). In the taxonomic tree, class stands above order. Linnaeus's decision to let a plant's stamens determine class and its pistils order was a purely artificial invention with no empirical justification. His writings romanticized the union of stamens and pistils, resulting in a heterosexualization of plants that reinforced traditional notions of gender hierarchy and incorporated a binary gender system into 'objective truths'.[2]

The interest in plant sexuality coincided with the rise of materialism in the study of animals and humans in the eighteenth century. Zoologists and anatomists exacted sexual difference in the bodily flesh. Again, following the work of Linnaeus, zoologists categorized an entire class of animals into mammals. This, on the one hand, drew on a long-established recognition since the ancient Greek philosopher Aristotle (384–322 BCE) that the female breast lactates, but, on the other, spoke to the heightened iconicity of women as nurturing fecund agents in the era of Enlightenment politics.[3] Moreover,

---

1 Carolus Linnaeus, *Systema naturae, 1735* (Nieuwkoop, Netherlands: B. de Graaf, 1964).
2 Londa Schoebinger, *Nature's Body: Gender in the Making of Modern Science* (Boston: Beacon, 1993), 11–39.
3 Schoebinger, *Nature's Body*, 39–74.

medical writers began to downplay a model of sex in which women were seen as an imperfect version of men – a view that had circulated since the time of the ancient Greek physician Galen (129–216 CE). In this so-called 'one-sex model', men and women shared the same bodily sex, with the only difference being that the female reproductive organ was an inverted version of the male. In the eighteenth century, however, this worldview imploded for epistemological and political reasons. In its stead, medicine came to foreground a 'two-sex model', which represented male and female biology as radically divergent opposites.[4] A key example of this contrast came with the spread of female skeletons (for the first time) throughout Europe between the 1730s and the 1790s to display the essential differences between female and male anatomy.[5]

The struggle over power between men and women reached a new height on the eve of modernity. While taxonomic and materialistic impulses can be considered intrinsic, or internal, to the production of empirical knowledge, they unfolded in tandem with the ways in which men began to relate to nature differently in order to justify sexism and other kinds of subordination. The new principle of classification implied hierarchy. Men of science extended such moral authority of nature into the social realm in order to maintain gender inequality. Differences in bodily sex helped to rationalize claims about why men were a better fit for performing certain public and political roles and, by extension, why women were more appropriately relegated to the domestic sphere. The potent and symbolic meaning of the female breast, for instance, not only defined an entire class of animals but also denoted human superiority in mastering this bestial inference in wider cultural depictions. A desire to uncover what was 'natural' fuelled an entire way of knowing and organizing social relations, which by the late eighteenth century buttressed new ideas about sexual complementarity, republican motherhood, and Mother Nature itself.

None of these developments can be understood outside the context of imperialism. Taxonomy in natural history addressed the growing need for understanding the abundant natural resources found abroad as European powers competed for expansion. When scientists such as Linnaeus gave 'local' species a new, Latin name, they implied that the native naming system carried no 'universal' scientific value. Here, military imperialism and cultural

---

4 Thomas Laqueur, *Making Sex: Body and Gender from the Greeks to Freud* (Cambridge, MA: Harvard University Press, 1990).
5 Londa Schoebinger, *The Mind Has No Sex? Women in the Origins of Modern Science* (Cambridge, MA: Harvard University Press, 1989), 189–213.

Scientific Sex in the Modern World

imperialism positioned themselves on a continuum. Empirical thinkers around the world were no less invested in understanding the interaction between different natural entities. The Ming dynasty naturalist Li Shizhen (1518–93), for example, catalogued five non-males and five non-females in his *Bencao gangmu* or *Compendium of Material Medica* (1578–96), but his criterion for normative sexual expression rested on reproductive capacity alone.[6]

At the peak of European imperialism in the nineteenth century, Western knowledge systems imposed a hegemonic import on most corners of the world.[7] In the Ottoman Middle East, one of the first books that instigated a revolution in medical knowledge – towards modern anatomical knowledge – was *Hamse-i Şânizâde* (Five Books of Şânizade, 1820), a five-volume treatise by Şânizade Mehmet Ataullah (1771–1826). In coastal East Asia, British missionary physician Benjamin Hobson (1816–73) published the first Mandarin text in modern anatomy: *Quanti xinlun* or *A Treatise on Anatomy* (1851). Fluent in the Chinese language, Hobson provided detailed descriptions of male and female reproductive anatomy, as well as multiple illustrations of its surrounding area in the body to give the reader both a cross-sectional perspective and a more complete impression. Out of the range of terms that Hobson used to introduce human reproductive anatomy to the Chinese, many remain in use today.[8] In other areas of the world, the modern biomedicalization of childbirth accompanied colonial conquests and the post-colonial struggle for sovereignty. In Congo, for example, Indigenous notions of reproduction encompassed a broader set of social and cultural practices, which curtailed the popularity of maternity wards.[9]

Race, Evolution, and Eugenics

The centrepiece of nineteenth-century science was the emergence of evolutionary thinking. Evolution holds that biodiversity acquires shape over time

---

6 Charlotte Furth, 'Androgynous Males and Deficient Females: Biology and Gender Boundaries in Sixteenth- and Seventeenth-Century China', *Late Imperial China* 9, no. 2 (1988): 1–31.

7 Hegemonic import, of course, does not mean a complete overhaul. In the context of late twentieth-century China, for instance, the development of men's medicine or *nanke* constituted an important movement to retain medical pluralism. See Everett Yuehong Zhang, *The Impotence Epidemic: Men's Medicine and Sexual Desire in Contemporary China* (Durham, NC: Duke University Press, 2015).

8 Howard Chiang, *After Eunuchs: Science, Medicine, and the Transformation of Sex in Modern China* (New York: Columbia University Press, 2018), 70–124.

9 Nancy Rose Hunt, *A Colonial Lexicon: Of Birth Ritual, Medicalization, and Mobility in Congo* (Durham, NC: Duke University Press, 1999).

according to a universal set of laws. The English naturalist Charles Darwin (1809–82) provided robust evidence for a scientific theory of biological change that departed from the view that God created each species independently.[10] According to Darwin, variation in life forms depended on *natural selection*, a process that preserved those heritable traits most advantageous to a species' survival. Since reproduction sat at the centre of hereditarian concerns, evolutionary biology was from the outset tied to debates about sexuality. In fact, before Darwin, scientists had already been studying the diversity of the human race in fields such as phrenology and physical anthropology. Even in his time, Darwin's theory was not always accepted; contending views flourished and sometimes overshadowed Darwinism into the twentieth century. But perhaps the most important legacy of the evolutionary revolution was the birth of eugenics, with varying programmes of implementation across the world.

In the first half of the nineteenth century, Western scientists developed a programme to study race systematically. The taxonomic, materialistic, naturalistic, and imperialist tendencies of empirical knowledge generated a fixation on viewing the body as an indicator of human difference. Between the 1820s and 1840s, this fixation contributed to the rise of a field of pseudoscience called phrenology (Figure 15.1). Phrenologists located the seat of mental faculties and intelligence in the shape and size of the cranium. They used the variation in skull sizes to condone traditional ideas about sex difference. According to the German physician Johann Spurzheim (1772–1836), 'certain mental powers are stronger, and others weaker in men than in women, and vice versa'.[11] This view was further perpetuated in the field of physical anthropology, which matured in full force by the mid-century. Physical anthropologists elaborated on the classification of races by physical structures. They also singled out women's shorter limbs, larger pelvises, menstrual physiology, facial angle, among other traits, as the basis of sex difference (as well as their physical and social inferiority). Within the larger context of imperialism and slavery, both phrenology and physical anthropology explained human difference in terms of not only visible bodily traits, but also an implicit ranking of mental capacity and degree of civilization.

Therefore, when Darwin proposed his theory of evolution, scientific thinkers had begun to move away from a purely taxonomic and descriptive practice and towards a meta-conceptual approach to understanding the

---

10 Charles Darwin, *On the Origins of Species* (London: John Murray, 1859).
11 Quoted in Cynthia Russett, *Sexual Science: The Victorian Construction of Womanhood* (Cambridge, MA: Harvard University Press, 1989), 18.

Scientific Sex in the Modern World

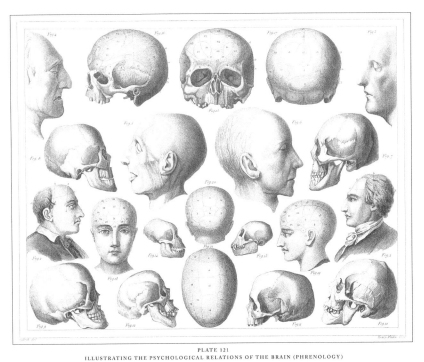

PLATE 121
ILLUSTRATING THE PSYCHOLOGICAL RELATIONS OF THE BRAIN (PHRENOLOGY)

Figure 15.1 A plate illustrating the psychological relations of the brain (phrenology) (1851). Source: Bauhaus1000/Digital Vision/Getty Images, 1173380813.

development of vital functions. With respect to sexual difference, Darwin found himself at a dead end, because many of the so-called 'secondary sex characteristics' held no intrinsic value to survival. In fact, some examples, such as the colourful feathers of male birds or the large decorative antlers of certain deer, may be dangerous and cumbersome. To explain the counter-intuitive existence of these features, Darwin proposed a parallel theory of *sexual selection*. Interestingly, while Darwin gave female animals the choice in sexual selection, he awarded the power of sexual choice to males among human beings.

Even though the theory came from Darwin, sexual selection immediately faced resistance. Some questioned the aesthetic authority Darwin assigned to female animals; others questioned its separation from natural selection. The leading contending voices were Patrick Geddes (1854–1932) and J. Arthur Thomson (1861–1933). In *The Evolution of Sex* (1889), the two Scottish biologists argued that secondary sex characteristics should be more adequately understood as *constitutional* maleness and femaleness: signs not instruments, expressive not functional.[12] Primary sex cells, in their reading, assumed the contrasting qualities of passiveness (the ovum) and activeness (the sperm). Geddes and Thomson's central thesis, along with other conventional Victorian assumptions about gender difference, surfaced in such landmark texts as *Man and Woman* (1894) by the English sexologist Havelock Ellis (1859–1939).[13] Also disputing Darwinian evolution, the German embryologist Ernst Haeckel (1834–1919) elaborated a biogenetic law that compared women to children and savages.[14]

In the nineteenth and twentieth centuries, the view of the French naturalist Jean-Baptist Lamarck (1744–1829) presented the major theoretical alternative to Darwinian evolution. In Lamarck's view, the inheritance of acquired characteristics was possible, and the environment could induce a change in trait that could then be passed on to succeeding generations – a process known as *transmutation*. By 1900, Darwin's theory, the key rival to Lamarckism, had gained widespread support, especially in the Anglophone and Germanophone worlds. However, this would not have been possible without the concrete knowledge of how heredity worked. Two geneticists unlocked this secret for Darwinism: a German, August Weismann (1834–1914), and an Austrian, Gregor Mendel (1822– 84). Their work, often synthesized into the Weismann-Mendel thesis, showed that the germ plasm alone was responsible for the transmission of the hereditary material. Against this 'hard' view of heredity, neo-Lamarckism proposed a theory of evolution driven by a slow, purposeful process. More importantly, this 'soft' view of heredity provided a solution for the existing uncertainties in genetics and what some scientists considered as the exaggerated claims of the Weismann-Mendel model.

The competing schools of hereditarian thinking surfaced most visibly in the different eugenics programmes implemented across the world. Eugenics, coined by the British scientist Francis Galton (1822–1911), was a movement that attempted to achieve better breeding by utilizing hereditary knowledge. Between the 1880s and the 1940s, there were two general circuits in global circulation: the Northern circuit and the Latin circuit. The former dominated eugenics thinking in North America and parts of Western Europe (especially Britain and Germany), reaching as far as East Asia, which espoused the

---

12 Patrick Geddes and J. Arthur Thomson, *The Evolution of Sex* (London: Walter Scott, 1889).

13 Havelock Ellis, *Man and Woman: A Study of Human Secondary Sexual Characters* (1894; London: Walter Scott, 1897).

14 Russett, *Sexual Science*, 51.

Weismann-Mendel model;[15] the latter characterized a loose network of scientists spanning from Italy and Spain to parts of Latin America (especially Brazil and Argentina) where neo-Lamarckism dictated societal views of evolution.[16] Eugenics promoted measures that could either encourage the breeding of fitter races (positive eugenics) or discourage the reproduction of unfit individuals (negative eugenics). In the Northern circuit, involuntary sterilization gradually became a hallmark of the increasing draconian character of negative eugenics: roughly 70,000 individuals were sterilized in the United States between 1907 and 1945, for example.

In contrast, the new field of biotypology typified the negative approach to eugenics in the Latin circuit. Implicit in the neo-Lamarckian perspective was an optimistic expectation that reforms of the social milieu would result in permanent improvement. Endorsing this vision, the Italian endocrinologist Nichola Pende (1880–1970) coined biotypology in 1922 as the scientific study of somatic and psychic individual types. The nature of this new science was classificatory, and it combined approaches from criminology, anthropology, endocrinology, and psychology to forge ideal types of men and women. An Institute of Biotypology was founded in Genoa in 1926, providing a model for the establishment of the Argentinian Association of Biotypology, Eugenics, and Social Medicine in 1932. After the Italian Institute was relocated to Rome in 1935, it anticipated examining 70,000 individuals a year. The signature activity of these institutes was the issuing of the 'biotypological card', which carried information about an individual's morphology, psychology, and behaviour. This kind of personality card was adopted by eugenicists in Argentina, Brazil, and Mexico in the 1930s. Among the individuals targeted for correction by Pende were those showing ambiguous secondary sex characteristics and homosexual behaviour. He introduced hormone therapy to normalize gender and sexual expression.[17] In the late 1940s, Pende's biotypology informed the sexological discourse about necrophilia and other sexual perversions in Peru.[18] (See also Chapter 6 by Mirela David in Volume IV of this work.)

---

15 Phillipa Levine and Alison Bashford, 'Introduction: Eugenics and the Modern World', in *The Oxford Handbook of the History of Eugenics*, ed. Alison Bashford and Phillipa Levine (Oxford: Oxford University Press, 2010), 3–24.

16 Nancy Leys Stepan, '*The Hour of Eugenics*': *Race, Gender, and Nation in Latin America* (Ithaca, NY: Cornell University Press, 1991).

17 Chiara Beccalossi, 'Types, Norms and Normalization: Hormone Research and Treatments in Italy, Argentina and Brazil, c. 1900–1950', *History of the Human Sciences* 34, no. 2 (2021): 113–37.

18 Paulo Drinot, 'Necrophilia, Psychiatry, and Sexology: The Making of Sexual Science in Mid-Twentieth Century Peru', *Journal of Social History* 56, no. 4 (2023): 782–804.

HOWARD CHIANG

Homosexuality and the Birth of a Forgotten World

The rise of evolutionary thinking merged with the interest in taxonomy, naturalism, materialism, and imperialism to form an interdisciplinary field of knowledge that came to be known as sexology in the closing decades of the nineteenth century. Initially, physicians took the lead in defining this new terrain of scientific knowledge, especially by claiming novel authority on problems of urban society that had heretofore fallen under the purview of law. By the turn of the twentieth century, sexology increasingly drew experts from other fields, including the natural and social sciences and, especially in the English context, literary and historical studies.[19] The vocabulary of sadism, masochism, fetishism, and other perversions underwrote the proliferation of sexual classification.[20] It was also around this time that circumcision became a medicalized procedure to prevent masturbation.[21] By the time that sexology had become a truly global science, the enterprise evolved into a tool of expansion for the modernization of nation-states. With varying consequences, the invention of homosexuality as a rubric anchored the heteronormalization of culture, citizenship, and history across most of the industrialized world.

Around the turn of the twentieth century, sexologists proposed three major frameworks for understanding homosexuality.[22] First, German medical doctors such as Richard von Krafft-Ebing (1840–1902) viewed homosexuality as an example of *nervous degeneracy*. Although Karl Westphal (1833–90) had already identified a case of 'contrary sexual feelings' in 1869, it was not until the publication of Krafft-Ebing's forensic psychiatric compendium, *Psychopathia Sexualis* (1886), that this view commanded widespread attention.[23] Influenced by evolutionary thinking, especially the French psychiatrist Benedict Morel's (1809–73) idea of degeneration, Krafft-Ebing argued

---

19 Heike Bauer, *English Literary Sexology: Translations of Inversion, 1860–1930* (New York: Palgrave Macmillan, 2009).

20 Arnold Davidson, *The Emergence of Sexuality: Historical Epistemology and the Formation of Concepts* (Cambridge, MA: Harvard University Press, 2001); Benjamin Kahan, *The Book of Minor Perverts: Sexology, Etiology, and the Emergence of Sexuality* (Chicago: University of Chicago Press, 2019).

21 Thomas Laqueur, *Solitary Sex: A Cultural History of Masturbation* (New York: Zone Books, 2003).

22 Jennifer Terry, *An American Obsession: Science, Medicine, and Homosexuality in Modern Society* (Chicago: University of Chicago Press, 1999), 42–3.

23 Karl Friedrich Otto Westphal, 'Die Conträre Sexualempfindung: Symptom eines neuropathitischen (psychopathitischen) Zustandes', *Archiv für Psychicatrie und Nervenkrankeiten* 2 (1869–70): 73–108; Richard von Krafft-Ebing, *Psychopathia Sexualis*, trans. F. S. Klaf (1903; New York: Stein & Day, 1965).

that sexual inversion represented an arrested stage of evolutionary development, because its characteristic of psychic hermaphroditism suggested a resemblance to lower-level life forms from which humans had evolved. Sexologists who shared this view pathologized homosexuality, pioneered the case study approach, and, in so doing, transferred the technology of control from law and religion to medicine.[24]

The German-Jewish physician and gay activist Magnus Hirschfeld (1868–1935) led a programme of sexual science that promoted the second framework, which viewed homosexuality as a *benign variation* of nature. Early advocates of this congenital view included the German jurist Karl Heinrich Ulrichs (1825–95), who first characterized same-sex erotic attraction as innate, and Austrian-born Hungarian journalist Karl Maria Kertbeny (1824–85), who coined the term 'homosexuality' in 1868. Building on these nineteenth-century efforts, Hirschfeld carried out a programme of social reform through the education and dissemination of sexual scientific knowledge. Hoping to overturn Paragraph 175, a provision of the German criminal code that criminalized homosexual behaviour, Hirschfeld formed the Scientific Humanitarian Committee (the world's first gay rights organization) in 1897, edited the *Yearbook of Sexual Intermediaries* from 1899 to 1923, and founded the Institute for Sexual Science in Berlin in 1919. Although Hirschfeld's institute was a private research centre, it served as a model for other similar entities. Most renowned was the world's first public university-based sexological institute, the Institute of Sexual Pathology, founded in Czechoslovakia in 1921.[25] Between 1931 and 1932, three sex consultant centres were opened in Tel Aviv.[26] In his research, Hirschfeld combined the methods of field interview, psychosocial questionnaire, statistical survey, and clinical case study. With a history of delivering expert opinions on sodomy cases in both the centre and the periphery of the German Empire, Hirschfeld genuinely believed in the achievement of greater tolerance by battling ignorance.[27] Many of the

---

24 Harry Oosterhuis, *Stepchildren of Nature: Krafft-Ebing, Psychiatry, and the Making of Sexual Identity* (Chicago: University of Chicago Press, 2000).

25 Katerina Liskova, '"Now You See Them, Now You Don't": Sexual Deviants and Sexological Experts in Communist Czechoslovakia', *History of the Human Sciences* 29, no. 1 (2016): 49–74, at 52. The Institute of Sexual Pathology was renamed the Sexological Institute in 1950.

26 Liat Kozma, 'Sexology in the Yishuv: The Rise and Decline of Sexual Consultation in Tel Aviv, 1930–39', *International Journal of Middle Eastern Studies* 42 (2010): 231–49.

27 Robert Tobin, 'Sexology in the Southwest: Law, Medicine, and Sexology in Germany and Its Colonies', in *A Global History of Sexual Science, 1880–1960*, ed. Veronika Fuechtner, Douglas E. Haynes, and Ryan M. Jones (Berkeley, CA: University of California Press, 2018), 141–62.

sexologists based in England, including Havelock Ellis and Edward Carpenter (1844–1929), endorsed a similar naturalizing outlook. Over time, Hirschfeld changed his view of colonialism, violence, and race, most likely as a result of his romantic involvement with a disciple-lover he met in Shanghai, Li Shiu Tong (1907–93).[28]

The third major framework for understanding homosexuality came from the school of psychoanalysis pioneered by Sigmund Freud (1856–1939). Unlike the degeneration or naturalization thesis, Freud and his followers espoused a purely *psychogenic* interpretation of human sexuality.[29] Rather than decoding the body (or the brain) for signs of mental deviation, psychoanalysts pointed to the mind's self-regulation as the fulcrum of explanation. They championed a 'polymorphous' notion of libido, or sex drive, and argued that 'all human beings are capable of making a homosexual object-choice and have in fact made one in their unconscious'.[30] Some of the most exemplary Freudian thinking on this topic appeared in *Three Essays on the Theory of Sexuality* (1905) and its subsequent editions. Notably, whereas other sexological views, including that of Krafft-Ebing, Ulrichs, Hirschfeld, Ellis, and Carpenter, all framed homosexuality as a minoritarian phenomenon, Freud's texts depicted it with a more universal predisposition.[31] While Freud himself insisted in a letter to an American mother in 1935 that homosexuality could not necessarily be cured through therapy, his conservative American followers launched a sweeping campaign that argued the exact opposite.[32] The interpersonal school of psychodynamic science, known as the neo-Freudians, offered alternative views on sexuality and even made an impact in the Asia Pacific.[33] (See also Chapter 5 by Alison Downham Moore in Volume I of this work.)

In the first half of the twentieth century, sexologists from around the world translated, challenged, and transformed these three competing epistemological

---

28 Heike Bauer, *The Hirschfeld Archives: Violence, Death, and Modern Queer Culture* (Philadelphia: Temple University Press, 2017); Laurie Marhoefer, *Racism and the Making of Gay Rights: A Sexologist, His Student, and the Empire of Queer Love* (Toronto: University of Toronto Press, 2022).

29 Katie Sutton, *Sex between Body and Mind: Psychoanalysis and Sexology in the German-Speaking World, 1890s–1930s* (Ann Arbor, MI: University of Michigan Press, 2019).

30 Sigmund Freud, *Three Essays on the Theory of Sexuality*, in *The Standard Edition of the Complete Psychological Works of Sigmund Freud*, Vol. 7, ed. James Strachey (1905; London: Hogarth, 1953–74), 145.

31 Kenneth Lewes, *The Psychoanalytic Theory of Male Homosexuality* (New York: Simon & Schuster, 1988).

32 Henry Abelove, 'Freud, Male Homosexuality, and the Americans', *Dissent* 33, no. 1 (1986): 59–69.

33 Howard Chiang, 'The Secrets of a Loyalist Soul: Psychoanalysis and Homosexuality in Wartime China', *GLQ: A Journal of Lesbian and Gay Studies* 29, no. 1 (2023): 61–76.

frameworks.[34] Similar to any other industrial city in the West, *fin-de-siècle* Buenos Aires witnessed a growing association of sex between men with female prostitution – in both elite and lay discourses – as signs of evolutionary regression against the backdrop of urban chaos and the pathos of civilization.[35] Between 1917 and 1933, Soviet public health commissar Nikolai Semashko (1874–1949) visited and learned from Hirschfeld's Institute.[36] Physicians in the Soviet Union promoted a diverse set of opinions on the nature of homosexuality – ranging from endocrinological to psychosocial.[37] Sexology thrived, too, in Meiji and modern Japan, where both Germanic and British influences were most pronounced. A translation of *Psychopathia Sexualis* appeared in 1894 under the sponsorship of the Japanese Forensic Medicine Association. Sex researchers such as Yamamoto Senji (1889–1929) promoted sexology as a system of both enlightenment and control;[38] feminist writers, including Ogura Seizaburō (1882–1941) and Hiratsuka Raichō (1886–1971), adapted free-love texts to disseminate new ideas about sex difference and gender equality.[39]

Likewise, in early twentieth-century China, a generation of sexologists, including Zhang Jingsheng (1888–1970) and Pan Guangdan (1899–1967), collected sex histories, psychoanalysed historical figures, and redefined same-sex desire through the vocabulary of homosexuality, which was translated into *tongxing lian'ai* in Chinese (and *dōseiai* in Japanese).[40] These East Asian iconoclastic thinkers inaugurated an era of sexual science in which the work of Ellis, Carpenter, Freud, and others braced potent discussions of sex education and eugenics.[41] In colonial Burma, sexologist P. Moe Nin (1883–1940) steered

---

34 Heike Bauer, ed., *Sexology and Translation: Cultural and Scientific Encounters across the Modern World* (Philadelphia: Temple University Press, 2015).

35 Pablo Ben, 'Global Modernity and Sexual Science: The Case of Male Homosexuality and Female Prostitution, 1850–1950', in *Global History of Sexual Science*, ed. Fuechtner et al., 29–50.

36 Dan Healey, *Homosexual Desire in Revolutionary Russia: The Regulation of Sexual and Gender Dissent* (Chicago: University of Chicago Press, 2001), 132–3.

37 Healey, *Homosexual Desire*, 126–51.

38 Gregory M. Pflugfelder, *Cartographies of Desire: Male–Male Sexuality in Japanese Discourse, 1600–1950* (Berkeley, CA: University of California Press, 1999); Sabine Frühstück, *Colonizing Sex: Sexology and Social Control in Modern Japan* (Berkeley, CA: University of California Press, 2003).

39 Michiko Suzuki, 'The Science of Sexual Difference: Ogura Seizaburō, Hiratsuka Raichō, and the Intersection of Sexology and Feminism in Early Twentieth-Century Japan', in *Global History of Sexual Science*, ed. Fuechtner et al., 258–78.

40 Chiang, *After Eunuchs*, 125–77.

41 Frank Dikötter, *Imperfect Conceptions: Medical Knowledge, Birth Defects, and Eugenics in China* (New York: Columbia University Press, 1998); Yuehtsen Juliette Chung, *Struggle for National Survival: Eugenics in Sino-Japanese Contexts, 1896–1945* (New York: Routledge, 2002); Sumiko Otsubo and James R. Bartholomew, 'Eugenics in Japan: Some Ironies of Modernity, 1883–1945', *Science in Context* 11, nos. 3–4 (2008): 545–65.

a heteronormative version of intimacy away from the contamination of *kilesa* (lust, evil desire, and defilements).[42] In the Persian world, under the influence of Western sexology, native conceptions of beauty and eros transformed from including to excluding the *amrad* figure: these beardless boys were erased from being an acceptable object of male desire in Iran.[43] Between the 1940s and 1960s, conceptions of homosexuality became the primary rubric for understanding transsexuality in Iran, displacing the earlier affinity between sex change and intersex conditions.[44] In Egypt, the psychoanalyst Yusuf Murad (1902–66) founded the *Journal of Psychology* or *Majallat 'Ilm al-Nafs*, which published Freudian interpretations of adolescent sexuality and homosexuality in the 1940s.[45] Increasingly, same-sex relations acquired social stigma and the status of deviance under the shadow of global imperialist aggression. A consistent pattern thus emerged in different regions across the early twentieth-century world: sexology provided nations with a tool of amnesia, namely, to 'forget' sexual diversity in the name of science. This management and alleviation of gender/sexual anxieties, what we might loosely call the heteronormalization of culture, became imbricated with claims to modernity.

Intersex, Trans, and the Rise of the Sex/Gender Binary

Despite the growing influence of Freud, new evidence from the life sciences convinced many researchers to continue the search for the biological basis of sexuality into the twentieth century. Discoveries of sex hormones, in particular, emerged as a bridge between debates in anatomy and genetics. In this process, the seat of maleness and femaleness shifted from gonads and chromosomes to the secretion of the endocrine glands.[46] The golden age of

---

42 Chie Ikeya, 'Talking Sex, Making Love: P. Moe Nin and Intimate Modernity in Colonial Burma', in *Modern Times in Southeast Asia, 1920s–1970s*, ed. Susie Protschky and Tom van den Berge (Leiden: Brill, 2018), 136–65, at 142.

43 Afsaneh Najmabadi, *Women with Mustaches and Men without Beards: Gender and Sexual Anxieties in Iranian Modernity* (Berkeley, CA: University of California Press, 2005).

44 Afsaneh Najmabadi, *Professing Selves: Transsexuality and Same-Sex Desire in Contemporary Iran* (Durham, NC: Duke University Press, 2014), 38–74.

45 Omnia El Shakry, *The Arabic Freud: Psychoanalysis and Islam in Modern Egypt* (Princeton, NJ: Princeton University Press, 2017), 77–8.

46 Nelly Oudshoorn, *Beyond the Natural Body: An Archeology of Sex Hormones* (New York: Routledge, 1994); Chandak Sengoopta, *The Most Secret Quintessence of Life: Sex, Glands, and Hormones, 1850–1950* (Chicago: University of Chicago Press, 2006). A parallel strand of brain organization theory, which posited the 'hard wiring' of male vs. female brains on the basis of pre-natal hormonal exposure, came to be consolidated by the 1970s. See

endocrinology – the 1920s and the 1930s – marked a paradigm shift in sexology, reaching unevenly into the Northern and Latin circuits of eugenics. More importantly, glandular science stimulated refreshing answers to two puzzles of human sexuality: sex ambiguity and sex metamorphosis. Coupled with surgical intervention, the administration of hormones suggested the possibility of managing sex differentiation artificially. The tension between minimizing and enabling sexual variation catalyzed a new science of intersexuality and transsexuality. By the 1950s, sexologists found the concept of biological sex insufficient; they expanded out of necessity its scientific definition to include *gender*, the psychological and social organization of sex.[47]

Ideas about sex transformation emanated from Europe to other places in the world. No other work assumed a greater international spotlight than the animal sex reversal experiments of the Austrian physiologist Eugen Steinach (1861–1944) in the 1910s. After transplanting ovaries into castrated male guinea pigs and testes into female guinea pigs, Steinach observed the development of opposite sex characteristics in his subjects. These studies soon became scientific classics as they confirmed the role of the glands' secretions in sexual development. Previously, geneticists had demonstrated the importance of chromosomes in sex-determination.[48] But with Steinach's work, scientists shifted the locus of sex differentiation to the endocrine system. Building on these studies, for example, both Hirschfeld and Pende sought to tinker with human sexual orientation by manipulating a person's hormonal level. In the Northern circuit, word of success in sex change experiments soon filled the American press and prompted a growing number of readers to seek medical intervention in altering their sex.[49] In the Latin circuit, the Spanish physician Gregorio Marañón (1887–1960) devised an elaborate theory of intersexuality to which he grouped hermaphroditism and homosexuality.[50] Marañón argued for a programme of hormonal treatment to adjust the sexual ambiguity of these intersexed states. His ideas critically informed the clinical approach to intersex management in places as far as Chile in the 1930s. East Asian writers also introduced the ideas of Steinach, but they did so by

Rebecca Jordan-Young, *Brain Storm: The Flaws in the Science of Sex Differences* (Cambridge, MA: Harvard University Press, 2010).

47 Bernice Hausmann, *Changing Sex: Transsexualism, Technology, and the Idea of Gender* (Durham, NC: Duke University Press, 1995).

48 Sarah S. Richardson, *Sex Itself: The Search for Male and Female in the Human Genome* (Chicago: University of Chicago Press, 2013).

49 Joanne Meyerowitz, *How Sex Changed: A History of Transsexuality in the United States* (Cambridge, MA: Harvard University Press, 2002).

50 Richard Cleminson and F. Vázquez García, *Hermaphroditism, Medical Science and Sexual Identity in Spain, 1850–1960* (Cardiff: University of Wales Press, 2009).

drawing on native examples of reproductive anomalies, such as eunuchs and hermaphrodites, to make accessible these foreign ideas about scientific sex change.[51]

Around the same time that these ideas took hold outside Europe, innovations in Western sexology drew inspiration from the non-Western world. In the Latin circuit, for example, the Latvia-born physiologist Alexander Lipschütz (1883–1980) introduced Marañón's theory to Chilean scientists. In the late 1920s, Lipschütz, Marañón, and others grounded the transnational circulation of sexology across the Iberian-American world in the famous case of the intersex patient 'O.B.B.', who was treated in Valparaiso, Chile. With Marañón's reference to the case, a multi-directional network of sexual science assumed salience across Latin America, Spain, and Central Europe.[52] Similarly, Hirschfeld's theory of transvestism crucially relied on a crude understanding of the *onnagata*, male actors who played female roles in Japanese Kabuki theatre. Here, Hirschfeld succeeded in delineating the notion of cross-gender identification and distinguishing it from same-sex sexuality. But by attributing to *onnagata* performers an innate inclination to adopt female roles, Hirschfeld invented a sexological category he assumed to hold universal value. Very quickly, his category spread to other nations in the Northern circuit. Yet it would not have been possible without his superficial, however intentional, engagement with Japanese culture.[53]

By the 1950s, the centre of gravity in sexual science had shifted to the United States. In the medical treatment of intersexuality and transsexuality in particular, American researchers promoted the new language of gender and its malleability. The psychologist John Money (1921–2006) at Johns Hopkins University gained international recognition for the protocols he developed to treat intersex conditions. He believed, erroneously, in the possibility of matching a child's sex of rearing (nurture) to fit the sex assigned at birth (nature). This model of gender malleability overturned not only the long-standing refusal to acknowledge the existence of human intersexuality in Western medicine, but also the lack of a robust and systematic apparatus for managing cases of children born with ambiguous genitalia.[54] In 1964,

---

51 Chiang, *After Eunuchs*, 178–235.
52 Kurt MacMillan, '"Forms So Attenuated That They Merge into Normality Itself": Alexander Lipschütz, Gregorio Merañón, and Theories of Intersexuality in Chile, circa 1930', in *Global History of Sexual Science*, ed. Fuechtner et al., 330–52.
53 Rainer Herrn and Michael Thomas Taylor, 'Magnus Hirschfeld's Interpretation of the Japanese *Onnagata* as Transvestites', *Journal of the History of Sexuality* 27, no. 1 (2018): 63–100.
54 Sandra Eder, *How the Clinic Made Gender: The Medical History of a Transformative Idea* (Chicago: University of Chicago Press, 2022).

Scientific Sex in the Modern World

psychiatrists Robert Stoller (1924–91) and Ralph Greenson (1911–79) at the University of California, Los Angeles (UCLA), coined the concept of *core gender identity* to refer to one's deep-seated identification as female or male.[55] The growing interest beyond genital morphology led to a clearer scientific demarcation of gender from sex.

The possibility that an individual's gender identity may be discordant with biological sex increasingly caught the attention of the endocrinologist Harry Benjamin (1885–1986), who popularized the medical treatment of transsexuality starting in the 1950s. Benjamin's thinking on the subject culminated in his magnum opus, *The Transsexual Phenomenon* (1966).[56] Yet if Money sought to manipulate a child's sex through rearing, or gender identification, Benjamin advocated the opposite approach: to correct an individual's sex to match their gender identity. Benjamin explicitly labelled the urge to transform one's physical sex 'transsexualism' and insisted that physicians should try their best to assist such individuals. Though he helped to relieve the discomfort of his patients mainly by prescribing hormones, Benjamin also corresponded with surgeons around the world to compile a list of possible surgical destinations for those who wanted them. The high-profile case that cemented Benjamin's interest in the subject was Christine Jorgensen (1926–89), an ex-GI who had travelled to Denmark for her sex re-assignment surgery in the early 1950s and rose to international stardom afterward.[57] Both Benjamin's work and Jorgensen's story commanded global interest. An exceeding number of readers wrote letters to Benjamin and Jorgensen from different regions of the world, and Jorgensen's saga sparked an unprecedented level of press coverage on medical sex change in places as far as Taiwan (as in the case of Xie Jianshun), Japan (the story of Nagai Akhiko), Mexico (the gender transition of Marta Olmos), Israel (the experience of Rina Nathan), and beyond.[58] This 'global Christine' phenomenon marked a turning point in the history of sexual science whereby ideas about the nature of the sex/gender binary enlivened a multi-directional discourse.

---

55 Ralph Greenson, 'On Homosexuality and Gender Identity', *International Journal of Psycho-Analysis* 45 (1964): 217–19; Robert Stoller, 'A Contribution to the Study of Gender Identity', *International Journal of Psycho-Analysis* 45 (1964): 220–6.

56 Harry Benjamin, *The Transsexual Phenomenon* (New York: Julian, 1966).

57 Meyerowitz, *How Sex Changed*.

58 Howard Chiang, *Transtopia in the Sinophone Pacific* (New York: Columbia University Press, 2021), 19–63; Ryan M. Jones, 'Mexican Sexology and Male Homosexuality: Genealogies and Global Contexts, 1860–1957', in *Global History of Sexual Science*, ed. Fuechtner et al., 232–57; Gil Englestein and Iris Rachimimov, 'Crossing Borders and Demolishing Boundaries: The Connected History of the Israeli Transgender Community, 1953–1986', *Journal of Modern Jewish Studies* 18, no. 2 (2019): 142–59.

HOWARD CHIANG

Cultural Truths and the Social Organization of Sexuality

In 1929, Havelock Ellis made a remark that stood evolutionary claims about the superiority of European civilization on their head. It appeared in the preface he wrote for British anthropologist Bronisław Malinowski's (1884–1942) *The Sexual Life of Savages in North-Western Melanesia*: 'we may even find that in some respects the savage has here reached a finer degree of civilization than the civilized man'.[59] Ellis's comment reflected a growing trend, beginning in the late 1920s, when researchers from across the social and medical sciences began to collaborate in a systematic investigation of culture as the leading determinant of gender and sexual variation. The rise of cultural anthropology joined a renewed scientific investment by colonial powers to reverse hierarchical templates of sexual practices and norms emanating from the metropoles. In response to the waning status of eugenics and hereditarian science, these cultural scientists stressed nurture over nature and society over biology. Not only did they collect evidence to support a more malleable understanding of gender and sexuality, but they also retooled the methods of social science to posit a new frame of sexual normality. The rise of this intellectual current – what historian Joanne Meyerowitz has called social constructionism – helped to shatter previously held assumptions about sexual pathology and deviance, including the 'disease' paradigm of homosexuality.[60]

Even though Freud and his followers insisted on a dynamic understanding of sex psychology, it was the work of Hirschfeld that can be seen as setting the precedent for this new approach to sexual science. In the world of sexology advanced by Hirschfeld, surveys, interviews, and data collection from the field were already important methods of conducting sex research.[61] In fact, many sexologists valued the insight of history and ethnology as much as the case studies approach of psychiatry and medicine.[62] But starting in the 1920s

---

59 Havelock Ellis, 'Preface', in Bronisław Malinowski, *The Sexual Life of Savages in North-Western Melanesia* (London: George Routledge, 1929), vii–xii, at xii.

60 Joanne Meyerowitz, '"How Common Culture Shapes the Separate Lives": Sexuality, Race, and Mid-Twentieth-Century Social Constructionist Thought', *Journal of American History* 96, no. 4 (2010): 1057–84.

61 Charlotte Wolff, *Magnus Hirschfeld: A Portrait of a Pioneer* (London: Quartet Books, 1986); Elena Mancini, *Magnus Hirschfeld and the Quest for Sexual Freedom: A History of the First International Sexual Freedom Movement* (New York: Palgrave Macmillan, 2010); Ralf Dose, *Magnus Hirschfeld: The Origins of the Gay Liberation Movement* (New York: Monthly Review, 2014).

62 Kate Fisher and Jane Funk, '"Let Us Leave the Hospital; Let Us Go on a Journey around the World": British and German Sexual Science and the Global Search for Sexual Variation', in *Global History of Sexual Science*, ed. Fuechtner et al., 51–69.

and especially the 1930s, it was the rise of cultural anthropology, psychometrics, and other more robust statistical sampling methods that shifted the tenor of sexology to challenge the rigid dichotomies of normality and deviance. In this regard, the writings of the Finnish anthropologist Edward Westermarck (1862–1939) were as widely read as, if not more so than, Freud's. Over the course of his career, Westermarck increasingly appealed to the empirical reality of sexual diversity as found in non-Western societies. His ethnographica data from Morocco confirmed Hirschfeld's thesis that the naturalization of heterosexuality was a false universal. Instead, Westermarck pushed for a scientific premise that considered sexual and cultural variability ordinary.[63]

The turn away from Darwinian evolution and towards cultural relativism was best exemplified in the rise of the Culture and Personality School. In the area of gender and sexuality, anthropologists Margaret Mead (1901–78) and Ruth Benedict (1887–1948), both students of Franz Boas (1858–1942) at Columbia University, pioneered a new vision of sexual liberalism through the study of cultural others. Based on fieldwork in Samoa and New Guinea, Mead began her career with a smashing success in demonstrating the cultural construction of adolescence. In the 1930s, Mead entered a dialogue with Benedict, her friend, mentor, and lover, by publishing *Sex and Temperament* (1935) as a response to Benedict's *Patterns of Culture* (1934).[64] Though at times holding different theoretical positions, Mead and Benedict shared similar views on the artificiality of American sexual mores. Each found evidence, whether it came from the Indigenous populations in the South Pacific or Native America, of women who behaved 'manly' or men who acted 'womanly' according to Western standards of the time. Contributing to a growing number of anthropological studies on what was then termed *berdache*, the socially sanctioned roles for cross-gender identification in American Indian tribes, Benedict defended the interpretation of homosexuality as a natural variation.[65] Whereas previous anthropologists considered *berdache* as signs of primitivity and inferiority, Benedict used it as evidence to

---

63 Ralph Fleck, 'Westermarck's Morocco: Sexology and the Epistemic Politics of Cultural Anthropology and Sexual Science', in *Global History of Sexual Science*, ed. Fuechtner et al., 70–96.

64 Ruth Benedict, *Patterns of Culture* (Boston: Houghton Mifflin, 1934); Margaret Mead, *Sex and Temperament in Three Primitive Societies* (New York: Morrow, 1935).

65 Contemporary queer Indigenous activists have argued for the replacement of the colonial category *berdache* with the more neutral concept *two-spirit*. The term *berdache* is retained here only to reflect the category used by the historical actors, especially the anthropologists, who studied them.

reverse such an assumption of cultural hierarchy, stressed the enlightening nature of these findings, and claimed that Western societies had as much to learn about human diversity from Indigenous communities as the other way around. Ultimately, Mead and Benedict construed maleness and femaleness as changing and non-discrete abstractions.[66]

It is important to note that even though Mead and Benedict highlighted the social organization of individual psychology and differences, their work resonated with the contemporaneous discovery in biochemistry that both male and female sex hormones can be detected in everyone's body. The sex continuum model thus reached its apex in the 1930s. During this time, the English anthropologist Edward Evan Evans-Pritchard (1902–73) began to collect information on male and female homosexuality among the Azande of South Sudan. From the 1950s on, his research called attention to the existence of institutionalized boy-wives in the Azande court, as well as woman–woman marriages in Nuer society. Based on his field notes from the 1930s, Evans-Pritchard published an essay called 'Sexual Inversion among the Azande' in *American Anthropologist* in 1970.[67] Evans-Pritchard's aim both resembled and departed from the ambition of the earlier cohort of Culture-and-Personality scholars. The similarity lay in a commitment to honouring the historical particularities of different cultures. But whereas Mead and Benedict challenged the accepted standards of Western sexuality, Evans-Pritchard disputed the anthropological claim that same-sex relationships were un-African – an assertion long maintained by ethnopsychiatrists including Frantz Fanon (1926–61).[68]

The questioning of sexual norms in the West entered an escalated phase with the international shock of the so-called 'k-bomb'. When most areas of the globe retreated to conventional gender norms after the Second World War, the Indiana University zoologist Alfred Kinsey (1894–1956) published his *Sexual Behavior in the Human Male* (1948) and *Sexual Behavior in the Human Female* (1953).[69] Together called the Kinsey reports, the two tomes provided

---

66 Lois Banner, *Intertwined Lives: Margaret Mead, Ruth Benedict, and Their Circle* (New York: Alfred A. Knopf, 2003).

67 E. E. Evans-Pritchard, 'Sexual Inversion among the Azande', *American Anthropologist* 72, no. 6 (1970): 1428–34.

68 Ezra Chitando, 'Anthropology in Africa South of the Sahara', in *The Global Encyclopedia of Lesbian, Gay, Bisexual, Transgender, and Queer History*, ed. Howard Chiang (Farmington Hills, MI: Gale, 2019), 61–9; Tiffany Fawn Jones, 'Ethnopsychiatry', in Chiang, *Global Encyclopedia of LGBTQ History*, 510–14.

69 Alfred C. Kinsey, Wardell B. Pomeroy, and Clyde E. Martin, *Sexual Behavior in the Human Male* (Philadelphia: W. B. Saunders, 1948); Alfred C. Kinsey, Wardell B. Pomeroy, Clyde E. Martin, and Paul H. Gebhard, *Sexual Behavior in the Human Female* (Philadelphia: W. B. Saunders, 1953).

surprising statistics of high level of homosexual tendency among the 18,000 white American men and women his team interviewed. Perhaps one of Kinsey's most important innovations was the seven-point heterosexual–homosexual rating scale (with 0 representing exclusively heterosexual and 6 exclusively homosexual). Kinsey's data indicated that only half of the total population of men surveyed were exclusively heterosexual all their lives. This left a largely unexplored conceptual space for treating bisexuality as the basis of identity.[70]

By the late 1950s, some mental health scientists were so convinced by Kinsey's findings that they began to reconsider their position on homosexuality.[71] American clinical psychologist Evelyn Hooker (1907–96) at UCLA administered psychological tests to 'normal' homosexual and hetero-sexual men, and found no difference in their psychological performance.[72] With pressure from both political activists and scientists themselves, the American Psychiatric Association (APA) decided to remove homosexuality from its list of mental disorders in 1973.[73] This would not have been possible without the work of Kinsey, Hooker, and others who reframed sexuality in terms of statistical rather than clinical normalcy.

Bombay in India became equally an important hub for challenging traditional sexual ideas in the mid-century. It was where the Indian eugenicist and physician Alyappin Padmanabha Pillay (1889–1957) edited the *International Journal of Sexology (IJS)* between 1947 and 1955.[74] The journal operated as a gateway for the circulation of sexual knowledge among an international network of experts, sexologists, and lay readers: Pillay corresponded with his contemporaries across the globe, and raised funds for the study of sexology in India. It was where Harry Benjamin published his first major findings on transsexualism, for instance. Similar journals had appeared elsewhere in Asia earlier in the century, including *Sexuality* and *Sexual Theory* in 1920s Japan and *Sex Science* in 1930s China, but they were published in the respective East Asian languages. None of their editors

70 Steven Angelides, *A History of Bisexuality* (Chicago: University of Chicago Press, 2001), 113.
71 Howard Chiang, 'Effecting Science, Affecting Medicine: Homosexuality, the Kinsey Reports, and the Contested Boundaries of Psychopathology in the United States, 1948–1965', *Journal of the History of the Behavioral Sciences* 44, no. 4 (2008): 300–18.
72 Evelyn Hooker, 'The Adjustment of the Male Overt Homosexual', *Journal of Projective Techniques* 21 (1957): 18–31; Evelyn Hooker, 'Male Homosexuality in Rorschach', *Journal of Projective Techniques* 22 (1958): 33–54.
73 Ronald Bayer, *Homosexuality and American Psychiatry: The Politics of Diagnosis* (New York: Basic Books, 1981); Jack Drescher and Joseph P. Merlino, eds., *American Psychiatry and Homosexuality: An Oral History* (New York: Routledge, 2007).
74 Sanjam Ahluwalia, '"Tyranny of Orgasm": Global Governance of Sexuality from Bombay, 1930s–1950s', in *Global History of Sexual Science*, ed. Fuechtner et al., 353–73.

reached a global readership. In contrast, the *IJS* was published in English, and as such it connected readers from places as varied as India, Pakistan, Israel, South Africa, Britain, Germany, United States, and Australia.

Trained in Western biomedicine, Pillay drew from his clinical work with Indian women to question dominant Western sexological views. On the subject of female orgasm, for instance, leading medical voices at the time construed the absence of vaginal orgasm as a central feature of frigidity. Even though the diagnosis of female hysteria as a psychological problem had begun to wane by this point (the APA dropped it from the *Diagnostic and Statistical Manual of Mental Disorders* or *DSM* in 1980), leading psychoanalysts and psychiatrists still adhered to the myth of vaginal orgasm.[75] Pillay challenged the view of frigidity as a neurotic condition with the following argument: Indian women rarely understood anything about orgasm immediately before or after marriage, and Indian men rarely comprehended the need for clitoral stimulation. Thus, the absence of orgasmic experience was not an ontologically neurotic symptom but cultural in origin.[76] As a vessel of cultural truths, the *IJS* taught its readers the contingency and partiality of Western sexual norms.

The Politics of Biology in the Era of Political Storms

Historians have argued that the decade of the 1970s harnessed a sexual revolution that reverberated into the twenty-first century, stimulating a rethinking of the work of nature and the importance of biology in body politics. In 1969, two American events fundamentally altered the relationship between sexual agents, research scientists, and health experts: the formation of the Boston Women's Health Collective (BWHC) and the Stonewall Riots.

In May 1969, a group of women in Boston held a workshop called Women and Their Bodies. They discussed matters relating to sexuality and the body, including pregnancy, abortion, and childbirth. In the process they echoed the frustration each felt with how little they knew about their own bodies. In 1970, they published *Women and Their Bodies*, expanded three years later into the first *Our Bodies, Ourselves* (*OBOS*), which has since been translated into at least thirty-three languages.[77] Some translations were selective: the Mandarin

---

75 Rachel Maines, *The Technology of Orgasm: 'Hysteria', the Vibrator, and Women's Sexual Satisfaction* (Baltimore, MD: Johns Hopkins University Press, 1999).
76 Ahluwalia, 'Tyranny of Orgasm', 361.
77 Boston Women's Health Collective, *Women and Their Bodies* (Boston: New England Free Press, 1970); Boston Women's Health Collective, *Our Bodies, Ourselves* (New York: Simon & Schuster, 1973).

Chinese version printed in Taiwan, for instance, left out the chapters on lesbianism, rape, self-defence, and abortion; others highlighted individualism and informed consent as crucial to reproductive rights. *OBOS* marked a departure from the male voices that dominated discourses surrounding women's health and sexuality, and its global circulation responded to the most immediate politics of a given time and place. Scholar Kathy Davis calls the text a 'feminist traveling theory', because women health activists around the world have adapted it to suit their local goals.[78] *OBOS* pioneered a methodological rigor in research protocols that accounted for gender, as most evident in the steady attention to diseases that affect women, such as breast cancer.

In late June 1969, a police raid on the Stonewall Inn, a gay bar in New York City, prompted unanticipated protests from the queer community. Often lauded as a milestone of the modern gay and lesbian movement, the Stonewall Rebellion sparked further demands by sexual minorities for rights and respect from authorities in the subsequent decades, including from medical authorities. Working with sympathetic scientists, gay and lesbian activists succeeded in persuading the APA to eliminate homosexuality from the *DSM*. When the HIV/AIDS pandemic struck in the 1980s, and the US and UK administrations took much more conservative stances on sexual morality, radicals in both countries formed the grassroots AIDS Coalition to Unleash Power (ACT UP) to pressure governments to release funds so that medical scientists could conduct research to end the epidemic (Figure 15.2).[79] Initially, the group focused on getting 'drugs into bodies', but it quickly broadened its agenda to include issues such as affordable healthcare and housing, gender inequity in healthcare, sex education, and clean-needle exchange programmes. By the end of the decade, ACT UP had internationalized, with chapters appearing in Canada, Europe, and Australia. Like the women empowered by the global dissemination of *OBOS*, gay and lesbian activists demanded a more systematic approach to managing the public health crisis directly from scientists. Both marked occasions when subjects of sexual science transformed themselves into activist-experts, leading and even challenging governments, the health profession, and pharmaceutical companies.[80]

---

78 Kathy Davis, *The Making of Our Bodies, Ourselves: How Feminism Travels across Borders* (Durham, NC: Duke University Press, 2007), 11.

79 Sarah Schulman, *Let the Record Show: A Political History of ACT UP New York, 1987–1993* (New York: Farrar, Straus and Giroux, 2021).

80 Steven Epstein, *Impure Science: AIDS, Activism, and the Politics of Knowledge* (Berkeley, CA: University of California Press, 1996).

Figure 15.2 ACT UP demonstrators protest and take over the Food and Drugs Administration headquarters in Rockville, Maryland, USA (October 1988). Source: Mikki Ansin/Archive Photos/Getty Images, 1213566352.

The appeal to nature and biology in the sexual sciences remains strong. In the late 1950s, American gynaecologist William Masters (1915–2001) and his assistant Virginia Johnson (1925–2013), founders of the Reproductive Biology Research Foundation (1964–94) in Saint Louis, Missouri, started to collect physiological data on human sexuality. In *Human Sexual Response* (1966) and *Human Sexual Inadequacy* (1970), they proposed a four-stage model of sexual response: excitement phase, plateau phase, orgasm, and resolution phase.[81] Whereas earlier generations of sex researchers such as Mead, Benedict, and Kinsey had re-oriented the focus of sexology to the social and cultural organization of sexuality, Masters and Johnson grounded their work in laboratory observation. Yet perhaps nowhere can the most enduring legacy of biological sexology in the late twentieth century be found than in the area of sexual orientation research. Gay scientists Simon LeVay (b. 1943) and Dean Hamer (b. 1951) in the United States have sought to establish a biological basis for human sexual orientation. Both claim to have found natural markers for

---

81 William H. Masters and Virginia E. Johnson, *Human Sexual Response* (New York: Bantam Books, 1966); William H. Masters and Virginia E. Johnson, *Human Sexual Inadequacy* (New York: Bantam Books, 1970).

male homosexuality: the former, in neuroanatomy, and the latter, in genetics.[82]

While these gay scientists have inherited the lofty ambition of Hirschfeld and others to naturalize homosexuality for a greater cause, a significant number of mental health professionals in countries across the globe have continued to advocate conversion therapy – a treatment that purportedly alters a person's sexual preference – into the twenty-first century. The history of the therapy can be traced to the behaviouralist experiments conducted by physicians Kurt Freund (1914–96) in 1950s Czechoslovakia and Nathaniel McConaghy (1927–2005) in 1960s Australia.[83] Since the 1990s, the APA has issued statements against the validity and practice of conversion therapy, and a dozen countries have prohibited it altogether, beginning with Brazil in 1999. And though the third edition of the *Chinese Classification of Mental Disorders* officially de-pathologized homosexuality in 2001, a group of doctors in China have persisted in claiming a high success rate in changing LGBTQ+ people's sexual orientation through such methods as therapy, hormonal treatment, drug injection, hypnosis, and electroconvulsive therapy.[84] Unlike China, where the leading proponents of conversion therapy have been medical professionals, in the United States and throughout eastern Europe, Africa, and the Middle East, the practice endures with the support of conservative Christians and Muslims.

Conclusion

The emergence of modern sexual science rested on a re-orientation in the emphasis of empirical knowledge towards taxonomy, materialism, naturalism, and imperialism. The evolutionary revolution of the nineteenth century gave the concept of race a new potency in human history and led to the birth of eugenics. These forces culminated in the formalization of sexology,

---

82 Simon LeVay and Dean H. Hamer, 'Evidence for a Biological Influence in Male Homosexuality', *Scientific American* 270, no. 5 (1994): 44–9. Scholars have criticized their studies: see William Byne, 'The Biological Evidence Challenged', *Scientific American* 270, no. 5 (1994): 50–5; Garland E. Allen, 'The Double-Edged Sword of Genetic Determinism: Social and Political Agendas in Genetic Studies of Homosexuality, 1940–1994', in *Science and Homosexualities*, ed. Vernon A. Rosario (New York: Routledge, 1997), 242–70; Jennifer Terry, 'The Seductive Power of Science in the Making of Deviant Subjectivity', in *Science and Homosexualities*, ed. Rosario, 271–95; Jordan-Young, *Brain Storm*.

83 Kate Davison, 'Cold War Pavlov: Homosexual Aversion Therapy in the 1960s', *History of the Human Sciences* 34, no. 1 (2021): 89–119.

84 Hongwei Bao, 'On Not to Be Gay: Aversion Therapy and the Transformation of the Self in Postsocialist China', *Health, Culture and Society* 3, no. 1 (2012): 133–49.

consolidated with the establishment of journals and professional societies, and this interdisciplinary field quickly became an international enterprise. Nonetheless, scientific elites around the world became obsessed with using the tools of sexology to tame gender and sexual diversity in the name of nationalism and modernization. In the first half of the twentieth century, this heteronormalization of global culture inadvertently pushed researchers to investigate further the notion of gender as a plastic variable distinct from sex. Social scientific methods afforded a new means to collect data from non-Western cultures and thus to challenge dominant norms in industrialized societies. Since the 1970s, a sexual liberation movement has swept the globe, but it has also brought back biology as a central dogma in sexual politics. In the twenty-first century, conservative doctors and religious figures have continued to defend the use of medicine for repressive purposes. When the US Supreme Court overturned *Roe v. Wade* and ended legal abortions in many states in July 2022, it was a clear sign that science will undoubtedly remain a contested domain in the future of reproductive and sexual justice.

Further Reading

Banner, Lois. *Intertwined Lives: Margaret Mead, Ruth Benedict, and Their Circle*. New York: Alfred A. Knopf, 2003.

Bashford, Alison, and Phillipa Levine, eds. *The Oxford Handbook of the History of Eugenics*. Oxford: Oxford University Press, 2010.

Bauer, Heike, ed. *Sexology and Translation: Cultural and Scientific Encounters across the Modern World*. Philadelphia: Temple University Press, 2015.

Bayer, Ronald. *Homosexuality and American Psychiatry: The Politics of Diagnosis*. New York: Basic Books, 1981.

Chiang, Howard. *After Eunuchs: Science, Medicine, and the Transformation of Sex in Modern China*. New York: Columbia University Press, 2018.

Transtopia in the Sinophone Pacific. New York: Columbia University Press, 2021.

Chung, Yuehtsen Juliette. *Struggle for National Survival: Eugenics in Sino-Japanese Contexts, 1896–1945*. New York: Routledge, 2002.

Cleminson, Richard, and F. Vázquez García. *Hermaphroditism, Medical Science and Sexual Identity in Spain, 1850–1960*. Cardiff: University of Wales Press, 2009.

Davis, Kathy. *The Making of Our Bodies, Ourselves: How Feminism Travels across Borders*. Durham, NC: Duke University Press, 2007.

Eder, Sandra. *How the Clinic Made Gender: The Medical History of a Transformative Idea*. Chicago: University of Chicago Press, 2022.

Epstein, Steven. *Impure Science: AIDS, Activism, and the Politics of Knowledge*. Berkeley, CA: University of California Press, 1996.

Fuechtner, Veronika, Douglas E. Haynes, and Ryan M. Jones, eds. *A Global History of Sexual Science, 1880–1960*. Berkeley, CA: University of California Press, 2018.

Healey, Dan. *Homosexual Desire in Revolutionary Russia: The Regulation of Sexual and Gender Dissent.* Chicago: University of Chicago Press, 2001.

Hunt, Nancy Rose. *A Colonial Lexicon: Of Birth Ritual, Medicalization, and Mobility in Congo.* Durham, NC: Duke University Press, 1999.

Jordan-Young, Rebecca. *Brain Storm: The Flaws in the Science of Sex Differences.* Cambridge, MA: Harvard University Press, 2010.

Laqueur, Thomas. *Making Sex: Body and Gender from the Greeks to Freud.* Cambridge, MA: Harvard University Press, 1990.

Lisková, Katerina. *Sexual Liberation, Socialist Style: Communist Czechoslovakia and the Science of Desire, 1945–1989.* Cambridge: Cambridge University Press, 2018.

Maines, Rachel. *The Technology of Orgasm: 'Hysteria', the Vibrator, and Women's Sexual Satisfaction.* Baltimore, MD: Johns Hopkins University Press, 1999.

Marhoefer, Laurie. *Racism and the Making of Gay Rights: A Sexologist, His Student, and the Empire of Queer Love.* Toronto: University of Toronto Press, 2022.

Meyerowitz, Joanne. *How Sex Changed: A History of Transsexuality in the United States.* Cambridge, MA: Harvard University Press, 2002.

Najmabadi, Afsaneh. *Professing Selves: Transsexuality and Same-Sex Desire in Contemporary Iran.* Durham, NC: Duke University Press, 2014.

Oosterhuis, Harry. *Stepchildren of Nature: Krafft-Ebing, Psychiatry, and the Making of Sexual Identity.* Chicago: University of Chicago Press, 2000.

Oudshoorn, Nelly. *Beyond the Natural Body: An Archeology of Sex Hormones.* New York: Routledge, 1994.

Richardson, Sarah S. *Sex Itself: The Search for Male and Female in the Human Genome.* Chicago: University of Chicago Press, 2013.

Rosario, Vernon A., ed. *Science and Homosexualities.* New York: Routledge, 1997.

Russett, Cynthia. *Sexual Science: The Victorian Construction of Womanhood.* Cambridge, MA: Harvard University Press, 1989.

Schoebinger, Londa. *Nature's Body: Gender in the Making of Modern Science.* Boston: Beacon, 1993.

Sengoopta, Chandak. *The Most Secret Quintessence of Life: Sex, Glands, and Hormones, 1850–1950.* Chicago: University of Chicago Press, 2006.

Stepan, Nancy Leys. *'The Hour of Eugenics': Race, Gender, and Nation in Latin America.* Ithaca, NY: Cornell University Press, 1991.

Sutton, Katie. *Sex between Body and Mind: Psychoanalysis and Sexology in the German-Speaking World, 1890s–1930s.* Ann Arbor, MI: University of Michigan Press, 2019.

Terry, Jennifer. *An American Obsession: Science, Medicine, and Homosexuality in Modern Society.* Chicago: University of Chicago Press, 1999.

16

Sexuality in Marxism and Socialism

JILL MASSINO

This chapter explores the interplay between sex and socialism in four milieus: as theorized by nineteenth-century socialist thinkers; in the Soviet Union from 1917 to the early 1960s; in Cold War Eastern Europe; and in socialist countries outside of Europe, namely China, Cuba, and Vietnam. It examines how sex was legislated, represented, and managed by the state, placing this analysis within the context of religious beliefs and cultural mores, Westernization and globalization, and generational change. Considering sexuality as both a procreative and a recreative practice, it demonstrates that concerns about regime consolidation, demographic growth, public health, and popular legitimacy, more so than commitment to gender and sexual equality or personal pleasure, shaped state approaches to sex. Yet while the state instrumentalized sex for the purpose of building socialism, some experts (physicians, sexologists, and psychologists) were genuinely devoted to enhancing citizens' knowledge of sexual health and satisfaction, eschewing ideological concerns. Meanwhile, socialist regimes had to contend with traditional values and religious influences, which were often contrary to the modernizing impulses and progressive policies states hoped to institute, and, as socialism wore on, younger generations who supported liberalizing tendencies. They also had to contend with external forces, such as the opening to Western culture, which occurred in Eastern Europe during the later Cold War, in China and Vietnam in the 1980s, and in Cuba in the 1990s. Thus, state policies and representations of sexuality varied across time and space, affecting individuals in different ways.

Sex and Socialism: Early Theorizations

The term 'socialism' was first coined in 1832 by Pierre Leroux, a French philosopher and prominent member of the Saint-Simonians, a political, social, and spiritual community established in Paris in the early 1830s. Retrospectively dubbed 'Utopian Socialists' by Karl Marx for their elevation of passions and non-violent approach to social transformation, the Saint-Simonians advocated the dismantling of all hierarchies and refashioning of social and sexual relations. Accordingly, repressive or restrictive institutions that enshrined male dominance and forestalled women's autonomy were to be abolished.

Utopian Socialism was a reaction to the cold rationalism and asceticism of Enlightenment philosophers, who glorified freedom and equality while abiding class, sexual, and racial hierarchies. For Charles Fourier (1772–1837), who was credited with coining the term 'feminism', equality of the sexes was essential for women's liberation and for social progress. Presenting sex as one among many needs, Fourier railed against the stigmatization of women's sexual pleasure and promoted their active and equal participation in sexual encounters. Fourier also regarded sexual identities as fluid and thus supported same-sex relations and expressions of androgyny. While Fourier's predictions about humanity and the natural world were often fanciful, his proposals were practised by communities in the United States. In a similar vein, the Saint-Simonian social reformer Barthélemy-Prosper Enfantin (1796–1864) criticized conventional marriage and monogamy. In an effort to experience 'what it is to be a woman', Enfantin, along with some male followers, practised celibacy, shared equally in household tasks, and sought to open up their personal feelings by means of continuous introspection and discussion. Only in this way, they reasoned, could socially prescribed gender roles (though they did not use this term) be understood and ultimately challenged.

Women socialists also contributed substantively to the early movement, though they focused less on sexuality and more on promoting social and gender equality. Flora Tristan (1803–44), a pioneer of socialist feminism, was the first thinker to connect women's liberation to the liberation of the labouring class. In her articles for the Utopian Socialist women's newspaper, *La tribune des femmes* (The Women's Tribune), Tristan outlined practical means for achieving women's (and girls') full equality, which included establishing universal childcare and schooling. Women's sexuality also featured in the newspaper, reflecting women's desire for increased agency. As one woman noted: 'For us the body is as holy as the spirit. Christian abstinence to us is completely ridiculous, even godless, because we cannot believe that the goal of God is to destroy His own work.'[1] Such candid discussions did not last long: in 1834, the French government forbade all oppositional organizations, and the paper was shut down.

While sex did not figure prominently in the works of the fathers of 'scientific socialism', Karl Marx (1818–83) and Friedrich Engels (1820–95), it was inherent in their broader critique of capitalism and patriarchal control. In their analysis, bourgeois men seek to enhance their status, wealth, and pleasure through women's bodies: those of their wives who provide heirs, those of working-class women who provide cheap labour, and those of prostitutes, who provide sexual gratification. Accordingly, women are instruments of reproduction, production, and pleasure, roles they cannot contest due their legal subordination and economic dependence on men. In *The Origin of the Family, Private Property and the State*, originally published in 1884, Engels expanded upon this analysis, arguing that patriarchy, like other hierarchies, was socially constructed and thus neither natural nor inevitable. As evidence he pointed to early matriarchal societies, asserting, 'The overthrow of the mother-right was the world historical defeat of the female sex. The man took command in the home also; the woman was degraded and reduced to servitude, she became the slave of his lust and a mere instrument for the production of children.'[2] Like Tristan, Engels linked women's liberation to social liberation, arguing that women's equality would be realized with their equal participation in paid labour and the abolition of private property. This in turn would transform the contractual basis of marriage, and partnerships based on love and companionship, rather than economic need, would prevail. The German writer and political figure August Bebel (1840–1913) expanded upon Engels's analysis in his best-selling *Women and Socialism* (1879). Published in several languages, the book similarly connected the transformation of sexual relations to the abolition of capitalism. No longer constrained by social conventions and inhibitions, under socialism, Bebel reasoned, men and women could express their sexual desires freely and pair with whomever they chose.

---

1 Signed by 'Les Femmes Nouvelles', in *La Femme Nouvelle*, 159, as quoted in Saskia Poldervaart, 'Theories about Sex and Sexuality in Utopian Socialism', *Journal of Homosexuality* 29, no. 2–3 (1995): 41–68, at 57.
2 Friedrich Engels, *The Origin of the Family, Private Property and the State* (London: Lawrence and Wishart, 1972), 125.

Sexuality in Marxism and Socialism

Sex in the First Socialist State

In November 1917 the first socialist state was founded – the Russian Soviet Republic – which, after a brutal civil war, became the Soviet Union (or Union of Soviet Socialist Republics, USSR). Formally a Marxist–Leninist state run by a vanguard of revolutionaries – the Bolsheviks – its leaders were ardently committed to transforming the societies under their direction, which included diverse national, ethnic, and confessional groups. These societies' understandings of gender and sexuality often diverged from one another as well as socialist prescriptions, a reality the Soviet leadership, propagandists, and authorities generally neglected.

The destruction and social dislocation wrought by the Russian civil war and famine had pronounced social implications, as women, desperate to feed themselves and their families, resorted to prostitution and soldiers perpetrated sexual violence as they captured towns and cities. Moreover, rates of casual sex increased among young people, contributing to rising rates of venereal disease, unwanted pregnancy, and child abandonment.

Asserting that sexual crisis was a threat to the body politic, the First People's Commissar of Public Health advocated a far-reaching sexual education and surveillance campaign.[3] Accordingly, a programme of sexual enlightenment (*polovoe prosveshchenie*) was devised, part and parcel of the broader Bolshevik project of social engineering and transforming everyday life (*byt*). Sexual enlightenment encompassed sexual hygiene as well as enforcing a code of moral and sexual conduct, with the aim of promoting 'normalcy' (mitigating or eradicating deviance in the name of the collective good). In the 1920s, various institutes, counselling centres, government divisions, and Communist Party organizations conducted research on sexual behaviour, disseminated pamphlets and newspapers, and organized mobile exhibitions, lectures, and plays on the 'sex question' and sexual hygiene. Workers, peasants, youth, and parents were targeted for these campaigns, with the latter being advised on how to educate their children on sexual health and hygiene.

Male sexual dysfunction, which seemingly reached epic proportions in the early 1920s, was of particular concern to Soviet authorities as men were appealing to doctors in record numbers, with some resorting to desperate measures, including suicide. According to some professionals, impotence was, at least in part, a function of the uncertainty, tumult, and stress produced

---

3 Frances Lee Bernstein, *The Dictatorship of Sex: Lifestyle Advice for the Soviet Masses* (Ithaca, NY: Cornell University Press, 2007), 4.

by the revolution and building socialism. Such stress, they argued, could lead to nervous exhaustion, and negatively affect political and social progress. As parallels were increasingly made between male potency and regime potency, doctors emphasized the urgency of destigmatizing afflictions such as impotence and minimizing anxiety and stress. That said, normality had its limits, and doctors drew a distinct line between acceptable sexual behaviour and depravity, claiming that excessive masturbation was among the most deviant sexual behaviours, causing impotence, paralysis, and even insanity – a belief advanced by some doctors and sex experts at the time in the West as well.

While socialism was predicated on the equality of the sexes, women's sexuality received comparatively less attention among doctors, underscoring the persistence of conventional beliefs regarding gender and sexuality. However, declining birth rates, as well as a genuine interest in women's sexuality, prompted some sexologists to focus on female pleasure. Women's lack of sexual fulfilment, experts argued, was primarily due to men's over-eagerness, selfishness, and lack of skill. This was not simply a personal matter, but a familial and social one, as it posed a threat to marital harmony, fidelity, and demographic growth. Yet, in the sexual enlightenment materials distributed to the population during the 1920s, no mention was made of women's sexual satisfaction, and women's sexuality was generally linked to reproduction and maternity.

The Bolshevik state relied heavily on visuals to transmit its messages, juxtaposing individuals who lived healthy sexual lives against those who did not. Although officially atheist, the state often appropriated religious tropes to make posters legible to a largely illiterate, yet devout populace. They also emphasized that good health, sexual or otherwise, was not an individual pursuit, but one with collective reverberations. Sanitary posters were designed to captivate, even shock the viewer, with graphic representations of syphilis sores and grave markers. The intent was both diagnostic and preventative: helping individuals identify problems on their bodies so they could seek medical care and deterring others from engaging in risky behaviours that would lead to such unfortunate outcomes.

While women were granted political and legal equality with men, they were expected to adhere to particular codes of dress and behaviour that reflected the asceticism of socialist ideology and the socio-cultural norms associated with their gender. Of particular concern during the early to mid-1920s was the 'Nepwoman', the Soviet counterpart of the Western 'new woman', depicted as a garish flirt who upset the sexual order by assuming the 'masculine' role of initiating sexual relations and engaging in casual sex.

Given the link between reproduction and women's sexuality, women who engaged in non-reproductive sexual behaviour – including prostitution or lesbianism – were portrayed as abnormal, even pathological, in propaganda and other sexual enlightenment materials. At the same time, prostitutes were portrayed as victims of economic circumstance and male lasciviousness, and because women still turned to sex work to support themselves and their families, selling sex was not criminalized, though brothel keeping and pimping were. Instead, in accordance with the belief that people could be rehabilitated, the state assigned former sex workers to dispensaries, which offered training in crafts and other skills. Yet, sex workers could still be charged with parasitism, vagrancy, violation of passport restrictions, and spreading venereal disease, the latter of which could carry a three-year prison sentence.

Just as punishment was a central feature of sexual enlightenment efforts, so too was discipline. While masturbation (in moderation) was seen as an acceptable means of satisfying sexual desire, it was also viewed as self-indulgent and thus antithetical to collectivist ideals.[4] Physicians were especially concerned with excessive masturbation, advising youth to 'sublimate' their sexual energy into sports and other activities. Doctors also advised against early sexual activity, believing that this could result in host of maladies, including anaemia, mental sluggishness, neurasthenia, nervousness, premature ageing, and muscular weakness, as well as negatively impacting on productivity, creativity, and memory. Some doctors even argued that postponing intercourse prolonged women's physical beauty. Accordingly, the recommended age for beginning sexual activity was twenty to twenty-three for women and twenty-three to twenty-five for men. As a corollary, doctors advised against early marriage, claiming that young people's sperm and ova were not fully developed – and thus of inferior quality – and that the young mother's body could not provide sufficient nourishment for the foetus, producing a feeble child prone to illness.

In light of these challenges, abstinence and sublimation were suggested as acceptable solutions to early sexual desire. Young people were advised to sleep with their hands above the covers, rise upon waking – so as not to engage in 'lazy behaviours' – avoid tight-fitting clothing, especially tight underwear, and reduce their intake of meat, spicy foods, and alcohol. Yet, here, too, distinctions were made according to gender, as experts claimed that teenaged girls and young women did not generally experience significant sexual desire – except for those who had been stimulated by erotic literature

4 Bernstein, *Dictatorship of Sex*, 142–4.

and were thus, according to one doctor, only 'half-virgins'. That said, maintaining abstinence beyond a certain age, particularly after age thirty, was considered problematic, leading to impotence or sexual weakness in males and bitterness, callousness, suspiciousness, and stinginess, among other traits, in females.

The militant climate of the post-Civil war period in Russia (after 1922) required abnegation, discipline, and sacrifice for the future, rather than pleasure and fulfilment in the here and now. Accordingly, what Frances Berenstein refers to as a 'sexless-sex' model dominated the educational materials distributed to the Soviet populace, rooted in the Bolshevik contention that sexual pleasure was a frivolous, bourgeois concern. This model distinguished between normal sexual behaviour and deviant sexual behaviour, and only peripherally engaged with the issue of sexual pleasure, if at all. Medical professionals mapped out appropriate and inappropriate levels of sexual curiosity. Excessive interest in sex was considered 'sick' and 'unhealthy', the result of poor upbringing, endocrine problems, and too much exposure to racy books, films, plays, and pictures. Drinking was also deemed potentially dangerous as it reduced inhibition and judgement, resulting in sexual encounters with unsavoury individuals, venereal disease, and rape. Sexual intercourse two to three times a week was presented as the ideal, with more frequent sexual activity leading to a host of problems, including anaemia, muscular weakness, decreased intellectual capability, melancholia, and digestive and heart issues.

Sexual pleasure was muted in public discourse due to the silencing of more 'radical' voices, particularly Aleksandra Kollontai (1872–1952), who briefly served as head of the People's Commissar for Welfare and founded, in 1919, the Zhenotdel (Women's Department). In line with Utopian Socialists, Kollontai argued that with the abolition of private property and women's full legal equality, women, like men, could enter into relationships based on mutual attraction, respect, and affection, rather than economic need. The result would be more profound and authentic unions: 'The greater the intellectual and emotional development of the individual the less place will there be in his or her relationship for the bare physiological side of love, and the brighter will be the love experience.'[5] Kollontai believed that such partnerships would be personally and mutually satisfying, as well as socially beneficial, since people would no longer be stuck in unfulfilling or abusive

---

5 Alexandra Kollontai, 'Theses on Communist Morality in the Sphere of Marital Relations', (1921) in *Alexandra Kollontai: Selected Writings*, trans. Alix Holt (London: Allison & Busby, 1977), 34.

relationships. Alongside the demise of conventional marriage, Kollontai envisaged that socialism would usher in an era of tolerance, in which same-sex unions would be free of social stigma.

Kollontai's view of sexuality was at odds with those of Vladimir Lenin (1870–1924), the head of Soviet government from 1917 to 1924. He and other Bolsheviks insisted upon self-discipline and an end to hedonistic behaviour, which he attributed, albeit falsely, to her writings. As Lenin remarked to German socialist feminist Clara Zetkin, 'Communism will not bring asceticism, but joy of life, power of life, and a satisfied love life will help to do that. But in my opinion the present widespread hypertrophy in sexual matters does not give joy and force to life, but takes it away. In the age of revolution that is bad, very bad.'[6] Lenin claimed that casually changing partners was 'bourgeois' and anti-revolutionary and that the instability produced by the transition to socialism required reinforcing conventional marital and family bonds.

Though in some ways conservative, in other respects the Bolshevik state's approach to gender and sexuality was progressive. In 1917 homosexuality (between consenting adult men) was decriminalized – despite the fact that Lenin considered same-sex relations deviant and, because they were non-procreative, contrary to the common good.[7] Lesbianism, by contrast, was not acknowledged in the new legislation due to prevailing beliefs regarding women's (comparative) lack of sexual desire. With the 1918 Code on Marriage, the Family, and Guardianship, the state replaced church marriages with civil ceremonies, liberalized divorce legislation, and equalized the status of legitimate and illegitimate children. While the new family law enabled women to extricate themselves from unsatisfying and abusive relationships, it also enabled men to flout their paternal responsibilities, and men increasingly initiated divorce proceedings after their wives became pregnant. Thus, easy divorce in some instances ironically facilitated the very behaviour – casual changing of partners – that Lenin had condemned. In the context of soaring unemployment and cuts in social services during the New Economic Policy (1921–8) women, particularly single mothers, faced dire poverty and some resorted to prostitution to feed themselves and their families.

Although pleasure did not appear very often in sexual enlightenment materials in the 1920s, it did appear on cinema screens, most notably in the

---

6 Clara Zetkin, 'Reminiscences of Lenin' (1924), www.marxists.org/archive/zetkin/1924/reminiscences-of-lenin.htm#h07.
7 At the same time, sodomy was criminalized in a number of the Soviet republics in the 1920s, including Azerbaijan, Uzbekistan, and Turkmenistan.

1927 Soviet film *Bed and Sofa* (*Tretya meshchanskaya*). The film depicted a love triangle between a woman, Liuda, her husband, Kolia, and his friend, Volodia, who moves in with the couple due to housing shortages in Moscow. While Kolia is away, Liuda begins a sexual relationship with Volodia, and sustains both – under the same roof – once Kolia returns. Discovering she is pregnant, but unsure of who the father is, Liuda, decides for and then against an abortion, and ultimately ends relations with both men, whom she finds domineering, preferring single motherhood. With its polyamorous content and feminist bent, the film offered a radical view of the sexual possibilities open to women under early socialism, echoing the writings of Kollontai.

Released after the advent of Joseph Stalin (1878–1953) to power, such progressive portraits did not last. As Stalin consolidated power in the late 1920s and early 1930s, he carried out a series of purges of the central party leadership, high-ranking military officials, and other groups deemed counter-revolutionary. A range of repressive measures were introduced that bore negatively on sexual expression and reproductive freedom. The year 1934 witnessed the criminalization of sodomy, with consensual sodomy punishable by deprivation of liberty for three to five years in prison, and 'forcible' sodomy punishable with five to eight years in prison or forced labour.[8] This law was implemented on the basis of 'national security', specifically the concern that because homosexuals had their own, private group, they were planning a plot against the government.

This was followed, in 1936, by the criminalization of abortion, justified on the basis that 'industrialization had done away with the social conditions making abortion necessary'. Reflecting the anti-intellectualism of new party elites, Stalin also did away with the science of sexology. Moreover, he filled the Soviet prison system, the Gulag, with individuals the state deemed anti-socialist, including common criminals, political prisoners, prostitutes, homosexuals, and lesbians. The Gulag was intended not only to punish but also to re-educate, and treatments were devised for particular groups.

After the death of Stalin in 1953, the Soviet state increasingly focused on health and resumed publishing sex education manuals, some written by sexologists in the Eastern bloc and translated into Russian and the other languages of the USSR. Sexualized images could also be found in Soviet magazines, as part of Premier Nikita Khrushchev's (1894–1971) thaw, a period from the mid-1950s to the mid-1960s when censorship and repression were relaxed. At the same time, invasive measures were implemented to examine,

---

8 Article 154a of the USSR Criminal Code, 1 April 1934 (SU No 15, art. 95).

Sexuality in Marxism and Socialism

often by force, individuals suspected of transmitting venereal disease, and convictions for sodomy increased due to new policing measures.

Approaches to Sex in Post-War Eastern Europe

After the Second World War, the Soviet Union expanded its influence across Eastern Europe, and tensions between the USSR and the United States and its allies in Western Europe increased. As in the USSR, socialist regimes in Eastern Europe promoted women's participation in paid labour, legislated equality between men and women, and supported women's autonomy through a host of subsidies. Although no grassroots efforts for sexual emancipation existed, the general trend over the course of socialist rule was towards less restrictive reproductive and sexual policies, with the exception of Romania and Albania.

Sexology was a prodigious field of study in several Eastern European countries during the 1920s and the 1930s; thus physicians and sexologists in Eastern Europe did not start with a blank slate after 1945. Their approach to sex required toeing the ideological party line, however. Of primary concern in the immediate post-war period was stemming the transmission of venereal diseases and promoting a healthy, civilized, and conscientious populace. In line with early Soviet approaches to sexual enlightenment, campaigns in Eastern Europe aimed to promote sexual health and hygiene and eradicate (or cure) deviant behaviours. Hedonistic attitudes were considered antithetical to the broader collective project of building socialism, as well as a threat to public health. Accordingly, individuals were advised against visiting prostitutes, engaging in debauched behaviour, and excessive sex – including masturbation. Moreover, young people were urged to postpone intercourse until they reached adulthood, with East German sexologist Rudolf Neubert recommending a 'healthy lifestyle, lots of movement in the fresh air, cleanliness' and 'wearing loose trousers'.[9] Neubert also encouraged youth to cultivate comradely relations with the opposite sex in the belief that intimate relationships in adulthood would be based on respect and companionship, rather than simply desire.

During the early years of socialist rule, sex manuals and articles provided general information on anatomy and physiology (nocturnal emissions and menstruation), as well as sexual health. Like earlier Soviet publications – and

---

9 Rudolf Neubert, *Die Geschlechterfrage: Ein Buch für junge Leute* (Rudolstadt, Germany: Greifenverlag, 1955), 65.

to some extent publications in the West – these were both descriptive and proscriptive, intended to inform readers *and* shape behaviour. Ideological but also cultural concerns often influenced what material was featured in them. Adolescent girls, for example, were warned about the dangers of youthful pregnancy and clandestine abortion. While designed as primers for young adults and teaching tools for parents, because the latter were often reticent to broach the topic of sexuality with their children, these manuals were not widely used to educate teens.

Starting in the 1960s, publications increasingly focused on pleasure, particularly female pleasure, as well as the emotional and psychological aspects of sex. Siegfried Schnabl's *Mann und Frau Intim* (Man and Woman, Intimately, 1969), a key text in East German sexual emancipation, emphasized the importance of foreplay in women's sexual satisfaction and suggested the best positions for women to achieve orgasm. The Polish *The Art of Loving*, authored by gynaecologist and sexologist Michalina Wisłocka, similarly provided an overview of basic sex positions and, in later editions, photographs of ways the penis could penetrate the vagina. Upon its publication in 1978, 100,000 copies – the entire print run – sold out in a matter of days, underscoring the book's popularity. The 1974 Hungarian *The ABC of Married Life* was also popular; it emphasized the importance of foreplay and identified the clitoris as the primary site of women's pleasure, though it was vague about female sexual stimulation and no diagrams were provided to aid readers. The Romanian sex manual *De Vorba cu tinerii* (Conversations with Youth), published in 1972, similarly focused on sexual health, hygiene, and pleasure, and included a discussion of various sex positions. However, in line with the conservatism of Romanian society and the regime's pro-natalist agenda, it cautioned against pre-marital sex (especially for women) and warned of the risks associated with abortion and using oral contraception.

While sex manuals enhanced people's knowledge about sexual health and pleasure, concern about sexual satisfaction was rooted in the larger aim of lowering divorce rates and increasing birth rates. It was also rooted in concern about infidelity, which was contrary to socialist mores. Accordingly, the work of sexologists, although often inspired by a genuine desire to improve marital harmony and sexual satisfaction, was also instrumentalized by Eastern European regimes to promote demographic growth and present a progressive face and, thereby, secure popular support.

Alongside manuals, socialist youth, women's, and health magazines featured pieces on sexuality. These ranged from articles by specialists (physicians and sexologists) to letters (ostensibly written by ordinary people) posing queries or seeking advice on issues related to sex. The East German youth magazine *Junge Welt* (Young World) and the Polish magazine *Etc.*, fielded questions about sexual hygiene and development and published exchanges between physicians and readers. In addition, the Romanian *Femeia* (Women) included a health column, which occasionally focused on sexual health and sexual pleasure. Information about sexuality and sexual health was also disseminated via radio, such as on the Czechoslovak 'Confidential Conversations' ('Důvěrné hovory'), a late-night radio talk show directed towards the heterosexual, married couple and hosted by sexologists who addressed sexual issues and fielded listeners' questions.[10]

Increased emphasis on women's sexual pleasure in socialist media, though instrumentalized for the purpose of demographic growth, was nonetheless progressive, validating women's right to sexual satisfaction. Yet such portraits often coexisted with traditional notions about gender and sexuality, manifest in everyday attitudes and behaviours. Thus, girls and boys were often differently socialized with respect to sexuality and relations with the opposite sex. Female youth in particular were urged to be alert to men's seduction strategies. An article in *Etc.*, for instance, informed readers about dances, where men sought to seduce naive female university students with their fancy cars and confessions of love. After such encounters, the girl returned starry-eyed to her dorm room never to hear from the man again – an outcome, the piece argued, that could leave lasting scars. Such episodes played out on cinema screens as well. The 1965 Czech New Wave film *Loves of a Blonde* features the story of a young woman, Andula, employed in a shoe factory in provincial Czechoslovakia, who falls for Milada, a Prague musician who plays at the factory dance. Seduced by this hip and talented city boy, Andula tracks him down at his parent's home (in Prague) where she learns, through eavesdropping, that the family wants her out. Rejected by Milada, she tearfully returns to the factory town. Similarly, *Femeia* included letters from young women complaining about men who romance one woman after another but never commit to any.[11] To minimize such encounters, the magazine's editors advised parents to disabuse themselves of the 'boys will be boys' approach to childrearing and teach their sons to value and respect girls as equal comrades. Additionally, mothers were instructed to teach their daughters the difference between love and lust

---

10 Kateřina Lišková, *Sexual Liberation, Socialist Style: Communist Czechoslovakia and the Science of Desire, 1945–1989* (Cambridge: Cambridge University Press, 2018), 138.

11 'Where Can I Find a Man that I Want to Marry?' *Femeia*, December 1976.

so they could discern a fling or affair from a genuine relationship based on mutual respect and love.[12]

Schools also included lessons on sex education, though the content and frequency varied throughout the bloc. In Hungary, seventh and eighth graders took 'education for family life', which included topics such as masturbation and caring for sick infants and children. According to surveys conducted in the 1970s, Hungarian youth were open and nuanced in their thinking about sexuality. In Poland, by contrast, pressure from the Catholic Church forced editors to water down sex ed manuals, and sex ed in school differed considerably from school to school. Lectures for young people also differed within the region: in East Germany, Minister of Justice Hilde Benjamin gave 'girls' talks' that offered a highly progressive view of gender and sexuality, while in Romania such talks, particularly after the criminalization of abortion in 1966, focused on the dangers of youthful sex, abortion, and pregnancy.

Meanwhile, sexologists focused their attention on women's sexual pleasure. In 1961 a conference on the female orgasm was organized in Czechoslovakia, and the term 'frigidity' was replaced with 'sexual disinterest', reflecting a more nuanced understanding of women's sexual pleasure. For Czech sexologist Josef Hynie, the problem lay in outmoded attitudes towards women and selfish husbands who viewed women as subordinates and 'vehicles for pleasure', thus ignoring their sexual needs and desires. Such beliefs, according to Hungarian gynaecologist Imre Aszódi, reflected a bourgeois mentality, wholly antithetical to socialist notions of equality. The solution was to educate youth about sexuality and to teach male youth to respect their partners, including their partners' sexual needs. Alongside selfishness, lack of experience and restraint also posed potential problems. According to Romanian endocrinologist Tudor Stoica, premature ejaculation, among other issues, could damage a woman's 'delicate physiological mechanism' and inhibit her ability to reach orgasm. Such an outcome could ultimately prove disruptive to marital harmony, producing resentment, resignation and, in some cases, prompt the wife – or the husband – to look elsewhere for sexual fulfilment.[13] It could also impede demographic growth, which was considered central to building a strong Romanian nation.

---

12 'Intimate Dialogue with My Daughter', *Femeia*, December 1966.
13 Tudor Stoica (1970) as quoted in Luciana Jinga, 'Science and Politics during the Cold War: The Controversial Case of Sexology in Communist Romania', *History of Communism in Europe* 9 (2018): 97–107, at 93.

By the early 1960s, sexologists suggested foreplay and sex therapy sessions to improve couples' sex lives. As Hynie claimed, 'The spouses who love each other and intensify each other's sexual pleasure with various peculiarities during intercourse should not be disparaged. One does not eat solely for caloric intake and essential nutrients but also for the enjoyment of food.'[14] Sexologists also encouraged women to be actively engaged in sex, communicating their needs to partners. By the mid-1970s, sexual therapy, based on the American sexologists William Masters and Virginia Johnson's approach, was adopted in Czechoslovakia by sexologist Stanislav Kratochvíl. To reduce anxiety, the approach encouraged the exploratory and experiential aspects of sex rather than performance and outcome.[15]

Poland was home to some of the leading sexologists in the Bloc, who tended to approach sexuality holistically, considering physical, psychological, and cultural factors and influences. At the same time, they often ascribed to essentialist and heterosexist notions. For instance, Michalina Wisłocka claimed that good sex was 'civilized and cultured sex', namely intercourse between a woman and a man (by which she meant wife and husband) who are both emotionally involved, mature, and open to parenthood.[16] Moreover, she claimed that women should assume a more passive role and men a more active role, advice she based on her ideas about unchangeable psychosexual differences between men and women:

> Our grandmothers claimed that 'man is the hunter and woman a bird he preys on. The more difficult to hunt, the more precious.' And that girls shouldn't take away from boys the pleasure of hunting a treasured prize. Look at the tremendously proud and delighted faces of men in magazines or on television triumphantly showing off the big fish they caught with their own hands. Their faces are a display of absolute happiness. He was the one to catch a fish that few can boast of.[17]

Similarly, the influential sexologist Zbigniew Lew-Starowicz advised that women taking the initiative can produce sexual dysfunction in men, as 'in our culture women's visible domination, their independence and self-confidence lessens their attractiveness'.[18]

---

14 Josef Hynie, 'Principy sexuálního chování a sexuální morálky' ('Principles of Sexual Behavior and Morality'), *Časopis lékařů českých* 108, no. 19 (1969): 553–6, at 555.
15 Stanislav Kratochvíl, 'Sex Therapy in an In-Patient and Out-Patient Setting', *Journal of Sex & Marital Therapy* 6, no. 2 (1980): 135–44.
16 Agnieszka Kościańska, *Gender, Pleasure, and Violence: The Construction of Expert Knowledge of Sexuality in Poland* (Bloomington, IN: Indiana University Press, 2021), 79–81.
17 Michalina Wisłocka, *Sztuka kochania* (The Art of Loving) (Warsaw: Iskry, 1978), 151–2.
18 Zbigniew Lew-Starowicz, *Etc.* (Warsaw: Iskry, 1975), 20.

In Czechoslovakia as well, distinct gender relations were considered essential for a good sex life – the result of family-centred discourse that emerged during normalization (after 1968) that located the home, rather than the public sphere, as the source of enjoyment. Sexologist Jaroslava Pondělíčková suggested that while women's emancipation had allowed them to experience sexual pleasure unbeknownst to their mothers and grandmothers, during the sex act women should assume a passive role.[19] Sexologist Jiří Mellan and psychologist Iva Šípová, authors of the highly popular sex manual *Young Marriage*, advanced similar claims: 'Intimate life is one of the situations where the undistorted personality manifests itself; intimate relationships reflect mutual relationships in the non-sexual realm. Partners can only have the roles in their sexual life which they occupy in their marriage.'[20]

Because state concern about women's sexual pleasure was rooted in demographic concerns, states promoted marriage in the belief this would increase the fertility rate. Yet, while Romania took a coercive approach, tightening divorce legislation on the heels of the criminalization of abortion, the East German state eased the divorce process, recognizing that marriage was not necessarily compatible with fecundity. As a corollary, 'sexual discord' became one of the grounds for divorce in East Germany, Czechoslovakia, and a number of other states. According to one divorce case in East Germany in 1966, 'In a sexual sense, there exists no harmony between the parties. The defendant [the husband] is absolutely egotistical, and only thinks of his own satisfaction . . . Because of it she has become nervous, and has developed a disinclination to engage in further sex with her husband.'[21]

Fertility Control and Homosexuality in Eastern Europe

While selfishness or inexperience on the part of male partners affected women's sexual pleasure, so too did challenges in controlling their fertility. Modern contraceptives such as the oral Pill and diaphragm were not widely accessible until the 1970s, and then unevenly in the region and primarily in

---

19 Jaroslava Pondělíčková-Mašlová, *Manželská sexualita* (Sexuality in Marriage) (Prague: Avicenum, 1986), 192.
20 Jiří Mellan and Iva Šípová, *Mladé manželství* (Young Marriage) (Prague: Avicenum, 1970), 75.
21 Paul Betts, *Within Walls: Private Life in the German Democratic Republic* (Oxford: Oxford University Press, 2010), 106–7.

urban areas. Consequently, women relied on *coitus interruptus* and abortion, which was illegal throughout Eastern Europe during the first decade of socialist rule. Thus, sex was often accompanied by fear of pregnancy. Yet because most states were focused on mass industrialization and promoting women into paid labour, they generally turned a blind eye to women who procured abortions from midwives or other practitioners. The exception was Albania, where abortion could garner a prison sentence, as in Romania after 1966.

In the 1950s, concern about the deleterious effects of illicit abortion on the health and future fertility of women facilitated the decriminalization of abortion (performed in state hospitals and clinics), throughout the region. In 1951, Yugoslavia became the first state in Eastern Europe to decriminalize abortion, followed by the USSR in 1955, and Poland, Hungary, Czechoslovakia, and Bulgaria in 1956. Exceptions were East Germany, which did not legalize abortion until 1972, Albania, which never decriminalized it, and Romania, which legalized abortion for a mere nine years (1957–66).

The legalization of abortion enabled many women to end unwanted pregnancies in a safe manner and easily control family size. For socialist regimes that depended on an ever-growing labour force to modernize the country, this produced concern. After briefly allowing abortion, Romania took extreme measures, subjecting women to forced gynaecological exams in factories and surveilling doctors in hospitals. In Yugoslavia, restrictions were more subtle: gynaecologists postponed abortion appointments, forcing women to seek the approval of a medical commission, which might delay the process to the point where an abortion could no longer be legally performed, or they shamed women into not having an abortion. Experts also peddled disinformation about contraceptives and correlated motherhood with happiness and commitment to the socialist collective. Meanwhile, childless couples – and even couples with one child – were portrayed as egotistical.

In the early years of socialist rule, homosexuality (among men) was a criminal offence in all countries in Eastern Europe, save Poland. Some of these laws were holdovers from the pre-socialist era, and others were implemented after socialist regimes assumed power. In line with much of Western Europe, homosexuality was considered deviant and perverse, and homosexuals could be – and often were – prosecuted by the authorities. Meanwhile, same-sex relations between women, while also considered deviant, were not criminalized in Eastern Europe.

Beginning in the 1960s, some countries in the region began adopting more progressive policies towards homosexuality. Ahead of many liberal democracies in the West, several Eastern European states decriminalized consensual sodomy: Czechoslovakia and Hungary in 1962; and East Germany and Bulgaria in 1968. This move reflected a significant shift in understandings of homosexuality, namely the belief that it was neither a choice nor curable and, therefore, should not be punishable by law. That said, state policies were not uniform in the region: Romania criminalized homosexuality in 1968 as part of its repressive pro-natalist policies and Albania did not decriminalize it until after the collapse of socialism. Moreover, media representations were uniformly heteronormative, and homosexuals continued to face social stigmas. In some cases, homosexuality was correlated with criminality, and homosexuals were considered 'unreliable elements' and surveilled by the security services or blackmailed and used as informants. Thus, decriminalization of homosexuality did not usher in an era of tolerance – let alone acceptance – among the authorities or the general public.

In Hungary, the Hungarian Penal Code of 1878, which remained in force until 1961, criminalized sexual acts between men, and from 1945 to 1961, approximately fifty-six individuals were charged for crimes against morality and socialism. With the decriminalization of homosexuality, the age of consent for same-sex relations between men was set at twenty (reduced to eighteen in 1978), significantly higher than the age of consent for heterosexual relations. This difference reflected official views that homosexuality primarily involved predatory adult men who tricked naive boys into relationships through promises of material goods and was thus a matter of morality and public safety. While it is unknown how many men identified as homosexuals in Hungary, given the continued stigma and surveillance that homosexuals – real or alleged – experienced, official registries indicated that by the late 1970s there were 50,000 known homosexuals in Hungary, with 45,000 in Budapest alone. After the onset of the AIDS crisis, the Hungarian government set up, in 1988, the first official organization for homosexuals and lesbians in Eastern Europe, Homeros-Lambda, largely to disseminate information about HIV/ AIDS to at-risk populations, whom the state began regularly screening for it. The 1980s also witnessed more sympathetic portraits of homosexuality on cinema screens, particularly with the 1982 film *Egymásra Nézve* (Another Way), based on a lesbian love story in the aftermath of the 1956 revolution.

Socialist Czechoslovakia retained pre-war legislation criminalizing homosexuality. The penalty for same-sex intercourse involving adults was imprisonment of up to one year, and between one and five years for a person who

Sexuality in Marxism and Socialism

engaged in sex with a minor. Meanwhile, men who paid or solicited money for sex with other men could face a jail term from six months up to three years. Finally, men who engaged in homosexual relations while married were placed in psychiatric hospitals in the belief that their 'deviant' behaviour was 'curable'. Doctors employed a range of approaches with self-identified homosexuals in these facilities, including aversion therapy and hormonal conditioning. In one research study carried out at the Sexological Institute in Prague in the 1950s, nausea was induced in male subjects who became aroused by images of men and testosterone was administered to the same subjects when presented with images of women. (Arousal was measured by a phalloplethysmograph, which calculated the volume of the penis.) These treatments allegedly 'cured' one-sixth of the subjects, who married women thereafter, though subsequent inquires found these unions to be unhappy. The doctor who performed the treatment, Kurt Freund, eventually concluded that homosexuality was incurable, and the state decriminalized homosexuality in 1961. By the 1970s, Czech medical professionals increasingly rejected the notion that homosexuality was a disease, and focused instead on improving the lives and social conditions of homosexuals. To that end, sexologist Dagmar Bártová founded the first socio-therapeutic group for homosexuals in Brno and Prague in 1976 and 1982, respectively.

Homosexuality was decriminalized in East Germany in 1968, except for sex between an adult and a minor (under the age of eighteen). Some medical professionals urged greater acceptance of non-heteronormative sexual orientations and discussed homosexuality in a nuanced, informed, and compassionate manner. Nonetheless, stereotypes about homosexuals remained. For instance, Rainer Werner's *Homosexualität* (Homosexuality, 1988) – the first official book about homosexuality in the German Democratic Republic (GDR) – was subtitled *Herausforderung an Wissen und Toleranz* (The Challenge of Knowledge and Tolerance), but still offered a clichéd portrait of homosexuals (arguing, for instance, that gay men made excellent hairdressers, waiters, and theatre actors), and suggested cross-dressers seek behavioural training.[22] Meanwhile, endocrinologist Günter Dörner asserted that homosexuality was the result of a mother's high level of stress during pregnancy, which led to increased levels of oestrogen in her son. As in Hungary, even after homosexuality was decriminalized in the GDR, members of the gay community were surveilled by the secret police (the Stasi) out

22 Josie McLellan, *Love in the Time of Communism: Intimacy and Sexuality in the GDR* (Cambridge: Cambridge University Press, 2011), 130.

of concern that gay rights groups would destabilize the regime. Moreover, the Stasi monitored military and other officials suspected of being homosexuals, and often blackmailed homosexuals, using them as informers. Homosexuals were generally absent from media portrayals of sexuality, though in 1979 a short documentary, *Tag für Tag* (Day after Day), which explored the relationship of a lesbian couple, was screened in East German cinemas.

In Poland homosexuality continued to be legal throughout the socialist period, however, due to cultural and religious mores it was generally unacceptable to the population at large. As with female sexuality, Lew-Starowicz's views about homosexuals were ambivalent. He emphasized the importance of therapy in affirming sexual orientation and expressed concern that the stigmatization of homosexuality produced alienation in young people, leading to drug and alcohol abuse and even suicidal tendencies. At the same time, he regarded same-sex attraction among men and women as unnatural and claimed that sexual orientation could be altered.[23] Polish magazines echoed these views, highlighting the challenges – and even dangers – homosexual male youth faced, while also emphasizing that sexual orientation is mutable.

Sexuality in Socialist Countries Outside of Europe

As in the Eastern bloc, approaches to sexuality in socialist countries outside of Europe were characterized by ambiguity, as policies both challenged or reinforced traditional cultural norms and practices. In China during socialist consolidation under Chairman Mao Zedong (early 1950s), the state legislated equality of the sexes and promoted women's engagement in all areas of life. It also abolished arranged marriage, granting women greater freedom in choosing a mate. Yet, as in the early Bolshevik state, sex and sexuality were presented as peripheral to the larger goal of constructing socialism, which required sacrificing desire for the common good. Accordingly, as in the USSR and post-war Eastern Europe, the emphasis was on sexual health and hygiene and reproduction, though only within the context of marriage. As a corollary, pre-marital and extra-marital sex were deemed immoral, and prostitution and concubinage were outlawed as relics from an earlier, exploitative era. While the 'Iron Girl' – the new female ideal under Mao, who, like her Stalinist

---

23 Zbigniew Lew-Starowicz, *Seks nietypowy* (Atypical Sex) (Warsaw: Instytut Wydawniczy Związków Zawodowych, 1988), 120.

counterpart, engaged in arduous work alongside men – was evidence of progressive gender politics in the productive sphere, patriarchal Confucian values remained pervasive in politics and family life.

With the introduction of the one-child policy (1979) and the Marriage Reform Law of 1980, official approaches towards sex were relaxed. Concerned about overpopulation, the leadership began to emphasise sex for pleasure instead of only for procreation. Additionally, pre-marital sex found increasing acceptance, as long as no children were produced, as did previously considered 'abnormal' behaviours such as masturbation and multiple partners. The market-oriented reforms of Deng Xiaoping in the 1980s and the broadening of the consumer sphere also facilitated more open discussions of sex in public forums and in music and literature.

Until recently, state policy towards homosexuality was uniformly repressive, and homosexuals, who were considered bourgeois and diseased, were charged with hooliganism. Current official policy towards homosexuality is more ambiguous and often described as the 'three nos': 'no approval; no disapproval; no promotion'. While in 2011 the Chinese Ministry of Public Security defined sexual orientation a personal choice and decriminalized homosexuality and the Chinese Society of Psychiatry no longer classifies it as a mental disorder, conversion therapy continues to be recommended. Meanwhile, same-sex partners may not marry, but as of 2017 they can become legal guardians for one another and make decisions about health and property.

LGBTQ+ individuals face marginalization in society more generally, as well as parental pressure to marry someone of the opposite sex. In some cases, they do, entering into phoney marriages, while continuing their authentic same-sex partnerships in private. At the same time, same-sex couples have become increasingly open about their relationships, especially in urban areas. Some LGBTQ+ organizations and services, such as HIV awareness campaigns targeting gay men, do work with local government departments, but they also get raided by police, especially if they are seen as a political threat. (For more on modern China, see Chapter 24 by Ting Guo in Volume III of this work.)

Cuba became a Communist state under the leadership of Fidel Castro after the 1959 Cuban Revolution. According to the Cuban Constitution, women and men were equal under the law and expected to contribute to the construction of socialism through paid labour; however, women were also expected to produce healthy offspring. Policies towards sexuality have been largely conservative, reinforcing patriarchal and heteronormative beliefs and attitudes. During the early years of socialist consolidation, the state encouraged young people to sublimate their desires and surrender their bodies to the revolution – not to one another – and sexual desire was presented as a male preserve. Thus, men's sexuality was vaunted while women's was considered relevant to the extent that it appealed to men and was related to reproduction. Indeed, in a nod towards early Utopian Socialist thinking, women were sometimes advised to use their sex appeal to inspire men to commit themselves to socialism.

The Federation of Cuban Women (Federación de Mujeres Cubanas, FMC), established in 1960, played an instrumental role in educating women about sexual health and hygiene and in securing women's rights, including the right to subsidized abortion on demand (in state facilities) in 1965. This measure significantly reduced the maternal mortality rate, given that abortion, along with traditional methods, was women's only source of fertility control. The FMC also helped usher in a new Family Code, adopted in 1975, which outlawed discrimination against women and girls, and declared that husband and wife were to share equal responsibilities in the household. In addition, the FMC organized community meetings, during which women were encouraged to post questions and discuss pressing issues, including those related to sexuality. The FMC's magazine, *Mujeres* (Women), which featured a section entitled 'Debates on Health', was instrumental in disseminating information about sexual health and hygiene, including to rural populations who were in most need of it.

In the 1970s, the National Commission on Sexual Education began offering health professionals, educators, and parents courses on sexuality, and Cuban television and radio aired education programmes on sexual health and hygiene. Moreover, popular science books by East German sexologists were translated into Spanish and became key sources of sex ed, including Siegfried Schnabl's *Man and Woman, Intimately*, which was published in Cuba in 1979. Selections from these books, which appeared in official magazines, presented sexuality as an important component of well-being for men and women alike, reflecting progress from earlier portraits in which women's sexual needs and desires were considered non-existent or shameful. In 1988, Masters and Johnson's *Human Sexual Response* was also published in translation in Cuba, though it was mainly read by medical professionals.

Homosexuality was criminalized in pre-revolutionary Cuba, although there was a small gay community in Havana. The situation worsened with the revolution: Castro and other revolutionaries combined traditional heterosexual masculinity with socialist morality and declared homosexuality

Sexuality in Marxism and Socialism

incompatible with revolutionary manhood. Homosexuals were presented as diseased victims of capitalist–imperialist propaganda who were potentially destabilizing to national security.[24] Deemed counter-revolutionaries, the state subjected self-identified or alleged homosexuals to public trials. At the university level, this involved a trial by one's peers, and because anyone who defended a homosexual risked having that same charge brought against themselves, many were forced to betray friends and colleagues. Individuals charged with homosexuality were expelled from university on the assumption that if permitted to earn a degree they would become 'homosexual architects who worked for the CIA, doctors who swindled old ladies, or agronomists and army officers who carried out economic sabotage against the Revolution'.[25] To root out homosexuals in the community, state authorities conducted raids of movie houses and nightclubs and relied on community surveillance. Once charged with homosexuality, individuals were expelled from study and barred from work, and some were sent to Military Units to Aid Production (UMAP) camps, where they performed forced labour along with others accused of 'counter-revolutionary activity' and 'asocial behaviour' such as members of religious sects, cultural figures, and peasants who resisted collectivization.

The late 1970s witnessed some progress: same-sex relations (between adults) were decriminalized and homosexuals could no longer be fired from cultural jobs. Nonetheless, Cuba remained an inhospitable place for sexual minorities well into the 1990s and many left during the Mariel exodus in 1980. In 1993, Fidel Castro declared homosexuality 'a natural tendency' and voiced his opposition to discrimination against sexual minorities. This was followed by a repeal of the government ban on allowing LGBTQ+ persons to serve openly in the military. Since the 2000s, LGBTQ+ people have been increasingly portrayed in film and television, and, with the 2022 Cuban Family Code referendum, same-sex marriage, as well as adoption by same-sex couples, is legal. Despite this, harassment has continued, with gay pride events abruptly cancelled and activists prohibited from leaving the country.

In the 1940s, a socialist and nationalist liberation movement developed in Vietnam under the leadership of Ho Chi Minh, which successfully defeated the French colonial government and established an independent country. A coup and further fighting led Vietnam to be divided into the socialist Democratic Republic of Vietnam in the north, led by Ho, and the Republic

24 Lillian Guerra, 'Gender Policing, Homosexuality, and the New Patriarchy of the Cuban Revolution, 1965–1970', *Social History* 35, no. 3 (2010): 268–89.
25 'iHay que hervirlos!', *Mella*, 7 June 1965, as quoted in Guerra, 'Gender Policing', 283.

of Vietnam in the south. War between the two and their allies lasted from 1955 to 1975, when the entire country was united as the Socialist Republic of Vietnam. With the advent of a unified, socialist Vietnam in 1976, equality between men and women was legally guaranteed. As in China, however, Confucian beliefs continued to influence how the state approached gender and sexuality, manifest in a restrictive moral code of behaviours for women. Accordingly, sexuality received little recognition outside of reproductive policies, and sexual desire was considered largely the preserve of men. Moreover, as the reproducer of the lineage, men are still considered superior to women, underscoring the salience of Confucian ideals.

With the free-market Renovation (*doi moi*) in 1986 – economic reforms similar to those in Deng Xiaoping's China – opportunities for sexual expression broadened, including for women, evident in more open discussion about sex in the media, especially among the younger generation. Despite proscriptions against pre-marital sex, there has been an increase in unmarried couples cohabitating in urban areas, a reality that women often conceal from their parents.

Given that parents generally do not discuss sex with their children, apart from urging abstinence, and there is no sex education in schools, young people rely on peers, internet blogs, and discussion forums for learning about sex. Concern about continued high rates of abortion (among the highest in the world), prompted the establishment of WeGrow Ed in 2019, which works to educate youth about sex and to develop a healthy relationship with their bodies and sexuality.

As in other socialist countries, homosexuality, like other state-defined 'social evils' such as extra-marital sex, pornography, prostitution, drug and alcohol addiction, gambling, and theft, was considered a threat to the collective good, and particularly to the health of adolescents. Into the twenty-first century, government-run media attributed increases in these behaviours to foreign influences, and presented them as a threat to the nation and race, citing the increase in HIV/AIDS in the country. Although there is no explicit mention of homosexuality in the Vietnamese penal code, only in 2022 did the government state that being gay, bisexual, or transgender is not deviant behaviour or a curable mental health problem. Moreover, the state only allows symbolic same-sex marriages; thus, same-sex couples do not enjoy the same legal protections under the Marriage and Family law as do heterosexual couples. Meanwhile, in 2015, the government amended the 2005 civil code, enshrining rights for transgender people and decriminalizing sexual reassignment surgery;

however, legal recognition of transgender status is dependent on the surgical procedure.

Urban centres in Vietnam have vibrant LGBTQ+ communities, and Gay Pride parades have occurred in Hanoi since 2012 and other cities thereafter. Moreover, LGBTQ+ issues are discussed in blogs and are featured in literature, film, and television. Despite this, LGBTQ+ youth face stigma, bullying, and, in some cases, violence. Moreover, teachers are often untrained and ill-equipped to handle cases of anti-LGBTQ+ discrimination, and their lessons frequently uphold the widespread myth in Vietnam that same-sex attraction is a disease.

Conclusion

State socialist approaches towards sexuality were ambiguous and varied over time and space. Policy and media depictions of sexuality were influenced by state expedience, namely modernization and the promotion of demographic growth. Although socialist regimes were not elected, popular attitudes and beliefs also influenced policy-making. Alongside increasing the fertility rate, socialist regimes focused on educating the populace about sexual health and hygiene and staving off behaviours they considered immoral or deviant, such as homosexuality and pre-marital sex. In this capacity, state policies were influenced by – or had to contend with, either through appropriation or refashioning – traditional norms and religious mores, with which a large share of the population identified, particularly during the early period of socialist consolidation.

Struggles over regime legitimacy also influenced state policies towards sexuality, as by the 1960s leaders had to contend with younger generations who eschewed the rigid and restrictive sexual policies of their parents and the early socialist period. In some cases, pressure for more liberal policies came from external forces, such as the opening up to Western culture, which happened to varying degrees in the Eastern Bloc during the Cold War, in China and Vietnam in the 1980s, and in Cuba in the 1990s. The impact of these processes changed – in some cases dramatically – state policies on women's sexuality, bodily autonomy, sex education, and same-sex relations. Abortion and homosexuality were decriminalized in most socialist states, and women's sexual pleasure became more prominent in public discourse about sex. Because sex was instrumentalized for the purpose of building socialism, state policies and representations of sexuality varied across time and space, affecting individuals in different ways.

Further Reading

Bebel, August. *Woman and Socialism*. Trans. Meta L. Stern. New York: Socialist Literature, 1910.

Bernstein, Frances Lee. *The Dictatorship of Sex: Lifestyle Advice for the Soviet Masses*. Ithaca, NY: Cornell University Press, 2007.

Biebuyck, Erin. 'The Collectivisation of Pleasure: Normative Sexuality in Post-1966 Romania'. *Aspasia* 4 (2010): 49–70.

Carleton, Gregory. *Sexual Revolution in Bolshevik Russia*. Pittsburgh, PA: University of Pittsburgh Press, 2004.

Dumitriu, Radu. *De vorbă cu tinerii: Probleme de educaţie a sexelor* (Speaking with Youth: Issues of Sex Education). Bucharest: Editura Tineretului, 1972.

Engels, Friedrich. *The Origin of the Family, Private Property and the State*. 1884; London: Verso, 2021.

Evans, Jennifer. 'Decriminalization, Seduction, and "Unnatural Desire" in the German Democratic Republic'. *Feminist Studies* 36, no. 3 (2010): 553–77.

Guerra, Lillian. 'Gender Policing, Homosexuality, and the New Patriarchy of the Cuban Revolution, 1965–1970'. *Social History* 35, no. 3 (2010): 268–89.

Hamilton, Carrie. *Sexual Revolutions in Cuba: Passion, Politics, and Memory*. Chapel Hill, NC: University of North Carolina Press, 2012.

Healey, Dan. *Homosexual Desire in Revolutionary Russia: The Regulation of Sexual and Gender Dissent*. Chicago: University of Chicago Press, 2001.

Herzog, Dagmar. 'East Germany's Sexual Evolution'. In *Socialist Modern: East German Everyday Culture and Politics*, ed. Katherine Pence and Paul Betts, 71–95. Ann Arbor, MI: University of Michigan Press, 2008.

Holt, Alix, ed. and trans. *Alexandra Kollontai: Selected Writings*. New York: W. W. Norton, 1980.

Hynson, Rachel M. 'Sex and State Making in Revolutionary Cuba, 1959–1968'. PhD dissertation, University of North Carolina at Chapel Hill, 2014.

Jackson, Stevi, Jieyu Liu, and Juhyun Woo, eds. *East Asian Sexualities: Modernity, Gender and New Sexual Cultures*. London: Zed Books, 2008.

Jeffreys, Elaine, ed. *Sex and Sexuality in China*. New York: Routledge, 2006.

Jinga, Luciana. 'Science and Politics during the Cold War: The Controversial Case of Sexology in Communist Romania'. *History of Communism in Europe* 9 (2018): 87–107.

Kirk, Emily J. 'Cuba's National Sex Education Program: Origins and Evolution'. *Cuban Studies* 49 (2020): 289–309.

Kościańska, Agnieszka, *Gender, Pleasure, and Violence: The Construction of Expert Knowledge of Sexuality in Poland*. Bloomington, IN: Indiana University Press, 2021.

Kulpa, Robert, and Mizielinska Joanna, eds. *De-Centring Western Sexualities: Central and Eastern European Perspectives*. Farnham, UK: Ashgate, 2011.

Kurimay, Anita. *Queer Budapest, 1873–1961*. Chicago: University of Chicago Press, 2000.

Kurimay, Anita, and Judit Takács. 'Emergence of the Hungarian Homosexual Movement in Late Refrigerator Socialism'. *Sexualities* 20, nos. 5/6 (2017): 585–603.

Lew-Starowicz, Zbigniew. *Seks nietypowy* (Atypical Sex). Warsaw: Instytut Wydawniczy Związków Zawodowych, 1988.

Lišková, Kateřina. *Sexual Liberation, Socialist Style: Communist Czechoslovakia and the Science of Desire, 1945–1989*. Cambridge: Cambridge University Press, 2018.

McLellan, Josie. *Love in the Time of Communism: Intimacy and Sexuality in the GDR*. Cambridge: Cambridge University Press, 2011.

Moon, Joan. 'Feminism and Socialism: The Utopian Synthesis of Flora Tristan'. In *Socialist Women: European Socialist Feminism in the Nineteenth and Early Twentieth Centuries*, ed. Marilyn J. Boxer and Jean H. Quatert, 19–50. New York: Elsevier, 1978.

Neubert, Rudolf. *Die Geschlechterfrage: Ein Buch für junge Leute*. Rudolstadt: Greifenverlag, 1955.

Poldervaart, Saskia. 'Theories about Sex and Sexuality in Utopian Socialism'. *Journal of Homosexuality* 2, no. 2/3 (1995): 41–67.

Rofel, Lisa. *Desiring China: Experiments in Neoliberalism, Sexuality, and Public Culture*. Durham, NC: Duke University Press, 2007.

Takács, Judit. 'Disciplining Gender and (Homo)sexuality in State Socialist Hungary in the 1970s'. *European Review of History: Revue européenne d'histoire* 22, no. 1 (2015): 161–75.

Wisłocka, Michalina. *Sztuka kochania* (The Art of Loving). Warsaw: Iskry, 1978.

17

Feminism and Modern Sexuality

VICTORIA HESFORD

When the American silent screen star Theda Bara declared in 1914 that she was 'in effect a *feministe*', she was asserting a relation between being a sex symbol and women's social and economic empowerment.[1] Both her *femme fatale* screen persona and her success as an actress (at the height of her fame she was Fox Studio's biggest star) signalled to her audience a different, and presumably for her many female fans, a more appealing way of being a woman – one not determined by domesticity but shaped by the technological innovation, commodity culture, and commercial capital of a mass-mediated public sphere. As a neologism, 'feminism' circulated widely in the 1910s as a word that would speak of, and for, a new and diverse constituency of women whose legibility as women was formed through the individualistic, mass societies of colonial modernity and whose claims to political agency were more expansive than those of the woman's rights movement of the nineteenth century. Like Bara, these 'new women' were defined by their relationship to capital and through race rather than kinship, and as the twentieth century continued, they would increasingly fashion themselves as sexual and social subjects through commodity culture and political activism rather than marriage and motherhood.

The relationship between feminism and sexuality in the long twentieth century is both complex and multifaceted. As the queer studies scholar Benjamin Kahan writes, the 'overlapping, unrationalized, diachronic, synchronic, collaged, messy contours of sexuality' emerged as a capacious discursive domain from the mid-nineteenth century to the mid-twentieth

---

1 Quoted in Nancy F. Cott, *The Grounding of Modern Feminism* (New Haven, CT: Yale University Press, 1987), 13.

century.[2] Whether sexuality is understood as congenital or acquired, specific to men or different for women, defined by object choice or aim, central to the character of an individual or the health of a population, it is a highly contested and messy set of discourses and institutional practices. Feminism is similarly impossible to define as a coherent ideology or political praxis. At once a historically specific political and cultural phenomenon emerging in the first decades of the twentieth century, feminism is also a highly differentiated transnational event that belies a single origin, set of beliefs, or constituency.

Organized around two key figures – the modern girl and the feminist-as-lesbian – this chapter explores the complexity of the historical relationship between feminism and sexuality through what Valerie Traub identifies as two recurrent themes of the history of sexuality as it pertains to 'female bodies, experiences, and representations': 'the relation of women's erotic ties to their political subjectivity – that is, to feminism', and the 'potential threat that female–female eroticism poses to patriarchal relations and male dominance'.[3] That is, I trace the connections between the commodification and politicization of women's sexuality as two axes around which the unsettled and generative relationship between modern sexuality and feminism revolves.

The Modern Girl

As the authors of the collective research project on *The Modern Girl Around the World* argue, the distinctively stylized figure of the modern girl 'simultaneously appeared around the globe in the 1920s and 1930s' largely as a consequence of the rise of international advertising agencies.[4] Recognizable through the standardized iconography of the ads she populated, the modern girl was also the product of the leisure activities and cultural and social aspirations of millions of young women from New York to New Delhi. As a representation and as an emergent subjectivity, the modern girl was a contested figure around which discourses of nationalism,

---

2 Benjamin Kahan, *The Book of Minor Perverts: Sexology, Etiology, and the Emergences of Sexuality* (Chicago: University of Chicago Press, 2019), 137. See also David M. Halperin, *How to Do the History of Sexuality* (Chicago: University of Chicago Press, 2002), and Valerie Traub, 'The Present Future of Lesbian Historiography', in *A Companion to Lesbian, Gay, Bisexual, and Transgender Studies*, ed. George Hagerty and Molly McGarry (Oxford: John Wiley & Sons, 2007), 124–45.

3 Traub, 'Present Future', 134.

4 Alys Eve Weinbaum, Lynn M. Thomas, Priti Ramamurthy, Uta G. Poiger, Madeleine Yue Dong, and Tani Barlow, eds., *The Modern Girl Around the World: Consumption, Modernity, and Globalization* (Durham, NC: Duke University Press, 2008), 25.

white supremacy, and colonial modernity circulated. Common to all her manifestations, however, was her association with 'sexual transgression'.[5] Whether viewed with suspicion or wonder, the modern girl figured as a departure from the 'proper' domain of femininity – the home and marriage – signalling instead a desire for dating, romantic love, and pre-marital sex. Her appeal, or threat, was predicated on her claiming of a publicity independent of social and familial obligations; she lived for pleasure and consumption rather than work and duty.

In visual and textual representations, the modern girl was drawn, and later photographed, according to a distinctive aesthetic: bobbed hair, an elongated or slender body posed in a relaxed or informal setting, and an 'open, easy smile'.[6] Her svelteness and frankness of expression suggested a physical and social confidence that invoked her sexual independence and attractiveness. The commodities she advertised – cosmetics, toiletries, items of clothing associated with leisure – were signs of her sexual appeal as well as her capacity for self-transformation and self-creation. Although differently invoked depending on where and what she was advertising, the modern girl was also a racialized figure. She became a key marker of the distinction between what Maria Lugones calls the 'dark and lighter side' of the 'colonial / modern gender system'.[7] While the lighter side idealized biological dimorphism and 'heterosexualism' in the guise of a 'civilizing' whiteness, the darker side projected fears of gender instability, sexual aggression, and biological atrophy onto the 'primitive' Black and Brown races of the Global South. Within the colonial contexts of the 1920s and the 1930s, the modern girl was often incorporated into a politics of respectability that drew upon and rearticulated the dark and lighter side of the colonial / modern gender system. In South Africa, for example, the modern girl became a contested figure of pan-Africanism in the 1930s, her modernity signalling on the one hand the racial uplift of a newly crafted African political and cultural identity, and on the other the debasements of an imported white Western sexuality.[8] In China, by contrast, the modern girl figured in the writings of the anti-Confucian, anti-imperialist, and nationalist May Fourth Movement in the 1910s as an ambivalent embrace of Western sexological thought. She became a 'scientized' symbol of modern China's break from Confucianism and its kinship system,

5 *Modern Girl*, ed. Weinbaum et al., 16.   6 *Modern Girl*, ed. Weinbaum et al., 13.
7 Maria Lugones, 'Heterosexualism and the Colonial / Modern Gender System', *Hypatia* 22, no.1 (2007): 186–209, at 202.
8 Lynn M. Thomas, 'The Modern Girl and Racial Respectability in 1930s South Africa', in *Modern Girl*, ed. Weinbaum et al., 96–119.

as well as an emblem of China's incorporation and acceptance of Western capitalism. For many of the May Fourth writers, the modern girl was a useful figure for exploring the contradictions of modernity – in both economic and sexual terms.[9]

The productive variability of the modern girl as a representational and social category was an effect, paradoxically, of her standardization through the mass media. She symbolized femininity across racial and class hierarchies and national borders precisely because she trafficked in the selling and buying of commodities. At the same time, the fantasy through which these commodities were advertised to their female consumers was predicated on a mostly implicit and sometimes explicit recognition of their transformation into wage-earners, white-collar professionals, and consumers of commodities. The characteristics that make the modern girl appealing – her physical vitality, informality, social independence, confidence, and self-regard – were also indicators of her potential and actual economic power. That is, the sexual transgressiveness with which the modern girl was associated was an effect of the autonomy and individuality she promised as a new subject of economic power.

The modern girl, of course, bears close resemblance to 'the new woman', a figure who first emerges in the mid- to late nineteenth century when middle- and upper-middle-class women began to claim a public voice through an appeal to civic duty and moral responsibility. By the turn of the twentieth century, a younger generation of new women rejected the self-effacement of these older 'warriors for social justice' and made more positive claims for sexual, political, and social autonomy.[10] It was these women who would begin to call themselves feminists in the 1910s, recognizing in the newness and imprecision of the word a language that could represent a more expansive desire for social and self-transformation than had been articulated by the women's rights and suffrage movements. As the historian Nancy Cott argues, feminism was 'a semantic claim to female modernism', asserted by its adherents as a breaking away from the old nineteenth-century women's movement and towards a future in which the changes women sought would be both more 'profound' and more revolutionary than those of the

---

9 Sarah E. Stevens, 'Figuring Modernity: The New Woman and the Modern Girl in Republican China', *NWSA Journal* 15, no. 3 (2003): 82–103.

10 Caroll Smith-Rosenberg, 'Discourses of Sexuality and Subjectivity: The New Woman, 1870–1936', in *Hidden from History: Reclaiming the Gay and Lesbian Past*, ed. Martin Duberman, Martha Vicinus, and George Chauncey, Jr. (New York: New American Library, 1989), 264–81, at 267.

women's rights movement.[11] Rather than acting out of a civic duty or sense of moral responsibility, these new feminist women understood their domain of action to be both political and cultural: the self and social transformation they sought would require a radical contestation of the separate spheres ideology of the previous century and the self and collective reinvention of an increasingly visible heterogenous mass of women.

Historians debate whether modern girls and new women were in fact representations of the same women. For the *Modern Girl* research group, the two figures operate more as 'heuristic devices' for thinking through the historical changes they reference rather than as representatives of empirically distinct groups of women. Although 'contemporaries identified the New Woman with reform and with social and political advocacy' and the modern girl with the 'frivolous pursuits of consumption, romance, and fashion', the distinction between political activism and participation in commodity culture was less clear in practice: many new women were also 'avid consumers and passionate advocates of "free love", and Modern Girls embraced a variety of political projects including socialism and nationalism'.[12] In contrast, the historian Miriam Silverberg argues that new women and modern girls were, in the case of modern Japan specifically, but also more broadly, different figures. For Silverberg, new women were deemed more of a social threat by male elites due to their prominence as intellectuals and social theorists. It was their political advocacy in conjunction with their status as artists, writers, and journalists that made new women active participants in the mass-mediated public spheres of their societies rather than simply consumers of them.[13]

The debates over the distinction between new women and modern girls are indicative of the inherent instability between culture and politics in the mass-mediated public sphere of the 1910s and the 1920s. If, as Nancy Cott argues, 'Woman's sphere was both the point of oppression and the point of departure for nineteenth-century feminists' with 'Womanhood ... their hallmark', then by the 1910s the notions of 'woman's sphere' and 'womanhood' determined less who women were and what kinds of public and social activity they could pursue.[14] Instead, the public and semi-public spheres of work and play – the factory, office, settlement house, college campus, print media, cinema, department store, and city street – became the domains in

---

11 Cott, *Grounding of Modern Feminism*, 15.   12 *Modern Girl*, ed. Weinbaum et al., 9–10.
13 Miriam Silverberg, 'After the Grand Tour: The Modern Girl, the New Woman, and the Colonial Maiden', in *Modern Girl*, ed. Weinbaum et al., 354–61.
14 Cott, *Grounding of Modern Feminism*, 20.

Feminism and Modern Sexuality

which a diverse and transnational constituency of women variously fashioned themselves as cultural subjects and social actors. The more profound and revolutionary changes sought by the newly anointed feminists of the 1910s would come precisely from their ability to be both new women and modern girls – that is, subjects who could traverse the dark and lighter side of the colonial/modern gender system and disturb the boundaries of a naturalized and racialized womanhood through their self-fashioning and collective public engagement.

As a semantic claim to female modernism, then, feminism both depended on and actively participated in the politicization and commercialization of the private sphere. As a result, feminism was a key contributor to the making public of intimate, private life. In this regard, it was not alone. By the turn of the twentieth century, scientific and medical discourses, along with public health and sociological analyses, all contributed to a profusion of expert knowledges on the sexual, emotional, and domestic lives of increasingly measured and managed national populations. Sexology was at the forefront of this epistemological activity. Emerging in the mid- to late nineteenth century, sexology was, by the 1910s, a highly influential if also contradictory set of medical and scientific theories of human sexuality. As the cultural and literary historians Lucy Bland and Laura Doan argue, sexology was nothing if not ambitious in its desire 'to produce an exhaustive classification of the multiple aspects of sexuality, tracing its etiology, scrutinizing its fantasies, its fetishes and the numerous pleasures of the body, and constructing new pathologized individual identities, such as the homosexual, the pervert, sadist, masochist, and frigid woman'.[15] This will-to-know on the part of sexology's mostly medical and scientific practitioners, and their exhaustive massing of evidentiary and theoretical material also meant, as Kahan argues, that the emergence of modern sexuality was riven by 'radical instability, unevenness, and messiness'.[16] This profusion of sexological discourse – its messiness – also provided fertile if contradictory ground for the explanations and arguments feminists would use to make their claims for social autonomy and economic independence. (For more on modern sexology, see Chapter 15 by Howard Chiang in this volume.)

Indeed, the contested status of female sexuality within the discourses of sexology allowed for political manoeuvre and vagueness on the part of feminists and provided a (limited) array of explanatory frameworks with which

15 Lucy Bland and Laura Doan, eds., *Sexology Uncensored: The Documents of Sexual Science* (Chicago: University of Chicago Press, 1998), 2
16 Kahan, *Minor Perverts*, 2.

feminists could make arguments for social and economic independence. For example, elite Western gender non-conforming women such as the English author Radclyffe Hall (1880–1943) could draw upon sexological theories of the congenital invert to explain and justify their masculine gender presentation, refusal to marry, sexual intimacy with other women, and public presence as social reformers and intellectuals. Hall's contemporaries, the American artist and writer Djuna Barnes and the English author Virginia Woolf, on the other hand, assumed an acquired model of sexuality in their literary explorations of female sexuality as either situational or based on the singular object of desire rather than a naturalized gender dimorphism.[17]

The confusion between acquired and congenital theories of sexuality also shaped the debates between socialist, anarchist, and liberal feminists over the revolutionary potential of free love. Emma Goldman (1869–1940), the American anarchist activist and thinker, linked the unfettered expression of sexual desire to women's freedom from social customs and institutions. Rather than reject the call of sexual or maternal love, as Goldman accused bourgeois feminists of doing in the name of equality, women should 'insist upon' their own 'unrestricted freedom' by 'listening to the voice of [their] nature'. Sexual freedom was, for Goldman, freedom from social convention and state regulation and depended on women rejecting the 'superficial equalization of human beings' in order to be 'oneself . . . in oneness with others'.[18] Although women's 'nature' remains an enigmatic notion in Goldman's thinking, her emphasis on freeing women from social convention in order for them to be themselves 'in oneness with others', suggests an understanding of sexuality as a potentially transformative life force. In contrast, Alexandra Kollontai (1872–1952), the Russian labour activist and first commissar for social welfare in Lenin's Bolshevik government, argued that the solution to the proletarian woman's economic and social oppression was state-supported maternal care, communal childcare, and free access to abortion and contraception. Without this kind of state aid and support, according to Kollontai, free love would likely lead to destitution for most working-class women. Sexuality, for Kollontai, was both economically determined and socially mandated, its supposed naturalness neither the most important aspect of its influence on women's lives, nor the source of their future freedom.[19]

17 Kahan, *Minor Perverts*, 17–18.
18 Emma Goldman, 'The Tragedy of Women's Emancipation' (1906), in *The Essential Feminist Reader*, ed. Estelle B. Freedman (New York: Modern Library, 2007), 173, 169.
19 Alexandra Kollontai, 'The Social Basis of the Woman Question' (1909), in *The Essential Feminist Reader*, ed. Freedman, 175–81.

For the mostly upper-middle-class intellectual and professional women who formed the New York feminist salon Heterodoxy in the early twentieth century, free love was most often associated with an individualistic desire for self-exploration and expression. As the American journalist and suffragist Rheta Childe Dorr wrote in remembrance of her participation in Heterodoxy in the years 1912–17, 'We thought we discussed the whole field, but we really discussed ourselves.'[20] Dorr's wry acknowledgement echoes the Chinese writer Ding Ling's famous portrayal of a young urban Chinese woman in the 1920s in the short story 'Miss Sophia's Diary'. Sophia struggles to understand and express herself, caught between a desire to free herself from tradition and the difficulty of doing so. In her conflicted subjectivity and sense of dissatisfaction with what the world has to offer her, Sophia represents the modern woman in ways that would have been very familiar to Dorr and her friends. For Ling, however, as for many of her May Fourth contemporaries, Sophia's self-obsessive tendencies were ultimately indicative of her lack of a political perspective rather than a sign of her emergent feminism.

As European sexological thought migrated to East and South Asia, it became a resource for nationalists and political progressives wishing to contest traditional kinship systems. Yet, as the historian Tze-Ian D. Sang writes, the appeal of sexological thought for May Fourth intellectuals ironically resulted in 'a regimentation of desire' that was, in some ways, just as constrictive of women's sexual expression as the more traditional feudal models they were contesting.[21] In their celebration of a scientized heterosexuality as the marker of a new, more modern China, the May Fourth intellectuals reclassified homoerotic and homosocial practices as psychological perversions and physical abnormalities. For women this meant both the invention of a new category – 'female same-sex love' – in the 1910s and the 1920s and its simultaneous pathologization.

Despite the unsettled profusion of circulating discourses concerning the causes and effects of sexuality in the early decades of the twentieth century, a common set of related associations began to form around the political claims of feminists: sexual transgressiveness (an explicit sexual expressiveness, interest in same-sex or interracial sexual relations, or sex outside of marriage), economic independence, and an increasingly assertive presence in the public sphere. The modern girl made these associations legible as aspirations to women seeking escape from the claims of family and as a warning to

20 Quoted in Cott, *Grounding of Modern Feminism*, 39.
21 Tze-Ian D. Sang, *The Emerging Lesbian: Female Same-Sex Desire in Modern China* (Chicago: University of Chicago Press, 2003), 15.

nationalist and state institutions of power. She also made it possible for feminists to become recognizable social types or figures in their own right – the modern girl's frank enjoyment of commodities and leisure differentiating her from the intellectualism and middle-class specificity of feminist political discourse. To think of the modern girl in relation to feminism, then, is to also highlight the diversity of women as political and social actors in the early twentieth century. The uneasy, temporary, alliance between bourgeois intellectual women who self-identified as feminists, and the working-class immigrant and Black women who formed political identities as community and labour activists, 'girl-strikers', and suffragists in the United States in the 1910s, is evidence of the contradictory ways in which sexual transgressiveness, economic independence, and an assertive presence in the public sphere could play out for different constituencies of women. For bourgeois white feminists it meant (relative) social power as heads of households, professionals, and public intellectuals. For Black and other women of colour and immigrant women who used their limited access to commodities to fashion distinct styles of femininity and protest, it often meant a notorious publicity and attendant risk of violence. But whether the political or social identity was feminist, girl striker, wayward Black girl, or new woman, the fashioning of each was dependent on and made use of a commercialized public sphere in which women operated as icons and agents of sexual modernity.

The Feminist-as-Lesbian

If American cinema's first sex symbol, Theda Bara, could declare herself in 1914 a *feministe*, by the mid-twentieth century, cinema offered a much more ambivalent legacy for feminist self-fashioning. Although cinema had, by the advent of the Second World War, become a dominant cultural domain for the creation of a hypervisible and transmissible modern femininity, it had done so largely at the expense of an expansive notion of women as political actors and social agents. Hollywood cinema provided women cinema goers with variations on a theme: an array of studio-produced hypersexualized and objectified movie stars who operated as sites (and sights) of cultural anxiety about women's increasing public presence as social agents and subjects. While women might copy the gestures and styles of movie stars, or perhaps imagine themselves in the *mise en scènes* of the films they saw, they would not see reflected back to them the complexity of their lives as modern subjects. Rather, both cinema and early television mostly invited women to identify with a series of clichés through which they were offered the compensatory pleasures of sentimental feeling or comic acquiescence to bourgeois patriarchal power and control.[22]

Such representations did not go unnoticed. As Betty Friedan famously argued in 1963, American women were, by the 1950s, the unhappy representatives of a deeply dysfunctional society, one that demanded strict adherence to a rigid gender ideology and complete capitulation to the pleasures and distractions of consumerism. Friedan's identification of a 'problem that has no name' or 'malaise' afflicting women resonated with her largely white middle-class readers because she located the problem in feelings and psychic discomfort rather than in economic or social inequality. The 'strange stirring ... sense of dissatisfaction' and 'yearning' felt by women was, according to Friedan, the result of cultural and social coercion rather than material deprivation or social marginalization.[23] They were unhappy, in other words, rather than oppressed – their restless unease and lack of purpose an effect of being other-directed by advertisements, the media, and experts demanding they enact and uphold a highly sexualized and objectified ideal femininity.

The targets of Friedan's critique of women's predicament were American Freudianism and mass culture. Friedan identified both as highly influential and pernicious purveyors of the feminine mystique. On the one hand, Freudianism offered an 'overly sexualized version of femininity' which, by the mid-twentieth century, meant medical and psychoanalytic practitioners diagnosing distinctly female pathologies – frigidity, lesbianism, nymphomania – as the result of women's failure to achieve the regular experience of what was touted as normalcy: matrimonial vaginal orgasms and healthy pregnancies.[24] On the other hand, mid-century mass culture was awash in sensationalistic stories of women's sexual and psychic perversion, which only further entrenched the association of femininity with a deeply problematic and potentially threatening sexuality. Friedan's solution to this suturing of sexuality to femininity was to prise them apart: women's happiness, she argued, would come from creative and professional pursuits independent of, if somehow also in harmony with, a sexually satisfying and loving marriage.

---

22 See Mary Ann Doane, *The Desire to Desire: The Woman's Film of the 1940s* (Bloomington, IN: Indiana University Press, 1987).

23 Betty Friedan, *The Feminine Mystique* (1963; New York: Dell, 1975), 1.

24 Jane Gerhard, *Desiring Revolution: Second-Wave Feminism and the Rewriting of Twentieth Century American Sexual Thought* (New York: Columbia University Press, 2001), 89.

Yet the success of *The Feminine Mystique* had less to do with Friedan's solution to women's unhappiness, which was as contradictory as the problem the book was attempting to explain, and more to do with the way it amplified the cultural fantasies and anxieties about women's sexual and social agency. Friedan's account of the 'sickly' sexual phantasies enveloping women in the post-war years was one of many that enforced the idea that, by the mid-twentieth century, sex was not only increasingly 'on display' in the public sphere but also integral to people's success or failure as social subjects.[25] In the United States, mass media publications such as *Playboy* magazine, first published in 1953, and Helen Gurley Brown's bestseller *Sex and the Single Girl*, published in 1963, were leading exemplars of a popularization of sexual expression outside of marriage. For the urban young professionals who were the primary target audience for these publications, being good at sex and having it often became synonymous with a healthy and successful social life, while the 'single's life' would ensure material success and the freedom to express their sexual desires when and how they wanted. In addition, the American scientific studies of Alfred Kinsey in the 1950s and of Masters and Johnson in the 1960s, both of which reached a mass audience through intense media interest, separated sexual behaviour from identity (and reproductive function) by accumulating a wealth of ethnographic and physiological data on the variety of human sexual activity and biophysical processes.[26] If these studies demonstrated that sexual practice did not map neatly onto the homo/hetero binary through which post-war societies in North America and western Europe increasingly organized sexuality, they nevertheless continued the modern assumption that sex was at the centre of people's sense of themselves and their relationships with others.

For women in the 1950s and the 1960s, the increasingly overt and pathologizing association of sexuality with femininity, in conjunction with the 'sexualization of public culture' more generally by the early 1960s, created a set of contradictory social pressures that proved an important catalyst for the rise of the women's liberation movement. As the historian Jane Gerhard argues, 'much of what galled women into feminism [in the 1960s] was precisely the sense of injustice forged in and through all things sexual'.[27]

---

25 Friedan, *Feminine Mystique*, 263.
26 Alfred C. Kinsey, Wardell B. Pomeroy, Clyde E. Martin, and Paul H. Gebhard, *Sexual Behavior in the Human Female* (1953; Bloomington, IN: Indiana University Press, 1998); William H. Masters and Virginia E. Johnson, *Human Sexual Response* (Toronto: Bantam Books, 1966).
27 Gerhard, *Desiring Revolution*, 3.

For the many young, white middle-class women who would become women's liberationists in North America and western Europe, popular culture and social commentary had created an impossible demand – that they be sexually available but not sluts, that their sexual desires should be healthy and 'normal' but not unadventurous or boring, and that they would, eventually, get married and have children. In contrast, lesbians, sex workers, working-class women, and women of colour were the targets of sensationalistic media exposés that pathologized them as sexual predators or social outcasts whose participation in urban sex and drug underworlds threatened the social order. These were the women made infamous by the American artist Valerie Solanas's *SCUM Manifesto* in 1968, the text of which offered women's liberation a thrilling refusal of middle-class femininity – a refusal, moreover, that was predicated on the rejection of sex as a means to individual or collective freedom.

Whether pathologized or idealized, the sexualized woman was an animating and absorbing social and cultural figure by the late 1960s. As the film studies scholar Damon Young writes: 'In the second half of the twentieth century, women and queers [were] at the centre of proliferating images and narratives of sex becoming public', a publicity which 'crystallized the tensions between, on the one hand, a new idea of the sexual subject as autonomous and independent and, on the other, enduring conceptions of the social as heterosexual and generational'. For Young, these tensions manifested themselves most acutely, in the case of women, in cinema's increasingly explicit depiction of the female orgasm – a depiction that tended to rely on the representational schema of sexual difference (the close-up of a woman's face) while also suggesting women's pleasure as 'freed from its relational trappings'.[28] The female orgasm, of course, also became the locus of radical feminist disagreements with post-war American Freudianism and was transformed by women's liberationists, most notably by the American activist Anne Koedt, into a highly contested and overtly politicized symbol of women's potential liberation from heteropatriarchal social relations.[29]

In one very simple sense, then, women's liberation responded to the widespread sexualization of women, and of public culture in general in the post-war years, by politicizing sexuality. One of the most famous and influential examples was the American writer and activist Kate Millett's 1970

---

28 Damon R. Young, *Making Sex Public and Other Cinematic Fantasies* (Durham, NC: Duke University Press, 2018), 17, 23.

29 Anne Koedt, 'The Myth of the Vaginal Orgasm' (1968), in *Radical Feminism*, ed. Anne Koedt, Ellen Levine, and Anita Rapone (New York: Quadrangle Books, 1973), 198.

bestseller, *Sexual Politics*. Echoing the ambition and interdisciplinary approach of the French philosopher Simone de Beauvoir's *The Second Sex*, published in 1949, *Sexual Politics* set out to 'formulate a systematic overview of patriarchy as a political institution' by attributing its 'historical and social constancy' to the 'political aspect' of sex.[30] Millett defined 'coitus' as the 'charged microcosm' of 'psychological feelings, social relations, and cultural values' through which the political, understood as 'power-structured relationships, arrangements whereby one group of persons is controlled by another' through 'techniques of control', operated.[31] Millett's argument that sexual relations were a locus for the production and maintenance of social power echoed the French philosopher Michel Foucault's near contemporaneous definition of sexuality as a 'dense transfer point for relations of power'.[32] However, unlike Foucault, Millett also argued that sex, and women, would be freed from their subjection to power through a radical transformation of those relations:

> It may be that a second wave of the sexual revolution might at last accomplish its aim of freeing half the race from its immemorial subordination – and in the process bring us all a great deal closer to humanity. It may be that we shall even be able to retire sex from the harsh realities of politics, but not until we have created a world we can bear out of the desert we inhabit.[33]

In locating the source of women's subjugation in sex as well as their potential emancipation, Millett understood sexuality as the primary site of women's claims to a political collectivity. Women's freedom would come through their contestation of and emancipation from the affective and social obligations of family life and the coercive psychological demands of heterosexuality. But as Kate Millett's utopian linking of women's freedom with the freeing of sex from politics at the end of *Sexual Politics* also suggests, sexuality was simultaneously idealized as a field of human experience that could potentially liberate women from *all* forms of social and economic subjugation – including those of race and class.

The contradictory understanding of sex as both the source of women's subjugation and their future liberation was evident across the international spectrum of women's liberation movements, including those in Europe, Japan, and South America, as well as the United States. Pamphlets and

---

30 Kate Millett, *Sexual Politics* (1970; New York: Ballantine Books, 1978), xi.
31 Millett, *Sexual Politics*, 31.
32 Michel Foucault, *The History of Sexuality*. Vol. 1: *An Introduction*, trans. Robert Hurley (1976; New York: Vintage Books, 1990), 103.
33 Millett, *Sexual Politics*, 363.

newsletters from different groups circulated through transnational leftist media networks, and a widespread cross-fertilization of ideas created a common, if differently oriented, focus on sexual liberation for women. In Japan, the *uman ribu*, or woman's lib movement, argued that women's erotic freedom was central to their social and economic liberation from the traditional family structure. An emphasis on access to free reproductive services for women as well as the creation of alternative communal spaces and households formed part of *uman ribu*'s protest against marriage and family life.[34] In Germany, lesbian activists championed erotic freedom, and pointed out the intrinsic connections between homophobia, racism, and institutionalized violence by the state.[35]

Reproductive justice and the articulation of the connections between imperialism, capitalism, and women's sexual oppression were also formative elements of the Third World Women's Alliance's (TWWA) intersectional and internationalist approach to women's liberation. Formed in 1970 in New York City by the Black Woman's Alliance and a group of Puerto Rican women activists, the TWWA foregrounded women's sexual and reproductive freedom within the context of an intersectional analysis of the racist and sexist conditions of (colonial) capitalism. For example, Frances Beal, one of the founders of the TWWA, argued in her widely circulated essay 'Double Jeopardy: to be Black and Female' (1970) that the economic and psychological exploitation of Black women was predicated on a 'genocidal' attempt by the white 'ruling-class elite' to control and ultimately extinguish Black and Brown peoples through forced sterilization. For Beale and her TWWA allies, the sexual and reproductive freedom of Black and Brown women was central to any anti-capitalist and anti-imperialist women's liberation movement.

The American activist Sue Katz's 'Smash Phallic Imperialism', another widely circulated essay from 1970, also captures the effective conjoining of a critique of capitalism and sex in women's liberation. Unlike the intersectional analyses offered by *uman ribu* and TWWA, however, Katz articulated her critique through a rhetorically charged opposition between straight and lesbian sexuality. In identifying sex as 'an institution' that reflected the 'same

---

34 See James Welker, 'From Women's Liberation to Lesbian Feminism in Japan', in *Rethinking Japanese Feminisms*, ed. Julia C. Bullock, Ayako Kano, and James Welker (Honolulu: University of Hawai'i Press, 2018), 50–67; and Setsu Shigematsu, *Scream from the Shadows: The Women's Liberation Movement in Japan* (Minneapolis, MN: University of Minnesota Press, 2012).

35 See Miriam Frank, 'Lesbian Life and Literature: A Survey of Recent German-Language Publications', *Women in German Yearbook* 10 (1994): 219–37.

ideology as other major institutions' in an oppressive, capitalist society such as the United States, Katz argued that sex was 'goal oriented, profit and productivity oriented' and a 'product' that women have had to 'turn out' for the economic and social benefit of men. All sex acts between men and women, Katz asserted, ultimately led to the 'Great Penetration and the Big Come', which left women frustrated and unsatisfied – literally had by a sexual system that used and objectified them for the economic and social benefit of men. The standardization of intercourse – suggested by the exaggerated and absurdist phrasing of Katz's description – became the trap of an exploitative relation through which women, or more particularly perhaps, their vaginas, became the objects through which heterosex was enacted as a contractual, productive, and reproductive relation. Echoing Solanas's description of sex as the exploitative ruse of America's 'money-work system', Katz concluded that for women to be free of the interrelated oppression of capitalism and heterosexuality they had to reject sex in favour of a 'sensuality' between women: 'For me, coming out meant an end to sex.'[36]

'The personal is political' became the phrase that both invoked and enabled the politics of women's liberation as a politics of sexuality that was also, as Katz's polemic exemplifies, often a simultaneous critique of capitalism and the gendered dynamics of the colonial modern nation-state. At the same time, the phrase was also suggestive of the contradictions of women's liberation's politicization of sexuality. What counted as the personal became an area of contestation and disagreement between Black and women of colour feminists and white feminists, as well as between straight and lesbian feminists. That is, the personal became the fault line through which some (white, Western, and middle-class) women could position themselves as sexual subjects while others (Black, women of colour, and poor women) were often used as signs or symbols of sexual pathology. The struggle to find a language that could give form to the problem of the personal as a *political* problem is evident in much of the early theorizing of women's liberation. Indeed, many of the texts of the emergent women's liberation movement were preoccupied with locating the source of women's oppression in feelings of sexual exploitation and dissatisfaction, and by 1970 the critique of psycho-sexual relations between men and women dominated the theoretical and polemical output of radical feminism.

---

36 Sue Katz, 'Smash Phallic Imperialism' (1972), in *Out of the Closets: Voices of Gay Liberation*, ed. Karla Jay and Allen Young (New York: New York University Press, 1992), 259–62, at 259.

Conversely, non-exploitative sexual and emotional relationships with others were either implied or invoked – increasingly in the form of lesbianism – as a practice of social and sexual freedom. In 'Smash Phallic Imperialism', for example, Katz asserts as an alternative to 'sex' a 'non-institutionalized' and 'creative' physical and emotional intimacy between women: 'it is touching and rubbing and cuddling and fondness. It is holding and rocking and kissing and lickin' with the only goal closeness and pleasure.' This creative, non-standardized, physical and emotional intimacy between women is also presented by Katz as a form of feminist political activity – it is a 'collective experience growing out of our struggle'.[37] Collective living and communal eroticism also formed part of the lesbian feminist political practice of the Gay Women's Liberation (GWL) group. Founded in 1969 in San Francisco and with strong connections to the Black Panther Party, GWL worked to transform lesbianism into a practice of political resistance. Prioritizing a local, multi-issue, coalitional politics, GWL attempted to create 'new intimate bonds that blurred sexual relationships, comradeship, and other bonds of family' through a community-oriented 'collective defense' approach to lesbian feminism.[38]

The conjoining of the sexual and the political in the figure of the lesbian became an explicit and transformative event for feminism in the early years of the women's liberation movement. Although lesbian feminism emerged transnationally in the early to mid-1970s out of a multi-dimensional, multi-racial, anti-racist, and anti-sexist leftist politics, the symbolic power of the feminist-as-lesbian was associated primarily with the white women's liber-ation groups covered by the mainstream media. As the historian Emily K. Hobson notes, the mainstream fixation on 'white girls gone wrong' tended to push Black and women of colour lesbian feminists out of view.[39] The feminist-as-lesbian also tended to circulate in the media as a figure of ridicule (of white women's liberationists) in contrast to the revolutionary woman, usually portrayed as the dangerous and threatening Black militant or Third World guerrilla fighter. Through contrasting depictions of the feminist-as-lesbian and revolutionary woman, the media tended to dismiss the import-ance of sexual politics while sensationalizing the threat of Black and women of colour radicalism. For women's liberation this meant the effective

---

37 Katz, 'Smash Phallic Imperialism', 260.
38 Emily K. Hobson, *Lavender and Red: Liberation and Solidarity in the Gay and Lesbian Left* (Berkeley, CA: University of California Press, 2016), 50.
39 Hobson, *Lavender and Red*, 48.

representational bifurcation of an ostensibly straight multi-racial militant feminist politics from an assumed white, bourgeois, lesbian feminism.

The manifesto 'The Woman-Identified-Woman' (1970) written by the Radicalesbians, a group formed in New York City in 1970, perhaps more than any other early position paper, captures the contradictory impulses inherent to the affective and representational force of the lesbian as a figure of women's sexual and social liberation:

> What is a Lesbian? A Lesbian is the rage of all women condensed to the point of explosion. She is the woman who, often beginning at an extremely early age, acts in accordance with her inner compulsion to be a more complete and freer human being than her society – perhaps then, but certainly later – cares to allow her.

Invoking the pathologization of the lesbian in mid-century clinical psycho-analysis and pulp sexology, the paper describes the 'tortuous journey through a night that may have been decades long' of a woman at odds with society and its expectations of her. Yet instead of meeting an early death, her typical fate in mid-century lesbian pulp fiction, this lesbian is a heroic, wilful being struggling to be true to her 'inner compulsion'. As she walks her lonely path through life, her alienation forces her to 'evolve her own life pattern' and to 'question and analyze what the rest of her society more or less accepts'. As the lesbian finds herself 'on the other side' of her 'tortuous journey through [the] night' of social ostracization and alienation, she gains 'the liberation of self, the inner peace, the real love of self and of all women'.[40]

As 'the rage of all women condensed to the point of explosion', the lesbian operates in the essay as a metaphor, not just for a feminist revolution, but also for the necessary blasting of the status quo – the radical transformation of affect – needed to incite and enact that revolution. At the same time, the essay utilizes the phrase 'woman-identified-woman' to mitigate the threat of women's rage and their rejection of the normal and the conventional. The predatory, highly sexualized lesbian of mid-century pulp fiction and sexology is transformed – through her politicization – into a woman who ultimately rejects the label lesbian as 'inauthentic': Lesbian is 'a word, the label, the condition that holds women in line'. When society is no longer organized in terms of men's oppression of women, when 'sexual expression is allowed to follow feelings, the categories of homosexuality and heterosexuality would

---

40 Radicalesbians, 'The Woman-Identified-Woman', in *Radical Feminism*, ed. Koedt, Levine, and Rapone, 240.

disappear'.[41] The turn away from lesbian and towards 'woman-identified-woman' is also, then, a turn away from all sex roles and, indeed, all categories of social division. The liberation and 'real love of self' will come, not through identification with the lesbian as social outcast or as sexual deviant, that is, through an identification with her unfeminine, asocial characteristics, but through her transformation into a woman who 'coincides' with other women in their collective discovery of their 'authentic selves'.[42] Here, the lesbian's association with social independence – from family claims and marriage – becomes a means to figure women's freedom but in such a way that the familiarity of women as a category of identity is maintained. Rejecting femininity as man's 'image of us' will not lead to strange, unfeminine, people who cannot be recognized through the familiar images of sexual difference, but to more 'authentic' or 'real' versions of women.

In locating a utopian notion of sex in a liberation from gender or sex roles, radical feminist thinkers such as the Radicalesbians, Millett, and Koedt argued that sexual and therefore social freedom could only happen beyond sex roles and, conversely, that women's sexual oppression was on account of their sex roles – on account of their being women. That is, in the attempt to disaggregate sex from social roles, or gender, these thinkers tended to reassert the relation between them. This is the paradox of sexual difference Solanas sought to negate through her call for the annihilation of men and which the Radicalesbians recognized but could not overcome in 'The Woman Identified Woman' when they asserted that the 'essence of being a "Woman" is to get fucked by men'. As Damon Young argues in relation to the cinematic depictions of sex in the 1960s and the 1970s, the 'insuperable aporia' of women both as the (orgasmic) face of a newly fashioned liberal sexual autonomy and as the objectified figure of sexual difference meant that the contested and unsettled relation between sex and gender was the fraught epicentre of making sex public.[43] For women's liberation, this making sex public also entailed the production of a politics that became focused on 'the personal' as the domain of feelings, intimacy, and the reproduction of heterodomesticity. That is, making sex visible through the symbolic figure of the lesbian in the early years of women's liberation meant the politicization and exposure of what being 'fucked by men' cost women psychically, emotionally, socially, and economically.

41 Radicalesbians, 'The Woman-Identified-Woman'.
42 Radicalesbians, 'The Woman-Identified-Woman'.
43 Young, *Making Sex Public*, 53.

The indirection and variety of associations between feminism and lesbianism for most of the twentieth century – from spinsterhood, frigidity, and celibacy, to promiscuity, criminality, and female masculinity – gave way in the early 1970s to an overly determined relation: the feminist-as-lesbian. As a figure that explicitly symbolized the radical feminist critique of heterosexuality, marriage, and the family claim, the feminist-as-lesbian also helped make public the domain of 'the personal' as the site of women's sexual and psychic subjugation. This projection of a politicized lesbianism, and the claim to a commonality of women's experiences it tended to assume and enact, however, also made 'the personal' the scene of disagreement and debate among feminists and between white women of the Global North and Black women and women of colour of the Global North and South.

For example, making sex public for Black women and women of colour often entailed the threat of their continuing objectification and abjection in a white-dominated world. At the same time, the sexualization of the public sphere in the 1960s and the 1970s also provided cultural imaginings of and by Black and Brown female sexual subjects that expanded the possibilities of an explicitly racialized sexuality. The US blaxploitation films starring Pam Grier in the early 1970s conjoined an assertive Black female sexuality with the iconography of an unapologetic Black nationalism. Similarly, hard-core pornography of the 1970s 'Golden Age' era included films with an all-Black cast and offered stories for their multi-racial audience that were as much about the fictionalization and performance of race as they were about sex. Watching the explicit sexualization of the Black female body provided the opportunity for Black women to take pleasure in 'the ecstatic possibilities of racialization' as much as it provided them with an opportunity to critique or oppose their objectification through disidentification. By understanding representations of the sexualized Black female body as generative of a contradictory and complex iconography, Black feminist theory scholars such as Jennifer Nash have expanded the politics of sexuality in Black and women of colour feminism. Rather than understand themselves as simply the victims of objectification and abjection, Black and Brown women might also enact and enjoy a proprietary performance and consumption of their own racialized sexuality.[44]

Across the globe, feminists faced diverse social and political contexts that determined forms of resistance, though the links between social and sexual

---

44 Jennifer Christine Nash, *The Black Body in Ecstasy: Reading Race, Reading Pornography* (Durham, NC: Duke University Press, 2014), 3.

autonomy meant that feminism and lesbianism remained intertwined. In France, for example, the *Mouvement de libération des femmes* provided a safe space for lesbians to come out in the 1970s.[45] Yet the personal costs of coming out varied substantially. Lesbian feminists in the former East Germany in the 1980s took advantage of their more privileged position between the freer democratic western Europe and more restrictive socialist eastern Europe to create networks for women across political lines.[46] In the dictatorships in Latin America in the 1970s and the 1980s, in contrast, feminists and lesbians risked violence and death in pursuing freer lives.[47] Feminist movements across the world nevertheless faced the same challenges of integrating concerns of race and class with those of gender: in the UK, the movement fractured over issues of immigration, religious fundamentalism, poverty, and conflict with police, which affected women of colour much more than white women.[48] In Latin America, Indigenous and lesbian feminists challenged the dominant liberal feminism over its resistance to incorporating issues of race, sexuality, and class, and called for a wider and more complex feminism.[49]

The question of sexual autonomy – what it is and for whom – continues to shape feminism today, for lesbians and all women-identified people: in the United States and United Kingdom, in Malaysia and the Philippines, in Namibia and South Africa, in Costa Rica and Chile.[50] From the #MeToo movement to the confrontations between transphobic and pro-trans feminisms, to the ongoing fights for reproductive justice, the contestation of the category 'women' and how women understand the cultural and social possibilities for their self-fashioning as sexual and gendered subjects, set the parameters for feminism as a transnational project of social transformation. The feminist-as-lesbian emerged as a consequence of the politicization of sexuality by radical feminists in the 1970s. She also became a type, a figure,

45 Christine Bard, 'Lesbianism as Political Construction in the French Feminist Context', in *The Women's Liberation Movement: Impacts and Outcomes*, ed. Kristina Schulz (New York: Berghahn, 2019), 157–77.

46 Maria Bühner, 'The Rise of a New Consciousness: Lesbian Activism in East Germany in the 1980s', in *The Politics of Authenticity: Countercultures and Radical Movements across the Iron Curtain, 1968–1989*, ed. Joachim C. Häberlen, Mark Keck-Szajbel, and Kate Mahoney (New York: Berghahn Books, 2019), 151–73.

47 Juanita Diaz-Cotto, 'Lesbian-Feminist Activism and Latin American Feminist *Encuentros*', in *Sexual Identities, Queer Politics*, ed. Mark Blasius (Princeton, NJ: Princeton University Press, 2001), 73–95.

48 Sheila Jeffreys, *The Lesbian Revolution: Lesbian Feminism in the UK, 1970–1990* (London: Routledge, 2018), esp. ch. 8.

49 See Ángela Ixkic Bastian Duarte, 'From the Margins of Latin American Feminism: Indigenous and Lesbian Feminisms', *Signs* 38, no. 1 (2012): 153–78.

50 See Monika Reinfelder, ed., *Amazon to Zami: Towards a Global Lesbian Feminism* (London: Cassell, 1996).

that simultaneously limited the implications of that politicization. As a figure imagined and depicted as a particular type of woman, the feminist-as-lesbian could not represent the complexity of sexuality as a conglomeration of psychological feelings, social and economic relations, and cultural values, nor could she adequately symbolize the meaning of sexual and social autonomy for all women. Yet, today, she also works as an apparition, to borrow Terry Castle's term for the cultural presence of the lesbian in modernity, of feminism's effective contestation of heterosexuality as the basis for women's legibility and viability as social subjects. By making the personal political and through her projection of social autonomy, the feminist-as-lesbian participated in the production of an idea of sex liberated from the social contract and from the gender binary – of sex for pleasure rather than reproduction, and for friendship, community, and social transformation rather than coupledom. If these ideas remain aspirational or partial in their ambition for many feminists today, they nevertheless form an important legacy in the ongoing and expansive struggle for women's social and sexual freedom.

Further Reading

Bullock, Julia C., Ayako Kano, and James Welker. *Rethinking Japanese Feminisms.* Honolulu: University of Hawai'i Press, 2018.

Castle, Terry. *The Apparitional Lesbian: Female Homosexuality and Modern Culture.* New York: Columbia University Press, 1995.

Cott, Nancy F. *The Grounding of Modern Feminism.* New Haven, CT: Yale University Press, 1987.

Doan, Laura. *Fashioning Sapphism: The Origins of Modern English Lesbian Culture.* New York: Columbia University Press, 2001.

Duarte, Ángela Ixkic Bastian. 'From the Margins of Latin American Feminism: Indigenous and Lesbian Feminisms'. *Signs* 38, no. 1 (2012): 153–78.

Gerhard, Jane. *Desiring Revolution: Second-Wave Feminism and the Rewriting of Twentieth Century American Sexual Thought.* New York: Columbia University Press, 2001.

Hartman, Saidiya. *Wayward Lives, Beautiful Experiments: Intimate Histories of Riotous Black Girls, Troublesome Women, and Queer Radicals.* New York: W. W. Norton, 2019.

Halperin, David M. *How to Do the History of Sexuality.* Chicago: University of Chicago Press, 2002.

Hesford, Victoria. *Feeling Women's Liberation.* Durham, NC: Duke University Press, 2013.

Hobson, Emily K. *Lavender and Red: Liberation and Solidarity in the Gay and Lesbian Left.* Berkeley, CA: University of California Press, 2016.

Jagose, Annamarie. *Orgasmology.* Durham, NC: Duke University Press, 2012.

Kahan, Benjamin. *The Book of Minor Perverts: Sexology, Etiology, and the Emergences of Sexuality.* Chicago: University of Chicago Press, 2019.

Lugones, Maria. 'Heterosexualism and the Colonial/Modern Gender System'. *Hypatia* 22, no. 1 (2007): 186–209.

Marcus, Sharon. *Between Women: Friendship, Desire, and Marriage in Victorian England*. Princeton, NJ: Princeton University Press, 2007.

Millett, Kate. *Sexual Politics*. 1970; New York: Ballantine Books, 1978.

Mitra, Durba. *Indian Sex Life: Sexuality and the Colonial Origins of Modern Social Thought*. Princeton, NJ: Princeton University Press, 2020.

Nash, Jennifer Christine. *The Black Body in Ecstasy: Reading Race, Reading Pornography*. Durham, NC: Duke University Press, 2014.

Penn, Donna. 'The Sexualized Woman: The Lesbian, the Prostitute, and the Containment of Female Sexuality in Postwar America'. In *Not June Cleaver: Women and Gender in Postwar America, 1945–1960*, ed. Joanne Myerowitz, 358–81. Philadelphia: Temple University Press, 1994.

Radner, Hilary, and Moya Luckett, eds. *Swinging Single: Representing Sexuality in the Sixties*. Minneapolis, MN: University of Minnesota Press, 1999.

Reinfelder, Monika, ed. *Amazon to Zami: Towards a Global Lesbian Feminism*. London: Cassell, 1996.

Rupp, Leila. 'Sexuality and Politics in the Early Twentieth Century: The Case of the International Women's Movement'. *Feminist Studies* 23, no. 3 (1997): 577–605.

Sang, Tze-Lan D. *The Emerging Lesbian: Female Same-Sex Desire in Modern China*. Chicago: University of Chicago Press, 2003.

Shigematsu, Setsu. *Scream from the Shadows: The Women's Liberation Movement in Japan*. Minneapolis, MN: University of Minnesota Press, 2012.

Smith-Rosenberg, Carroll. 'Discourses of Sexuality and Subjectivity: The New Woman, 1870-1936'. In *Hidden from History: Reclaiming the Gay and Lesbian Past*, ed. Martin Duberman, Martha Vicinus, and George Chauncey, Jr., 264–80. New York: New American Library, 1989.

Traub, Valerie. 'The Present Future of Lesbian Historiography'. In *A Companion to Lesbian, Gay, Bisexual, and Transgender Studies*, ed. George Hagerty and Molly McGarry, 124–45. Oxford: John Wiley, 2007.

Vicinus, Martha. *Independent Women: Work and Community for Single Women, 1850–1920*. Chicago: University of Chicago Press, 1985.

Weinbaum, Alys Eve, Lynn M. Thomas, Priti Ramamurthy, Uta G. Poiger, Madeline Yue Dong, and Tani E. Barlow, eds. *The Modern Girl around the World: Consumption, Modernity, and Globalization*. Durham, NC: Duke University Press, 2008.

Young, Damon R. *Making Sex Public and Other Cinematic Fantasies*. Durham, NC: Duke University Press, 2018.

18

Post-Colonialism and Sexuality

ANNE HARDGROVE

Post-colonialism arose as an interdisciplinary field following the meteoric impact of Edward Said's *Orientalism* (1978). Said argued that as the colonizing Occident or West created knowledge about the Orient or East, it projected its own fantasies and fears and created an image of overly sexualized colonized people. Post-colonialism also invites similar introspection into internal colonialism: of aboriginal peoples under settler colonialism, and people of colour in white-majority societies. As an analytical tool, post-colonialism is Janus-faced, looking towards the past and a reconsideration of colonialism as well as to the present in documenting and disentangling both colonial and decolonial roots of contemporary society. Post-colonialism examines the culture of colonialism by re-reading colonial texts through a decolonizing eye, providing tools to examine some dilemmas of post-colonial societies that are in part tied to their colonial roots. Literary scholars and literature have provided much cross-fertilization with historical scholarship, as both fields attempt to assess the biases and outcomes of colonial domination. This chapter very selectively outlines some of post-colonial scholarship's major contributions to understanding sexuality in colonial contexts, ranging from the Americas to Africa and Asia, and is organized roughly chronologically. The chapter attempts, in the spirit of post-colonialism, to identify and de-centre colonial metanarratives while offering insights into a spectrum of practices of resistance and accommodation.

Sexual and Early Colonial Encounters

Sexuality is not just a by-product of colonialism, but is at the heart of empire. So from post-colonialism's start, sexuality has been a major area of research and theory. The experience of sexuality under colonialism radically transformed ideas and practices concerning bodies, gender roles and identities, and sexual practices, for both colonized and colonizer, colony and metropole. During colonialism, and indeed well after, the Occident simultaneously created itself as a space of sexual purity and idealized domesticity, establishing itself as a norm in opposition to what was rendered sexually impure, uncivilized, or animalistic in the colonies. The colonial importation and imposition of certain 'civilizing' Christian ideas of sexual modesty and shame grafted unevenly onto local understandings. Europeans generally attempted to enforce heteronormativity (an assumption about their own society, selectively ignoring other behaviours), and stigmatized otherwise unremarkable and normalized sexual practices and ideas which might appear progressive or permissive today. Colonial rule also typically produced a culture of rape, wherein a phobia of white women being raped by Brown or Black men grew out of the very opposite of what happened generally, namely, the social acceptability of white men forcibly bedding women of colour. Colonialism itself can be described as a sexual conquest of the West over the rest, where 'manly' Europeans overpowered and emasculated 'effeminate' Others, offering them a false opportunity for respectability by accepting the violation.

Historically constructed ideas of sexual and racial purity formed an integral aspect of the methods by which politics, knowledge, and identity became enmeshed in colonial encounters, colonial governance, and colonial culture. Historical specificity is key. Cohabitations between colonizer and colonized in early periods of empire led to elaborate social stratification in some societies, and the production and policing of a colour line in others. Such relationships eventually became the basis of anti-colonial nationalisms. Across colonialisms, children born of interracial unions by their very existence represented a challenge to the colonial order. But different metropolitan societies found different solutions to interrace dilemmas, also varying by period. In the early English colonies, interracial children were generally enslaved, while the early Spanish colonies developed an elaborate system of social castes for interracial individuals. All systems of nomenclature and recognition of racially mixing systems at their very root share the intention of preserving the appearance of purity of European bloodlines, at least as much as possible.

Post-colonial scholarship has shown that colonialism and sexualities in the pre-modern and modern worlds were never monolithic, in time or in space or in scale. Most post-colonial theorists focus on British or French colonialism. Yet to examine these trends in isolation from earlier colonizations distorts many global contexts and histories. In the early modern era, Portugal and Spain were the earliest colonizers, followed by the Dutch, then Britain and France. The United States often dodges the formal label of colonizer. Yet US global interventions, and its internal colonization of captive and Indigenous peoples of colour within its own borders, arguably justify its inclusion in this narrative. In fact, most nation-states have exercised brutal practices of internal colonialization to discipline non-white or non-normative bodies, whose very presence resists incorporation into the sexual citizenship of the imagined national community.

Early Modern Colonialisms and Sexualities

Early modern empires are rich sites of historical investigation, important precursors to later colonialisms which have been more central to the postcolonial analysis. European royalty, sponsors of voyages overseas, were famously preoccupied by lineage and blood lines, even to the point of inbreeding. For ordinary people, detailed registers of marriages, births, and baptisms, documenting family lineages, were maintained by Christian church officials, a practice continued in colonial expansion. Highly selective interpretations of Christian morality created categories of normative sexual practices, denouncing sex outside of marriage and stigmatizing and criminalizing births outside of marriage, paid sex work, and 'unnatural' same-sex relations. Cross-dressing, non-conformity to gender stereotypes, nonheteronormative practices including masturbation and men having sex with men or women having sex with women – now understood as gender expression, identity, self-pleasure, and forms of queerness – were targeted by laws of church as well as state. European attitudes against non-normative sexualities came to the colonies, where they were met by local conventions often at odds with colonial moralities.

Early modern empires saw the creation of colonial trading networks, gradually expanded and formalized by treaties and conquest, and with them came the adoption of new forms of sexual understanding among colonizers and colonized. Indeed, the policing of sexuality through identity and sexual differences helped control local populations and build the bureaucracy of imperial states within the colonies. European men having sex with local, Indigenous, and/or enslaved women was an integral part of economic, political, and trade relations. Kerry Ward's *Networks of Empire* details how the forced labour practices of the Dutch East India Company trafficked humans between Batavia (modern Jakarta, Indonesia) and the South African Cape, profiting from the criminalization of large swaths of society, including some for sexual practices deemed deviant by the burgeoning colonial state. Post-colonial scholars, who have mostly focused on sexuality within the boundaries of a colonized nation and its metropole, have sometimes eclipsed major global historical movements, such as the massive European commodification of African people through slavery. Yet centuries of brutal European enslavement and transportation of African men and women in the transatlantic world, along with the attempted enslavement and genocide of Indigenous peoples in the Americas and Australia, fomented deep ideas about power, race, sexuality, and cultural superiority.

The end of colonialism throughout the Americas did not mark a sharp break with the rise of nationalism because largely the same set of Europeanized people stayed in power. In the Americas especially, nationalist myths enshrined romanticized accounts of an Indigenous woman serving as a translator or guide for the white conqueror, including Malintzin/Dona Marina/La Malinche for Mexico, and Pocahontas and Sacagawea for the United States. Such narratives created an archetypal figure of the female Indigenous collaborator as both mother and whore. Octavio Paz, referring to the fact that the historical La Malinche conceived a son by the conquistador Cortés, famously lamented that Mexican people are quite literally the unwitting children of rape. The agency of women to control or bargain their own sexuality under unequal power relations is doubtful. Ramon Gutierrez documents the restructuring of Pueblo culture in New Mexico with the arrival of the Spanish, noting how the Spanish rejected local attitudes and practices we might see today as progressive. Yet Mary Louise Pratt's theory of the contact zone reminds us that colonial domination was far from total. Pratt's work captures moments of resistance and accommodation on the part of the colonized, providing evidence that no conquest was ever complete or all-encompassing. This double-consciousness of colonial subjects between collaboration and resistance is a fruitful area of post-colonial research.

It is helpful to look across both centuries of time and space to discover what was unique about the ways that colonialism created nomenclature and boundaries about sexual knowledge and practices. Centuries of unevenly tolerant Moorish government in the Iberian peninsula saw limited inter-marriage between Jews, Muslims, and Christians. Muslim women were not allowed to marry Christian or Jewish men, although Christian or Jewish women could marry Muslim men by converting to Islam. After the last Moorish state was conquered by Christians in 1492, such inter-religious family lineages became a problem, and authorities increasingly insisted on 'purity of blood' (*limpieza de sangre*), meaning no Muslim or Jewish ancestors, for Christians seeking any social privilege. Similar conditions existed in early modern Portugal.

In the early modern era, Portugal and Spain were the earliest colonizers, and these notions were translated to the mixed European, Indigenous, and African populations of their colonies. Post-colonial thinkers often refer to colonial knowledge formation, by which they mean how ideas and ideologies were met not only with resistance but also with hybridity, syncretism, and mimicry. Under Portuguese and Spanish colonialism, sexual conquest, cohabitation, political power, and social identity went hand in hand. Ann Twinam describes how highly elaborate but localized systems of social hierarchies developed to describe the bi-racial offspring of African, Indigenous, and European parentage, and were important markers of social, religious, and political rankings. Bi-racial and multi-racial identities became formalized into thirty-two unique social categories, based on the purported amounts of Indigenous, European, and African ancestry in each. (One of these terms, *mestizaje*, denoting having half European and half Indigenous American ancestry, is now often used as a general term for mixed-race identity.) Portuguese observers of social stratification in India – practised according to clusters of family lineages – applied the word 'caste' (*casta*) to them, and it became the term used in Latin America for these racial categories.

Neither colonizer nor colonized was a blank slate. Ideas of sexuality within Latin American societies did not, of course, begin with colonization, but drew upon older histories. Aztecs, Mayas, and Incas – only the latest of Indigenous empires in the Americas – had their own sexual values and customs, and behind them were those of the earlier peoples of the Americas they were heir to. (See Chapter 9 by Rosemary Joyce in this volume.) Sexual knowledge developed in the uneven landscape of colonial cultures demonstrates how uneasily the old and new fit together. In many Indigenous American societies individuals born and raised in one gender identity might choose another. (See Chapter 14 by Jen Manion in Volume I of this work.) Indigenous languages had varied terms for such individuals, though we now use the general term 'two-spirit'. Yet such individuals became known in Spanish colonial society by the pejorative term *bardaxa* or *bardaje* (better known in French as *berdache*), a word implying sexual prostitute, derived from the Arabic word *bardaj*, meaning slave, in turn taken from Persian. This is not to say that all examples of *berdaches* should be celebrated as early forms of gender fluidity. One important insight of post-colonial thinking is to resist the temptation to translate and collapse categories across time and space. Prisoners of war were sometimes forced to become *berdaches* and clothe themselves as women, as a form of humiliation accompanying their punishment.

Sexual and racial purity literally mapped on locality, and cartography itself became part of a sexualized landscape. For the Spanish themselves, 'creole' and 'peninsular' were important demarcations of one's birthplace in the new or old world, respectively. The divide took on increased importance in the 1780s in the burgeoning independence movements. The Spanish governors sought to have top officials come exclusively from those born in Spain, to ensure that those new colonial-turned-national leaders would be full-blooded Europeans. After independence in Mexico in 1810, the political slogan 'Todos somos Mexicanos' ('We are all Mexicans') attempted to instil nationalism by blurring distinctions of birth right and parentage between citizens at a popular level. Intellectuals took their cultural cues less from Spain, and more from a new metropole, France, as the centre of intellectual and artistic production. It was a rejection of Spain, but not of its racial and sexual hierarchies, and throughout Mexico's independence era, European ancestry remained privileged over *mestizaje* and Indigenous.

Post-colonial scholars strategically take note also of silences, as evidence not that sexual relations across races did not occur, but that such relationships were not socially sanctioned. The early English conquest in North America and the Caribbean, like the Spanish, was oriented around settler colonialism. From the Mayflower on, many Europeans came in already-formed family units, as religious freedom seekers. Many more came individually and unmarried: as adventurers, indentured servants, soldiers, and convicts. As the English expanded the trafficking of African slaves for plantation work, sexual relationships between white male masters and enslaved Black women, however unequal, became normalized and ubiquitous. Indeed, other types of relationships were difficult to impossible: American slavers purposely divided people with shared languages to thwart rebellion, and ruthlessly divided families on the slave auction block. Unlike the Spanish, Anglo society formally recognized no offspring of bi-racial parentage. So expanding historical sources beyond the official archives, to incorporate inter-generational knowledge of kinship networks and modern genetic information, has helped historians bring such relationships to light.

As Ann Twinam outlines, the English language developed no words to describe the children of different racial backgrounds. Instead, the infamous 'one-drop' rule created a colour line in Anglo societies, optimizing for the benefit of white slaveowners the legal enslavement of bi-racial children and enslaved mothers. Prominent slave-owning politicians, including US presidents George Washington and Thomas Jefferson, went to extraordinary lengths to maintain their slave populations, including people who were their lovers and children. In practice, colourism – the granting of privilege based on skin tone – especially within the family, was the ultimate judge of future prospects. As Winthrop Jordan notes, individuals who could purchase their freedom and were light-skinned did pass into white society, though with a hefty price: the severing of social ties with Black-identified family.

The rape culture of slavery derived from American slavery created a societal norm of white men having sexual access to enslaved Black women. Yet it was Black people, both women and men, who were cast as hypersexualized. At the same time that white men routinely raped Black women, a widespread paranoia about Black men attacking white women became an established truth, with little substantial reality to back it up. White women were seen as the protectors and standard-bearers of whiteness, on whose virtue rested the fragile architecture of white supremacy. The discourse of white women being raped by Black men was a powerful trope, based upon a projection of white men's sexual conquest to Black male bodies. The unspoken logic was that Black men, given the opportunity, would surely ravish white women's bodies; because that is exactly what many powerful white men already did to Black women.

English expansion into India during the seventeenth and eighteenth centuries followed a pattern of single men migrating for employment with the British East India Company. Unlike their earlier counterparts in the Americas and elsewhere, early English colonists in India did not have religious conversion as a central concern. The earliest Europeans living in India under employment of the East India Company were also quite different from their later 'British Raj' counterparts of the nineteenth and early twentieth centuries. They were deeply integrated into Indian society – men adopted local clothing, spoke Indian languages, sometimes converted to Islam or lived as Hindus, cohabitating and sometimes marrying local women and having children with them. English colonial servants, particularly in princely states where the British ruled indirectly through local sovereigns, lived as prominent people in their local environment and adopted traditional signs of social status, with some men keeping harems.

This British colonial experience in India saw extensive coupling of English and Scottish men with female Indian *bibis*, legal or common-law wives of East

India Company officials. Postmodern scholars have sought to bring these unexpected relationships to light. Durba Ghosh's research on legal wills shows that at least one-third of European men in India through the late 1700s had Indian wives. Children born of such unions presented awkward choices. Fathers who were affluent enough, and whose children were light-skinned enough, sometimes sent their children to live with relatives and take their places in England. William Dalrymple's fascinating research focuses on James Kirkpatrick, a British regent for the princely state of Hyderabad, who married a highly ranked Muslim princess; his children were sent to Britain for school and to live, separated from their heartbroken mother. Many mixed-race offspring of dual Indian-British parents remained in India, however, they and their descendants eventually becoming an ethnic community of Anglo-Indians. Anglo-Indians were frequently met with social derision, their very existence seen as an offensive affront to the endogamous sensibilities of both British and Indian elite.

Inventing Sexuality in the Metropoles

It was not just in colonized places where sexuality changed. Post-colonial studies recognize that metropoles, along with colonies, were themselves transformed from the colonial encounter. Within the metropole, as in the colony, intersections of race and sexuality reflected the dynamics of colonial pasts and presents. To be sure, the European homelands of the colonizers were themselves never pristine white spaces. Michael Fisher traces how Indians had travelled and lived in Britain since at least 1600, that is, for as long as the British had organized their own forays to India. Centuries of East Indian Bengali sailors, known as *lascars*, worked on sailing vessels between Asia and Europe. Some Lascars settled in the British Isles, marrying British women and integrating into British society. Native Americans also travelled and settled in Europe. Matoaka, the historical Pocahontas, was baptized under the name Rebecca, married the settler John Rolfe, and returned with him to England in 1616. Even European royalty included non-white court-iers – and possibly more. France's Louis XIV's wife Maria Theresa of Spain (1638–83) had as a close confidant the African man Nabo, with whom she is rumoured to have had an illegitimate daughter, eventually sent off to live in a convent. Queen Victoria herself had Abdul as an advisor, confidant, and close friend. Any representations of Europe as exclusively white are certainly excluding evidence to the contrary.

By critically examining the language of these colonial encounters, in the metropoles as well as by authorities in the colonies, post-colonial scholars have made critical interventions in the intersections of colonialism and sexuality, seeing colonial rule as being a productive space of knowledge, including knowledge of sexuality. Commonly accepted 'facts' – or unsubstantiated rumours – derived from the colonizer's view of the world are now to be understood as situated within a context of both subjugation and resistance. This focus on colonial discourse – ways of speaking, simply put – has led to breakthroughs in issues of subjectivity, agency, and accommodation and in recognizing anti-colonial actions and thinking.

Some of the most path-breaking work on sexuality in post-colonial studies places both metropole and colony under a single analytical lens. Ann Laura Stoler fruitfully argues that the colonies served as metropolitan laboratories of modernity – that the shaping of colonial societies through legislative action and attempts at social hegemony prefigured similar shifts in the societies of the colonizers. At the same time, the metropoles became distorted mirrors of modernity, juxtaposed as 'pure' and 'ideal' societies against exoticized representations of 'primitive' and 'savage' life in the colonies.

In review essays such as this, individual lives can easily become eclipsed by theoretical language and generalizations. So I wish to look at the life and death of Saartje Baartman, who has emerged as perhaps *the* key symbol of sexuality and post-colonialism. From the time of her birth in the 1770s until about 1810, Sara Baartman lived an ordinary existence in Southern Africa. Like many Khoekhoe tribal women, Sara became a mother and worked to support herself. But the last five years of her life thrust Sara onto a global stage. She was taken to England and exhibited as an object of racialized sexual difference in London's Piccadilly Circus as the 'Hottentot Venus'. ('Hottentot' was an ethnic slur for Khoekhoe, while 'Venus' referred to her exotic sexuality as seen through Western eyes.) Like many colonial subjects, we know little about Sara's own view of her situation: we do not know if she was free or enslaved, and we do not know if she had any choice in her display.

Baartman's exhibition says much more about the British than about her or her people. The British had ended their slave trade in 1807, although slavery continued to 1834. The people of London would have been very familiar with Black people, mostly from their own enslaved domestic and factory labour, though also with free African Americans and Caribbeans. Some might have seen performances of Shakespeare's play *Othello*, its leading role played always by white actors made up to look like Africans (though in 1814 played for the first time with a 'tawny' skin tone make-up to much controversy), and a character that was both hypersexualized and criminalized, with the play thus serving as a warning not to let dark-skinned others into polite society.

Sara's body was rendered exotic and erotic due to her prominent breasts and hips and elongated vaginal labia, which produced a sensationalized, sexualized, and racialized difference in the gaze of her audiences. The exhibition of Sara occurred in the context of public displays of flora and fauna from Britain's colonies, along with anatomically different people from Britain's own society. Audience members jeered and gawked at Sara, who bristled against such insults. Some men went as far as poking her body with their walking canes, along with women who jabbed at Sara with their parasols. In hindsight, these Britons were being educated not just on the appearance of an ethnic Khoekhoe woman, but also in learning to see the colonized dark body as inferior and overly sexualized. The exhibition of Sara Baartman was billed at the time as a scientific, sexual, and racial wonder. Here was a woman whose sexual organs, breasts, and buttocks provided audiences with a living spectacle of the differences between white and black.

By displaying Baartman as an anatomical specimen, her exhibitors staged literal performances of European mastery over colonized people. Most European intellectuals perceived the world at that time as being scaled according to degrees of civilization and superiority, with ideas about racial, intellectual, and sexual difference being primary criteria of judging whether societies ranked higher-up or lower-down. The Khoekhoe people on the South African frontier had been enslaved and coerced into forced labour under Dutch and then British colonialism. In fact, Cape Colony was only definitively conquered by the British in 1806, and was just beginning to be developed as one of the newest colonial holdings, and that meant the removal or enslavement of the Khoekhoe who lived there.

Capitalism was a driving force in the people who bought, sold, shipped, and displayed Sara. Her procurers hoped to profit from the sale of tickets to public exhibitions, and ultimately the commodification of her body. Sara was first displayed in the Slave Lodge in Cape Town, before being sold and relocated to London. She appeared in numerous exhibitions, where people paid two pence for a chance to view her. Sara later was displayed in similar exhibitions in Paris, where she died. Sara's death did not mean the end of the commodification and display of her body. The exhibition of her body, as a marker of sexual difference, would extend well beyond her live display on stage. After Sara's death her body was dissected, and her sexual organs reproduced in moulded casts. These body casts along with her skeleton stayed on display to the public until the late 1970s before being relegated to storage. In fact, her remains held at the Museum of Man (Musée de l'homme) in Paris were classified as 'animal' – a sad reminder of how she had been treated as less than human. Only in 2002, nearly 200 years after her death, were Sara Baartman's remains finally returned to South Africa. (For more on Baartman, see Chapter 11 by Jennifer Boittin in Volume I of this work.)

The display of Sara Baartman was not the first incident of the colonial fixations on sexuality, and nor does Sara herself represent an essential prototype. Nonetheless, her story provides us with some of the underlying post-colonial themes of the commodification of sexuality. As British audiences were schooled to see dark skin and colonized bodies as overtly sexualized, they also learned new ways to see themselves. By projecting their fears and desires onto an exoticized and eroticized body, they learned to see themselves – and their whiteness – as superior, cultured, chaste, and beautiful compared with the people Europeans colonized. The exhibition of Sara served to contextualize physiological difference as hierarchical and representative of the relative levels of civilization. By exhibiting someone as a prototype of a people and as an example of manufactured difference, the audience's gaze also reflected back on themselves, as being superior and setting a civilizational norm. Exhibitions of sexualized colonial subjects such as Sarah Baartman created literal displays of white mastery over Brown and Black bodies.

Legislating Sexuality

As colonialism evolved to more direct local rule, especially in the nineteenth century, anxieties over sexuality became fertile grounds upon which colonial legislation was enacted and colonial identities were formed. Debates over polygamy, dowry, child marriage, widows, clitoridectomy, prostitution, and sodomy became a part of both criminal and civil legal codes. These legislative efforts had both intended and unintended effects in terms of shaping identities and creating criminalities. Ultimately, the regulation of sexuality through the power of the colonial state helped to hypersexualize colonial subjects and to foster metropolitan superiority.

British India provides an excellent example of these processes at work. European colonial rule lasted throughout the nineteenth century there, unlike most parts of Africa and Asia, and the size of the colony – it includes the modern nations of Bangladesh, India, Myanmar, Pakistan, and Sri Lanka – means that its government extended over a large and diverse population. The British government took direct control of the region from the East India

Company in 1858. It is considered the start of the British Raj, which lasted until 1947. Even before the Raj, British military forces took increasing control of all parts of the region, Christian missionaries were increasingly active, and British-run administrations were growing in complexity.

British India provides an excellent example for another reason: some of the canonical texts in post-colonial studies focus on the region. Lata Mani's and Gayatri Spivak's work on *sati*, a word used to mean the burning of widows but which literally means the widow herself, show how the practice became a 'contentious' point, to use Mani's word, between colonizer and colonized over the question of a widow's sexuality. The danger was that a widow might move property from her first marital family to a second marital family if she remarried. If she did not remarry, her marital family had to continue to support her, though she no longer provided a tangible benefit to them. Through *sati*, a once-rare religious ritual, the otherwise sexually available widow was turned into a goddess by immolating herself on her husband's funeral pyre – and, once dead, she was no longer a social or economic problem. Spivak's early work centred on the role of the subaltern, that is, the groups silenced and denied agency in past colonial societies and in the historical sources written in and preserved from these societies. The administrators of British rule in India prioritized texts over practice, and these texts almost always presented only high-caste Brahman perspectives to the exclusion of other groups. The debates over *sati* were argued – inscribed, metaphorically – onto the bodies of women, without ever asking women for their thoughts. Control over women's bodies through the regulation of *sati* became a politicized debate between Westernized views of individuality and Hindu views of traditional religious practice. Spivak's own answer to her question 'Can the Subaltern Speak?' was ultimately that no, a *sati*'s voice could not be heard through colonial archives. Academic interlocuters – trained in reading across the grain through postmodern analysis – would have to speak for her.

Throughout the nineteenth century, the British passed increasing numbers of laws intended to reform Indian society, particularly women's sexuality, though often with injurious effects. Indian reformer and journalist Rammohan Roy (1772–1833) was among the early champions of the ban on *sati*. Roy came from a Bengali family of *kulin* Brahmans, whose ideas of endogamy were extreme. Families married off *kulin* daughters as babies to *kulin* grooms, even if they had married before, in order to assure that proper marriage laws were followed. Some *kulin* men had dozens of wives, and might meet them on only very rare occasions. Roy worked within his *kulin* community to reform such practices, which made him aware of issues related to widows generally. Textual evidence was again considered paramount, and Hindu scriptures were scrutinized for arguments both pro and con. The British passed a highly ineffectual Hindu Widows' Remarriage Act in 1856, appeasing wealthy families by allowing widows to remarry only as long as any immovable property did not change hands, and the widow's original marital family's wealth and property holdings remained intact. As Lucy Carroll shows, however, the impulse for the Act came from India's high-caste Brahman families only, for whom wealth transfer was a deal-breaking concern. For the majority of Indians outside the Brahman caste, the taboo on widow remarriage never existed. Instead, widow remarriage and property transfer were the norms. After the law passed, though Brahman widows continued rarely to remarry, most other widows were impoverished, because the law forbade them to keep any assets upon remarriage, and *sati* provided a means of escaping a life of poverty.

Other British laws disadvantaged women. Veena Talwar Oldenburg's work on dowry in the Punjab region of colonial India documents the disparaging language used by colonial officials in describing the elaborate weddings and dowries that were common. Oldenburg masterfully connects the increase in marriage expenses to changing terms of colonial land tenure, which lacked flexibility in case of calamity, and drove many families to foreclosure. Dowry is a transfer of wealth from the bride's family to the groom's family upon marriage, ostensibly remaining the bride's property, although Oldenburg demonstrates that, in practice, that was rarely the case. As the British implemented higher and less flexible taxation schemes, real and prospective land foreclosures increased family reliance on dowries as a stable source of income to help avoid insolvency. Oldenberg's other work on the courtesans of the northern city of Lucknow illustrates a similar brushstroke of colonial influence. Women courtesans, once recognized as an educated, property-owning, and profit-earning group, saw their status change from elite performers to marginalized prostitutes.

Illicit sexualities have absorbed the attention of many postmodern scholars of India, because they often reveal internal inconsistencies in colonial regimes. European colonists often established, organized, and maintained official military-serving brothels for its soldiers throughout the nineteenth century, for example. In British India, military divisions procured and coerced young women and girls, who often came from very poor families in rural areas. These military-run brothels were entirely under the aegis of the colonial state, which did everything from recruitment to establishing prices for various sexual acts. The business of sex for pay was both informal and formal. A major legislative effort of the colonial state, echoing policies in the metropole but devised specifically for the colonial context, was the control and surveillance of the native prostitute. This control was reinforced by the implementation of the Contagious Diseases Acts of 1864, 1866, and 1869, as shown by Philippa Levine. Across the British Empire, troops had fallen ill with sexually transmitted ('venereal') diseases, rendering them unfit for the physical demands of soldiery. Yet military commanders put the onus against disease spread onto the sex workers. Sex workers were confined to certain areas, subject to involuntary inspections, often in public places such as railway platforms, and could be detained to order to receive treatment.

In British India, as in most colonial societies, the importation of anti-sodomy laws helped spread prejudice against same-sex love. Post-colonial scholars working on queer sexualities have demonstrated how colonial legislation against same-sex desire and acts planted the seeds of homophobia among the colonized. Anjali Arondekar investigates queer archival sites of sexuality in her innovative research, using examples from colonial India. Pornography, law, anthropology, and literature worked together to produce sexual knowledge at the same time as it silenced, disciplined, and limited queerness and other sexualities deemed outside of social norms. As Arondekar writes, explorer, and eventual co-founder of the London Anthropological Society, Captain Richard Burton's reporting about the boy-brothels of the western port city of Karachi got him expelled from the British army. This was perhaps because he seems to have had sex with some of the boys there, though he claimed he had been commanded to write the report, and after he submitted it in 1845 all copies were destroyed. Burton's life work helped launch the academic discipline of anthropology, even while it demonstrated the uneasy nature of colonial knowledge of sexuality.

Burton's story reminds us that besides attempting to justify European rule by virtue of the need to civilize sexually deviant colonial subjects, one of the most fraught concerns of colonial governance was to tame the unsettled margins of its own populations, to hide away misfits who might blemish any appearance of European supremacy. Ideas of sexual normalcy and sexual deviance for Europeans, too, were in part fashioned in the colonies. Arondekar also examines the lawsuit brought against a gender-variant entertainer identified only as Khairati in 1884, a resident of a village in the Moradabad district of northern India. Khairati was likely a *hijra*, the public entertainers born and raised male but who chose female lives for themselves, known for bringing congratulatory blessings to auspicious events, such as weddings or the birth of a child. Jessica Hinchy explores the British colonial approach to *hijra* in more detail. Located outside of normative procreative heterosexuality, North Indian *hijra* were made subject to legislation of 1871, the Registration of Criminal Tribes and Eunuchs. Disparaged as ungovernable and amoral, *hijra* were seen as corrupting public spaces with obscenity. *Hijra* structures of kinship, of guru and disciple relationships, were equated with forms of slavery. Educated upper-middle-class Indian men, writing editorials to newspapers, echoed the colonial libellous stereotypes that *hijras* kidnapped, castrated, and enslaved Indian boys. Colonial knowledge of *hijra*, like all forms of sexuality, was shaped by elite members of Indian society, albeit with certain differences. Hinchy maintains that while Indian elite commentary on *hijra* engaged in critique and disparagement, the level of moral panic was far less compared with that expressed about courtesans and prostitutes. In writing post-colonial histories of gender-variant communities, Hinchy draws upon translation and transgender studies to consider the 'compulsion' of using universally translatable terms, which flattens out the cultural richness and historical specificity of gender and sexual identities.

Sexuality and Anti-Colonial Nationalisms

While resistance to colonial rule existed throughout the colonial era, anti-colonial nationalist movements challenged colonial rule, especially from the 1920s on. They were in part practical movements for political independence – and while the earliest colonies had achieved independence long before that, and some still exist, most colonies around the world gained independence between the late 1940s and the 1960s. Anti-colonial nationalism was also a philosophical movement, and its proponents debated the role of violence in gaining independence, the tensions between different ethnic and religious groups within post-colonial states, and democracy as a model for government – they also reflected on the legacy of colonialism on local societies, including colonial re-shaping of sexual values and traditions.

Post-colonial scholars have identified how anti-colonial nationalists challenged the discourse of colonial masculinity woven throughout European rule, for example. Kristen Hoganson documents the contrasts created in the US press during the Spanish-American war (1898) between the chivalrous American male and the degraded, even degenerate, Cuban and Filipino males as pretexts for the US annexation of the Cuba and the Philippines. Mrinalini Sinha shows how British colonial rule in the region of Bengal, India, gendered colonizer and colonized as 'manly' Europeans versus 'effeminate' Bengalis.

The same contrasts existed in colonial Australia between settlers and Indigenous populations; post-colonialism has rendered visible how the colonized subject across the globe was rendered weak, feminized, and powerless vis-à-vis the strong, commanding, and masculine European.

Sinha's more recent work moves from the late nineteenth century into the early twentieth, through an analysis of gendered themes in Katherine Mayo's *Mother India* (1927), a book written to counter the independence movement in India. Katherine Mayo (1867–1940), an American muck-raking journalist, represented a voice which was complicit in both endorsing white nationalism and propagating colonialism. Throughout her corpus of work, Mayo demonstrated a strong bias against minority populations, based on false and exaggerated dangers that people of colour posed to the public, through sexuality and public health. Mayo opposed both non-white and Catholic immigrants, as part of her ardent support for white supremacy. She particularly feared both Indian and Black immigration to the United States, championing Asian Exclusion Acts which prevented Chinese and other immigrants from obtaining citizenship rights. Mayo favoured strengthening police forces, portraying them as national heroes who protected white women from immigrant and Black Americans, who lacked self-control. And she supported US involvement in the Philippines on the basis that the people were incapable of ruling themselves. In *Mother India*, Mayo attempted to show how backward India was in its treatment of women, and that Indian men could not therefore be trusted to run their own country. Mayo's mischaracterization of women in Indian society, particularly around issues of public health and hygiene, led her to argue that the ultimate problem was Hindu men's unbridled sexuality, which lay at the root of India's ills: child marriage, rape, prostitution, venereal disease, homosexuality, and an overall inability for self-rule. Similar arguments were made about Chinese, African, and Indigenous Australian men's treatment of women – and always to the same effect: justifying white supremacy and the continued need for colonial rule.

Mahatma Gandhi (1869–1948), probably the most famous anti-colonial nationalist, himself joined into the debates launched by Mayo. Gandhi represented a different model of masculinity than the feminized male of colonial discourse, or the hypersexualized male of Mayo's book. He famously embraced celibacy. Control of desire, Gandhi maintained, would render Indians fit to rule their own nation. Gandhi's sexuality was not without its own contradictions: his wife opposed his vow, and in his seventies he slept naked with young women, including his own grandniece, to test his self-control. Joseph's Lelyveld also described Gandhi's close relationship with a friend Herman Kellenbach, with whom Gandhi lived for a year in South Africa. (Though Lelyveld's book does not use words 'gay' or 'bisexual', the legislature in Gandhi's home state of Gujarat was quick to ban the book, showing that the legacy of colonial attitudes against homosexuality runs deep within modern Indian political discourse.) Anti-colonial masculinities often ignored women's self-determination. Sun Yat-sen (1866–1925), leader of the Chinese revolt against the European-dominated Qing emperors, had two wives simultaneously and at least three concubines. Ho Chi Minh (1890–1969), an advocate and fighter for Vietnamese independence from France, married a Chinese woman in 1926, saying he needed someone 'to keep house'. Nonetheless, these new figureheads for nationalist manhood offered symbols of strength and self-determination to their supporters.

The rhetoric of cultural superiority and inferiority worked not only to diminish and dismiss the possibilities for self-rule in colonies but also for self-government among Indigenous peoples within countries. Settler colonialism, such as took place in twentieth-century United States, Canada, and Australia, sought to break up, and in Margaret Jacob's word, 'pathologize', Indigenous families. Aboriginal and Native American children were removed from their mothers and families and placed in boarding schools. As Jacobs notes, the very presence of Indigenous peoples served as an impediment to the imagined racial purity of white cultures. Removing children was an attempt to separate people from their land and from the kinship networks which tied people to homelands, cloaked in the language of assimilation. Residential schools attempted to 'uplift' Indigenous children, taken forcibly from their families, with white culture. White women found power by participating in these removal strategies, staffing residential schools and using Indigenous domestic servants in their homes. As discoveries of mass graves on the grounds of Indigenous boarding schools attest, though, strategies of forced removal were an essential part of the white genocide of local inhabitants.

The cult of domesticity for white and wealthy households that typifies white societies in the first half of the twentieth century stands in stark contrast to the dismantling of families who did not fit the racial and class definitions of civilization. As in colonial societies, women of colour were often marked as instigators of sexual immorality, ignoring the government policies that undermined Indigenous family cohesion and economic self-sufficiency and drove these women into casual sexual relationships and sex work, and ignoring, too, the white men who were the likelier sexual predators.

The mid-twentieth century brought a major world war and eventual end to colonialism in much of the world. The conflicts of this era provide examples of how militaries contended with the sexual drives of soldiers, providing outlets ranging from military leave to organized brothels to the sexual abuse of women and men in their own ranks. Military officials often reasoned that official brothels limited the amount of sexual violence on the general population, controlled the spread of sexually transmitted diseases in order to keep soldiers' health robust, and kept morale high, even though these benefits came at the expense of local populations. Japan's horrific exploitation of Korean and Taiwanese 'comfort women' during the Second World War has become a key focus of scholarly activism and criticism, perhaps because living survivors hoped for recognition, if not justice. The Japanese imperial army maintained a notorious system of brothels for its soldiers. Women in regions under Japanese rule were recruited, often forcibly, to serve as sex slaves for soldiers, and known as 'comfort women', a Japanese euphemism for prostitute. The unwillingness and reluctance of the Japanese government to acknowledge what had happened, claim responsibility, and issue an apology or reparations meant their existence was unrecognized until the 1980s and is still a matter of contention.

The violence of colonial independence is also only lately coming to light. The decision to splinter British India along religious lines between Muslims and Hindus at the end of colonial rule resulted in widespread violence across India but especially in Bengal and Punjab, two states divided, with parts of each joining both India and Pakistan. Uncertainty about the exact location of the border, communal tensions between Hindus, Muslims, and also Sikhs in Punjab, and the impending loss of immovable wealth created widespread anger, fear, and uncertainty. Men beating each other resorted to stripping their adversaries, to check for circumcised Muslims or uncircumcised Hindus. Over 100,000 women on each side of the border were raped by men of the 'other' religion, rendering them impure and tainted – unacceptable to their natal families and unmarriable in the eyes of others. Saadat Hasan Manto's *Khol Do* (*Open It*), published in 1948, is a sobering testament to the banality of rape in the partition. Only now are some details becoming known. Some families have admitted to oral historians the killing of female family members before the onslaught of violence, in an attempt to maintain the honour of the family. Some exploited women remained with their violators, choosing religious conversion to create kinship bonds since returning to their families, especially with children, was an impossibility. Extensive repatriation schemes launched by both India and Pakistan after the Partition, intended to return women to their rightful nation, were largely met with silence from the affected women, declining to uproot themselves from a settled domestic existence, however violent the origins.

Sexuality in the Post-Colony

By the late 1960s, most former colonies around the world had become independent, though a few remain to this day, especially in the Caribbean and Pacific. All former colonies struggled with reconciling rapid political and social changes with the legacy of colonial rule amid attempts to restore earlier native customs and cultures. Using examples mostly from Africa, where formal colonialism ended most recently, the continued impact of sexuality on national identity can be demonstrated.

The colonial era in Africa began mostly later than elsewhere, but as in the previous examples from Latin America and Asia, colonial governance in Africa was predicated upon and legitimized itself through the governance of sexuality, especially women's sexuality. A pioneering scholar is Anne McClintock. She argues that African colonies became theatres for the performance of imperialism and domesticity, reinforcing patriarchy and white supremacy. McClintock helpfully reminds us that as much as imperialism represented man's conquest of feminized spaces, this projection of European superiority contained many cracks, where reminders of the insecurities of colonial regimes are very much apparent. Other post-colonial scholars have followed this lead. Nancy Rose Hunt shows how colonialization in the Belgian Congo came with the same cult of white domesticity, where Africans were instructed to reinvent their lives along European models. But she characterizes the colony as 'a nervous state', obsessed with fertility and infertility, sexually transmitted diseases, medical interventions, and native healing. Lynn Thomas shows how women's bodies in Kenya became the site upon which the colonial regime sought self-legitimization, in particular, through control of reproductive technologies, including abortion access, premarital pregnancies, midwifery, and female genital cutting. And Luise White's study of prostitution in the colonial city of Nairobi, Kenya, shifts the emphasis away from the registration and regulation of colonial prostitution to an examination of how the colonial regime provided the context of both migrant labour in which prostitution flourished and how Kenyan women engaged in the casual labour of sex work as a means to support themselves and their families.

The era of independence offered a new model of colonial inhabitants as manly fighters, but displayed equal internal contradictions. Some, such as Kwame Nkrumah of Ghana, who had been educated in the United States and Britain, had sexual lives like those recommended by Europeans: he married Fathia Ritzk of Egypt, and they had three children. Others, such as Jomo Kenyatta of Kenya – who practised polygamy – led more traditionally African sexual lives. Most held to the philosophy sometimes called *négritude*, first formulated by French-speaking Black writers of the 1930s, and which by the 1960s was also known as the Black Consciousness Movement, and in the United States as Black Power, a reclaiming of pride in African cultural traditions and working against the colonial discourse on the culture inferiority of Africans. Despite the presence of many important women in the African independence movements, the rhetoric against the colonial contempt for African masculinity gave rise to exaggerated claims to manliness, even to a violent masculinity in the context of the wars of independence.

The appeal of a powerful hypermasculinity is not unique to Africans. Collected essays by Ronald Jackson and Murali Balaji include similar hypermasculinities at work in Jamaica, Peru, and Turkey. But it has had a major consequence for the policing of gay sexuality, particularly among men in post-colonial African nations. The colonial imposition of anti-sodomy laws served to stigmatize same-sex relations as amoral. In challenging the characterization of their societies as effeminate and weak, some African leaders continued to enforce colonial legislation, or introduced new laws based on ultraconservative Islamic traditions. And while many Christian denominations have denounced the homophobic Christian past, these African leaders have found moral and financial support from anti-gay American evangelicals, whose influence has grown in Africa in recent decades. Some post-colonial African nations, including Uganda, Mauritania, Sudan, and parts of Nigeria and Somalia, have instituted a death penalty when apprehending same-sex lovers, though not all have been actually executed for it. In total, thirty-six African nations have some laws against homosexuality, though twelve do not – and among those twelve, some have specifically decriminalized homosexuality in recent years: Lesotho, Mozambique, Angola, Botswana, and South Africa. Here, too, Africa is not unique. Post-colonial regimes in Iran, Saudi Arabia, and Yemen have introduced the death penalty for homosexual acts, and several others impose harsh prison sentences – most justified by anti-Western sentiment. The lives of gender and sexual non-conformists, like the lives of women, still bear the scars of colonialism.

Conclusions

Sexuality and post-colonialism has helped historians write new histories of the discipline and rule of sexual bodies under colonialism. Far from being only a process of economic extraction, colonialism shaped the ways that we see, know, and experience sexuality and race, gender, and nationality. Modern scientific techniques, especially in tracing DNA and genetics, provide separate confirmation of sexual relationships across cultures, slave societies, and colonizer and colonized. Among African Americans, common ancestors are found most often through the male lines of European heritage, confirming the ubiquity of widespread sexual relationships among white men and Black women. In some Indian and British families, DNA testing often confirms the family lore of English or Indian ancestors, respectively. The ubiquity of genetic connections through shared European ancestors, and the relative absence of African ancestors, is proof that sexual relations were unequal. White men had access to Black and Brown women's bodies, but there were very few if any relationships between Black and Brown men with white women. What science and genetics cannot answer, however, are infinite unanswerable questions of consent and desire, power and silence. Some maintain that DNA is evidence of rape, while other scholars argue that subjected women used their reproductive powers to move up socially, and tried for better conditions for their children. Unfortunately, the answer to Gayatri Spivak's provocative question, whether the subaltern sexual subject can speak, must remain no.

Post-colonial sexual modernity not only offers a critique of our colonial past, but also opens doors for new interpretations of tradition. Many people deploy post-colonial thinking in re-imagining cultural knowledge. In the twenty-first century, girls of Indian descent in countries across the globe train in classical dance traditions under the umbrella term of *bharatnatyam*. Whereas British once denigrated these dances as part and parcel of prostitution, post-colonial subjects have brought back once-scorned traditions. Training in Indian dance is a way of connecting with one's culture, and recitals for family and friends are often even offered in the social halls associated with Hindu temples, albeit for more of a debutante event showcasing the skill, beauty, and self-discipline of the student.

Post-colonialism continues to provide rich context and vocabulary and analytical tools for decolonizing knowledge and debate over sexual issues including same-sex marriages, transgender identities, sex as paid labour, and much more in formerly colonized societies and their metropoles, along with the internal colonization of Indigenous people and people of colour. Post-colonialism and sexuality make important contributions in dialogue with other areas of scholarly research, including feminism and intersectionality, migration, globalization, transnational history, spatial analyses, and nationalist revival.

Further Reading

Alter, Joseph. *Gandhi's Body: Sex, Diet, and the Politics of Nationalism.* Philadelphia: University of Pennsylvania Press, 2000.

Arondekar, Anjali. *For the Record: On Sexuality and the Colonial Archive in India.* Durham, NC: Duke University Press, 2009.

Butalia, Urvarshi. *The Other Side of Silence: Voices from the Partition of India.* Durham, NC: Duke University Press, 2000.

Dalrymple, William. *White Mughals: Love and Betrayal in Eighteenth-Century India.* New York: Viking, 2003.

Fisher, Michael, Shompa Lahiri, and Shinder S. Thandi. *A South Asian History of Britain: Four Centuries of Peoples from the Indian Subcontinent.* Westport, CT: Greenwood, 2007.

Ghosh, Durba. *Sex and the Family in Colonial India: The Making of Empire.* Cambridge: Cambridge University Press, 2008.

Gutierrez, Ramon. *When Jesus Came, the Corn Mothers Went Away: Marriage, Sexuality, and Power in New Mexico, 1500–1846.* Stanford, CA: Stanford University Press, 1991.

Hinchy, Jessica. *Governing Gender and Sexuality in Colonial India: The Hijra, c. 1850–1900.* Cambridge: Cambridge University Press, 2019.

Hoganson, Kristen L. *Fighting for American Manhood: How Gender Politics Provoked the Spanish-American and Philippine-American Wars.* New Haven, CT: Yale University Press, 1998.

Jackson, Ronald L., and Murali Balaji, eds. *Global Masculinities and Manhood.* Champaign, IL: University of Illinois Press, 2011.

Jacobs, Margaret. *White Mother to a Dark Race: Settler Colonialism, Maternalism, and the Removal of Indigenous Children in the American West and Australia, 1880–1940.* Lincoln, NE: University of Nebraska Press, 2011.

Jordan, Winthrop. *White over Black: American Attitudes toward the Negro, 1550–1812.* Durham, NC: University of North Carolina Press, 1968.

Lelyveld, Joseph. *Great Soul: Mahatma Gandhi and His Struggle with India.* New York: Alfred A. Knopf, 2011.

Levine, Philippa. *Prostitution, Race, and Politics: Policing Venereal Disease in the British Empire.* New York: Routledge, 2003.

Mani, Lata. *Contentious Traditions: The Debate on Sati in Colonial India.* Berkeley, CA: University of California, 2007.

McClintock, Anne. *Imperial Leather: Race, Gender and Sexuality in the Colonial Conquest.* New York: Routledge, 1995.

Mohanty, Chandra Talpade. 'Under Western Eyes: Feminist Scholarship and Colonial Discourses'. In *Feminist Postcolonial Theory: A Reader*, ed. Reina Lewis and Sara Mills, 49–74. Hoboken, NJ: Taylor and Francis, 2013.

Oldenburg, Veena Talwar. *Dowry Murder: The Imperial Origins of a Cultural Crime*. Oxford: Oxford University Press, 2002.

'Lifestyle as Resistance: The Case of the Courtesans of Lucknow, India'. *Feminist Studies* 16, no. 2 (1990): 259–87.

Pratt, Mary Louise. *Imperial Eyes: Travel Writing and Transculturation*. New York: Routledge, 1992.

Said, Edward. *Orientalism*. New York: Pantheon Books, 1978.

Sculley, Pamela, and Cliff Crais. *Sara Baartman: Publisher, Performer, Prisoner*. Cape Town: University of the Western Cape Press, 2007.

Sinha, Mrinalini. *Mother India*. Ann Arbor, MI: University of Michigan, 2000.

Spivak, Gayatri. *A Critique of Postcolonial Reason: Toward a History of the Vanishing Present*. Cambridge, MA: Harvard University Press, 1999.

Stoler, Ann Laura. *Tensions of Empire: Colonial Cultures in a Bourgeois World*. Berkeley, CA: University of California Press, 1997.

Thomas, Lynn M. *Politics of the Womb: Women, Reproduction, and the State in Kenya*. Berkeley, CA: University of California Press, 2003.

Twinam, Ann. *Public Lives, Private Secrets: Gender, Honor, Sexuality and Illegitimacy in Colonial Spanish America*. Stanford, CA: Stanford University Press, 1999.

Walsh, Judith. *Domesticity in Colonial India: What Women Learned When Men Gave Them Advice*. Lanham, MD: Rowman & Littlefield, 2004.

Ward, Kerry. *Networks of Empire: Forced Migration in the Dutch East India Company*. Cambridge: Cambridge University Press, 2009.

White, Louise. *The Comforts of Home: Prostitution in Colonial Nairobi*. Chicago: University of Chicago Press, 1990.

Index

Page numbers in *italics* refer to content in figures.

ABC of Married Life, The (1974), 350
Abina (Mansah), 165–6
Aboriginal Australians, 404
abortion, 289–90, 348, 350, 352, 355, 360, 362, 406
abstinence, 84, 345–6, 349, 362
Abu'l Fazl, 83
aclla women, 195
Adam and Eve narrative, 256–7, 277
adultery
  African traditions, 177
  ancient Egypt, 27, 38
  ancient Near East, 50, 51, 52–3
  Buddhism, 234, 235–6
  Christianity, 271
  Islam, 301–3
  Oceanic traditions, 208, 212
  pre-modern China, 130
  pre-modern Japan, 154
  socialism, 350
  South Asian traditions, 75, 80
Aeschines, 106
African traditions, 158–60
  adolescence, 161–3
  children and parenthood, 166–7
  elite alliances and politics, 168–70
  feminism, 368
  intimate partnerships, 171–4, 332
  marriage, 163–6, 168–9, 173–4, 176
  post-colonialism, 406–7
  power, healing, and danger, 174–8
Agathon, 106
age of consent, 83, 356
Ahmed, Leila, 309–10

AIDS Coalition to Unleash Power (ACT UP), 335, *336*
Ājīvika school of thought, 64
Ajootan, Aileen, 102
akam poetry, 78–9
Aki no Yo no Nagamonogatari (A Long Tale for an Autumn Night, 1377), 152
Alcman, *Partheneia*, 109
Alexander, Jacqui, 209
Alexeyeff, Kalissa, 226
Al-Ghazālī, *The Revival of the Religious Sciences*, 299
Al-Hibri, Azizah, 311
Alī ibn Nasr, *The Encyclopedia of Love*, 308
Ali, Kecia, 299, 300
Al-Jāhiz, 305
Al-Rāzī (Rhazes), *The Book of Coitus*, 307–8
American Psychiatric Association (APA), 333, 335, 337
Americas, colonial, 391–4
Americas, pre-colonial, 392–3
  Mexica and Maya in Mesoamerica, 185–94
  North American gender fluidity, 196–8
  queering Andean history, 195–6
  sources and biases, 181–5
Anacreon, 89–90
anal sex, 106, 127, 176, 212, 264, 265, 304
ancestral mating systems, 2–7
ancient Greece
  erōs in philosophy and medical texts, 91–6
  erōs in poetry, 88–91
  erotic imagery, 96–102, *98*
  female sexuality, 107–10
  male sexuality, 103–6, *105*
  slavery, 110–12

411

Index

ancient Near East, 43–6
  criminal law, 59–61
  gender norms and inequality, 51–2
  marriage, 52–4, 55–7
  politics and religion, 56–9
  reproduction, 46–8
  sexual bodies, 48–50
  slavery, 52, 54–6
ancient Rome
  erōs in philosophy and medical texts,
    93–4, 95–6
  erōs in poetry, 89, 91
  erotic imagery, 97–102, *99*, *100*, *103*
  female sexuality, 107–10
  male sexuality, 27, 103–6
  slavery, 110–12, 276
Andean traditions, 195–6
Andrews, Lorrin, 206
Anglo-Muhammadan law, 301
Angola, 176
Another Way (dir. Károly Makk, 1982), 356
Apocalypse of Peter (second century), 287
Appu narrative (Hittite text), 47–8
Aquinas, Thomas, 273, 279
  Summa Theologiae (1485), 280–1
Archilochus, 89
Argentina, 321, 325
Aristophanes, 101, 104, 107, 109, 111
Aristotle, 254, 280, 315
  The Generation of Animals, 95, 273
Arondekar, Anjali, 401–2
arranged marriage, 52, 163, 236, 358
ars erotica, 126, 131
Asaṅga, 240
Asante state, 174
Asante, Molefi, 407
Ascertaining the Vinaya: Upāli's Questions, 240
Asclepiades, 110
Åshede, Linnea, 102
Ashurbanipal, King of Assyria, 56
Aśvaghoṣa, *The Teaching on the Ten Non-*
  Virtues, 235
Aszódi, Imre, 352
Atharva Veda, 67–8, 69
Augustine of Hippo, 275–7, 279, 288, 289
Australia, 217, 337, 403, 404
Azande people, 332

Baartman, Sarah, 158, 396–8
Babur, Mughal emperor, 83
Badran, Margot, 310
Ba-Ila people, 163
Bantu people, 161, 162, 164, 168

Bara, Theda, 366
Barlas, Asma, 310
Barnes, Djuna, 372
Bártová, Dagmar, 357
bathhouses, 27–8, 98, *100*
Batwa people, 168
Bauer, Thomas, 294–5, 305
Beal, Frances, 'Double Jeopardy' (1970), 379
Beauvoir, Simone de, *The Second Sex*
  (1949), 378
Bebel, August, *Women and Socialism*
  (1879), 342
Bed and Sofa (dir. Abram Room, 1927), 348
bedchamber arts, 119–20, 125, 129, 131
Belgian Congo, 406
Bemba people, 174
Ben Azzai, Shimmon, 262–3
Benedict, Ruth, *Patterns of Culture* (1934), 331–2
Benjamin, Harry, 329, 333
Benjamin, Hilde, 352
Berenstein, Francis, 346
Besnier, Niko, 226
bestiality, 60, 69, 177, 301
bhakti spiritualism, 79
Biafran Igbo people, 169
Bible. *See* Christianity; Jewish traditions
biotypology, 321
birth control, 287–9, 350, 354–5
birth rates, 11, 344, 350, 354
bisexuality, 333
Black Woman's Alliance, 379
Bland, Lucy, 371
blaxploitation films, 384
Blood Bowl Sutra, 151, 154
Boas, Frank, 8
bodhisattvas, 239–40
bodies, sexual, 48–50, 69–70, 148–50, 245–6,
  274, 397. *See also* sexual science
body modification, 162
Book of the Dead, 30, 35
Booth, Charlotte, 25
Bossler, Beverly, 128
Boston Women's Health Collective (BWHC),
  334–5
Boudhiba, Abdalwahab, 297
Boyarin, Daniel, 268
Brahman caste, 399–400
Brahmanical traditions, 63–4, 67–8
Brazil, 284, 321, 337
bride service, 163–4
bridewealth, 163–5, 174
Britain, 286, 394–5, 396–8, 402
  legislation in India, 398–402

412

Index

brothels, 30, 111–12, 345, 400–1, 405
Brown, Helen Gurley, *Sex and the Single Girl* (1963), 376
Buddha, 69, 81, 228, 231, 234–5, 237
Buddhaghosa, 239
Buddhism, 64, 228–9
  altruistic sexuality in Mayahana texts, 239–40
  celibacy and *Vinaya* texts, 68–70, 230–4
  non-normative sexualities, 237–9
  pre-modern China, 122–3, 233–4
  pre-modern Japan, 137–8, 142, 144–50, 151–3, 234
  problem of sex, 229–30
  rules for lay people, 234–7
  Tantric sex, 81, 240–3
  Tibetan reformulations, 243–7
Buenos Aries, 325
Buganda, 166, 167, 170, 176
Bugwere Kingdom, 171
Burma, 325–6
Burton, Richard, 401
Busoga Kingdom, 166

Cabezón, José Ignacio, 237
Cakrasamvara Tantra, 242–3
Calvin, John, 287
Canada, 404
Cannon, John, 288
Cape Colony, 397
capitalism, 223, 342, 369, 379–80, 397
Carpenter, Edward, 324
Cārvākas school of thought, 64
caste systems, 72, 389, 392
Castle, Terry, 386
castration, 49–50, 299
Castro, Fidel, 360–1
Cato the Elder, 110, 112
celibacy
  African traditions, 170, 176
  Buddhism, 68–70, 230–4
  Christianity, 274–6, 279, 282, 285
  Islam, 298
  Jewish traditions, 262–3
  pre-colonial Americas, 187
  pre-modern Japan, 147
  South Asian traditions, 64, 68–70, 72, 84, 403–4
censorship, 129, 159, 348
Central Sabi people, 162, 164, 174, 177
challenge hypothesis, 16
chastity, 122, 123, 289–90
Chiang, Howard, 128–9, 202

chigo (acolytes), 151–3
Chikunda people, 177
child abuse, 290–1
childbirth, 141–2, 151, 317
childhood gendering, 186–7, 219, 328
child-rearing. *See* parenthood
Childs, Margaret, 152
China, modern, 325, 337, 358–9, 368–9, 373, 404
China, pre-modern
  Buddhism, 122–3, 233–4
  comparative histories, 131–3
  homoerotic relations, 123–4, 126, 129–30, 132
  institutions and practices, 119–24
  limitations in scholarship, 124–31
  terminology and epistemology, 115–19
Christianity
  antiquity, 271–9
  early modern world, 282–5, 390, 391–2
  homophobia, 132, 407
  medieval Europe, 279–82
  modern legacies, 286–91
  Oceanic traditions, 202–3
    Hawai'i, 203, 205, 206–9
    Papua New Guinea, 213–14, 216–17
    Samoa, 219–20, 222
Chumash people, 197
Church of England, 284
Cilappatikāram (fifth century), 78–9
cinema, 84, 348, 351, 356, 358, 374–5, 377
circumcision, 162, 322
class
  African traditions, 167
  ancient Near East, 55–6
  feminism, 374, 378
  Indigenous Americas, 189
  Oceanic traditions, 204–5, 218–19
  South Asian traditions, 74
Clement of Alexandria, 37, 275
clothing, 107–8, 148
Codex Mendoza (*c.* 1541), 186–7
cohabitation, 283–4, 362, 389
coitus interruptus, 287–8, 299, 355
colonialism, 284–5. *See also* Oceanic traditions; post-colonialism
  Africa, 165–6, 406
  Americas, 182–3, 391–4
  feminism, 368–9
  Islam, 301, 309
  South Asia, 83–4
Columella, 110
comfort women, 405
concealed ovulation, 5–6
concubines, 120–1, 300–1, 358

413

Index

Confucianism, 138–9, 153–4, 359, 362, 368
Congo, 317
consent, 38, 53, 233, 236, 281–2
consumerism, 369, 370
Contagious Diseases Acts (1960s), 401
contraception. *See* birth control
conversion therapy, 337, 357, 359
Cook, James, 202, 205
cooperative breeding, 14–16
Cott, Nancy, 369–70
creation myths. *See* mythology
Cuba, 359–61, 402
cultic practices, 58–9
cultural anthropology, 330–2
Culture and Personality school, 331–2

Dalrymple, William, 395
dance, 188, 408
Danhomè, 177
Daoism, 117, 123, 245
Darwin, Charles, 318–20
Davidson, James, 106
Davis, Kathy, 335
Day after Day (dir. Volker Koepp, 1979), 358
degeneration, 322–3
Demosthenes, 106
Demotic papyri, 23, 26, 29
Deng Xiaoping, 359
desire
 ancient Egypt, 24–8
 ancient Greece and Rome
  erōs in philosophy and medical texts, 91–6
  erōs in poetry, 88–91
  erotic imagery, 96–102, *98, 99, 100, 103*
  female sexuality, 107–10
  male sexuality, 103–6
  slavery, 110–12
 Buddhism, 230, 232, 237, 239–40, 247
 Christianity, 282
 Islam, 299
 Jewish traditions, 256–7
 pre-modern China, 117–18, 123, 132
 pre-modern Japan, 139, 142–3, 144–8
 socialism, 360, 362
 South Asian traditions, 63–4, 67, 71, 73–6
Dharmapadda, 234
Dharmaśāstras, 64, 71–3
Didache (first century), 289
Ding Ling, 'Miss Sophia's Diary' (1928), 373
division of labour, 7–8, 13
divorce
 ancient Near East, 55
 Christianity, 271, 282–3

Islam, 300, 301
 Jewish traditions, 258
 pre-modern China, 121
 pre-modern Japan, 153
 socialism, 347, 350, 354
Doan, Laura, 371
domination, 91, 103–4, 215–16, 223
Dorner, Gunter, 357
Dorr, Rheta Childe, 373
Dover, Kenneth, 87, 103–5
dowers, 298, 299–300
dowries, 120, 122, 400
Dumitriu, Radu, *De Vorba cu tinerii* (1972), 350
Dutch East India Company (VOC), 390–1

East India Company (EIC), 394–5, 399
Eastern Europe, 349–54
effeminacy, 37, 39–40, 273–4, 402–3
Egypt, ancient, 22–3
 desire and pleasure, 24–8
 homoerotic relations, 34–8, 39–40
 prostitution, 29–31
 public sex and festivals, 28–9
 representations of sex, 31–4
 sexual violence, 38–9
Egypt, modern, 326
El-Arish naos (Egypt), 39
Elbert, Samuel, 205
Eliezer, Rabbi, 253–4, 255–6, 265
Elkunirsha and Ashertu, 52
Ellis, Havelock, 210, 324, 330
 Man and Woman (1894), 320
Encratites, 274
endocrinology, 321, 326–8
endogamy, 72, 399
Enfantin, Barthélemy-Prosper, 341
Engels, Friedrich, 342
Engishiki (c. 927), 150–1
Epic of Gilgamesh, 43, 52
Epicureanism, 93–4
erotica
 ancient Egypt, 31–3
 ancient Greece and Rome, 96–102, *98, 99, 100, 103*
 ancient Near East, 49
 Indigenous Americas, 189–90, 195–6
 pre-modern China, 130
 South Asia, 64–7, 81–2
Esarhaddon, King of Assyria, 56
Etc. (Polish magazine), 351
Ethiopia, 168, 172–3
eugenics, 318, 320–1, 327
eunuchs, 49–50, 275

414

Index

Evans-Pritchard, Edward, 332
evolutionary legacy, 1–2
  ancestral mating systems, 2–7
  human mating cross-culturally, 8–11
  multi-male/multi-female societies, 7–8
  parenting and family systems, 11–16
evolutionary thinking, 317–20, 322–3
exogamy, 211
extra-pair paternity, 11

family. *See also* marriage; parenthood
  African traditions, 163–5
  Christianity, 282
  colonial societies, 399–400, 404, 405
  evolutionary legacy, 7–9, 11–16
  Islam, 297–8, 301
  Oceanic traditions, 208–9, 211, 219–20
  pre-modern Asia, 52, 120–1, 153
  socialism, 347
Fanon, Frantz, 332
fatherhood, 12–14, 16
Faure, Bernard, 144, 148
feagaiga relations, 219–20
Federation of Cuban Women (FMC), 360
female genital cutting, 162, 406
female homoerotic relations, 18–19
  African traditions, 161, 164–5, 172–3,
    176–7, 332
  ancient Egypt, 28, 37–8
  ancient Greece and Rome, 109–10
  Buddhism, 69
  Christianity, 286–7
  feminism, 373, 374–86
  Indigenous Americas, 188
  Islam, 303, 304–5, 308
  Jewish traditions, 265–7
  Oceanic traditions, 205–6, 214
  pre-modern China, 124, 126, 129–30
  sexual science, 322–6, 331–3
  socialism, 345, 347, 355, 356, 358, 359,
    360–1, 362
female orgasm, 95, 299, 307, 334, 352, 377
female pleasure
  African traditions, 162, 216
  ancient Greece and Rome, 90, 108
  Islam, 299, 307–8
  socialism, 341, 344, 350, 352–4
  South Asian traditions, 75
Femeia (Romanian magazine), 351–2
femininity, 70, 76–80, 81, 194, 368, 369, 375, 383
feminism, 195, 366–7
  feminist-as-lesbian, 374–86
  Islamic traditions, 293, 300, 309–11

Jewish traditions, 269
  modern girl, 367–74
  sexual science, 325, 334–5
  socialist feminism, 341–2
fertility
  African traditions, 167, 176
  ancient Near East, 48, 49
  ancient Rome, 111
  Jewish traditions, 258–63
  Oceanic traditions, 207
  pre-modern Japan, 142, 151
  South Asian traditions, 65–6
festivals, 28–9, 30
Figiel, Sia, 224
filial piety, 123
fiqh (Islamic jurisprudence), 295–6, 299–300,
  301, 310
First Story of Setne, The (fourth century BCE),
  26, 30
Fisher, Michael, 395
Florentine Codex, The (sixteenth century), 182–4
fornication, crime of, 208, 283, 301–3
Foucault, Michel, *The History of Sexuality*
  (1976–2018), 23, 34, 104, 131, 267,
  293, 378
Fourier, Charles, 341
France, 385, 397–8
Franke, Patrick, 306
free love, 372–3
Freeman, Derek, 221–3
Fresco of Priapus (Pompeii), 99
Freud, Sigmund, 211, 324, 330
Freudianism, 324, 375, 377
Freund, Kurt, 337, 357
Friedan, Betty, *The Feminine Mystique* (1963),
  375–6
frigidity, 334, 352
Fujiwara no Yorinaga, *Taiki* (twelfth
  century), 152
Furth, Charlotte, 126, 131

Gaius, 111
Galen, 96, 107, 307, 316
Galton, Francis, 320
Gandhi, Mahatma, 84, 403–4
Gāthā Sattasaī (Sat), 76–7
Gauguin, Paul, 225
gay liberation movement, 286, 335, *336*
Gay Women's Liberation (GWL), 381
Geddes, Patrick (with J. Arthur Thomson),
  The Evolution of Sex (1889),
  319–20
gender equality, 341–2, 349

415

Index

gender hierarchy
  ancient Near East, 51–2
  capitalism, 342
  Christianity, 272, 273–5
  Islam, 297–8
  pre-modern Japan, 143–4
  sexual science, 315, 316
Genshin, *Ōjōyōshū* (*Treatises on Rebirth*)
  (985), 152
Gerhard, Jane, 376
Germany, 322–4, 354, 355, 357–8, 379, 385
Ghosh, Durba, 395
Gilgamesh, Enkidu and the Netherworld, 47
Glassman, Hank, 151
Gnosticism, 274, 278, 288
Gold Coast Colony, 165–6
Goldin, Paul R., 126
  The Culture of Sex in Ancient China (2002),
   127–8
  'Sexuality: Ancient China' (2015), 130, 132
Goldman, Emma, 372
Goldstein, Melvyn, 239
Great Perfection literature, 246
Greece. *See* ancient Greece
Greenberg, David, 127
Greenson, Ralph, 329
Gregorian Reforms, 279–80
Gregory of Nyssa, 276
Gṛhyasūtras, 70
Gulik, Robert Hans van, 124–6, 129
  Erotic Colour Prints of the Ming Period (1951),
   124–5
  Sexual Life in Ancient China (1961), 124–5, 131
Gutierrez, Ramon, 391
Gutzwiller, Kathryn, 109
Guyana, 10
Gyatso, Janet, 246

hadīth, 295, 298
Hadza people, 15
Haeckel, Ernst, 320
halakhah (Jewish law), 250–1, 260, 263, 264, 267
Hall, Radclyffe, 372
Hallett, Judith, 110
Halperin, David, 106
Hamer, Dean, 336–7
harems, 75, 394
Hatshepsut, Egyptian pharaoh, 33
healers, 175–7
health, 96, 118, 245, 254–5, 335, 344, 350–1, 360
Herdt, Gilbert, 215–17
Hermaphroditus, 101–2, *103*
Herodotus, 29, 58–9

Herophilus, 95–6, 107
Hesiod
  Theogony, 88
  Works and Days, 107
hetairai (courtesans), 30
Heterodoxy (New York City club), 373
Hevajra Tantra, 242
Hidatsa people, 197–8
Hidayatullah, Aysha, 293
hijras, 83, 401–2
Hillel school of thought, 254, 259
Hinchy, Jessica, 402
Hindu Widows' Remarriage Act (1856), 400
Hinduism, 63–4, 82, 243, 245, 399–400
Hinsch, Bret, *Passions of the Cut Sleeve* (1990),
  126–7
Hippocratic corpus, 94–5, 107
Hiratsuka Raichō, 325
Hirschfeld, Magnus, 323–4, 327, 328, 330–1
Hittite Laws, 60
HIV/AIDS, 213, 214–15, 217, 289, 335, 356, 362
Ho Chi Minh, 404
Hobson, Benjamin, *A Treatise on Anatomy*
  (1851), 317
Hobson, Emily K., 381
Hodgson, Marshall, 295
Hoganson, Kristen, 402
Holiness Code, 264–5, 267–8, 273
Homer
  Iliad (*c.* 750 BCE), 88
  Odyssey (*c.* 700 BCE), 88–9
homoerotic relations. *See* female homoerotic
  relations; male homoerotic relations
honji suijaku, 137–8
Hooker, Evelyn, 333
hormone therapy, 321, 327–8
Huna, Rav, 266
Hunt, Nancy Rose, 406
Hymn of Iddin-Dagan, The (*c.* 1900 BCE), 59
Hynie, Jozef, 352–3

Ibn Sīnā (Avicenna), *The Canon of
  Medicine*, 308
Igat Hope, 217–18
Iggeret ha-Kodesh (*Holy Letter*), 261–2
illegitimate children, 55, 347
image of God, 260–1, 272
imperial knowledge systems, 316–17
impotence, 48, 178, 299, 343–4
impurity, 58, 142–3, 150–1, 405
Inandik vase, 47
incest, 59–60, 140, 177, 204–5, 212–13, 219,
  301

Index

India, 301, 333–4, 394–5, 398–404, 405–6, 408. *See also* South Asian traditions
Indigenous Americans, 18, 196–8, 395, 404
Indus civilization, 66
inheritance, 47, 55, 56, 59, 168–9, 301
initiation practices, 161–3, 215–16
Inka society, 195
Institute for Sexual Science (Berlin), 323, 325
intercrural sex, 105, 206, 306
International Journal of Sexology (IJS) (1947–55), 333–4
interracial unions, 285, 389
intersex, 101–2, 192, 206, 265, 291, 326–9
Inuit people, 10–11
Iran, 303, 326, 407
Ireland, 289–90
Islam, 82–3, 293–6, 407
    feminist interpretations, 293, 300, 309–11
    illicit sex in Muslim law, 301–6
    marriage in Muslim law, 298–301
    medicine and erotology, 306–9
    Qur'an and Sunna, 296–8
Iyanaga, Nobumi, 147–8

Jackson, Ronald, 407
Jacobs, Margaret, 404
Jacoby, Sarah, 245
Jainism, 64, 68
Japan, modern, 325, 328, 370, 379, 405
Japan, pre-modern, 136–9
    bodies and gender instability, 148–50
    Buddhism, 137–8, 142, 144–50, 151–3, 234
    Confucianism, 138–9, 153–4
    Kami Way, 136, 139–44, 150–1
    male homoerotic relations, 151–3
    purity and pollution, 142–3, 150–1
    sexual desire, 139, 142–3, 144–8
Jātaka tales, 70, 235, 237
Jayadeva, *Gitagovinda* (twelfth century), 80
Jefferson, Thomas, 394
Jerome, 275, 278
Jewish traditions, 250–2
    homoerotic relations, 263–8
    marriage, 252–8, 266
    procreation, 258–63
Jing Fang, 116
John Cassian, 279
John Chrysostom, 273–4
Johnson, Virginia, 336, 353, 360, 376
Jordan, Winthrop, 394
Jorgensen, Christine, 329

Journal of Psychology (Majallat 'Ilm al-Naf) (1945–53), 326
Jovinian, 275
Junge Welt (German magazine), 351
Juvenal, 106

Ka'ahumanu, 203, 205, 207–8
Kabbalah, 255
kabuki theatres, 328
Kahan, Benjamin, 366–7, 371
Kalakaua, King of Hawai'i, 209
Kamakau, Samuel, 206–7
Kāmasūtra, 73–6, 77
Kamehameha I, King of Hawai'i, 203
Kamehameha III, King of Hawai'i, 204–5
Kami Way, 136, 150–1
Kanaka'ole, Kaumakaiwa, 206
Kapul Champions, 217–18
Katz, Sue, 'Smash Phallic Imperialism' (1970), 379–81
Kauanui, J. Kēhaulani, 203–4, 207, 209
kāvya texts, 73, 76
Kazembe, 169
Kellenbach, Herman, 404
Kenya, 173, 406–7
Kenyatta, Jomo, 407
Kēopūolani, 203, 205, 207
Kertbeny, Karl Maria, 323
Khairati, 401–2
Khandro, Sera, 245, 246
Khoekhoe people, 396–8
Khrushchev, Nikita, 348–9
Kihara, Yuki, 224–5
Kinsey, Alfred, 332–3, 376
Kirkpatrick, James, 395
Koedt, Anne, 377
Kojiki (712), 137, 139–44, 150
Kollontai, Alexandra, 346–7, 372
Krafft-Ebing, Richad von, *Psychopathia Sexualis* (1886), 322–3, 325
Kramer, Heinrich, *Malleus Maleficarum* (1486), 279–80
Kratochvíl, Stanislav, 353
kulin Brahmans, 399–400
Kumano nuns, 151
Kumulipo narrative, 204
Kyōkai, 144

La Malinche, 391
La tribune des femmes (1832–4), 341–2
labia lengthening practice, 162
Lake Nyanza societies, 165, 175–6
Lamarck, Jean-Baptist, 320

417

Index

Lambeth Conference, 287, 288
Landa, Diego de, *Relación de las Cosas de Yucatan* (c. 1566), 182
Laqish, Resh, 268
lascar sailors, 395
Latai, Latu, 222
Laws of Hammurabi, 60
Laws of Ur-Namma, 60
Leach, Timothy, 217–18
Lelyveld, Joseph, 404
Lenin, Vladimir, 347
Lepani, Katherine, *Islands of Love, Islands of Risk* (2012), 213–15
Leroux, Pierre, 341
Letter of Barnabas (c. 70–132), 289
LeVay, Simon, 336–7
Levine, Philippa, 401
Lew-Starowicz, Zbigniew, 353, 358
LGBTQ+ movements, 269, 335, 336, 363
Li Shiu Tong, 324
Li Shizhen, *Compendium of Material Medica* (1578–96), 317
Lieven, Alexandra von, 38
Lili'uokalani, Queen of Hawai'i, 203, 207
Linnaeus, Carl, *Systema naturae* (1735), 315, 316
Lipschütz, Alexander, 328
Livy (Titus Livius), 107
Lombard, Peter, 281
London Missionary Society, 218
Lotus Sutra, 148–9
love, 272, 308–9
Loves of a Blonde (dir. Milos Forman, 1965), 351
loyalty, 108–9
Lu, Weijing, 129, 130
Lucretius, 94
Lugones, Maria, 368
Luther, Martin, 282, 283

magical rituals, 48
Mahābhārata, 70–1
Mahāvīra, 68
Mahayana Buddhism, 239–40
Maimonides, 261
  Mishneh Torah, 254–5, 267
Majjhima Nikāya, 232
Makushi people, 10
Malagasy people, 164
male gaze, 108
male homoerotic relations, 18–19
  African traditions, 161, 171–2, 173–4, 176, 332, 407
  ancient Egypt, 27, 34–7, 39–40
  ancient Greece and Rome, 104–6

ancient Near East, 50, 60
British India, 401
Buddhism, 233, 236
Christianity, 273–4, 280, 284, 285, 286–7
Indigenous Americas, 188, 190, 191
Islam, 303–5, 307, 308–9
Jewish traditions, 263–5, 267–8
Oceanic traditions, 205, 206–7, 212, 214, 215–16, 217
pre-modern China, 123–4, 126–7, 132
pre-modern Japan, 151–3
sexual science, 322–6, 331–3, 336–7
socialism, 347, 348, 355–8, 359, 360–1, 362
South Asian traditions, 69, 75–6, 83–4
Malinowski, Bronisław, *The Sexual Life of Savages in North-Western Melanesia* (1929), 210–13, 330
Malo, David, 206–7
Mānava Dharmaśāstra, 70, 71–2
Mani, Lata, 399
Mann, Susan, *Gender and Sexuality in Modern China* (2011), 128, 129, 130, 132
Manto, Saadat Hasan, *Khol Do* (1948), 405
Manu law codes, 70
Manyōshū, 152
Mao Zedong, 358–9
Marañón, Gregorio, 327–8
Marcion, 274
Maria Theresa of Spain (wife of King Louis XIV of France), 395
marriage. *See also* adultery; divorce
  African traditions, 163–6, 168–9, 173–4, 176
  ancient Greece and Rome, 102, 105, 107–8
  ancient Near East, 52–4, 55–7
  Buddhism, 234–5, 236
  Christianity
    early modern world, 282–5
    pre-modern times, 271–2, 275–6, 281–2
  colonialism, 394–5
  evolutionary legacy, 7, 9–11, 17, 18
  Islam, 295
    Muslim law, 298–301
    Qur'an and Sunna, 296–8
  Jewish traditions, 252–8, 266
  Oceanic traditions, 204, 208–9, 211, 216–17, 218, 222
  pre-modern China, 120–3
  pre-modern Japan, 143, 153–4
  socialism, 345, 347, 358, 361
  South Asian traditions, 64, 70–2, 399–400
Martial, 110
Marx, Karl, 341, 342
Mary (mother of Jesus), 277–8, 281–2

418

Index

masculinity
  ancient Greece and Rome, 103–6
  colonialism, 402–4, 407
  Oceanic traditions, 215
  pre-modern China, 122
  pre-modern Japan, 143
  socialism, 360–1
  South Asian traditions, 67, 70–1, 83
Masters, William, 336, 353, 360, 376
Masterson, Mark, 106
masturbation, 190, 212, 322
  Buddhism, 69, 233
  Christianity, 280, 287–8
  Islam, 305–6
  socialism, 344, 345, 349, 359
Matamba, 169
mate guarding, 16–17
May Fourth Movement (1919), 368–9, 373
Maya people, 14, 15, 185–94
Mayo, Katherine, *Mother India* (1927), 403
McClintock, Anne, 406
McConaghy, Nathaniel, 337
Mead, Margaret
  Coming of Age in Samoa (1928), 1, 221–3
  Sex and Temperament (1935), 331–2
medical texts, 94–6, 117–18, 148, 306–8
Meleisea, Leasiolagi Malama, 222
Mellan, Jiří, and Iva Sípová, *Young Marriage* (1970), 354
Menander, 110
Mendel, Gregor, 320
Meskell, Lynn, 22–3, 25, 34, 35
Mesoamerica, 185–94, 392–3
Mesopotamia. *See* ancient Near East
Mexica people, 185–94
Mexico, 321, 391, 393. *See also* Mesoamerica
Meyerowitz, Joanne, 330
Middle Assyrian Laws, 60
midrashic exegesis, 265–6
Millett, Kate, *Sexual Politics* (1970), 377–8
Mir-Hosseini, Ziba, 303, 310–11
Mishnah, 253–8, 259–60, 264–5
missionaries, 202, 203, 205, 206, 208–9, 222, 284–5, 291
Moche people, 195–6
modern girl, 367–74
Moe Nin, P., 325–6
Money, John, 328
monogamy, 3–7, 9, 13, 154, 234
Monte Albán (Mexico), 192
Moravians, 285
Morel, Benedict, 322

Mormons, 285
Morocco, 331
Mughal Empire, 82–3
Muhammad, 296, 298, 302, 309
Mujeres (Cuban magazine), 360
Murad, Yusuf, 326
Murasaki Shikibu, *The Tale of Genji* (c. 1008), 152
Musawah, 310–11
Musonius Rufus, Gaius, 93
Myrne, Pernilla, 308
mythology
  ancient Egypt, 28, 32–4, 35, 38–9
  ancient Greece and Rome, 88–9, 101–2
  Oceanic traditions, 204, 205–6, 212–13, 224
  pre-modern Japan, 139–44, 150
  South Asian traditions, 67–8, 70–1

Nā Mamo o Hawai'i, 209
Nachituti's Gifts narrative, 169
nadītu priestesses, 59
Nahi'ena'ena, 204–5
Najmabadi, Afsaneh, 293
Namibia, 176
Nash, Jennifer, 384
nationalism, 84, 338, 373, 391, 393, 402–6
natural world, 209–10, 314–17
Ndongo, 169
necrophilia, 321
Needham, Joseph, 125, 131
négritude movement, 407
Neubert, Rudolf, 349
New Economic Policy (NEP), 347
New Woman, 369–71
Niankhkhnnum-Khnumhotep relationship, 36
Nihon ryōiki (c. 822), 144–7
Njinga, Queen of Ndongo, 169–70
Nkabinde, Nkunzi, 177
Nkrumah, Kwame, 407
North Nyanza people, 166, 171
Nossis, 109
Nsenga people, 164
Nsukka Igbo people, 174–5
Nthunya, Mpho 'M'atsepo, 172
nuclear family, 2, 8–9, 208
nudity, 48–9, 99–101, 175
Nyanja-Cewa people, 167
Nyiramongi, Queen-Mother of Rwanda, 170

Oceanic traditions, 201–3
  Hawai'i, 203–10
  Papua New Guinea, 210–18
  Samoa, 218–25

419

Index

Ogura Seizaburō, 325
okwalulá abaana ceremony, 167
Oldenburg, Veena Talwar, 400
one-child policy, 359
Oneida Community, 285
one-sex model, 316
onnagata, 328
Onyonyo Muru Nwanga Women's War
    (1926), 175
oral sex, 75–6, 106, 212, 215–16
orgasm. *See* female orgasm
Orientalism, 126
Origen, 275
Orthodox Churches, 284, 286–7, 289
Our Bodies, Ourselves (1970), 334–5
Ovid, *Metamorphoses*, 101–2, 110
ovulation, 5–6

Padmasambhava, 244
Pakistan, 303, 405–6
Pāli Sutras, 235, 237
Pan Guangdan, 325
pandakas, 238–9
Papua New Guinea, 210–18
Papyrus Turin 55001, 31–2
Papyrus Westcar, 27
parenthood, 7–8, 11–16, 166–7, 211,
    351–2
Parkinson, Richard, 35
Pashupati seal, 66
Pausanias, 106
Paz, Octavio, 391
pederasty, 92–3, 104–6, *105*, 151–3, 215–16,
    305, 309
Pende, Nichola, 321, 327
penitential books, 281
Peter Damian, *Book of Gomorrah* (1051), 280
phallic imagery, 97, *98*, *99*, 142, 190
Philippines, 402, 403
Philo Judaeos, 262
philosophy, 91–4
photographs, 225
phrenology, 318, *319*
physical anthropology, 318
Pillay, Alyappin Padmanabha, 333–4
pimping, 121, 345
Plato
    Gorgias, 106
    Phaedrus, 92, 108
    Symposium, 91–2, 101, 104, 106,
        109–10
Plautus, *Poenulus*, 111
Playboy (1953–present), 376

Pliny the Elder, 101
Pocahontas (Matoaka), 395
Poland, 352, 353, 358
pollution, 142–3, 150–1, 216, 217, 278–9, 281
polyandry, 7, 67–8, 120, 204
polygyny
    ancient Near East, 54
    Buddhism, 234
    Christianity, 284, 285
    evolutionary legacy, 2, 3–5, 6, 7, 9
    Islam, 297
    Oceanic traditions, 204, 212, 213, 218
polymorphous perversity, 324
Pondělíčková, Jaroslava, 354
Pope Benedict XVI, 286
Pope Francis, 284, 289
Pope John Paul II, 288–9, 291
Pope Paul VI, *Humanae vitae* (1968), 288
Pope Pius XI, 275, 288
pornography, 384
Portugal, 168, 169, 392
post-colonialism
    anti-colonial nationalisms, 402–6
    early colonial encounters, 388–90
    early modern colonialism, 390–5
    inventing sexuality in metropoles,
        395–8
    legislating sexuality, 398–402
    post-colony sexuality, 406
poverty, 167, 284, 347
power relations, 74–5, 378, 391
power, sexual, 174–8
prātimoksa vows, 230–1, 240
Pratt, Mary Louise, 391
Praxitales, 'Aphrodite of Knidos' (fourth
    century BCE), 101
procreation. *See* reproduction
prostitution
    African traditions, 173, 406
    ancient Egypt, 29–31
    ancient Greece and Rome, 111–12
    ancient Near East, 52
    Buddhism, 235, 237
    Christianity, 272
    colonialism, 217, 400–1, 406
    Islam, 301
    pre-modern China, 120–2
    socialism, 343, 345, 347, 349, 358
    South Asian traditions, 74, 83
Ptolemy I, Egyptian pharaoh, 30
Ptolemy IV, Egyptian pharaoh, 30
Pueblo people, 391
Pukui, Mary, 205

Index

Purāṇas, 64, 70–1
Pyramid Texts, 34

Quack, Joachim Friedrich, 30
Qur'an, 295, 296–8, 302, 304, 305,
    310
Quraishi-Landes, Asifa, 311

race
    colonialism, 389, 392, 393–4, 396–8, 403,
        404, 408
    feminism, 368–9, 374, 378, 379, 381–2, 384–5
    sexual science, 318
Radicalesbians, 'The Woman-Identified-
    Woman' (1970), 382–3
Ralston, Caroline, 203
Rāmāyana, 70, 82
Ramesses III, Egyptian pharaoh, 36
Ramesses IV, Egyptian pharaoh, 29–30
Ramsey, Michael, 286
Rappo, Gaétan, 147
Rashi, 257
religion. *See* Buddhism; Christianity; cultic
    practices; Hinduism; Islam; Jewish
    traditions
reproduction
    ancestral mating systems, 3
    ancient Greece and Rome, 93, 95–6, 108,
        111
    ancient Near East, 46–8
    Christianity, 273, 280, 288
    Indigenous Americas, 194, 197
    Islam, 297
    Jewish traditions, 258–63
    pre-modern China, 118
    pre-modern Japan, 141–2, 143
    sexual science, 317
    socialism, 358–9, 360
    South Asian traditions, 64
reproductive fluids, 34, 215, 242, 245, 261–2,
    307
Ṛg Veda, 67
Richlin, Amy, 104
ritual sex, 174, 215–16, 241–3
Rocha, Leon, 132–3
Roe v. *Wade* (1973), 289, 290
Rolfe, John, 395
Roman law, 251
Rome. *See* ancient Rome
Roy, Rammohan, 399–400
Rufus of Ephesus, 307
Russia. *See* Soviet Union (USSR)
Rwanda, 170

sacramental sex, 240–3
sacred marriage, 59
sacred prostitution, 58–9
sadomasochism, 74–5, 77
Sahagun, Fray Bernardino de, 182–3
Said, Edward, *Orientalism* (1978), 388
Saint-Simonians, 341
Saiva groups, 243
'Salmakis Inscription' (second century
    BCE), 102
Sambia people, 215–17
same-sex marriage, 18, 209, 266, 361
Samoa, 1, 218–25
San people, 174
Sang, Tze-lan, 129–30, 373
Sânizade Mehmet Ataullah, *Hamse-i Şânizâde*
    (1820), 317
Sappho, 38, 90, 109
sati (widow burning), 399–400
Saudi Arabia, 407
Savanna Pumé, 9, 13, 15
Schnabl, Siegfried, *Mann und Frau Intim*
    (1969), 350, 360
Schoeffel, Penelope, 222
scientia sexualis, 131
Second World War (1939–45), 405
Sefer ha-Hinukh (thirteenth century), 259, 260
Semashko, Nikolai, 325
Semonides, 107
Seneca, 93, 108
Sennacherib, King of Assyria, 56
Senwosret I, Egyptian pharaoh, 33
servants, 124
setsuwa narratives, 144–7, 148, 149–50
sex change, 116, 327–8, 329
sex education, 161–2, 325, 343, 352, 360
sex manuals, 119–20, 125, 129, 131, 261–2, 348,
    349–50
sex therapy, 353, 358
sex tourism, 209
sexless-sex model, 346
Sexological Institute (Prague), 357
sexual debt, 253–6, 263
sexual dimorphism, 3–5, 7
sexual pleasure. *See* female pleasure
sexual science
    cultural truths and social organization,
        330–4
    homosexuality, 322–6, 331–3, 336–7
    intersex. Trans. and gender binary, 326–9
    politics of biology and sexual revolution,
        334–7, *336*
    pre-modern times, 94–6, 131, 280, 306–8

Index

sexual science (cont.)
  race, evolution, and eugenics, 317–21, *319*
  sexing nature, 314–17
sexual selection, 319–20
sexual violence
  African traditions, 163
  ancient Egypt, 38–9
  ancient Near East, 53–4
  ancient Rome, 91, 111
  Buddhism, 236
  Christianity, 290–1
  colonialism, 389, 394, 405–6
  Islam, 301
  pre-modern China, 122, 124, 128
  pre-modern Japan, 143
  South Asian traditions, 71, 74–5, 84–5
Shakers, 285
Shakespeare, William, *Othello*, (*c.* 1603), 396–7
Shammai school of thought, 254, 259
Shankman, Paul, 223
shari'a law, 301, 310–11
Shepherd of Hermas, The (*c.* 120 CE), 276
Shi'a, 298
Shinjō, *Juhō yōjinshū* (1268), 147
Shinran, 147
Shona people, 161, 171–2
Silverberg, Miriam, 370
Simi, Noumea, 'What are we?' (1992), 224
sin, concept of, 132, 276–7, 279, 281,
  287
Sinha, Mrinalini, 402–3
Sissa, Giulia, 23
slavery
  African traditions, 165–6, 168–9
  ancient Egypt, 30
  ancient Greece and Rome, 91, 110–12
  ancient Near East, 52, 54–6
  Christianity, 276, 284
  Islam, 297, 300
  post-colonialism, 390–1, 393–4, 402,
    405
social class. *See* class
social constructionism, 330
social motherhood, 166
socialism
  early theorizations, 341–2
  Eastern Europe
    birth control and homosexuality,
      354–8
    post-war approaches, 349–54
  non-European nations, 358–63
  Soviet Union (USSR), 343–9
Sodom narrative, 303–4

sodomy, 83, 206, 217, 280, 348, 401,
  407
Solanas, Valerie, *SCUM Manifesto* (1968),
  377, 383
Sommer, Matthew, 124
Soranus, 96, 107
Sotho people, 161, 165, 172
South Africa, 176–7, 368, 397
South Asian traditions, 63–4
  Dharmaśāstra traditions, 71–3
  heterodox and epic-Purānic traditions,
    68–71
  Kāma tradition, 73–6
  later developments, 82–5
  non-Sanskrit love poetry, 76–80
  pre- and post-historic context, 64–7
  Tantric sex and visual art, 80–2
  Vedic-Brahmanical thought systems,
    63–4, 67–8
South Kyoga, 166
Soviet Union (USSR), 325, 343–9
Spain, 261, 392–3
Spanish-American War (1898), 402
Spivak, Gayatri, 399, 408
Spurzheim, Johann, 318
Stalin, Joseph, 348
Standard Cross-Cultural Sample, 9
Steinach, Eugen, 327–8
sterilization, 321, 379
Stewart, Christine, 217
stirpiculture, 285
Stoica, Tudor, 352
Stoicism, 92–3, 275
Stoler, Ann Laura, 396
Stoller, Robert, 329
Stonewall Riots (1969), 286, 335
Story of Petese, Son of Peletum, The (first or
  second century CE), 27
Strabo, 31
Strīvivartavyākarana Sūtra, 239–40
Subhā Jivakambavanikā, 69–70
Suburban Baths (Pompeii), 98, *100*
Sulpicia, 91, 109
Sun Yat-sen, 404
Sunjata Epic (thirteenth century), 163
Sunna, 295, 298, 302
Sunnis, 298
supernatural sex, 177–8
Suppiluliuma I, Hittite king, 57
Swanson, David, 207

Tabalu subclan, 211
Tachikawaryū, 147–8

Index

Tale of the Herdsman, The (Egyptian text), 33
Talmudic tradition, 255, 256, 260, 263, 265, 266–7, 268
Tamasese Ta'isi Efi, Tui Atua, 224
Tamil love poetry, 78–9
Tantric sex, 80–1, 240–7
Tanzania, 15, 173, 178
taupou marriages, 222
taxonomy, 314–17
Tcherkézoff, Serge, 220, 223
Teaiwa, Teresia, 209
Temple of Dionysus (Delos), 97, *98*
Tertullian, 274, 278
testis size, 5, 7
testosterone, 16, 357
Theognidea, 89
Theognis, 104
Therīgāthā, 68–9
Third World Women's Alliance (TWWA), 379
Thomas, Lynn, 406
Tibet, 243–7
Tibullus, 91
Torah, 250, 254–5, 257, 262–3
transgenderism, 18
  African traditions, 160, 169–70
  ancient Greece and Rome, 101–2
  British India, 401–2
  Christianity, 291
  Indigenous Americas, 190–2, 196–8, 392–3
  Oceanic traditions, 206, 217, 220, 224–5
  sexual science, 326–9
  South Asian traditions, 70, 83
  Vietnam, 362–3
Traub, Valerie, 367
Tristan, Flora, 341
Trobriand people, 210–15
Trojan War myth, 88–9
Tsogyal, Yeshe, 244
Tukulti-Ninurta I, Assyrian king, 46
Turke, Paul, 14–15
Twinam, Ann, 392, 393
two-sex model, 316
two-spirits, 18, 196–8

Uganda, 166–7, 171
Ulpian, 111
Ulrichs, Karl Heinrich, 323
uman ribu, 379
United States of America (USA), 9, 18–19, 221, 341

Christianity, 285, 286, 289, 290
  feminism, 376
  post-colonialism, 402, 403, 404
  sexual science, 321, 328–9, 332–3, 334–5
Utopian Socialism, 341–2, 360

Valentinus, 274
Valerius Maximus, 108
Vedas, 63–4, 67–8
veiling, 108, 272, 278
venereal disease, 207, 343, 344, 349, 401
Venus figurines, 65
Victoria, Queen of England, 395
Vietnam, 361–3, 404
Vimalakirti Sutra, 149
Vinaya Pitaka, 69, 229–33, 237–9
Virgil, *Aeneid* (19 BCE), 89
virginity, 51, 71, 85, 218, 221, 222, 237, 274, 275–6, 277–9

Wadud, Amina, *Qur'an and Woman* (1999), 310
Walatta Petros, 172–3
Ward, Kerry, *Networks of Empire* (2008), 390–1
Warren Cup (*c.* 30 BCE–30 CE), 99
Washington, George, 394
WeGrow Ed (Vietnamese sex education), 362
Weinbaum, Alys Eve, *The Modern Girl Around the World* (2008), 367, 370
Weismann, August, 320
Wendt, Albert, *The Mango's Kiss* (2003), 223–4
Werner, Reiner, *Homosexualität* (1988), 357
Westermarck, Edward, 331
Westphal, Karl, 322
wet dreams, 278–9
White, Luise, 406
widowhood, 122, 174, 212, 399–400
Williams, Craig, 106
Winkler, John, 106
Wislocka, Michalina, *The Art of Loving* (1978), 350, 353
women's liberation movement, 376–83
Woolf, Virginia, 372

Xenophon, *Oeconomicus*, 108, 110

Yamamoto Senji, 325
Yamato family, 138, 139
Yao, Ping, 129–30
Yaśodharā (wife of Buddha), 235

423

Index

Yemen, 407
Yeshe, Thubtan, 246–7
Yishak, Ethopian emperor, 168
yoga, sexual, 244–7
yoginī tantras, 241–3
Yohanan, Rabbi, 268
Young, Damon, 377, 383
Young, Serenity, 235
yù terminology, 115–16

zāiyì system, 116
Zambia, 163
Zeno of Citium, 92–3
Zhang Jingsheng, 325
Zimbabwe, 163, 176
Zoroastrianism, 251
Zulu people, 161, 164
Zulu, Shaka, 170

CONTENTS TO VOLUMES I, III, AND IV

Volume I: General Overviews

1 · The History of the History of Sexuality
MATHEW KUEFLER

2 · The History of Sexuality and Anthropology
JOAN VENDRELL FERRÉ

3 · The History of Sexuality and Women's History
JUDITH A. ALLEN

4 · The History of Sexuality and LGBTQ+ History
EMILY SKIDMORE

5 · The Impact of Sigmund Freud on the History of Sexuality
ALISON M. DOWNHAM MOORE

6 · Michel Foucault's Influence on the History of Sexuality
MICHAEL C. BEHRENT

7 · Queer Theory and the History of Sexuality
RIIKKA TAAVETTI

8 · The Sexual Body in History
KIM M. PHILLIPS

9 · Marriage and Families in the History of Sexuality
MERRY E. WIESNER-HANKS

CONTENTS TO VOLUMES I, III, AND IV

10 · Class in the History of Sexuality
HELEN SMITH, WITH MATHEW KUEFLER AND MERRY E. WIESNER-HANKS

11 · Sexuality and Race: Representations, Regulations, and Sentiments
JENNIFER ANNE BOITTIN

12 · Male Homoerotic Relations in History
DOMINIC JANES

13 · Desire, Love, and Sex between Women in Global History
LEILA J. RUPP

14 · Trans and Gender Variant Sexualities in History
JEN MANION

15 · The Sale of Sex in History
MAGALY RODRÍGUEZ GARCÍA

16 · Sexual Violence in History
LISA FEATHERSTONE

17 · Sexual Science in History
SEAN M. QUINLAN

18 · Sexuality and Emotion
KATIE BARCLAY

19 · Erotic Art in World History
Y. YVON WANG

20 · Erotic Literature in History
JAMES GRANTHAM TURNER

21 · The Material Culture of the History of Sexuality
CHRIS BRICKELL

22 · Public History and Sexuality
MELINDA MARIE JETTÉ

CONTENTS TO VOLUMES I, III, AND IV

Volume III: Sites of Knowledge and Practice

1 · Sex in Athens in the Fifth and Fourth Centuries BCE
JAMES ROBSON

2 · Sex in Rome in the First Century BCE and the First Century CE
AVEN MCMASTER

3 · Sex in Constantinople in the Sixth Century CE
SHAUN TOUGHER

4 · Sex in Chang'an in the Eighth and Ninth Centuries CE
PING YAO

5 · Sexuality in Baghdad in the Ninth and Tenth Centuries CE
KAREN MOUKHEIBER AND NADIA MARIA EL CHEIKH

6 · Sex in Heian-kyō (Kyoto) in the Tenth through Twelfth Centuries CE
JOSHUA S. MOSTOW

7 · Sex in Iceland in the Fourteenth and Fifteenth Centuries CE
AGNES S. ARNÓRSDÓTTIR

8 · Sex in Florence in the Fifteenth Century
IAN FREDERICK MOULTON

9 · Sexuality in Tenochtitlan in the Early Sixteenth Century
MIRIAM LÓPEZ HERNÁNDEZ

10 · Sex in Sixteenth-Century Istanbul
SELIM S. KURU

11 · Sex in Geneva in the Sixteenth Century
JEFFREY R. WATT

12 · Sex in Eighteenth-Century Edo (Tokyo)
ANGELIKA KOCH

13 · Sex in Eighteenth-Century Paris
NINA KUSHNER

CONTENTS TO VOLUMES I, III, AND IV

14 · Sex and Sexuality in Eighteenth-Century Philadelphia
MERRIL D. SMITH

15 · Sex in Nineteenth-Century Cairo
MARIO M. RUIZ

16 · Sexual Pleasures and Perils in Nineteenth-Century London
PAUL R. DESLANDES

17 · Sex in Manila in the Late Nineteenth and Early Twentieth Centuries
RAQUEL A. G. REYES

18 · Sex in Lagos from the Mid-Nineteenth to the Mid-Twentieth Century
NDUBUEZE L. MBAH

19 · Sex in Bombay in the Late Nineteenth and Early Twentieth Centuries
ADITI SEN

20 · Sexuality in a Distant Metropolis: Buenos Aires from the Late Nineteenth to the Mid-Twentieth Century
PABLO BEN AND SANTIAGO JOAQUÍN INSAUSTI

21 · Sex in Early Twentieth-Century Berlin
ANNETTE F. TIMM

22 · Sex in Sydney in the Twentieth Century
FRANK BONGIORNO

23 · Toronto the Good, Toronto the Gay: Sex and Morality in the Twentieth Century
TOM HOOPER

24 · Sex in Shanghai in the Twentieth Century: Intimate Negotiations
TING GUO

25 · Sex in Twentieth-Century Rio de Janeiro
JAMES N. GREEN

Volume IV: Modern Sexualities

1 · Sexuality and Capitalism
ADRIANA ZAHARIJEVIĆ

CONTENTS TO VOLUMES I, III, AND IV

2 · Colonialism and Modern Sexuality
PENNY RUSSELL

3 · Gender, Migration, and Sexuality in the Modern World
KALPANA HIRALAL

4 · 'Pornography', 'Obscenity', and the Suppression of Libertine Literature
JAMES GRANTHAM TURNER

5 · Sexuality and the Print Media in the Modern World
GRETCHEN SODERLUND

6 · Eugenics, Public Health, and Modern Sexuality
MIRELA DAVID

7 · Sexuality and Consumerism in the Modern World: The Business
of Pleasure
ERIKA RAPPAPORT AND JULIE JOHNSON

8 · Sex Education in the Modern World
CRIS MAYO AND LAUREN BIALYSTOK

9 · Birth Control and Reproductive Rights in the Modern World
DARSHI THORADENIYA

10 · The Impact of the World Wars on Modern Sexuality
CORNELIE USBORNE AND LEE ARNOTT

11 · Sexualities and Dictatorships of the Twentieth Century
CRISTINA SCHEIBE WOLFF

12 · Sexuality in Post-war Liberal Democracies
BARBARA BROOKES

13 · The Sexual Revolution
DAGMAR HERZOG AND YANARA SCHMACKS

14 · Sex Tourism: Fluid Borders of Meanings and Practices
AMALIA L. CABEZAS

CONTENTS TO VOLUMES I, III, AND IV

15 · The History of AIDS Since 1981: Medicine, Politics, and Societies
in a Pandemic

MANDISA MBALI

16 · Sex Trafficking in the Modern World

ANAMARIA MARCON VENSON AND JOANA MARIA PEDRO

17 · Sex, Law, and Domestic Violence against Women in the Modern
World

CONCEIÇÃO GOMES

18 · Sexuality under Attack Now

ANDREA PETŐ